ERIE COUNTY, NEW YORK
OBITUARIES

AS FOUND IN THE FILES OF THE
BUFFALO AND ERIE COUNTY
HISTORICAL SOCIETY

Compiled by
Martha and Bill Reamy

HERITAGE BOOKS
2009

HERITAGE BOOKS
AN IMPRINT OF HERITAGE BOOKS, INC.

Books, CDs, and more—Worldwide

For our listing of thousands of titles see our website
at
www.HeritageBooks.com

Published 2009 by
HERITAGE BOOKS, INC.
Publishing Division
100 Railroad Ave. #104
Westminster, Maryland 21157

Copyright © 1992 Martha and Bill Reamy

All rights reserved. No part of this book may be reproduced or transmitted in any form or by any means, electronic or mechanical, including photocopying, recording or by any information storage and retrieval system without written permission from the author, except for the inclusion of brief quotations in a review.

International Standard Book Numbers
Paperbound: 978-1-58549-641-9
Clothbound: 978-0-7884-7596-2

TABLE OF CONTENTS

Preface v

Obituary Records 1

Gazetteer 305

Index 309

PREFACE

The Buffalo and Erie County Historical society is pleased to cooperate with Martha Reamy and Pipe Creek in publishing part of the "deaths file" located in our library.

Library staff at the Society have for many years produced an index to obituaries published in Buffalo newspapers. This is a card file, alphabetical by last name, and is updated daily.

The file was begun in the 1800s, when an intrepid researcher went through all newspapers extant and indexed every death notice, going back to 1812. Of course, not every issue of every newspaper published in Buffalo was still available at the time this was done, but it is a fairly complete index from the 1840s forward.

This book lists those cards from our index for deaths from the earliest listings (ca. 1811) through 1880. The deaths before 1868 can be found in *Early Settlers of New York State, Their Ancestors and Descendants*, edited by Janet Wethy Foley and published in 9 volumes from 1934 to 1942. Listings through about 1984 are available on microfilm from the Church of the Latter Day Saints, which filmed them in 1985, and, of course, the complete index to the present day is available for public searching in the Society library.

Some early listings have no newspaper citation. We do not know where this information came from; possibly it was found on gravestones or in some published source, such as a count history. Since death dates are given for these listings, it is sometimes - but not always - possible to find death notices by searching newspapers for a few days after the date.

We no longer index every death notice, but only true obituaries; that is, only paragraph write-ups published separately from the columns of notices. This has been the practice for most of the 20th century; there are simply too many notices now for us to do them all.

Many of the citations for the 1800s are for a death notice, not an obituary; that is, for a two-line notice that gives only the name and date of death and perhaps the age. A notice normally does not give names of children or parents, or the burial place.

Copies of obituaries/death notices can be made from our newspaper microfilm. We have a printer that prints only a negative copy; that is, the print is white on a black background. With this type of copy, photographs do not print well. Copies may be ordered by mail; contact the Society library for fees for this service. Turn-around time is usually within two weeks. If no citation is given and we must search the newspapers for a notice, we limit the time spent to 30 minutes. If more time is required, we provide a list of local researchers who can be hired.

The deaths file and other genealogical materials are available for on-site use. At the present time the Society library is open to the public Wednesdays, Thursdays and Fridays from 10 to 5 and Saturdays from 12 to 5; it is closed on holidays. There is a daily use fee for non-members.

The Buffalo and Erie County Historical Society is located at 25 Nottingham Court, Buffalo, NY 14216; telephone 716-873-9644.

    Mary F. Bell
Director of Library and Archives
Buffalo and Erie County Historical Society

April 3, 1992

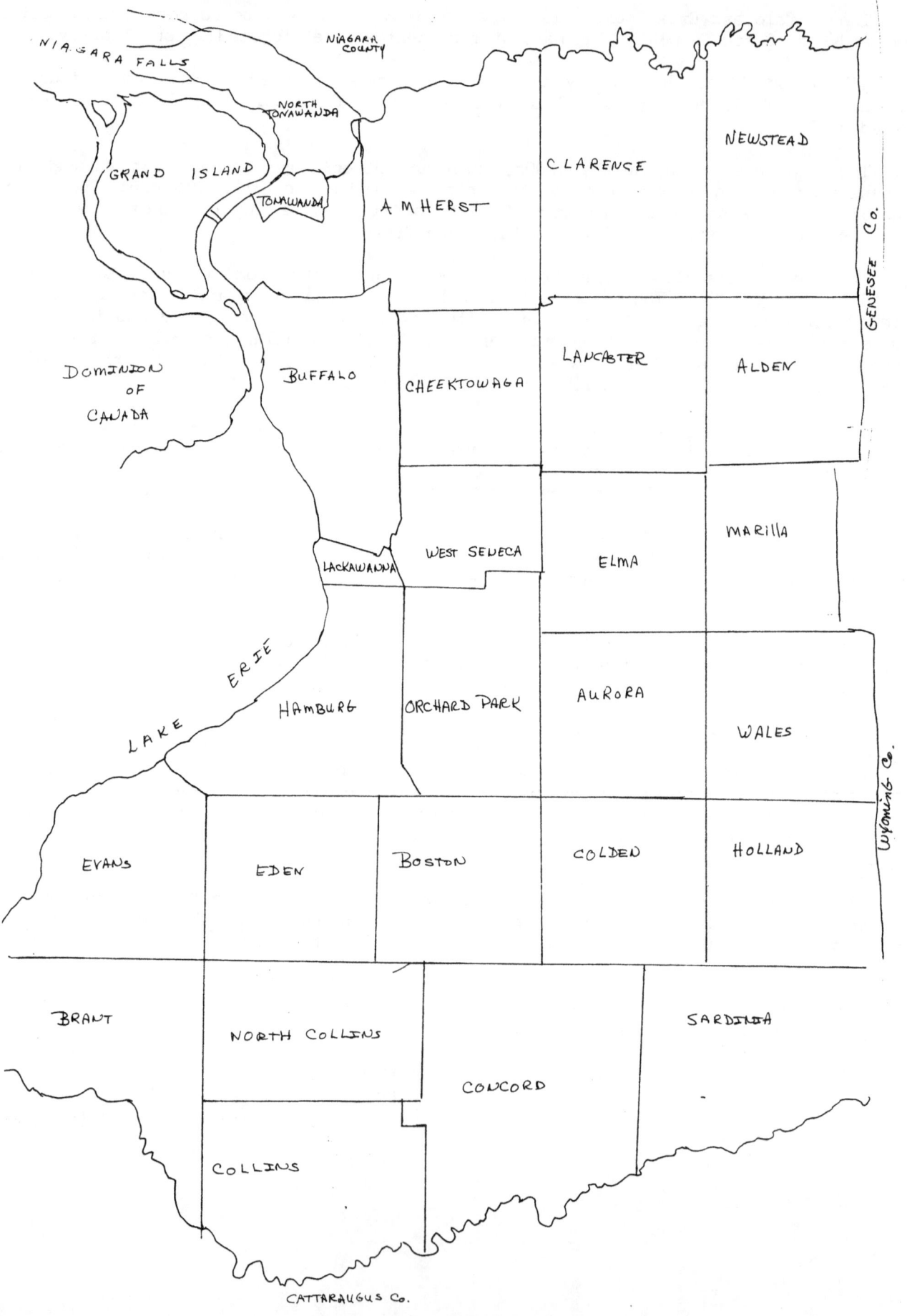

OBITUARY RECORDS OF FORMER RESIDENTS OF ERIE COUNTY, NY

Aarons, Aaron, April 16, 1871, age 67.
Abbey, Delia Jane, only dau. of Austin, Feb. 1879, age 23.
Abbey, Hermon A., Lancaster, NY, Sept. 5, 1879, age 25.
Abbott, Abram, Buffalo, Sept. 1, 1859, age 49.
Abbott, Annie, wife of James, Buffalo, Jan. 30, 1866, age 25.
Abbott, Caleb, Jan. 13, 1885, age 35.
Abbott, Caleb C., Colden, NY, Feb. 14, 1868, age 46 y, 7 m, 4 d.
Abbott, Charles Francis, March 10, 1873, age 30.
Abbott, Charles S., East Hamburgh, NY, Aug. 15, 1879.
Abbott, Chauncey, Hamburgh, NY, Nov. 23, 1834, age 36.
Abbott, Chauncey B., Hamburgh, Nov. 2, 1851, 20, at Springville, NY.
Abbott, Miss Eliza M., Abbotts's Corners, NY, March 5, 1855, age 20; in Oregon, IL.
Abbott, Elizabeth Frawley, Sept. 28, 1876, wife of James.
Abbott, Ella S., East Hamburgh, NY, Jan. 16, 1879, age 27.
Abbott, Evelyn C., wife of G. S., of Buffalo, Sept. 20, 1867, age 49, in Chicago.
Abbott, Franklin B., Buffalo, Aug. 20, 1840, age 29.
Abbott, George W., Hamburgh, NY, Sept. 20, 1845, age c. 38.
Abbott, Henry, East Hamburg, NY, June 16, 1879, age 84 y, 3 m.
Abbott, Margaret, Buffalo, October 15, 1847, age 67.
Abbott, Mrs. Prudence, Buffalo, late of Michigan City, Sept. 1855, age 56 in Chicago. See *Commercial Advertiser* of Sept. 7.
Abbott, Deacon Samuel, Hamburgh, NY, Oct. 2, 1846, age 68.
Abbott, Seth, Hamburgh, NY, June 8, 1831, age c. 63.
Abbott, Sophia, wife of Samuel, Aug. 16, 1838.
Abbott, Sophia, wife of Samuel, East Hamburgh, NY, Dec. 31, 1843, age 68.
Abbott, Susan, wife of Daniel, Hamburgh, NY, Sept. 9, 1829, age 60.
Abbott, Wm. W., Buffalo, 22 May 1864, age 45.
Abel, John H., March 18, 1875, accident; age 26 y, 11 m; taken to Rochester, NY.
Abell, Eliza Lee, wife of William H., March 21, 1868, age 48.
Abell, Elizabeth, wife of C., Sept. 29, 1879, age 35.
Abell, Eunice E., Feb. 20, 1875, taken to Fredonia.
Abell, Louise R., Oct. 11, 1869, 4th dau. of the late Thomas G., taken to Fredonia, NY.
Abell, Rhoda Hawks, wife of Col. Thomas G., Buffalo, Feb. 18, 1862; taken to Fredonia, NY.
Abell, Col. Thomas G., May 8, 1857, 66; taken to Fredonia, NY.
Abell, William O., April 1873, 25; eldest son of William H.; d. in Milan, TN; bur. in Buffalo.
Abernathy, Capt. Andrew, Oct. 9, 1877, age 47; drowned at Point au Pelee, Ontario. Shipwreck.
Abraham, George, June 18, 1879, drowned in Niagara River on April 19, age 24.
Abraham, Patrick, March 10, 1877, Co. Almshouse, age 70.
Abrahams, Abram, Buffalo, July 16, 1866, age 50.
Abrahams, Emma, Oct. 2, 1871, sister of Mrs. Hiram Extein.
Ackard, Mrs. Frances, Cheektowaga, NY, June 14, 1878, railroad accident.
Ackerman, Caroline, dau. of P. I., Cheektowaga, NY, Dec. 4, 1863, age 14 y, 8 m, 4 d.
Ackerman, Mary Elizabeth, wife of P.J., April 19, 1873, age 23 y, 1 m, 5 d.
Ackerman, Phillip Jacob, Cheektowaga, NY, April 8, 1872, age 65.
Ackerman, Rosana Fields, wife of Philip, Buffalo, Oct. 19, 1867, age 26; dau. of Robert Fields of Buffalo; d. in village of Webster.
Ackley, Marietta, sister of Mrs. E. Roberts, d. in Buffalo, 13 May 1859; taken to Rochester, NY.
Ackley, Richard, almshouse, March 24, 1879, age 52.
Ackley, Zebulon, Clarence, Jan. 1813, age 39.
Acton, Henry, Buffalo, Sept. 13, 1862, age 51.
Adair, Emma Edwards, formerly Mrs. Chadduck, March 9, 1872, age 37.
Adair, Robert, Buffalo, May 31, 1851, age 23.
Adams, Mr., Oct. 12, 1872, age 14.
Adams, Adeline A., Jan. 26, 1875, age 80.
Adams, Agnes, wife of John, Buffalo, Oct. 28, 1843, age 67.

Adams, Alexander of Scotland, res. Buffalo, Sept. 22, 1845, age 21 y, 1 m, 7 d.
Adams, Alma, widow of B. C. of Beloit, Buffalo, July 4, 1863, age 57. Dau. of Alvan Dodge of Buffalo.
Adams, Betsey, wife of John I., Buffalo, April 13, 1835, age 27, at Burlington Flats.
Adams, Charles A., Clarence, brother of Dr. N. H. (US Navy) and Dr. A. B. of Warsaw, Aug. 28, 1869.
Adams, Charles C., Dec. 31, 1874, age 34.
Adams, Charlotte, Buffalo, June 27, 1842, age 42; dau. of John Cooper of Washington, DC.
Adams, Mrs. Charlotte T., June 1873, in 63rd year; taken to North Adams, MA.
Adams, Mrs. Christiana, Buffalo, March 26, 1858, age 74 y, 8 d; of Perthshire, Scotland.
Adams, E. Stanley, formerly of Buffalo, Jan. 20, 1875, age 47.
Adams, Elijah C., formerly of Erie Co., Feb. 27, 1877, age 71 y, 3 m, 22 d. Died at Indian Bay, Monroe Co., AR.
Adams, Eliza H., wife of E. C., Cheektowaga, Feb. 15, 1841, age 28.
Adams, Eliza Jane, wife of Hon. W. H., June 12, 1855, age 58, at Lyons, NY.
Adams, Erasmus, East Aurora, NY, July 28, 1878, in 88th year.
Adams, Esther, wife of Asahel, Buffalo, Aug. 19, 1823, age 58.
Adams, Frances, wife of George, Sept. 17, 1874, age 20.
Adams, Frederick H., Jan., 1873, 24. Found dead. Taken to Angola.
Adams, Hannah, Buffalo, Nov. 5, 1861, age 70 y, 6 m.
Adams, Mrs. Harriet, April, 1874, age 80.
Adams, Hugh, late of Edin., Scotland, Buffalo, Machinist, Sept. 27, 1865, age 35.
Adams, Hiram, Buffalo, Aug. 18, 1864, age 61.
Adams, Dr. Isaac Newton, Sept. 19, 1847, age 27, formerly of Hinesburgh, VT.
Adams, Mrs. Jane M., formerly of Buffalo, Jan. 15, 1878, age 90 y, 7m. D. near Belleville, KS.
Adams, John, Oct. 7, 1864, age 56, in New York; bur. at Fort Plain, NY.
Adams, John, Sen., father of John, Jan. 28, 1845, age 71, in High St., Paisley, Scotland.
Adams, John Jr., Sept. 28, 1850, age 28, in Sacramento, CA.
Adams, Joseph, Jan. 28, 1840, age 74, in Collins, NY.
Adams, Joseph, June 4, 1863, age 70, at Mill Point, Ottawa Co., MI.
Adams, Mrs. Louisa, Evans, March 22, 1874, age 79; wife of Luther.
Adams, Mrs. Maria, March 6, 1880, age 78.
Adams, Mary, Aug. 31, 1877, age 29; wife of W. F.
Adams, Milan, Oct. 29, 1863, age 61.
Adams, Dr. N., Clarence, Surgeon, US Navy, Nov., 1869. Bur. in Clarence, NY, Nov. 30, 1869.
Adams, Nathaniel W., clerk in U.S. Treasury Dept., Dec. 24, 1851, age 29, in Washington, DC.
Adams, Nelson, Aug. 18, 1845, age 45.
Adams, Robert, Nov., 1871; sailor.
Adams, Susan, wife of Elijah, Cheektowaga, Feb. 25, 1861, age 41.
Adams, Mrs. Victoria, May 26, 1878.
Adams, Wm., Sept. 1, 1828, age 35.
Adams, Wm., Colden, NY, Oct. 25, 1835, age 40.
Adams, Wm. Henry, April 13, 1867, age 31.
Adamy, Benjamin, May 17, 1872, age 61.
Addington, Mrs. Almeda, Aurora, NY, Oct. 25, 1872, age 21 y, 10 m, 12 d.
Addington, Almeda, Aurora, NY, Sept. 17, 1848, age 51.
Addington, Hawxhurst, Potter's Corners, East Hamburgh, NY, Feb. 13, 1870, age 85. Brother of Isaac of Aurora and Samuel H. of Buffalo.
Addington, Isaac, Aurora, Sept. 29, 1870, age 75.
Addington, Samuel H., Jan. 23, 1864, age 72. Taken to Suspension Bridge.
Addison, Robert Jr., of London, England, Aug. 4, 1858, age 25, d. in New York.
Adkins, Lieut. Asahel, Dec. 1812, age 40, Swift's Regiment.
Adler, John, Aug. 11, 1879; dropped dead in street.
Adler, Joseph, March 20?, 1878, age 59 y, 7 m.
Adler, Max, Aug. 21, 1879, age 68 y, 4 m.
Adolph, George, Cheektowaga, NY, Dec. 2, 1872, age 42. Killed on railroad in Buffalo.
Aechner, Elizabeth, June 22, 1874, age 55.
Agard, Joshua, Concord, Sept. 1860, age 72.

Agen, Catharine, wife of James, Sept. 1814, age 40.
Agen, James, April 1815.
Agins, Euphemy, June 7, 1878, age 63 y, 8 m.
Agins, Florence Estelle, Aug. 13, 1873, age 19 y, 6 m; youngest dau. of David.
Agins, Marietta V., Dec. 17, 1876, age 30 y, 7 m.
Ahearn, Johanna, widow of Thomas, Feb. 11, 1878, age 78.
Ahern, P., Oct. 6, 1879; d. at Jefferson, TX, formerly of Buffalo.
Ahlheim, Katherine, wife of John, Feb. 20, 1879, age 29 y, 7 m.
Ainger, Mrs. Julia, Dec. 15, 1874, age 19 y, 4 m, 15 d.
Aiplie, John, Nov. 26, 1878.
Akely, George C., Brant, NY, Aug. 14, 1864, age 55.
Albee, Christina, July 23, 1879, age 79 y, 7 m, 9 d.
Alberger, Franklin A., Aug. 24, 1877, age 52 y, 6 m, 10 d.
Alberger, Job, Nov. 30, 1863, age 63.
Albert, Joseph, Hamburg, Nov. 1844, age 66.
Albertson, Jennie Atwater, wife of William F., Aug. 12, 1879, age 24.
Albrecht, Anton, June 28, 1879, age 51.
Albro, Mrs. Martha, mother of Mrs. John Benson, Jan. 4, 1862, age 75 y, 12 d.
Albro, Steven, Nov. 29, 1866, age 78.
Aldrich, Mrs. Annie D., West Concord, April 1860, age 19.
Aldrick, Henry B., Dec. 8, 1879, age 39 y, 18 d.
Aldrich, James, March 14, 1858, age 70, d. in Prescott, WI.
Aldrich, Newell, Boston, Dec. 21, 1879, age 59.
Alexander, Mrs., wife of Capt. S., April 20, 1850, age 26; d. in New Orleans.
Alford, William S., March 14, 1877, age 45.
Alger, Jane, widow of John, mother of Seth Clark, Aug. 27, 1867, age 75.
Allbury, Alice, wife of Robert, June 1, 1844, age 24.
Allen, Mrs. ---, wife of Horace, July 17, 1831.
Allen, Alexander 2nd, native of Scotland, Feb. 16, 1853, age 45.
Allen, Alexander, Oct. 20, 1877, age 47.
Allen, Mrs. Alice N. Smith, wife of George E., June 13, 1879, age 28y, 6 m, 2 d.
Allen, Anthony, Nov. 19, 1871, age 35.
Allen, Capt. Archiband, Dec. 1, 1840, age 40; in Lake commerce.
Allen, Caroline B., wife of Philo, June 24, 1845, age 21.
Allen, Catharine, wife of Capt. Levi, June 2, 1858, age 55.
Allen, Catherine, wife of John P., March 16, 1876, age 48.
Allen, Charles H., Oct. 14, 1851, age 38.
Allen, Charlotte Griswold, Feb. 21, 1877, age 64; wife of C.T.
Allen, Dr. E. G., formerly of Cleveland, March 16, 1876.
Allen, Edward B., son of George W., Dec. 6, 1863, age 20.
Allen, Eliza, widow of Capt. Archibald, Sept. 2, 1853, age 44.
Allen, Eliza Minerva, wife of William R., Nov. 11, 1838, age 28.
Allen, Mrs. Elizabeth, mother of Isaac Halloway, Nov. 18, 1862, age 76.
Allen, Miss Emily, June 7, 1842, age 23.
Allen, Mrs. Emily, formerly of Buffao, March 16, 1879, age 78.
Allen, Ethan, Wales, 1846, age 65. See *National Buffalo Pilot*, May 4, 1846.
Allen, Eunice, mother of Mrs. E. B. Forbush, June 28, 1861.
Allen, Fanny, wife of Stephen, Jan. 25, 1836, age 44.
Allen, George W., formerly of Buffalo, July 31, 1879, age 77.
Allen, Harding, son of Job of North Bedford, MA, Dec. 4, 1839, age 37, 9.
Allen, Miss Harriet, dau. of Levi, Nov. 26, 1856, age 21, 6.
Allen, Harriet E., widow of Gen. B., of Batavia, sister of E.B. Seymour of Buffalo, May 25, 1867, age 73.
Allen, Henry E., Nov. 29, 1865, age 46.
Allen, Hiram Pratt, son of Orlando, Oct. 14, 1859, age 24.
Allen, Horace of Springfield, MA, Nov. 30, 1838, age 44. Farmers Hotel.
Allen, Ira W., West Seneca, NY, formerly of Buffalo, Aug. 13, 1877, age 52.
Allen, Isaac, Collins, NY, June 8, 1879, age 85 y, 9 m, 12 d.
Allen, Jabez Jr., Aurora, NY, June 25, 1876, age 22.
Allen, James, M.D., Whites Corners, NY, Oct. 7, 1852, age 46.

Allen, James, March 13, 1878, age 53.
Allen, Jeremiah, b. 1765, d. 1851, bur. N. Ridoe [sic], Revolutionary Soldier.
Allen, John Gilbert, formerly of Buffalo, d. in Richmond, Province of Quebec, Jan. 12, 1875, age 41.
Allen, John H., March 8, 1879, age 25.
Allen, John Platt, son of George W., formerly of Buffalo, April 7, 1873, age 27 y, 10 m.
Allen, John T., father of George W., and Carlisle T., Aug. 17, 1857, age 80.
Allen, Joseph, Oct. 27, 1850, age 44. Died in Cincinnati.
Allen, Julia Wood, wife of Henry E., May 5, 1864, age 36.
Allen, Julius W., April 9, 1840, age 33.
Allen, King P., Hamburgh, NY, June 2, 1867, age 59.
Allen, Mrs. Lewis F., 1880
Allen, Lloyd, engineer of Steam Bunker Hill, May 4, 1847, age 26.
Allen, Louisa, Jan. 15, 1854, age 44.
Allen, Lucy, wife of John, Oct. 10, 1872, age 41.
Allen, Lydia G., wife of Jacob, formerly of Buffalo, Sept. 4, 1878, age 73.
Allen, Margaret Cleveland, wife of Lewis F., Sept. 13, 1879.
Allen, Marietta, wife of Crayton, Jan. 9, 1862, age 37.
Allen, Miss Mary, sister of George W., Oct. 31, 1838, age 26; d. in Johnstown, OH.
Allen, Miss Mary, June 2, 1845, age 21.
Allen, Miss Mary, Prospect Hill, Feb. 17, 1862, age 50.
Allen, Mary, wife of W. P., Hamburgh, Nov. 30, 1859; d. at New Albion, NY.
Allen, Mary Louisa, wife of George W., May 11, 1839, age 33.
Allen, Michael, tailor, Oct. 20, 1879, General Hospital (chloroform).
Allen, Orlando, Feb. 14, 1862, age 30. Born in Buffalo, died in Cairo, IL.
Allen, Orlando, husband of Marilla Adeline Pratt, Sept. 4, 1874, age 71.
Allen, Otis, Nov. 1860. Buried 17th.
Allen, Patience, Hamburgh, NY, Feb. 1813, age 45.
Allen, Philip Kissam, formerly of Buffalo?, Jan. 2, 1874, age 32 y, 5m, 19 d. Son of the late Charles H. D. in St. Louis, bur. in Buffalo.
Allen, Phineas, Alden, July 11, 1858, age 77.
Allen, Rebecca, wife of Dr. James, White's Corners, NY, Sept. 9, 1852, age 42.
Allen, Richard C., eldest son of Lewis F., Black Rock, NY, Dec. 15, 1855, age 24.
Allen, Richard L., formerly of Buffalo, d. in Stockholm, Sweden 1869; brother of Hon. Lewis F.
Allen, Mrs. Sally, mother of Henry E., May 4, 1864, age 81.
Allen, Mrs. Sally, Nov. 23, 1872.
Allen, Sarah, mother of Orlando and Charles H., Feb. 6, 1847, age 68.
Allen, Silas, formerly of Buffalo, d. at Kalamazoo, MI, brother of Levi; Jan. 19, 1873, age 65.
Allen, Silas T., master of Schooner *Beaupre*, July 21, 1843, age 24.
Allen, Sophronia, formerly of Buffalo, d. at Rock Stream, Yates Co., NY, wife of Ralph, Aug. 29, 1868.
Allen, Thomas Gilchrist, Nov. 18, 1857, age 26; d. in Detroit, buried in Buffalo.
Allen, Walter I., March 22, 1879, age 70.
Allen, William F. Jr., of Cleveland, Aug. 1, 1849, age 36.
Allen, Zadoc G., Nov. 8, 1874, age 64; taken to East Hamburgh, NY.
Allinder, Mrs. Ann, North Buffalo, Dec. 1873, in 44th y.
Allis, Raphael, Austrian sailor, accidently killed, Dec. 2, 1873, age 33.
Allison, Mrs. Elizabeth, April 24, 1870, age 85.
Allison, Rev. George M., Oct. 22, 1872, age 53.
Allison, Peter, Jan. 1832, age 33.
Allman, Francis, April 17, 1859, age 39.
Allman, George F., Oct. 27, 1870, age 43.
Allman, John, Nov. 17, 1879, age 57.
Allmendinger, Fanny, wife of Charles F., March 11, 1857, age 37.
Almy, Mrs. Mary, mother-in-law of Samuel A. Bigelow, Sept. 30, 1857, age 81. Taken to Pavilion Center.
Alport, Isabella Musson, wife of E.S., April 5, 1869, age 44; taken to Toronto, Ontario.
Alston, Henry, sailor, Aug. 21, 1873, age c. 45.

Altman, Adelaide, wife of Jacob, Feb. 13, 1863, age 43.
Alward, Rev. Henry C., formerly of Buffalo, d. at Battle Creek, MI Feb. 9, 1874, age 43.
Amann, Maggie, dau. of Christine, May 10, 1876, age 21.
Ambrose, John, Dec. 2, 1871, age 54.
Ambrose, Mary, Dec. 25, 1875, age 35.
Ambrose, Mrs. Odelia, April 25, 1874, age 88 y, 7 m, 4 d.
Amerman, Albert Livingston, Sept. 13, 1879, age 19.
Ames, Ashley, Angola, sailor, lost overboard, Sept. 17, 1871.
Amidon, Nelson, May 22, 1865, age 58. Died in Sparta, MI.
Amlah, John, March 5, 1878, age 46.
Amsden, Mary Pitts, Aug. 12, 1873, age 37 y 9 m; wife of Ira R.
Amsdill, Abner, Hamburg, Aug. 11, 1850, age 90 y, 5 d. Rev. soldier.
Anderle, Francis, musician, Dec. 1, 1877, age 42.
Anderson, Alexander, Akron, Aug. 22, 1871, age 34.
Anderson, Alexander S., Dec. 16, 1871, age 56. Taken to Greenwood Cemetery.
Anderson, Capt. Andrew, Sept. 17, 1868, d. at Galveston, TX.
Anderson, Carl F., Feb. 6, 1874, age 29.
Anderson, Caroline, wife of Cyrus H., Mar. 7, 1837, age 33.
Anderson, Charles, June 9, 1875, age 41 y, 4 m.
Anderson, Clara C., Co. Almshouse, Oct. 28, 1876, age 46.
Anderson, Mrs. Eliza, mother of H. S., May 4, 1867, age 80. Taken to Brooklyn.
Anderson, Miss Elizabeth, Sept. 10, 1864, age 29; d. in Waterford, PA, bur. in Buffalo.
Anderson, Hannah (colored), Aug. 14, 1879, age 102, Erie Co. Almshouse.
Anderson, James, father of Mrs. Thos. Carr, Aug. 27, 1864, age 80.
Anderson, Capt. James, Feb. 18, 1865, age 63.
Anderson, John, Black Rock, Aug. 26, 1854, age 56.
Anderson, John, July 12, 1879, age 105, Co. Almshouse.
Anderson, John H., son of James, Jan. 6, 1850, age 25.
Anderson, Jonas, Sept. 28, 1879, age 31, almshouse.
Anderson, Maria, wife of Cyrus K., Sept. 10, 1839, age 29.
Anderson, Marian C., July 23, 1877, age 53.
Anderson, Rebecca Jones, wife of Robert H., Jan. 29, 1876, age 38 y, 9 m.
Anderson, Capt. Robert, Jan. 30, 1879, age 58.
Anderson, Mrs. Sarah, Newstead, NY, June 7, 1835, age 80.
Anderson, Sarah Dickson, wife of James, Aug. 14, 1873, age 60.
Anding, Amelia Buhler, wife of Adam, March 25, 1869, age 22.
Andre, Azuba, wife of William, Boston, NY, Mar. 24, 1847.
Andre, William, County Clerk, Oct. 14, 1861, age 68.
Andrews, Andrew, died in London, England, April 30, 1866. See *Com. Adv.* June 23, 1866.
Andrews, Charles, Jan. 23, 1868, age 43.
Andrews, D. B. of Elyria, OH, April 4, 1849.
Andrews, David B., Oct. 18, 1860, age 40.
Andrews, Elisha, of Otsego Co., NY, May 1814, age 56.
Andrews, Elizabeth, widow of R., Aug. 14, 1879, age 83.
Andrews, Ellen, Sept. 23, 1875, sister of Mrs. H. P. Dudley.
Andrews, George H., April 3, 1867, age 28.
Andrews, Josiah, Sardinia, NY, Nov. 21, 1876, age 90.
Andrews, Maria Phillips, wife of William, H., April 24, 1856. Taken to Albany.
Andrews, Marvin C., July, 1877, age 53.
Andrews, R., July 14, 1868, age 67 y, 11 m, 25 d.
Andrews, Richard, father of H. P. Dudley, Sept. 8, 1864.
Andrews, Robert F., July 14, 1868, age 68.
Andrews, Capt. S. C., April 1, 1865, age 43; taken to Detroit.
Andrews, Susan, widow of Richard, Dec. 22, 1865, age 76.
Andrews, Mrs., wife of William A., Jan. 8, 1839, age 29.
Angles, Daniel, April 23, 1860, age 85.
Anguish, John, Dec. 1812, age 21.
Annis, Ezakiel, Dec. 17, 1865, age 68 y, 19 d.
Annowski, John Frederick, April 4, 1872, age c. 80.
Ansdell, Robert, Hamburgh, NY, March 5, 1841, age 52.

Ansley, Mrs. Mary E., dau. of late Albertus L. Lynde, March 19, 1866, age 30; d. at Augustus, GA.
Ansted, Louis, Nov. 8, 1876, age 36.
Ansteth, Bertha Louisa Schultz, wife of M., Lancaster, March 1, 1875, age 31; bur. in Buffalo.
Ansteth, George, March 23, 1878, age 68.
Appleby, Capt. James, Oct. 22, 1858, age 76.
Appleby, Mary, wife of James, Sept. 24, 1846, age 57.
Archer, Abel, Sept. 24, 1860, age 51.
Arey, Isabel Caroline, formerly of Buffalo, dau. of Rev. Dr. Charles Arey, Oct. 23, 1877, age 22 y, 3 m; d. in Salem MA.
Argus, George, March 8, 1876, age 56 y, 10 m, 16 d.
Argus, George, Nov. 24, 1878, age 41.
Argus, Louisa, July 17, 1872, age 22.
Argus, Margaret, wife of Joseph, Dec. 23, 1878, age 33 y, 5 m, 16 d.
Arkenburgh, Mrs. Jane A., May 25, 1844, age 25.
Armbruster, Martin M., July 5, 1879, age 32 y, 7 m.
Armitage, David, Cheektowaga, NY, formerly of Yorkshire, England, March 3, 1870, in 64th year.
Armitage, Isaac, Toll-gate keeper, April 9, 1879, age 68.
Armitage, Lydia, wife of James, May 2, 1867, age 20.
Arms, Jeanette E., wife of Richard A., June 7, 1831, age 23.
Arms, Richard, March 1862. Buried March 12.
Arms, William C., formerly of Buffalo, second son of the late Richard of Buffalo, Sept. 18, 1873 in 31st year; d. in Hong Kong China.
Armstrong, Adaline Jane, wife of Charles, March 13, 1844, age 25.
Armstrong, Alonzo, Oct. 29, 1875, age 45.
Armstrong, Alonzo, Evans, Aug. 4, 1879, age 69 y, 11 m, 10 d.
Armstrong, Ann, wife of Christopher, Dec. 29, 1858, age 28.
Armstrong, Mrs. Ann, Feb. 9, 1879, age 78.
Armstrong, B., Jan. 10, 1849, age 63 y. 9 m.
Armstrong, Charles, March 14, 1863, age 48.
Armstrong, James Albert, formerly of Buffalo, March 10, 1874, age 68 y, 3 m, 1 d; d. in Detroit, MI.
Armstrong, John W., May 21, 1864, age 72.
Armstrong, Mary A., wife of Hiram I., Aug. 1, 1866, age 26.
Armstrong, Nancy, dau. of William H. of Lockport, March 29, 1869, age 56; taken to Lockport, NY.
Armstrong, Richard V., Feb. 7, 1870, age 25.
Armstrong, Sally, wife of Capt. B., Aug. 18, 1843, age 58 y 4 m.
Armstrong, Saloma, mother of Charles B., Feb., 1873, age 84.
Armstrong, Thomas A., July 25, 1861, age 25.
Armstrong, William C., formerly of Buffalo, Aug. 22, 1879; d. at Luray, MO.
Arnholt, Henry, April, 1878, age 58.
Arnold, Aldrich, Hamburgh, NY, June 21, 1823, age 50.
Arnold, Ellen J. Kerr, wife of George, Nov. 3, 1878, in 29th y.
Arnold, Estella A., wife of Daniel, July 27, 1879, age 54.
Arnold, John, Dec. 13, 1879, age 80.
Arnold, Julia B., dau. of the late W. W., Aug. 2, 1875.
Arnold, Louisa C., wife of Jacob, Dec. 13, 1841, age 33.
Arnold, Millie A., dau. of the late William W., July 28, 1870, age 23.
Arnold, Ruth, wife of Oliver H., East Hamburgh, NY, Sept. 21, 1853, age 49.
Arnold, Susanah, wife of Lewis, Hamburgh, Dec. 10, 1822, age 24.
Arnold, William W., Feb. 13, 1869, in 47th y; taken to Victor, NY.
Arrowsmith, Nicholas, Sept. 1814, age 24.
Ash, Robert, Feb. 4, 1870; d. in Hamilton, Ontario, bur. in Buffalo.
Ashfield, Mrs. Ann, formerly of Buffalo, June 2, 1870, age 62; d. at Syracuse, NY.
Ashley, James, Sept. 4, 1834, age 21.
Ashley, Jane, wife of William M., Nov. 5, 1857, age 38; d. at Erie, PA.
Ashley, Mrs. R., aunt of Mrs. A. Van Slyke, Nov. 24, 1870.

Ashley, Mrs. Dorothy, Feb. 13, 1873, age 86.
Ashman, Amaziah, Concord, June 13, 1861, age 75 y, 10 m.
Ashton, Mrs. Elizabeth, June 25, 1867, age 66.
Ashton, Isaac, July 30, 1867, age 54.
Ashton, James, Dec. 28, 1847, age 45.
Aspell, Katie, Oct. 13, 1878, age 24 y. 4 m.
Athearn, Cyrus, Sept. 9, 1854, age 63; d. in Charlestown, MA.
Athearn, Mrs. Lydia S., formerly of Buffalo, March 19, 1877, age 80 y, 8 m.
Atkins, Anna, widow of Samuel, Dec. 1822, age 57.
Atkins, Joel, Oct. 26, 1852, age 43 y, 10 m.
Atkins, Mary, widow of Asahel, Dec. 4, 1821, age 34.
Atkins, Samuel, Dec. 6, 1812, age 50.
Atkins, Samuel R., July 24, 1839, age 42; b. Aug. 29, 1797 at Fort Stanwix, NY.
Atkins, Mrs. Thomas I., March 26, 1826.
Atkins, Thomas I., Ransom's Grove, Clarence, NY, Aug. 6, 1831, age 50.
Atkins, Welthy, widow of Samuel R., mother of Barton, Mrs. I. B. Scott and E. E. Clark, April 20, 1856, age 63.
Atkins, Samuel R., born Aug. 29, 1797 at Fort Stanwix, NY, July 24, 1839, age 42.
Atkinson, Thomas, Sept. 18, 1879, age 22.
Atloff (Adloff, Adolff), John, Elma, April 2, 1878. Murdered by Carl Mauke, who was executed May 14, 1880.
Atterbury, Samuel, East Hamburgh, NY, Sept. 4, 1874, age c. 50.
Attherton, Samuel, May 26, 1876, age 23 y, 10 m, 5 d.
Atwater, Elizabeth Emerson, wife of S. T., formerly of Buffalo, res. in Chicago. D. in Buffalo, April 11, 1878 in 66th year.
Atwater, Henry C., died in New Haven, CT, July 8, 1845, age 39.
Atwater, Louisa I., Principal of School No. 4, Oct. 1861, age 40. Taken to Bergen.
Atwater, Panthea, widow of Moses of Canandaigua, March 23, 1850, age 84.
Atwood, Aaron, Jr., P.M., Evans, July 13, 1843, age 35.
Atwood, Elizabeth M., wife of Henry, Lancaster, NY, Aug. 13, 1869.
Ault, Minerva E., wife of James, May 26, 1852, age 29.
Aumock, Mary E., wife of Dr. A. P., Aug. 15, 1848, age 23.
Auberry, Mrs. Magdalena, Sept. 17, 1873, age 81.
Auch, Frederick, June 23, 1877, age 85; accident.
Auchinleck, Alexander, July 8, 1875; d. at Key West, FL.
Ault, Minerva E., dau. of James R., May 24, 1872, age 20 y, 7 d.
Aurere, Alfred F., May, 1877, age 46; d. at St. Catherines, Ontario; bur. in Buffalo.
Austin, Anna Lapham, widow of Benjamin H., Feb. 4, 1876, age 76 y, 6 m, 11 d.
Austin, Benjamin H., July 13, 1874, age 75 y, 5 m, 10 d.
Austin, Deacon Edmund, July 22, 1858, age 61.
Austin, Elizabeth, wife of John, April 24, 1879, age 25.
Austin, George H., Eng. of Propellor *Montezuma*, Aug. 12, 1849, age 30.
Austin, Hiram E., Springville, Oct. 1, 1866, age 34.
Austin, Mrs. Mary, Sept. 12, 1879, age 69 y, 2 m, 5 d.
Austin, Perry, Tonawanda, NY, April 14, 1853.
Austin, Phebe, wife of Seth, Feb. 3, 1863, age 71.
Austin, Sarah Jane, eldest dau. of Benj. H., Nov. 14, 1857, age 20 y, 9 m, 25 d.
Austin, Stephen G., June 19, 1872, age 81.
Austin, William A., formerly of Buffalo?, April 3, 1878, age 67; d. at North Melbourne.
Averel, Zerah, Sept. 1828, age 36.
Averell, Ann B., wife of Capt. James M., Jan., 1869, age 68.
Averill, Capt. James M., Jan. 14, 1869.
Averill, Capt. James M., Oct. 13, 1873, age 66.
Avery, Mrs. Caroline, formerly of East Hamburgh, NY, March 6, 1872, age 50; d. at Rockford, IL.
Avery, Catharine, wife of George, June 17, 1873, age 68.
Avery, Ella D., March 2, 1880, age 25.
Avery, George, May 11, 1876, age 76 y, 8 m.
Avery, George W., April 4, 1861, age 30.
Avery, George W., May 16, 1879, age 50. Found drowned May 18, missing since 16th.

Avery, Park, North Collins, Dec. 15, 1867, age 69 y, 7 m, 24 d.
Avery, Sarah W., wife of C. L., sister-in-law of Mrs. S. S. Fish, formerly of Buffalo, Sept. 29, 1869; d. in Brooklyn.
Avery, Thomas Sr., March 20, 1872, age 56.
Ayatt or Hyatt, Charles, from Sherbrook, L.C., Nov. 19, 1850, age 49.
Ayer, George, M.D., Dec. 7, 1877, age 56.
Ayer, Corporal Ira of 116 Reg. N.Y. V., East Hamburgh, NY, Sept. 15, 1863, age 23 y, 6m.
Ayer, Captain James, of 116 Reg. N.Y. V., Evans, NY, May 22, 1863, age 49 y, 9m.
Ayer, Julia M., wife of Col. Ira, Evans, NY, Aug. 1861, age 53.
Ayer, Putnam, East Hamburg, NY, March 20, 1870, age 63.
Ayer, Richard, Boston, NY, Jan. 11, 1858, age 25.
Ayer, Sophronia, widow of Charles, Boston, NY, Aug. 1, 1863, age 48.
Ayers, Mary, wife of George B., formerly of Buffalo, Feb. 1, 1878; d. in Philadelphia.
Ayetskey, Chas. Henry, only son of Mrs. Anna E. Wing, May 23, 1862, age 20. Killed in front of Richmond.
Aykroyd, Edward, Aug. 16, 1866, age 29.
Aylesworth, Mrs. Clarissa, March 21, 1837, age 44. Dau. of late Benj. Hodge.
Aylsworth, Lina, 2nd dau. of George, Clarence, NY, Feb. 4, 1874, age 23.
Aylsworth, William of Columbia Co., NY, Clarence, Sept. 1826, age 42.
Aylworth, Hazard D., Wales, Jan. 26, 1844, age 60.
Ayrault, Jas. Nicholas, son of Nicholas of Geneva, NY, Aug. 15, 1845, age 25.
Ayres, Cordelia M., wife of William B., Aug. 13, 1854, age 33 y, 8 m.

Baade, Louisa A., wife of William F., eldest dau. of H. C. Persch, Feb. 16, 1871, age 26 y, 1 m.
Baade, William F., June 4, 1877, age 44.
Babbet, ---, Revolutionary soldier, Nov. 4, 1849, age 82.
Babcock, Alfred C., Dec. 22, 1877 age 30.
Babcock, Christopher, Feb. 25, 1875, age 61.
Babcock, Miss Emily L., June 1, 1847, age 23.
Babcock, Hon. George R., Sept. 22, 1876, age 70.
Babcock, Mrs. George R., 1877.
Babcock, Heman P., M.D., of Oakland, CA, formerly of Buffalo, son of the late George R., Dec. 27, 1878, age 38. D. & bur. in Buffalo.
Babcock, James, Cheektowaga, Dec. 28, 1858, age 75; bur. in Buffalo.
Babcock, Jane M., wife of John D., April 5, 1847, age 59.
Babcock, Lois, widow of James, Cheektowaga, NY, Oct. 15, 1871, age 81; bur. in Buffalo.
Babcock, Mary Potter, widow of George R., Sept. 20, 1877, age 62.
Babcock, Deacon Orrin, Eden, NY, Aug. 15, 1872, age 65.
Bachelder, Enoch W., Aug. 3, 1870, age 72.
Bachert, Jacob, firm of Bachert Bros., June 1872.
Bachman, Josephine, dau. of Adam, Sept. 10, 1877, age 24 y, 3 m, 24 d.
Bachmane, Peter, Alden, March 1, 1872, age 36.
Backman, Charles O., May 19, 1873, d. at Detroit, MI.
Backus, Jennie, wife of D.C., Dec. 8, 1873, age 27; d. at Petrolia, Butler Co., PA.
Backus, Julia, Sept. 30, 1879, age 76.
Bacon, Agnes E., wife of Charles E. and oldest dau. of C. F. S.
Bacon, Amos, father of Mrs. A. S. Kingsley, Feb. 9, 1865, age 87 y, 3 m, 18d.
Bacon, Augustus P., youngest son of Henry, Sept. 27, 1861, age 28; d. at Saratoga Springs, NY.
Bacon, Mrs. Catharine, April 8, 1875, age 19.
Bacon, David F., Alden, June 2, 1871, age 65.
Bacon, Henry, formerly of Buffalo, father of Charles E., May 15, 1874, age 84; d. at Saratoga Springs, NY.
Bacon, Mrs. Henry, formerly of Buffalo, Nov. 14, 1874, age 73; d. at Minneapolis, MN.
Bacon, Deacon Joshua, Holland, NY, May 5, 1828, age 69.
Bacon, William H. of Williamsburgh, NY, Aug. 15, 1866; d. in Chicago.
Badger, Mrs. Hannah, Lancaster, NY, April 12, 1852, age 37.
Badus, Frederick, at Co. Almshouse, May 12, 1877, age 62.
Baecher, Joseph, Jan. 7, 1879, age 50 y, 9 m, 28 d.

Baeher, Henry O., formerly of Buffalo, April 3, 1878, age 61; d. at Syracuse.
Baer, John, April 1, 1878, age 41.
Baethig, Dr. Henry, Dec. 5, 1871, age 62.
Baetzhold, Esther, wife of August, Feb. 24, 1869, age 38.
Bagley, George W., Oct. 31, 1867, age 27.
Bagnall, Capt. Benj., June 13, 1859, age 46; born in Plymouth, MA.
Bagnall, Harriet Newell, wife of Samuel, Oct. 14, 1866, age 50 y, 10 m.
Bagnall, Nellie M., dau. of the late Benjamin, Aug. 24, 1878, age 37 y, 11 m, 9 d.
Bagnall, Samuel W., Feb. 26, 1869, age 53 y, 7 m.
Bailey, Alonzo T., Sept. 6, 1876, age 37 y, 6 m, 26 d.
Bailey, David C., Jan. 19, 1841, age 25; d. in Fayette, MS.
Bailey, Dr. Dyer, ? Hamburgh, NY, Aug. 28, 1837, age 29.
Bailey, Mrs. Elizabeth (widow), March 16, 1873, aged c. 45.
Bailey, Frances C., wife of Rev. George W., Nov. 8, 1880, age 51 y, 2 m.
Baily, Freeman, Boston, NY, Nov. 18, 1862, age 65.
Bailey, Capt. Gilbert, Holland, NY, Jan. 13, 1852, age 59.
Bailey, Gordon, April 11, 1876, age 83.
Bailey, Joshua, March 24, 1853, age 40.
Bailey, Josiah B., March 26, 1876, age 64.
Bailey, Julia A., widow of Samuel, Lancaster, NY, Nov. 10, 1874, age 39.
Bailey, Lettice A., Sardinia, wife of Horace, Nov. 27, 1873, age 48.
Bailey, Miss Lois, Clarence, NY, March 18, 1817, age 23.
Bailey, Miss Maggie, Boston, NY, May 4, 1866, age 27.
Bailey, Mrs. Mary P., widow of Gordon, Oct. 4, 1880, age 88.
Bailey, Samuel, Lancaster, Sept. 1, 1874, age 51 y, 2 m; suicide.
Bailey, William, Nov. 7, 1860, age 56.
Bain, Edwin, formerly of Buffalo, March 25, 1872, age 36; d. at Cheltenham, England.
Bain, James, at Co. Almshouse, Aug. 1, 1878, age 71.
Bain, Louisa McPherson, wife of Alexander, July 9, 1852, of Wick, Scotland.
Bain, Miss Lucy E., April 14, 1865, age 27 y, 9 m, 14 d.
Bain, Mrs. Lucy Lane, Oct. 9, 1878, age 87 y, 6 m, 11 d.
Bain, Mrs. Mary, Sept. 1, 1878, age 49; drowned.
Bain, William, Capt. of Schooner *Onondaga*, Sept. 9, 1875; drowned at Chicago in the gale wrecking his vessel.
Bain, William, Sept. 5, 1877, age 33; colored. Drowned, deck-hand on the Propeller *China*.
Baird, Capt. Billy, oldest settler of Buffalo at time of death; July 29, 1856.
Baken, Hannora, Feb. 28, 1879, age 38 y, 10 m.
Baker, ---, Hamburg, Dec. 30, 1813. Killed at battle of Black Rock.
Baker, Midshipman Albert L. Jr., U.S. Navy, March 3, 1864, age 20.
Baker, Hon. Albert L., May 22, 1873, in 58th year.
Baker, Annie M. Watson, wife of William H., Dec. 3, 1873, age 35.
Baker, Artemus, brother of Moses Seneca, Nov. 29, 1859, age 57.
Baker, Bethia, wife of Capt. Theophilus, Eden, NY, May 13, 1836, age 86.
Baker, C. Lasvia, East Aurora, NY, March 29, 1875, age 50; wife of Rev. C. S.
Baker, Mrs. Catherine, April 8, 1875, age 19.
Baker, Charles Everett, only son of Darius O., formerly of Buffalo, May 1, 1872, age 25 y, 10 d; d. at Auburn, NY.
Baker, Sergeant Chas. H., 112 Reg. N.Y.S.V., June 4, 1864, age 22. Killed at Cold Harbor.
Baker, Charles H., M.D., Sept. 1, 1878, age 61.
Baker, Clifford A., formerly of Buffalo, March 8, 1879, age 48; d. in Chicago, bur. in Buffalo.
Baker, Cynthia M., wife of Isaac E., Hamburgh, NY, March 28, 1849, age 36.
Baker, Daniel, Potters Corners, East Hamburgh, NY, Dec. 26, 1874, age 66.
Baker, Darius O., formerly of Buffalo, July 12, 1873, age 57 y, 5 m, 12 d; d. in Auburn, NY.
Baker, Delana, wife of Chauncey, Newstead, NY, May 13, 1857, age 31.
Baker, Diana, May 13, 1879, age 58 y, 10 m.
Baker, Dorcas, wife of Moses, Nov. 3, 1846, age 51.
Baker, Edmond, son of Moses, July 26, 1849, age 26.
Baker, Edward B., East Hamburg, Dec. 20, 1862, age 47.

Baker, Eleanor, wife of Obadiah, dau. of Milton Bull, May 2, 1854, age 23.
Baker, Elisha D., Nov. 24, 1842, age 24; bur. in Hamburgh, NY.
Baker, Elizabeth, wife of Elisha, E. Hamburgh, NY, Feb. 20, 1838, age 63.
Baker, Elizabeth, wife of Freeman, West Falls, May 14, 1861, age 30 y, 3 m, 16d.
Baker, Elizabeth, wife of Isaac, Hamburgh, Mar. 26, 1833, age 26.
Baker, Elizabeth, wife of William, July 14, 1872, age 25.
Baker, Elizabeth, Aug. 26, 1876, age 40.
Baker, Mrs. Elizabeth, mother of Mrs. C.F. Miller, March 11, 1878, age 83.
Baker, Elizabeth A., wife of Alfred, June 28, 1874, age 20.
Baker, Mrs. Elvira, East Aurora, Dec. 2, 1878, age 68.
Baker, Emily, wife of S. O., dau. of F. Shuster, Dec. 28, 1865, age 27.
Baker, Emily Earl, wife of George P., Jan. 13, 1860, age 24; d. at Water Valley.
Baker, Emma, wife of James H., Dec. 11, 1880, age 39.
Baker, Florence L., wife of Clifford A., May 16, 1872, age 25.
Baker, Francis Mary, April 1861.
Baker, Frederick, June 5, 1857, age 29.
Baker, Gaius P. or Garris P., W. Hamburgh, Feb. 28, 1870, age 72.
Baker, Hannah, wife of William H., Nov. 3, 1871, age 45.
Baker, Henry L., West Aurora, NY, Aug. 25, 1838, age 39.
Baker, James M., son of Albert L., March 8, 1872, age 34.
Baker, Jane, Potter's Corners, April 14, 1879, age 70; suicide.
Baker, Mrs. Jane, Aug. 10, 1880, age 80; bur. at South Yarmouth, MA.
Baker, John, Sept. 10, 1868, age 62.
Baker, John P., 86 Reg. N.Y.S.V., Alden, Oct. 27, 1864, age 28.
Baker, John S., son of Dr. Chas. H. Collins, Mar. 11, 1862, age 18. Died in Military Hospital at Frederick, MD.
Baker, M. Lafayette, son of Moses, Jan. 12, 1847, age 22. Drowned off Patagonia, from whaling ship *Canton*. Sailed from New Bedford Aug. 17, 1846.
Baker, Leander, Jan. 11, 1847, age 30.
Baker, Levi, Dec. 1818, age 40.
Baker, Lydia, Feb. 7, 1866, age 58.
Baker, Magdalena, widow of Daniel, Jan. 30, 1876, age 63.
Baker, Margaret, wife of Israel, Hamburgh, NY, April 20, 1835, age 45.
Baker, Margaret, wife of William, July 20, 1872, age 61.
Baker, Margaret Louisa, June 12, 1873, age 23 y, 5 m, 18 d; taken to Belleville, Ont.
Baker, Martin, Jan. 31, 1860, age 27.
Baker, Miss Mary, Feb. 15, 1862, age 30; d. in Chicago.
Baker, Mary A., March 7, 1870, age 64.
Baker, Mary Ann, wife of Darius O., March 9, 1838, age 20. Formerly of St. Johns, New Brunswick. Dau. of Hiram Smith.
Baker, Mary Frances, youngest dau. of Geo. W., April 27, 1861, age 21y, 11 m.
Baker, Mary Louisa, wife of Clifford A., July 2, 1867, dau. of W. Ward Wheeler of Detroit.
Baker, Moses, Sept. 3, 1865, age 70 y, 1 m, 12 d.
Baker, Phila Putnam, wife of George W., Aug. 31, 1875, age 75.
Baker, Phoebe A., wife of George L., July 22, 1879, age 44.
Baker, Randall, April 26, 1843, age 73.
Baker, Sarah E., Nov. 13, 1866, age 22.
Baker, Sarah H., wife of Isaac, formerly of East Hamburgh, NY, May 14, 1877.
Baker, Capt. Theophilus, Rev. Patriot, Eden, April 14, 1838, age 90. Native of Yarmouth, Barnstable Co., MA.
Baker, Thomas H., laborer, Nov. 13, 1879; sudden death, age 40.
Baker, William, April 5, 1853, age 32.
Baker, William, March 20, 1876, age 24 y, 6 m, 2 d.
Balcam, Mary M., wife of Vine, Feb. 4, 1865, age 39, of Kendall, Orleans Co., NY.
Balch, Charles, son of Dan, Aug. 7, 1845, age 26, of Newburyport, MA.
Balch, Mrs. Mary Ann C., July 23, 1829, age 23.
Balcom, Mrs. Abigail, Dec. 2, 1862, age 79.
Balcom, James Alonzo, oldest son of Abijah W., May 24, 1862, age 22 y, 5 m, 5 d; d. at Ellery Center, Chautauqua, NY.

Balcom, Mr. P., father of Philo A., Hamburgh, NY, March 18, 1852, age 78. Revolutionary soldier.
Balcom, Philo A., May 4, 1879, age 72.
Baldauf, John, a German, March 8, 1874, age 69.
Baldwin, Charles S., firm of Maynard and Baldwin, Feb. 21, 1851, age 40.
Baldwin, David Newstead, Dec. 21, 1849, age 24.
Baldwin, David, Buffalo, May 24, 1859, age 42.
Baldwin, Daniel, March 6, 1869; age 60.
Baldwin, George L., Hamburg merchant, May 10, 1826, age 26.
Baldwin, Hannah I., wife of C. H., Town Line, July 2, 1851, age 29.
Baldwin, Henry D., Aug. 31, 1861, age 33.
Baldwin, Isaac, April 9, 1876, age 99.
Baldwin, Jennie A., wife of Wm. M., July 8, 1859, age 23 y, 7 m. Only child of J. H. Rutterfield of Buffalo; d. in Newark, NJ.
Baldwin, L., Newstead, Jan. 25, 1875, age 77.
Baldwin, Lucy Caroline, wife of Daniel, Jan. 28, 1846, age 35.
Baldwin, Mary Augusta, Jan. 21, 1843, age 20.
Baldwin, Nancy, wife of Isaac, May 3, 1875, age 86.
Baldwin, Rachel, wife of Capt. Ira, Dec. 3, 1848, age 52, of Ithaca, NY.
Baldwin, William, May 10, 1877, age 64.
Baldy, Charlotte, only dau. of C. M., Aug. 25, 1865, age 24 y, 10 m, 25 d; d. in Hudson City, NJ.
Baldy, Christopher M., May 9, 1870, age 58.
Baldy, Mrs. Marietta, Aug. 24, 1873, age 57.
Baldy, Mary Ann, dau. of Wm., Feb. 21, 1852, age 23.
Baldy, Mary Ann, wife of Wm., Nov. 23, 1854, age 44.
Baldy, William, June 10, 1860, age 51.
Bale, Lois Loton, wife of George T., May 2, 1867, age 20.
Baley, Nathan, Clarence, NY, July 25, 1821, age 21.
Balfour, Agnes, widow of William, mother of Mrs. Wm. Ferguson, Nov. 4, 1869, age 89.
Ball, Ashley H., formerly of Buffalo, Jan. 1879; d. at Portland, OR.
Ball, John N., Dec. 30, 1869, age 42.
Ball, John S., Newstead, March 22, 1845, age 61.
Ball, Laura, wife of Timothy, July 11, 1871.
Ball, Mathias, father of Joseph, June 15, 1870, age 90.
Ball, Mrs. Sarah, Newstead, NY, June 26, 1873, age 81 y, 1 m, 13 d.
Ball, Sheldon, 1838.
Ball, William, father of Rev. G. H. of Buffalo, Tonawanda, March 9, 1866, age 88.
Ballard, Elias, Collins, NY, 1840, age c. 35.
Ballard, Col. James, Aurora, NY, Aug. 9, 1852; d. in Jackson, MI.
Ballmeier, Frederick, June 25, 1879, age 55; killed on R.R.
Ballou, Levi, July 29, 1878, age 67.
Ballou, Martha, widow of Levi, Sept. 13, 1878, age 74.
Baltz, Magdalena, wife of George, July 26, 1873.
Baltz, Peter, Sept. 29, 1877, age 38 y, 6 m, 29 d.
Baltz, Peter, father of Hon. George, Feb. 11, 1878, age 77.
Baltzer, Valentine, Feb. 5, 1879.
Bamberg, William H., Sept. 13, 1878, age 35 y, 2 m, 6 d.
Bamlet, George J., April 20, 1874, age 38.
Bancroft, Mrs. Emily B., dau. of William Ketcham, formerly of Buffalo, Dec. 4, 1869, age 33. D. in San Francisco, CA., bur. Buffalo.
Bandell, Elizen, March 1, 1879, age 63.
Bangasser, Frederick J., Jr. May 22, 1874, age 22 y, 6 m.
Bangasser, George, April 3, 1871, age 77.
Bangasser, George T., April 19, 1875, age 27 y, 6 m.
Banker, Charles, May 15, 1879, age 60 y, 2 m; found dead.
Banks, Anna, wife of Levi A., April 8, 1857, age 25 y, 2 m, 8 d.
Banks, Elizabeth, May 3, 1871, age 22.
Bannister, Eliza, wife of John, Nov. 11, 1871, age 58.
Banta, J. W., July 10, 1863, age 53 y, 7m.

Bantam, Capt. John S., formerly of Buffalo, Jan. 6, 1878; d. at Lacrosse, WI.
Bapt[i]st, W., Dec. 31, 1879, age 29.
Barber, Cyrena, wife of Rowell, Hamburgh, NY, June 14, 1850, age 31.
Barber, J. Leroy, Whites Corners, NY, April 11, 1865, age 25.
Barber, Mary, wife of Daniel, Nov. 4, 1868, age 59.
Barber, Orson, Co. Almshouse, Feb. 23, 1879, age 63.
Barber, Thomas, b. 1762, d. 1837, bur. Williamsville, Revolutionary Soldier.
Barber, Wm. B., North Evans printer, Dec. 18, 1865, age 30; bur. in Buffalo.
Barckley, Mary L., wife of William, Feb. 12, 1877, age 49.
Bardol, Mary M., March 23, 1877, age 67.
Bardwell, Hiram, Co. Almshouse, Jan. 10, 1879, age 60.
Bardwell, Jonathan S., May 19, 1852, age 68. Died while returning to Troy from residence of son in Brant, NY.
Bardwell, Mary E., Brant, NY, wife of Smead, Oct. 16, 1875.
Barger, Benjamin S., Aug. 28, 1852, age 35.
Barger, Lewis, Dec. 3, 1853, age 24; taken to Westfield, NY.
Bark, Capt. Peter Evans, Ocean and Lake Capt., Nov. 3, 1863, age 62. Born in Gottenburg, Sweden.
Barker, Abby Coit, formerly of Buffalo, widow of George B., Feb. 6, 1874; d. at Norwich, CT.
Barker, Addison, Wales, April 23, 1839, age 20.
Barker, Alden, March 10, 1879, age 75; taken to Kingsville, OH.
Barker, Anna G., wife of Pierre A., July 2, 1865. Mother of Mrs. Philander Hodge; d.in Warsaw, IL.
Barker, Catherine E., formerly of Buffalo, widow of Jacob A., Oct. 21, 1875; d. at Litchfield, CT, bur. in Buffalo.
Barker, Cynthia Pratt, South Wales, widow of Gideon, Oct. 2, 1877, age 83.
Barker, Ellen, wife of D.B., Hamburgh, NY, June 22, 1878, age 41.
Barker, George, South Wales, June 1873, age 46; d. at Orange Bluff, FL; bur. at South Wales.
Barker, George Payson, Jan. 29, 1868, age 33; d. in Norwich, CT.
Barker, Gideon, South Wales, Sept. 3, 1868, age 75 y, 5 m.
Barker, Jacob A., June 2, 1859, age 66.
Barker, Margaret, wife of Zenas, Hamburgh, June 18, 1815, age 36.
Barker, Martin, Jan. 29, 1880, age 34; d. at East Buffalo Freight yards.
Barker, Mehitabel, Dec. 31, 1878, widow of William, Dec. 31, 1878, age 92.
Barker, Minerva N., widow of Nathan B., Feb. 7, 1877.
Barker, Nancy, Hamburgh, NY, Jan. 1, 1822, age 31.
Barker, Nathan B., teacher, Dec. 4, 1873, age 62.
Barker, Orton C., Feb. 19, 1879; suicide.
Barker, Phoebe D., wife of George W., Springville, July 17, 1872.
Barker, Pierre A., formerly of Buffalo, Jan. 4, 1870, age 80; d. at Natchez, Miss. at the residence of his son.
Barker, Rhoda, wife of Judge Z., Hamburg, Jan. 1814.
Barker, Rosina H., wife of Michael H., Gowanda, NY, Nov. 28, 1849, age 42.
Barker, Mrs. Sarah of Nantucket, Sept. 30, 1843, age 53.
Barker, Miss Sophia, Mar. 3, 1837, age 29.
Barker, William, Nov. 27, 1844, age 51.
Barker, Zenas, b. 1765, d. 1834, bur. Buffalo, Revolutionary Soldier.
Barker, Zenas Ward, formerly of Buffalo, April 10, 1879, age 88; Sandusky, OH.
Barlow, L. Maria, June 7, 1880.
Barnard, Albert, Sept. 1, 1849, age 37; d. in Batavia, NY.
Barnard, Dorothy, wife of Selah, Cayuga Creek, Oct. 2, 1831, age 45. Dau. of Gen. Othniel Taylor of Canandaigua.
Barnard, Elizabeth A., widow of Albert, April 4, 1875, age 56.
Barnard, Ellen A., widow of Frank, Oct. 10, 1874, age33 y, 9 m, 3 d.
Barnard, Frank J., March 26, 1874, age 32.
Barnard, Frank S., Jan. 15, 1876, age 39.
Barnard, Ira H., Hamburg, May 18, 1871, age 88.
Barnard, George N., Hamburgh, NY, Mar. 19, 1859, age 38.
Barnard, wife of Ira, Hamburgh, NY. Aug. 28, 1862, age 80.

Barnard, Louis J., Dec. 29, 1876, age 33; railroad accident.
Barnard, Mrs. Margaret, Feb. 11, 1864, age 64 y, 7 m, 13 d.
Barnard, Mrs. Martha, March 8, 1874, age 76.
Barnard, Mary Jane, wife of Ira, Hamburgh, Aug. 10, 1839, age 20.
Barnard, Selah, Nov. 18, 1855; d. at Grand Rapids, MI.
Barnard, Susan Adelia, wife of Othniel FitzHenry, Williamsville, NY, Feb. 28, 1843, age 31.
Barnard, Susan M., wife of Edward C., Aug. 23, 1843, age 38; d. in New Bedford.
Barnard, O. T. H., Williamsville, NY, 2d son of the late Judge Selah, June 28, 1876, age 68 y, 7 m, 10 d; d. in Newark, NJ, bur. in Williamsville.
Barnes, Bradford R., July 17, 1849, age 23.
Barnes, Delia Marsh, widow of Dr. Josiah, Dec. 16, 1875, age 66 y, 2 m.
Barnes, Mrs. George, Aug. 1838, age 40; bur. the 22d.
Barnes, George A., son of Bradford, July 10, 1858; d. in Murfresboro, TN.
Barnes, Henry, Dec. 21, 1862, age 49.
Barnes, Henry S., April 27, 1874, age 51; taken to Hartford, CT.
Barnes, Isabella, wife of George M., March 10, 1868, age 31; d. in Albany.
Barnes, Jacob L., Jan. 14, 1873, age 54.
Barnes, Jonathan D., son of W. T., Oct. 3, 1861; drowned in Troy.
Barnes, Dr. Josiah, June 1, 1871, age 67 y, 5 d.
Barnes, Miss Lavinia H., Feb. 26, 1854.
Barnes, Lucy L., wife of Jacob L., Jan. 24, 1865, age 33 y, 2 m, 1 d.
Barnes, Mahitable, wife of Seth, Newstead, NY, Feb. 2, 1849, age 76.
Barnes, Mrs. Maria, June 17, 1857, age 61; d. at Rock Island, IL.
Barnes, Minerva, wife of Jacob L., March 1, 1850, age 26. Sister of R. H. Best.
Barnes, Morris O., Feb. 5, 1867, age 67; d. in Corfu, Genesee Co., NY.
Barnes, Moses, July 25, 1822, age 45.
Barnes, Myra H., July 24, 1878, age 38.
Barnes, Rachel, wife of Bradford, Nov. 10, 1863, age 72.
Barnes, Sara, at Home for the Friendless, Jan. 8, 1880, age 75.
Barnes, Stephen, Jan. 30, 1826, age 45.
Barnes, Susan, wife of Joseph, July 4, 1866, age 55 y, 7 m.
Barnes, William H., May 3, ---, age 38.
Barnes, William Josiah, Nov. 19, 1875, age 29 y, 9 m, 26 d.
Barnes, William T., Dec. 13, 1861, age 59; d. at Delaware Water Gap, NJ.
Barnes, Malvina, wife of Irvina, June 1, 1832, age 20.
Barnes, Mrs. Susan A., dau. of Robert Patterson, July 4, 1854, age 47.
Barnett, James, Feb. 13, 1874, age 63 y, 9 m, 26 d.
Barnett, Mrs. Mary, May 7, 1877, age 54.
Barnett, Penelope, wife of James, Jan. 11, 1874, age 70.
Barnett, William A., April 25, 1875, age 34.
Barney, Danford N., formerly of Buffalo, March 8, 1874; d. in New York.
Barney, Hiram H., teacher, July 27, 1879; d. at Wyoming, OH, formerly of Buffalo and East Aurora, NY.
Barnhart, John, May 30, 1880, age 58.
Barnum, Alice C., dau. of George G. and Ellen, May 24, 1880, age 26.
Barnum, Austin, Oct. 29, 1870, age 70.
Barnum, Mrs. Charlotte, Sept. 12, 1869, age 72.
Barnum, Ezra S., formerly of Buffalo, father of Stephen O. of Buffalo, Feb. 20, 1878, age 86; d. in Utica.
Barnum, George C., son of E. S. of Utica, NY, Jan. 25, 1851. Died at Jackson Creek, CA.
Barnum, Hannah, wife of Austin, March 24, 1868, age 70.
Barnum, Henry F., son of S. O., April 4, 1876, age 29.
Barnum, John Parsons, March 29, 1876, age 56.
Barnum, Richard S., brother of S. O., Jan. 17, 1865; d. in Chicago.
Barnum, Samuel G., Feb. 21, 1849, age 63 y, 6 m.
Baron, Abial, Lancaster, NY, May 11, 1847, age 45.
Barr, Mrs. Agnes, mother of William, Niagara Falls, Nov. 27, 1872, age 74; bur. in Buffalo.
Barr, Charles J., May 4, 1872, age 54.
Barr, Charles W., only son of Augustus, May 28, 1865, age 21.
Barr, Malvina E., Williamsville, NY, widow of Charles, Oct. 19, 1874.

Barr, Marion, widow of Rudolph, May 27, 1853, age 67.
Barr, Rudolph, Dec. 20, 1836, age 55.
Barras, Charles M., formerly of Buffalo, March 31, 1873, age 47.
Barras, Sallie St. Clair, wife of Chas. M., April 9, 1867, age 36.
Barrell, Lydia R., Evans, July 6, 1865, age 45.
Barrell, John Hudson, Evans, NY, Oct. 25, 1864, age 31; d. at River Side, LA.
Barrell, Henry, Evans, NY, July 23, 1874, age 43 y, 10 m, 11 d.
Barrett, George, Almshouse, June 20, 1880, age 28.
Barrett, Johanna, wife of Patrick, Jan. 25, 1871, age 40.
Barrett, Joseph, saloon keeper, Dec, 8, 1870, age 60.
Barrett, Henry L., Aug. 3, 1850, age 25.
Barrett, Jeremiah, Marilla, March 22, 1864, age 74.
Barrett, Wm., c. age 50, stranger here; d. at G. W. Black's, Cor. Evans and Terrace, Sept. 16, 1848. Said had a family near Sackett's Harbor.
Barritt, Zillah D., widow of Ransom, Akron, Feb. 6, 1871, age 78.
Barron, Josephine, Holland, NY, Dec. 13, 1871, age 45.
Barrow, Carrie, March 7, 1876, age 24; suicide.
Barrow, Sarah, wife of James, Clarence, NY, Feb. 10, 1861, age 40.
Barrows, Gersham, Stanley, July 4, 1861, age 27.
Barrows, La Vancha, wife of A. Z., Feb. 2, 1870, age 43 y, 3 m, 5 d.
Barrows, Thomas Jr., Oct. 14, 1879, age 66.
Barrows, Warren J., Eden, Dec. 10, 1872, age 27.
Barrows, William F., Aug. 4, 870, age 80; d. at Fort Monroe, VA, bur. in Buffalo.
Barry, Caroline Matilda, widow of John M. and mother of Gen. Barry.
Barry, Katherine W., widow of Gen. William F., Dec. 17, 1879.
Barry, Linus F., July 26, 1876, age 42.
Barry, Mary, wife of Mathew, April 11, 1875, age 34.
Barry, Mary N., wife of Augustus B., Jan. 28, 1857. Of Rock Island, IL.
Barry, Mrs. Sarah E., Aug. 10, 1842; d. at Monmouth, IL.
Barry, Timothy, June 1, 1872, age 49.
Barry, William, May 27, 1887, age 42.
Barry, Maj. Gen. Wm. F., July 18, 1879, age 61; d. at Ft. McHenry, Baltimore harbor, formerly of Buffalo.
Barstow, Samuel of Detroit, July 12, 1854, age 41.
Bartell, Mrs. Victor, July 27, 1880, age 65.
Barth, Catharine, Oct. 6, 1871, age 51.
Barth, Fulton, July 1872.
Barth, Henry, Co. Almshouse, Feb. 22, 1877, age 34.
Barth, Julia, only child of J. A. & Catherine, Feb. 11, 1875, age 19 y, 7 m, 3 d.
Barth, Lawrence, Lancaster, Aug. 5, 1875, age 26; suicide.
Barth, Mrs. Maria, Nov. 4, 1877, age 52; railroad accident.
Bartholomew, Adaline, wife of Chauncey, Feb. 8, 1848, age 40.
Bartholomew, Ann, Lancaster, NY, Oct. 27, 1877, age 72.
Bartholomew, Esther Ann, dau. of Chauncey, Nov. 4, 1845, age 20.
Bartholomew, John A., Buffalo formerly, Feb. 18, 1879; d. in Chicago.
Bartholomew, Matilda, May 20, 1857, age 20 y, 6 m.
Bartholomew, Sarah Sophia, Nov. 17, 1854, age 21.
Barthow, (*name supposed), Nov. 30, 1875: d. at Alden Centre.
Bartles, Daniel, blacksmith, Sept. 2, 1873, age 31.
Bartlett, Arvilla, wife of Allen, Aurora, NY, Sept. 25, 1858, age 29.
Bartlett, Mrs. Caroline S., dau. of Wm. H. Corbin, West Aurora, NY, March 14, 1855.
Bartlett, Helen J., wife of Allen, Willink, NY, Oct. 2, 1865, age 29.
Bartlett, Henry, Clarence, Aug. 9, 1814, age 45.
Bartlett, Captain John, formerly Coxsackie, Green Co., July 22, 1836, age 65.
Bartlett, Lois, wife of Elliott, Aug. 16, 1873, age 73.
Bartlett, Martha, April 18, 1871, age 27.
Bartlett, Mary, widow of J. M., Clarence, July 6, 1875.
Bartlett, Mrs. Mary A., Oct. 22, 1863, age 47; taken to Hadley, MA.
Bartlett, Thomas B., brother of Dr. F. W., Jan. 12, 1859. Formerly of and taken to Kingston, MA.

Bartlett, Victor, d. in Brooklyn, Oct. 26, 1843, age 27.
Bartley, Betsey Elizabeth, wife of Samuel, Colden, NY, Sept. 30, 1852, age 48.
Barton, Alice L., granddau. of John Lock, Sept. 26, 1875, age 20.
Barton, Alma Taylor, widow of Theodore D., Jan. 10, 1877, age 63; d. at Golden's Bridge, Westchester Co., NY.
Barton, Mrs. Clara, formerly of Buffalo, Sept. 6, 1876; suicide.
Barton, Emma S., wife of Pliny F., Aug. 11, 1860, age 62.
Barton, Harriet L., wife of L. H. and dau. of J. Lock, June 17, 1864, age 29.
Barton, Harriet R., widow of Col. James L., Nov. 20, 1879, age 71.
Barton, Hiram, lawyer, Feb. 10, 1880, age 69.
Barton, James H., Oct. 25, 1878, age 57.
Barton, Hon. James L., Oct. 6, 1869, age 74.
Barton, John B., late of Providence, RI, father of Mrs. George Coit, May 6, 1869, age 84.
Barton, Joseph A., Aug. 23, 1875, age 66.
Barton, Mrs. Mary, Nov. 3, 1861, age 64.
Barton, Phineas, Feb. 17, 1866, age 69.
Barton, Pliny F., March 22, 1864, age 58.
Barton, Sarah Maria, wife of Col. James L., Dec. 2, 1851, age 53.
Barton, Sheldon T., formerly of Buffalo, youngest son of the late Col. James, Jan. 9, 1876, age 39. D. in New Orleans, bur. Buffalo.
Barton, Susan, wife of Phineas, June 11, 1857; d. in New York. Buried in Buffalo.
Barton, T. B., d. in Galt, Canada West, June 6, 1853. Organist of Trinity Church, Galt.
Barton, Theodore D., June 24, 1863, age 54.
Bartoo, Silas, b. May 21, 1742, d. Nov. 7, 1831, bur. Eden Valley Cemetery, Eden, NY; soldier of the Revolution.
Bartoo, Deacon J. L., Evans, NY, Oct. 19, 1870, age 66 y, 1 m.
Bartow, John, d. in Washington, D.C. Lawyer, employed in Dept. of Interior, Dec. 8, 1857, age 44.
Bartram, Hannah Maria, wife of Henry, June 13, 1845, age 33.
Bashford, Ex-Gov. Coles, formerly of Erie Co., April 1878; d. at Prescott, AZ.
Basinger, William P., son of Jacob B., Jan. 23, 1875, age 28; suicide.
Basket, Charles Thomas, Englishman, Oct. 15, 1840, age 56.
Bass, Samuel Savil, Marilla, NY, Nov. 18, 1859, age 25 y, 4 m. 4d.
Bassett, Abby F., sister of Gustavus and Thomas, Nov. 23, 1854.
Bassett, Daniel K., June 21, 1877, age 57.
Bassett, Jason, architect, Oct. 27, 1850, age 41.
Bassett, Mary, wife of Col. Jason, July 28, 1849, age 40.
Bassett, Dea. Nathaniel T., Evans, NY, Feb. 6, 1863, age 64.
Bassett, Susan Bartlett, wife of Gustavus, Feb. 17, 1847, age 31.
Bastian, Michael, Holland, NY, Sept. 16, 1872, age 58.
Bastian, Robert C., April 14, 1850, age 38.
Batchelder, Amos, formerly of Sutton, MA, Dec. 23, 1866, age 62.
Batchelder, Edroy A., May 15, 1872, age 22 y, 5 m, 15 d.
Bateman, Capt. Frank E., formerly of Buffalo, March 1877.
Bates, John, Dec. 11, 1858, age 56.
Bates, Mark, formerly of Buffalo, Jan. 15 or 16, 1879, age 37; d. in Philadelphia.
Bates, Mary, widow of John, Dec. 3, 1864, age 64.
Bates, Mrs. Mary Ann, April 14, 1871, age 57.
Bates, Sally G., widow of Phineas P. of Canandaigua, Oct. 4, 1863, age 83.
Bath, Mrs. Louisa E., Feb. 2, 1876, age 82.
Bath, Pauline, wife of Thomas Jr., Dec. 15, 1874, age 28.
Bath, Thomas E. Jr., Jan. 16, 1876, age 35.
Batt, Joseph, Cheektowaga, NY, July 29, 1872, age 83 y, 2 m, 19 d.
Battel, Bridget, wife of Henry Sr., Nov. 3, 1877, age 69.
Battell, Cyrus, Engineer and Steamboat Inspector, Jan. 26, 1840, age 40.
Battell, Mrs. Mary Fuller, niece of Miss Clara Cutler, Dec. 25, 1859.
Batten, James, Aug. 9, 1862, age 35.
Battey, George H., April 12, 1880, age 31.
Batty, Hannah, wife of David, Hamburgh, NY, Aug. 19, 1839, age 50; d. in Huntsville, Madison Co., IN.

Bauer, Eva, wife of Peter, May 1874, age 45.
Bauer, John, April 7, 1879, age 79 y, 10 m.
Bauer, Louise, wife of George F., March 3, 1868; d. in Stuttgart, Germany.
Bauer, Mary, dau. of Peter, Oct. 14, 1880, age 24; d. at Wellsvillle.
Bauer, Peter, Jan. 31, 1877, age 55.
Bauermeister, John Henry, April 1, 1867, age 53.
Bauld, Isabel, widow of John, Dec. 21, 1880, age 50.
Baule, Mrs. J., Oct. 14, 1871, age 34.
Baumgardner, Christian, Almshouse, June 3, 1880, age 50.
Bavavinski, Adeline, April 23, 1874, age 24.
Baxter, Flora, wife of John, Oct. 24, 1873, age 40.
Baxter, George P., eldest son of Peter, printer, Aug. 26, 1859, age 19.
Baxter, James B., Oct. 1865. Funeral 29th.
Baxter, Peter, Sept. 23, 1878, age 61.
Baxter, Thomas, formerly of Buffalo, April 6, 1876, age c. 45; accidently drowned at Hamilton, Canada.
Bayliss, Rev. James E., formerly of East Aurora, NY, Oct. 5, 1875, age 34; d. at Grand Rapids, MI, bur. East Aurora, NY.
Bayliss, Rev. Samuel, Feb. 12, 1879, age 68; d. in Brooklyn, bur. in Buffalo.
Beach, Aaron, b. 1761, d. June 17, 1846, bur. Cambria, NY, soldier of the Revolution.
Beach, Bennett, Cheektowaga, Feb. 3, 1851, age 45.
Beach, Charles, railroad conductor, Jan. 21, 1880; d. at Attica, crushed by cars.
Beach, Charles Rollin, Sept. 12, 1826, age 38.
Beach, Charles W., Hamburgh, Sept. 25, 1873, age 23 y, 2 m, 25 d.
Beach, Hannah, Hamburgh, NY, wife of Harry, March 1, 1872, age 62 y, 8 m, 23 d.
Beach, Henry C., Co. A, 116 Reg. N.Y.S. Vol. Hamburgh, NY, Oct. 13, 1863, age 28; d. at St. Louis Hospital.
Beach, John, Feb. 17, 1824, age 28.
Beach, Mrs. Ortha, mother of Mrs. O. O. Newton, Nov. 17, 1878, age 78.
Beach, Mrs. Ruth Ann, mother of Col. W. F. P. Taylor, Oct. 5, 1854, age 72.
Beach, Seth, April 28, 1836, age 32.
Beach, William, Williamsville, July 3, 1873, age 69.
Beach, William H., printer, Dec. 7, 1879, age 61; bur. in Rochester.
Beadle, Rev. Dr. E., formerly of Buffalo, Jan. 13, 1879; d. in Philadelphia.
Beadle, William, Feb. 19, 1877, age 34.
Beal, Mary L. Evans, Nov. 27, 1853, age 49.
Beale, Edward C., Jan. 9, 1871, age 34.
Beale, Miss Emily, June 14, 1859.
Beale, Mary C., Dec. 6, 1871, age 64.
Beales, Elizabeth, formerly of Buffalo, wife of William John, Nov. 5, 1873. Killed by her husband at Fort Erie, Ontario; bur. in Buffalo.
Beale, Edward C., Jan. 1871.
Beals, John W., June 17, 1846, age 55.
Beals, John W., Sept. 3, 1852, age 36 10.
Beals, Mrs. Julia R., April 8, 1857, age 65.
Beamer, James, prisoner in the Penitentiary, Nov. 1, 1878, age 25.
Beamus, Jotham, Rev. Soldier, Hamburgh, NY, Mar. 1813, age 53.
Bean, Aaron, Jan. 18, 1852, age 55.
Bean, Harriet, wife of Dixon, formerly of Buffalo, Oct. 30, 1874; d. in Chicago.
Bean, Josephine, wife of William M., June 8, 1866, age 30 y, 7 m, 28 d.
Bean, Luke Andrew, Aurora, Jan. 5, 1858, age 51 y, 8 m.
Bean, Lauranie, wife of Aaron, May 25, 1843, age 40.
Bean, Milo Inigo, Aurora, NY, May 29, 1862, age 57.
Beard, David Holbrook, Nov. 6, 1853, age 27.
Beard, Eliza, widow of David, March 1, 1852, age 60.
Beard, Flora Johnson, wife of Wm. H., Nov. 17, 1859, age 20.
Beard, Miss Parthenia, Aug. 15, 1847, age 34.
Beardsley, Abraham, Jan. 25, 1864, age 48 10.
Beardsley, Jerusha, wife of Hazard, Eden, Oct. 21, 1824.
Beardsley, Lewis, formerly of Conneaut, OH, Oct. 10, 1868, age 38.

Beardsley, Salmon W., b. 1759, d. 1824 or 1825, bur. Eden Center, Revolutionary soldier.
Beardsley, Samuel B., Eden, Dec. 28, 1875, age 65 y, 8 m, 16 d.
Beardsley, Sarah, Oct. 7, 1829.
Barry, Mrs. Ann, Dec. 25, 1862, age 68.
Beare, Charles H., July 2, 1869, age 26 y, 7 m.
Beattie, Charles A., son of John, Sept. 12, 1871, age 24 y, 4 m, 23 d.
Beatty, Susan, wife of Charles, Sept. 16, 1865, age 22 y, 5 m.
Beaugrand, Emeline L., wife of Capt. John B., June 5, 1850, age 28.
Beaupre, Louis, June 11, 1886, age 58 y, 6 m.
Beaver, Elizabeth, wife of Nicholas, Oct. 20, 1865, age 41 y, 5 m.
Beaver, Magalana, North Collins, wife of Nicholas, July 20, 1868; age 70 y, 10 m, 25 d.
Beck, Henry, April 4, 1816, age 27.
Beck, Johanna, March 8, 1880; age 60 y, 8 m.
Becken, Ferdinand C., Feb. 18, 1865, age 43 y, 9 m, 28 d.
Becker, Christian, Jan. 24, 1869, age 88 y, 28 d.
Becker, Conrad, West Seneca, July 25, 1871, age 53.
Becker, Mrs. Frances, April 27, 1859, age 77.
Becker, Frank, formerly of Buffalo, March 27, 1878, age 42; d. at Erie, PA.
Becker, John, Jan. 3, 1876.
Becker, Mary Elizabeth, widow of Anthony, April 24, 1880, age 52 y, 10 m, 4 d.
Becker, Peter, Sept. 2, 1879, age 35.
Beckett, Robert, Nov. 24, 1873, age 38.
Beckle, Caroline, July 4, 1876, age 42 y, 11 m, 10 d.
Beckley, Julia, wife of John, Jan. 7, 1879, age 43.
Beckris, George Henry, Sept. 25, 1880, age 72 y, 4 m, 22 d.
Beckwith, Ezekiel, Tonawanda, NY, July 24, 1856, age 66.
Beckwith, Francis Westley, son of Capt. James L., Sept. 15, 1875, age 28 y, 5 m, 1 d.
Beckwith, Harry K., formerly of Buffalo, March 11, 1879, age 38; d. at Leroy, NY.
Beckwith, Oliver W., M.D., Angola, NY, June 4, 1875, age 57.
Beckwith, Samuel, Nov. 1813, age 34.
Bede, Rev. Father Peter, Aug. 1870.
Bedford, Charlotte, widow of John, West Seneca, NY, July 30, 1880.
Bedford, John, West Seneca, NY, Sept. 9, 1873, age 65.
Beebe, Lemuel T., March 14, 1870, age 40.
Beebe, Sylvanus L., Oct. 19, 1878, age 22 y, 1 m, 13 d.
Beebee, Alfred, Springville, NY, Feb. 1851, age 34.
Beebee, Erastus, May 28, 1843, age 46.
Beebee, Julia, wife of Ebenezer, Cheektowaga, NY, April 26, 1843, age 27.
Beebee, Lorinda, wife of E., Jan. 26, 1843, age 40.
Beebee, Silas H., son of Erastus, March 18, 1852; d. in Oregon, IL.
Beecher, ---, wife of Eneas, Oct. 5, 1816. From Ontario Co.
Beecher, Elsie M. Curtis, widow of Hiram L., Oct. 3, 1879, age 74 y, 11 m.
Beecher, Hiram S., Dec. 12, 1876, age 73.
Beecher, Lucy Nichols Smith, wife of James C., March 19, 1868, age 25.
Beecher, William Henry, LaSalle, IL, formerly of Ellicottville, July 6, 1879, age 58.
Beelfus (or Beilforis, Beilfuss), Albert, May 16, 1880, age 36; accident.
Beeman, ---, wife of Col. Samuel, Clarence, May 16, 1841, age 52 y, 2 m, 27 d.
Beeman, Miss Permelia, dau. of Joshua, Clarence, NY, Feb. 25, 1870.
Beeman, Col. Samuel, Clarence, Aug. 1, 1876, age 89 y, 5 m.
Beers, Dr. A. H., formerly of Buffalo, physician, Jan. 5, 1869; d. in Litchfield, CT.
Beers, Belinda Webster, widow of the late Hon. Seth P., Jan. 4, 1868, age 81; d. in Litchfield, CT.
Beegan, Daniel, Oct. 23, 1876, age 93.
Beers, Anthony, May 26, 1835, age 46.
Behan, Margaret, wife of Michael, June 2, 1879, age 32.
Behan, Patrick, Feb. 1874, age 20.
Beider (or Buder), Augusta, Almshouse, Feb. 18, 1880, age 65.
Beidinger, William, Nov. 29, 1858, age 39.
Beigg, Alfred, laborer employed by Sheldon Pease?, April 6, 1870, age 24.
Beile, Carl, seaman, July 12, 1876, age 23; d. on the steamship *Holland*.

Beirne, Mrs. Margaret, Oct. 16, 1877, age 70.
Beiser, Catherine, widow of Adolph, Nov. 12, 1878, age 46.
Beiser, Frederick, May 22, 1872, age 38 y, 6 m.
Beiser, L. P.A., July 11, 1870; d. on voyage from NY to Europe, bur. at sea.
Belden, Benjamin, formerly of St. Johnsburg, VT, Sept. 2, 1861.
Belden, Charles H. Bishop, only son of Dexter, April 1, 1878.
Belden, E. Dexter, eldest son of Dexter, Sept. 28, 1865, age 27.
Belden, Fanny Maria, wife of Dexter, May 27, 1869.
Belden, Webster, Oct. 19, 1880, age 27 y, 4 m.
Belding, Jonathan, b. 1760, d. 1850, bur. Pakin, Revolutionary soldier.
Belknap, Cyrus, Father of Mrs. J. L. Barnes, Feb. 10, 1859, age 60. D. in Haldimand, bur. in Buffalo.
Belknap, Halsey S., brother of Mrs. Jacob L. Barnes, Jan. 22, 1865, age 22 2. D. in Centralia, IL, bur. in Buffalo.
Bell, Andrew, Revolutionary soldier, Newstead, NY, Oct. 25, 1845, age 91. [Another card: Bell, Andrew, b. June 30, 1755, d. Oct. 25, 1845, bur. Newstead, NY.]
Bell, Elizabeth, wife of David, Dec. 12, 1866, age 47.
Bell, Edwin, Dec. 19, 1873, age 63.
Bell, Helen M., Nov. 30, 1873, age 39; wife of Lafayette W. Taken to Holland, Erie Co., NY.
Bell, Mr. L. W., Holland, NY, Nov. 14, 1877; d. in Buffalo.
Bell, Mrs. M. I. of St. Louis, Feb. 16, 1869; taken East.
Bell, Mary, widow of William, March 10, 1872, age 70.
Bell, Robert W., Sept. 24, 1877, age 36.
Bell, Salmon, pastor Baptist Church, Clarence, NY, Nov. 1815.
Bell, William, Jan. 11, 1870, age 76.
Bellinger, Salinda, wife of Peter P.E., Nov. 1, 1870, age 53; taken to Little Falls, Herkimer Co.
Bellinger, Mrs. Varion, mother of Mrs. Capt. Radcliffe, April 9, 1867.
Beltz, Susie A., wife of W. H., Aug. 19, 1878, age 21 y, 11 m, 24 d.
Bement, Mrs. I., d. in Detroit, July 25, 1847, age 45.
Bement, Mr. J., July 28, 1849, age c 45; d. in Detroit.
Bement, William H., June 13, 1864, age 47. Died at Cuba, NY.
Bemis, Asaph S., Dec. 13, 1823, age 34.
Bemis (Bemue), Gothan, b. Jan. 1760, d. March 24, 1813, bur. Orchard Park, NY, soldier of the Revolution.
Bemis, John, Sept. 8, 1868, age 21; d. in the General Hospital.
Bemish, Richard, Dec. 9, 1871, age 53.
Bencinger, John, Feb. 5, 1876, age 66 y, 9 m.
Bender, Elizabeth, wife of Hon. P. H., July 13, 1879, age 42.
Bender, George, Lancaster, NY, Feb. 5, 1872.
Bender, George Frederick, Nov. 7, 1869, age 72. Father of Ph. H. and Louis L. Bender.
Bender, Herman, Alden, NY, June 8, 1871, age 38.
Benedict, Maj. Charles Oscar, formerly of Buffalo, Oct. 24, 1872, age 53; d. at Saratoga Springs, NY.
Benedict, Ezra T., Jan. 1, 1868, age 54.
Benedict, Frank, May 14, 1878; d. at Union Springs. Wife [sic] of D. V.
Benedict, Joel H., Water Valley, Dec. 23, 1865, age 53.
Benedict, Rev. Judson D., formerly of Aurora, NY, April 18, 1874, age 66. D. at Fenwick, Ontario; bur. Tonawanda.
Benedict, Julia Stambach, wife of Alfred, June 11, 18671, age 28.
Benedict, Phebe, wife of Joel H. July 12, 1854, age 48.
Benedict, Sarah R. Cone, wife of George C., Dec. 8, 1872; taken to Utica.
Benewitz, Charles, April 30, 1873, age 69.
Benham, Col. S.C., East Aurora, NY, Oct. 12, 1876, age 47.
Benham, William G., Sept. 24, 1877, age 38; sent East.
Benjamin, D. Spencer, Sept. 5, 1860, age 23.
Benjamin, George W., Dec. 24, 1859, age 25.
Bennet, Elnathan, Cheektowaga, NY, March 24, 1863, age 74.
Bennet, James, Lancaster, NY, May 4, 1860, age 62.

Bennet, Alva, Nov. 10, 1850, age 41.
Bennet, Hayes, Black Rock, NY, Sept. 1815, age 45.
Bennet, Henry A., Postmaster at Black Rock Dam, Feb. 26, 1856, age 38.
Bennet, James E. D. at Utica, Nov. 10, 1844, age 35.
Bennet, Mrs. May, Sept. 10, 1867, age 68.
Bennet, Nathaniel G., eldest son of Philander, firm of Marvin & Bennett, 1841, age 22.
Bennet, Mrs. Phebe Ann, April 17, 1850, age 39.
Bennet, Philander, July 22, 1863, age 68.
Bennet, Samuel W., Dec. 18, 1865, age 40 y, 3m.
Bennet, Susan Barton, wife of Seymour, May 29, 1865, age 27 y, 6m.
Bennet, Thankful, wife of James, Lancaster, NY, Nov. 22, 1853.
Bennett, Alexander, Jan. 27, 1879, age 45 y, 6 m, 6 d.
Bennett, Alice, wife of Andrew, Feb. 28, 1875, age 39.
Bennett, Andrew, Nov. 24, 1877, age 46 y, 2 m, 26 d.
Bennett, Mary, wife of Hon. Joseph, Evans, Feb. 3, 1879, age 70.
Bennett, Mary A. Winspear, wife of D. Chapin, Cheektowaga, Nov. 17, 1880, age 56.
Bennett, Mr. P. A. (or R.), May 1, 1878.
Bennett, William, from England, Almshouse, Nov. 5, 1880, age 52.
Benny, George Eugene, son of Francis, Aug. 11, 1875, age 19 y, 8 m, 4 d.
Benseoler, Mrs. Jane Talman, Wales, Jan. 29, 1859, age 31.
Benson, Bradley, 6th Wisconsin Bat., son of E. W. of Buffalo, Feb. 22, 1865. D. at Nashville, TN.
Benson, Gen. Elias Willard, father of D.D. & O.P., formerly of Buffalo, Nov. 27, 1874, age 77; d. at Medina, MI.
Benson, Mrs. Elizabeth, April 10, 1855, age 75 y, 6m.
Benson, Harriet C., widow of John, Sept. 6, 1880, age 56.
Benson, John, Sept. 6, 1849, age 71.
Benson, John, Feb. 18, 1870, age 51.
Benson, John, July 4, 1877, age c. 30: accident.
Benson, Kate, wife of John, April 28, 1875.
Benson, Silas, Nov. 18, 1871, age 60.
Benstead, Richard, Sept. 21, 1870, age 53.
Bent, Mrs. Jane E., April 6, 1871, age 31.
Bentel, Kate, wife of Charles, Sept. 30, 1880, age 61 y, 7 m, 20 d.
Benter, Frederick C., Feb. 19, 1880, age 40 y, 10 m.
Bentley, Alonzo C., formerly of Buffalo, Dec. 27, 1870, age 62; d. in Green Bay, WI.
Bentley, Charles A., Hamburgh, NY, July 20, 1880, age 29; accidental death.
Bentley, James R., Jan. 9, 1870, age 64.
Bentley, William P., engineer, Dec. 11, 1880, age 56; killed on railroad.
Bentzinger, Mrs. Anna M., April 14, 1880, age 79.
Benzinger, Mrs. Magdalena A., May 30, 1880, age 73 y, 12 d.
Berg, A. V., April 14, 1876, age 42.
Bergh, Christian S., Feb. 27, 1873, age 39; d. at Spring Lake, Mich.; bur. in Buffalo.
Bergmann, Charles, March 22, 1877, age 62; suicide.
Bergtold, Daniel, East Aurora, Nov. 15, 1865, age 29 y, 7 m, 6 d.
Bergtold, Mrs. Margaret, Sept. 3, 1864, age 64 y, 8 m, 8 d.
Bernisch, Anthony, Jan. 14, 1873, age 69.
Berry, Elizabeth E., Sept. 28, 1869.
Berry, Frances, wife of Matthew, Aug. 23, 1880, age 36.
Berry, Hannah, widow of Joseph, Nov. 5, 1880, age 78.
Berry, Henry, Aug. 15, 1872, age 22.
Berry, Major Jack, an old and distinguished chief of the Seneca Tribe, Buffalo Creek Reservation, July 3, 1839.
Berry, James, Sept. 17, 1866, age 66 y, 2 m, 21 d.
Berry, Mrs. James, widow of James, May 7, 1880, age 70.
Berry, Luther O., June 26, 1872, age 24.
Berry, Sarah, dau. of the late James, April 24, 1870.
Berry, Thomas, father of Mrs. M. White and Mrs. D. A. Bowen, Nov. 15, 1870, age 74 y, 7 m.
Berryman, Mrs. Anna Sophia, eldest dau. of Mrs. Catherine Deveraux, Feb. 16, 1860, age 27.
Berryman, Charles, an Englishman, Oct. 7, 1833, age 23.

Berryman, Elizabeth, widow of Capt. John, Dec. 1, 1880, age 47.
Bertling, Eva Magdalena, wife of John, March 12, 1866, age 19.
Berryman, Capt. John, May 7, 1868, age 38.
Berryman, Mary A. Duggan, wife of James, July 3, 1873.
Berryman, William, brother of the late Capt. John, May 15, 1869, age 21; d. in Mackinac, bur. in Buffalo.
Berthker, Edward, Aug. 5, 1873, age 27 or 29; Erie Railroad employee.
Bertling, Helena, wife of Reinhard, June 30, 1878, age 71; drowned.
Bertrand, Joseph P., Feb. 19, 1855, age 19 y, 11m.
Bertrand, Mary, widow of Michael, Feb. 22, 1858, age 69 y, 11m.
Bertrand, Michael, printer, June 20, 1856, age 28 y, 3m. D. in Toronto.
Besancon, Frank, Aug. 3, 1878, age 72 y, 7 m, 3d.
Besse, Caroline Eliza, eldest dau. of John, Wales, March 16, 1843, age 22.
Besse, John, Wales, Oct. 8, 1851, age 53.
Besser, Johanna Christiane, widow of Johann G., Aug. 24, 1878, age 74 y, 4 m, 1 d.
Besser, John B., Amherst, Aug. 13, 1828, age 55.
Besser, Maria, wife of Ernst, Dec. 21, 1877, age 33.
Bessmer, John, June 1, 1873, age 42; suicide.
Best, Charles M., Oct. 24, 1876, age 25.
Best, Henry, April 7, 1878, age 25; accident.
Best, Honor, wife of Joseph, Oct. 22, 1876, age 57.
Best, Jane, widow of Capt. William, mother of R. H. and William F., July 18, 1855, age 72.
Best, Captain William, Tonawanda, Jan. 19, 1854, age 84.
Best, Mrs. Sylvinia, June 3, 1873, age 55; taken to Pine Plain, NY.
Best, William F., May 24, 1869, age 54.
Bestow, Capt. Job, Williamsville, June 11, 1865, age 73.
Bestow, Lurenah, widow of Job of Hinsdale, MA, mother of Captain Job of former place, April 14, 1835, age 72.
Bettinger, J. Edward, Aug. 22, 1876, age 21 y, 6 m.
Bettinger, Joseph R., son of Stephen, June 23, 1880, age 27.
Bettis, Mary E., dau. of Stephen, Oct. 5, 1851, age 21.
Bettis, Stephen, d. in Westfield, NY Nov. 19, 1850, age 50.
Betts, Frederick J., Oct. 12, 1879, age 77.
Bettys, ---, wife of G., Clarence, NY, Dec. 23, 1817, age 30.
Betz, Heinrich, July 1, 1876, age 52; suicide.
Betz, Peter, March 5, 1874, age 67.
Beveridge, Julia Louisa, wife of Robert C., formerly of Buffalo, July 23, 1873, age 25; d. at Rouseville, PA.
Beverly, Mrs. Mary, June 10, 1869, age 91.
Bewz, Nicholas, Co. Almshouse, May 12, 1877, age 80.
Beyer, Barbara, widow of Philip, Jan. 31, 1872, age 90.
Beyer, Fritz, formerly of Buffalo, March 2, 1878, age 43; d. in Detroit.
Beyer, Henrietta S., wife of William H., dau. of C.F. Soldan of Syracuse, June 7, 1869, age 25 y, 8 m.
Bibaman, Catherine, wife of Jacob, March 25, 1879, age 56 y, 6 m, 15 d.
Bicicle, Philip, April 28, 1880, age 56, drowned, probably suicide.
Bickerstaff, Anne, wife of Francis, Hamburg, Dec. 29, 1871, age 73.
Bickerstaff, Frederick, Dec. 1, 1873, age 57.
Bickerstaff, Marie Constantia, dau. of Francis, West Hamburgh, NY, Feb. 14, 1864, age 22.
Bicksler, Jonas, Hamburg, Aug. 9, 1877, age 58.
Bidwell, Benjamin, Dec. 21, 1862, age 72; father of Brig.-Gen. Daniel Davidson Bidwell; bur. Forest Lawn.
Bidwell, Charles S., July 6, 1878, age 52.
Bidwell, Brig. Gen. Daniel D., Oct. 19, 1864, age 48; killed in Battle of Cedar Creek; bur. Forest Lawn.
Bidwell, Emily, wife of John H., Aug. 15, 1854, age 36 years, 1 month, 23 days.
Bidwell, Emma H. Frazer, wife of Charles H., Sept. 17, 1866, age 23 y, 4 m, 8 d.
Bidwell, Frances M., Oct. 18, 1869, age 21 y, 10 m, 18 d; dau. of J. N.
Bidwell, Rev. Ira G., formerly of Buffalo, Dec. 25, 1878, age 42.
Bidwell, Jane, March 4, 1875, age 83 y, 7 m, 2 d, widow of Benjamin.

Bidwell, John H., March 21, 1866, age 56.
Bidwell, Maria N., wife of J. N., April 4, 1865, age 41 y, 4m, 17d.
Bidwell, Olive, widow of John H., d. at Bay City, MI, formerly of Buffalo, April 23, 1880.
Bidwell, Phineas, Nov. 5, 1835 in Stockton, NY, age 77; Revolutionary Soldier.
Bidwell, Susan H., wife of Daniel D., Jan. 25, 1851, age 26.
Bidwell, Virginia, wife of B. S., Aug. 18, 1859.
Biege, Philip, March 13, 1878, age 73; County Almshouse.
Bier, Frederica, March 27, 1876, age 47; County Almshouse.
Bierma, Henry, May 17, 1865, age 35.
Biesenthal, Solomon, April 9, 1878, age c. 64.
Bigden, Henry, son of Robert, May 25, 1862, age 26. D. at Water Valley, West Hamburgh, NY.
Bigden, Mrs. Libbie C., Feb. 3, 1869, in 26th year.
Bigelow, Fanny E. B., wife of W. H. of Freeport, IL, formerly of Buffalo, dau. of Hon.
    Daniel Bowen, Aug. 13, 1861.
Bigelow, George, Sardinia, April 28, 1875.
Bigelow, Milly, wife of Dr. E. A., formerly of Buffalo, June 10, 1843.
Bigelow, Samuel Allen, May 2, 1878, age 80 y, 6 m.
Bigelow, Samuel Olney, formerly of Buffalo, July 19, 1873, age 34; d. in Utica, NY, bur.
    Cleveland, OH.
Bigelow, Samuel S., formerly of Buffalo, Dec. 31, 1850, age 31.
Bigge, Albert W., Sept. 2, 1876, age 26 y, 4 m, 25 d.
Biggs, John, May 27, 1849, age 49.
Bigham, Jane, wife of John, June 17, 1878, age 75.
Bignell, Elizabeth, formerly of Buffalo, widow of John, postmaster, Quebec, May 10, 1862,
    age 75.
Bill, Asahel, Buffalo Town, Oct. 19, 1836, age 37.
Bill, Maria Louisa, Cold Spring, NY, March 13, 1852, age 22.
Billey, William E., formerly of Buffalo, Sept. 29, 1878, age 65; d. at Weedsport, NY.
Billings, Alfred, Jan. 4, 1840, age 22.
Billings, Catharine A., widow of Dr. J. A., June 18, 1862.
Billings, Capt. Francis P., March 11, 1865, age 55.
Billings, Libbie, Dec. 8, 1878, wife of Henry F.
Billings, Mary Ann, wife of Theodore D., Aug. 30, 1837, age 23. D. at South Dearfield, MA.
Billings, Parker, March 1829, age 50.
Billings, Susan, formerly of Buffalo, Jan. 5, 1869, age 37. Wife of Charles F., dau. of
    Harlow French. D. in Milwaukee, bur. in Buffalo.
Billyard, Sophronia, wife of Francis, Newstead, Jan. 28, 1873, age 61 y, 6 m, 1 d.
Bindemann, Frederick William, Jan. 25, 1873, age 35.
Bingeman, Caroline Pfeifer, wife of John, Oct. 4, 1869, age 26 y, 11 m.
Bingham, Bartley F., Jan. 25, 1875.
Bingham, Belle, July 29, 1879, age 10 y, 6 m; bur. Forest Lawn.
Bingham, Mary, mother of Mrs. James McGinness, Oct. 31, 1861, age 72.
Bingham, Mrs. Mary, Lancaster, NY, Jan. 11, 1874, age 94.
Bingham, Susan, Jan. 19, 1868, age 38.
Bingham, William Stanford, Aug. 25, 1870, age 39.
Binks, Reuben, Jan. 12, 1875, age 78.
Birch, Charles W., Feb. 22, 1858, age 22 y, 9 m.
Bird, Amelia S., wife of George W., July 27, 1876.
Bird, Ellen, at Co. Almshouse, March 14, 1876, age 27.
Bird, Henry, Co. Almshouse, April 21, 1877, age 28.
Bird, Dr. J. Herman, formerly of Buffalo, eldest son of W.A., March 4, 1871; d. at Sioux
    City, IA; bur. in Buffalo.
Bird, Joanna M., wife of W. A., Black Rock, NY, April 11, 1837, age 34.
Bird, Mrs. Mary, Jan. 12, 1853, age 47.
Bird, Miss Mary M., Oct. 7, 1870, age 74; taken to Westfield.
Bird, Col. Nathaniel. Revolutionary soldier, Hamburg, Jan. 11, 1847, age 84. Native of
    New Marlborough, MA.
Bird, William A., Aug. 19, 1878, age 81.
Birge, Daniel O., July 25, 1846, age 21. Formerly of Buffalo, d. at Carlyle, IL.
Birk, John, Feb. 14, 1880, age 21 y, 4 m, 25 d.

Birk, Mary, wife of Jacob, Dec. 8, 1879, age 57 y, 3 m, 4 d.
Birkenstock, Fred A., April 17, 1886, age 66.
Birmingham, John, April 21, 1878, age 51.
Bisantz, Anthony, April 16, 1875, age 28; bur. Pine Hill.
Bisantz, Mary Magdalena, May 4, 1878, age 63 y, 5 m, 2 d.
Bisgood, William A., Nov. 18, 1863, age 22 y, 5 m, 18 d.
Bishop, A. B., wife of Christopher F., Sept. 25, 1854, age 28.
Bishop, Calvin, April 1, 1852, age 46.
Bishop, Caroline, wife of Nathaniel, July 24, 1867, age 42 y, 1 m.
Bishop, Edward Francis, son of DeFrancis T., Colden, July 8, 1869, age 20 y, 10 m, 8d.
Bishop, Dr. Francis T., Colden, March 12, 1864, age 57. Native of Basingstoke, Hampshire, England.
Bishop, Frederick A., March 13, 1874, age 26 y, 15 d; suicide.
Bishop, Henry, Tonawanda, NY, March 30, 1874.
Bishop, James, Oct. 27, 1869, age 36 y, 7 m.
Bishop, James D., Cheektowaga, NY, Nov. 23, 1880, age 74.
Bishop, Maria L. B., wife of Albert W., Jan. 14, 1860, age 24.
Bishop, Samuel L., Aug. 5, 1849, age 24.
Bissell, Dorothy, Lancaster, NY, Nov. 2, 1844, age 78.
Bissell, Capt. Elias, Clarence, NY, Feb. 1813, age 55.
Bissell, Elias, Lancaster, NY, June 16, 1880, age 86.
Bissell, Elias, b. 1759, d. 1815, bur. Lancaster, NY; Revolutionary soldier.
Bissell, Elihu, Lancaster, Feb. 20, 1874, age 72; d. in Rochester, bur. in Lancaster, NY.
Bissell, Dr. Harry H., Sept. 16, 1858, age 62.
Bissell, Lucy G., wife of Elias, Lancaster, Dec. 21, 1873, age 69.
Bissell, Rosette, wife of Elihu, Lancaster, April 29, 1846, age 32.
Bittner, Ernst, June 5, 1874, age 52; suicide.
Bivens, Margaret, wife of E. D., Clarence, NY, May 19, 1846.
Bivens, Thomas, Clarence, Oct. 3, 1832, age 40; d. in MI of cholera.
Bivins, William, Clarence, NY, Oct. 31, 1872, age 19 y, 11 m, 12 d. Son of the late Homer.
Bixby, Daniel, White's Corners, NY, Oct. 20, 1860, age 54.
Bixby, Maria Charlotte Beare, wife of Robert S., East Aurora, NY, March 1862, age 65.
Bixby, Robert, father of James, Oct. 8, 1865, age 81. Taken to Lewiston.
Black, Capt. Braddock, North Evans, NY, Feb. 4, 1851, age 54.
Black, Caroline, wife of Lytle, Oct. 5, 1877, age 32 y, 9 m, 8 d.
Black, Elisha M., only child of Braddock, Evans, NY, Jan. 29, 1851, age 20 y, 5 m.
Black, Elizabeth G., wife of Robert, bookseller, Sept. 8, 1857, age 46. Formerly of Brechin, Scotland.
Black, James, March 11, 1876, age 40; car-driver, drowned.
Blackley, Rebecca Harvey, Oct. 21, 1873, age 23; wife of Edward.
Blackman, George, Marilla, May 26, 1864, age 60. Formerly of Chautauqua County.
Blackman, George S., Lancaster, NY, Dec. 17, 1852. D. in Cincinnati, bur. in Lancaster.
Blackmond, Edwin F. Sr., Dec. 30, 1868, age 59.
Blackmond, Francis W., eldest son of Edwin T., Black Rock, NY, July 26, 1860, age 26 y, 11 m, 9 d.
Blackmore, Priscilla, wife of John, Grand Island, Feb. 14, 1879, age 43; d. at Petrolia City, PA.
Blackmur, Anna, April 19, 1872, age 24 y, 5 m, 28 d; wife of Edward.
Blackston, William, M.D., Lancaster, NY, Oct. 27, 1852, age 42 y, 10 m. Formerly of Baltimore, MD.
Blackwood, Atchinson N., brother of Mrs. Charles W. Hopkins, May 11, 1855, age 23.
Blackwood, Mrs. Hannah, Jan. 27, 1879, age 84.
Blackwood, Sarah B., May 21, 1878.
Blain, Eliza, April 6, 1875, widow of Oscar.
Blain, Mrs. Eliza, Feb. 12, 1879, age 63.
Blain, Rev. Jacob, March 28, 1880, age 88 y, 2 m.
Blaine, John, Sept. 1871.
Blair, Mrs. Nancy, Dec. 25, 1877, age 74.
Blake, Mrs., June 8, 1835, age 85.
Blake, Mrs. A. D., Dec. 5, 1839, age c. 51.

Blake, Ithamar, June 9, 1835, age 84.
Blakeley, Edward, Co. F., 116 NY Vol., Boston, NY, May 24, 1864, age 19.
Blakeley, Edwin E., Elma, March 13, 1864, age 22 y, 6 m.
Blakeley, Robert L., in U.S. Army, March 4, 1863, age 17 y, 6 m, 4d. D. at Vicksburg.
Blakeley, Sally, wife of Joseph, Arora, Aug. 1842, age 62.
Blakely, Annie M., wife of Joseph, Jr., Oct. 24, 1874, age 35 y, 6 m, 19 d.
Blakely, Charlotte, wife of Erastus, Aurora, NY, April 1836, age 21.
Blakely, David, West Falls, NY, April 9, 1871, age 84 y, 1 m, 9 d.
Blakely, Deacon Isaac, Aurora, NY, April 21, 1849, age 73.
Blakely, Joseph, East Aurora, NY, March 4, 1863, age 81.
Blakely, Joseph W., eldest son of William, May 15, 1864, age 19 7 6.
Blakely, Sarah, wife of Robert, March 20, 1871.
Blakely, Mrs. William E., Aurora, NY, Feb. 19, 1865, age 43.
Blakeslee, Adaline, wife of G. W., March 12, 1845, age 30.
Blanchard, Mrs. Mary, Eden Valley, NY, Aug. 3, 1873, age 73.
Blanchard, Philinda A., wife of G. G. of Jamestown (Chautauqua Co.), Clarence, NY, April 15, 1848, age 23.
Blanchard, Ruth E. T., wife of A. A., Sept. 14, 1857, age 34. D. at Hanover, NH.
Blanchard, William D., April 26, 1866, age 34. D. at Jamestown, bur. in Buffalo.
Blaney, James D., April 28, 1877, age 73.
Blassdell, William Henry, Sept. 18, 1858, age 36.
Blatchford, Daniel, June 27, 1848, age 65.
Blatchford, Capt. Daniel, Co. E., 179th Reg. NY Vol., June 18, 1864, age 32. Killed in battle of Petersburg; bur. Buffalo.
Blauvelt, Maria, wife of John, Oct. 30, 1874, age 62.
Bleiler, Albert E., 116th Reg. NY Vol., March 30, 1867, age 21 y, 3m.
Bleiler, Casper, Sr., Jan. 26, 1878, age 63 y, 28 d.
Bleiler, George, March 26, 1858, age 40.
Bleiler, Magdalen, March 22, 1879, age 63; wife of Casper.
Bleier, Mathias, April 30, 1858, age 36.
Bliss, Florence, Feb. 17, 1872, age 20 y, 10 m.
Bliss, Lieut. Col. John, Nov. 22, 1854 at St. Augustine, FL, age 66. Bur. Forest Lawn.
Bliss, Joseph, Oct. 1837, age 23. D. at father's home, Ludlow, MA.
Bliss, Dr. Judah, formerly of Hartford, CT, Nov. 30, 1845, age 69.
Bliss, Letitia Matilda, April 21, 1864, Erie, PA, age 82. [Dau. of Andrew Ellicott & Sarah Brown. Wife of Lieut. Col. John Bliss. Bur. in Forest Lawn.]
Bliss, Mary, dau. of Wm. Lovering and Mary, wife of John Horace Bliss, Nov. 7, 1848. D. at Mammoth Cave, KY, bur. in Buffalo.
Bliss, Mrs. S., Aug. 4, 1873, age 43 y, 10 m, 17d.
Blocher, Catharine, Clarence Centre, Jan. 6, 1871, age 75. Widow, mother of John Blocher of Buffalo.
Blocher, Emanuel, Clarence, April, 1878; d. in Nebraska, bur. in Clarence, NY.
Blocher, Peter, Harris Hill, NY, Oct. 7, 1877, age 65.
Block, Conrad, at Co. Almshouse, Aug. 16, 1876, age 65.
Block, Julius, d. at Meadeville, Aug. 23, 1879, age 35 y, 6 m, 28 d; suicide.
Blocker, David N., Clarence, NY, Jan. 17, 1880, age 48.
Blodget, Margaret, wife of Isaac, Wales, NY, May 4, 1831, age 67.
Blodgett, Betsey, widow of Lewis, Hermitage, Oct. 22, 1880, age 84.
Blodgett, Mrs. Elizabeth, Brant, NY, March 13, 1866, age 66.
Blodgett, Mrs. Emeline, Alden, NY, Feb. 24, 1879, age 67.
Blodgett, J., formerly of Buffalo, March 24, 1873, age 44; d. in Cortland, NY.
Blodgett, Maria, wife of William H., formerly of Buffalo, Feb. 29, 1876; d. in Washington, DC.
Blodgett, Miss Mary Ann, Alden, NY, May 24, 1853, age 38.
Bloeser, Mrs. Clara Louise, April 18, 1876, age 22 y, 9 m, 17 d; dau. of George Kreiner.
Bloker, Andrew F., Williamsville, NY, Dec. 31, 1879, age 52.
Bloker, Henry S., Williamsville, NY, Oct. 25, 1878, age 23.
Blood, Mrs. Caroline P., widow of Ira D., formerly of Buffalo, Dec. 10, 1879, age 47.
Blood, Henrietta, dau. of David, May 29, 1853, age 26.
Blood, Ira D., formerly of Buffalo, Aug. 20, 1870; d. Rochester, MN.

Blood, James R., April 28, 1879, age 49.
Blood, Louisa, wife of Ira D., May 28, 1857, age 23. Taken east.
Bloomer, Tooker T., March 7, 1867, age 52.
Bloomfield, Louisa M., wife of N. J., dau. of Ansel Mills, March 31, 1851, age 36.
Blossom, Charlotte Strong, Sept. 13, 1879, age 65; wife of Thomas Blossom.
Blossom, Edward H., son of the late Ira, formerly of Buffalo, Feb. 24, 1876, age 28; d. at Clifton Springs.
Blossom, Eunice J., widow of Col. Ira A., formerly of Buffalo, Oct. 20, 1875, age 72; d. Norwalk, CT.
Blossom, Ira A., Oct. 27, 1856, age 66.
Blossom, Ira H., Jan. 11, 1855, age 32.
Blossom, Mrs. Jane Hillman, Feb. 5, 1877, aged 81.
Blossom, Laura B., wife of Ira H., April 12, 1853, age 24.
Blossom, Samuel F., brother of Ira A. and Thomas of Buffalo, Amherst, Dec. 15, 1840. Late of Monmouth, ME.
Blossom, Samuel H., April 13, 1880, age 48 y, 7 m.
Blossom, Miss Sarah E., June 22, 1853, age 25.
Blossom, Mrs. Thomas, Sept. 15, 1879, age 65.
Blount, Jonathan, b. 1758, d. 1828, bur. Clarence, NY; Revolutionary Soldier.
Bluett, Mrs. Mary, lately of Leixlip, Ireland, Feb. 18, 1851, age 60.
Blum, Mrs. Anna M., Jan. 9, 1874, age 21.
Blum, Peter, Oct. 14, 1869, age 55 y, 7 m.
Blume, Henry, accident, Wolcott Bush, March 24, 1879, age c. 40.
Blumenthal, Maurice, Sept. 7, 1872, age 40.
Blust, Stephen, accident, Hamburgh, laborer, April 4-5, 1880.
Boalch, George T., Oct. 2, 1870, age 33.
Boalch, William P., March 17, 1875, age 30 y, 11 m, 5d.
Boardman, Amanda P., formerly of Buffalo, Aug. 5, 1878, age 73. Wife of William G. D. at Saratoga Springs; bur. in Albany Rural Cemetery.
Boardman, Edward E., April 24, 1872, age 24; taken to Darien Centre.
Boardman, Elijah, March 6, 1869, in 74th y; taken to Akron, NY.
Boardman, Fannie M., wife of Dr. John, Aug. 22, 1867.
Boardman, John, March 20, 1858, age 74.
Boardman, Mrs. Nancy, Newstead, March 18, 1846, age 84.
Boardman, Sarah Parmelee, widow of Samuel, Dec. 12, 1860, age 72.
Boas, Samuel, Jan. 29, 1873, age 55.
Bochoer, Rev. Father Charles, formerly of Buffalo, Aug. 1878, age c. 50; d. in New Orleans.
Bodamer, Gottleib F., Jan. 24, 1879, age 68 y, 10 m, 24 d.
Bodemer, Jacob, Erie Co. Almshouse, March 27, 1877, age 83.
Bodine, ---, wife of Abram, Clarence, Jan. 17, 1879, age past 70.
Bodine, Mary E., wife of Cornelius, Clarence, NY, March 14, 1879, age 31.
Bodkin, Ellen, wife of Patrick, May 17, 1872, age c. 40.
Boeckel, Carrie C., Oct. 5, 1874, age 30 y, 24 d.
Boese, Charles, formerly of Tonawanda, NY, May 21, 1872; suicide at Saginaw, MI.
Bogart, Martin S., Sept. 10, 1868, age 41; d. at Venice Center, Cayuga Co., NY.
Bogert, Lawrence K., Nov. 24, 1873, age 69.
Bogert, Mary A., dau. of James B., granddaughter of L. K., Jan. 4, 1860.
Boggan, Michael, April 1, 1876, age 46.
Boggiano, Margaretta, wife of Anthony, March 22, 1877.
Boggis, Elizabeth, wife of William, June 27, 1868.
Boggis, William, Jan. 1, 1876, age 69.
Boggs, Mary H., Sept. 30, 1873, age 58.
Boggs, Thomas, sailor, drowned, July, 1874.
Bogley, Betsey C. (E.?), March 18, 1880, age 77.
Bogue, Mrs. G. C., widow of Rev. H.P.B., Feb. 18, 1880, age 80; d. at Avon.
Bogue, Rev. H., Jan. 1872, age 75.
Bohl, Louis, March 16, 1871, age 45.
Bohr, John Henry, Feb. 25, 1871, age 52.
Boice, Mrs. Rose Anna, wife of Isaac, Oct. 27, 1860, age 57.
Boies, Eber, formerly of Aurora, NY, March 8, 1873, age 87.

Boies, Hannah, Aurora, Sept. 19, 1870, in 87th y; widow of Deacon Joel.
Boies, Deacon Joel, Aurora, Feb. 16, 1845, age 61.
Boies, Versalia M., formerly of Buffalo, April 17, 1877, age 43 y, 2 m, 16 d; wife of Hon. Horace, d. at Waterloo, IA.
Boilletat, G., Nov. 1875.
Boillotat, Dominique, June 7, 1868, age 46 y, 4 m, 5 d.
Boland, Francis, Nov. 20, 1876, age 80.
Boland, Mrs. Frank, Sept. 29, 1873, age 26.
Boland, Honora, wife of William, Oct. 10, 1854, age 46.
Boland, James, Oct. 18, 1873, age 41.
Boland, Mrs. Martin, March, 1878, age 72.
Boldt, Mrs. Dora M., Aug. 14, 1880, age 71 y, 4 m, 21 d.
Boldt, Ernst, Jan. 11, 1874, age 36.
Boldt, Helen Gutwasser, wife of C.F.H., July 25, 1870.
Bole, Archibald, late from Ireland, Oct. 1823, age 24.
Boles, Barney, Oct. 6, 1873, age 71.
Bolger, Frank, Aug. 14, 1874, age 41.
Boll, Mrs. Eureka, Feb. 20, 1873, age 22.
Bolle, August, Nov. 17, 1878, age 54.
Boller, Mrs. Margaretha, May 7, 1877, age 64 y, 5 m, 22 d.
Bolton, Henry D., Feb. 6, 1838, age 40.
Bolz, Mrs. Elizabeth, widow, Feb. 9, 1877, age 61.
Bond, Albert, Sept. 4, 1862, age 21.
Bond, Mrs. Betsey, Aurora, NY, Aug. 19, 1855, age 72.
Bond, Charles P., Aug. 25, 1864, age 35.
Bond, Harriett, wife of William W., Aurora, Jan. 8, 1840, age 27.
Bond, Huldah, June 30, 1872, age 61 y, 9 m; wife of Oliver. D. at Sheboygan, WI, bur. in Buffalo.
Bond, LaForrest, only son of Oliver, Aug. 28, 1864, age 27.
Bond, William W., East Aurora, NY, Jan. 23, 1879, age 69.
Boniface, James T., Detroit, MI, Feb. 17, 1878, age 75. Father of Georgia; taken to London.
Bonnar, Charlotte, dau. of William H., Oct. 15, 1870, age 23; d. at King, Ontario, bur. in Buffalo.
Bonnar, George L., Oct. 26, 1876, age 21 y, 9 m.
Bonnar, William H., Jan. 12, 1864, age 48.
Bonnar, William H., Oct. 16, 1872, age 22.
Bonner, Mary, wife of T. E., Nov. 20, 1835, age 26.
Bonney, Charles, d. at LeRoy, April 30, 1849, age 22.
Bonney, Eliza, wife of Zoroaster, Feb. 3, 1857, age 43.
Bonney, Horace, July 28, 1869, age 62 y, 3 m; brother of Zoroaster & David; taken to Brockport.
Bonney, Josephine, Feb. 9, 1871, age 27; youngest dau. of Zoroaster.
Bonney, Zoroaster, Nov. 26, 1876, age 74.
Booker, Sabina M., Dec. 10, 1875; wife of B. W.
Booman, Mrs. Mary W., wife of Capt. John W., May 17, 1879, age 53.
Boomer, Lavinia, wife of Dr. Samuel, Dec. 6, 1822, age 30.
Booram, Cornelius, d. in Washington, DC, bur. in Buffalo, Feb. 24, 1864, age 54.
Boordman, Philip, killed by a falling tree, East Elma, NY, April 14, 1880.
Boorham, Abraham, May 27, 1848, age c. 45.
Boorman, Mary, wife of Richard, Aug. 19, 1876, age 50.
Booth, Mrs. Diana, Feb. 18, 1880, age 24; accident or suicide.
Booth, James W., May 23, 1876, age 45.
Booth, Jennie E., Lancaster, Oct. 1, 1879, age 3 y, 1 m, 7 d.
Booth, John, Dec. 28, 1880, age 67.
Borcharding, Herman, April 24, 1875, age 44; accident.
Borden, Mrs. Vashti, July 27, 1865, age 87; taken to Rochester.
Bordew, R., Tonawanda, NY, April 9, 1872.
Bordwell, Benjamin R., Feb. 22, 1867, age 70 y, 5 m.
Bordwell, Catharine G., wife of Dennice, March 4, 1856, age 27; dau. of Daniel Grider.
Bork, Charles, laborer, Sept. 20, 1880.

Borman, Peter, June 9, 1867, age 32.
Borst, Mrs. Mary, March 13, 1873, age 38.
Bosch, Anton, April 20, 1878, age 65.
Bosche, John, June 1, 1861, age 69 y, 8 m.
Bosseler, Jacob, April 19, 1877, age 31.
Boston, Carrie, wife of William, April 20, 1874, age 25.
Bostwick, Major Lucius A., formerly of Buffalo, Jan. 2, 1863, age 52; d. in Hillsdale, MI.
Bostwick, Mary B., Lancaster, June 2, 1862, age 75; formerly of Bennington, VT.
Bosworth, Sarah, widow of Benjamin of Bristol, RI, Nov. 26, 1849.
Bosworth, Susanna, wife of Samuel, Sept. 18, 1832, age 42.
Botsford, Caroline, wife of Jerome, Sept. 19, 1868, age 52.
Bouck, Mrs. Margaret, Lancaster, NY, July 6, 1875, age 77.
Boughton, --- Mr., Black Rock, NY, Aug. 29, 1820.
Boughton, Mrs. Abigail, April 9, 1844, age 64.
Boughton, James, Feb. 3, 1872, age 56.
Bourkhart, Louisa, Jan. 22, 1879, age 22; dau. of Frank.
Bourne, Rev. George, 1845.
Bouyon, Josephine Monnin, wife of Paul, formerly of Buffalo, Oct. 5, 1873, age 38; d. in St. Louis, MO, bur. in Buffalo.
Bovet, Mrs. Mary Augusta, March 16, 1879, age 85.
Bovington, Jane A., wife of E.E. of Chicago, Jan. 16, 1861, age 33.
Bow, Mrs. Ellen, Dec. 3, 1878, age 38.
Bowan, Sarah, wife of Jason, East Aurora, March 15, 1880, age 69.
Bowden, Miss Ann Jane, Dec. 27, 1868, age 38; taken to Whites Corners, NY.
Bowden, James of Mina, Chautauqua Co., March 10, 1847, age 55.
Bowe, James, Jan. 13, 1878, age 44.
Bowen, Anstress, wife of Palmer, Aurora, NY, Jan. 12, 1852, age 49.
Bowen, Caleb, East Buffalo, Nov. 14, 1865, age 83.
Bowen, Caroline A., Sept. 6, 1850, age 20.
Bowen, Daniel A., Jan. 12, 1879, age 55.
Bowen, Dennis, April 21, 1877, age 58.
Bowen, Eliza, wife of Thomas, Dec. 28, 1848.
Bowen, Emily S., dau. of Jason T., East Aurora, NY, Oct. 13, 1870, age 34.
Bowen, Frederick, July 28, 1843, age 31.
Bowen, George, Feb. 12, 1838, age 80.
Bowen, Georgiana, Jan. 31, 1868, age 39, wife of Lucius M.
Bowen, Mrs. Goodrich J., Dec. 13, 1872.
Bowen, Harriet Callard, wife of Goodrich J., Dec. 13, 1872.
Bowen, Henry W., East Aurora, Aug. 17, 1876, age 35; son of Samuel W.
Bowen, James, formerly of Aurora, merchant, Dec. 6, 1843, age 27; d. at Yorkshire, Cattaraugus Co., NY.
Bowen, John (or James Bowns), Jan. 15, 1877, age c. 37.
Bowen, Jonathan, East Aurora, Aug. 23, 1869, age 87 y, 26 d; father of Dennis Bowen of Buffalo.
Bowen, Joseph, Colden, May 13, 1869, age 55.
Bowen, Deacon Joshua, Holland, NY, May 5, 1828, age 79.
Bowen, Lemuel B., West Falls, NY, Oct. 2, 1865, age 20 y, 10 m.
Bowen, Lucy, wife of Daniel, June 12, 1871, age 69.
Bowen, Lucy Ann Morgan, eldest dau. of Daniel, April 1, 1851, age 29.
Bowen, Mary E., June 9, 1878, age 25; wife of Goodrich J.
Bowen, Sarah Berry, wife of Daniel A., Aug. 14, 1877, age 48 y, 18 d.
Bowen, Sophia, wife of George W., Feb. 21, 1849, age 51; d. at Whitehall.
Bowen, Susan A., wife of John, East Aurora, NY, March 31, 1861, age 46; sister of Dr. George H. Latham.
Bowen, Vashti, wife of Jonathan, Aurora, NY, Nov. 19, 1857, age 79; mother of Capt. Isaac and Dennis.
Bower, Hannah Louise, wife of Philip, Nov. 2, 1866, age 27 y, 5 m.
Bower, Magdelane, wife of Jacob Sr., Oct. 23, 1867, age 57 y, 8 m, 3 d.
Bowers, Michael, at General Hospital, June 7, 1880, age 75.
Bowes, Charlotte McConkin, wife of John, April 12, 1871, age 40.

Bowes, John, Co. Almshouse, Jan. 8, 1878, age 58.
Bowes, Margaret, Oct. 17, 1880, age 48.
Bowie (or Bowil), Lydia A., wife of William D., Aurora, NY, April 17, 1864, age 44.
Bowie, William Day, East Aurora, NY, Sept. 25, 1876, age 62.
Bowles, Bowles, Dec. 12, 1874, age 32.
Bowles, Capt. John C., Co. D., 74th Reg., May 14, 1865, age 33. Taken to Bedford, PA.
Bowles, Minnie, wife of Charles I., Dec. 20, 1878, age 22.
Bowman, Capt., officer of Rev. Army, Clarence, June 29, 1822, age 82; bur. in Harris Hill Cemetery, Town of Clarence, NY.
Bowman, Isaac F., Williamsville, NY, Aug. 22, 1821, age 40.
Bowman, Sgt. Maj. Julius Eli, youngest son of Eli H., Oct. 6, 1864, age 18 y, 5 m, 6d. D. in Beverly Hospital, NJ. Taken to Harris Hill, NY.
Bowman, Mary, wife of Benjamin, Lancaster, NY, Jan. 26, 1850, age 70.
Bowman, Sarah, wife of George, June 4, 1880, age 28.
Boy, Frederick, native of Germany, Dec. 22, 1872, age 44.
Boyce, Benjamin, Evans, NY, June 21, 1869, age 73.
Boyce, Charles, July 21, 1874; d. in State Prison at Auburn, NY.
Boyd, Mrs. Ann, Aug. 31, 1863, age 64.
Boyd, Charlotte Baker, wife of Wm., East Hamburgh, NY, April 24, 1860, age 35.
Boyd, David, d. at Erie, PA, Nov. 25, 1853, age 63.
Boyd, David, West Aurora, NY, June 20, 1872, age 73.
Boyd, George W., Dec. 17, 1879, age 29 y, 1 m, 17 d.
Boyd, Harlow, Sardinia, NY, June 5, 1846, age 32.
Boyd, Henry, Griffin's Mills, Oct. 11, 1871, age 31 y, 6 m, 20 d.
Boyd, Mrs. Hugh, Dec. 7, 1872, age 37.
Boyd, Isabella, wife of David, Jan. 18, 1853, age 62.
Boyd, James, Jan. 8, 1860, age 44.
Boyd, Mrs. Jane, Aug. 9, 1849, age 46.
Boyd, Robert, Aurora, NY, Oct. 11, 1874, age 40.
Boyd, Robert D., March 10, 1871, age 68.
Boyd, Thomas, Oct. 10, 1867, age 56.
Boyd, William, March 28, 1857, age 39.
Boyd, William D. or B., West Alden, June 9, 1874, age (52) or 74.
Boyden, Charles F., June 8, 1876, age 38 y, 8 m.
Boyer, William, Oct. 28, 1872, age 27.
Boyland, Ann, Dec. 1, 1880, age 68.
Boylaw, Mary, Sept. 21, 1880, age 40.
Boyle, Hugh, May 30, 1875, age 72.
Boyle, James, July 6, 1873.
Boyle, John, Sept. 28, 1880, age 59.
Boynton, Charles, Sept. 24, 1852, age 75.
Boynton, Charles William son of Charles, brother of T. N., Dec. 29, 1857, age 53, d. in New York.
Boynton, Polly, May 26, 1873, age 90; widow of Charles.
Boynton, Thomas Franklin, April 9, 1876, age 67.
Bozze, Catharine, wife of Dominick, Sept. 15, 1877, age 41.
Brace, Curtis L., April 28, 1869, age 51.
Brace, Frederick Gelston, son of the late Curtis, Feb. 12, 1872, age 20.
Brace, Julia Ann, wife of Orange, Jan. 23, 1837, age 27.
Brace, Laura, dau. of Lester and Tamma, Dec. 6, 1848, age 30.
Brace, Lester, 1869.
Brace, Lester, Dec. 8, 1871, age 82.
Brace, Tamma, wife of Lester, May 20, 1869, in 77th year.
Bracken, William R., Dec. 1, 1880, age 39 y, 5 m.
Bradford, Amanda, wife of Thomas, April 23, 1847, age 22. Formerly of Cold Spring, Putnam Co., NY.
Bradford, John L., Sept. 19, 1868, age 55.
Bradford, William R., formerly of Abbotsford, C. E., Oct. 10, 1867, age 35 y, 7 m.
Bradie, Mrs. Elizabeth, May 24, 1875, age 80 y, 8 m.
Bradish, Bridget Kimmit, wife of John, April 5, 1872, age 25.

Bradley, Adeline H., wife of Benjamin, July 13, 1853, age 34.
Bradley, David L., Springville, July 1, 1830, age 32. D. at Jacksonville, FL.
Bradley, Elias A., June 4, 1868, age 73.
Bradley, James, May 13, 1874, age 30; railroad accident.
Bradley, James Ward, April 25, 1869, age 24 y, 10 m, 14 d; telegraph operator; head of the "Telegraph Institute" in Buffalo.
Bradley, Mary, wife of Philo, Sept. 3, 1871, age 40.
Bradley, Sophia, widow of Elias A., April 29, 1871, age 67.
Bradner, Lester, Dansville, Livingston Co., NY, Aug. 17, 1872, age 82.
Bradshaw, Thomas P., July 31, 1879, age 59.
Bradt, Levi, July 7, 1874, age 40 y, 9m.
Brady, Charles B., son of Capt. John R., Boston, NY, Nov. 25, 1860, age 35.
Brady, Mrs. Elizabeth, mother of Capt. John R., East Hamburgh, NY, June 16, 1854, age 92.
Brady, Capt. John R., East Hamburgh, NY, Nov. 22, 1863, age 63.
Brady, Mary Ann, wife of Capt. John R., Hamburgh, NY, July 15, 1848, age 31.
Brady, Patrick, Dec. 6, 1879; found dead.
Brady, Thomas, Nov. 7, 1877, age 85.
Bragg, Margaret, wife of George, Aug. 15, 1838, age 31.
Bragg, Seneca, Co. C., 24th N Y Cav., Aurora, April 27, 1864, age 28, eldest son of George S., d. at Camp Stoneman Hospital, DC.
Braids, Mrs. Catherine, Feb. 26, 1871, age 66.
Braids, Clara E., May 5, 1874, age 20; dau. of William.
Braids, Edward, Feb. 8, 1879, age 37.
Braids, Elizabeth C., May 24, 1876, wife of William.
Brainard, Mrs. Cornelia, mother-in-law of J.G. and the late Capt. W. P. Stone, May 1, 1854, age 68.
Brainard, Henry Clay, son of J. G., Dec. 25, 1877.
Brainard, Joshua G., May 15, 1880, age 69 y, 11 m.
Brand, H. Maria, wife of Gardner, Springville, NY, June 15, 1846, age 25.
Brandel, Frank, Aug. 27, 1878, age 21 y, 9 m.
Brandel, Mrs. Mary, March 23, 1871, age 85.
Brandon, Maggie Loretta, Aug. 14, 1877, age 22.
Brandt, Col. John, Brandford, U.C., Aug. 27, 1832. Celebrated Chief of the Six Nations and member of Upper Canada Parliament; d. of cholera.
Brandt, William, Nov. 10, 1878, age 72 y, 8 m, 18 d.
Brathwaite, Maria, wife of John C., April 11, 1866, dau. of Dr. James Hunter of Ann Arbor.
Bratt, Nicholas, Newstead, NY, May 11, 1864, age 64.
Brayman, Dwight, son of Henry, Hamburgh, NY, June 16, 1838.
Brayman, Henry, May 2, 1853, age 62.
Brayman, Maria, wife of Henry, April 16, 1852, age 57. Taken to Abbott's Corners, NY.
Brayman, Miss Sarah, dau. of Daniel, Hamburgh, NY, Aug. 31, 1855, age 38.
Brayton, Flora Russell, wife of Charles E., South Wales, NY, Feb. 22, 1875; d. in Chicago, taken to South Wales.
Brayton, Philip F., Providence, RI, Sept. 27, 1850, age 41.
Brazier, Francis, May 19, 1874, age 24.
Brechtel, Charles, April 25, 1879, age 80 y, 10 m, 7 d.
Brechtel, John, Sr., Feb. 5, 1879, age 76 y, 9 m, 15 d.
Brechtel, Julie, June 22, 1879, age 22 y, 3 m, 20 d.
Brechtel, Louisa R., April 18, 1872, age 27 y, 8 m, 15 d.
Breck, Theresa, May 9, 1880, age 21 y, 10 m, 17 d.
Breckenridge, Stephen P., Aug. 1, 1857, age 42.
Bredel, Mrs. Betsey, Nov. 18, 1878; suicide.
Breed, Ann, wife of F.W., Aug. 14, 1876.
Breed, Casper, Tonawanda, NY, July 7, 1874, age 33; drowned.
Brees, John, July 14, 1873.
Breier, Conrad, Aug. 12, 1878, age 74 y, 9 m.
Breitwieser, Jacob, Aug. 19, 1869, age 26; found shot through the head, in his room.
Bremiller, Mrs. Mary Ann, Hamburgh, NY, March 22, 1874, age 74. Accidently killed on the Buffalo & Jamestown Railroad.
Breneman, Charles, West Seneca, July 27, 1873; suicide.

Brennan, Andrew, Dec. 22, 1873, age 66.
Brennan, Bernard, Oct. 22, 1878, age 36.
Brennan, D. M., May 27, 1873; drowned.
Brennan, Emma R., March 6, 1869, age 34; dau. of the late Jesse Ketcham.
Brennan, Florence, Aug. 12, 1875, accident.
Brennan, Mrs. Honora, Nov. 15, 1880, age 65.
Brennan, Jane, July 28, 1875, age 66.
Brennan, Matthew, May, 1872, age c. 60; suicide.
Brennan, Patrick, Sept. 3, 1878, age 67; at Co. Almshouse.
Brennan, William, Lake Engineer, May 13, 1880, age 42.
Brennen, John, almshouse, Oct. 2, 1880, age 69.
Brent, Benjamin, July 15, 1877, age 65 y, 11 m, 16 d.
Brett, Mary, wife of John, March 15, 1871, age 24.
Bretton, Matilda, widow of Thomas, Sept. 13, 1875, age 52.
Brewster, Cortland, Oct. 1, 1874, age 51; taken to West Troy, NY.
Brewster, Ezra E., Jan. 20, 1874, age 47 y, 6 m.
Brewster, Samuel C., of Syracuse, formerly of Buffalo, Aug. 27, 1871, age 72; d. at
    Syracuse, NY.
Brtian, Mrs. Ellen C., Feb. 22, 1875, age 86.
Brick, Theresa A., wife of Anthony, Oct. 31, 1878, age 42.
Brick, Valentine, May 11, 1878; accident.
Brideson, Ann, wife of Augustus C., Oct. 4, 1880, age 62.
Bridge, Joseph A., Jan. 14, 1869, age 51.
Bridge, Lucius, formerly of Buffalo, Oct. 5, 1859, age 31. D. in Rochester.
Bridges, Mrs., formerly Mrs. Daley, Sept. 8, 1854, age 54, of Batavia, Kane Co., IL,
    formerly of Buffalo.
Bridges, Thomas, May 22, 1878, age 36.
Bridgman, Henreitta M. Humphrey, wife of J. W., Dec. 8, 1865, age 25 y, 6 m.
Brierley, Hannah, Jan. 23, 1876, age 76 y, 11 m, 18 d; widow of William.
Brierley, William, Sept. 12, 1863, age 73 y, 4 m, 10 d.
Brierley, William H., son of the late William, Dec. 2, 1876, age 48.
Brierly, Catharine Maria, Sept. 23, 1870, age 49.
Briggs, Alpha, wife of Morey P., Boston, NY, March 22, 1855, age 55.
Briggs, Charles C., formerly of East Hamburgh, NY, Dec. 8, 1869, age 62; d. at Oil Creek,
    PA.
Briggs, Mrs. Clarissa A., Dec. 26, 1860, age 63 y, 7 m, 15 d.
Briggs, Ebenezer, Lancaster, NY, Oct. 18, 1872, age 42.
Briggs, Ebenezer G., Lancaster, NY, Jan. 25, 1875, age 68. Wife d. on Saturday last.
Briggs, Eliza, widow of Thomas, Aug. 7, 1873, age 67; d. at Lockport, bur. in Buffalo.
Briggs, Eliza M. Lindsley, wife of Ebenezer G., Lancaster, NY, Jan. 23, 1875, age 60.
Briggs, Ephraim, b. May 13, 1753, d. June 13, 1843, bur. Sardinia, NY, soldier of the
    Revolution.
Briggs, J. C., May 24, 1867.
Briggs, James, June 20, 1876, age 27; suicide.
Briggs, John, U.S. Vol., Black Rock, NY, June 1812.
Briggs, John C., East Hamburgh, NY, May 11, 1874, age 73 y, 8 m.
Briggs, Joseph A., Feb. 12, 1866, age 37 y, 7 m, 3 d.
Briggs, L. Jeannette, wife of Alexander J., Dec. 13, 1864, age 34 y, 14 d.
Briggs, Morey P., Boston, NY, Jan. 24, 1875, age 79.
Briggs, Oliver, of the Society of Friends, Hamburgh, NY, Aug. 21, 1822, age 72.
Briggs, Thomas, March 24, 1869, age 64.
Brigham, Pierpont, Sept. 12, 1852, age 67.
Brightman, Johnson, Rev. soldier, Hamburgh, NY, Feb. 6, 1841, age 84.
Brigs, Maria T., widow of Isaac of Skaneateles, NY, Aug. 14, 1837, age 34.
Brimmer, Harriet, wife of Martin, Boston, NY, Jan. 1, 1833, age 28, dau. of James Wadsworth
    of Geneseo.
Brinkman, Christopher, April 7, 1873; killed on railroad.
Brinkman, John, Jan. 24, 1874, age 35.
Brinkman, Maria, wife of Henry, June 25, 1874, age 39.
Brinkworth, Francis, Feb. 24, 1874, age 53.

Brintnal, Sophia, wife of Phineas, Nov. 24, 1870, age 66.
Brintnall, Phineas, Sept. 17, 1880, age 87 y, 11 m.
Briscoe, Edward, formerly of 100th Regt., May 10, 1866, age 40.
Bristol, Miss Addie, June 24, 1867, age 26 y, 4 d; taken to Newark, N.J.
Bristol, Cyrenius Wells, son of C. C., formerly of Buffalo, Aug. 7, 1878; d. in Philadelphia, PA.
Bristol, Dan., Jan. 30, 1867, age 85.
Bristol, Diana M. Shuart, wife of Henry, Aug. 1, 1867.
Bristol, Harrison, formerly of Buffalo, Oct. 28, 1871; d. at Watsonville, CA.
Bristol, Jessie, dau. of Cyrenius C., Jan. 19, 1864, age 22.
Bristol, Julia E. C., Aug. 16, 1874, age 27; taken to Xenia, OH.
Bristol, Mrs. Maria, Sept. 20, 1872, age 68 y, 6m; taken to Newark, Wayne Co., NY.
Bristol, Martha Hayden, wife of Cyrenius C., Feb. 17, 1866, age 55.
Bristol, Mary J. McLeish, wife of T.M., Oct. 13, 1872, age 29.
Bristol, Dr. Moses, Nov. 6, 1869, age 88.
Bristol, Polly Lockwood, widow of Daniel, Feb. 28, 1879, age 92.
Britt, Catharine, March 22, 1880, age 55.
Britt, Catherine, Oct. 28, 1879, age 94.
Britt, James Joseph, April 4, 1876, age 21 y, 7 m, 13 d.
Britt, John V., Aug. 1, 1878, age 21; railroad accident.
Brittan, ---, wife of John, Clarence, NY, Dec. 1812, age 55.
Brittin, Charles, Sardinia, March 17, 1865, age 37 y, 11 m, 12 d; taken to Malta, DeKalb Co., IL.
Brittin, Wm. D., son of Lewis, July 26, 1852, age 23.
Britton, Anna, wife of Andrew, July 7, 1865, age 28.
Britton, Henry T., d. in Battle of Perryville, 1862.
Britton, Lucinda, wife of N., Oct. 1, 1853, age 43.
Britton, Nicholas, Nov. 18, 1875, age 61.
Britton, Thomas, Aug. 2, 1871, age 52.
Broad, Mary Ann, dau. of Thomas, Nov. 22, 1878.
Brock, Mrs. Bertha, wife of Henry E., Sept. 1, 1879, age 65.
Brock, Jacob, May 17, 1874, age 33.
Brock, Julius, Feb. 26, 1878, age 48.
Brodhead, William W., Dec. 17, 1866, age 69.
Brodie, Mary, wife of James, Evans Centre, Feb. 13, 1874, age 56.
Brodie, William, Aug. 13, 1825, age 33; late from Scotland.
Brogan, George, North Evans, Oct., 1871.
Brokenbourgh, A., April 5, 1876, age 66.
Bronner, Henry, Sept. 15, 1871, age 32 y, 11 m.
Bronner, Philip L., April 19, 1847, age 40.
Bronson, Edwin T., grain dealer & miller, Nov. 14, 1880, age 62; d. in Oswego, formerly of Buffalo.
Bronson, Mrs. Nancy, March 18, 1857, age 77, mother of Isaac C. of Warsaw and of Mrs. Samuel Cramer of Buffalo; taken to Warsaw.
Brooker, Charles H., Nov. 13, 1875, age c. 50; accident.
Brooks, Mrs., Black Rock, Sept. 1827, age 56
Brooks, Alonzo, March 20, 1864, age 36.
Brooks, Mrs. Cyrus, Nov. 8, 1879, age 50 y, 2 d; d. at Cohoes, NY.
Brooks, Frederick J., March 28, 1872, age 27.
Brooks, Helen, widow of Hon. Wells, Feb. 26, 1872, age 57; d. at Olean, bur. in Buffalo.
Brooks, Hon. John, Colden, June 7, 1858, age 69.
Brooks, Rev. Lemuel, Springville, Sept. 18, 1835, age 57.
Brooks, Lester, July 22, 1878, age 76 y, 8 m.
Brooks, Margaret, wife of Sheldon, July 20, 1876, age 39 y, 2 m.
Brooks, Margaret Louise, wife of George, Feb. 18, 1880, age 25.
Brooks, Preston, son of Wells, Oct. 29, 1860, age 23.
Brooks, Robert, West Seneca, NY, Aug. 27, 1857, age 58.
Brooks, Sarah, dau. of late Wells, Jan. 6, 1864, age 25.
Brooks, Wells, Dec. 23, 1859, age 54.
Brooks, William, Elma, Aug. 8, 1878, age 67; suicide.

Brookway, William, Wales, July 23, 1869, age 68.
Brosart, Catherine B., widow of Charles L., June 6, 1878, age 74 y, 6 m, 21 d.
Brosart, Charles L., Nov. 30, 1874, age 71 y, 8 m.
Brother, Frederick, Aug. 2, 1872, brewer.
Brothers, Annie L. Newell, wife of John L., Oct. 28, 1865, age 20 y, 1 d.
Brothers, Mrs. C., Dec. 31, 1879, age 83 y, 2 m.
Brothers, Lewis, Sept. 19, 1860, age 63.
Brothers, Mrs. M. Dortha, Oct. 3, 1866, age 50 y, 7 m, 19 d.
Brothers, Philip, Aug. 12, 1880, age 43 y, 8 m, 14 d.
Brouner, Christina, widow of George L., Nov. 27, 1870, age 85 y, 9 m, 10 d.
Bourner, Susan A., wife of C., Jr., May 16, 1872, age 30 y, 8 m.
Brown, Mr., Williamsville, NY, April 1814, age 27.
Brown, Addie, dau. of the late Charles, July 12, 1874, age 26.
Brown, Agnes, wife of John M., May 19, 1873, age 38.
Brown, Alice Ann, wife of Capt. Neil, Jan. 3, 1870, age 34.
Brown, Ann, wife of Robert, Clarence, Dec. 2, 1846, age 35.
Brown, Anna Stewart, dau. of Edward, May 30, 1871, age 19 y, 6 m.
Brown, Artemus, father of C. Wheeler, May 25, 1845, age 67; taken to Newstead.
Brown, B., April 16, 1878, age 48.
Brown, Benjamin, Aug. 25, 1875, age 72.
Brown, Benjamin F., April 2, 1856, age 40; firm of Clark and Brown.
Brown, Betsey, wife of Henry, April 25, 1879, age 34.
Brown, Catherine, wife of William, April 1858, bur. April 9.
Brown, Catharine E., wife of George V., March 19, 1849, age 25; d. at West Dearborn, Mich.
Brown, Charlotte Caroline, widow of Eleazer, March 27, 1844, age 41.
Brown, Charlotty, widow of Jeremiah, Aurora, June 3, 1865, age 71.
Brown, Mrs. Christian, Clarence, Feb. 28, 1876, age 86; accident.
Brown, Christina, Co. Almshouse, Dec. 6, 1877, age 38.
Brown, Cody S., Sept. 2, 1873, age 28.
Brown, Cornelia L., only dau. of Mrs. Phebe P., Sept. 28, 1863; teacher.
Brown, Lieut. Cyrus, 1863.
Brown, Daniel, Oct. 25, 1869, age 30 y, 1 m.
Brown, Dr. David S., Jan. 14, 1877, age 27; taken to Albion.
Brown, Dexter B., Aurora, Jan. 1, 1830, age 58; formerly of Vt.
Brown, E. R., Grand Island, April 21, 1860, age 65.
Brown, Eliza, wife of Col. Orange T., Aurora, March 14, 1850; d. at Tinmouth, Rutland Co., VT.
Brown, Eliza, wife of Noah H., Newstead, March 11, 1859, age 26.
Brown, Mrs. Elizabeth, Aug., 1875, age 70 y, 11 m.
Brown, Elizabeth Burgess, wife of Thomas, Oct. 27, 1875.
Brown, Emily, dau. of Henry, Dec. 30, 1874, age 20 y, 3 m.
Brown, Fanny W., wife of Joseph W., Feb. 28, 1844; bur. in East Hamburgh, NY.
Brown, Fanney W., wife of Alexander H., Feb. 16, 1857, age 29.
Brown, Frances S., dau. of James C., Nov. 12, 1877, age 21.
Brown, Frederick, formerly of Buffalo, Oct., 1875; killed in accident at Elmira.
Brown, George, Jan. 25, 1863, age 42; formerly of Edinburg, Scotland.
Brown, Gottlieb, Nov. 28, 1880, age 38; hung himself.
Brown, Capt. Hallam Frederick, 1867.
Brown, Hannah, mother of J. C. Brown and Mrs. Pitman, Nov. 3, 1869, age 77.
Brown, Hannah R., wife of Joseph E., Feb. 9, 1873, age 41.
Brown, Harriet, wife of Sylvester, Dec. 5, 1859, age 48; late of Rochester, NY and taken there.
Brown, Harriet, wife of Alvah, Oct. 4, 1863, age 42.
Brown, Henrietta, wife of David Paul, Aug. 10, 1848, age 26.
Brown, Henry, Co. Almshouse, Feb. 2, 1876, age 48.
Brown, Hiram, Eden, June 22, 1870, age c. 60; suicide by shooting.
Brown, Jacob, Oct. 6, 1880, age 35.
Brown, Jane, wife of E. D., Aug. 13, 1872, age 37.
Brown, Jay, Co. Almshouse, March 30, 1877, age 29.
Brown, Jeremiah, father of Charles of Buffalo, Aurora, NY, May 21, 1860, age 69.

Brown, Jeremiah, Co. Almshouse, Aug. 10, 1876, age 68.
Brown, Dr. Jeremiah N., Sept. 18, 1874, age 40; d. in Utica, bur. in Buffalo.
Brown, Dr. John, Lancaster, NY, Feb. 27, 1852, age 60.
Brown, John, formerly of Aurora, NY, Oct. 17, 1868, age 88 y, 6 m; d. at Prophetstown, IL.
Brown, John, formerly of Buffalo, Feb. 19, 1873, age 77; d. at Westfield, NY.
Brown, John, car workman, April 8, 1880.
Brown, John H., Dec. 8, 1817, age 25.
Brown, John H., Nov. 16, 1863, age 51.
Brown, John James, eldest son of Wm., March 30, 1867.
Brown, Joseph P., Jan. 26, 1860, age 29 8. D. at Aspinwall, NY.
Brown, Mrs. Juliette, 2nd dau. of Adiel Sherwood, Oct. 13, 1849, 32 y, 4 m.
Brown, Kate Howard, dau. of George V., Aug. 17, 1863.
Brown, Dr. Levi, Clarence, March 1817, age 39; d. at Salem, Washington Co., NY.
Brown, Lewis E., March 27, 1860, age 32.
Brown, Lloyd (colored), Jan. 21, 1879, found dead.
Brown, M., Williamsville, April, 1814, age 27.
Brown, Martha, Newstead, widow of J. J., March 13, 1869, age 72.
Brown, Mary, wife of Lorenzo, Jan. 17, 1855, age 54; d. at Green Bay, WI.
Brown, Mary, wife of George, Sept. 17, 1859, age 39.
Brown, Mary, March 2, 1871, age 25.
Brown, Mary, Erie Co. Almshouse, March, 1877, age 29.
Brown, Mary, Jan. 9, 1879, age 39.
Brown, Mary Alvina, wife of William D., April 7, 1880, age 42 y, 10 m, 17 d.
Brown, Mary Ann, wife of John F., April 18, 1849, age 19. Dau. of Capt. Levi Allen.
Brown, Mary E., wife of J. F. and dau. of A. Robinson, formerly of Marilla, Sept. 16, 1871; d. at Washington, IA.
Brown, Mary Jane, wife of George E., Evans Center, NY, May 15, 1859, age 20.
Brown, Mary Jane, wife of Samuel, Jan. 16, 1870, age 41.
Brown, Mary L., wife of C. Wheeler, formerly of Buffalo, May 17, 1865, age 47; d. at Jackson, MI.
Brown, Mary R., wife of John S., formerly of Buffalo, Aug. 8, 1878, age 72; d. at Lawrence, KS.
Brown, Mehitable W., wife of Enos R., Clarence, June 3, 1845, age 38.
Brown, Myron E., Nov. 27, 1879, age 52; suicide.
Brown, Nancy A., wife of Alexander H., May 24, 1880, age 57 y, 7 m, 4 d.
Brown, Nancy R., wife of Horace, July 18, 1844.
Brown, Neal, March 4, 1866, age 69.
Brown, Olivia C., wife of William O., March 9, 1853, age 37.
Brown, Col. Orange T., Aurora, NY, April 30, 1853, age 52.
Brown, Ovid, March 5, 1844, age 27; d. in Rochester.
Brown, Robert, formerly of Clarence, NY, Aug. 19, 1880, age 71; d. at Okemos, MI.
Brown, Robert R., son of R. R., April 17, 1850.
Brown, Mrs. Rosa S., mother of the late Cody S., Sept. 20, 1873, age 53.
Brown, Russell Searle, March 26, 1844, age 41.
Brown, Samuel, Sept. 11, 1863, age 73.
Brown, Miss Sarah, dau. of Phebe, Sept. 27, 1860. Prin. of School No. 7.
Brown, Sewell, Hamburgh, NY, March 27, 1848, age 55.
Brown, Sophia C., Yonkers, NY., widow of John D, mother of Mrs. Seth B. Grosvenor, Dec. 12, 1870; bur. in Buffalo.
Brown, Stoddart, April 3, 1835, age 35; formerly of Burlington, VT.
Brown, Mrs. Susanna, Nov. 28, 1870, age 82.
Brown, Sylvester, Nov. 14, 1874, age over 60; d. on a sleeping-car near Boston, MA.
Brown, Thomas, uncle of Sheriff Brown, of Buffalo, Clarence, NY, Jan. 11, 1841, age 65.
Brown, Thomas J., Dec. 12, 1862.
Brown, Uriah C., Clarence, July 27, 1821.
Brown, William, Englishman, May 13, 1856, age 70.
Brown, William, son of Samuel, June 14, 1862, age 30; d. in San Francisco, CA.
Brown, William, June 3, 1868, age 33.
Brown, William, March 29, 1873, age 53.
Brown, William C., March 14, 1879, age 21.

Brown, William L., Oct. 20, 1871.
Brown, William O., Feb. 25, 1871, in 70th y; d. at Yonkers, bur. in Buffalo.
Brown, Rev. William Steill, d. in Columbia, TX, Aug. 4, 1835. Former pastor of Unitarian Church, Buffalo. An Englishman.
Brown, William W., Feb. 12, 1878, age 70.
Brown, William W., Sept. 11, 1879, age 63 y, 5 m, 9 d.
Browne, Peres E., Jr., Dec. 22, 1869, age 21 y, 10 m, 14 d.
Brownell, J., Feb. 13, 1880, age 42; bur. at Gowanda.
Brownell, Lucia Emilie, wife of Isaac W., Sept. 1, 1861; taken to Greenwood.
Brownell, William, Hartland, Niagara Co., March 2, 1870, age 84; taken to Hartland.
Browner, James, Sept. 29, 1877.
Browning, Catharine Delaney, wife of Thomas H., March 30, 1844, age 27.
Browning, John, 1st Sgt. Co. K, 2 Reg. Art., May 4, 1839. In army 16 years.
Browning, Martha E., May 23, 1871.
Browning, Martha F., wife of Potter, June 10, 1842, age 43.
Browning, Potter, late of "Lovejoy House," Buffalo, March, 1853; bur. March 30.
Browning, Mrs. Sarah, widow of late Barnard B., Nov. 24, 1879, age 68.
Brownson, Eunice P., April 7, 1880, age 81.
Bruce, Albert A., Gowanda, Jan. 30, 1869, age 26; d. at Gowanda.
Bruce, Alice S., wife of George, Lancaster, July 23, 1855, age 59.
Bruce, Jacob, Lancaster, April 24, 1850, age 61.
Bruce, F. M., eldest son of E. K., June 27, 1876, age 25 y, 10 m, 3 d; d. in Chicago, bur. in Buffalo.
Bruce, Fannie M., dau. of B., Sept. 9, 1880, age 24 y, 6 m, 4 d.
Bruce, Jacob, Lancaster, April 24, 1850, age 61.
Bruce, James, Dec. 16, 1872, age 21.
Bruce, Mrs. Jane, July 5, 1846, age 79 y, 10 m.
Bruce, Jesse, Oct. 13, 1845, age 79.
Bruce, Oliver S., brother of E. K., Jan. 23, 1856, age 32; d. in Toledo, bur. in Buffalo.
Bruce, Thankful M., widow of Jacob, Lancaster, NY, Oct. 30, 1864, age 69. Mother of E. K. of Chicago and R. F. of Buffalo.
Bruce, W., Sept. 13, 1872, age 53 y, 9 m; taken to Lancaster, NY.
Brugier, Elizabeth Magdalena, Almshouse, Feb. 13, 1876, age 30.
Bruin, Charles, Leicestershire, England, Feb. 6, 1870, age 42.
Bruley, Godfrey, Sept. 12, 1877, age 52.
Brum, Thankful, April 14, 1875, age 76.
Bruman, Mrs. C., Dec. 5, 1871, age 47.
Brumley, Mrs. Lydia, at Home of the Friendless, June 2, 1879, age 90.
Brunck, Lieut. F., Nov. 7, 1867, age 26; d. at Ft. Morgan, Mobile Bay.
Brunck, Dr. Francis C., March 9, 1887, age 77.
Brundage, Clark, Jan. 3, 1879; railroad accident.
Brunton, James A., brother-in-law of Israel Gillett, Feb. 8, 1848, age 22.
Brunton, Mrs. Jane, Feb. 21, 1879, age 80; d. in NY City, bur. in Buffalo.
Brush, Edgar C., June 23, 1827, age 22.
Brush, Elizabeth S., wife of John, Jr., Oct. 30, 1876, age 25 y. 10 m.
Brush, Emma C., wife of Henry B., Dec. 1, 1867, age 21.
Brush, Lorinda A., wife of Alexander, Nov. 13, 1862, age 22.
Brush, Lucia, wife of Hiram, formerly of Buffalo, Jan. 14, 1875.
Brush, Nathaniel H., Feb. 8, 1870, age 48.
Brush, Phebe, Jan. 30, 1873, age 77.
Bryant, Deacon Abner, July 20, 1853, age 65.
Bryant, Anna F., wife of Deacon Abner, Jan. 8, 1867; d. in Detroit, bur. in Buffalo.
Bryant, Catharine Howard, wife of Isaac F. and eldest dau. of Henry Howard, Nov. 27, 1856, age 25.
Bryant, Mrs. Elizabeth L., Jan. 19, 1852, age 55.
Bryant, Emily P., mother of William C., July 17, 1864, age 52.
Bryant, Maria T., wife of Warren, Dec. 23, 1835, age 22; d. in Clinton, Oneida Co., NY.
Bryant, Reuben, father of William C., Jan. 17, 1863, age 70 y, 6 m.
Bryant, Miss Welthy, Dec. 19, 1833, age 49.
Bryant, William, May 16, 1845, age 25, musician.

Bryson, Henry, April 3, 1880, age 56.
Bryson, Jane, wife of William, July 9, 1852, age 44.
Bryson, Jane, eldest dau. of William, May 28, 1863, age 28.
Bryson, Mary A., Jan. 21, 1872.
Bryson, William, Sr., June 1, 1869, age 66.
Bryson, William, Oakland, CA, formerly of Buffalo, May 9, 1879.
Bubell, Barbary, widow of Michael, June 25, 1879, age 79.
Buchanan, Fanny, widow of Robert S., Dec. 23, 1880, age 84 y, 5 m, 9 d.
Buchanan, Robert G., May 16, 1872, age 78.
Buchard, Edward, Jan. 28, 1873, switchman.
Bucher, Mrs. N., Jan. 16, 1878; d. at Weedsport, bur. in Buffalo.
Buchser, Mrs. Susanna, wife of Jacob, June 9, 1872, age 35.
Buck, Frederick, July 7, 1820.
Buck, Jennie C., wife of H. T., April 7, 1874, age 30; taken to Troy, PA.
Buck, Martha, widow of Thomas, April 22, 1870, age 69.
Buckland, John A., formerly of Ellington, CT, Aug. 3, 1853, age 43. Drowned at Black Rock.
Buckland, Julia A. Turner, wife of Andrew I., dau. of Chester P. Turner, Nov. 25, 1869, age 33 y, 7 m, 10 d.
Buckley, Michael, Co. Almshouse, Oct. 23, 1877, age 75.
Buckley, William, July 8, 1854, age 52.
Bucklin, Charles, Sgt. in Capt. Matteson's volunteers, Black Rock, NY, July 14, 1812.
Bucklin, Charles, formerly of Hartford, CT, Aug. 24, 1823, age 37.
Budd, Capt. Thomas A., U.S.N., March 22, 1862, in 49th y; killed at Mosquito Inlet, FL, while in command of U.S. Steamer *Penguin*.
Buddenburg, George A., son of J.B.J., May 19, 1872, age 22 y, 6 m, 23 d.
Budlong, Serg. Thomas H., of 67th Pa. Vols., July 2, 1863, age 29; killed in battle of Gettysburg. Brother of Mrs. Charles P. Clapp of Buffalo.
Budroe, John M., White's Corners, Oct. 28, 1869, age 28.
Buehl, Louisa M., wife of Christian, Oct. 2, 1863, age 21 y, 8 m, 17 d; dau. of George Voltz.
Buesch, Henry, May 28, 1844, age 61.
Buettler, Mathias, Sept. 3, 1873, age 52.
Buffam, Amy, wife of Richard, Colden, NY, Oct. 7, 1837.
Buffam, Mary, wife of Richard, Holland, NY, Dec. 18, 1819, age 49.
Buffum, Richard, fromerly of Elma, NY, Dec. 17, 1878; d. near Freeport, IL.
Bugbee, Alvan, Gowanda, merchant, May 25, 1849, age 50.
Bugbee, Jane A., wife of Alvin W., dau. of Alfred W. Wilgus, Jan. 21, 1848, age 22.
Bugbee, Louisa, wife of A. W., dau. of Martin Daley, Nov. 21, 1851.
Bugbee, Oliver, April 5, 1879, age 74.
Bugbee, Sarah Walker, wife of O., July 20, 1858, age 52.
Bugbur, Alain W., formerly of Buffalo, Aug. 9, 1877; d. in Chicago.
Buhlman, Joseph M., shoemaker, April 30, 1880, age 46 (?); shot by Indians and d. at Silver City, NM, formerly of Buffalo.
Bugler, James, Aug. 22, 1880, age 38 y, 5 m.
Bugler, John, April 13, 1870, age 40.
Bulger, John M., Aug. 12, 1863, age 34.
Bugler, William A., Feb. 9, 1879, age 25; railroad accident.
Bull, Absalom, Feb. 21, 1866, age 69.
Bull, Cadwallader, son of Absalom, Aug. 23, 1863, age 36.
Bull, Eunice, mother of George B., Aug. 21, 1867, age 96; bur. in Bath, Steuben Co., NY.
Bull, Frances C., wife of Charles, Jan. 28, 1839, age 42.
Bull, Frederick B., son of George W., Aug. 15, 1872, age 26.
Bull, George B., March 4, 1873, age 62.
Bull, George W., Dec. 26, 1879, age 70.
Bull, Harriet L., wife of Hugh L., dau. of late Judge Rochester, Dec. 13, 1854, age 33.
Bull, Jabez Benedict, Jan. 26, 1871, age 65 y, 5 m.
Bull, Jessie A., Nov. 28, 1880, age 37; d. and bur. at Geneva.
Bull, Katharine M., Sept. 30, 1870, age 20 y, 9 m; dau. of Jabez B.
Bull, Mrs. Maria, March 21, 1874, age 43.
Bull, Maria Lindsey, widow of Absalom, Black Rock, NY, June 13, 1869, in 70th year.

Bull, Mary, eldest dau. of Jabez, Feb. 24, 1865, age 23.
Bull, Mary Denniston, Sept. 10, 1864, age 22.
Bull, Mary E., wife of E. C., April 28, 1876, age 38.
Bull, Miles J., formerly of Buffalo, Sept. 28, 1872, age 34; d. at Olean, NY.
Bull, Milton W., East Hamburgh, March 25, 1864, age 66 y, 11 m.
Bull, Mrs. Sarah, Feb. 19, 1865, age 90. Taken to Orange Co.
Bull, Sarah Elizabeth, wife of J. B., Dec. 13, 1864, age 45.
Bull, Sarah G. Vail, wife of Dr. A. T., March 7, 1876, age 49; taken to Middletown, NY.
Bull, William, Oct. 6, 1878, age 72.
Bull, William B., Aurora, NY, Jan. 24, 1877, age c. 30; suicide.
Bullard, Joseph, March 27, 1875, age 38.
Bullis, Benjamin, Aurora, NY, July 3, 1859, age 80. His wife d. May 3, 1859, age 83.
Bullis, Dorothy, wife of Hiram, East Hamburgh, NY, Oct. 20 or 26 1853, age 54.
Bullis, Lewis M., Elma, NY, Dec. 3, 1868, age 65.
Bullock, Louisa, wife of Samuel, March 8, 1864, age 32.
Bullock, William of Berkshire, England, East Evans, NY, Sept. 3, 1869, age 85.
Bullymore, Henry J., Oct. 25, 1871, age 23.
Bullymore, Jane, wife of Joseph, July 26, 1843, age 24.
Bullymore, Mary L. Giddings, wife of Thomas R., Dec. 29, 1872, age 32.
Bullymore, Thomas, Feb. 9, 1866, age 53.
Bullymore, Adj. William, eldest son of Richard, May 8, 1862, age 20. D. at Fortress Monroe,
    bur. in Buffalo.
Bulson, Alanson, J., Aug. 4, 1872, age 27.
Bulson, Alexander, father of Daniel R., Angola, NY, Feb. 17, 1866, age 73.
Bulson, Mrs. Margaret, mother of D.B., Nov. 25, 1870, age 78.
Bulson, Peter, formerly of Buffalo, Nov. 9, 1865, age 55; d. at Rouseville, PA.
Bump, Phebe, wife of Jonathan, Boston, Dec. 27, 1843, age 56.
Bundy, Harlan E., formerly of Angola, April 16, 1880, age 38; d. at Streator, IL.
Bundy, Jonathan, Marilla, Dec. 25, 1872, age 47.
Bundy, Lavina, wife of Sanford, Evans, Feb. 7, 1847, age 64.
Bundy, Rinaldo, Marilla, Feb. 7, 1865, age 46.
Bunker, Abner B., formerly of Buffalo, July 19, 1865, age 49; d. in Cleveland, OH, bur. in
    Buffalo.
Bunker, Lavina, wife of A. B., May 1, 1863, age 46.
Bunnell, Adaline, Lancaster, April 30, 1847, age 37.
Bunnell, Matilda, wife of Levi, May 21, 1853, age 61.
Bunting, Eliza M., Eden, dau. of Joseph and Lucinda, Aug. 11, 1880, age 42.
Bunting, Levi, Eden, Oct. 21, 1872, age 89 y, 7 m.
Bunting, Prince A., Eden, Sept. 22, 1874, age 31.
Bunting, William H., only son of Mrs. John Roberts, Jan. 10, 1863, age 32; d. at Flint, MI.
Burbach, Jacob, of 100th NY Vol., Sept. 12, 1878.
Burbanck, Capt. Jesse, Master of the *Caledonia*, Dec. 1812, age 51.
Burch, Albert, Oct. 4, 1877, age 22; drowned from the Schooner *Nettie Weaver* on Lake Huron.
Burchill, Margaret, March 22, 1870; sister of Mrs. J. W. Leach and Susan Burchill.
Burdett, Capt. Benj., Cayuga Island, April 2, 1855, age 45.
Burdett, Grace D., wife of James D., Aug. 29, 1876, age 42.
Burdette, Ophelia J. Scudder, wife of John, Cayuga Island, Sept. 2, 1873.
Burdick, Clark, Clarence, March 20, 1879, age 80 y, 9 m.
Burg, Mary Ann, wife of John, Feb. 7, 1879, age 31 y, 10 m, 7 d.
Burgard, Caroline Young, wife of John, July 20, 1878, age 60 y, 2 m, 22 d.
Burgard, Mrs. Katherine, May 2, 1876, age 83.
Burger, Rev. Otto, March 19, 1874, age 45.
Burger, William J., Sept. 30, 1870, age 72.
Burgess, Mrs. Ann, Aug. 17, 1877, age 81; d. at St. Johns, New Brunswick.
Burgess, Cynthia S., wife of R. W., April 1, 1853, age 27. Youngest dau. of James Baldwin;
    d. in Washington, DC.
Burgess, Henry, June 19, 1872, age 52.
Burgess, Isaac, b. 1762, d. 1855, bur. N. Ridge; Revolutionary soldier.
Burgess, Mrs. Isabella, Feb. 5, 1874, age 54.
Burgess, James, March 14, 1875, age 62.

Burgess, John A., Dec. 5, 1880, age 51.
Burgess, Mary Ann, wife of Henry, June 25, 1868.
Burgs, Christian, formerly of Buffalo, April 22, 1878, age 49; d. at Reading, PA.
Burk, John, Oct. 29, 1876, age 40; drowned.
Burke, Andrew, Nov. 10, 1880, bookseller; d. in NY City, formerly of Buffalo.
Burke, Mrs. Bridget, June 2, 1876, age 53.
Burke, Bridget, wife of Michael, Oct. 15, 1880, age 40.
Burke, Catherine, Oct. 22, 1878, age 76.
Burke, D., General Hospital, Sept. 5, 1880, age 55.
Burke, Edmund J., Jan. 1877.
Burke, Capt. Edward, April 8, 1842, age 68.
Burke, Edwin P., son of the late Dr. Ulic Burke, formerly of Buffalo, April 10, 1873, age 27; d. at Albany.
Burke, Frances Jane, wife of Charles G., Sept. 7, 1876, age 34.
Burke, George, Lancaster, Nov. 19, 1858, age 51.
Burke, George, May 26, 1878, age 22; railroad accident.
Burke, Hannah, Co. Almshouse, Nov. 10, 1877, age 40.
Burke, J. Edmund, Jan. 15, 1877, age 46.
Burke, Johannah, widow of John, Oct. 15, 1875, age 33.
Burke, John, Oct. 20, 1873, age 24 y, 6 m.
Burke, Dr. John J., May 10, 1874, age 26 y, 3 m, 2 d; d. at San Bernardino, CA; bur. in Buffalo.
Burke, Margaret, wife of William, May 25, 1869, age 50.
Burke, Mary E., July 14, 1880, age 49.
Burke, Capt. Nicholas J., Jan. 21, 1872, age 31; taken to Cleveland, OH.
Burke, Mrs. R. B., late of Lee, Onondaga Co., Aurora, NY, May 19, 1837, age 46.
Burkhard, Mrs. Catherine, April 1, 1878.
Burkshaw, Mary Ann, wife of George, Dec. 17, 1873, age 36.
Burlin, Anna, dau. of J. Burlin, Feb. 9, 1813, age 19.
Burlin, Francis, Sept., 1823, age 58.
Burmell, Susan, wife of Jacob, Eggertsville, July 7, 1872, age 30.
Burnet, William, West Aurora, NY, Oct. 3, 1854.
Burnett, Charles, missed Feb. 9, 1880; found drowned April 5. From Randolph, Cattaraugus Co., NY, age 44.
Burnett, Capt. Charles H., March 10, 1860, age 58.
Burnett, Harris H., Aug. 11, 1852, age 42.
Burnett, Sarah G. Lansing, wife of Gen. H.S., formerly of Buffalo, Feb. 11, 1877.
Burnham, Elisha Hyde, late of Newstead, May 20, 1869, in 68th year; d. at Toledo, OH. For many years a res. of Black Rock, NY.
Burnham, James N., Aurora, Feb. 5, 1840, age 24; attorney.
Burnham, Capt. John, Rev. Patriot, Oct. 7, 1837, age 79.
Burns, ---, wife of Patrolman Robert, May 26, 1878, age 25.
Burns, Andrew, Aug. 24, 1850, age 73.
Burns, Miss Ann A., Jan. 20, 1854, age 28 y, 3 m, 4 d.
Burns, Anna M., dau. of James, April 21, 1872, age 21 y, 2 m, 8 d.
Burns, Mrs. Catharine Stevens, July 21, 1880, age 80; d. at LaCrosse, WI, formerly of Buffalo.
Burns, Charles C., May 29, 1865, age 25.
Burns, Daniel, Aug. 29, 1874, age 27.
Burns, Dennis, March, 1859; d. at Sisters of Charity Hospital.
Burns, Elizabeth, wife of George L., June 3, 1864. Dau. of Joseph, sister of Arthur Christey.
Burns, Elizabeth, wife of Daniel, Oct. 26, 1867, age 32; dau. of Sila Usher.
Burns, George B., July 19, 1873, age 53.
Burns, Mrs. Jane McCarthy, widow of Theodore, Feb. 26, 1880, age 33.
Burns, John, Feb. 26, 1871, age 68.
Burns, L. W., formerly of Buffalo, Sept. 16, 1878, age 49. Brother of John C. and W. P.; d. in New Orleans.
Burns, Lois, widow of John, Dec. 17, 1873, age 68 y, 7 m.

Burns, Margaret, wife of Michael, Jan. 9, 1866. Dau. of George Shiels, late of Earlstown, Berwickshire, Scotland.
Burns, Mary H., Dec. 15, 1854, age 38 y, 6 m, 28 d.
Burns, Matthew, Black Rock, July 4, 1832, age 30; drowned.
Burns, Rhoda A., wife of Alexander, Clarence Centre, NY, Jan. 26, 1878, age 50.
Burns, Robert, June 10, 1876, age 34.
Burns, Robert C., Co. A, 44th Reg. N.Y. Vol., formerly of Buffalo, July 5, 1863, age 19 y, 8 m, 25 d. Wounded at Gettysburg.
Burns, Miss Sarah J., May 13, 1855, age 26.
Burns, Thomas, Nov. 29, 1878, age 22 y, 10 d.
Burns, Thomas, March 23, 1880, age 28.
Burnside, Elenor Noble, wife of Arthur, March 1875, age 44 y, 2 d.
Burnum, Samuel, Sept. 11, 1852; d. at Sisters of Charity Hospital.
Burr, E. Prosser, eldest son of the late Emmet D., Oct. 18, 1877, age 21; d. in New York City.
Burr, Electa, wife of Levi C., Colden, Feb. 16, 1848, age 28.
Burr, Emmet D., formerly of Buffalo, Jan. 18, 1876; bur. in Buffalo.
Burr, Frank, Cheektowaga, Nov. 24, 1880, age 23; d. at Boston, NY.
Burr, Licious H., March 8, 1865, age 23 y, 5 m, 6d.
Burr, Lois, widow of Moses, Aug. 28, 1849, age 78. Mother of Mrs. R. H. Maynard of Buffalo; d. in Hartford, CT.
Burr, Sidney, March 8, 1863, age 64.
Burrell, Henry, Sept. 4, 1879, age 47. Sudden death; ink manufacturer.
Burrell, Lyman, Feb. 12, 1880, age 68; at City Hospital.
Burridge, George, cook of the tug *Compound*, May 12, 1872, age 28.
Burroughs, Ann, Wales, Feb. 22, 1872; dau. of the late Joseph.
Burroughs, Jane, widow of Joseph, Wales, NY, May 4, 1873, age 78.
Burroughs, Joseph, Wales, March 7, 1870, age 82.
Burrows, Amasa A., Sept. 28, 1863, age 35; late of Barnardstown, Franklin Co., MA.
Burrows, Julia M., dau. of Roswell S., Sept. 14, 1878.
Burrows, Latham A., Sept. 25, 1855, age 63.
Burrows, Latham A., Jr., Sept. 7, 1847, age 28.
Burrows, Mrs. Latham A., Nov. 11, 1860, age 66.
Burrows, Sarah A., eldest dau. of L. A., Aug. 6, 1848, age 25; d. in Parma, Monroe Co., bur. in Buffalo.
Burrows, William H., Dec. 6, 1865, age 36.
Burrus, Mary Jane, wife of L. G., April 4, 1865, age 31. Eldest dau. of John Dickey of Buffalo; d. in Hudson City, NJ, bur. in Buffalo.
Burt, Alvin, b. 1761, d. 1841, bur. East Aurora; Revolutionary soldier.
Burt, General David, Aug. 9, 1848, age 58.
Burt, Elizabeth, wife of George L., Wales, NY, Oct. 7, 1856.
Burt, Francis F., brother of H. B., June 18, 1850, age 25; d. in Eldorado, CA.
Burt, Frederick, Aug. 13, 1837, age 31.
Burt, Frederick N., eldest son of the late Gen., Aug. 6, 1854, age 22.
Burt, George, Sept. 24, 1835, age 34.
Burt, George L., Dec. 31, 1873, age 71; taken to Aurora, NY.
Burt, Henrietta E., wife of Henry B., Jan. 6, 1859, age 44.
Burt, Henry B., Jan. 1868.
Burt, Lt. William J., 33rd N.Y. Ind. Battery of Light Artillery; d. at Camp Barry, Washington, DC, April 18, 1864, age 22. Bur. in Buffalo.
Burt, Zenas, Nov. 14, 1854, age 74; taken to Cambridge, PA.
Burth, Christopher, March 14, 1876, age 29.
Burtis, Arthur, D.D., March 23, 1867, age 60. D. at Oxford, OH; bur. in Buffalo.
Burtis, Grace E., widow of Rev. Arthur, D.D., April 29, 1876, age 71.
Burton, Jacob, March 3, 1873, age 33.
Burton, Joel W., May 1, 1878, age 65.
Burton, L., Hamburgh, Sept. 30, 1874, age 52.
Burton, Lucia Clark, wife of J. H., May 28, 1873; d. at Nice, France.
Burton, Lucretia L., wife of Silas, Hamburgh, NY, Sept. 7, 1850, age 59.
Burton, Mary A., mother-in-law of Edward Farmer, June 16, 1856, age 82.

Burton, Moses, Nov. 28, 1865, age 70.
Burton, Silas, formerly of Buffalo (1824-1850), Sept. 17, 1866, age 75; d. at Coldwater, MI.
Burton, William, May 31, 1872, age 80; taken to Cleveland.
Burts, Margaret, wife of Robert, Amherst, NY, March 25, 1844.
Burnell, Ann, wife of Dr. B., Sept. 14, 1838, age 41.
Burnell, Bryant, M.D., Sept. 8, 1861, age 65.
Burnell, Catharine Ann, wife of Dr. Elliott Burnell and eldest dau. of Pierre A. Barker, April 25, 1836, age 23.
Burnell, Lurinda, wife of Alfred, Alden, NY, May 15, 1846, age 26.
Burwell, Maria T., widow of Dr. Bryant Burwell, Aug. 3, 1875, age 75.
Burz, John A., Sr., Boston, NY, Feb. 3, 1865, age 65.
Busbridge, Sarah, wife of John, Aug. 14, 1880, age 60 y, 2 m, 7 d.
Buse, Mrs. Sophia, Williamsville Road, Oct., 1878, age 77; funeral Nov. 2.
Bush, Adam, North Buffalo, Nov. 19, 1865, age 76.
Bush, Mrs. C., Amherst, July 29, 1871, age 54.
Bush, Charles E., May 29, 1877, age 33.
Bush, Charles Seymour, son of G. Webster, Aug. 29, 1854, age 21 y, 2 m, 10 d.
Bush, Charlotte H., Nov. 27, 1854.
Bush, Elizabeth A., widow of John, Oct. 12, 1877, age 57.
Bush, George R., Nov. 8, 1874, age 34.
Bush, George Webster, formerly of Buffalo, Oct. 4, 1874, age 74; d. at Rahway, N.J.
Bush, Hannah F., wife of John, June 11, 1858, age 70.
Bush, Henrietta C., wife of Ephraim, July 12, 1860, age 28, d. at Angels, LA.
Bush, John, Sept. 22, 1873, age 80.
Bush, Joseph, Nov. 10, 1828, age 80.
Bush, Julia, wife of W., April 10, 1880, age 21 y, 6 m, 3 d.
Bush, Steuben, June 27, 1849, age 32; d. at Deer River, Lewis Co.
Bush, William, Dec. 21, 1879, age 27; d. at Hornellsville.
Busher, Capt. Martin, Sept. 10, 1870, age 42 y, 2 m.
Busher, Sarah J. Husted, wife of F. W., Sept. 11, 1875, age 22 y, 4 m, 8 d.
Bussmann, ---, wife of Anton, Lancaster, March 24, 1879.
Buswell, Henry, April 30, 1842, age 26; d. in Albany.
Butcher, Edward, Jan. 28, 1873, switchman.
Butler, Mrs. A., Dec. 7, 1842, formerly of the Eagle St. Theater.
Butler, Andrew J., Nov. 4, 1876, age c. 56; taken to Lockport.
Butler, Mrs. Ann, March 11, 1878, age 57 y, 2 m, 4 d; d. in Bradford, PA.
Butler, Edwin of Columbus, OH, May 26, 1842, age 27.
Butler, Eliza A., wife of Frederick J., Nov. 30, 1854, age 33.
Butler, F. P., wood engraver, March 12, 1850, aged c. 30; d. at Angola, NY, taken to Rochester.
Butler, George, harness-maker, May 25, 1872, age c 47.
Butler, Harriet N., wife of Theodore, Jan. 5, 1869, in 54th y.
Butler, Henry F., Dec. 15, 1880, age 28.
Butler, Hope, Aug. 6, 1876, age c 90; at Buffalo General Hospital.
Butler, James, May 30, 1873, age 46.
Butler, James, Nov. 14, 1879, age 82; sudden death.
Butler, James, July 26, 1880, age 23 y, 4 m.
Butler, Capt. James M., June 7, 1877, age 64.
Butler, Julia Ann, widow of Samuel M., Alden, NY, Dec. 19, 1879, age 69.
Butler, Margaret, wife of James, June 26, 1868, age 52.
Butler, Mary Jane, wife of Charles W., March 13, 1858, age 27.
Butler, Morris, Jan. 11, 1875.
Butler, Mrs. Sarah, July 27, 1854, aged 55.
Butler, Sarah H. Latimer, wife of Morris, Dec. 29, 1852, age 34. Recently of Buffalo, d. in Farmington, IL.
Butler, Theodore, April 22, 1876, age 69.
Butler, Dr. Wm. H., Feb. 5, 1854, age 34; d. in Washington.
Butman, Clarissa A., wife of William, formerly of Buffalo, Nov. 18, 1871, age 48; d. at Fulton, IL.

Butman, Martha A., wife of Charles A., May 10, 1874.
Butterfield, Daniel W., Feb. 19, 1842, age 32.
Butterfield, Esther, wife of Robert, Alden, NY, May 13, 1862, age 56.
Butterfield, George K., June 15, 1864, age 45 y, 11 m.
Butterfield, Mrs. S. Wiborg, formerly of Williamsville, Feb. 22, 1876.
Butters, John, Dec. 14, 1876, age 65.
Butters, Susan E., dau. of John, Sept. 14, 1865, age 31.
Butterworth, Mr., formerly of MA, now Springville, NY, Aug. 29, 1828, age 60.
Buttolph, Abigail N., widow of John P., Buffalo Plains, Jan. 5, 1874; taken to VT.
Butts, Carrie L., wife of S.B., June 1, 1876, age 41.
Butts, Riley, from Lexington, Greene Co., Aug. 21, 1828, age 38.
Buxton, Mrs. Harriet E., widow of Braley K., Hamburgh, NY, June 23, 1880, age 57 y, 3 d.
Buyer (Boyer), Segt. Jacob, b. 1747, d. 1825, bur. Newstead; Revolutionary soldier.
Byers, Elizabeth, Nov, 1874, age 32; found drowned.
Byers, Nellie, wife of Robert L., Jan. 27, 1873, age 29 y, 2 m, 2 d.
Byrne, Mrs. Eliza, April 5, 1875, age 22.
Byrne, Hugh, March 2, 1880, age 74.
Byrne, James, Jan. 15, 1876, age 75.
Byrne, Julia, May 26, 1880, age 72; at Sisters of Charity Hospital.
Byrne, Mrs. Mary, mother of Supt. John Byrne, Sept. 3, 1875, age 67.
Byrne, Sarah, Aug. 18, 1879.
Byrne, William, from Kilkenny, Ireland, Jan. 28, 1857, age c 30.
Byrnes, John, Sept. 14, 1873.
Byron, Mrs. Ann, Aug. 5, 1880, age 76.

Cadwallader, Mary Ann C., widow of Michenor, Oct. 16, 1866, age 71. D. in Chicago, bur. in Buffalo.
Cadwallader, Michenor, Feb. 9, 1864, age 66.
Cady, Henry V., of Monticello, Sullivan Co., May 11, 1835, age 27.
Cady, John, March 16, 1844, age 31.
Cady, Maurice, Alden, March 18, 1873, age 80; accidently killed on railroad.
Cahill, Ellen, wife of Thomas, Aug. 31, 1877, in 20th y.
Cahill, Mrs. Mary, May 24, 1875, age 70.
Cahill, Michael, Aug. 12, 1876, age 50; Erie Co. Almshouse.
Cahill, Patrick, April 16, 1878, age 34 y, 7 m.
Cahiil, Patrick, Aug. 18, 1880, age 29 y, 7 m.
Cahill, William, Sept. 23, 1874; killed by his brother Joseph.
Cain, Catharine, wife of Jesse, March 5, 1846, age 41.
Cain, Michael, June 22, 1873, age c 60.
Calder, Arthur, April 20, 1853, age 27.
Caldwell, John, July 10, 1879, age 33 y, 2 d.
Caldwell, Maria, widow of Samuel, Oct. 4, 1872, age 69.
Caldwell, Samuel, Sept. 22, 1849, age 52.
Caldwell, Samuel, July 9, 1874, age 55.
Caldwell, Samuel, Jr., Dec. 18, 1857, age 22.
Caleb, Capt. Elijah H., Nov. 30, 1869, age 56; d. at Buffalo General Hospital.
Calhoun, Rev. Simeon Howard, missionary, Dec. 14, 1876, in 73rd y.
Caligan, Nellie Cunningham, wife of John E., formerly of Buffalo, Aug. 5, 1878; d. at Castile, NY; bur. in Buffalo.
Caligan, Susan Lee, wife of Charles, Sept. 26, 1877, age 53 y, 3 m, 16 d.
Calkins, Betsey, wife of Delavan, Aurora, NY, July 19, 1862, age 36.
Calkins, Elizabeth, widow of Deacon Calkins of Holland, NY, June 5, 1838, age 80.
Calkins, Elizabeth A., wife of Moses, Colden, NY, May 14, 1871, age 51.
Calkins, James, Aug. 18, 1852, age 31 y, 9 m, 13 d.
Callahan, Bridget A., wife of Michael, April 23, 1879, age 32 y, 4 m.
Callahan, Edward, Aug. 2, 1877, age 35.
Callahan, Honora, June 26, 1868.
Callahan, John, March 30, 1876, age 48; taken east.
Callahan, John D., son of William, formerly of Hamburg, March 25, 1870, age 28. D. in Mobile, AL, bur. Buffalo.

Callahan, Margaret A., wife of Richard, Sept. 9, 1875, age 35.
Callamore, Eliza., April 21, 1869, age 69.
Callen (or Callon), John, Tonawanda, NY, Aug. 14, 1873, age 72.
Callan, Margaret, June 14, 1878, age 76.
Callanan, Honoria, M. Lonergan [sic], wife of Cornelius, Aug. 14, 1868, age 48 y, 11 m, 29 d.
Callanan, James, July 1, 1880; d. Middletown, PA.
Callard, Elizabeth, wife of A., April 9, 1849.
Callard, Henry, Aug. 7, 1843, age 32.
Callard, Mary Jane, widow of Capt. George, May 4, 1862, age 37.
Callendar, Samuel N., Dec. 27, 1880, age 80.
Callender, Deacon Amos, Jan. 19, 1857, age 77.
Callender, Mrs. Amos (formerly Mrs. Thomas C. Griffith), formerly of Buffalo, May 3, 1874, age 76; d. in Chicago.
Callender, Harriet, wife of Deacon Amos, April 8, 1844, age 61.
Callender, Nancy, wife of Samuel N., Sept. 21, 1867, age 66.
Callender, Rebecca, wife of Amos, Sept. 14, 1817, age 37.
Callender, Samuel N., 1880.
Callery, Edwin, Sept. 17, 1873.
Callinan, Margaret, April 23, 1879, age 51.
Calvert, George, Dec. 20, 1869, age 54.
Calvin, Mrs. Mary A., Dec. 29, 1873, age 55; d. Cleveland, OH.
Cemeron, Elizabeth Smith, wife of Gilbert, Nov. 11, 1877, age 57.
Cameron, James, May 18, 1852, age c 75.
Cameron, Mrs. Jane, Aug. 29, 1863, age 78.
Cameron, John, June 6, 1848, age 34.
Cameron, John, formerly of Buffalo, Sept. 26, 1860, age 62; d. at Memphis.
Cameron, Margaret, widow of Walter, July 4, 1869, age 70.
Cameron, Walter A. J., Dec. 9, 1861, age 59.
Cameron, William, Evans, Nov. 4, 1872, age 54. Found dead in a field c 2 miles from Angola.
Camin, George, Aug. 26, 1880; killed near Hall's station by fall from cars.
Camp, Asahel, Aug. 23, 1844, age 40.
Camp, Asahel, Gowanda, Aug. 9, 1865, age 68.
Camp, Betsey, wife of Deacon L., Evans, NY, Sept. 25, 1844, age 68.
Camp, Daniel, Hamburgh, Dec. 13, 1849, age 83.
Camp, Mrs. Emily, Hamburgh, Feb. 6, 1847.
Camp, H. B., M.D., Hamburgh, March 25, 1845, age 38.
Camp, Dr. Joseph, March 12, 1851, age 54; taken to Pittsford, Monroe Co.
Camp, Merlin, April 1, 1846, age 45.
Camp, Olive M., widow of Dr. H. B., Hamburgh, Feb. 5, 1847, age 38.
Camp, Rhoda, widow of Maj. John G., formerly of Buffalo, July 23, 1876, age 79.
Camp, Thuel, Aug. 23, 1835, age 45.
Campbell, Aletha G. Dallas, wife of Augustus T., Feb. 20, 1874, age 19.
Campbell, Ann, wife of Capt. Daniel, June 4, 1871, age 35.
Campbell, Anna, April 29, 1880, age 45; dropped dead in street.
Campbell, Catharine, sister of Maurice and James, Oct. 24, 1875.
Campbell, Ella V., wife of Robert, March 21, 1874, age 22.
Campbell, Ellen M., wife of Henry C., Aug. 21, 1855, age 20 y, 9 m.
Campbell, Frances A., wife of Colin, formerly of Buffalo, Aug. 9, 1878, age 36; d. at Tarrytown, bur. in Buffalo.
Campbell, Hon. Henry M., formerly of Buffalo, Jan. 23, 1842, age c 60; d. in Detroit, MI.
Campbell, Hugh Park, May 26, 1877, age 27; taken to Waterford, PA.
Campbell, Huldah, wife of Rufus H., formerly of Clarence, NY, Dec. 31, 1843, age 30; d. at Harbor Creek, PA.
Campbell, James, Feb. 24, 1875, age 67.
Campbell, Jane, wife of Alexander, Dec. 10, 1872, age 55.
Campbell, Mrs. Jane, Aug. 22, 1873, age 71.
Campbell, Jason J., only son of M. A., Aug. 11, 1849, age 19 y, 3 m.
Campbell, John A. B., Oct. 1, 1877, age 48 y, 9 m, 7 d.
Campbell, John B. Cheektowaga, Jan. 1, 1875, age 62 y, 3 m, 8 d.

Campbell, Laura B., wife of Charles J., near Williamsville, Jan. 11, 1842, age 24.
Campbell, M. A., March 28, 1863, age 62.
Campbell, Mrs. Martha, Sept. 18, 1860, age 82; Bath, Steuben Co.
Campbell, Robert M., June 18, 1866. Drowned in Lake Erie.
Campbell, Sarah A., wife of Walter, Sept. 1, 1852, age 33.
Campbell, Sarah Jane, wife of C. J., Feb. 24, 1846.
Campbell, Thomas, March 5, 1871, age 62.
Campbell, Thomas, Aug. 30, 1880, age 22; d. County Hospital at Chicago, formerly of Buffalo. Accident.
Campbell, W. R., Nov. 5, 1877, age c 32; railroad accident.
Campbell, William, only son of Walter, May 5, 1862, age 21; d. in Chesapeake Hospital, VA.
Campbell, Capt. William, Oct. 12, 1865, age 53; d. in Erie, PA, bur. in Buffalo.
Campbell, William, Dec. 1, 1870, age 56.
Campian, Catherine, Nov. 24, 1874, age 40.
Canan, William, Sept. 7, 1876, age 86; Erie Co. Almshouse.
Cand, James, Aug. 17, 1852, age 60.
Candee, Dean, Jan. 9, 1874, age 50 y, 3 m.
Candee, Eber, Evans, Feb. 8, 1875, age 89 y, 11 m, 3 d.
Candee, Emily Elizabeth, wife of Charles E., Hamburgh, Aug. 31, 1864, age 26. Dau. of James Moore; d. at Dunkirk.
Candee, Julia Jenings, wife of Joseph, Jan. 13, 1875, age 61 y, 6 m, 12 d.
Candell, Mrs. Hannah, wife of Rev. Henry, June 30, 1879, age 73 y, 6 m, 6 d.
Candler, Hannah C., wife of Capt. William, Jan. 13, 1839.
Caney, Mary, wife of David, Oct. 3, 1880, age 25.
Canfield, C. H., of Wellsville, MO, formerly of Buffalo, Nov. 1, 1872, age 60. D. at Batavia, NY.
Canfield, Dennis, b. 1763, d. 1846, bur. Hamburg; Revolutionary soldier.
Canfield, Dennis, East Hamburgh, NY, May 5, 1875, age 84.
Canfield, Hannah, wife of Jared, dau. of Robert Hough, May 2, 1862, age 36.
Canfield, Horace, April 23, 1866, age 72; d. at Canandaigua, bur. in Buffalo.
Canfield, Mrs. Polly, Hamburg, April 1, 1874.
Canfield, Sylvester, formerly of Buffalo, Sept. 8, 1852; d. at Sacramento, CA.
Canfield, Thomas, Feb. 16, 1876, age 32.
Cannan, John, Nov. 14, 1878, age 29.
Cannell, John, April 28, 1873, age 45.
Cannell, William H., son of Thomas, July 15, 1858, age 26; d. at River Side.
Cannon, Annie, wife of Peter, July 28, 1880, age 65.
Cannon, Harriet Louise, wife of George S., Dec. 12, 1870, age 28 y, 25 d.
Cannon, James, June 12, 1870, age 53.
Cannon, Mrs. Naomi, April 29, 1880, age 64.
Cannon, Peter F., Dec. 25, 1880, age 23 y, 5 m.
Cantlin (Kenderlink or Cantlan), Patrick, Sept. 11, 1872, coroner's inquest.
Cantwell, Margaret, Nov. 10, 1860, age 21.
Cantwell, Lt. Thomas J., Jan. 6, 1869, age 26.
Canty, Catherine, wife of John C., July 10, 1866.
Canty, Margaret L., wife of Eugene, Dec. 20, 1872, age 51.
Canty, Thomas, Jan. 16, 1875, age 47.
Carall, Charles S., Jan. 1, 1869; steward of Steamer *S. D. Caldwell*.
Carberry, Mrs. Jane, July 31, 1879, age 73.
Card, James, father of William, Aug. 27, 1852.
Card, William, Jan. 21, 1860, age 41.
Carey, Catherine, wife of Richard J., Oct. 3, 1874, age 43.
Carey, Clarissa, wife of Murray B., Dec. 23, 1861, age 41 y, 7 m, 19 d.
Carey, Edmund, June 19, 1873, drowned.
Carey, Mrs. Grace, April 12, 1879, age 59 y, 10 m.
Carey, Luther H., Boston, Dec. 21, 1874, age 74.
Carey, Mrs. Margaret, March 15, 1870, age 37.
Carey, Martha, wife of Samuel, April 8, 1868, age 79.
Carey, Patrick, Oct. 18, 1878, age 55.

Carey, Richard, b. Jan. 15, 1758, d. Dec. 18, 1841, bur. Patchin, NY; soldier of the Revolution.
Carey, Richard J., Feb. 3, 1876, age 50; suicide.
Carey, Samuel, formerly of Buffalo, Sept. 12, 1874, age 84; d. in Philadelphia.
Carey, Sarah A., March 28, 1880.
Carey, Sarah H., wife of John, May 17, 1871, age 55.
Carhart, Jeremiah, Aug. 1868.
Carhart, Nancy H., wife of Jeremiah, dau. of Niles Jerauld of Eden, NY, March 30, 1847, age 27.
Carl, Jane Eliza, wife of Peter, dau. of Jacob Lyons, April 3, 1849, age 21; d. in Herkimer County, bur. Buffalo.
Carleton, James, formerly of Providena, Feb. 22, 1880; d. at General Hospital.
Carley, Joseph, Oct. 3, 1872, age 56.
Carlisle, Mrs. Mary, Sept. 20, 1857, age 60.
Carmar, Abraham, b. 1760, d. 1848, bur. Clarence Center, NY; Revolutionary Soldier.
Carmer, Julius, formerly of Clarence, Jan. 6, 1874; d. near Middletport, NY.
Carmichael, Henry S., Dec. 26, 1865, age 41; d. in New York City, bur. in Buffalo.
Carnahan, Isaac V., Sept. 12, 1874, age 61; taken to Cincinnati, OH.
Carney, Barnabas, Sardinia, Feb. 13, 1874, age 71.
Carney, Delia, Sept. 16, 1878, age 21 y, 16 d.
Carney, John F., March 17, 1879, age 38 y, 9 m.
Carney, Louis, July 1, 1878, age 78.
Carney, Mary, wife of Wm., Sept. 10, 1872, age 22 y, 1 m.
Carney, Michael, March, 1871.
Carney, Sarah H. Carey, wife of John, May 17, 1871.
Carney, William, Nov. 6, 1877, age c 40; injuries by two men.
Carnichey, Mary J., Aug. 19, 1879, age 20; suicide.
Carpenter, Mrs., Aurora, NY, Oct. 22, 1873.
Carpenter, Abbie, wife of Frank S., March 22, 1874, age 34; taken to Perry, Wyoming Co.
Carpenter, Carnot, son of William A. of Buffalo, an artist, Dec. 27, 1853, age 33.
Carpenter, Elizabeth, wife of the late William A., Jan. 2, 1868, age 81.
Carpenter, George W., 24th Cavalry, Sept. 2, 1864, age 27; d. at City Point.
Carpenter, Harriet, wife of John, Wales, Feb. 22, 1831, age 36.
Carpenter, Hattie L. Catlin, wife of M.D., East Evans, NY, Sept. 9, 1873.
Carpenter, Hezekiah H., Jan. 1, 1849, age 48; formerly of Le Roy, Genesee Co., NY. Firm of G. D. Smith & Co.
Carpenter, James A., Nov. 17, 1879, age 47 y, 7 m, 9 d.
Carpenter, Jennie M., widow of John H., July 1, 1878, age 52.
Carpenter, John, East Aurora, Dec. 29, 1868, age 78.
Carpenter, John H., Jan. 21, 1863, age 44.
Carpenter, Joseph, Holland, Feb. 13, 1846, age 25. Son of Isaac of Franklinville, late of U.S. Army.
Carpenter, Lucinda, wife of S.W., June 13, 1887, age 76.
Carpenter, Robert N., July 31, 1880, age 40.
Carpenter, Samuel E., June 18, 1854, age 46.
Carpenter, Mrs. Sarah, Lancaster, Jan. 24, 1847, age 71.
Carpenter, Miss Susan Harriet, dau. of John, Wales, NY, Dec. 25, 1853, age 20.
Carpenter, Thurstone, Lancaster, NY, Jan. 11, 1863, age 42 y, 4 m.
Carpenter, William Allison, Dec. 25, 1858, age 78.
Carpenter, William L., formerly of Buffalo, Sept. 1, 1868, age 54; d. in Washington, DC.
Carr, Abraham J., Feb. 27, 1847, age 39.
Carr, Elder Clark, Concord, March 13, 1854, age 88.
Carr, Clark M., formerly of Erie Co., April 17, 1876, age 71; d. in Galesburg, IL.
Carr, Delia Ann, wife of Clark M., Nov. 22, 1839, age 30.
Carr, Emanuel M., Aug. 11, 1877, age 77.
Carr, Isabel, wife of E. M., Aug. 27, 1867, age 49. Formerly manager of National Theater, New York City.
Carr, Jenett, dau. of the late John, March 7, 1878, age 20.
Carr, John, Nov. 14, 1814, age 40.
Carr, John, Feb. 14, 1877, age 23.

Carr, John C., East Hamburg, Sept. 6, 1876, age 84.
Carr, Maria, June 6, 1878, age 70.
Carr, Mary, wife of Peter, July 26, 1876, age 55; railroad accident.
Carr, Patrick, Jan. 29, 1880, age 46.
Carr, Mrs. Rebecca, Dec. 31, 1872, age 96.
Carr, Sylvia, wife of George, March 28, 1850, age 47.
Carr, Thomas, son of Rev. Charles, March 10, 1876, age 36; d. in WV.
Carr, William, eldest son of Charles, May 9, 1866, age 29.
Carr, William Edward, carpenter, Dec. 3, 1873, age 45; accidental death.
Carreau, Mrs. Cordelia C., May 28, 1874.
Carrick, Margrett, June 18, 1873, age 62.
Carrier, Elizabeth, wife of David, Evans, Dec. 1855, age 78.
Carroll, A., July 24, 1880, age 38. Death by accidental poisoning at Bradford, PA.
Carroll, Annie E., wife of Patrick, July 1, 1880, age 43.
Carroll, Cornelius, Aug. 28, 1877, age 62 y, 9 m.
Carroll, Edward, Sept. 20, 1879, age 34; found drowned, missing since Sept. 17.
Carroll, Edward, Feb., 1880, age 40.
Carroll, Edward, Co. F, 4th Reg. MA Vol., Aug. 31, 1863, age 18; Foxborough, MA.
Carroll, John P., April 5, 1879, age 30 y, 8 m, 8 d.
Carroll, John S., Feb. 21, 1868, age 68.
Carroll, Julia, wife of Thomas, Jan. 5, 1867, age 56.
Carroll, Kittie L. Cotter, wife of J.W., Sept. 16, 1873, age 20.
Carroll, Mary A., wife of Capt. James, June 7, 1877.
Carroll, Michael, Nov. 29, 1873, age 40; engineer of Propeller *Oneida*.
Carroll, Michael, April 18, 1875, age 65.
Carroll, Patrick, Nov. 22, 1877, age 69; Erie Co. Almshouse.
Carroll, Patrick, April 5, 1878; accidental death.
Carroll, Philip, March 17, 1877, age 65.
Carroll, Sarah, March 12, 1853, age 27.
Carroll, Thomas, Jan. 12, 1873, age 30.
Carroll, William, Dec. 4, 1863, age 29.
Carruthers, Sarah, wife of George, May 9, 1852, age 48.
Carson, Mrs., March 20, 1862.
Carson, John A., Oct. 20, 1874, age 37; d. in Cleveland, OH, bur. in Buffalo.
Carson, John A., Dec. 1, 1875, age 38.
Carson, Mary, widow of Joseph, June 10, 1874, age 60 y, 7 d.
Carsons, Isaiah, Nov. 4, 1854, age 44.
Carswell, Allen, April 28, 1869, age 63.
Carswell, Susan P., wife of Allen, mother of Mrs. Walter Reeve, July 10, 1862, age 43 y, 6 m, 2 d.
Carter, Annie, wife of John P., Dec. 24, 1880, age 42.
Carter, Mrs. Eliza., March 29, 1879, age 61.
Carter, William R., car machinist, Jan. 15, 1880, age 33. Collision of locomotive and street car.
Cartwright, Mrs. Mary Ann, mother of E. of Buffalo, Sept. 1, 1867, age 77; Derbyshire, England.
Cartwright, Sophia S. Rouse, wife of Burr E., Aug. 27, 1875, age 19.
Cartwright, William, of Shropshire, England, Colden, NY, May 23, 1854, age 74.
Caruthers, William J., formerly of Buffalo, Jan .31, 1874, age 20 y, 6 m; killed on the Mississippi Railroad.
Carver, Catharine E., wife of Jerome G., Critteneden, NY, July 19, 1869, age 40.
Carver, Julia, wife of Lafayette, Aurora, Dec. 7, 1833, age 22.
Carwin, J. H., 1863.
Cary, Mr. C. R., merchant, June 11, 1836.
Cary, Calvin, Eden, Dec. 30, 1813; killed in Black Rock Battle.
Cary, Dansford A., Boston, Nov. 19, 1868, age 35 y, 4m.
Cary, Demareus, widow of Asa, Boston, April 17, 1863, age 91.
Cary, Jeremiah, Dec. 16, 1865.
Cary, John, Jan. 24, 1875, age 35.
Cary, Michael, Feb. 14, 1872, age 75.

Cary, Orphana, wife of Truman, Boston, NY, April 28, 1864.
Cary, Richard, soldier of Revolutionary and War of 1812, Boston, NY, Nov. 29, 1841, age 84.
Cary, Recompense, Revolutionary Soldier, Lancaster, Jan. 13, 1837, age 81. [Another card: Cary, Recompense, b. 1756-7, d. Dec. 13, 1836, bur. Lancaster, NY, soldier of the Revolution. Jan. 13, 1837, age 81.]
Cary, Deacon Truman, Boston, Sept. 6, 1879, age 88 y, 3 m, 6 d.
Cary, Trumbull, June 20, 1869 in Batavia, N.Y.
Caryl, Alexander Hamilton, June 21, 1879, age 67; d. at Groton, MA, formerly of Buffalo.
Caryl, Benjamin, Nov. 8, 1856, age 83 y, 27 d.
Caryl, Benjamin D., June 2, 1873, age 68; d. at Canadaigua, bur. in Buffalo.
Caryl, Catharine, wife of Jonathan, Eden, Aug. 1845, age 76.
Caryl, Lucian W., M.D., April 15, 1837, age 31; d. at Fredonia.
Caryl, Lucian E., conductor, March 4, 1880, age 32 y, 8 m, 6 d.
Caryl, Susanna, wife of Capt. Benj., Mar. 1, 1846, age 69 y, 6 m.
Caryl, Thomas F., Eden, Sept. 13, 1856, age 32?.
Caryl, Dr. William Oscar, formerly of Buffalo, Aug. 28, 1837, age 25; d. at Fredonia.
Case, Betsey, dau. of Maj. Manning Case, April 3, 1829, age 20.
Case, Catherine B., wife of A. J., late of London, Ontario, Jan. 6, 1870, in 27th year.
Case, Edward L., Feb. 12, 1877, age 29.
Case, Eliza Ann, wife of Hugh M., Crittenden, May 30, 1861, age 33.
Case, Frances Davenport, formerly of Buffalo, wife of E. C., Jan. 1878; d. at Newton, NJ.
Case, Harriet, wife of S. S., Aug. 22, 1836.
Case, James A., son of Joseph G., Nov. 6, 1858, age 36; d. in Utica, bur. Buffalo.
Case, James Ely, Alden, Aug. 17, 1875, age 63.
Case, John A., June 1, 1879, age 59.
Case, Lucy, widow of Maj. Manning Case, Jan. 11, 1861, age 83 y, 4 m.
Case, Maj. Manning, Oct. 29, 1843, age 68.
Case, Margaret, wife of Whitney A., dau. of Isaac D. Felthousen of Schenectady, Jan. 10, 1851, age 25 y, 15 d.
Case, Mary (or Carr), wife of Patrick, May 1, 1871, age 36.
Case, Orange of Monticello, Aug. 25, 1849, age 23.
Case, Squire S., formerly of Buffalo, March 30, 1878, age 77; d. at Maunston, WI.
Casey, Betsey, mother of Mrs. James Demarest, Nov. 3, 1851, age 75.
Casey, Cornelius, Feb. 19, 1873, age 54.
Casey, Edward, Oct. 31, 1872, age 23.
Casey, Eliza M., Dec., 1880, age 47.
Casey, Edward, Sept. 8, 1863, age 31.
Casey, John P., Sept. 30, 1875; d. in Bay City, MI, bur. Buffalo.
Casey, Martin, Feb. 10, 1877, age 55; drowned.
Casey, Thomas, Dec. 12, 1877, age 26.
Casey, Mrs. Winney, May 13, 1874, age 40.
Cash, Miss Hattie A., Evans, March 29, 1872, age 32.
Cash, John P., son of Whiting, Evans, NY, Aug. 20, 1849, age 22 y, 5 m.
Cash, Persis, wife of Whiting, Evans, NY, Aug. 27, 1864, age 71.
Cash, Whiting, Evans, NY, Dec. 1867, age 75.
Caskey, Joseph, master of Schooner *Atalanta*, Aug. 18, 1834, age 35.
Casler, Mary Ann Gillbride, wife of Gillbride [sic], Nov. 9, 1879, age 27.
Casper, Theobald, Oct. 10, 1873, age 72.
Cass, Rebecca, wife of William S., Oct. 2, 1875, age 60.
Cassaday, Alexander, Dec. 12, 1874, age 21 y, 6 m.
Cassaday, Robert, Feb. 4, 1878.
Cassaday, William S., Jan. 9, 1878, age 28.
Cassel, Leon T., Williamsville, Feb. 13, 1878, age 16; accidental.
Cassidy, Bernard, Amherst, March 2, 1850, age 45; bur. Buffalo.
Cassidy, John, Sept. 21, 1850, age 33.
Cassidy, John, East Aurora, NY, June 30, 1876, age 65 y, 4 d.
Castine, Jane, colored, June 1, 1830, age 119. Born at Nine Partners, NY 1711; d. Erie Co. Poor House.
Castle, Fanny A., wife of D.B., Sept. 17, 1871, age 55.
Castle, Hiram S., June 3, 1855, age 32.

Castle, Ida A., dau. of Lewis S., May 30, 1877, age 19 y, 6 m, 22 d.
Castle, Phoebe, formerly of CT, May 11, 1843, age 58.
Castle, Thomas, April 18, 1872, age 23.
Castleton, Rev. John, Griffins Mills, May 22, 1862, age 81.
Caston, John, Co. Almshouse, Jan. 25, 1878, age 75.
Caswell, Dominico, known as Sandy, June 11, 1848.
Caswell, Miss Maria B., Jan. 26, 1874, age 58.
Caswell, William R., Alden, Sept. 7, 1833.
Cation, John, March 28, 1874, age 53.
Cation, Margaret, wife of John, Dec. 22, 1871.
Catlin, Rev. Oren, East Evans, Aug. 11, 1849, age 55.
Catlin, Miss Sophia M., East Evans, Sept. 9, 1878, age 31 y, 8 m, 27 d.
Catterson, Mrs. Margaret A., April 26, 1878, age 63 y, 9 m, 23 d.
Caudell (or Candell), Rev. John, March 1, 1863.
Caughey, David V., formerly of Buffalo, Aug. 13, 1866, age 47 y, 4 m, 12 d; d. in Erie, PA.
Caughey, John, June 5, 1875, age 65.
Caughlin, Miss Sally, Aurora, Ny, May 6, 1838, age 22.
Caulfield, Mary, wife of Peter, Elma, NY, Jan. 20, 1876, age 65.
Caufield, Peter, Elma, July 26, 1879, age 83.
Cavalli, Charles, late of Buffalo, Jan., 1869; d. in Milwaukee, WI.
Cavanagh, Francis, Nov. 27, 1880, age 52.
Cavanah, Ann, wife of John, Oct. 8, 1866, age 51.
Cavanaugh, David, Oct. 19, 1880, age 44; killed by cars in Canada.
Cavanaugh, Johanna, wife of Jeremiah, Feb. 9, 1875, age 52.
Cavanaugh, John, Jan. 18, 1871, age 50; drowned.
Cavanaugh, Mary, wife of Daniel, Jan. 6, 1880, age 40 y, 6 m, 5 d.
Caverly, Cornelius, July 24, 1870, age 32; d. at Petroleum Centre, PA, bur. in Buffalo.
Chace, Eber C., Aug. 29, 1870, age 64; suicide by hanging.
Chadbourne, Lt. Theodore Lincoln, May 9, 1846, age 24. Formerly attached to the garrison
    at Fort Niagara; killed at the Battle of Resaca de la Palma, Mexico.
Chadderden, James, Dec. 24, 1870, age 44; taken to Marilla.
Chaddock, Herbert L., Dec. 13, 1870, age 28; d. at LeRoy, NY.
Chadduck, Mrs. VanDyke, wife of David S., July 14, 1855, age 51.
Chaderdon, James, Marilla, July 27, 1877, age 81.
Chadwick, Adeline, wife of Prof. Edmund of Starkey, Yates Co., NY, March 18, 1873, age 46
    y, 6 m, 5 d. For 12 years preceptress of Starkey Seminary, NY.
Chadwick, Cecil, Oct. 7, 1874, age 23 y, 11 m.
Chadwick, H. H., Dec., 22, 1875, age 62; funeral at Westmoreland.
Chaffee, Ezra, Boston, NY, Sept. 7, 1858, age 54.
Chaffee, Hollis W., formerly of Alden, NY, April 17, 1879, age 67; d. near Great Bend, KA
    [KS ?]
Chaffee, Louise Lockwood, wife of Freelon, Oct. 4, 1880, age 33 y, 9 m, 18 d.
Chaffee, Stephen, b. Jan. 23, 1757, d. Jan. 23, 1819, bur. Springville, NY; Soldier of the
    Revolution.
Chalk, Mrs. Amy, Sept. 21, 1863, age 68.
Chalk, John S., Nov. 13, 1832, age 38.
Chalker, Mary, widow of Randolph W. of Guilford, CT, Oct. 14, 1848.
Challen, Joseph W., Canada, June 13, 1872, age 27; suicide.
Challis, Enos, b. 1753, d. 1815, bur. Holland; Revolutionary Soldier.
Chamberlain, A., Sept. 3, 1858, age 46.
Chamberlain, A. J., Dec. 19, 1854, age 49.
Chamberlain, Alonzo, Oct. 10, 1858, age 36 y, 6 m.
Chamberlain, Catherine, wife of Jonathan, Aug. 15, 1860, age 30.
Chamberlain, Culver T., July 15, 1869, age 38.
Chamberlain, David, formerly of Buffalo, Nov. 29, 1852, age 53; d. in Louisville, Clay Co.,
    IL.
Chamberlain, Mr. D. P. H., formerly of Buffalo, Aug. 11, 1856, age 20 y, 4 m; d. in
    Charleston, SC.
Chamberlain, Hannah, wife of Sylvester, Dec. 20, 1851, age 65.

Chamberlain, Capt. Horace P., son of Sylvester, Feb. 4, 1838, age 23. In Texan Army; d. at Galveston Island, TX, serving with the Texan army.
Chamberlain, Hunting S., Nov. 20, 1867, age 56.
Chamberlain, John, Sr., June 1, 1867, age 76.
Chamberlain, Luther, Alden, Aug. 31, 1833, age 50.
Chamberlain, Merritt, July 30, 1835, age 23; late of Forestville, Chautauqua Co., NY.
Chamberlain, Nancy A., widow of Alonzo J., Aug. 23, 1871, age 63.
Chamberlain, Sallie, widow of John, May 26, 1873, age 77.
Chamberlain, Samuel Miller, Nov. 13, 1874, age 47.
Chamberlain, Sylvester, July 14, 1862, age 79.
Chamberlayne, Mary Florence, dau. of E. L., Nov. 20, 1871, age 20.
Chamberlin, Asahel, Dec. 6, 1828, age 38.
Chamberlin, Deacon John, Sardinia, Dec. 23, 1869, age 77.
Chamberlin, Lydia, wife of Asahel, July 8, 1853, age 34.
Chamberlin, Mary, widow of John, Sardinia, July 29, 1871, age 80.
Chamberlin, R. B., Oct. 30, 1843; formerly of Buffalo, d. in Mobile, AL. Late steward of Steamer *New World*.
Chambers, Miss Flora M., May 1857.
Chambers, Hannah Butler, wife of Dr. Hiram, Feb. 4, 1865, age 46.
Chambers, Isaac J., Feb. 3, 1880, age 43 y, 1 m, 21 d.
Chambers, Mary, May 27, 1872, age 81.
Chamot, Catharine, July 30, 1865, age 71.
Chamot, Catherine, wife of Frederick, April 28, 1872, age 61.
Champion, Daniel, May 28, 1859, age 33.
Champlin, Miss Hannah, Feb. 28, 1878, age 90.
Champlin, M. Jennie Howell, wife of Thos. A. T., Aug. 22, 1856, age 21 y, 10 m.
Champlin, Minerva Lydia, wife of Capt. Stephen of U.S. Navy, June 8, 1859, age 61.
Champlin, S. Raymond, April 21, 1868, age 45; d. at St. Paul, MN.
Champlin, Commodore Stephen, Feb. 20, 1870, in 81st year. Only remaining commanding officer in the battle of Lake Erie at time of his death.
Champlin, William B., brother of O.H.P., May 3, 1876.
Chandler, Albert F., only son of A. W. of Colden, NY, Nov. 20, 1862, age 24; d. in Annapolis Hospital, MD. Enlisted in Porter Gerard's Buffalo, Co. B, Cavalry.
Chandler, Amy, wife of Lyman, Willink, NY, Sept. 21, 1868, age 70 y, 4 d.
Chandler, Edgar, Elma, NY, Jan. 3, 1874, age 39 y, 2 m, 22 d.
Chandler, Elvira, widow of James D., May 18, 1871, age 43 y, 1 m, 25 d.
Chandler, Emily, dau. of Oira and Louise, East Hamburgh, NY, June 18, 1874, age 36.
Chandler, Isaac, Rev. Soldier, Hamburgh, NY, Feb. 26, 1841, age 76.
Chandler, Isaac Percy, son of O., Jan. 3, 1870, age 28 y, 10 m, 20 d.
Chandler, James D., son-in-law of Waterman Perkins, Westfalls, April 29, 1869, age 43 y, 5 m, 18 d.
Chandler, Lavina E., Willink, Jan. 10, 1870, age 28 y, 3 m, 17 d; d. at Spring, Crawford Co., PA.
Chandler, Mrs. Maria M., Colden, April 4, 1868, in 53d y.
Chandler, Patience, wife of Isaac, Hamburg, Nov., 1814, age 40.
Chandler, Percy, Jan. 3, 1870, age 29.
Chapel, William R., Boston, NY, May 17, 1875, age 43.
Chapin, Andrew A., merchant of New York, July 31, 1857, age 26; d. in Utica.
Chapin, Dr. Cyrenius, Feb. 20, 1838, age 66.
Chapin, Mrs., wife of Dr. Daniel, Dec. 1812.
Chapin, Brig.-Gen. Edward Payson, May 27, 1863 at Port Hudson, LA in 32nd year; bur. at Waterloo, NY.
Chapin, Elias, Rev. Soldier, Evans, NY, Feb. 4, 1839, age 87. Native of Somers, CT.
Chapin, Hannah B., wife of R., July 30, 1851.
Chapin, Hollis, June 13, 1852, age 58; d. in Alden, NY, bur. in Buffalo.
Chapin, Capt. James, Black Rock, NY, Sept. 24, 1832, age 46.
Chapin, John, Clarence, NY, April 1839.
Chapin, Maria, wife of Cooley S., March 16, 1853, age 35.
Chapin, Martha Amelia, wife of Rev. Henry, Alden, Nov. 26, 1844, age 27.
Chapin, Mary, widow of Col. William, May 13, 1862.

Chapin, Mary Josephine, wife of E.D., formerly of Buffalo, July 1, 1875; d. in Covington, KY, bur. Buffalo.
Chapin, Seth, merchant, Nov. 12, 1826, age 36.
Chapin, Sylvia, widow of Seth, dau. of Dr. Cyrenius Chapin, Dec. 1, 1831, age 36.
Chapin, Sylvia, widow of Dr. Cyrenius, Oct. 1, 1863, age 96.
Chapin, Theodore, June 29, 1854, age 54; taken to Rochester, NY.
Chapin, Col. William W., Buffalo Plains, June 20, 1857, age 73.
Chapman, Catherine, wife of E.W., Clarence, NY, Feb. 18, 1877, age 25 y, 1 m, 8 d.
Chapman, Dudley, Clarence, NY, Feb. 16, 1873, age 86 y, 9 m, 1 d.
Chapman, Harvey, April 30, 1878, Co. Almshouse.
Chapman, John, son of George L., Oct. 17, 1854, age 24.
Chapman, Margaret, wife of George L., July 6, 1855, age 43.
Chapman, Mrs. Palexamy, April 16, 1845, age 45.
Chapman, Mrs. Ruth, Nov. 27, 1858, age 85.
Chapman, Sophie Arey, Jan. 23, 1868, age 28.
Chapman, William, March 10, 1878, age 70; Co. Almshouse.
Chappell, Bruce, May 5, 1868, age 34.
Chappell, Mrs. Elizabeth, No. 34 Folsom, Feb. 9, 1873, age 81.
Chappell, Mary A., wife of R. C., Dec. 27, 1849, age 18.
Chappell, Nathan L., Jan. 11, 1879, age 82 y, 9 m.
Chard, Mary, wife of William, June 14, 1854, age 51.
Chard, William, Nov. 25, 1854, age 49; d. at Canton, OH, bur. in Buffalo.
Charles, George, June 26, 1867, age 52.
Charles, Nelson P., Jan. 30, 1869, age 26.
Chase, Alanson, East Humburgh, NY, Dec. 17, 1880, age 77.
Chase, Anna Aykroid, wife of Edward, Nov. 5, 1871, age 20.
Chase (or Chace), Annette, Oct. 5, 1875, age 20; suicide.
Chase, Mrs. Clarissa, mother of William H. and Charles E., Lancaster, NY, April 18, 1860, age 75.
Chase, David V. R., Feb. 6, 1877, age 84.
Chase, Mrs. Elizabeth, June 26, 1843, age 53.
Chase, George R., Oct. 22, 1879, age 64; d. at Auburn, NY, formerly of Buffalo.
Chase, Harriet, wife of Charles E., formerly of Buffalo, June 14, 1870, age 41; d. in Chicago, eldest dau. of William Wells of Buffalo.
Chase, Jacob, Jan. 1873, age 55.
Chase, James, Holland, July 19, 1845, age 59.
Chase, James H., Oct. 18, 1863, age 49.
Chase, Jonathan E., Oct. 25, 1878, age 56 y, 9 m.
Chase, Miss Josephine, Dec. 19, 1873, age 19 y, 11 m.
Chase, Louisa A., wife of J. L., May 11, 1855, age 30 y, 6 m., 11 d. Died at St. Catharines.
Chase, Mary Ann, Amherst, Aug. 7, 1835, age 24.
Chase, Mary S., wife of Rev. George L. of St. Cloud, MN, dau. of R. H. Heywood of Buffalo, Sept. 22, 1866, age 25. Died in Venier, OH, born in Buffalo.
Chase, Prudence, wife of Alanson, East Hamburgh, NY, Sept. 24, 1863, age 60.
Chase, Rachel E., widow of Jacob, Oct. 10, 1872, age 43 y, 9 m.
Chase, Capt. Robert B., on board schooner *Pilgrim*, Aug. 17, 1849, age 52.
Chase, Capt. Samuel, Aug. 12, 1844, age 40.
Chase, Sarah R., widow of David V. R., June 1, 1878, age 78.
Chase, Susan, wife of Thomas B., Aug. 22, 1849, age 31.
Chasselet, Alexander, Tonawanda, NY, Aug. 5, 1849, age 69.
Chatfield, Mrs. M. A., June 18, 1871, age 41.
Chatterdon, Lewis, Spring Brook, NY, April 29, 1852, age 92.
Cheeseboro, James, b. Jan. 1762, d. March 24, 1848, Alden, NY; soldier of the Revolution.
Cheeseman, William, Hamburgh, NY, Dec. 30, 1813. Killed at Battle of Black Rock.
Cheeseman, William, Oct. 1, 1880, age 75.
Cheever, George N., formerly of Whitesborough, Sept. 22, 1848, age 26.
Cheney, A. H., form of Seward, Bentley & Cheney, Jan. 17, 1870; d. in Mobile, AL.
Cheney, Eliza, wife of Orlando W., Feb. 13, 1872, age 24 y, 3 m, 2 d.
Cheney, Greenleaf E., Jan. 19, 1880, age 24.

Cheney, James B., May 18, 1879, age 26.
Cheney, William H., Sept. 17, 1877, age 31 y, 6 m.
Cherevoy, George H., May 20, 1864, age 41; d. in Santa Cruz, Cuba.
Cherry, Mrs. Jane, Feb. 19, 1860, age 69.
Cherry, Moses, formerly of Buffalo, Feb. 4, 1870, age 61; d. at Oswego, IL.
Chessman, William, 1880.
Chester, Edward J., April 3, 1875, age 28; accidental death.
Chester, Elizabeth Stanley, wife of Rev. Dr. A. T., Sept. 22, 1875, age 61 y, 1 m, 17 d.
Chester, Friendly Dean, wife of Augustus, Oct. 27, 1852; d. in Attica, NY.
Chester, Hattie C. Sage, wife of Charles, Feb. 8, 1866, age 24.
Chester, John, Aug. 16, 1871, age 65; d. at Plainfield, NJ, bur. in Buffalo.
Chesterman, Constantie, Jan. 6, 1869, age 38.
Chew, Sarah E., wife of Francis W., May 9, 1843, age 20.
Chichester, David, father of J. L. and Lewis, Nov. 17, 1874, age 85; taken to Rochester, NY.
Chidsey, Charles H., Sept. 22, 1869, age 50; taken to Painesville, OH.
Chilcott, Benjamin F., East Hamburgh, NY, April 30, 1867.
Chilcott, Charles Henry, March 1, 1880, age 20 y, 10 m, 2 d.
Chilcott, Evan G., Aurora, March 31, 1852, age 51.
Chilcott, Rachel, wife of Amos, East Hamburgh, NY, March 23, 1880, age 78.
Chilcott, William, July 20, 1873, age 43.
Child, Cornelia, dau. of Hon. Jonathan of Rochester, Oct. 3, 1856, age 24.
Child, Helen M., wife of Perley A., dau. of Pascall P. Pratt, April 14, 1867; d. at West Exeter, Otsego Co., NY, b. in Buffalo.
Child, Hon. Jonathan, father-in-law of A. P. Nichols, Oct. 27, 1860. Of Rochester and buried there.
Childs, Marcia N., wife of Isaac, Springville, NY, Oct. 23, 1861, age 33 y, 7 m, 2 d.
Chipman, Silas, formerly of Boston, MA, Innkeeper, Aug. 20, 1829, age 32.
Chipman, Tillitha C., formerly of Buffalo, wife of John B., Dec. 13, 1852, age 26; d. in Rochester, NY.
Chittenden, Harlow W., formerly of Buffalo, July 24, 1872, age 55; d. in Syracuse, NY.
Chittenden, Martin, Surrogate of Erie Co., Sept. 4, 1832, age 28. Cholera.
Chittenden, Thomas, Feb. 7, 1875, age 54.
Chittenden, William E., Feb. 15, 1880, age 72; d. in Cleveland, formerly of Buffalo.
Chitterling, H., April 26, 1878, age 50 y, 2 m, 15 d.
Choate, Eli W., Lancaster, NY, April 10, 1872, age 61 y, 11 m.
Choate, Fidelia E., wife of E. W., Lancaster, NY, June 1, 1847, age 33.
Choate, Harry E., May 6, 1868, age 30.
Choate, Mrs. M., mother of R. M. of Buffalo, Williamsville, NY, Nov. 5, 1873, age 76?.
Choate, Vesta A., wife of W. H., July 24, 1870, age 30; taken to Gardiner, ME.
Chowings, Henry Cotton, sexton of St. John's Church, Aug. 26, 1867, age 71.
Chowings, Mary Ann, wife of Henry C., Sept. 7, 1856, age 28.
Chowings, Susan, widow of Henry C., March 29, 1877, age 83.
Chretien, Barbara Gertrude, wife of George, April 30, 1873, age 22.
Chretien, Charles, April 28, 1876, age 64 y, 2 m, 15d.
Chretien, Emelia Walter, wife of Joseph, Jan. 19, 1873, age 24 y, 4 m, 4 d.
Chretien, John, April 3, 1873, age 55.
Chretien, Joseph A., Oct. 9, 1878, age 30 y, 8 m.
Christ, Elenore, wife of Carl, Sept. 12, 1879, age 44.
Christ, John, Co. Almshouse, July 12, 1879, age 92.
Christey, John, printer, Jan. 31, 1851, age 27 y, 3 m.
Christey, Joseph, father of Arthur, Feb. 21, 1863, age 73.
Christian, Maria L., June 2, 1860, age 20.
Christie, Jane, March 8, 1873, age 67; taken to Stamford, Ontario.
Christie, Dr. P., Surgeon in U.S. Navy, March 4, 1853, age 63.
Christoff, H., formerly a merchant of Worms, Germany, Dec. 27, 1836, age 45.
Christoph, Mary, wife of E. G., April 17, 1877, age 24 y, 4 m, 16 d.
Christopherson, Christopher, Clarence, NY, April, 1878; drowned.
Christy, Joseph L., Brant, July 18, 1873, age 65.
Chukland, Samuel, Newstead, Feb. 6, 1842, age 66.

Church, Almira, wife of Ralph, Jan. 31, 1848, age 36.
Church, Anna, wife of Ralph, April 5, 1854, age 43.
Church, Edwin, Oct. 2, 1854, age 23.
Church, George, Co. Almshouse, June 14, 1877, age 22.
Church, Capt. John, Collins, April 24, 1832, age 50.
Church, Rev. Livius S., formerly of Buffalo, Nov. 5, 1873.
Church, Mary M., wife of Alvah, July 26, 1866, age 44.
Church, Ralph, April 27, 1871, age 63.
Church, Mrs. Sarah P., dau. of the late F. S. Craig, sister of A. F. Craig of Buffalo, White's Corners, NY, Feb. 10, 1870, age 33.
Church, William M., 1st Lt. in Wheeler's Battery, 33rd NY, Feb. 15, 1869, age 39; taken to Lockport, NY.
Churchill, Amelia L., wife of F. G., Feb. 5, 1869, age 34 y, 6 m.
Churchill, Calista Ann, wife of Putnam, Oct. 31, 1843, age 38.
Churchill, Clark H., Feb. 23, 1876, age 23 y, 8 m.
Churchill, Elmira, wife of Julius M., dau. of Gen. L. I. Roberts, West Seneca, Nov. 25, 1868, age 38.
Churchill, Harriet, wife of Charles, Sept. 25, 1850, age 32.
Churchill, Hattie, wife of Frank P., Sept. 23, 1872; taken to Sardinia, Erie Co., NY.
Churchill, Jennie R. Hoyt, wife of Rev. M. A., formerly of Buffalo, Dec. 17, 1875, age 28; d. at Yokohama, Japan.
Churchill, Lydia, wife of Putnam, June 5, 1830, age 30.
Churchill, Nellie, wife of Emmet L., Oct. 22, 1879, age 29.
Churchill, Olive, widow of John, Sept. 7, 1861, age 62. Sister of Aaron Rumsey. Taken to Portland, Chautuqua Co., NY.
Churchill, Philo, May, 1862; suicide.
Churchill, Putnam, formerly of Buffalo, Nov. 11, 1874, age 78; d. at Elyria, OH.
Churchyard, Ruth S., wife of Joseph, Oct. 4, 1878, age 47.
Clabaux, Augustus, Dec. 6, 1855, age 33 y, 4 m.
Clabeaux, Francois T., Nov. 16, 1871, age 75.
Clabo, Elizabeth Ernst, wife of Peter, Oct. 29, 1862, age 33 y, 8 m, 3 d.
Clempet, Mrs. Alice, Nov. 19, 1880, age 48.
Clampffer, Mrs. Ann E., April 12, 1855, age 41.
Clancy, Mrs. Ann Bailey, Oct. 14, 1860, age 66.
Clancy, Nellie, dau. of P. J., Oct. 10, 1878.
Clancy, Thomas, March 11, 1874, age 35.
Clancy, William B., Oct. 5, 1864, age 45; d. in Philadelphia of wounds received at front in Petersburg, b. in Buffalo.
Clapp, Artemas, formerly of Norton, Mass., Aug. 9, 1834, age 25.
Clapp, Mrs. Eliza S., Jan. 12, 1871, age 82 y, 10 m.
Clapp, Frank W., only son of Lewis, Lancaster, NY, July 7, 1863, age 20 y, 8 m, 6 d. Of 44th Reg. Band. D. in South Framington, MA.
Clapp, Hattie E., Lancaster, NY, eldest dau. of Lewis, Nov. 14, 1869, age 25.
Clapp, Julius, merchant, Aug. 22, 1849, age 38
Clapp, Mrs. Keziah, mother of A. M., Sept. 4, 1862, age 73.
Clapp, Mrs. Lydia, June 19, 1879.
Clar, Michael, Jan. 1873.
Claraluna, Charles Bartholomew, Oct. 2, 1863, age 40. Son of the late Rev. Bartholomew Claraluna of Switzerland. Brother-in-law of Hon. Eli Cook.
Clarey, Roger, July 19, 1875, age 72. Killed by a mule on a canal boat near West Troy, bur. in Buffalo.
Claris, John, Oct. 9, 1856, age 45.
Clark, Mrs., Hamburgh, NY, Mar. 1814, age 50.
Clark, Abraham, Evans, NY, April 25, 1864, age 74.
Clark, Adah Sabin, wife of Zenas, April 24, 1867, age 64.
Clark, Adam, Cold Springs, NY, Sept. 26, 1874, age 46.
Clark, Albert A., East Granby, CT, July 2, 1857, age 18.
Clark, Mrs. Almira, mother of Mrs. B. H. Austin, Jr., Oct. 26, 1869, age 53.
Clark, Ambrose, Aug. 10, 1878, age 62.
Clark, Dr. Archibald, late of Buffalo, Nov. 1846; d. at Little Fort, IL.

Clark, Belinda, wife of William, Feb. 11, 1871, age 79 y, 11 m, 20 d.
Clark, Benjamin, Drum Major of Swift's Regiment, Dec. 1812, age 21.
Clark, Benjamin. Rev. Soldier, [bur.] Lancaster, NY, Feb. 28, 1843, age 83. Son James said age 85 was correct. [Another card says b. 1759, d. 1842.]
Clark, Benjamin, June 19, 1878, age 80.
Clark, Betsey Pember, wife of James, Lancaster, NY, Sept. 22, 1879, age 92 y, 1 m, 8 d.
Clark, Caroline Elizabeth, wife of Geo. R., Feb. 23, 1870, age 39.
Clark, Caroline P., wife of Richard W., April 4, 1858, age 52.
Clark, Catharine, April 24, 1837, age 20.
Clark, Catharine, wife of W. A., June 19, 1842, age 27; d. at Clarence, NY.
Clark, Catherine M., Oct. 10, 1879, age 64.
Clark, Celinda, wife of Harvey, Lancaster, NY, Sept. 11, 1867, age 67.
Clark, Charles W., formerly of Buffalo, April 8, 1874, age 25; drowned in Baltimore, MD.
Clark, Daniel C., eldest son of Horace, March 11, 1851, age 33; d. in Brooklyn.
Clark, David Augustus, son of D. N., Nov. 14, 1857, age 21 y, 6 d.
Clark, David N., July 27, 1880, age 75.
Clark, Delia, dau. of Henry, Lancaster, Aug. 20, 1845, age 26.
Clark, Mrs. Electa, mother-in-law of William O. Brown, Nov. 21, 1856, age 68.
Clark, Elisha, May 3, 1857, age 65.
Clark, Eliza, wife of Erastus, June 6, 1863, age 33.
Clark, Emeline E., dau. of Stephen, March 1, 1853, age 42.
Clark, Enice, widow of Hon. Staley N., Corry, PA, June 23, 1873, age 77; d. at Corry, bur. in Buffalo.
Clark, Erastus W., July 22, 1876, age 63.
Clark, Ezra, Marilla, Sept. 25, 1870, age 73.
Clark, F. C., brother-in-law of William O. Brown, July 9, 1854, age 35; d. in Chicago, bur. in Buffalo.
Clark, Frances E., widow of Major Satterlee, Dec. 13, 1864.
Clark, George A., July 23, 1843, age 36.
Clark, Gustavus, Feb. 18, 1871, age 85; taken to Clarkson.
Clark, Harriet, widow of Daniel, Dec. 17, 1874, age 55.
Clark, Hattie E., wife of Edward, East Hamburgh, NY, Oct. 22, 1878, age 23 y, 8 m, 22 d.
Clark, Heman, Sept. 29, 1843, age 23.
Clark, Heman W., Jan. 9, 1830, age 35.
Clark, Henry, Aug. 9, 1848, age 52.
Clark, Henry, son of Hon. John, recently of Hamburgh, NY, Dec. 14, 1862, age 25; d. in Cherry Free, Venengo Co., PA.
Clark, Henry S., formerly of Buffalo, Dec. 21, 1874, age 52; d. at Northampton, MA.
Clark, Herbert H., son of Alfred, Oct. 10, 1867, age 24.
Clark, Hiram, teacher, Evans Center, NY, Jan. 17, 1858, age 31.
Clark, Horace, Clarence, May 1812, age 18.
Clark, Horace, Nov. 4, 1852, age 57; d. at Pompey, Onondaga Co., bur. in Buffalo.
Clark, James, June 17, 1877; drowned at Albion, Orleans Co., bur. in Buffalo.
Clark, James, Lancaster, Oct. 16, 1879, age 84 y, 7 m, 4 d.
Clark, Mrs. Jane B., Feb. 7, 1875, age 41 y, 8 m.
Clark, Johanna, Sept. 17, 1871, age 35.
Clark, John, Clarence, Apgil 1812, age 74.
Clark, John, formerly of Portsmouth, NH, May 24, 1842, age 50.
Clark, John, Collins Centre, Sept. 29, 1844, age 77.
Clark, John, June 21, 1869, age 39.
Clark, John, Dec. 4, 1872, age 35.
Clark, Dr. John W., Nov. 25, 1872, age 73.
Clark, Deacon Joseph, Lancaster, NY, May 10, 1853, age 67.
Clark, Kate Worcester, wife of Myron H., Lancaster, NY, Jan. 1, 1875, age 38; bur. in Buffalo.
Clark, Kittie L., wife of Orton S., Aug. 5, 1877, age 38.
Clark, Laura, wife of Henry, postmaster, Sept. 14, 1845, age 47.
Clark, Laura B., wife of William A., March 28, 1849, age 22.
Clark, Lavina, wife of W. S., Eden, NY, Dec. 25, 1836, age 53.
Clark, Lot, Dec. 18, 1862, age 71.

Clark, Maria R., wife of Almond, Oct. 8, 1851, age 46; d. at Dansville.
Clark, Martin R., July 20, 1880, age 49, son of Zenas; d. at Irving, KS, formerly of Buffalo.
Clark, Mary, wife of Dr. Sylvester, Boston, NY, April 29, 1840, age 56.
Clark, Mary, widow of John, Nov. 24, 1862, age 63.
Clark, Mary D., wife of Charles, Feb. 21, 1856, age 27. Taken to Clarkson, Monroe Co.
Clark, Mary E., wife of Charles S., Feb. 19, 1852, age 25.
Clark, Melinda, widow of Stephen, March 3, 1853, age 62.
Clark, Melinda Candee, wife of Horace, May 31, 1851, age 57; d. near Peoria, IL, bur. in Buffalo.
Clark, Michael, July 22, 1867, age 71 y, 3 m, 16 d.
Clark, Olive, wife of Benjamin, Lancaster, NY, Aug. 15, 1833, age 70.
Clark, Oliver H., Feb. 14, 1853, age 32.
Clark, Reuben, b. 1759, d. 1844; bur. Chestnut Ridge, soldier of the Revolution.
Clark, Reuben, April 12, 1853, age 25.
Clark, Robert, Feb. 24, 1870, age 40.
Clark, Samuel, July 10, 1841, age 53.
Clark, Sarah, sister of Dr. J. W., Juy 12, 1849.
Clark, Sarah A., widow of Justus, Oct. 4, 1871, age 43.
Clark, Sarah N. Gould, wife of Alexander L., April 17, 1874, age 53.
Clark, Seneca A., Sept. 21, 1879, age 45.
Clark, Seth, Dec. 7, 1875, age 61; suicide.
Clark, Sophia, wife of Benjamin, Feb. 25, 1837, age 34. Formerly of Elbridge, NY.
Clark, Stephen, June 17, 1848, age 63.
Clark, Stephen C., Director in Buffalo Steam Engine Works, Aug. 8, 1845, age 36; d. at Middlesex, Mercer Co., PA.
Clark, Stephen E., eldest son of Erastus, June 17, 1863, age 20 y, 4 m, 13 d.
Clark, Dr. Sylvester, Boston, NY, April 26, 1843, age 58.
Clark, Capt. Thomas, July 5, 1878, age 58.
Clark, Ursula, late of Hartford, CT, Aug. 5, 1827, age 24.
Clark, William, June 1, 1863; drowned near the old lighthouse.
Clark, William, late of North Collins, Oct. 8, 1863, age 32; d. at Princeton, WI.
Clark, William, father of Orange W., Aug. 19, 1874, age 84.
Clark, William A., formerly of Buffalo, March 3, 1877, age 65; d. in Philadelphia, bur. in Buffalo.
Clark, Gen. William Hyde, Oct. 10, 1872; d. at Dubuque, IA.
Clark, William S., July 3, 1845, age 59.
Clarke, Miss, formerly of Buffalo, Aug. 1880; suicide at sea.
Clarke, Alfred, July 20, 1880, age 66.
Clarke, Archibald S., Clarence, Nov. 28, 1821, age 44.
Clarke, Catharine E., wife of Cyrus, Feb. 17, 1872.
Clarke, Charles, Oct. 27, 1857, age 35; d. at Murray, Orleans Co.
Clarke, Charle E., formerly of Buffalo, May 13, 1875, aged 63 y, 9 d; d. in Millerstown, PA, bur. in Buffalo.
Clarke, Chloe Sears, wife of Col. Dudley, Feb. 19, 1867, age 65.
Clarke, Col. Dudley, Sept. 22, 1871, age 78; d. in Pulaski, NY., bur. in Buffalo.
Clarke, E. I., formerly of Buffalo, Nov. 27, 1869, age 47.
Clarke, Rev. E. W., formerly pastor of Cottage Baptist Church in Buffalo, June 21, 1856, age 35; d. at Arcade, Wyoming Co., NY.
Clarke, Elizabeth Stone, wife of Charles S., March 18, 1868, age 42.
Clarke, Frederick C., son of John of Norwich, England, April 1864, age 39; funeral April 22.
Clarke, Mary Anna, wife of Charles E., Lancaster, NY, March 2, 1869, age 56.
Clarke, Rev. Walter, b. April 5, 1812, d. May 23, 1871, age 59; taken to Hartford, CT.
Clarkson, Charles, Jan. 8, 1872, age 25; taken to Maumee, OH.
Clarkson, Emma Wadsworth, wife of George P., Sept. 3, 1871.
Clary, Joseph, lawyer, April 11, 1842, age 50.
Clary, Mary, Dec. 11, 1875, age 76.
Clause, Mrs. Mary Eva, Sept. 21, 1880, age 73.
Clawson, Benjamin F., April 29, 1865, age 24.

Clay, John, July 10, 1850, age 60.
Cleary, James, Dec. 12, 1879, age 69 y, 7 m.
Clemens, Aaron, April 1878, age 25.
Clemens, Christian, Almshouse, Nov. 2, 1879, age 59.
Clement, Mary Elizabeth, wife of Jesse, May 23, 1858, age 38; d. at Dubuque, IA.
Clemmens, or Clemons, Miss Ann, June 2, 1876, age 80; d. at Pembroke, Genesee Co., NY.
Clemons, Elizabeth, wife of Col. Alfred, Feb. 13, 1858, age 53; sister of Col. Alanson Palmer.
Cleveland, Eliza, wife of Palmer, Amherst, April 28, 1820, age 26.
Cleveland, Jennette R., July 18, 1855.
Cleveland, Margaret, Black Rock, widow of William, formerly of Norwich, CT, mother-in-law of Lewis F. Allen, Aug. 13, 1850, age 84.
Cleveland, Palmer, formerly of Buffalo, Jan. 2, 1873, age 79; d. at Alton, IL.
Cleveland, Serepta, wife of Palmer, formerly of Buffalo, May 4, 1869; d. at Alton, IL.
Cleveland, William, husband of Margaret, Aug. 18, 1837, age 67. [Card reads: "Norwich, Conn. Aug. 18, 1837 in Black Rock at the residence of his son-in-law, Lewis F. Allen, age 67."]
Cliff, Jane E., wife of John W., March 20, 1873, age 33 y, 5 m; d. and bur. at Niagara City, Ontario.
Clifford, Johanna, wife of James, May 8, 1875.
Clifford, John, March 15, 1857, age 62.
Clifford, Julia A., widow of John, Feb. 13, 1863; d. in Detroit, MI, b. in Buffalo.
Clifton, Henry, Aug. 12, 1877, age 57; d. at Beaver Island (at St. James), Lake Michigan.
Clinch (or Church), Charles, Black Rock, Sept. 23, 1828, age 35.
Cline, Mrs. M., April 3, 1879, age 46.
Clingen, Margaret McKernan, wife of William, Sept. 30, 1866.
Clink, Louisa H. Pfeiffer, wife of George, Sept. 23, 1880, age 20 y, 2 m.
Clinton, Major DeWitt, formerly of Buffalo, Aug. 13, 1873, age 40 y, 4 m. Eldest son of George W.; d. at St. Paul, MN, bur. in Buffalo.
Clinton, George DeWitt, May 5, 1877, age 51.
Clinton, Henry P., Feb. 17, 1870, age 41; d. at Socorro, NM., bur. in Buffalo.
Clinton, Mrs. Jane Rutherford, widow of Thomas, Dec. 8, 1880, age 80.
Clinton, Sarah W., wife of Spencer, Oct. 6, 1880.
Clinton, Thomas, Black Rock, NY, May 1835, age 40.
Clor, Catherine, wife of Michael, Aug. 11, 1857, age 42.
Clor, Michael, Jan. 17, 1873, age 60.
Close, Catharine, wife of Jerome B., Sept. 18, 1871, age 42.
Close, Emily B., wife of Emery, Feb. 1, 1880, age 44 y, 8 m, 25 d.
Close, Jerome B., May 7, 1879, age 56, formerly of Buffalo; d. in Washington, DC.
Close, Thomas, Sept. 28, 1873.
Clough, Horace, Evans, NY, Feb. 3, 1864, age 72 y, 11.
Clough, Parthenia, widow of Horace, Evans, NY, April 21, 1865, age 72.
Cluer, Heman M., Angola, May 2, 1859, age 72 y, 10 m.
Cluff, William, b. July 16, 1828, in Worcestershire, England, d. March 29, 1860.
Coak, Jones, Nov. 27, 1862, age 40.
Coates, Charlotte F., Dec. 26, 1867; d. at Norwich, CT.
Coates, Lydia H., wife of James J., March 2, 1872, age 26; bur. at North Collins, NY.
Coates, Zebulon, b. 1763, d. 1849, bur. Olcott; soldier of the Revolution.
Coatsworth, Caleb, Dec. 22, 1858, age 69.
Coatsworth, Caleb, Aug. 10, 1870, age 59 y, 6 m, 26.
Coatsworth, Jane, Jan. 12, 1862, age 79.
Coatsworth, Jane F., wife of C., July 21, 1849, age 32.
Coatsworth, John, d. a few weeks since in Canada, late of this village; *Niagara Journal*, Jan. 18, 1820.
Coatsworth, John, March 8, 1866, age 53.
Coatsworth, Joseph, March 30, 1879, age 72.
Coatsworth, Molly Graham, widow of Caleb, May 1863, age 68; funeral May 13.
Coatsworth, Thomas, June 28, 1833, age 54.
Coatsworth, William, March 25, 1860, age 28.
Coatsworth, William Edgson, Sept. 5, 1873, age 24.

Cobb, Adeline, wife of Frank, June 21, 1862, age 35.
Cobb, Annie E., wife of A. R., Oct. 26, 1862.
Cobb, Carlos, formerly of Buffalo, Sept. 16, 1877, age 62; d. at Tarrytown, NY.
Cobb, Charlotte Callender, wife of Oscar, April 12, 1867, age 34.
Cobb, David, July 28, 1878, age 83.
Cobb, Elenor, Black Rock, NY, wife of Zenas, July 29, 1853.
Cobb, Emeline Field, wife of Carlos, Nov. 26, 1875; d. in New York, bur. in Buffalo.
Cobb, George, son of Francis, Feb. 7, 1878, age 24 y, 8 m, 8 d.
Cobb, Gideon, formerly of Buffalo, Aug. 14, 1864, age 73; d. at Brighton Hill near Rochester, NY.
Cobb, Miss Mary M., Spring Brook, Dec. 21, 1871, aged 31 y, 7 m.
Cobb, Perez, Dec. 21, 1869, age 79.
Cobb, Samuel, formerly of St. Johns, New Brunswick, Feb. 25, 1839, age 47.
Cobb, Samuel T., March 20, 1865, age 42.
Cobb, Sarah, widow of Dr. John of Ogden, Monroe Co., July 27, 1844, age 66; taken to Ogden.
Cobb, Mrs. Sarah, Oct. 31, 1869, age 79.
Cobb, Shelby H., March 15, 1874, age 27 y, 8 m.
Cobb, Thomas S., Nov. 25, 1871.
Cobb, William H. H., April 26, 1873.
Cobb, Zenas, March 20, 1856, age 78.
Cobleigh, A. M., dancing master, Nov. 21, 1879, age 69.
Cobleigh, Reuben, Rev. Soldier, Hamburgh, Feb. 15, 1847, age 87.
Cobley, Rhoda, wife of Oliver, Eden, NY, April 11, 1835, age 35.
Coburn, Paul, Oct. 2, 1849, age 37.
Coburn, Sarah, wife of Theodore, Sept. 22, 1862, age 71.
Coburn, Theodore, Dec. 8, 1849, age 61.
Cochrane, Andrew G. C., May 28, 1872, age 63.
Cochrane, Mrs. E. C., Aug. 14, 1871.
Cochrane, Rev. Joseph G., formerly of Springville, NY, Nov. 2, 1871, age 54; d. at Oroomiah, Persia.
Cochrane, Samuel, Springville, NY, Oct. 19, 1845, age 61.
Cochrane, Thomas A. C., son of A. G. C., Feb. 27, 1870, age 38; d. in Brooklyn, N.Y., bur. in Buffalo.
Coichrane, William, July 20, 1873, age 62; d. in Brooklyn, NY.
Cockle, Robert B., Sept. 13, 1874, age 73; taken to Abbotts Corners, NY.
Codd, Hannah, sister of the late Robert, March 21, 1867; taken to Toronto.
Codd, Lucy, wife of Thomas F., Aurora, NY, March 17, 1852, age 17 y, 5 m.
Codd, Robert, June 9, 1865, age 72.
Coddington, William, April 29, 1880, age 76.
Coe, Bela D., Nov. 26, 1852, age 62; d. in London, England, b. in Buffalo, Feb. 11, 1853.
Coe, Charlotte, wife of Thomas D., native of Fulham, near London, England, Jan. 4, 1833, age 36; d. at the Cantonment near Williamsville.
Coe, John, Williamsville, NY, July 25, 1871, age 71.
Coe, John A., Dec. 31, 1819, age 28.
Coe, Thomas, May 21, 1838, age 80; d. at the Cantonment near Williamsville.
Coe, William, Williamsville, NY, April 9, 1874, age 75.
Coester, John, Sept. 12, 1872, age 62 y, 11 m, 29 d.
Coff, Sarah, Co. Almshouse, March 22, 1878, age 60.
Coffee, Annie, May 16, 1880, age 21 y, 2 m, 8 d.
Coffey, John, Feb. 14, 1872, age c. 42.
Coffey, Thomas, Nov. 14, 1865, age 47.
Cofflin, Charles A., June 26, 1872, age 54; taken to Phelps, NY.
Cogan, Miss Ellen, April 4, 1871, age 25 y, 6 w.
Cogan, James, Dec. 30, 1870, age 53.
Cogan, James, Nov. 20, 1874, age 26.
Cogan, Margaret, March 3, 1878, age 20.
Cogger, Mrs. Mary Ann, Sept. 4, 1840, age 41.
Cogswell, Albert Smith, late of Peterborough, NH, son of Henry T., Sept. 13, 1848, age 21.
Cogswell, Eliza, dau. of Henry F. of LeRoy, Jan. 3, 1855, age 23.
Cogswell, George W., April 22, 1854, age 24; d. at LeRoy, NY, bur. at Buffalo.

Cogswell, William Henry, son of Henry F. of Buffalo, March 1858, age 32; d. in Hudson, MI.
Cointot, Xavier, June 23, 1879, age 56 y, 8 m.
Coit, Alfred S., Dec. 4, 1862, age 24.
Coit, George, May 9, 1865, age 75; early resident of Buffalo.
Coit, Hannah T., wife of George, March 11, 1835, age 44.
Coit, Rev. John T., pastor of St. Peter's Church, Rochester, Jan. 23, 1863, age 38; d. in Albion, NY, b. in Buffalo.
Coit, Mary S., wife of George, Feb. 14, 1840, age 34.
Coit, Capt. Oliver, Dec. 16, 1843, age 72; d. at Greswate, CT.
Coke, Mary Ann, formerly of Buffalo, wife of John, March 27, 1874, age 61; d. at Lyons, Wayne County, NY.
Colborn, Sylvester, April 26, 1841, age 78.
Colborn, Emily Louise, only dau. of R. H., Feb. 26, 1860.
Colburn, Jeremiah, Aug. 11, 1820, age 21.
Colburn, John Gray, Boston, MA, May 30, 1856, age 55.
Colburn, Laura P., widow of William M., Oct. 21, 1874, age 52; taken to Schenectady.
Colburn, Louisa H., formerly of Buffalo, wife of George C., late of New York, June 11, 1855. Dau. of Erastus Sparrow. D. at San Francisco.
Colburn, Phebe L., wife of James, Evans Centre, NY, May 11, 1872, age 46.
Colby, Mrs. Elizabeth S., Aug. 17, 1853, age 32.
Colby, Ezekiel, b. 1768, d. 1848, bur. HOlland; Soldier of the Revolution.
Colby, Jonathan, Holland, NY, April 1, 1880, aged 91 y, 6 m, 2 d.
Cole, Aaron, Springville, NY, May 29, 1862, age 73.
Cole, Almira, wife of William W., formerly of Wales, March 17, 1864, age 32; d. at Armawan, Henry Co., IL.
Cole, Daniel, formerly of Williamsville, NY, Jan. 8, 1879, age 64 y, 2 m, 11 d; d. at Alden, NY.
Cole, Mrs. Eliza Jane, Oct. 6, 1875, age 45 y, 7 m, 6 d.
Cole, George, Aug. 20, 1862, age 40; d. at Sisters of Charity Hospital.
Cole, Jeremiah, Buffalo?, Nov. 1878; killed in Detroit, MI.
Cole, John, Revolutionary Soldier, Wales, NY, Aug. 13, 1837, age 75. [Another card: John Cole, b. 1763, d. 1837, bur. Wales Center, Soldier of the Revolution.]
Cole, Mrs. John, Wales, NY, Nov. 20, 1844, age 35.
Cole, John W., East Aurora, Dec. 13, 1880, age 56 y, 4 m, 5 d.
Cole, Joshua P., March 16, 1866, age 49; taken to Lancaster, NY.
Cole, Niles, Wales, NY, April 17, 1846, age 50.
Cole, Phebe, widow of John, Wales, NY, Feb. 12, 1847, age 78.
Cole, Robert W., Oct. 22, 1878, age 59.
Cole, Mrs. Sally Ann, April 23, 1871, age 78.
Cole, Mrs. Sarah C., Springville, NY, Dec. 18, 1852, age 80.
Colegrove, Eliza, wife of Dr. B. H., Sardinia, NY, Sept. 28, 1852, age 45.
Coleman, Abigail, wife of Charles H., Sept. 11, 1847, age 53.
Coleman, Ann, wife of John C., Sept. 8, 1863, age 34.
Coleman, Catherine, wife of Jeremiah, Sept. 24, 1878, age 29.
Coleman, Charles, Aug. 11, 1863, age 52; d. at Chatham Four Corners, Columbia Co., NY.
Coleman, Charles H., Feb. 25, 1880, age 92.
Coleman, Mrs. Emma, July 27, 1873, age 39.
Coleman, Mrs. Jeremiah, Jan. 26, 1873.
Coleman, Lewis L., Nov. 29, 1874, age 56 y, 9 m, 7 d; taken to Dunkirk, NY.
Coleman, Mary Ann, wife of Capt. William, June 29, 1875, age 31 y, 10 m, 20 d.
Coleman, William B., June 5, 1869, age 57.
Coles, Elsie Ann, wife of Henry, dau. of Jeremiah Harrett, April 23, 1870, age 20 y, 1 m, 12 d.
Colgrove, Dr. Bela H., Sardinia, NY, March 19, 1874, age 76 y, 11 m.
Colie, Amanda, wife of Samuel D., July 9, 1878.
Colie, Catharine W., dau. of Samuel D., Feb. 10, 1875, age 19 y, 5 m, 20 d.
Colie, Edwin T., son of Oliver S., July 1874, age 36 y, 7 m, 2 d.
Colie, Elizabeth, wife of Samuel, Aug. 29, 1848, age 66.
Colie, Emily A., wife of Samuel D., Jan. 17, 1870, age 46.

Colie, Samuel, April 1, 1850, age 70; formerly of Springfield, NJ.
Colin, F. Xavier, Aug. 26, 1880, age 78.
Colin, Josephine, native of France, Feb. 4, 1879, age 73.
Collamer, Job, Asst. Supt. N.Y. Central R.R., Nov. 7, 1861.
Collard, Eunice, wife of Nathan, Hamburgh, NY, Dec. 1812, age 19.
Colleman, Hulda, Co. Almshouse, Aug. 9, 1878, age 52.
Collette, Andrew, Co. Almshouse, March 19, 1877, age 57.
Collette, L., formerly of Buffalo, wife of Lambert, Dec. 22, 1851.
Collette, L. N., Jan. 21, 1865, age 74.
Collette, Leon, Jan. 16, 1870, age 45 y, 5 m, 9 d.
Colley, Elvira M., wife of D. D., Sept. 28, 1847, age 19; taken to Cowlesville, Wyoming Co., NY.
Collignon, Arminia, wife of John C., April 26, 1880, age 49.
Colligon, Lewis, Jan. 28, 1854, age 33.
Colling, Charles H., July 27, 1858, age 23; d. in Utica, NY.
Collini, Mary Elizabeth, March 24, 1847, age 24. Native of Stockholm, Sweden.
Collins, Bridget, widow, Sept. 17, 1876, age 60.
Collins, Dennis, March 2, 1877, age 68.
Collins, Mrs. Ellen, Dec. 10, 1874, age 23.
Collins, Mrs. Ellen, March 30, 1878, age 89; railroad accident.
Collins, Ellen, wife of Dennis, formerly of Buffalo, Jan. 27, 1880; d. in Chicago.
Collins, Frances H., widow of Thomas, May 25, 1874, age 74; taken to Sardinia, NY.
Collins, Georgia, formerly of Buffalo, wife of Frank, Oct. 16, 1877, age 27 y, 3 m; d. at Moravia, NY.
Collins, Jane, Co. Almshouse, April 19, 1876, age 28.
Collins, Jennie, wife of John, Sept. 10, 1878, age 26.
Collins, Joihannah, wife of Daniel, Sept. 11, 1879, age 46.
Collins, John, Black Rock, Dec. 5, 1846, age 42.
Collins, Capt. John, March 31, 1874, age 32.
Collins, John, April 5, 1877, age 42.
Collins, John H., Feb. 22, 1876, age 28.
Collins, John J., July 26, 1878, age 58.
Collins, Kate, dau. of Jeremiah, of Desertserges, Cork Co., Ireland, Sept. 5, 1863.
Collins, Kate, Sept. 6, 1863, age 30.
Collins, Lizzie, Aug. 20, 1866.
Collins, Mary Ann, wife of John J., Sept. 27, 1872, age 45.
Collins, Mary Anne, wife of Thomas, July 28, 1877.
Collins, Maurice, Oct. 17, 1876, age 65.
Collins, Michael, son of Patrick, Jan. 31, 1873, age 41.
Collins, Michael, Feb. 11, 1880, age 35.
Collins, Thomas, April 21, 1873, age 80 y, 7 m, 25 d; taken to Sardinia, NY.
Collopy, Edward or William, generally known as "William Moore," Aug. 20, 1874, age c. 30.
Colquehoun, John, Feb. 10, 1874, age 79.
Colquhoun, Christina, widow of John, Dec. 3, 1877, age 79.
Colson, Charles W., Feb. 15, 1864, age 36; d. in Chicago, IL.
Colson, Julia H., wife of Frederick K., dau. of Chauncey Bartholomew, July 31, 1864, age 25.
Colson, Sarah A., wife of Augustus; Dec. 18, 1862, age 57; d. in Brooklyn, Long Island.
Colson, Mrs. Wilhelmina, Aug. 4, 1835, age 60.
Colston, Margaret, wife of James, Dec. 25, 1852, age 35.
Colt, Peter H., merchant, Dec. 1, 1812, age 42.
Colton, Catharine W., wife of R. P., Oct. 12, 1863; taken to Brockville, Canada West.
Colton, Elizabeth, July 31, 1832, age 65; wife of Joseph.
Colton, George, April 10, 1869.
Colton, Henry, Oct. 27, 1848, age 40.
Colton, Manly, March 14, 1852, age 56.
Colton, Mary A., wife of Manly, May 11, 1847, age 45.
Colton, Royal, formerly of Buffalo, merchant, brother of Manly and Henry of Buffalo. D. in St. Louis, Nov. 7, 1850, age 49.
Colvin, Alexander, native of Scotland, Aug. 11, 1852, age 50.

Colvin, Amos, Hamburgh, NY, Jan. 10, 1833, age 78.
Colvin, B. Barton, formerly of Buffalo, Jan. 27, 1873, age 47; d. at Kirkwood, MO.
Colvin, Hannah, East Hamburgh, NY, widow of Major Luther, March 17, 1852, age 71.
Colvin, Jacob, Hamburg, April 2, 1842, age 60.
Colvin, Sarah, widow of Amos, East Hamburgh, May 23, 1875, age 88.
Colvin, Susan S., widow of Zina of Lewistown, Aug. 30, 1863.
Colyer, Lavinia P., wife of Dr. Charles W., Sept. 1, 1867, age 37.
Comaford, Patrick, June 9, 1873, age 63.
Comesford, Bridget Fahay, wife of H. G., Sept. 3, 1858, age 25 y, 3 m.
Commerford, Mrs. Mary, Jan. 6, 1873, age 42.
Compton, Ann, Aug. 17, 1873, age 68.
Compton, George B., son of late Lewis, Nov. 11, 1880, age 33; d. at Chicago.
Compton, Harmon B., Sept. 2, 1848, age 23.
Compton, Letitia, wife of Lewis, Feb. 24, 1837, age 20.
Compton, Lewis, Aug. 18, 1868, age 56.
Comstock, Dr. Albert, formerly of Buffalo, May 15, 1876, age 74; d. at Mt. Kisco, Westchester Co., NY.
Comstock, Col. Andrew, April 9, 1839, age 53.
Comstock, Anna E., wife of Marcus L., Jan. 23, 1860, age 31.
Comstock, Caroline, widow of George, March 16, 1870, age 53 y, 8 m.
Comstock, Catharine Jane, wife of Martin, Feb. 18, 1859, age 37.
Comstock, Edward M., July 9, 1868, age 45.
Comstock, George, Oct. 27, 1860, age 49.
Comstock, Harriet A., wife of Martin, Nov. 21, 1865, age 34 y, 6 m.
Comyn, Patrick, Jan. 4, 1877, age 34.
Conant, Jane Uretta Bliss, wife of Allen E., March 14, 1875, age 50 y, 8 m.
Conant, Tirzah Ann, wife of R. M., Aug. 8, 1848, age 25.
Concklin, Naomie, wife of Mathew, Clarence, NY, Sept. 12, 1873, age 65.
Congdon, Abigail D., wife of Capt. John, April 27, 1853, age 33.
Congdon, Dr. Benjamin C., Aug. 22, 1828, age 37.
Congdon, Dr. Israel, Collins, June 21, 1846, age 40.
Congdon, William, Sept. 2, 1826, age 35.
Conger, Hon. Anson G., Collins Center, NY, Feb. 13, 1880, age 67.
Conger, Betsey, North Collins, wife of Noel, May 28, 1860, age 60 y, 1 m, 5 d.
Conger, Stephen, North Collins, NY, Jan. 25, 1877, age 63.
Conifeild (or Carifield), Mary, Nov. 28, 1876, age 23.
Conk, Mrs. Francis, Feb. 16, 1844, age 42.
Conkey, D. S., Sept. 1827. D. on the line of the Welland Canal, Tonawanda.
Conkey, Mary, wife of Col. David S., Clarence, NY, May 31, 1823, age 25.
Conklin, Burnett, Nov. 28, 1880, age 76 y, 9 m; d. at Griffins Mills, formerly of Buffalo.
Conklin, Hart S., Jan. 11, 1850, age 21 y, 9 m; d. at Sacramento, CA.
Conklin, Lewis M., Aurora, NY, Oct. 28, 1873, age 67.
Conklin, Patrick, July 20, 1878, age 35.
Conkling, Aurelian, May 27, 1861, age 42 y, 1 m.
Conkling, Frederick A., son of Aurelian, Oct. 12, 1866, age 25 y, 8 m; d. in New York.
Conley, Elizabeth, wife of Terence, Sept. 4, 1878, age 42.
Conly, Vilera, wife of William R., Clarence, NY, March 24, 1835, age 27.
Connat, Joseph, July 13, 1873, age 84.
Connell, John, July, 1872.
Connell, Richard, Dec. 24, 1880, age 77.
Connelley, Mrs. Mary, Jan. 25, 1865.
Connelly, Edward, son of Edward, May 3, 1875, age 17. Both suffocated by gas.
Connelly, Edward, May 3, 1875, age 50; suffocated by gas.
Connelly, John, Oct. 19, 1872; drowned.
Connelly, John, Oct. 27, 1877, age 55; railroad accident.
Connely, D., 1st Serg., Co. E, 154 Reg. N.Y. Vol., age 29. Newspaper notice, Feb. 4, 1864.
Conner, Ellen Cooley, wife of Michael, Akron, March 30, 1874, age 24 y, 6 m; d. at Looneyville.
Conner, John, Clarence, Oct. 29, 1815, age 22; formerly of Williamstown, VT.
Conners, Mrs. Mary, July 29, 1863, age 32.

Conners, Mary, Co. Almshouse, July 13, 1876, age 30.
Conners, Mrs. Michael, Buffalo Plains, March 6, 1879.
Conners, Patrick, Co. Almshouse, Aug. 11, 1879, age 73.
Conners, Richard, Oct. 12, 1878, age 27.
Connolly, Mrs. Anna J., Oct. 18, 1878, age 52 y, 2 m.
Connoly, Dorah Fitzgerald, wife of Thomas, formerly of Buffalo, March 1878; d. at St. Paul MN.
Connor, Mrs. Isabella, eldest dau. of the late John Finney, formerly of Buffalo, Dec. 1, 1871, age 43 y, 2 m, 13 d; d. in Chicago.
Connors, John, May 28, 1873, age 53.
Conroy, Bernard, Angola, March 9, 1877, railroad accident.
Conry, Catherine, May 11, 1873, age 52.
Constant, Rev. John, [of] Co. Cork Ireland, Sept. 2, 1868, age 70; d. in Hospital of the Sisters of Charity.
Constantine, Louis A., Nov. 12, 1874, age 86.
Conway, John, March 30, 1872, age 23.
Conway, Mrs. Rosa, Oct. 11, 1878, age 84 y, 24 d.
Conway, Thomas, March 23, 1874, age 46; accident.
Conway, Thomas, Nov. 20, 1880, age 49.
Cook, Mrs. Almira, Dec. 14, 1879, age 40.
Cook, Anna, wife of Capt. Raphael, Williamsville, NY, Jan. 17, 1815, age 54.
Cook Benjamin H., Feb. 27, 1876, age 56; taken to Canastota.
Cook, Betsy, wife of Benjamin, Jr., Jan. 14, 1837, age 40.
Cook, Caroline Whitney, wife of Josiah, March 23, 1873; taken to Palmyra.
Cook, Catharine, mother of Hon. Eli and Josiah, April 15, 1860, age 74.
Cook, Hon. Eli, Feb. 25, 1865.
Cook, Elisha, formerly of Buffalo, Dec. 31, 1871, age 49; d. in San Francisco, CA.
Cook, Elizbaeth, wife of James, March 21, 1855, age 29.
Cook, Elizabeth, wife of William, formerly of Buffalo, July 9, 1869, age 58; d. at Andrian, MI.
Cook, Emma, July 2, 1878, age 27.
Cook, George, Alden, March 9, 1876, age 24; accident, killed by the falling of a tree at Marilla.
Cook, Harriet, wife of Charles L., Aug. 20, 1844, age 25.
Cook, Henry, Aug. 14, 1871.
Cook, Hiram H., eldest son of Col. E. W., Springville, NY, Sept. 18, 1858, age 22.
Cook, Israel, father of Capts. David and Seyman, Eden, Sept. 5, 1857, age 79; native of Rutland, VT
Cook, Capt. James, formerly of ME, Jan. 22, 1862, age 47 y, 9 m.
Cook, John, April 10, 1866, age 44.
Cook, John, Nov. 8, 1868, age 40.
Cook, John, July 22, 1874, age 22; drowned.
Cook, John L., Oct. 4, 1869, age 73.
Cook, Joseph Edward, Nov. 23, 1880, age 38 y, 1 m, 29 d.
Cook, Kate, wife of Joseph, Jan. 15, 1871, age 35; taken to Lockport, NY.
Cook, L. D., Nov. 27, 1868, age 42; d. at Pavilion, Genesee Co.
Cook, Lucinda Manville Mabie, wife of William H., March 31, 1874, age 62.
Cook, Lyman, formerly of Buffalo, Dec. 23, 1870, age 61 y, 3 m; d. in San Francisco.
Cook, Mary, widow of Jonathan, June 14, 1871, age 80; taken to Sardinia, NY.
Cook, Mary A., wife of Eli, Sept. 23, 1849, age 33; d. in Syracuse, bur. in Buffalo.
Cook, Mary E. Wilcox, wife of John Cook, Aug. 1, 1880, age 33; d. at Denver, CO, formerly of Buffalo.
Cook, Patrick, Feb. 15, 1878, age 55.
Cook, Peter, March 9, 1872, age 23.
Cook, Peter, Jan. 29, 1874, age 54.
Cook, Capt. Raphael, Rev. soldier, Innkeeper, April 15, 1821, age 65.
Cook, Robert, Dec. 27, 1812, age 29.
Cook, Thomas, Sept. 5, 1870, age 60.
Cook, Thomas, June 14, 1876, age 25.
Cook, Walter D. N., formerly of Buffalo, Feb. 13, 1833, age 33; d. in New York.

Cook, William, July 7, 1879, age 39 y, 10 m.
Cook, William P., Aug. 15, 1865, age 28.
Cooke, Isaac, b. 1738, d. 1810, bur. Lewiston; Soldier of the Revolution. (Niagara Co.)
Cooke, John, formerly of Buffalo, March 6, 1875, age 74; d. in Lyons, Wayne Co., NY.
Cooke, Lemuel, b. 1762, d. 1839, bur. Lewiston (Niagara Co.); soldier of the Revolution.
Cooley, C. H., Aug. 5, 1863, age 28; d. in Chicago, bur. in Buffalo.
Cooley or Corley, Joseph, Dec. 1867, funeral 31st.
Cooley, Sally, Jan. 3, 1868, age 53.
Cooney, James, brakeman, Sept. 13, 1880. Not res. of Erie Co., belonged at Irvington, PA; accident.
Cooney, Peter C., Sept. 8, 1874, age 26; d. in Chicago, bur. in Buffalo.
Coons, D. M., June 3, 1870, age 44.
Coons, Mary Barbara, wife of George, Feb. 15, 1874, age 51.
Cooper, Adalade Louise, wife of Lt. P. H. of U.S. Navy, Juy 11, 1868, age 21.
Cooper, Amelia B., wife of Young, June 14, 1876, age 33.
Cooper, Charles, Englishman, musician, Feb. 20, 1843, age 42.
Cooper, Charles M., Aug. 11, 1847, age 32.
Cooper, David, July 5, 1880, age 69 y, 6 m.
Cooper, Mrs. Eliza, March 26, 1880; d. at Elk Rapids, MI, formerly of Buffalo.
Cooper, Hannah E., widow of Joseph, March 25, 1865, age 87 y, 5 m, 12 d.
Cooper, John, Tonawanda, March 10, 1863, age 43; d. in Jersey City, bur. Tonawanda.
Cooper, Joseph, b. 1757, d. 1844, bur. Holland; Soldier of the Revolution.
Cooper, Joseph, April 19, 1852, age 69.
Cooper, Mrs. Louisa Augusta, formerly of Buffalo, dau. of Pierre A. Barker, Oct. 11, 1843, age 24; d. at Holly Springs, MS.
Cooper, Margaret, Co. Almshouse, March 14, 1876, age 37.
Cooper, Mary M., dau. of William, Boston, NY., Jan. 24, 1848, age 20 y, 4 m.
Cooper, Seth, formerly of Buffalo, March 11, 1877, age 67.
Cooper, Watts, of Horsham, Sussex, England, March 16, 1863, age 61.
Cooper, William, Jan. 31, 1855, age 67.
Cooper, William, formerly of Settle, Yorkshire, England, June 25, 1876, age 72.
Cootes, Anna, Sept. 23, 1880, age 20.
Coots, Caroline, wife of William A., March 8, 1839, age 23
Coots, Carrie M., eldest dau. of Wm. A., April 4, 1860, age 22; d. in Louisville, KY, bur. in Buffalo.
Coots, William A., formerly of Buffalo, March 11, 1875, age 65; d. at St. Joseph, MI
Copeland, Mrs. Caroline, formerly of Buffalo, Feb. 11, 1863, age 73; d. in Brooklyn, NY.
Copeland, Jenny A., April 29, 1872, age 20.
Coppock, Catharine, East Hamburgh, NY, Nov. 14, 1874, age 46; bur. in Buffalo.
Coppock, Mary L., wife of W. R., Black Rock, NY, June 11, 1851.
Coppock, William R., Sept. 17, 1863, age 58.
Corbett, Elijah, father of William G., Oct. 23, 1857, age 91.
Corbett, Emeline, wife of William G., Nov. 2, 1843, age 24.
Corbett, George (Thomas), laborer, Aug. 23, 1871.
Corbett, Mary, wife of Elijah, April 4, 1847, age 76 y, 9 m.
Corbin, Mrs. Betty, widow of John, formerly of Erie Co. near Hamburgh, NY, Jan. 10, 1880, age nearly 100.
Corbin, David, b. 1757, d. 1846, bur. N. Collins; Soldier of the Revolution.
Corbin, Edith Russell, wife of Peter, Dec. 6, 1867, age 67.
Corbin, Fayette H., 2nd son of W. H., Aurora, NY, Nov. 22, 1862, age 30.
Corbin, Mary E., dau. of W. H., Aurora, NY, June 26, 1863, age 25.
Corbin, Peter, June 6, 1874, age 80 y, 5 m.
Corbin, Thomas R., youngest son of Peter, Oct. 1872; d. at Quincey, IL.
Corbin, William H., Willink, Oct. 21, 1868, age 69.
Corcoran, Bridget, wife of Martin, April 4, 1870, age 57.
Corcoran, Cornelius, Aug. 27, 1878.
Corcoran, John, formerly of Buffalo, Nov. 16, 1875; d. at Minneapolis, MN, bur. in Buffalo.
Corcoran, Mrs. P. F., Sept. 21, 1877, age 31.
Corcoran, Thomas, Nov. 23, 1874.
Cordukes, William, native of Yorkshire, England, April 2, 1843, age 29.

Corey, Capt. Philip, d. 1834; d. in town of Hartland, Niagara Co.; soldier of the Revolution (Niagara *Courier*, March 5, 1834.)
Corely, Caroline M., Sept. 26, 1873, age 62; taken to Ithica.
Corey, Augustus F., formerly of Buffalo, Jan. 27, 1878, age 74; d. at Elmira, NY.
Corley, John, Feb. 8, 1869, age 86; taken to Ithaca, NY.
Corlis, Samuel, Holland, NY, April 27, 1863, age 79.
Cormick, Annie Quinn, formerly of Buffalo, dau. of the late Joseph, Aug. 2, 1876; d. at Ashtabula, OH, bur. in Buffalo.
Cornell, Albert, Springville, NY, Aug. 9, 1866, age 25.
Correll, Henry V., Dec. 25, 1873, age 22,; railroad accident, taken to Lewiston, NY.
Cornell, Jane, wife of George E., Oct. 4, 1867, age 41; taken to Auburn, NY.
Cornell, Paul D., Dec. 14, 1868, age 58; taken to Auburn.
Cornell, Samuel W., July 23, 1865, age 76.
Cornell, Sarah Douglas, wife of S. G., July 26, 1877.
Corning, Jasper, formerly of Buffalo, Nov. 16, 1869, age 77; d. in city of New York.
Corning, John, formerly of Buffalo, Nov. 17, 1878; d. at San Fernandino, CA.
Corning, Margaret, widow of Jasper, formerly of Buffalo, Jan. 1, 1874, age 81.
Cornish, Mrs. Jane, Feb. 8, 1867, age 78.
Cornish, Orlando J. M., Jan. 30, 1853, age 53.
Corns, Charles, May 29, 1867, age 38.
Corns, Mrs. Sarah A. (Pearson), Feb. 21, 1867, age 35.
Cornue, Josephine, Nov. 22, 1880, age 72; sudden death.
Cornwall, Sally, wife of W. W., Concord, March 22, 1846, age 48.
Cornwall, William, formerly of Buffalo, March 5, 1840; d. in Detroit.
Cornwell, Edward L., son of the late Francis E., May 25, 1877, age 29; d. at Utica, taken to Albany.
Cornwell, Francis E., lawyer, Nov. 2, 1869, age 47.
Cornwell, Levinus, Sardinia, Nov. 3, 1878, age 87.
Cornwell, Mary A. Weeden, wife of W. C., Hamburgh, NY, Sept. 15, 1874, age 35.
Corp, Charles R., Jan. 14, 1862, age 44 y, 3 m.
Corridon, Thomas, May 1, 1874, age 29; taken to Galt, Ontario.
Corrigan, Maj. Alfred McQuin, 9th N.Y. Cav., May 28, 1864, age 24 y, 4 m, 17 d; d. at Point Lookout Hospital of wounds received in front of Richmond.
Corrigan, Frederick M., Sept. 29, 1862, age 20. Lost at sea, near Australia.
Corriston, Edward, Nov. 8, 1879, age 82 y, 6 m.
Corriston, William, Nov. 6, 1876, age 42.
Corwin, Sergt. James H., Nov. 1863. D. in the hospital in Washington, bur. Nov. 11 in Buffalo.
Corwin, Jesse K., Black Rock, NY, of Scott's 900 Cavalry, June 9, 1863. D. in hospital Leonardstown, MD, bur. in Buffalo.
Corwin, Miles, formerly of Aurora, NY, July 1, 1875, age 58; d. in Summit Two., Crawford Co., PA.
Corwin, Rockwell B., March 4, 1858, age 25 y, 4 m.
Corwin, Simeon Bryant, Nov. 21, 1869, age 60 y, 2 m.
Corwin, Sophia, Oct. 22, 1875, age 67.
Cosgrove, Anna McDermot, wife of William, Oct. 7, 1871, age 41.
Cosgrove, Torrance, Nov. 17, 1864, age 92.
Cosgrove, William, July 19, 1880, age 52.
Costello, Jane, wife of Thomas of the Emerald Hotel, July 11, 1849, age 35.
Costello, John B., July 19, 1871, age 50.
Costello, Peter, July 2, 1874, age 26; drowned.
Cotrell, John, Springville, June 23, 1866, age 65.
Cott, Charlotte, wife of George, Feb. 21, 1876, age 21 y, 6 m, 2 d.
Cotter, C. B., formerly of East Aurora, July 1873, age 59; d. at Saginaw, MI.
Cotter, John, late of San Francisco, CA, Jan. 15, 1856, age 43; d. in Buffalo.
Cotti, Jacob, grandfather of Alexander Martin, Oct. 29, 1863, age 79.
Cotti, Regina Federspiel, widow of Jacob, Sept. 5, 1878, age 86.
Cottier, Lt. Elisha B. (or P.), 116 Reg. N.Y. Vol., Aug. 21, 1863, age 31 y, 9 m, 2 d; d. at Baton Rouge, LA, bur. in Buffalo, Feb. 14, 1864.

Cottier, Franklin H., youngest son of Hugh, Jan. 25, 1869, age 20 y, 6 m, 13 d.
Cottier, Hugh, Sept. 17, 1878, age 58.
Cotton, Abigail, April 23, 1845, age 79.
Cotton, Camantha, wife of Daniel H., Oct. 1, 1861, age 57 y, 7 m. Dau. of Alvan Dodge, of Buffalo; d. at Richland, Jackson Co., IA.
Cotton, Miss Eliza Grosvenor, Oct. 4, 1870, age 70; eldest and adopted sister of Rev. Dr. Grosvenor Heacock.
Cotton, George W., March 27, 1878, age 82.
Cotton, Keziah, wife of Capt. Rowland, June 13, 1820, age 57.
Cotton, Capt. L. H., formerly of Buffalo, Jan. 4, 1878, age 74; d. at Harrisburg, AR.
Cotton, Martin S., May 22, 1870, age 45.
Cotton, Mrs. Sarah, April 28, 1844, age 20.
Cotton, Sophia Brooks, wife of Elisha G., Elma, NY, March 31, 1865, age 78 y, 2 d.
Cotton, Ward, Dec. 20, 1812, age 50. [Another card: Cotton, Ward, b. 1762, d. Dec. 20, 1812, age 50; bur. Buffalo; Soldier of the Revolution.]
Coughlin, Mrs. Ann, Nov. 30, 1874, age 50.
Coughlin, Catharine J. Reynolds, wife of Michael, Jan. 31, 1877, age 24.
Coughlin, Cornelius, April 9, 1880, age 24.
Courson, Isaac D., March 25, 1877, age 32 y, 6 m; taken to Niagara Falls.
Courtney, Mrs. Emma, Oct. 14, 1873, age 32.
Courter, Hamilton, late of Buffalo, Oct. 30, 1873, age 44; d. at Cobleskill, Schoharie Co., NY.
Courtney, Diana M., July 18, 1880, age 39.
Courtney, William, formerly of Toronto, Canada, May 7, 1866, age 51 y, 8 m.
Cousins, Hattie C., wife of William of Warren, PA, Aug. 5, 1866, age 35.
Covell, Minnie, wife of Ezra M., Feb. 26, 1876, age 24.
Coveney, Jeremiah, April 11, 1873, age 64.
Coveny, Sarah, wife of Robert, June 10, 1851, age 31.
Covert, George, formerly of Buffalo, Nov. 17, 1875, age 78.
Covert, Mrs. George, formerly of Buffalo, Nov. 11, 1875, age 74; d. at Ithaca, NY.
Covey, Hon. Lorenzo D., Akron, Feb. 16, 1877.
Coville, Dorcas, widow of Peter, Oct. 23, 1875, age 78.
Coville, Capt. Stephen, Huntsburgh, OH, Oct. 1, 1866, age 46; formerly of Buffalo.
Covney, Robert, Nov. 27, 1864, age 50.
Cowan, Anna E., wife of Charles H., March 14, 1858, age 25.
Cowan, Hugh, Nov. 11, 1865, age 26 y, 5 m.
Cowan, James, April 8, 1874, age 23.
Cowan, Samuel Adams, formerly of Buffalo, son of Robert of Jamestown, NY, printer, March 2, 1861, age 26; d. in Warren, PA.
Cowans, Peter, March, 1880.
Cowery, Susan, March 26, 1879, age 28.
Cowgill, Joseph C., March 19, 1852, age 34; d. in Detroit.
Cowing, Abigail, widow of John, March 17, 1836, age 70.
Cowing, Calvin, father of H. O. and E. H. of Buffalo, Feb. 3, 1859, age 73.
Cowing, Fordyce, June 16, 1869, age 69.
Cowing, Frank Wilton, youngest son of H.O., Sept. 19, 1876, age 23.
Cowles, Absalom or Abraham, Feb. 15, 1838, age 38.
Cowles, Harriet, wife of E. W., Sept. 5, 1872, age 27 y, 6 m, 12 d; d. in Cleveland, OH, bur. in Buffalo.
Cowles, John, April 5, 1872, age 69.
Cowles, Louisa F. Birdsey, wife of Seth G., Feb. 29, 1872, age 28.
Cowles, Samuel H., July 4, 1865, age 34.
Cowles, Sarah A., formerly of Buffalo, widow of Samuel H., Feb. 5, 1879, age 40; d. in Chicago, dau. of the late Henry A. White.
Cox, Albert W., Oct. 31, 1880, age 56.
Cox, Catherine, Feb. 11, 1880, age 72.
Cox, John F., May 28, 1868, age 58.
Cox, Martin, April 22, 1877; sudden death. (See Knox, Warren L.)
Coyle, Sarah, native of Ireland, Sept. 30, 1869, age 40.
Coyne, James, May 5, 1880, age 66.

Coyne, R. Emmet, March 9, 1879, age 27.
Cozzens, Corp. John S., Nov. 1864.
Cozzens, Levi, father of Mrs. S. Kingsley, Feb. 12, 1873, age 86 y, 5 d; taken to Utica.
Crabner, Frederick, April 18, 1878.
Craft, Mrs. Almira, July 30, 1874, age 38.
Crafts, Jane E., widow of Willard, April 3, 1874, age 70; taken to Utica.
Crahe, Orrin, Nov. 1827, age 35.
Craig, Edward W., April 13, 1880, age 46.
Craig, Francis S., April 13, 1864, age 51; formerly of Hamburgh.
Craig, James D., April 5, 1853; d. in New York City.
Craig, James F., son of William H., Nov. 25, 1874, age 21 y, 5 m, 13 d.
Craig, Laura L., widow of Francis S., June 2, 1867.
Craig, Mary, mother of Francis S., Big Tree Corners, Hamburgh, NY, Dec. 16, 1865, age 87.
Cramer, Adam, Dec. 14, 1877, age 82; railroad accident, Grimesville Station.
Cramer, Capt. Charles D., Tonawanda, Feb. 9, 1878, age 40.
Cramer, Jacob, youngest son of Peter, Oct. 27, 1864, age 26. D. at City Point, VA from battle wounds; bur. in Buffalo.
Cramp, William, Pine Hill, July 10, 1876; sun stroke.
Crandall, Lodema, Dec. 17, 1880, age 53.
Crandall, Luke, Revolutionary Patriot, Collins, Aug. 1832. [Another card: Crandall, Luke, b. 1754, d. Aug. 1, 1832, bur. Collins, NY; Soldier of the Revolution.]
Crandall, Mrs. P. M., Canandaigua, dau. of Nathan Calhoun of Pittsford, Sept. 30, 1848.
Crane, Miss Amanda, dau. of Mrs. Ruth Crane, April 27, 1851.
Crane, Amy A., wife of Willie J., April 18, 1879, age 35.
Crane, George B., joiner, June 5, 1859, age 48.
Crane, Hannah, wife of Thomas, Crittenden, NY, Nov. 11, 1875, age 60.
Crane, James, April 14, 1869, age 61.
Crane, John, East Aurora, NY, Jan. 15, 1879.
Crane, Sarah, widow of George B., Feb. 1, 1873, age 65.
Crane, Thomas, Aug. 16, 1838, age 52.
Crane, Thomas, formerly of East Aurora, NY, Nov. 7, 1878, age 34; d. in Lawrence, KS.
Crary, Betsey, wife of L. P., Williamsville, NY, Sept. 24, 1821, age 31.
Crary, Mrs. Betsey, Sept. 19, 1857, age 56; taken to Cattaraugus Co.
Crary, Jane A., wife of Oscar F., dau. of Benjamin Bidwell, July 24, 1862, age 41.
Crary, Gen. Leonard P., Black Rock, NY, March 6, 1836, age 43.
Crary, Leonard, Menasha, WI, formerly of Buffalo, Sept. 13, 1857, age 40.
Crary, Maria E., dau. of Dr. Spencer Crary of Columbus, IN, April 17, 1860, age 20.
Crate, Susan, wife of James, April 6, 1878.
Crawford, Mr., Amherst, Nov. 29, 1823; killed by the falling of a tree, age 30.
Crawford, Charles, Oct. 10, 1872, age 43.
Crawford, Mr. Emory O., Feb. 27, 1877, age 40.
Crawford, Mrs. Elizabeth, July 29, 1879, age 70.
Crawford, H. H., Feb. 26, 1863, age 37.
Crawford, Henry, Aurora, March 28, 1835, age 40; Justice of the Peace in Buffalo.
Crawford, Letitia, widow of Charles, Oct. 1, 1877, age 47.
Crawford, Miss Martha, Holland, April 27, 1879, age 75 (?); sudden.
Crawford, Mrs. Mary, Oct. 3, 1864, age 49.
Crawford, Samuel L., Prince Edward Islands, Nov. 12, 1862. Late carpenter's mate of Steam Frigate *Mississippi*.
Crawford, William, almshouse, May 24, 1880, age 93.
Creciat, Simon, Sept. 17, 1880, age 61.
Crego, Elizabeth C., wife of Francis, Feb. 22, 1855, age 48.
Crego, Lois, sister of Mrs. John H. Hebard, Oct. 9, 1864, age 27 y, 6 m.
Crego, William D., formerly of Buffalo, Aug. 11, 1866, age 36; d. in Chicago.
Creighton, William, May 17, 1870, age 69.
Cremar, Joseph, late mate of Steamer *Lexington*, Feb. 1, 1843, age 22.
Cremer, Mary Ann, wife of James, Black Rock, NY, Oct. 16, 1849.
Cremer, Thomas J., Jan. 7, 1870, age 23; d. in Cleveland, OH, bur. in Buffalo.
Crenkahn, August, insane, from Co. Almshouse, found dead near Lancaster, NY, Jan. 9, 1880, age 44.

Criner, Joseph, laborer, July 19, 1878; sunstroke.
Criqui, Elizabeth, widow of Anthony, April 10, 1877, age 70.
Crocker, Ellen, wife of William, dau. of Charles H. Waite, Aug. 16, 1865, age 20.
Crocker, Ellen, wife of John, Dec. 25, 1880, age 50.
Crocker, Emma, wife of James, Sept. 11, 1849, age 56.
Crocker, George L., Aug. 23, 1860, age 62.
Crocker, James, Feb. 4, 1861, age 70.
Crocker, Leonard, Jan. 2, 1870, age 66.
Crocker, Nathaniel, Aug 15, 1855, age 98.
Crocker, Saray Aylworth, wife of William, Nov. 14, 1868, age 39; taken to Wales, NY.
Crocker, Mrs. William, only dau. of Aaron Rumsey, Feb. 14, 1861, age 36.
Croley, Catherine, Sept. 7, 1875, age 45.
Crolius, Huldah, widow of John, formerly of New York City, May 2, 1858, age 75.
Cromwell, Luther, b. 1762, d. 1839, bur. Collins; Soldier of the Revolution.
Cronin, Mrs. Ann, wife of Patrick, May 12, 1879, age 34.
Cronin, Anna, wife of James, March 11, 1872, age 32.
Cronin, Ellen, Co. Almshouse, April 8, 1877, age 51.
Cronin, Jeremiah, Aug. 24, 1879, age 79.
Cronin (Kronin), Mrs. Kate, Nov. 26, 1880, age 65; sudden death.
Cronin, Margaret, May 23, 1878, age 59.
Cronyn, Anna L., Aug. 30, 1877, age 21.
Cronyn, Catharine, Nov. 26, 1880, age 58.
Cronyn, Jeremiah, June 7, 1875, age 29.
Cronyn, Mrs. Mary, Dec. 13, 1862, age 81.
Crook, Mr., Revolutionary Patriot, Aurora, NY, Dec. 29, 1838.
Crook, Charles, b. 1754, d. 1834, bur. Holland; Soldier of the Revolution.
Crook, Dolly, wife of Benjamin, Holland, NY, June 22, 1841, age 46.
Croos, Thomas, b. 1751, d. 1838, bur. E. Aurora; Soldier of the Revolution.
Crooker, Abigail, widow of William, Dec. 13, 1844, age 64.
Crooker, Chiloe Ann, wife of George, Aug. 18, 1864, age 49.
Crooker, Jane, wife of Capt. Erastus, Oct. 29, 1860, age 45.
Crooker, Mrs. Louisa K., Oct. 31, 1875, age 54.
Crooker, William, June 3, 1855, age 54.
Crooks, Alice, Co. Almshouse, Feb. 9, 1878, age 30.
Crooks, James Ramsay, sailor, Oct. 4, 1863, age 53.
Crosby, E. W., Sr., Jan. 20, 1877, age 60.
Crosby, Jane L., wife of Chauncey, Feb. 24, 1876, age 45 y, 7 m, 5 d.
Crosby, Laura B., wife of O. T., Alden, Dec. 16, 1866, age 67.
Crosby, Mrs. Letitia, Dec. 18, 1848.
Crosby, Sarah E., July 21, 1874, age 32; d. at Birmingham, MI, taken to Cuba, NY.
Crosier, John A., Aug. 4, 1852, age 20 y, 4 m.
Crosier, John M., March 26, 1866, age 65.
Crosier, Minerva, wife of John M., July 21, 1850, age 45 y, 4 m.
Crosier, William Henry, Dec. 27, 1851, age 23 y, 3 m; d. at Jacksonville, FL.
Crosman, John, Jan. 13, 1874, age 53.
Crosman, Kittie E., wife of Irwin H., Nov. 15, 1874, age 29; taken to Batavia.
Cross, Alphonso, Feb. 17, 1873, age 63.
Cross, Mrs. Elizabeth, sister of Mrs. B. L. Derrick, Oct. 1, 1867, age 59.
Cross, Dr. Erastus, April 17, 1849, age 80. Formerly of Darien, Genesee Co. and bur. there.
Cross, Hannah, June 7, 1872, age 89.
Cross, Mrs. J. R., Aug. 19, 1866, age 30.
Cross, Jane, wife of Rev. Joseph, D.D., formerly Rector of St. John's Church of Buffalo, Sept. 29, 1870; d. at Nolin, Ky.
Cross, Mary Ann, wife of Aviral, Feb. 23, 1849, age 24.
Cross, Mary M., wife of William and dau. of R. Irish, formerly of Colden, Oct. 22, 1877; d. at Pine Island, MN.
Cross, Sophia, wife of E. T., dau. of Jabez Otis, Westfield, MA, Aug. 7, 1850, age 42; taken to Darien.
Cross, Sylvester, Nov. 30, 1878, age 25; railroad accident.
Cross, Urania, wife of Daniel, June 5, 1850, age 53.

Crossland, John F., Aug. 7, 1875, age c. 45; accidental death.
Crossley, Catherine, Nov. 12, 1877, age 50; railroad accident.
Crossley, James, Feb. 8, 1870, age 32 y, 2 m.
Crossley, John T., Aug. 29, 1863, age 51 y, 11 m.
Crossley, Joseph J., Jan. 13, 1873, age 25 y, 5 m.
Croswell, Addison M., only son of Jacob, Black Rock, NY, Aug. 15, 1844, age 21.
Croswell, Jacob, Feb. 28, 1857, age 58.
Crow, Almond, Hamburgh, NY, Jan. 12, 1849, age 54.
Crow, Miss Florilla, Nov. 1813, age 18.
Crow, Jedidah, sister of Olive, Hamburgh, Feb. 22, 1852, age 26.
Crow, William, Hamburgh, NY, son of Almond, Jan. 19, 1849, age 21.
Crowder, Elizabeth, Black Rock, NY, Jan. 27, 1867, age 84.
Crowder, Jane, wife of Jacob, Feb. 13, 1865, age 44 y, 11 m, 13 d.
Crowe, Ellen, wife of Patrick, Oct. 15, 1874, age 45.
Crowe, Thomas, Aug. 23, 1872, age 28.
Crowell, James W., March 30, 1879, age 42.
Crowing, Henry Colton, engraver, late of Buffalo, Oct. 13, 1857, age 31; d. in St. Louis.
Crowl, Ansel, Oct. 14, 1849, age 47.
Crowl, Charles M., Sept. 20, 1874, age 37; taken to Adams Basin.
Crowl, Sarah A., May 12, 1876, age 34; taken to Adams Basin.
Crowley, Mrs., Sept. 23, 1878, age 34; kerosene accident.
Crowley, Daniel, late of Buffalo, Oct., 1873, age 26; stabbed, killed in Sandusky.
Crowley, Daniel J., Dec. 10, 1876, age 24; taken to Boston, MA.
Crowley, Dennis, Aug. 4, 1880, age 65.
Crowley, Mrs. Ellen J. G., wife of J. G., March 10, 1872, age 27.
Crowley, Joanna, wife of Michael, May 16, 1873, age 42.
Crowley, Miss Kate F., Aug. 8, 1876, age 21 y, 9 m, 4d.
Crowley, Lyman, Wales, NY, Oct. 30, 1844, age 53.
Crowley, Mary, Co. Almshouse, July 19, 1879, age 70.
Crowley, Mary A., Nov. 13, 1880, age 22 y, 3 m, 6 d.
Crowley, Mary L., wife of Timothy, Jan. 29, 1879, age 48.
Crudden, James, May 9, 1875, age 70.
Cruice, Thomas, Sr., April 19, 1876, age 70.
Cruinkshank, Janet, wife of John K., dau. of James Wilson Boke, March 7, 1863.
Crump, Elizabeth, wife of Benjamin, Colden, NY, Sept. 1877, age 74.
Cruthers, Thomas, Jan. 18, 1859; d. in Lancaster, NY; formerly of and bur. in Buffalo.
Cruttenden, Charles R., White's Corners, NY, Dec. 19, 1865, age 30.
Cruttenden, Edward, Black Rock, NY, July 26, 1849, age 42.
Crydenwise, Isaac, Clarence, NY, Jan. 1813, age 35.
Cuddebeck, Moses, Alden, NY, Dec. 18, 1870, age 76.
Cuddon, James, Feb. 17, 1851, age 35.
Cuff, Francis, Sr., Feb. 21, 1878, age 58 y, 6 m.
Culbertson, Julia A., dau. of James A., Hamburgh, NY, Sept. 6, 1861, age 25.
Cullen, Harry, Marilla, Jan. 6, 1875; accidental death.
Cullen, Owen of Hornellsville, July 3, 1873, age 35.
Culliman or Cullinan, Ellen, wife of Michael, Oct. 5, 1876, age 38 y, 7 m.
Culliny, Patrick, Crittenden, Jan. 6, 1878, age c. 30; railroad accident.
Culver, John, Oct. 29, 1840, age 35; d. at the "Hydraulics."
Cumberland, Robert, March 13, 1877, at General Hospital.
Cumings, William H., General Freight Agent, March 3, 1880, age 51.
Cumming, Mrs. Elizabeth, July 6, 1863.
Cumming, John T., son of James, Aug. 25, 1876, age 20.
Cummings, Ann, wife of B. L., Nov. 22, 1860, age 38; taken to Rochester, NY.
Cummings, Clara Z. Richardson, wife of U., March 22, 1867, age 33.
Cummings, George, Nov. 27, 1873, age 33 y, 7 m, 27 d.
Cummings, Haffield, Dec. 30, 1849, age 51.
Cummings, Hezekiah, Akron, Dec. 18, 1872, age 70.
Cummings, Homer H., Oct. 31, 1877, age 42.
Cummings, Jennie Henderson, wife of Frank, formerly of Buffalo, April 21, 1877, age 24; d. at Woodcock, PA.

Cummings, Joshua (colored), Oct. 21, 1872, age 67.
Cummings, Lottie Bell, wife of A. A., formerly of Buffalo, Sept. 9, 1876; d. in Soquel, CA.
Cummings, Mrs. Martha, Oct. 9, 1852 in New Canaan, NH, age 101 y, 5 m, 7 d.
Cummings, Phebe, widow of Haffield, April 15, 1851, age 49.
Cummings, Mrs. S. A., formerly of Clarence, NY, Sept. 11, 1878, age 71; d. at Dallas, MI.
Cummings, Sarah Ann, wife of William S., March 27, 1871, age 48; taken to State Line, Chautauqua Co.
Cummins, Mrs. Maria, Sept. 28, 1879, age 64.
Cunningham, Elizabeth S., wife of H. S., July 26, 1863, age 28.
Cunningham, Ira, formerly of Lancaster, NY, Oct. 10, 1873, age 82; d. at Elyria, OH.
Cunningham, Isabel, Dec. 8, 1875, age c. 30.
Cunningham, Mary, Dec. 4, 1878, age 70.
Cunningham, Peter, Nov. 2, 1875, age 29.
Cunningham, Phebe, wife of Layton, Lancaster, NY, March 7, 1852, age 84.
Cunningham, William, June 20, 1875, age 33.
Curran, Ellen, wife of James, Sept. 12, 1880, age 55.
Curran, Peter, Sept. 23, 1879, age 52; d. in Green Bay, WI or Bay City, MI.
Curran, Robert, Concord, Nov. 7, 1865, age 85.
Curren, Eliza Armstrong, wife of Thomas, April 12, 1872.
Currie, Fannie, dau. of Alexander and Sarah, Sept. 19, 1869, age 21.
Currier, Joseph, Nov. 8, 1867, age 53; taken to Arcade.
Currier, Susannah, wife of Col. Abner, Holland, NY, Aug. 8, 1850, age 64.
Curry, Emma J., wife of William C. of Erie, PA, Feb. 8, 1865, age 45.
Curry, Francis F., Dec. 17, 1876, age 52 y, 3 m, 14 d.
Curry, Mary A., wife of F. F., May 23, 1875, age 38 y, 6 m.
Curry, Mrs. Nancy, May 31, 1868, age 77.
Cursons, Hannah, eldest dau. of Josiah, Feb. 6, 1854, age 22 y, 11 m.
Cursons, Olive, widow of Josiah, Sept. 1, 1862, age 53.
Curtenius, Edward A., 1st Lt., 15th Regt. U.S. Inf., Nov. 9, 1862, age 26 y, 2 d. D. at home of his father, John L.
Curtenius, John L., formerly of Buffalo, July 26, 1871; d. in Utica.
Curtenius, Mrs. Mary Foster, widow of John L., Nov. 25, 1880, age 78; d. at Utica, formerly of Buffalo.
Curtis, Almon, Sardina, NY, Jan. 29, 1861, age 70 y, 11 m, 16 d.
Curtis, Blake, Black Rock, Aug. 1827, age 38.
Curtis, Eliza, wife of J. A., July 17, 1849, age 30.
Curtis, Elizabeth S., dau. of O., formerly of Buffalo, Dec. 19, 1869, age 33; d. at Ripley, NY.
Curtis, Franklin J., Oct. 29, 1870, age 39.
Curtis, Philena, wife of Robert C., Black Rock Dam, July 26, 1854.
Curtiss, Mrs. Almira, mother of Peter, Sept. 18, 1848, age 81.
Curtiss, C. M., June 4, 1877, age 28.
Curtiss, Cynthia J., widow of Peter and dau. of the late George Palmer, July 31, 1871, age 53.
Curtiss, Eliza F., wife of Peter, Feb. 16, 1845, age 43.
Curtiss, Etta Bennett, wife of Dr. R. I., Angola, NY, Aug. 6, 1868, age 34.
Curtiss, Henry A., Sept. 21, 1873, age 69.
Curtiss, Ida, wife of William H. M. D., Angola, NY, June 11, 1876, age 23.
Curtiss, Capt. J. S., Feb. 11, 1872, age 46.
Curtiss, Olive, wife of Frederick A., Clarence, NY, May 18, 1814, age 39.
Curtiss, Peter, Jan. 11, 1862, age c 66; d. in Farmington, CT, b. in Buffalo.
Curtiss, Pony, Dec. 12, 1872, age 40.
Curtiss, Sarah Ann, Feb. 8, 1857, age 30 y, 8 m.
Curtiss, Ailpha, wife of Henry A., April 27, 1873; d. at Huntington, WV, bur. in Buffalo.
Curwin, Dennis, Almshouse, April 7, 1880, age 42.
Chusing, Mrs., Aug. 1816.
Cushing, Ellen M., wife of Alanson S., Feb. 13, 1869, age 38.
Cushing, Emily H., wife of Lysander, Water Valley, Feb. 18, 1874, age 54 y, 9 m.
Cushman, A. S., Eden Center, NY, Aug. 9, 1878, age 44 y, 8 m; bur. in Buffalo.
Cushman, Elsey, wife of Josiah, Oct. 25, 1826, age 38.

Cushman, Mrs. Mary E., formerly of Buffalo, sister of Dr. C. C. and Joseph E. Haddock, May 21, 1842 in Bangor, ME, age 33.
Cusick, Lt. Nicholas (Kaghnatshon), Tuscarora Res., Soldier of the Revolution. [No dates given.]
Cuthbert, Richard, Burr, King's Co., Ireland, Oct. 28, 1866, age 66.
Cuthbert, Susan, Nov. 27, 1866, age 24 y, 4 d.
Cutler, Deacon Caleb, Holland, NY, June 11, 1851, age 80.
Cutler, Calvin, Tonawanda, March 17, 1880, age 79 y, 5 m, 24 d.
Cutler, Charles, Jan. 2, 1858, age 30. Formerly of Buffalo; d. at Wyoming, IA.
Cutler, Christopher, Sept. 17, 1861, age 37.
Cutler, Mrs. Clarinda, Dec. 13, 1873, age 74.
Cutler, Mrs. Doty, Sept. 6, 1833, age 64.
Cutler, Electa, wife of S. J., Mill Grove, March 18, 1873, age 52; taken to Batavia, NY.
Cutler, Hector, Dec. 4, 1849.
Cutler, Huldah R., wife of Samuel J., Aug. 22, 1860, age 32.
Cutler, Ida H., wife of Asa, Oct. 29, 1862, Prairie Mound, MI.
Cutler, Lydia, wife of Abner, June 9, 1873, age 65.
Cutler, Sarah Ann, wife of Samuel J., May 27, 1851, age 28.
Cutler, Susan Ware, March 11, 1873, age 69.
Cutter, Ammi Winship, March 28, 1869, age 53.
Cutter, Charles Sidney, son of A. W., Sept. 25, 1862, age 21.
Cutter, George W., Aurora, June 2, 1869, age 52.
Cutting, Frances, adopted dau. of Thomas C., July 28, 1853.
Cutting, Harvey T., Jan. 16, 1878, age 59.
Cutting, Maria, wife of Thomas S., Oct. 14, 1878, age 41.
Cutting, Mary Ann, wife of Thomas C., April 26, 1845, age 30.
Cutting, Sarah, wife of Harvey T., June 6, 1850, age 34.

Daboll, Nathan, Groton, Conn., author of Daboll's Arithmetic, March 9, 1818, age 68.
Daetsch, Annie M., wife of Conrad, Sept. 22, 1879, age 58 y, 4 m.
Dagner, Thomas, laborer, Sept. 28, 1872, age 40.
Dahlke, Frederick, fisherman, Dec. 6, 1877, age 61. Drowned, body recovered April 6, 1877 [sic].
Dailey, Patience, Jan. 30, 1826, age 78.
Daily, Mrs. Julia, Dec. 28, 1876, age 90.
Dalche, Ferdinand, July 21, 1876, age 50; drowned.
Dales, Mrs. Mary, April 4, 1840, age c. 50.
Daley, ---, widow of Martin, Nov. 18, 1853, age 58.
Daley, Caroline, dau. of Martin, Aug. 29, 1840, age 24.
Daley, Cornelia, dau. of Martin, Dec. 28, 1850, age 22 y, 10 m.
Daley, David, Aug. 14, 1855, age 49.
Daley, John, Oct. 31, 1880, age 25.
Daley, Martin, Aug. 10, 1852, age 64.
Daley, Mary, wife of Charles, Feb. 11, 1879, age 55; suicide.
Daley, Phebe, dau. of late Martin, Dec. 9, 1858.
Daley, William, d. at Northern Hotel, Albany, Sept. 29, 1840.
Dalman, John, May 6, 1873, age 26; accidently killed on NYC Railroad.
Dalton, Richard, Sept. 8, 1877, age 59; accidental death.
Daly, Bridget, widow of James, April 4, 1873, age 50.
Daly, Elizabeth or Mrs. Day, Holland, NY, March 6, 1877, age 39.
Daly, Ellen, Feb. 6, 1874, age 70.
Daly, John T., May 1877, age 53.
Daly, Olinda M., [wife of R. H.], formerly of Buffalo, April 28, (?), 1865, age 41; d. in Chicago.
Daly, Patrick, Sept. 1, 1872, age c. 43; drowned.
Dalzell, Samuel, brother of William, Oct. 26, 1872, age 43; d. in Brooklyn, bur. in Buffalo.
Damainville, August, merchant, Feb. 24, 1862, age 51.
Dembach, Clara, wife of E. W., July 25, 1875, age 20 y, 4 d.
Damon, Sarah Lovejoy, wife of Hiram, Oct. 17, 1858, age 40.
Dampbill, Ens., killed in battle of Niagara, 1814.

Dana, Mrs. Mary, mother of Mrs. S. A. Fobes, Nov. 4, 1852, age 89.
Danahan, Catherine, Co. Almshouse, Oct. 10, 1879, age 44.
Danahy, Elizabeth Patterson, wife of Dennis, Jan. 16, 1879, age 35.
Danbrook, William, milkman, Aug. 13, 1880, age 47; drowned.
Danforth, Dwight, New York City, brother of J. B. of Buffalo. D. 1850, on passage from San
    Francisco to Panama, age 37.
Danforth, James B., Aug. 28, 1852, age 37.
Danforth, Loring, Oct. 11, 1869, age 56.
Danforth, Louisa, formerly of Erie Co.; d. at Grand Rapids, MI, March 20, 1859, age 22.
Danforth, Louisa W., widow of Loring, Feb. 16, 1870, age 49.
Danforth, Mary Mills, eldest dau. of Loring, Feb. 1, 1867, age 20.
Daniel, Bertles, blacksmith, Sept. 2, 1873, age c. 30.
Daniel, John M., Feb. 20, 1871, age 51 y, 2 m.
Daniel, Marinda, wife of J. M., June 16, 1864, age 32 y, 5 m.
Daniels, Betsey, wife of Henry, Amherst, NY, Nov. 3, 1830, age 37.
Daniels, Charles W., April 16, 1878.
Daniels, Henry, Amherst, July 24, 1835, age 43.
Daniels, Mrs. James, July 6, 1879, age 52.
Daniels, Mary E., wife of William, Oct. 10, 1878, age 20 y, 10 m.
Daniels, Mary J. Porter, wife of Hon. Charles, Dec. 20, 1866, age 37.
Dann, Jesse C., Nov. 6, 1876, age 74; taken to Little Falls, NY.
Danner, Elizabeth C., dau. of the late J. Hellriegel, Feb. 10, 1874, age 34.
Danner, Mrs. Mary J. R., March 10, 1880, age 28 y, 3 m, 1 d.
Danner, Peter, July 14, 1876, age 57.
Danner, Philip H., March 11, 1873, age 31.
Danser, Rachel, wife of Jacob, Clarence, NY, June 7, 1824.
Dantzer, P. M., formerly of Buffalo, Oct. 27, 1878; d. at Indianapolis, IN, bur. in Buffalo.
Darbee, Charles Rollin, son of John C., West Falls, Oct. 21, 1870, age 52.
Darbee, Charlotte, wife of Wallace L., Oct. 25, 1869, age 34 y, 6 m.
Darbee, Eliza C., wife of Wallace L., East Hamburgh, NY, April 29, 1862, age 31 y, 10 m,
    14 d.
Darbee, Harriet, wife of Nathan N., Colden, NY, Oct. 6, 1865, age 65.
Darbee, Jedediah, West Falls, Feb. 10, 1866, age 75 y, 2 m, 6 d.
Darby, Albert A., son of John C., Aug. 1863, age 40 y, 11 m, 17 d.
Darby, Jerediah, Aurora, Oct. 9, 1828, age 72. [Another card: Darby, Jedediah, b. 1757, d.
    1828, bur. Griffins Mills, Soldier of the Revolution.]
Darby, Mrs. Margaret, mother of Mrs. Loring Pierce, Nov. 5, 1845, age 76.
Darby, Nathaniel H., Aurora, NY, April 14, 1877, age 46.
Darcy, Charles, Oct. 13, 1876, age 42.
Darcy, Mrs. Daniel, March 13, 1848, age 34.
Darcy, Daniel, Aug. 5, 1863, age 61.
Darcy, Daniel, formerly of Buffalo, Aug. 30, 1876, age 38; d. at Utica, bur. in Buffalo.
Dargan, Patrick, Aug. 14, 1871, age c. 32.
Dark, Lucinda Edith, wife of John, Sept. 23, 1872, age 32.
Darling, Anna, widow of Jonathan, Dec. 3, 1867.
Darling, Charles H., of Brighton, England, Oct. 31, 1872, age 23 y, 7 m, 12 d.
Darling, Jonathan, Oct. 4, 1866, age 58.
Darrett, George, Dec. 1812, age 25.
Darrigan, Richard, Drum Major, 49th Regt., N.Y. Vol., Nov. 5, 1862, age 19.
Darrow, Avery D., East Aurora, May 27, 1880, age 74 y, 6 m, 17 d.
Darrow, Caroline M., widow of George W., May 18, 1873, age 55; taken to Madison Co.
Darrow, Charles, formerly of Buffalo; d. at Camanche, IA, Jan. 4, 1850, age 31.
Darrow, Elijah, formerly of Stonington, CT, Aug. 21, 1842, age 67.
Darrow, George W., Oct. 3, 1871, age c. 55.
Darrow, Henry P., Aug. 2, 1852, age 44.
Darrow, Philena, wife of Avery; d. Sept. 29, 1852, age 45.
Darrow, Sophy E., wife of Harvey C., July 13, 1870, age 36.
Dart, Allen K., Hamburgh, NY, April 21, 1875, age 53.
Dart, Dr. Ashbel, Nov. 8, 1844, age 50.; d. in Conneaut, OH, b. in Buffalo.
Dart, Dotha D., wife of Joseph, May 10, 1865, age 56.

Dart, Ellen Dotha, dau. of Joseph, Aug. 26, 1876.
Dart, Joseph, Sept. 28, 1879, age 80.
Dart, or Doat, Mary, Black Rock, NY, Nov. 9, 1848, age 28 y, 10 m.
Dart, Miranda, wife of Rev. Freeman, Boston, NY, June 25, 1844, age 38.
Dascomb, Hiram, April 25, 1872, age 49.
Dascomb, William, Hamburgh, NY, Sept. 8, 1862, age 72.
Dashide or Dashiell, John R., of Somerset Co., England, Dec. 12, 1849, age 37.
Daugherty, John, May 15, 1861, age 66.
Daul, Edward, son of Andrew, March 23, 1877, age 20 y, 7 m, 8 d.
Dausch, Mrs. Magdalena, Jan. 31, 1871, age 53.
Davenport, Charles Y., Nov. 16, 1875, age 50.
Davenport, Orrin, Lancaster, NY, Feb. 25, 1857.
Davenport, William Henry Harrison, formerly of Buffalo, July 1, 1877; d. at Sidney, New South Wales.
Davidson, Rev. Alexander, Sept. 29, 1870, d. at Governor's Island, NY Harbor.
Davidson, Anne Trainor, wife of Samuel, West Seneca, NY, from Kirkcudbrightshire, Scotland, Dec. 9, 1864, age 40 y, 26 d.
Davidson, George B., late of Newton, Lower Fall, MA, May 9, 1876, age 47.
Davidson, Helen Shaw, wife of Edgar, dau. of Henry T. Gillett of Buffalo, Sept. 3, 1860; d. in New York City, bur. Buffalo.
Davidson, Henrietta, wife of Douglas N., 2d dau. of David Hawkins, Feb. 13, 1851, age 22 y, 1 m.
Davidson, Louise C., wife of John B., March 16, 1877, age 47.
Davidson, Capt. William C., May 1875.
Davies, Joseph, Feb. 27, 1862, age 49.
Davies, Dr. Richard John, from Carlow, Ireland, Aug. 17, 1851.
Davies, Thomas of England, March 12, 1876, age 29.
Davis, A. C. or Robert G., Angola, Aug. 21, 1874, age c. 30. Killed by the cars. First conductor of L.S. & M.S. Railroad.
Davis, Allen J., eldest son of William, April 14, 1870, age 22 y, 9 m, 13 d.
Davis, Rev. Asahel, Nov. 15, 1876, age 85 y, 1 m.
Davis, Clarissa, wife of Noah, Nov. 22, 1849, age 36.
Davis, Mrs. D. C., mother of Dr. W. R. Crumb, April 25, 1873, age 69.
Davis, Edward B., son of W. of Leroy, NY, Nov. 17, 1864, age 33.
Davis, Eliza Jane, only dau. of Jacob, Dec. 31, 1850.
Davis, Emily, widow of William, North Collins, NY, Jan. 4, 1874, age 52 y, 27 d.
Davis, Miss Eunice, dau. of John, Hamburgh, Feb. 3, 1842, age 21.
Davis, Fanny, wife of Louis, March 26, 1880, age 62.
Davis, Frederick A., railroad conductor, May 12, 1872.
Davis, George, Elma, Sept. 23, 1866, age 30 y, 1 m.
Davis, George, July 23, 1879; d. at Elizabeth, NJ, formerly of Buffalo.
Davis, Hattie E., formerly of Buffalo, wife of Orion L., Aug. 12, 1872, age 30; d. at Lockport, NY.
Davis, Henry M., Aug. 7, 1876, age 43.
Davis, Horace, only son of widow Laura, Aug. 22, 1842, age 23.
Davis, Isaac D., Oct. 25, 1859, age 38.
Davis, Jacob, formerly of Buffalo, Aug. 1873, age 79; d. at Niagara Falls.
Davis, Jacob J., Dec. 4, 1875, age 34 y, 14 d.
Davis, James H., June 21, 1879, age 52.
Davis, James M., Spring Brook, NY, Feb. 1, 1874, age 54; suicide at Elma.
Davis, John, East Hamburgh, NY, Feb. 8, 1855, age 68.
Davis, John, Nov. 30, 1870, age 58.
Davis, John, Jr., March 15, 1876, age 31 y, 4 m.
Davis, John, Aurora, May 23, 1880, age 70 y, 27 d. Accident, runaway horse.
Davis, Joshua, b. 1761, d. 1825, bur. Holland; Soldier of the Revolution.
Davis, Josiah, Revolutionary Soldier, Nov. 12, 1848, age 87. [Another card: Davis, Josiah, East Hamburgh, NY, Nov. 12, 1848, age 84th year (Born 1761?), Revolutinary Soldier.]
Davis, Julia Ann, wife of William, Jan. 29, 1839, age 29.
Davis, Mrs. Laura, June 12, 1862, age 71; d. in New York City, bur. in Buffalo.
Davis, Dr. Louis L., Boston, NY, June 9, 1875, age 61 y, 9 m, 6 d.

Davis, Lucy B. Kelly, wife of William, formerly of Aurora, NY, Dec. 11, 1872, age 60; d. in Rockton, IL.
Davis, Mrs. Maria, July 14, 1863, age 84; d. at the "Church Home."
Davis, Maria Elizabeth, Nov. 4, 1878, age 21 y, 3 m.
Davis, Martha E., wife of John H., Dec. 12, 1872, age 35.
Davis, Mary Ann, wife of George, Oct. 16, 1868, age 56; d. in Brooklyn.
Davis, Mary C., July 21, 1876, age 24 y, 8 m.
Davis, Matilda, wife of Rev. A., April 5, 1848, age 50.
Davis, Peter or Dewis, Aug. 21, 1876, age 20; drowned.
Davis (or Davies), Mrs. Prudence, Aug. 13, 1846, age 69.
Davis, Richard of Youghal, Ireland, Oct. 21, 1872, age 38.
Davis, Robert, mate of the Steamer *Illinois*, Sept. 24, 1843.
Davis, Miss Sarah of Chippewa, Ontario, Canada, Sept. 2, 1854, age 24.
Davis, Sarah, wife of William H., Elma, NY, April 24, 1864, age 28.
Davis, Shelden, Jan. 24, 1826, age 40.
Davis, Thomas, July 2, 1874, age 23.
Davis, Thomas, Aug. 26, 1875, age 43 y, 9 m, 23 d.
Davis, William, June 13, 1871, age 55.
Davis, William, May 18, 1872, age 64.
Davis, William, April 28, 1875, age 72.
Davis, William H., alias William Caswell, Sept. 25, 1872, age c. 40. Killed at the foot of Bird St. by the collision of two canal boats.
Davis, William H., May 28, 1874, age 63.
Davis, William H., Jr., Oct. 15, 1868, age 24.
Davis, William P., Feb. 16, 1872, age 21.
Davison, Catharine, widow of William C., May 8, 1877, age 65 y, 6 m.
Davison, Major Daniel S., Nov. 4, 1833, age 46.
Davison, Mrs. Emily, Dec. 21, 1865, age 24 y, 6 m.
Davison, George W., father of Capts. William C. and B. F., April 30, 1854, age 83 y, 8 m, 10 d.
Davison, Mrs. S. C., Sept. 18, 1869, age 75.
Davison, Thomas, b. 1757, d. 1840, bur. Chestnut Ridge (Niagara Co.); Soldier of the Revolution.
Davison, William C., June 14, 1858, age 24.
Davison, Capt. William C., May 17, 1875, age 69.
Davock, John W., July 17, 1853, age 41.
Davock, John W., July 4, 1871.
Daw, Caroline, wife of William, Sept. 12, 1871, age 65 y, 5 m, 23 d.
Daw, Henry, Aug. 19, 1864, age 69 y, 2 m.
Daw, Mrs. Mary, widow of Henry, July 16, 1879, age 84.
Dawes, William, Dec. 26, 1879, age 47.
Day, Abigail, wife of Ebenezer, Oct. 31, 1870, age 78.
Day, Mrs. Almira, Jan. 1, 1859, age 46.
Day, Betsey, wife of Elijah, Tonawanda, NY, Feb. 17, 1831, age 41.
Day, David M., Dec. 12, 1839, age 48. Formerly one of the publishers of the Whig and Journal of Buffalo.
Day, David M., May 18, 1856, age 35.
Day, David P., Oct. 25, 1871.
Day, Delia L., formerly teacher in School No. 5, Buffalo, Aug. 5, 1861, age 25; d. in Lockport, NY.
Day, Ebenezer, father of Hiram C. and David F., March 16, 1871, age 88.
Day, Edward, engineer, June 10, 1875; accidental death, killed by the explosion of the Tug *R. R. Hefford*.
Day, George, plumber, Dec. 2, 1853, age 45.
Day, Mrs. Hannah, found dead in bed, March 17, 1878.
Day, John S., printer, formerly of Buffalo, Nov. 14, 1851, age 35; d. in Chicago.
Day, Lester, Nov. 12, 1874, age 65; taken to Otis, MA.
Day, Lydia, wife of Thomas, Sept. 3, 1850, age 55.
Day, Mary, wife of John, April 24, 1880, age 42 y, 7 m.
Day, Nancy S., widow of David M., Feb. 6, 1854, age 59.

Day, Mrs. Nettie Vedder, wife of William A., Concord, Erie Co., Feb. 7, 1880, age 28 y, 4 m, 5 d.
Day, Norris W., Oct. 6, 1861, age 35.
Day, Orrin E., Aug. 19, 1859, age 53.
Day, Mrs. Susan, Jan. 10, 1864, age 65.
Day, Thomas, June 15, 1873, age 83.
Day, Thomas Henry, Co. C, 116 Reg., youngest son of Thomas of Buffalo, May 16, 1864; d. in General Hospital, New Orleans.
Dayton, Alice M. Campbell, wife of Dr. L. P., Jan. 19, 1873, age 30 y, 6 m.
Dayton, Grace Holley, North Buffalo, wife of Dr. L. P., youngest dau. of late Myron Holley, July 2, 1865.
Dayton, Isaac, Nov., 1812, age 50.
Dayton, Maria Louise, wife of M.W., Springville, NY, Nov. 11, 1855.
Dayton, Hon. Nathan, Lockport, NY, April 1859.
Dayton, Deacon William, Alden, NY, Sept. 23, 1871.
Dea, Mrs. Margaret, July 11, 1877.
Deacon, Ann, wife of Jacob, April 21, 1864, age 64.
Deacon, Jacob, Feb. 25, 1865, age 64.
Deacon, Mrs. Mary, March 30, 1880, age 44 y, 3 m.
Deacon, William R., Nov. 2, 1870, age 36.
DeAlba, Don Pedro, Nov. 1835.
Dean, Abram P., April 12, 1862, age 64.
Dean, Miss Clarissa, Sept. 27, 1873, age 63; taken to Oneida, NY.
Dean, Delia, dau. of Jonathan, June 25, 1878.
Dean, Jonathon, Eden, NY, Oct. 21, 1879, age 88 y, 5 m, 20 d.
Dean, Rachel K., wife of Dr. Stephen, East Hamburgh, NY, April 7, 1852, age 47 y, 6 m.
Dean, Sarah S., East Hamburgh, NY, wife of Dr. Stephen, Oct. 16, 1862; taken to Saratoga.
Dean, Dr. Stephen, April 7, 1869, age 72 y, 6 m, 21 d; taken to East Hamburgh, NY.
Deane, Mrs. Mary, May 28, 1855, age 36.
Debbitt, Mrs. Elizabeth, April 1, 1878, age 65.
Deck, Anthony, May 5, 1880, age 74 y, 5 m, 25 d.
Decker, Everett B., July 12, 1878, age 23.
Decker, Rachel, wife of Billens, West Falls, March 10, 1852, age 61 y, 1 m, 21 d.
Dee, William H., formerly of Buffalo, April 17, 1875, age 55. Killed by the cars in Chicago, accidental death.
Deeves, Mary, widow of William, Jan. 28, 1876, age 53.
Deeves, William, Sept. 2, 1859, age 48.
DeForest, Antoinette, June 23, 1849.
DeForest, Charles L., May 15, 1875, age 37.
DeForest, Clarissa Jane, wife of C.H., Sept. 3, 1849, age 35.
DeForest, Levi W., Aug. 28, 1877, age 21 y, 9 m, 4 d; railroad accident.
Degenhard, Charles G. (Prof.), Aug. 1867.
Degner, Henrietta, wife of Charles, May 19, 1879, age 69 y, 3 m, 17 d.
Degraff, David, Dec. 3, 1864, age 20.
DeGraff, Harry F., Sergt., March 31, 1865, age 23; killed before Petersburg.
DeGraff, James H., Feb. 19, 1863, age 22 y, 3 m.
DeGraff, John, Jan. 14, 1856, age 40.
DeGrood, Henry, March 21, 1878, age 67 y, 6 m.
DeHaas, Dr. Charles, formerly of Buffalo, April 21, 1875, age 58.
Deiteschell, Vincent, June 30, 1873, age 53; suicide.
Dekert, Henry, sailor, Nov. 16, 1871, age c. 40; drowned.
Delahunt, Mrs. Margaret, Nov. 30, 1879, age 70.
DeLaney, James, Aug. 22, 1852.
Delaney, Charles G., Oct. 15, 1877, age 58.
Delaney, Joel, son of Thomas and Arteruina D., April 1, 1880, age 24 y, 1 m, 8 d.
Delaney, John, July 23, 1874, age 27.
Delaney, Nicholas, Jan. 28, 1877, age 43.
Delaney, William, Nov. 26, 1873.
Delano, Miss, Sept. 1827, age 22.
Delano, Elisha, Oct. 10, 1827, age 64.

Delano, Frances W., wife of David B., Sept. 18, 1874; taken to Rochester, NY.
Delano, Mary, wife of Elisha D., Jan. 21, 1827, age 60.
Delany, William, Nov. 8, 1875, age c. 50.
Delenhanty, John, Dec. 24, 1870, age 29.
Dell, Thomas, carpenter, Nov. 18, 1872, age 45.
Dellamere, Mrs. Jane, Jan. 31, 1856; d. in Philadelphia.
Dellenbaugh, Edward F., son of Dr. Frederick, Oct. 7, 1878, age 26 y, 7 m.
Dellenbaugh, Samuel, physician, June 17, 1879, age 73 y, 3 m, 19 d.
Dellinger, Victor, brother-in-law of Jacob Fox, April 12, 1860, age 96; of Napoleon's Old Guard, a resident of Buffalo for 28 years.
Dellury, John, Aug. 1, 1875, age 28.
Dellury, Margaret, dau. of Thomas, Dec. 2, 1877, age 21 y, 7 m.
Delong, Charles, Cornell, VT, Oct. 14, 1850; d. at Southern Hotel.
Delong, Frances E., wife of John, March 25, 1853, age 28.
Deltman, Frederick, Aug. 5, 1879, age 55.
Demarest, Eliza Sanders, wife of William C., March 3, 1876.
Demarest, Elizabeth P., widow of James and mother of William C. and James F., March 5, 1870, age 69.
Demarest, James, Jan. 18, 1868, age 77.
Demmer, Jacob Sr., Feb. 25, 1872, age 55.
Demmons, James E., marble worker, Aug. 24, 1880, age 44.
Demond, Emma, wife of Alpheus, Nov. 4, 1877, age 32.
Dempsey, John, April 6, 1878, age 30.
Dempsey, Theresa, June 6, 1880, age 60 y, 6 m, 17 d.
Demster, William, June 23, 1860, age 44.
Demus, Nancy, Co. Almshouse, Sept. 23, 1877, age 65.
Demuth, John, Sept. 26, 1870, age 27 y, 6 m.
Demuth, Louis John, July 13, 1875, age 30 y, 2 m, 3 d.
Dene, Blass L., East Eden, NY, Dec. 9, 1873, age 45.
Denel, Myron, Aug. 26, 1880, age 58; d. at Iberia Parish, LA, formerly of Buffalo.
Denham or Densham, Fanny, wife of J.B., Aug. 1, 1851, age 26.
Denio, John R., formerly of Buffalo, Jan. 19, 1871, age 47; d. in San Francisco, CA.
Denison, Miss Eliza, Jan. 20, 1871.
Denison, Frederick D., formerly of Buffalo, Jan. 22, 1879.
Denison, Henry H., oldest son of late E. H., Aug. 29, 1854; brother of Mrs. Joseph Dart.
Denison, John S., Marilla, March 1879, age 60.
Denison, S. S., East Hamburgh, NY, Oct. 29, 1872, age 66 y, 6 m.
Denison, Sopronia F., April 29, 1875, age 81.
Denison, Thomas, Sept. 4, 1854, age 74.
Dennis, Jeanie, wife of Daniel, April 11, 1879, accident by fire.
Dennis, Mary, wife of Arad, July 25, 1835, age 49 y, 7 m; formerly of Hamburgh, NY.
Dennis, Peter, Aug. 21, 1876, age 20; drowned.
Dennis, Robert, ex-soldier, March 10, 1870; d. at Buffalo General Hospital of disease from exposure during the war.
Dennison, Albert G., May 22, 1861, age 22 y, 10 m.
Dennison, Betsey P., widow of John M., May 4, 1849, age 47 y, 8 m.
Dennison, Chester, Holland, NY, June 26, 1841, age 30.
Dennison, John M., Jan. 14, 1849, age 66 y, 8 m.
Dennison, Mary P., wife of William, May 20, 1850, age 56.
Dennison, Rebecca, dau. of John M., Oct. 27, 1852, age 23.
Dennison, Royal, Wales Center, Nov. 8, 1879, age 45 (?), accident.
Dennison, Thomas B., Sept. 5, 1849, age 22.
Dennison, William, Nov. 27, 1852, age 68.
Denny, Mrs. Catherine, Dec. 23, 1873, age 62.
Denny, Louisa E., wife of George, March 24, 1878, age 60.
Densham, Margaret M., widow of Capt. John A., Sept. 26, 1858, age 28.
Densmore, Mrs. Annie D., June 26, 1873, age 68.
Densmore, John, July 20, 1876, age 75.
Denter, Mary, wife of Lewis A., Dec. 23, 1879, age 48 y, 7 m, 10 d.
Denton, Robert, May 6, 1869, age 75.

Denton, Dr. William, Sept. 23, 1853, age 27; d. at Algonac, MI, formerly of Buffalo.
Denz, Matthew, Dec. 17, 1879, age 58.
Deoremus, Mrs. Hattie, dau. of J. Berry, July 14, 1872, age 45.
Deprinske, Lorenzini, Feb. 16, 1875, age 32; accidental death.
DePue, Mrs. Mary L., Nov. 21, 1878, age 78.
Depuy, Mrs. Henry W., wife of private secretary of Governor of New York, Sept. 29, 1853, age 34; d. on passage from Chicago to Buffalo.
DePuy, Hon. Henry Walter, formerly of Buffalo, Feb. 2, 1876.
Derby, George H., Sept. 15, 1852, age 30.
Derick, Ephraim, Revolutionary pensioner, Clarence, NY, Sept. 28, 1832, age 76. [Another card: Derrick, Empraim, b. 1756, d. 1832, bur. Clarence Chollow; Soldier of the Revolution.]
Dermody, Matthew, March 26, 1853, age 42.
Derr, Elizabeth, wife of John L., May 9, 1874, age 36 y, 1 m, 17 d.
Derrick, Bryant B., formerly of Buffalo, 1877, age 44; d. in NV.
Derrick, Bybie L., April 10, 1865, age 69.
Derrick, Frederick R., youngest son of B. L., Dec. 1, 1864, age 27 y, 4 d.
Derrick, Levi Felton, formerly of Buffalo, Oct. 20, 1863, age 35; d. in Clarence, WI.
DeRuth, Bernhard G. E., Dec. 8, 1878, age 59.
Deshler, John G., Jan. 9, 1878, age 58; d. in Columbus, OH.
Deshler, M. Louise, widow of Hon. John G., formerly of Buffalo, Feb. 12, 1878; d. in Columbus, OH.
Deshler, Margaret Nashee, wife of D. W., of Columbus, OH, June 1, 1854, age 45.
Desilrey, Thomas Miles, Feb. 20, 1867, age 25.
Despar, John, Jan. 16, 1831, age 59.
DeSpies, Ailletta Van DeSande, wife of Gustate, Jan. 15, 1860.
DeStaebler, Louis, Jan. 15, 1872, age 37.
Detamble, Emanuel, Jan. 23, 1879; drowned.
DeTamble, Jacob, son of Peter, April 27, 1878, age 24 y, 5 m.
Detine, Emily, Dec. 31, 1879, age 46 y, 8 m.
Detloff (Detlapp/Detlopp), Frederick, Aug. 27, 1873, age 49.
Dette, Johanna Elizabeth Dorothea, widow, Jan. 7, 1845, age 63.
Duell, Charles B., 2nd Lt. of Co. C, 65th Regt., April 3, 1875.
Deuel, Dulcena, wife of Charles, Jan. 1, 1859, age 28 y, 5 m.
Deuel, Harriet Lockwood, wife of Merritt, East Hamburgh, NY, July 3, 1872.
Deuel, Maria L., wife of Charles, East Hamburgh, NY, June 9, 1872, age 53.
Deuel, Mary E., wife of Samuel L., June 30, 1874; taken to East Hamburgh, NY.
Deuel, Isaac, East Hamburgh, NY, Nov. 22, 1867, age 66.
Deuel, Jennettee Cutter, wife of Merrit, Sept. 5, 1863, age 28.
Deuel, Joseph, Jr., Hamburgh, NY, July 30, 1863, age 29.
Deuel, Miss Louisa, East Hamburgh, NY, Aug. 27, 1863, age 40; d. in Buffalo, taken to East Hamburgh.
Deuel, Millard F., Feb. 17, 1874, age 34.
Deuel, Phebe, widow of Joseph, East Hamburgh, March 16, 1878, age 92 y, 5 m.
Deuel, Sarah, widow of Isaac, East Hamburgh, Oct. 7, 1874, age 72.
Deuel, William J., Oct. 18, 1867, age 67.
Deutchendor, F. or J., Oct. 7, 1875; accidental death. Killed at Elmira, bur. in Buffalo.
Deuthal, Carl, formerly of Buffalo, Sept. 29, 1878, d. in New Orleans.
Deuther, Ann, wife of George A., March 21, 1854, age 36.
Deuther, Anna M., Oct. 1877, age 27; bur. Oct. 3.
DeVeaux, Maria Woodruff, April 23, 1815, age 19. First wife of Judge Samuel DeVeaux. Bur. in LeRoy Cemetery, re-interred in St. Davids, Ontario, 1863.
Devening, Catharine, wife of Daniel, Jr., Jan. 22, 1844, age 28.
Devening, Susanna Hellriegal, wife of Dr. D., Jan. 29, 1859, age 37 y, 2 m, 7 d.
Devenport, Emily, wife of Horace, Lancaster, Jan. 5, 1865, age 64.
Dever, Andrew, June 16, 1877, age 67; d. at S.C. Hospital.
Deveraux, Elizabeth B., wife of Capt. Elisha S., Tonawanda, NY, Sept. 5, 1839, age 37.
Deveraux, E. Story, March 6, 1852, age 29.
Deveraux, Ruth, wife of Capt. Elisha S., Tonawanda, NY, 1838, age 40. Formerly of Marblehead, MA.

Deverell, Joseph H., son of T., June 12, 1878, age 22 y, 10 m.
Deverell, Tarelton, Depot Master N.Y.C., June 25, 1879, age 49.
Devine, Mrs. Bridget, wife of Thomas, Jan. 11 or 12, 1880, age 50 (?); found drowned.
Devine, James, Almshouse, Sept. 2, 1880, age 30.
DeVine, Mary Eliza Beale, wife of Charles H., Dec. 29, 1864.
Devine, Thomas, Oct. 15, 1880, age 52.
Devlin, Daniel, Sept. 17, 1870; found dead in bed.
Devlin, Sister Philomena, Sister of Mercy, Jan. 4, 1868.
Dewein, Anna Mary, wife of Frederick, May 4, 1869, age 49 y, 5 m, 16 d.
Dewel, Milton, son of Benjamin, Hamburgh, June 4, 1849, age 27.
Dewey, Jeanette, wife of S. B., July 10, 1871, age 58.
Dewey, Norman M., son of Norman R., Lancaster, NY, Aug. 29, 1853, age 21 y, 8 m, 19 d; d. at Natchez, MS.
Dewey, Lt. O. S., July 1867.
Dewey, Orville S., Feb. 1868.
Dewey, Trumand, Evans, June 2, 1853, age 67.
Dewitt, A. N., April 5, 1864, age 50.
Dewitt, Mrs. A. N., April 9, 1864, age 35.
Dewitt, James V., formerly of Buffalo, firm of Dewitt, Dudley and Co., Oct. 1, 1852, age 29; d. at Watertown, WI.
Dewitt, John, Jan. 29, 1873, age 35 y, 3 m, 5 d.
Dewitt, Mary Smith, dau. of Edward, Aug. 5, 1874, age 35 y, 2 m, 11 d.
Dexter, John, Nov. 15, 1879, age 36; found drowned.
Deyoung, Joseph J., Nov. 23, 1871, age 56.
Diamond, Henry S., formerly of Buffalo, Jan. 7, 1879; d. in Chicago.
Diamond, Maggie, Feb. 6, 1879, age 45; d. at B. G. Hospital.
Dibble, Champlin, formerly of New Haven, Conn., April 28, 1835.
Dibble, Ebenezer, Springville, Sept. 1846, age 58.
Dibble, Eliza B., wife of Clark, Wales, NY, July 1821, age 20.
Dibble, Mary, wife of R. E., Sept. 9, 1851; d. in New York City, b. in Buffalo.
Dick, James Albert, son of Rev. Robert, Jan. 2, 1870, age 29.
Dick, John, Cheektowaga, Oct. 19, 1860, age 79.
Dick, John, East Aurora, Oct. 24, 1873, age 40.
Dick, Joseph B., Willink, Nov. 3, 1871, age 47.
Dick, Lucy A., wife of W. H., Feb. 15, 1873, age 38; bur. at Cheektowaga, NY.
Dick, Mary F., youngest dau. of Rev. Robert, Aug. 10, 1873, age 20.
Dickerson, Mrs. Harriet, Dec. 2, 1874, age 70.
Dickerson, Pheoebe, wife of William, Aug. 22, 1866, age 40 y, 10 m, 21 d; late of Buffalo. D. at Port Washington, Long Island.
Dickerson, Walter J., Nov. 27, 1869, age 21 y, 6 m.
Dickerson, William J., Dec. 5, 1879, age 53, 9 m.
Dickes, Ann, wife of Ralph, Dec. 4, 1878, age 60.
Dickey, Margaret, wife of Anderson, Oct. 20, 1855, age 37.
Dickey, Thomas, Oct. 13, 1850, age 28.
Dickie, John H., brother of J. G., formerly of Buffalo, Sept. 28, 1870; d. in Brooklyn.
Dickinson, Abel B., April 30, 1871, age 57; taken to Herkimer Co.
Dickinson, Mrs. Ann, Nov. 1, 1873, age 64.
Dickinson, Mrs. Chloe, formerly of Berlin, CT, Alden, NY, Aug. 22, 1859, age 90. Mother of Mrs. Horace Stanley.
Dickinson, Eugene, son of A.B., Jan. 26, 1867, age 25. Taken to Herkimer County, NY.
Dickinson, Henry, Aug. 14, 1838, age 52.
Dickinson, Ira, one of the oldest settlers, March 27, 1836, age 52.
Dickinson, Mrs. Matilda, April 8, 1863, age 80; mother of Mrs. C. P. Churchill.
Dickinson, William, Dec. 23, 1872, age 58.
Dickman, George, April 20, 1867, age 51.
Dickman, Henry, d. at Erie Co. Penitentiary Aug. 13, 1880, age 25.
Dickson, Miss Esther, dau. of the late Capt. Wm., Feb. 26, 1872.
Dickson, Hiram, Aug. 7, 1875, age 57.
Dickson, Jennette McKnight, Nov. 1, 1876, age 26 y, 6 m.
Dickson, John H., son of Capt. Dickson, Sept. 18, 1865, age 24 y, 4 m.

Dickson, John W., Jan. 4, 1879, age 47.
Dickson, Mary A., widow of Capt. Wm. D., May 31, 1879, age 69.
Dickson, Robert J., Sept. 11, 1878, age 35.
Dickson, Capt. William, Jan. 20, 1865, age 65.
Dickinson, Varsel, b. 1735, d. 1833, bur. Warsaw (Wyoming Co.), Soldier of the Revolution.
Dickson, William F., Nov. 11, 1871, age 26 y, 11 m, 7 d.
Diebold, Charles Augustus, April 20, 1873.
Diebold, Mrs. Magdalen, March 17, 1880, age 51 y, 5 m, 22 d.
Dieboldt, Margaret, wife of Bernard, Aug. 14, 1870, age 39 y, 9 m, 13 d.
Diebolt, Katie Ginther, dau. of George, Dec. 20, 1877, age 24 y, 1 m, 20 d.
Diegelman, Lawrence, Nov. 18, 1872, age 40.
Diehl, Frederick, April 29, 1880, age 39 y, 4 m, 22 d.
Diehl, Peter, Blossomville, Dec. 28, 1875; accidently killed.
Diemer, Mrs. John, Aug. 1, 1872, age 38.
Dietrich, Mrs. Carl, Oct. 5, 1873.
Dietrich, Daniel, March 11, 1857, age 36.
Dietrich, Jacob, forge workman, April 5, 1880, age 35; d. from injuries by boiler explosion.
Dietrich, John M., Feb. 16, 1870, age 27.
Dietrich, Peter, April 7, 1876, age 61 y, 9 m.
Dietz, Lenhard, March 3, 1879, age 66.
Dietz, Maria, wife of Julius, Aug. 29, 1878, age 31.
Dietzer, Mrs. Christina, mother of Daniel, Feb. 19, 1875, age 73.
Dietzler (or Deitzle), Mrs. Margaret, June 22, 1876, age 66.
Dighton, George, Conductor of L.S. & M.S. Railway, Sept. 25, 1873.
Dill, Capt. Isaac S., April 21, 1863, age 46.
Dillane, Mary, wife of James, Jan. 16, 1877, age 38.
Diller, John, July 28, 1880, age 52 y, 6.
Dillon, Ann, wife of James, Jan. 12, 1872, age 33.
Dillon, Edward H., Dec. 29, 1880, age 34.
Dillon, John, March 30, 1873, age 51.
Dillon, John J., Feb. 14, 1878, age 32.
Dillon, Mary, widow of John, June 15, 1876, age 53.
Dillon, Richard, Sept. 29, 1875; accidental death.
Dimery, John, Dec. 2, 1857, age 30.
Dimick, Capt. Merenius, Sept. 18, 1871, age 63.
Dimon, Henry S., Feb. 1879.
Dimond, Flora, wife of Charles A., April 15, 1873, age 20 y, 6 m.
Dimond, Mrs. Jane, Dec. 5, 1862, age 56.
Dimond, Jane Smyth Cossens, wife of Henry S., Feb. 11, 1863, age 39; d. in Bridgewater, Somerset, England.
Dimond, Robert, Jan. 7, 1874, age 48.
Dimonski, John, Nov. 18, 1877; railroad accident.
Dindruff, Mary Ann Walter, formerly of Buffalo, Sept. 1, 1872, age 35; d. at Lockport, NY.
Dingens, Frank L., May 29, 1873, age 31 y, 11 m.
Dingens, George, b. in Alsace, France, April 26, 1842, age 37.
Dingens, John, Dec. 26, 1848, age 38 y, 10 m.
Dingman, John G., Evans, Oct. 14, 1869, age 72.
Dinkel, Mrs. Barbara, wife of Thomas, May 14, 1879, age 56; violent death.
Dinkel, Thomas, June 24, 1879, age 61. Suicide, having killed his wife. See Barbara D.
Dinnin, Cynthia, wife of J. R., June 11, 1874, age 50.
Dinsmore, Harriet G. Snow, wife of A., May 12, 1855, age 26.
Dinsmore, Phebe Dow, Sept. 6, 1852, age 38.
Dinwoodie, John, Lancaster, NY, July 15, 1866, age 84; late of Earlstown, Berwickshire, England.
Dinwoodie, John Jr., Lancaster, NY, Dec. 26, 1852, age 38; b. in Buffalo.
Dirstine, Jacob, Williston, March 29, 1877, age 60.
Dislar, Johannah, widow of John Burke, Oct. 15, 1875, age 34.
Dissett, Bridget, wife of Joseph, Jan. 28, 1880, age 43.
Dissett, Rosanna M. Kilroy, wife of Capt. H., Oct. 23, 1875, age 28.
Ditsmars, Mrs. Ann, March 26, 1851, age 58.

Ditto, Laura Sydney, June 18, 1880, age 20 y, 4 m, 23 d.
Dixon, George W., Nov. 27, 1874, age 84 y, 11 m.
Dixon, Joseph, July 13, 1874, age 54.
Dixon, Thomas, June 4, 1879, age 43.
Dizard, Elizabeth, wife of James, July 14, 1861, age 35.
Dizert, James, Jan. 10, 1864, age 48.
Doane, Anna, Eden, Aug. 5, 1872, age 72.
Doat, George, Sept. 23, 1867, age 81 y, 7 m, 23 d.
Doat, Mary, Nov. 9, 1848, age 28 years, 10 months.
Doat, Thomas, Oct. 14, 1868, age 46 y, 6 m.
Dobbin, Mrs. Rachel, mother of Mrs. J. W. Newkirk, Tonawanda, NY, Sept. 12, 1851, age 88 y, 7 m.
Dodd, Susan, wife of William, Nov. 17, 1854.
Dodd, William D., May 19, 1871, age 50 y, 3 m, 21 d.
Dodds, Stephen V., Feb. 1873, age 69.
Dodds, Thomas G., Aug. 13, 1872, age 43 y, 4 m.
Dodds, William H., member of Union Cornet Band, July 16, 1861, age 25.
Dodge, Almira, dau. of Harry, Alden, NY, June 30, 1854, age 32; formerly of Clayton Co., IA.
Dodge, Alonzo, Black Rock, Sept. 26, 1828, age 24.
Dodge, Alphonso, April 8, 1858, age 31 y, 5 m, 29 d; d. in Cleveland, OH, b. in Buffalo.
Dodge, Alvin, Black Rock, NY, Jan. 14, 1847, age 65.
Dodge, Azariah, Nov. 27, 1826, age 45.
Dodge, Charles H., April 15, 1846, age 33.
Dodge, Charles V., son of the late Elam, Sept. 30, 1872, age 28; d. N.Y. City, bur. Buffalo.
Dodge, Charlotte, wife of Wayne, Clarence, NY, July 31, 1864, age 46.
Dodge, Elam, merchant, Black Rock, NY, Sept. 14, 1847, age 37.
Dodge, Emily P. Hotchkiss, wife of Leonard, Dec. 31, 1872, age 25 y, 1 m.
Dodge, George, eldest son of Alvan L. of Clarence, NY, late of Buffalo, April 5, 1865, age 34; d. at Minneapolis, MN, b. in Buffalo.
Dodge, George Clinton, Alden, NY, Feb. 19, 1856, age 31 y, 6 m.
Dodge, John G., April 13, 1862, age 65; d. in St. Louis, bur. in Buffalo.
Dodge, Mrs. Mary, June 2, 1829, age 41.
Dodge, Mrs. Mary, widow, mother of Alvan L. and J. W., Sept. 23, 1867, age 84.
Dodge, Mary E., wife of Hampton, July 11, 1870, age 49.
Dodge, R. C., Jan. 9, 1854, age 47.
Dodge, Ruth H., wife of Alvan L., Feb. 25, 1878, age 80.
Dodge, Washington C., Black Rock Dam, Nov. 5, 1855, age 25.
Dodsworth, Mrs. Sarah, wife of William, Aug. 10, 1879, age 64.
Doelman, Jane, wife of Myron, April 21, 1877, age 27 y, 8 m, 3 d.
Doetterl, George, June 27, 1877, age 64.
Doherty, Elizabeth, Sept. 27, 1871, age 33.
Dolan, Ellen, wife of James D., May 2, 1870, age 49.
Dolan, Michael, Oct. 7, 1874, age 70.
Dolan, Patrick, March 28, 1875, age 65. Found in the water March 28.
Dolan, Sarah Ann, May 18, 1879, age 21 y, 5 m, 2 d.
Dolan, Thomas, Nov. 18, 1880, age 72.
Dolan, William, Dec. 15, 1879, age 59.
Dole, Abigail S., wife of Benjamin, Nov. 20, 1848, age 44.
Dole, Adelia, wife of Anthony, Sept. 13, 1859, age 22 y, 6 m.
Dole, Charlotte, wife of John A., Aug. 22, 1852, age 48 y, 1 m, 16 d.
Dole, James B., 2d son of Francis, Evans Center, NY, April 11, 1866, age 28 y, 7 d.
Dole, John A., formerly of Buffalo, Jan. 1870; d. in Philadelphia; bur. in Forestville, Chautauqua Co. Jan. 19.
Dole, Linua, Eden, Sept. 12, 1880, age 87.
Dole, Patrick, Aug. 25, 1838, age 34.
Dole, Stephen, Jan. 1813, age 28.
Dolen, Harry T., Nov. 27, 1849.
Doll, Frederick, Nov. 7, 1867, age 62 y, 9 m.
Doll, Frederick, April 3, 1871, age 35.

Doll, Mary Ann, Jan. 18, 1879, age 70 y, 4 m, 10 d.
Doll, Michael, Jan. 5, 1857, age 42 y, 6 m.
Doll, Sebastian, Nov. 28, 1880, age 46 y, 2 m, 20 d.
Dolly, Jacob, Co. Almshouse, Dec. 28, 1877, age 48.
Dolmage, Miss Florence Merion, Aug. 18, 1875, age 26 y, 5 m.
Domaneas, Edward, July 15, 1878, age 85.
Domedian, Jacob, Feb. 23, 1868, age 58 y, 6 m.
Domedion, George, May 29, 1875, age 21 y, 2 m, 7 d.
Dominoes, Mary Gibson, wife of Edward, Jan. 28, 1876.
Dominy, Felix, Dec. 20, 1868, age 69; taken to East Hampton, Long Island.
Donaldson, James, moulder in Mayhews Foundery, Oct. 5, 1847, age 42.
Donaldson, James D., Oct. 20, 1876.
Donavan, Michael T., March 13, 1869, age 55.
Doney, Mrs., Clarence, Aug. 17, 1815, age 60.
Doney, Harry, Clarence, Aug. 11, 1872, age 88.
Doney, Mary, wife of Henry, Clarence, Jan. 19, 1871, age 87 y, 2 d.
Doney, Sarah, wife of Loring, Nov. 26, 1831, age 36.
Donius, Frank, Aug. 8, 1878, age 24; drowned.
Donlon, James, June 2, 1873, age 67.
Donn, Elizabeth, wife of Nicholas, Oct. 16, 1879, age 51.
Donnelly, Mrs. Mary, Oct. 1878, age 53 y, 2 m, 5 d.
Donnelly, Thomas F., April 21, 1880, age 23.
Donohue, Mrs. Ellen, of County Tirone, Ireland, Aug. 16, 1869, age 75.
Donohue, Mrs. Mary, Jan. 21, 1873, age 72.
Donohue, Michael, June 23, 1873, age 21; drowned.
Donohue, Michael J., Sept. 4, 1880, age 21; d. at Colville, PA, formerly of Buffalo.
Donohue, Patrick, Sept. 20, 1871, age 26; suicide in Batavia, formerly of Buffalo.
Donohue, Timothy, Co. Almshouse, May 17, 1876, age 52.
Dononghue, Jessie, wife of Hugh, July 19, 1870, age 49 y, 8 m.
Donovan, Mrs., Dec. 15, 1875, age 80.
Donovan, Cornelius, Dec. 27, 1875; drowned.
Donovan, Daniel, July 13, 1871, age 48.
Donovan, Ellen, sister of Miss S. E., April 10, 1869.
Donovan, Eva, wife of Dennis J., March 11, 1880, age 26 y, 8 m, 4 d.
Donovan, Mary, Co. Almshouse, Dec. 25, 1878, age 60.
Doody, Jeremiah, Jan. 20, 1880, age 35.
Doody, Thomas, Nov. 30, 1879, age 21.
Doolittle, Charles H., formerly of Buffalo, Oct. 1868; d. at Sherburn, NY, at res. of his sister.
Doolittle, Chauncey, formerly of Buffalo, June 4, 1871, age 70; d. at Warsaw, Wyoming Co.
Doolittle, Eliza M., wife of Charles, Jan. 1, 1861, age 49.
Doolittle, Lucy E., wife of Rev. Justus of North China Mission, dau. of Calvin Mills of Alden, Aug. 12, 1865, at Rutland, Jefferson Co., NY.
Doolittle, Miss Sarah, Cheektowaga, Oct. 12, 1869, age 63. Formerly of CT.
Dopkins, John K., brother-in-law of William Madison, Aug. 27, 1847, age 30.
Dorchester, Mrs., mother of Mrs. E. D. Efner, May 6, 1820, age 54; formerly of Utica.
Dorethy, Peter, Co. Almshouse, Aug. 2, 1877, age 45.
Dorland, Dr. Joseph, East Hamburgh, NY, March 21, 1873, age 74 y, 6 m, 11 d.
Dorland, Dr. Philip S., East Hamburgh, Aug. 15, 1866, age 29; d. in Chicago, bur. in East Hamburgh, NY.
Dorling, Joseph, May 24, 1878, age c. 40.
Dorman, Mrs. Anna A., Feb. 14, 1832, age 55.
Dorr, John, April 15, 1852, age 40; d. in Dunkirk, NY, formerly of Buffalo.
Dorr, Mary, wife of Frank J., March 16, 1873, age 21.
Dorr, Mrs. Nancy, July 4, 1853, age 66.
Dorr, Nellie, Feb. 6, 1869, age 22. Wife of John N. Taken to Greenwood Cemetery, Brooklyn, NY.
Dorret, Benjamin, Nov. 5, 1844, age 34.
Dorris, Louise E., wife of Philo W., Aug. 21, 1879, age 36.
Dorsey, James, Aug. 21, 1871.

Dorsheimer, Philip, April 11, 1868, age 71.
Dorsheimer, Sarah, widow of Philip, March 22, 1869.
Dorsheimer, William, father of P., Oct. 28, 1851, age 86.
Dorst, Emma L., dau. of Philip, Feb. 6, 1880, age 21 y, 2 m, 15 d.
Dorst, Jacob, Jan. 12, 1872, age 59.
Dorst, Mrs. Jacob, Dec. 31, 1880, age 63.
Dorst, John, father of Jacob, East Hamburgh, May 18, 1856, age 65.
Doty, Mrs., Feb. 12, 1877, age 65.
Doty, Ezra, b. 1760, d. 1840, bur. Lockport (Niagara Co.), Soldier of the Revolution.
Doty, John, Springville, NY, Nov. 29, 1843, age 91 y, 3 d. Revolutionary soldier at Bunker Hill, capture of Burgoyne, etc.
Doty, Joseph, Collins, Dec. 2, 1875, age 46; accidental death.
Doty, Maggie I., dau. of Rufus, May 2, 1866, age 21 y, 9 m, 23 d; d. in Lockport, NY, bur. in Buffalo.
Doty, Rufus, May 4, 1875, age 64; d. at Lockport, bur. Buffalo.
Doty, Russell, Aug. 14, 1852, age 52.
Doty, Thomas, Co. Almshouse, May 14, 1878, age 69.
Dotzler, George, May 2, 1876, age 20 y, 6 m.
Dougan, Thomas A., Co. Penetentiary, Aug. 9, 1876, age 38.
Dougherty, Capt. Edward N., Nov. 24, 1877, age 38; lost at sea.
Dougherty, Mrs. Isabella, mother of Mrs. D. N. Tuttle, Sept. 16, 1860, age 90.
Dougherty, James, Aug. 20, 1873, age 32; accidently killed on railroad.
Dougherty, Jane, wife of Alexander F., April 29, 1827, age 20.
Dougherty, Mrs. Mary, March 29, 1869, age 47; d. in N.Y. City, bur. Buffalo.
Douglas, John, Jan. 2, 1873; killed on the railroad.
Douglas, William, of "Doug's Dive," Nov. 28, 1878, age over 90.
Douglass, Agnes, eldest dau. of Robert, Aug. 11, 1870, age 21 y, 1 m, 15 d.
Douglass, William Henry, Dec. 1, 1875, age 59; d. in Albany, bur. in Lockport, NY.
Douw, Peter J., Oct. 20, 1879, age 68.
Dover, Annie E. Gurnes, wife of John H., Sept. 14, 1879, age 32.
Dover, Eliza, wife of George, Oct. 20, 1859, age 46.
Dover, Sarah Ann, wife of George, June 30, 1862, age 32.
Dow, Caroline E., wife of William F., Nov. 2, 1849, age 32.
Dow, Mrs. Carrie (nee Schmidt), formerly of Buffalo, April 5, 1872, age 25; suicide at East Saginaw.
Dow, Ellen, wife of William F., June 23, 1847, age 28 y, 7 m, 11 d.
Dowd, John, July 11, 1858, age 49.
Dowd, Rosana, wife of Bernard, Sept. 11, 1877, age 57.
Dower, Patrick, formerly of Buffalo, May 6, 1877, age 40; drowned.
Dowling, Sarah, Jan. 2, 1877, age 80.
Downes, David, Sept. 15, 1880, age 55.
Downs, Ann, wife of Edward, June 2, 1852.
Downs, Charles S., Nov. 7, 1873, age 34.
Downs, Edward, formerly of Buffalo, Sept. 28, 1871, age 61; d. in Brantford, Ontario, bur. Buffalo.
Downs, Francis S., July 9, 1874, age 65 y, 9 m, 3 d.
Dox, Edward R., formerly of Buffalo, April 16, 1862; d. in Geneva, NY.
Dox, Myndert M., late of U.S. Army, Sept. 8, 1830, age 42.
Doyle, David C., Nov. 27, 1878, age 31 y, 9 m.
Doyle, Elizabeth Ann (Ann Eliza), wife of Timothy, Oct. 11, 1873, age 35.
Doyle, James, Aug. 20, 1875, drowned.
Doyle, John, Jan. 18, 1847, age 35.
Doyle, John, ex-alderman, Aug. 4, 1878, age 38.
Doyle, Laurence, April 13, 1872, age 43; d. St. Louis, MO.
Doyle, Mary, Sept. 19, 1872, age 77.
Doyle, Michael, July 7, 1872, age 74.
Doyle, Patrick, Dec. 6, 1877, age 60; accidental death.
Doyle, Thomas, Almshouse, April 6, 1880, age 68.
Doyle, Timothy, Nov. 15, 1877, age 41 y, 8 m.
Drake, Mrs. Electa, Springville, NY, June 20, 1866, age 63 y, 6 m, 14 d.

Drake, Harriet, wife of John, Nov. 10, 1853, age 49.
Drake, John, Sept. 23, 1854, age 57.
Drake, Mary A. Ludlow, wife of Marcus M., Nov. 2, 1880, age 33.
Drake, William, Black Rock, NY, Sept. 15, 1828; formerly of Locke, Cayuga Co.
Draper, Sgt. J. W., Co. B, 10th NY Cav., May 17, 1863, age 33. D. in hospital at Aquia Creek, VA.
Draper, Mary, Elma, Aug. 28, 1858, age 78; formerly of Pelham, MA.
Draper, Miss Mary C., Lancaster, NY, March 20, 1847, age 28.
Draper, Seth C., Lancaster, NY, Nov. 24, 1861, age 40.
Drechler, Charlotte, Johannesberg, Dec. 14, 1877, age 78; railroad accident.
Dreher, Charles Jr., Oct. 16, 1873, age 23 y, 7 m.
Drennan, Miss Mary, Oct. 16, 1880, age 82.
Dresler, D. V., Colposteur of American Tract Society, April 20, 1850, age 35.
Drew, Austin M., letter carrier, Aug. 25, 1877, age 36; taken to Plymouth, MA.
Drew, Capt. Edward, Co. G, 1st Regt. Berdan's U.S. Sharpshooters, June 30, 1862 or July 1, age 28. Killed at battle of White Oak Swamp. (Death denied July 12; confirmed July 21.)
Drew, Eliza, wife of John, Feb. 4, 1844, age 36.
Drew, Elizabeth B. Wesley, widow of the late Capt. Edward, June [no year given.]
Drew, George H., formerly of Buffalo, Jan. 4, 1869; d. at Nagasaki, Japan.
Drew, Sarah Ann, wife of John, Aug. 7, 1849, age 34.
Driggs, Mrs. Harriet Benedict, wife of Roswell W., Tonawanda, NY, March 14, 1880, age 40.
Driggs, Lucy Ann, wife of Uriel, Tonawanda, NY, June 2, 1868, age 70 y, 3 m, 23 d.
Driggs, Uriel, Tonawanda, Nov. 25, 1829, age 50.
Driggs, Uriel B., youngest son of Uriel, Tonawanda, NY, Dec. 13, 1859, age 24 y, 7 m, 2 d.
Driscoll, Charles M., March 26, 1875, age 27.
Driscoll, Mrs. Johanna, April 29, 1864, age 58 years.
Driscoll, Mrs. Margaret, March 29, 1875, age 28.
Driscoll, Patrick, Oct. 12, 1872, age 34.
Druer, Andrew, Dec. 6, 1875, age 35; suicide.
Druar, John, North Buffalo, Aug. 15, 1872, age 62 y, 6 m, 25 d; d. in Cleveland, OH, bur. Buffalo.
Druar, Margaret, Aug. 31, 1873, age 68.
Drullard, Eliza, wife of George, March 5, 1849, age 35.
Drullard, Francis, June 19, 1868, age 87; d. at London, Canada W.
Drullard, Francis O., son of Soloman, Aug. 6, 1869, age 31.
Drullard, Margaret, widow of Francis, Jan. 4, 1871, age 84.
Drullard, Ralph, Nov. 7, 1866, age 33 y, 10 m.
Drummer, Mary, July 8, 1877, age 26.
"Dublin," Thomas Hamilton, near Buffalo, laborer, May 23, 1872; killed on the railroad.
Dubois, Agnes, wife of J. B., March 16, 1857, age 39 y, 6 m.
Dubois, Alfred, Aug. 24, 1840, age 25.
Dubois, Alfred, son of James B., Sept. 30, 1869, age 28 y, 3 m, 21 d.
Dubois, George T., youngest son of James B., Feb. 16, 1876, age 24 y, 3 m.
DuBois, James B., April 29, 1878, age 67.
Dubois, Samuel H., March 1876, age 63.
Dubois, Sarah Sherod, wife of Philo, March 4, 1868, age 51.
Dubois, Tobias, Wales, NY, July 26, 1874, age c. 40; suicide.
DuBril, Joseph, Co. Almshouse, Dec. 23, 1878, age 79.
Duchene, Mary Metz, wife of Lucius, Dec. 29, 1874, age 32.
Duck, Jane, wife of Dr. D., late of London, Aug. 9, 1831.
Duckmore, George, Aug. 11, 1875, age 20; drowned.
Duckmyer, Mathias, Aug. 11, 1875, age 20; drowned.
Ducro, Mrs. Gertrude, April 1878, age 83.
Dudley, Mrs., May 1875.
Dudley, Caroline, wife of Thomas J., Aug. 17, 1844, age 40.
Dudley, Edward, Feb. 15, 1871, age 51.
Dudley, George E., Sept. 7, 1860, age 30. Prof. of Mathematics, State Normal School, Ypsilanti, MI; taken to Bath, Steuben Co., NY.
Dudley, Hannah S., wife of Stephen, Nov. 26, 1853, age 47 y, 4 m, 15 d.

Dudley, James G., formerly of Buffalo, Nov. 25, 1872, age 44 y, 8 m.
Dudley, John E., May 15, 1863, age 49 y, 4 m.
Dudley, John L., formerly of Buffalo, March 19, 1846, age 37; d. at Leon, Cattaraugus Co.
Dudley, Joseph Dana, July 16, 1880, age 57 y, 9 m.
Dudley, Mary Ann, wife of Joseph D., June 8, 1851, age 27.
Dudley, Moses T., Sept. 13, 1864, age 39.
Dudley, Stephen, senior partner of S. Dudley and Sons, Aug. 11, 1856, age 58 y, 15 d.
Dudley, Thomas J., Nov. 4, 1875, age 75 y, 3 m.
Dudley, Thomas J., Jr., lawyer, formerly of Buffalo, July 15, 1879, age 58; d. at Cedar Rapids, IA.
Dudley, William C., Eden, Dec. 30, 1813. Killed at Battle of Black Rock.
Duel (or Deuel), Albert T., Nov. 29, 1880, age 47.
Duel, Miss Fanny, formerly of Buffalo, Oct. 16, 1869, age 64; d. at Evans Center, NY, at res. of Daniel E. Mosher.
Duel, Phebe, widow of Benjamin, East Hamburgh, NY, Nov. 10, 1865, age 71.
Duer, Betsey, wife of William, East Hamburgh, Oct. 9, 1875, age 69.
Duer, Catharine, wife of Edward, Hamburgh, NY, Sept. 9, 1841, age 72; formerly of Mohawk, Montgomery Co., NY.
Duer, Edward, East Hamburgh, Jan. 29, 1854, age 81.
Duer, Miss Polly, April 5, 1814, age 19.
Duer, William, East Hamburgh, NY, Sept. 27, 1876, age 78.
Duff, Archibald M., Dec. 31, 1861, age 54 y, 4 m; formerly of Perthshire, Scotland.
Duff, George W., son of Frank, Sept. 3, 1878, age 19 y, 5 m, 9 d.
Duff, James, April 17, 1870, age 35 y, 8 m, 27 d.
Duff, Margaret, widow of A. M., Nov. 28, 1862, age 50 y, 9 m.
Duff, Peter, July 9, 1861, age 22 y, 6 m.
Duffy, Edward, Springbrook, Nov. 18, 1874, accident death.
Duffy, Mrs. Eliza, March 27, 1872, age 54.
Durry, James, Feb. 27, 1878; d. at Courtland, NY.
Duffy, Mrs. John, May 12, 1878, age 67.
Duffy, Joseph, May 2, 1865, age 56; formerly of Cheshire, England.
Duffy, Thomas F., April 1879.
Duffy, William, Aug. 17, 1866, age 61.
Dugan, Roger, March 29, 1879, age 70.
Duggan, Abigail, Jan. 10, 1878, age 55.
Duggan, Henry P., June 15, 1880, age 24 y, 10 m, 7 d.
Duggan, P. M., Jan. 20, 1878, age 58.
Duggan, Patrick, March 13, 1876, age 79.
Duhemy, Patrick, March 3, 1877, age 55.
Dukenfield, Enoch S., Jan. 20, 1877, age 19 y, 9 m, 26 d.
Dukes, John, June 12, 1869, age 60.
Dukes, John Q., April 2, 1870, age 36 y, 2 m.
Dukes, William H., June 17, 1867, age 32.
Dulanty or Duhalanty, Thomas, Oct. 27, 1873, age 48
Dumbolton, Samuel, Willink, NY, Dec. 1812 in Buffalo. [Another card: Dumbleton, John, b. 1744, d. 1812, bur. Hamburg; Soldier of the Revolution.]
Dumont, Eleanor D., wife of Waldron, Dec. 11, 1854, age 37; taken to Geneva, NY.
Dumoulin, Mary A., eldest dau. of Joseph and Mary A. Nechter, June 9, 1879.
Dunakin, Samuel, Sept. 1813, age 25.
Dunbar, Albert, Jan. 14, 1873, age 33.
Dunbar, Edwin, Aug. 12, 1872, age 69.
Dunbar, Frances L., wife of George W., Dec. 3, 1873, age 22 y, 10 m, 22 d.
Dunbar, Hannah H., wife of Thomas, Sept. 14, 1865, age 49; taken to Dedham, MA.
Dunbar, J. Jewett, Aug. 7, 1874, age 38 y, 2 m, 9 d.
Dunbar, Julia, wife of Lyman, Dec. 30, 1832, age 34; formerly of Berlin, CT.
Dunbar, Lyman, Dec. 9, 1855, age 65; formerly of Plymouth, CT.
Dunbar, Mary E., wife of Robert, June 16, 1867.
Dunbar, Mary M. Gibson, wife of Robert, Sept. 22, 1863.
Dunbar, Minnie E., dau. of Robert, May 15, 1874, age 20.
Dunbar, Sarah Maria, wife of Robert, Dec. 9, 1849, age 38.

Dunbar, Susan Merrill, wife of Edwin, Aug. 23, 1861, age 53.
Dunbar, William J., July 29, 1868, age 26.
Duncan, Emilia Willis, North Buffalo, wife of John, Dec. 11, 1873.
Duncan, James, Dec. 24, 1865, age 43.
Duncan, Mrs. Rebecca, Dec. 29, 1873, age 73; taken to Chicago.
Duncan, Robert, Nov. 23, 1877, age 31.
Dungey, Mrs. Isabella, Oct. 21, 1876, age 67 y, 5 m.
Dunham or Dennert or Donnert, John, Co. Almshouse, May 18, 1877, age 20.
Dunham, William, Dec. 12, 1871, age 83; taken to Newstead.
Dunkel, Othella, dau. of Jacob A., Aug. 28, 1872, age 20 y, 8 m.
Dunlap, Horace, formerly of Buffalo, Feb. 28, 1873, age 73; d. at Leavenworth, KS.
Dunlap, John, July 15, 1872, age 25; accidently killed.
Dunlap, Lucy P., wife of Horace, Nov. 9, 1868, age 64 y, 5 m; d. at Leavenworth, KS.
Dunlap, Rebecca J., May 1, 1871, age 30.
Dunlop, Hannah, wife of James, Dec. 19, 1854, age 46 y, 5 m.
Dunmeyer, Lottie, wife of Louis, Titusville, PA, Feb. 26, 1871; d. at Titusville, bur. in Buffalo.
Dunn, Mrs. Anne, Dec. 1878, age 65.
Dunn, David, Black Rock, NY, Sept. 1824, age 42.
Dunn, Mrs. Ellen, Feb. 13, 1854, age 48.
Dunn, John, Jan. 2, 1875, age 45; accidental death.
Dunn, John P., Oct. 21, 1852, age 43.
Dunn, John P., Oct. 17, 1877, age 51 y, 4 m, 26 d.
Dunn, Kittie, Aug. 12, 1871.
Dunn, Mary, March 25, 1857, age 70.
Dunn, Mary A., wife of Taylor, July 15, 1880; d. at Penn Yan, formerly of Buffalo.
Dunn, Mary Ann, May 12, 1872, age 21.
Dunn, Obediah, son of Rosanna McDonald, Oct. 29, 1846, age 22.
Dunn, Samuel, Aug. 15, 1878, age 72.
Dunn, Thomas O., formerly of Buffalo, May 9, 1874, age 53; d. at Selby Flat, CA.
Dunne, James W., formerly of Buffalo, April 23, 1858; d. at Springfield, IL.
Dunning, Anna, wife of Martin D., Black Rock, May 19, 1824, age 19.
Dunning, William R., July 19, 1864, age 45.
Dunning, William W., oldest son of William R., June 18, 1865; age 21 y, 6 m, 27 d. Captain at Newberne, NC; d. in Andersonville Prison.
Dunston, Mrs. Thomas A., Nov. 7, 1879.
Dunton, Almon, Lancaster, NY, April 1, 1871, age 45; taken to Chautauqua Co.
Durfee, Mary W., wife of Philo, Nov. 8, 1861, age 48.
Durick, James, Nov. 28, 1853, age 51; d. at Springfield, NY, bur. in Buffalo, Forest Lawn.
Durick, Jeremiah R., formerly of Buffalo, Feb. 2, 1866; d. at Shasta, CA.
Durick, Lavinia, widow of James, March 31, 1865, age 68.
Durkee, Mrs. Betsey, mother of N. B. Thorp of Buffalo, Clarence, NY, Aug. 16, 1857, age 73.
Durkee, Hannah A., Alden, widow of Ziba, March 17, 1872, age 75.
Durkee, Isabel, dau. of Phebe H., July 22, 1868, age 20.
Durkee, Mary Elizabeth, wife of George B., Alden, NY, dau. of Daniel Hibbard of Black Rock, NY, Jan. 15, 1865, age 37.
Durkee, Mrs. Mary Waldo, mother of George and Mrs. John J. Gibbsons, Harmony, Chautauqua Co., May 14, 1869, age 79; bur. in Buffalo.
Durkee, Rodney, son of Rudney of Suspension Bridge, NY, Aug. 27, 1868, age 31.
Durkee, Sarah J., wife of Dwight, formerly of Buffalo, Sept. 12, 1867, age 37; d. in St. Louis.
Durkee, Thomas, Holland, Aug. 9, 1869, age 82.
Durkee, Ziba, Alden, Dec. 17, 1853, age 60; d. at York, PA.
Durney, Thomas, Oct. 27, 1876, age 70.
Durr, Mrs. Jennie Archer, May 17, 1862, age 25.
Durrie, Johanna, widow of Horace, Aurora, Cayuga Co., dau. of Daniel Steele of Albany, Aug. 13, 1849.
Dusenbury, Benjamin, June 23, 1862, age 77.
Dusenbury, Elizabeth, wife of Erastus, May 26, 1863, age 32.
Dusenbury, Erastus F., Dec. 19, 1870, age 42.

Dusenbury, Hiram, Jan. 28, 1878, age 54.
Dusenbury, Jeremiah, Aurora, Feb. 19, 1852, age 62.
Dusenbury, Mary, wife of E. F., April 6, 1860, age 23.
Dusenthal, William, April 1872.
Dussinger, Nicholas, Nov. 8, 1875; accidental death.
Dustin, William R., Sept. 9, 1871, age 33; d. in Detroit, bur. Buffalo.
Duthie, Ellen, dau. of James, Jan. 23, 1869.
Duthie, James, son of James of Buffalo, Dec. 22, 1865, age 20; d. at Fergus, Canada West; bur. in Buffalo.
Dutton, Carlton, June 20, 1862, age 50; formerly of Rochester, NY.
Dutton, Carrie M., wife of Wert O., Alden, NY, July 22, 1874.
Dutton, Edward Bates, Dec. 1, 1860, age 23 y, 8 m.
Dutton, Elizabeth Kendall, widow of Carlton, Sept. 4, 1869, age 42.
Dutton, Lydia, wife of James, Jan. 25, 1812, age 55; formerly widow Powers of Newtown.
Dwight, G. P. Barker, only son of T. C., Black Rock, Aug. 3, 1838.
Dwight, Seth, April 3, 1825, age 55; recently from Utica.
Dwight, Timothy C., formerly of Buffalo, Jan. 19, 1875, age 69.
Dwyer, James, Sept. 20, 1878.
Dwyer, John B., formerly of Buffalo, March 1, 1877; d. at Carondelet, MO.
Dwyer, Mary (or Ellen), wife of Michael, March 25, 1879.
Dyer, Andrew, June 19, 1878, age 23 y, 8 m, 23 d.
Dyer, Charles H., Nov. 1874, age 35 y, 5 m.
Dyer, Mrs. Harriet, Jan. 18, 1879, age 68.
Dyer, Mary E., May 17, 1873, age 30 y, 7 m.
Dyer, Sylvanus, Oct. 1, 1823, age 24; formerly of Sangerfield, Oneida Co., NY.
Dygert, Ida, dau. of J. W., Feb. 20, 1874, age 27; d. in Chicago, bur. Buffalo.
Dynes, Jane, Feb. 4, 1873, age 84.

Eagan, Mrs. Johannah, mother of John C., June 16, 1878, age 64.
Eagan, John, July 4, 1874, age 68.
Eagen, Mrs. Ann, Sept. 22, 1872, age 41.
Eardley, Ann, March 20, 1880, age 73 y, 10 m.
Eardley, Bryan, April 8, 1872.
Eardley, John, March 24, 1868, age 29 y, 1 m, 2 d.
Earl, Benjamin, Aurora, May 18, 1835, age 40.
Earl, Deborah M., Nov. 5, 1880, age 81 y, 3 m, 8 d.
Earl, John, Willink, Jan. 1813, age 45.
Earl, Oliver, Aurora, March 1, 1847, age 45.
Earl, Stephen H., Hamburgh, Nov. 14, 1840, age 74.
Earl (or Eales or Eeles), William, April 27, 1880, age 45 y, 10 m; found dead in bed.
Earl, William P., Abbott's Corners, NY, Dec. 6, 1878, age 79.
Earll, Willard, formerly of New York, Oct. 12, 1849, age 37; d. at the "Phelps House."
Ernest, Mr. F. S., July 20, 1878, age 28; sunstroke.
Easley, Amy C., wife of William T., Feb. 10, 1880; d. at Pine Wood, TN, formerly of Buffalo.
East, Ann Jane, only dau. of James, Dec. 29, 1865, age 33.
East, Elizabeth, wife of James, Nov. 1, 1868, age 72.
East, Sarah Jane, wife of William R., Sept. 4, 1874, age 31.
Easterly, Daniel, Nov. 27, 1872.
Eastley, Andrew, Lancaster, NY, Oct. 26, 1871, age 22.
Eastman, Cyprian D., Black Rock (Cold Springs), NY, Sept. 10, 1852, age 44.
Eastman, Mrs. Marilla, Black Rock, NY, Sept. 11, 1852, age 38.
Eastman, Dr. Sandford, formerly of Buffalo, Jan. 8, 1874, age 53; d. at Riverside, CA, bur. in Marshall, MI.
Eastman, Sarah A., wife of Dr. Sanford, March 23, 1864.
Easton, Antoinette D., wife of James T., Aug. 26, 1858, age 39; taken to Canajoharie, NY.
Eastwick, Mrs. Catharine, July 30, 1861, age 68.
Eastwick, Capt. John, April 18, 1862, age 44 y, 4 m.
Eaton, Alexander T., Sept. 19, 1852.
Eaton, Alonzo K., Jan. 12, 1849, age 36; d. in New York.
Eaton, Anna F., wife of C. S., Oct. 25, 1868.

Eaton, Anna Maria, widow of Hon. Lewis, Dec. 8, 1879, age 84 y, 3 m.
Eaton, Augustine, formerly of Buffalo, Jan. 21, 1860, age 57 y, 3 m.; d. in New York.
Eaton, Horace, North Buffalo, Nov. 15, 1863, age 47.
Eaton, Lewis, Aug. 22, 1857, age 68.
Eaton, Lewis L., July 18, 1862.
Eaton, Myron C., formerly of Buffalo, Sept. 16, 1851; d. at Fond du Lac, WI.
Eaton, O. B., July 30, 1869, age 52; taken to Rochester, NY.
Eaton, Rufus, Springville, Feb. 1845, age 74.
Eaton, Sarah E. Leavitt, wife of R. of Albany, Jan. 6, 1860.
Eaton, Rev. Sylvester, Pastor of 1st Presbyterian Church of Buffalo, May 14, 1844, age 54; d. in Troy.
Eaton, Miss Zadia Louisa, dau. of Lewis, April 8, 1851.
Eberhardt, Rudie or Reuben, Aug. 20, 1877, age c. 20; railroad accident.
Eberhart, Christian, July 10, 1857, age 45 y, 6 m.
Ebner, Boniface, laborer, July 30, 1879, age 45.
Eck, Louis, Lancaster, May 25, 1875; suicide.
Eckardt, Henry, Aug. 9, 1870, age 84; found dead in his bed.
Eckert, Frederick, April 1874, age 22.
Eckhardt, Catherine, wife of John, Feb. 26, 1874, age 39.
Eckhart, Frances M., wife of Jacob, March 29, 1872, age 35.
Eckley, Edward, June 27, 1858 at Clifton Springs, NY, age 37; bur. in Buffalo.
Eckley, William H. E., Jan. 22, 1857, age 34.
Ecob, John, East Hamburgh, NY, Aug. 6, 1866, age 38.
Eddy, Hannah, wife of David, East Hamburgh, Feb. 16, 1844, age 66.
Eddy, Hosea, East Hamburgh, NY, Jan. 26, 1843, age 71.
Eddy, Hugh, May 26, 1849, age 37.
Eddy, Ira, formerly of MA, Springville, NY, April 14, 1826.
Eddy, Jacob, Hamburgh, July 19, 1825, age 77.
Eddy, Lucinda M., wife of Amazi, Boston, NY, March 5, 1862, age 25.
Eddy, Nancy, wife of Hosea, East Hamburgh near Potter's Corners, NY, March 3, 1862, age 81 y, 6 m.
Eddy, Deacon Nathan, East Aurora, NY, April 26, 1867, age 69.
Eddy, Osmer, Boston, NY, May 21, 1849, age 54.
Eddy, Mrs. Phebe, Boston, NY July 25, 1868, age 61.
Edes, Lucy J., wife of Alonzo B., Nov. 7, 1875, age 35; taken to Oneida Co.
Edgarton, Maria Louisa, wife of Orrin, Aug. 18, 1847, age 34.
Edge, Edward, Aug. 25, 1875, age 74.
Edge, Mary, wife of Edward, Nov. 12, 1872, age 66.
Edgerton, Almira S., wife of Orrin, May 6, 1841, age 43.
Edgerton, Emily J., wife of Julius, late of Buffalo, Sept. 10, 1849, age 21; d. in Detroit, MI.
Edgerton, Maria J., wife of Julius, Aug. 15, 1848, age 27.
Edmonds, Frank, Almshouse, May 21, 1880, age 50.
Edmonds, Mary A., wife of Thomas, July 30, 1870, age 56.
Edmonds, Thomas J., Jan. 17, 1872, age 33.
Edmunds, Eliza J., widow of Dr. James J., Sept. 29, 1876, age 60 y, 8 m.
Edmunds, Fitch C., brother of Dr. J.J., May 15, 1865, age 34.
Edmunds, Deacon James, b. Feb. 25, 1762, d. May 19, 1846, bur. Hartland, NY; Soldier of the Revolution.
Edmunds, James J., M.D., Aug. 26, 1869, age 50.
Edmunds, James J. Jr., son of the late Dr. J. J., June 24, 1874, age 24 y, 7 m.
Edmunds, Louisa, Jan. 13, 1847, age 54.
Edmunds, Mary A., wife of Nelson W., Jan. 14, 1874, age 45.
Edmunds, Nelson W., Jan. 14, 1879, age 51.
Edwards, F. H., 1st mate of Schooner *A. B. Moore*, Oct. 4, 1873; drowned at Milwaukee, WI.
Edwards, Henry E., Dec. 21, 1875, age 24; taken to Pike, Wyoming Co.
Edwards, John N., laborer, April 26, 1879, age 40.
Edwards, Marcia, formerly of Buffalo, wife of L. B., Dec. 6, 1836; d. at Fredonia, Chautauqua Co.
Edwards, Mary Ann, wife of W., June 18, 1874, age 42.

Edwards, Richard H., Sept. 3, 1865, age 45 y, 5 m, 8 d; d. at Springfield, Illinois; bur. in Buffalo.
Edwards, Robert, July 25, 1872.
Edwards, William, East Aurora, Dec. 26, 1876, age 65.
Eelbeck, Junius H., Nov. 28, 1864, age 54.
Eeles, Catharine C., Nov. 11, 1878, age 69 y, 10 m.
Eeles, Eliza A., wife of William A., Nov. 11, 1874, age 31.
Eeles, William, formerly of Buffalo, Feb. 27, 1858, age 48; d. in Baltimore, MD.
Eels, Sergt. Edward, Co. C, 116th N.Y. Vol., Alden, July 22, 1863, age 24; d. in hospital at Camp Niagara, Baton Rouge, LA.
Eels, Mrs. Hannah, Boston, NY, Sept. 16, 1859, age 83.
Efner, Elijah D., July 4, 1873, age 82.
Efner, Sophia, widow of E., Aug. 14, 1876, age 80.
Egan, John, Jan. 22, 1871, age 33.
Egan, Mrs. Margaret, June 8, 1875, age 27.
Egarton, Mercy, March 12, 1858, age 72.
Egelston, Alanson, son of Alanson, Lancaster, NY, Dec. 15, 1852, age 21 y, 6 m, at Alexandria, VA.
Egelston, Lanson, Lancaster, NY, Aug. 13, 1856, age 74.
Egelston, Malvina A., wife of E., Lancaster, Dec. 14, 1873, age 63.
Egelston, Nathaniel; son of Lanson, Lancaster, NY, Aug. 27, 1843, age 29.
Eggelston, Adaline, eldest dau. of Eri, Lancaster, April 17, 1851 at Randolph, Cattaraugus Co.
Egger, Ernest, Aug. 5, 1868, age 54.
Eggers, Charles, only son of Ernest, July 23, 1863, age 20 y, 8 m, 18 d; d. in Rochester, by falling from a railroad train.
Eggers, Conrad, March 20, 1876, age 51.
Eggers, Henrietta, widow of Ernst, Nov. 30, 1880, age 62.
Eggert, Benjamin F., merchant, Sept. 2, 1853, age 33 y, 5 m, 7 d.
Eggert, Christian, Williamsville, NY, Aug. 15, 1879, age 84.
Eggerts, C. M., Tonawanda, Aug. 9, 1861, age 30; d. at Eggertsville, NY.
Eggleston, Clarence, Co. Almshouse, May 1, 1878, age 23.
Eggleston, Eri, Cirttenden, NY, Oct. 3, 1877, age 69.
Eggleston, Hiram, Alden, NY, Feb. 14, 1870, age 62 y, 2 m, 29 d.
Eggleston, Matilda, wife of Seth, Clarence, NY, June 7, 1838, c. age 50.
Eggleston, Oliver, Aug. 7, 1872, age 23; drowned.
Egleston, Cornelius, March 10, 1845, age 23.
Ehlbeck or Elebeck, Henry N., colored, Jan. 8, 1876, age 30.
Ehle, Emma B., wife of Melvin, July 30, 1874, age 20 y, 18 d.
Ehrig, Mrs. Elizabeth, Sept. 22, 1876, age 52.
Ehrlich, Bertha, wife of Jacob, dau. of Barnett Lichtensten, Dec. 14, 1864, age 25 y, 9 m, 11 d.
Ehrmann, Dr. Louis, formerly of Buffalo, Oct. 29, 1853, at Farmington, IA.
Ehrnpforth, Charles G., Nov. 4, 1871, age 49.
Eichelsdoerfer, Michael, March 1878, age 48.
Eichenauer, John, April 21, 1875, age 62; suicide.
Eighme, Mary Anna, wife of Isaac, July 23, 1841, age 29.
Eisenberger, Katy, Nov. 29, 1873, age 27.
Eisenberger, Libbie, March 12, 1870, age 21 y, 3 m, 4 d.
Eissmann, John, Dec. 2, 1879, age 38; accidently killed.
Elder, Martin, Sept. 12, 1871, age 35; accidently killed.
Elderkin, Beulah, wife of William, Eden, NY, Aug. 16, 1838, age 57.
Elderkin, Sophia, wife of Alamath, Feb. 26, 1860, age 42; d. in Otsego, Otsego Co., NY.
Eldred, Almon, Clarence, NY, June 22, 1843, age 40.
Eldredge, Mr., June 30, 1835, age 45.
Eldredge, Solomon, Jan. 2, 1813, age 50.
Eldredge, Sylvanus, Dec. 5, 1812, age 49.
Eldridge, Benjamin, formerly of Buffalo, Feb. 6, 1879, age 78 y, 25 d.
Eldridge, Caroline Broun, wife of Samuel, April 28, 1879, age 66.
Eldridge, Eliza, wife of Benjamin, Aug. 3, 1875, age 68 y, 11 m, 3 d.

Eldridge, Elizabeth, wife of Zoeth, formerly of Buffalo, Oct. 7, 1869; d. at St. Joseph, MI.
Eldridge, Sarah, wife of Solomon, Oct. 7, 1811, age 50.
Eldridge, Willis H., son of John R., March 24, 1875, age 19.
Eley or Ely, Phelps, Buffalo Plains, July 2, 1872, age 33.
Eley, Samuel, Nov. 15, 1877, age 78.
Elgas, Mary M., Oct. 1, 1874.
Ellas, Sarah E., wife of F. S., Jan. 27, 1847, age 29.
Eller, Louise, wife of Christian, March 18, 1876, age 25; suicide.
Elles, Frederick W., son-of-law of H. Roop, Aug. 25, 1872, age 27.
Ellicott, Benjamin, Williamsville, NY, Dec. 10, 1827, age 63.
Ellicott, Joseph, late agent of Holland Land Co., Batavia, Aug. 19, 1826, age 66. D. at New York Asylum; bur. in Friends burial ground, later bur. at Batavia, NY.
Elliot, Augustus G., Springville, NY, Aug. 25, 1834, age 56.
Elliott, Anna, widow of John B., Aug. 9, 1870, age 52.
Elliott, Barnard, Nov. 4, 1876, age 46.
Elliott, Daniel, June 18, 1872, age c. 27; accidently killed.
Elliott, David, Aug. 3, 1848, aged c. 40.
Elliott, Edward, Jan. 2, 1878.
Elliott, Gilbert, Sept. 24, 1859, age 85.
Elliott, James, Oct. 6, 1872, age 24; d. in Erie, PA, bur. in Buffalo.
Elliott, John B., June 11, 1870, age 64.
Elliott, Maria T., widow of Bernard, April 20, 1879, age 48; accident by runaway team.
Elliott, Robert, July 1862, bur. the 16th.
Elliott, William, Nov. 30, 1877, age 65; at the Homeopethic Hospital.
Ellis, Mary, Aug. 17, 1877, age 53.
Ellis, Richard P., formerly of Buffalo, Sept. 7, 1874, d. in Rochester.
Ellis, Maj. William, 49th NY Vol., Aug. 1864, bur. the 11th.
Ellis, Dr. William, July 19, 1865.
Ellis, William, Nov. 18, 1880; killed by cars. (See John Sterling.)
Ellisworth, Col., May 1861.
Ellsworth, Ann Elizabeth, wife of Daniel P., March 6, 1849, age 46.
Ellsworth, Caroline, dau. of Daniel P., June 5, 1851.
Elmore, John J., 1st Engineer, Steamboat *Wayne*; funeral May 1, 1850.
Elsesser, Dorotha, wife of John, North Buffalo, Aug. 29, 1871, age 72.
Elwell, Joseph L., "Indian Doctor," Nov. 17, 1872, age 75.
Elwood, Mrs. Elizabeth H., June 27, 1872, age 49.
Elwood, George R., May 25, 1873, age 28.
Ely, Deacon Calvin, Cheektowaga, NY, March 25, 1877, age 77.
Ely, Elizabeth, wife of Samuel, May 12, 1872, age 74.
Ely, Emily, wife of Israel N., Lancaster, NY, May 3, 1858.
Ely, Israel, formerly of Lyme, CT, Cheektowaga, NY, Jan. 4, 1855, age 85. A resident of Buffalo and vicinity for 36 y.
Ely, Israel N., formerly of Lancaster, NY Jan. 27, 1873.
Ely, Mary A., wife of E. Selden, Cheektowaga, NY, Dec. 22, 1863.
Ely, Miss Mary Ann, May 5, 1839, age 32.
Emeigh, Anna, sister of Mrs. George B. Allen, Jan. 28, 1876.
Emeigh, Mrs., wife of Michael, April 5, 1853, age 49.
Emeigh, Francis A., Nov. 20, 1866, age 29.
Emeigh, Miss Sarah, dau. of Michael, Dec. 21, 1854, age 21.
Emerick, Caroline L., wife of Jacob, April 17, 1870, age 52.
Emerick, Mrs. Frederika, Aug. 29, 1851, age 59 y, 10 m.
Emerick, Jacob Jr., Nov. 17, 1873, age 20 y, 8 m.
Emerick, Louis, Jan. 3, 1880, age 64.
Emerson, Lydia Minerva, wife of Gen. Charles D., 2d dau. of Capt. Stephen Champlin, U.S. Army, March 2, 1863, age 37, at St. Paul, MN.
Emerson, Margaret Geddes, wife of Charles A., formerly of Buffalo, Oct. 13, 1875, age 63 y, 10 m; d. at Riga, NY, bur. in Lancaster, NY.
Emerson, Mary Ann, widow of Nathaniel, dau. of Thomas Rathbun, Nov. 26, 1859, age 35.
Emerson, Nathaniel, May 20, 1859 at Oshkosh, WI, bur. in Buffalo.

Emerson, Sarah Ann, wife of Nelson, Aurora, Nov. 27, 1839, age 26.
Emery, Cornelia J., wife of Edson F., Aug. 20, 1877, age 39.
Emery, Daniel F., formerly of Buffalo, July 12, 1876, age 68; d. at Portland, Ionia Co., MI.
Emery, James, Jan. 6, 1879, age 63.
Emery, Col. Josiah, South Wales, NY, Aug. 14, 1873, age 90.
Emery, Moses L., Aurora, NY, Aug. 2, 1840, age 25.
Emery, Susan, wife of Col. Josiah, Aurora, NY, Feb. 5, 1861, age 80 y, 3 m, 22 d.
Emmons, Alexander H., March 21, 1872, age 65.
Emmons, Carlos, M.D., Dec. 12, 1875, age 76 y, 5 m, 25 d; d. in Springville, NY.
Emmons, Frederick W., Jan. 14, 1856, age 46.
Emmons, Harriet, wife of Dr. Carlos, Springville, May 22, 1845.
Emmons, Lucy C., wife of A. H., Jan. 10, 1866, age 49.
Emslie, Emogene A., wife of Peter, Sept. 22, 1851, age 23.
Emslie, Marion, wife of George, April 15, 1879, age 46.
Enck, Benjamin, Williamsville, Oct. 15, 1879, age 87 y, 4 m, 25 d.
Endris, Gabrela, Feb. 4, 1879, age 72 y, 10 m, 20 d.
Engel, Herman, June 12, 1876, age 72.
Englehardt, Peter, March 18, 1879, age 28; railroad accident.
Engleman, Charles, Aurora, Nov. 21, 1871, age c. 46.
English, Abel, Hamburgh, Aug. 22, 1832, age 80.
English, Anna, Hamburgh, NY, widow of Abel, March 16, 1854, age 98; d. at Angelica, NY.
English, Ruth, wife of William, May 5, 1872, age 59 y, 7 m.
English, William, June 19, 1880, age 59.
Enos, Esther, wife of Elisha, Dec. 1812, age 28, Hamburgh, NY.
Enos, James, Aurora, June 26, 1842, age 74.
Enos, Laurens, Feb. 6, 1871, age 42.
Enos, Olive, widow of Harvey, Nov., 27, 1879, Colden, NY.
Enos, William L., Co. E, 100th N.Y. Vol., son of Capt. E. M. of Wales Center, Dec. 10, 1864, age 26, at Naval School Hospital, MD.
Enright, Honoria, June 6, 1877, age 37.
Ensfield, Catharine, wife of George, June 29, 1857, age 59.
Ensign, Charles, Dec. 3, 1880.
Ensign, Edward, brother of E.W., Aug. 31, 1868; d. at Clifton Springs, bur. Buffalo.
Ensign, Elisha, Sept. 12, 1852, age 68 in Chippewa, Canada West.
Ensign, Elisha W., Oct. 1, 1877, age 56.
Ensign, Elizabeth, youngest dau. of Elisha, Sept. 3, 1852, age 21.
Ensign, Olive, wife of Elisha, April 13, 1837, age 43.
Ensign, Royal, Hamburgh, NY, Jan. 25, 1835, age 30.
Ensworth, Dr. Azel, late of Rochester, NY, May 5, 1854, age 95.
Entwistle, Robert, Sept. 12, 1878.
Epperlee, Frederick, formerly of Buffalo, Oct. 23, 1870; d. in Cleveland, OH.
Erchbach, David, Grand Island, Jan. 21, 1874, age 23.
Erdman, Theodore, April 29, 1874.
Erickson, Elling, March 22, 1875, age 47 y, 6 m.
Erickson, Katie, dau. of the late Allen, June 6, 1875, age 19 y, 4 m.
Erisman, Martin, Dec. 17, 1872, age 74.
Erlenbach, Adam, March 18, 1876, age 41.
Ernst, Dora M., fore of J. Fred., July 29, 1874, age 24 y, 10 m, 29 d.
Ernst, Frances E., wife of Capt. J. Frederick, Jr., dau. of Samuel Haines, Sept. 16, 1867.
Ernst, Mrs. George D., June 10, 1873, age 35.
Ernst, John A., formerly of Buffalo, Aug. 16, 1873, age 29; d. in Chicago, bur. in Buffalo.
Ernst, Miss Kate, dau. of Christian, Cheektowaga, NY, Jan. 18, 1865, age 28 y, 9 m.
Ernst, Mrs. Mary Ann, July 1878, age 23.
Ernst, Michael, July 11, 1876, age 66 y, 1 d.
Ernst, Philip, July 24, 1870, age 72.
Ernst, William, April 3, 1870, age 26 y, 5 m, 25 d.
Errington, John, East Hamburgh, NY, April 9, 1876, age 38.
Erwin, Margaret E., wife of Henry C., formerly of MS, June 29, 1856, age 26.
Eschenfelder, Daniel, Aug. 3, 1874, age 25.

Escott, William, March 9, 1879.
Estabrook, Ebenezer H., Oct. 7, 1861, age 50.
Estabrook, John, Alden, Feb. 9, 1864, age 71.
Estabrook, Nehemiah, b. Aug. 27, 1749, d. 1826, bur. Alden, NY; Soldier of the Revolution.
Estee, J., Eden, March 31, 1861, age 73.
Ettinger, Michael, Aug. 21, 1874, age 59.
Eugent (or Nugent), James H., form. of Buffalo, May 21, 1875, age c. 25; railroad accident.
Euluer (or Euller), Mrs. Maria Annie, Nov. 5, 1850, age 37.
Eustaphieve, Alexander Alexis, Aug. 20, 1879, age 67.
Eustaphieve, Emily, wife of Alexander A., Oct. 10, 1872, age 53.
Eva, Margaret, wife of Adam, July 1, 1861, age 33.
Evans, Amelia LaGrange, wife of Lewis E., Sept. 14, 1874, age 45.
Evans, C. Galon, July 28, 1866, age 42.
Evans, Eliza Jane, wife of O. M., June 2, 1848, age 30.
Evans, Garrett, son of Lewis E., Aug. 28, 1872, age 24.
Evans, Jane A., wife of James C., April 29, 1870, age 66; d. at Lewiston, NY, bur. Buffalo.
Evans, John R., Dec. 5, 1861, age 54.
Evans, Labin, Sept. 11, 1823, age 45.
Evans, Letitia, June 4, 1841, age 79.
Evans, Lewis E., Williamsville, NY, Dec. 17, 1827, age 45.
Evans, Mrs. Margaret, March 19, 1872, age 90.
Evans, Margarett, April 25, 1880, dau. of Lewis.
Evans, Mrs. Mariam, Aug. 12, 1852, age 73.
Evans, Mary Ann, wife of Henry B., formerly of Williamsville, NY, Jan. 29, 1859, age 46, in East Troy, Walworth Co., WI.
Evans, Mary Ann, May 5, 1878.
Evans, Mary Jane, wife of Robert M., April 1872.
Evans, Mary S., wife of Henry B., May 16, 1876.
Evans, Moses, formerly of Skaneateles, NY, March 15, 1838, age 30.
Evans, O., formerly of Buffalo, photographer, June 22, 1878; d. at Titusville, PA, bur. Buffalo.
Evans, Robert, Aug. 29, 1867, age 30.
Evans, Sarah Ellicott Grant, wife of Edwin T., Aug. 7, 1873, age 35.
Evans, Sarah J., April 15, 1879, age 59.
Evans, Susan, wife of Evan B., April 3, 1864, in Niles, OH; bur. in Buffalo.
Evans, William, March 9, 1840, age 62.
Evans, William, brother of Richard, March 24, 1870, age 67.
Evans, William A., Aug. 21, 1880, age 63; d. at Lewiston, NY, formerly of Buffalo.
Evarts, Emily Louisa, wife of Henry, Oct. 9, 1876, age 34.
Evens, John, eldest son of Richard, Nov. 5, 1861, age 22, at Morris, IL; bur. in Buffalo.
Everett, Mrs. Polly, Jan. 13, 1858, age 87.
Everhart, Mary Ann, wife of Jacob, May 1, 1877, age 60 y, 10 m.
Evers, Capt. John P., Dec. 19, 1874, age 46.
Everson, John, Feb. 24, 1869, age 76 y, 21 d.
Everson, Mrs. M. H., March 2, 1872, age 67.
Eves, Mrs. Mary, June 22, 1874, age 81.
Ewart, Miss Elizabeth, April 6, 1878, age 20 y, 2 m, 15 d.
Ewell, Dexter, Alden, NY, Feb. 28, 1872, age 67.
Ewers, Charles, North Evans, NY, Dec. 4, 1871, age 75.
Ewing, Harriet Clark, wife of Benjamin, late of Toronto, July 26, 1872.
Exelby, Richard, March 27, 1873, age 42; funeral at Angola, NY.

Faber, Segt. John, Co. F, 65th NY Regt., Feb. 13, 1869, age 19.
Faber, Michael, June 27, 1872, age c. 28; found dead in Erie, PA.
Fahey, Joseph, Sept. 18, 1878, age 23 y, 9 m.
Fahey, Malachi, Dec. 28, 1876, age 42.
Fahey, Michael T., Dec. 2, 1879, age 20 y, 8 m.
Fahey, Patrick, May 7, 1872, age c. 23; shot by John Gaffney.
Failing, Catharine, wife of R., Tonawanda, NY, April 28, 1867, age 74 y, 6 m.
Failing, David, Wales, Nov. 30, 1862, age 70.

Failing, Richard, Tonawanda, NY, April 27, 1868, age 81.
Fairbank, James, Aurora, NY, Jan. 18, 1851, age 73.
Fairbanks, Dr. James F., East Aurora, NY, Sept. 10, 1879, age 50.
Fairbanks, Mary, wife of Willard, Feb. 13, 1840, age 31. [no card]
Fairbrother, Thomas, Indian Reservation, June 15, 1844, age 70.
Fairchild, Miss Betsey, July 2, 1833, age 21.
Fairchild, John, April 14, 1868, age 31.
Fairchild, Margaret, wife of Caleb, June 4, 1832, age 60.
Fairfield, James L., Dec. 27, 1875, age 45 y, 6 m.
Fairchild, Nathaniel, b. 1752, d. 1837, bur. Harris Hill; Soldier of the Revolution.
Fairfix (or Fairfax), Maria, April 21, 1879, age 70 or 66; sudden death.
Fairman, Franklin F., Dec. 14, 1860, age 50; bur. in Greenwood Cemetery, Brooklyn, NY.
Falconer, Miss Ruth Hughes, Tonawanda, NY, May 6, 1863, age 73.
Falconer, Miss Sarah M., Tonawanda, NY, Sept. 27, 1838, age 54; recently of New York, NY.
Fales, Henry, Grand Island, May 31, 1873, age 82 y, 11 m.
Fales, Maria, wife of Henry, Aug. 4, 1829.
Fallis, Mrs. Janet, Feb. 13, 1865, age 60.
Fallon, Edward, Co. Almshouse, Jan. 26, 1879, age 32.
Falvery, Ellen, wife of Michael, Sept. 10, 1874, age 34.
Falvey, Catherine, wife of Michael, Jan. 1, 1869, age 37.
Falvey, Mrs. Mary, April 1, 1874, age 69.
Famous, John A., Nov. 11, 1879, age 21; drowned in canal.
Fancher, Rufus, father of Mrs. Dr. Lockwood of Buffalo, Alden, Feb. 8, 1864, age 87.
Fanner, Mrs. Maria, Oct. 18, 1879, age 52 y, 10 m.
Fanning, Mrs. Amy, Black Rock, NY, March 17, 1832, age 58.
Fanning, Henrietta, sister of Mrs. James McKnight, Nov. 9, 1863.
Fanning, John, April 6, 1831, age 62.
Fanning, Capt. Jonathan, Revolutionary Soldier, Evans, NY, May 30, 1844, age 90. [Another
    card: Fanning. Capt. Jonathan, b. May 13, 1754, d. May 30-31, 1844, bur. Derby, NY;
    Soldier of the Revolution.]
Fanning, Rufus, Tonawanda, Sept. 27, 1875, age 75.
Fargo, Libbie M. Prendergast, widow of William G., Jr., Oct. 11, 1873, age 24.
Fargo, Marietta Perry, wife of Francis F., May 4, 1880.
Fargo, Orin W., Aug. 20, 1877, age 34.
Fargo, Tacie, wife of William C., mother of William G. and Jerome of Buffalo, Nov. 9, 1869,
    age 70; d. in Syracuse, bur. Buffalo.
Fargo, William C., father of William G. and Jerome F., Syracuse, March 16, 1878, age 87;
    bur. in Buffalo.
Fargo, William G., Jr., Dec. 30, 1872, age 27.
Farley, Michael, Jan. 28, 1874, age 26 y, 5 m.
Farmer, Mary, wife of William G., Oct. 28, 1874, age 52.
Farmer, Mrs. Robert, West Seneca, Dec. 6, 1874, age 48; funeral at White's Corners, NY.
Farmer, Terence, April 10, 1872, age 49.
Farmer, William, Aug. 4, 1865, age 71.
Farnham, Lt. Charles S., May 12, 1862, age 24, in Nelson Hospital, Yorktown; bur. in
    Buffalo.
Farnham, George D., Aug. 21, 1853, age 50; bur. Silver Creek, NY.
Farnham, Horatio N., formerly of Buffalo, Aug. 30, 1877, age 37; accident, d. at
    Minneapolis, MN.
Farnham, Leroy, May 19, 1866, age 66 y, 11 d.
Farnham, Lucy B., wife of Walter R., formerly of Holland, NY, May 15, 1876, age 57; d. in
    Bergen, NY.
Farnham, Pamelia S., wife of J. B., Dec. 5, 1845, age 25.
Farnham, Walter R., brother of Thomas of Buffalo, formerly of Holland, NY, June 28, 1876,
    age 59; drowned in St. Louis.
Farnham, William E., formerly of Buffalo, Sept. 24, 1878, age 33; d. at East Portland, OR.
Farnsworth, Mrs. Abigail, Sept. 8, 1862, age 69.
Farnsworth, Sarah, widow of Levi, Boston, NY, April 4, 1849, age 78.
Farnsworth, Sophia, wife of Thomas, Alden, NY, Sept. 11, 1862, age 58.
Farr, Abby, widow of Rinaldo, formerly of Buffalo, Sept. 29, 1871; d. in Brooklyn, NY.

Farr, Marietta Chase, wife of J. S., Lancaster, NY, Nov. 8, 1864, age 42 y, 7 m.
Farr, Mrs. Polly, mother of Rinaldo of Buffalo, Lancaster, NY, Aug. 21, 1859, age 74.
Farr, Ralston A., Aug. 1874, age 74.
Farr, Rinaldo, formerly of Buffalo, March 7, 1865, age 55; d. in Brooklyn, NY.
Farrand, Minerva P., wife of Augustus, dau. of William Paxson, East Hamburgh, NY, Sept. 16, 1850, age 23.
Farre, Mary Ann, Dec. 26, 1879, age 73.
Farrell, Andrew, Nov. 29, 1875, age c. 60.
Farrell, Ann, wife of Michael, Feb. 19, 1880, age 74.
Farrell, Annie, wife of Timothy, April 29, 1879, age 40.
Farrell, James, Jan. 12, 1876, age 54.
Farrell, Mary, wife of C.J., Oct. 1874, age 32.
Farron, Augusta Roach, wife of Augustus, Dec. 17, 1877, age 30.
Farthing, Mary Ann, Jan. 6, 1865, age 31.
Farthing, William, July 1877, age 52.
Farwell, Eldridge, Cheektowaga, NY, Jan. 27, 1864, age 52.
Farwell, Maj. Joseph, Oct. 23, 1813, age 41.
Farwell, Lucy S., wife of Eldridge, June 24, 1840, age 23 y, 11 m.
Farwell, William, father of Henry D., June 21, 1862, age 64; taken to NH.
Fasset, Elisha, Hamburgh, NY. June 25, 1844, age 61.
Fassett, Mary Ann, wife of A. D., Aug. 27, 1849, age 30.
Fattey, Louisa, wife of George L., Jan. 20, 1857, age 27.
Fauderlein, William, Dec. 24, 1870, age 40.
Faul, Elizabeth, wife of Gottfried, July 29, 1866, age 51 y, 11 m, 9 d.
Faulkner, Alice, wife of George, Oct. 4, 1880, age 53.
Faulkner, Caroline, widow of Morgan L., April 23, 1854, age 42 y, 7 m, 14 d.
Faulkner, James R., Jan. 18, 1879, age 46 y, 4 m; d. at Houston, TX, brought to Buffalo.
Faulkner, Morgan Lewis, March 9, 1845, age 40.
Faust, William N., July 5, 1869.
Faver, Margaret, wife of Peter, April 8, 1872, age 59.
Favor, Mrs. Mary Ann, wife of James, Dec. 26, 1879, age 72.
Faxon, Charles O., formerly of Buffalo, Jan. 27, 1870, age c. 47; d. at Clarksville, TN.
Faxon, Lt. Daniel E., June 19, 1862, age 27 y, 7 m, 13 d; in Hospital of 36th Regt. NY Vol., Fair Oaks, VA, bur. in Buffalo.
Faxon, Maj. Elihu J., May 3, 1863, age 24 y, 8 m, 8 d. Killed in battle at Fredericksburg, VA, bur. in Buffalo.
Faxon, Henry W., 24th N.Y. Cavalry, Sept. 11, 1864. Formerly of Buffalo Press. D. in Harwood Hospital, Washington.
Faxon, James, March 1870, age 62. US Consul at Curacoa since 1864; father of Maj. and Capt. Faxon who were killed in the Union Army during the late Rebellion; bur. in Buffalo.
Faxon, Lucy A., widow of Charles and sister of O. G. Steele, formerly of Buffalo, May 21, 1874; d. at Clarksville, TN.
Faxon, Henry, Almshouse, May 18, 1880, age 69.
Fay, Cyrus M., d. in San Juan, Dec. 12, 1850, age 45.
Fay, Jane M., wife of Amos F., March 10, 1859, age 36.
Fay, Dr. Levi, Aug. 12, 1877, age 84 y, 5 m; taken to Bergen, NY.
Fay, Luana, wife of Ward, March 2, 1870, age 34.
Fayfield, Franklin E., Nov. 14, 1880, age 26; d. at Jackson, MI.
Feason or Tearson, Frederick, Tonawanda, NY, June 18, 1872, age 26.
Featherston, Thomas, formerly of Sandy Hill, Washington Co., April 10, 1849, age 58.
Featherston, Thomas, Sept. 22, 1857, age 32 y, 5 m, 21 d.
Frederickson, Christian, Feb. 14, 1874, age 48.
Fee, George, April 4, 1869, age 29.
Feeney, Mary, wife of John, Jan. 4, 1876, age 45.
Feil, Rosina, wife of Gottleib, Jan. 19, 1874, age 44 y, 14 d.
Feist, Mathias, Aug. 11, 1880, age 76 y, 7 m.
Feist, Rosa, wife of John, Jan. 19, 1880, age 34.
Feldman, Rev. Henry, Pastor, St. Boniface Church, Nov. 30, 1880, age 55.
Filmore, Cyrus, b. 1758, d. Feb. 18, 1846, bur. East Aurora, NY; Soldier of the Revolution.
Flegemaker, Caroline B., widow of Dr. Joseph A., Jan. 2, 1879, age 64 y, 6 m.

Fellner, Magdalena, wife of Louis, Feb. 22, 1880, age 54 y, 9 m.
Fellows, Abraham, formerly of Troy, March 24, 1851, age 62.
Fellows, Dora Louise, wife of Adrian W., June 22, 1877.
Fellows, Edwin R., formerly of New London, CT, July 14, 1861, age 49.
Fellows, Harriet, widow of Abram, March 14, 1869, age 77.
Fellows, J. C., formerly of Buffalo, Feb. 28, 1879; d. in Brooklyn, NY, brought to Buffalo.
Fellows, James H., Dec. 29, 1863, age 44 y, 9 m, 22 d.
Fellows, Capt. John, March 24, 1874, age 61; d. at Ft. Erie, Ontario, bur. Buffalo.
Fellows, John H., Oct. 14, 1876, age 26 y, 5 m, 18 d; railroad accident.
Fellows, Mary Ann, wife of William R., July 16, 1846, age 24.
Fellows, Relief G., widow of Capt. John, formerly of Buffalo, April 8, 1880.
Feltes or Felton, Elizabeth, wife of Nicholas, Feb. 16, 1872, age 45.
Felton, Ellen Jane, wife of Charles E., June 13, 1872, age 33; d. in Chicago, bur. in Buffalo.
Felton, Mrs., Clarence, Jan. 1813, age 70.
Fenner, Clifford A., eldest son of Hon. Seth, East Aurora, NY, April 26, 1877, age 24.
Feno, Moses, Clarence, killed at Battle of Black Rock, Dec. 30, 1813.
Fenry, Michael, Aug. 8, 1872, age 28.
Fenton, Daniel, July 17, 1873, age 23.
Fenton, Sarah H., widow of Solomon, Brant, NY, Nov. 19, 1871, age 73.
Fenton, Solomon, Brant, NY, March 7, 1870, age 69.
Ferguson, James, Clarence, NY, Aug. 11, 1817, age 55.
Ferguson, James, formerly of Toronto, Canada, printer, July 30, 1859, age 19.
Ferguson, James A., formerly of Buffalo, Dec. 29, 1870, age 29; d. in St. Louis, taken to London, Ontario.
Ferguson, John, Nov. 5, 1847, age 28.
Ferguson, John B., Nov. 2, 1878, age 34 y, 9 m.
Ferguson, Mary, wife of Alonzo, Dec. 22, 1858, age 33.
Ferguson, Robert, a young blacksmith, April 23, 1845; d. of hydrophobia.
Ferguson, Sarah, widow of Andrew, Jan. 12, 1880, age 61.
Ferguson, Mrs. Susan, May 25, 1880, age 76.
Ferguson, Terrence, July 17, 1864, age 55.
Ferguson, William, master builder, Aug. 3, 1871, age 50; d. at Duluth, MN.
Fernlacher, John G., Sept. 13, 1879, age 50.
Fero, Abram, eldest son of Robert, June 28, 1853, age 28; d. in Chicago, bur. in Buffalo.
Fero, Alonzo, June 9, 1866, age 30.
Fero, Edward B., Dec. 20, 1869, age 26.
Fero, John, June 18, 1862, age 49 y, 10 m, 10 d.
Fero, Nancy Bilinger, mother of Robert, April 3, 1867, age 89.
Fero, Nancy Catharine, eldest dau. of Robert, Sept. 25, 1848, age 19 y, 6 m, 15 d.
Fero, O. Emerson, March 27, 1864, age 25.
Fero, Robert, May 28, 1873, age 71; d. at Alden, NY, bur. Buffalo.
Fero, Robert, Jr., Sept. 4, 1862, age 28 y, 6 m, 25 d.
Fero, Stephen R., son of Robert, May 11, 1861, age 29 y, 6 m, 13 d.
Ferrand, George L., Cheektowaga, Nov. 23, 1880, age 30 y, 4 m.
Ferrell, Capt. John, Oct. 29, 1857, age 29.
Ferrell, Merritt, youngest brother of Capt. John, Sept. 17, 1858, age 20 y, 4 m, 14 d.
Ferris, Charles W., Feb. 23, 1870, age 34.
Ferris, Edward, April 11, 1869, age 30.
Ferris, Ellen M., Nov. 1876.
Ferris, Helen M., dau. of Mrs. H. A. and the late Charles D., Nov. 26, 1876, age 33.
Ferris, Isaac W., late of Buffalo, East Hamburgh, NY, Aug. 5, 1851, age 24.
Ferris, Mrs. Margaret, widow of Isaac W., March 12, 1852.
Ferris, Mary L., dau. of Christopher, Nov. 2, 1872, age 31 y, 8 m.
Ferris, Nancy A., wife of Nathaniel P., formerly of Buffalo, Sept. 23, 1850 in Cincinnati.
Ferris, William B., Nov. 14, 1879, age 24; d. at Black River, MI, formerly of Buffalo.
Ferris, William W., Dec. 19, 1876, age 39.
Ferris, Dr. Zechariah, April 3, 1836, age 27.
Ferron, Thomas, Feb. 28, 1874, age 25.
Feth, John J., Oct. 11, 1880, age 85; sudden death.

Fettmiller, Philip, Co. Almshouse, Jan. 11, 1876, age 70.
Fetzer, George, Tonawanda, NY, Jan. 25, 1877.
Fickes, Francis, Feb. 4, 1866, age 38.
Fiedler, Christian, Oct. 7, 1874, age c. 38; d. from injuries.
Fiedler, Mary L., widow of Francis, July 4, 1877, age 51.
Fiedler, William, Jan. 20, 1873, drowned.
Field, Annie, wife of Charles, May 27, 1880, age 35.
Field, Deacon Asa, Clarence, Dec. 6, 1831, age 75.
Field, Betsey W., wife of Asa, July 9, 1832, age 27.
Field, Mrs. Charles, July 25, 1844, age 22.
Field, Charles B., 132nd Reg., N.Y. State Vol., brother of M. D. Field, April 30, 1865, age 58; d. at Davids Island Hospital.
Field, Capt. George P., U.S. Army, Sept. 21, 1846, age 33. Fell at the head of his company at Monterey, Mexico.
Field, H. A., wife of James, Lancaster, NY, Sept. 4, 1878.
Field, Jance C., wife of Capt. Charles, Nov. 22, 1841, age 41.
Fielder, Francis, Nov. 6, 1874, age 53.
Fielder, Louise, wife of Alexander and dau. of John Smith of Buffalo, formerly of Buffalo, March 30, 1870; bur. Buffalo.
Fieldman or Feldman, Antohny, July 13, 1870, age 69.
Fields, Charles, Almshouse, Jan. 7, 1880, age 46.
Fields, Mrs. Emma, Jan. 20, 1863, age 68.
Fields, Jane, Co. Almshouse, Feb. 15, 1879, age 42.
Fields, Thomas C., April 29, 1879, age 55.
Fields, William, Dec. 31, 1880, age 48.
Fields, William A., April 9, 1868, age 32.
Fields, William P., Nov. 31, 1845, age 65.
Fiescholtz, Andrew, March 12, 1873, age 60.
Filkins, Warren, Lancaster, March 30, 1862, age 55.
Fillmore, Rev. A. N., Aug. 23, 1880, cousin of Millard Fillmore; d. at Watkins NY. Vicinity of Buffalo.
Fillmore, Abigail Powers, wife of Hon. Millard, March 29, 1853, in Washington, D.C., bur. in Buffalo. Born March 13, 1798 at Stillwater, Saratoga Co., NY.
Fillmore, Almon H., late of Buffalo, Aurora, Jan. 17, 1830, age 25.
Fillmore, Col. Calvin, East Aurora, NY, Oct. 22, 1865, age 90.
Fillmore, Charles D., brother of Hon. Millard, July 27, 1854, age 36; d. St. Paul, MN.
Fillmore, Darius J., March 9, 1837, age 23; d. Aurora, NY.
Fillmore, Rev. Gleazen, D.D., Clarence, Jan. 26, 1875, age 85.
Fillmore, Jerusha, wife of Calvin, East Aurora, NY, Jan. 4, 1852, age 73 y, 9 m.
Fillmore, Lois, wife of Sherlock, Clarence, Feb. 4, 1844, age 46.
Fillmore, Lucy, wife of Simeon, Clarence, March 31, 1844, age 73.
Fillmore, Miss Maria P., Aurora, NY, dau. of Nathaniel, sister of Hon. Millard, July 2, 1843, age 23; d. at Adrian, MI.
Fillmore, Miss Mary Abbie, only dau. of Hon. Millard, July 26, 1854, age 22; d. at Aurora, NY, bur. in Buffalo.
Fillmore, Millard, March 8, 1874, age 74 y, 2 m, 1 d.
Fillmore, Nathaniel, father of Hon. Millard, East Aurora, NY, March 28, 1863, age 92.
Fillmore, Phebe, wife of Nathaniel, Aurora, April 2, 1831, age 49.
Fillmore, Simeon, Clarence, NY, May 1, 1848, age 84.
Fillmore, Susan, wife of Simeon, Clarence, Dec. 30, 1825, age 59.
Finch, Cynthia, widow of Ephraim, April 20, 1872, age 77.
Finch, Col. Ephraim, father of Mrs. Dr. William Treat, Oct. 18, 1863, age 66; d. High Street Hospital.
Finch, Eveline, wife of Andrew J., June 30, 1878, age 48.
Finch, Mrs. Mary, May 14, 1855, age 85.
Findlay, Ellen, dau. of James, Sept. 9, 1873, age 21.
Finegan, Frank A., Nov. 23, 1870, age 22.
Finegan, Joseph S., Jan. 24, 1870, age 23.
Fink, Mrs. Barbara, Feb. 28, 1880, age 64 y, 5 m.
Fink, Christian, mother of Mrs. M. Hottinger, June 12, 1867, age 74.

Fink, George, East Aurora, Aug. 14, 1876, age 54.
Finkenshaedt, Ferdinand L., formerly of Buffalo, May 9, 1879, age 27; d. in San Francisco.
Finkenstaedt, Margaret, wife of R., Jan. 23, 1872, age 32.
Finley, Alexander, Aug. 31, 1852, age 35.
Finley, Miss Eliza, sister of Mrs. A. Dickey, Oct. 24, 1867.
Finley, Ellen, wife of James, July 21, 1865, age 34.
Finley, George, Feb. 8, 1865, age 39.
Finley, James, July 21, 1865, age 71.
Finley, James, Colden, Sept. 17, 1871, age c. 80; d. in Buffalo.
Finley, James, May 22, 1872, age 34.
Finley, John, June 6, 1860, age 60.
Finley, John, April 10, 1874, age 41 y, 4 m.
Finley, William, July 22, 1876, age 30.
Finn, Catherine, Oct. 11, 1878, age 71.
Finnegan, Jessie, May 2, 1879, age 40; sudden death.
Finnigan, Hattie, Co. Almshouse, Sept. 22, 1879, age 25.
Finnick (or Finon), George, Oct. 25, 1872.
Firkins, Mrs. William, 575 No. Washington St., Black Rock, NY, July 14, 1873, age 30; accident.
Fischer, Paul, March 14, 1873, age c. 47.
Fish, Miss Adeline, dau. of Anson, East Hamburgh, NY, Aug. 14, 1852, age 20.
Fish, Daniel, East Hamburgh, NY, March 27, 1845, age 55.
Fish, Major H. H., April 1865, funeral April 8.
Fish, Harriet M., widow of the late James M., Feb. 12, 1868, age 35.
Fish, James M., Aug. 19, 1860, age 50; taken to Rochester.
Fish, John S., Dec. 20, 1874, age 36.
Fish, Joshua, June 12, 1860, age 72; taken to Rochester.
Fish, Lydia, East Hamburgh, NY, Aug. 5, 1852, age 77.
Fish, Mary, wife of Edward P., Feb. 20, 1868.
Fish, Miss Mary K., late of Chelsea, VT, Eden, NY, Jan. 31, 1832, age 28.
Fish, Platt S., East Hamburgh, NY, March 19, 1874, age 74.
Fish, Sally, wife of Anson T., East Hamburgh, NY, July 10, 1850, age 43.
Fish, Thomas, Hamburgh, Aug. 4, 1822, age 52.
Fish, Thomas M., formerly of Buffalo, Feb. 7, 1863, age 46; in Geneseo, IL.
Fisher, Barney, grocer, formerly of Buffalo, May 12, 1879, age 25.
Fisher, Corp. Charles M., 11th IN Vol., Oct. 19, 1864, age 18. Formerly of 21st N.Y.S.V. Killed at battle of Cedar Creek, VA, bur. in Buffalo May 23, 1865.
Fisher, Mrs. Cyrus M., dau. of Ripley, formerly of Buffalo, April 1873, age 39. Lost on Steamship *Atlantic*.
Fisher, Francis, Sept. 21, 1871, age 55 y, 6 m.
Fisher, Frederick, Clarence, NY, Nov. 30, 1873, age 23; suicide.
Fisher, George, son of Michael, June 15, 1870, age 22; d. in St. Louis, bur. Buffalo.
Fisher, Hannah, wife of James and mother of James H., June 9, 1865, age 68. Taken to Rochester.
Fisher, Jacob, Dec. 10, 1867, age 29 y, 3 m, 26 d.
Fisher, James, formerly of Buffalo, Aug. 9, 1877, age 82; d. in Rochester, NY.
Fisher, John, Oct. 2, 1878, age 25; railroad accident.
Fisher, John, Jr., Oct. 8, 1872, age 50; d. at Marshalltown, IA.
Fisher, John P., Feb. 1, 1875, age 46.
Fisher, Josephine, wife of Jacob P., June 2, 1862, age 24 y, 28 d.
Fisher, Mary, wife of Rev. D., Tonawanda, NY, Feb. 4, 1880, age 64 y, 11 m, 25 d.
Fisher, Mary Ann, wife of Martin, Dec. 25, 1867, age 67.
Fisher, Otto, 91st Regt. NY Vol., native of Prussia, Sept. 5, 1864, at Soldier's Rest.
Fisher, Ross, Co. Almshouse, July 2, 1878, age 37.
Fisher, William P., formerly of Buffalo, Aug. 22, 1862, age 25, in Hamilton, Canada West.
Fisk, Anna Mary, widow of Rev. Harvey, Gowanda, NY, March 24, 1872, age 66.
Fisk, Eliza, wife of William, Clarence, NY, May 27, 1829, age 29.
Fisk, Ezra, June 26, 1874, age 55; suicide.
Fisk, Mrs. Maria, eldest dau. of Gamaliel St. John, mother of Mrs. Orson Phelps, March 27, 1864, age 73.; d. in Cleveland, bur. Buffalo.

Fisk, Sylvanus, June 18, 1864, age 89 y, 4 m.
Fisk, Capt. William, Lancaster, NY, March 30, 1845, age 50.
Fiske, Charles, Jan. 28, 1876, age 30; d. at Los Angeles, CA, bur. in Buffalo.
Fiske, Delavan D., late of Buffalo, Lancaster, NY, Feb. 27, 1827, age 33.
Fiske, Mrs. Mary, mother of Mrs. James Allen, White's Corners, NY, Sept. 14, 1852, age 64.
Fiske, Susan, wife of William, Sept. 19, 1852, age 42.
Fiske, William, Dec. 4, 1873, age 67.
Fitch, Anna Palmer, wife of William C., Feb. 7, 1873, age 21.
Fitch, Augustus B., formerly of Buffalo, Oct. 15, 1880, age 46; funeral at Norton, CT.
Fitch, Rev. Charles formerly of Cleveland, OH, Oct. 14, 1844, age 40.
Fitch, Charlotte, wife of William, late of Batavia, NY, April 24, 1836, age 34. D. of consumption.
Fitch, Eliza H., wife of Augustus B., April 24, 1868.
Fitch, George, Collins Center, NY, Aug. 3, 1848, age 45.
Fitch, Henry S., formerly of Buffalo, Nov. 16, 1870, age 66; d. in Strongville, OH.
Fitch, Julia F., wife of William, 1846, age 33; d. in Darien, CT.
Fitch, Mrs. N. H., formerly of Norwich, CT, March 22, 1848, age 56.
Fitch, Sarah E., wife of Francis S., June 6, 1863, age 34.
Fitch, William, June 7, 1866, age 66.
Fitts, Dr. Franklin, Dec. 8, 1839, age 28.
Fitzgerald, Daniel, May 23, 1871.
Fitzgerald, Garrett, Jan. 8, 1875, age 70.
Fitzgerald, James, April 28, 1874, age 45; killed by Joseph Criqui.
Fitzgerald, James, Nov. 21, 1879, age 40.
Fitzgerald, John, March 8, 1878, age 92.
Fitzgerald, Mrs. Margaret, Lake View, Feb. 15, 1873, age 41; killed on L.S. & Michigan S. Railroad.
Fitzgerald, Margaret, April 7, 1880, age 68.
Fitzgerald, Mary, Co. Almshouse, Jan. 3, 1879, age 20.
Fitzgerald, Patrick, Sept. 14, 1875, age 40; drowned.
Fitzpatrick, Clara E., wife of Thomas, Aug. 24, 1866, age 31; taken to Painesville, OH.
Fitzpatrick, Edward, Lake View, Dec. 9, 1872, age 50.
Fitzpatrick, Frank, Aug. 21, 1877, age c. 50; killed by the cars.
Fitzpatrick, Jane, March 23, 1872, age 56.
Fitzpatrick, Martin, Jan. 29, 1879, age 65.
Fitzpatrick, Minerva, wife of Thomas, Aug. 10, 1853, age 31 y, 2 m.
Fitzpatrick, Thomas, Oct. 17, 1880, age 51.
Fix, Valentine, Grand Island, April 19, 1873; drowned.
Flach, Caroline, wife of Col. Richard, Jan. 6, 1879, age 51 y, 5 m.
Flach, Frederick C., March 13, 1873, age 23 y, 11 m.
Flagg, Edward M., Sept. 1833, age 27, in Columbus, OH.
Flagg, John B., formerly of Hartford, CT, June 27, 1856, age 58.
Flagg, L. B., widow of John B., Sept. 18, 1875, age 74.
Flagg, Mary, wife of Edmund, Oct. 16, 1830, age 19.
Flaherty, John, Feb. 27, 1870, age 25.
Flaherty, Morris, Feb. 12, 1875, age 25; accident.
Flanagan, Henry C., Feb. 25, 1880, age 38; d. at Jefferson City, MO, formerly of Buffalo.
Flanagan, James, June 13, 1868, age 23.
Flanagan, Patrick Henry, June 1877, age 21 y, 4 m.
Flanagan, Robert, April 9, 1868, age 21.
Flanigan, John, April 24, 1871, age 80.
Flannigan, Joseph, Aug. 16, 1852, age 6 m., 16 d.
Flannigan, Michael, May 25, 1867, age 52.
Flavin, Mary, Aug. 23, 1880, age 38.
Flay, William, Aug. 5, 1872, age 38.
Fleeharty, James, Oct. 14, 1867, age 38.
Fleeharty, Capt. John, Feb. 7, 1861, age 58; d. in Erie, PA.
Fleeharty, Lizzie M., wife of John, formerly of Buffalo, March 7, 1876; d. at East Davenport, IA.
Fleeman, Barbara, wife of Adam, North Buffalo, Oct. 1, 1870, age 46 y, 3 m, 8 d.

Fleeman, Louis C., son of Adam, Aug. 5, 1874, age 19 y, 2 m, 26 d.
Fleeman, Mrs. Magdalena, May 17, 1874, age 48.
Fleming, Edward C., Jan. 3, 1875, age 32.
Fleming, Eliza A., Dec. 13, 1880, age 69 y, 9 m, 13 d.
Fleming, James, son of the late John, May 28, 1872, age 35.
Fleming, John, Feb. 9, 1872, age 64.
Fleming, John, Jr., Dec. 5, 1861, age 28. [no card]
Fleming, Marie Harris, wife of Emmet, June 21, 1878, age 30.
Fleming, Mary, wife of John, Jan. 17, 1861.
Fleming, William H., Oct. 19, 1856, age 45.
Flersham, Mary Steele, Nov. 10, 1879; d. at Chicago, formerly of Buffalo.
Flersheim, Lemuel, Sept. 24, 1846, age 71.
Flershein, Mary Patterson, wife of George B., March 17, 1868, age 35.
Fletcher, Cotton, Hamburgh, NY, March 19, 1826.
Fletcher, John W., Nov. 20, 1876, age 65.
Fletcher, Mrs. Levi, Aug. 18, 1829, age 26.
Fletcher, Mrs. Mary, Sept. 25, 1879, age 76.
Fletcher, Samuel, Hamburgh, NY, Jan. 1826, age 67.
Fletcher, Squire H., Collins, NY, Feb. 6, 1854, age 82.
Fletcher, William, Nov. 20, 1876, age 55.
Fletcher, William, June 2, 1880, age 45.
Flett, Carrie E., wife of John, Nov. 12, 1876, age 28.
Flinders, George, Englishman, brewer, April 24, 1843, age 42.
Fling, Mrs. Hester, mother of John F. Titus, Oct. 19, 1878, age 86 y, 8 m, 9 d.
Flinn, Richard, Aug. 15, 1863, age 64.
Flint, Mrs. Abigail, Aug. 10, 1880, age 84.
Flint, Mrs. Eliza, Sept. 10, 1879, age 72; d. at Newark, NJ, formerly of Aurora, NY.
Flint, Harriet M., wife of Charles G., Sept. 1, 1869, age 57.
Flood, Christian, Jan. 28, 1878, age 80.
Flood, Joseph, Marilla, April 14, 1854, age 74 y, 6 m.
Flora, Joseph, Amherst, Aug. 12, 1871, age 56.
Flynn, Dennis, Co. Almshouse, April 27, 1877, age 48.
Flynn, Dennis, Oct. 8, 1880, age 42; found drowned 18th.
Flynn, Mrs. Honora, Jan. 30, 1874, age 67.
Flynn, Mrs. James, Dec. 12, 1878.
Flynn, Kate, teacher, April 11, 1871; taken to Arcade, Wyoming Co., NY.
Flynn, Nellie, Dec. 29, 1877.
Flynn, Thomas, July 28, 1880, age 63 y, 11 m, 23 d.
Fogarty, John, June 17, 1872, age 54.
Fogelsonger, Mary Heck, Oct. 8, 1879, age 20.
Fogelsonger, Wendell, Jr., Williamsville, June 23, 1878, age 39 y, 7 m, 22 d.
Foglesonger, Michael, Buffalo Plains, May 1837, age 74.
Foles, Silas A., Dec. 23, 1851, age 67.
Foley, Elizabeth, Dec. 1870, age 20.
Foley, James Bernard, eldest son of the late Bernard, Aug. 7, 1870, age 26 y, 1 m, 26 d.
Foley, John, July 6, 1872, age 22.
Folger, Mrs. B. H., Jan. 1, 1863, age 58.
Folger, Benjamin H., Dec. 2, 1861, age 63.
Folger, Charles, formerly of Buffalo, Nov. 28, 1873; d. at Lockport.
Folger, Edward F., formerly of Buffalo, June 2, 1875, age 51; d. in Baltimore, MD.
Folger, Sophia A., wife of Capt. T. P., formerly of Buffalo, July 16, 1852 in N. Y. City.
Folger, Capt. Thomas P., formerly of Buffalo, March 26, 1855; d. in Auburn, NY.
Follett, John E., Nov. 18, 1872, age 62.
Follett, Nancy F., wife of O., March 16, 1830, age 28.
Follmer, John, Tonawanta, NY, drowned in Tonawanta Creek, April 9, 1815.
Folsom, Burt, eldest son of D. E., Boston, NY, Sept. 24, 1878, age 24; d. at Red Rock, PA.
Folsom, Deacon Daniel, d. 1839, bur. Boston, NY.
Folsom, Elder Elijah, d. 1852, bur. Boston, NY.
Folsom, Rev. Jeremiah, d. 1823, bur. Boston, NY.; first settler.
Folsom, Noah, May 27, 1843, age 56.

Folsom, Oscar, July 23, 1875, age 37; accident.
Folsom, William, March 21, 1853, age 65.
Folsom, Winthrop, formerly of NH, Sept. 1827, age 64.
Folwell, Adelaide Young, Sept. 6, 1873; dau. of William W. D. in Waterloo, NY, bur. in Buffalo.
Fones, Louisa M., wife of W., Spring Brook, NY, Aug. 7, 1873, age 45 y, 1 m.
Fontaine, Drusilla Miles, wife of Eli, Nov. 14, 1877, age 55 y, 5 m, 10 d.
Foody, Michael, Co. Almshouse, June 23, 1877, age 36.
Foot, Edward, Co. Almshouse, March 1876, age 38.
Foot, Star, son-in-law of Sylvester Chamberlain, formerly of Buffalo, Nov. 14, 1862, age 62; d. in Chicago.
Foot, Teressa P., wife of Star, June 17, 1855, age 45.
Foot, William, Sept. 5, 1878, age 62.
Foote, Delia, sister of the late Hon. Thomas M., formerly of Buffalo, Jan. 18, 1878, age 73; d. in NY, bur. Buffalo.
Foote, Eliza, wife of R. S., March 14, 1860, age 53.
Foote, Eliza A., wife of John C., Sept. 11, 1871, age 65 y, 11 m, 11 d.
Foote, Julia A., wife of Dr. Thomas, dau. of Gen. Ethan B. Allen of Batavia, NY, June 28, 1853, age 33, in NY City, bur. in Buffalo.
Foote, Margaret, wife of Thomas M., July 27, 1849.
Foote, Maria Bird, widow of Dr. Thomas M., June 28, 1876.
Foote, Mrs. Rhoda, mother of William, Feb. 18, 1865, age 87 y, 8 m, 22 d. [no card]
Foote, Hon. Thomas, M.D., Feb. 20, 1858, age 49.
Foote, Thrina, wife of Clinton C., Aug. 6, 1850, age 69.
Foote, William, formerly of Buffalo, July 1877, age 74; d. at Dansville, Livingston Co., NY.
Forbest, Alexander, at the General Hospital, March 12, 1878, age 54; native of Perth, Scotland.
Forbes, Mrs. Catharine Janett, wife of D.S., Fredonia, NY, Feb. 24, 1875; d. in Buffalo, bur. Fredonia.
Forbes, Capt. Cleveland, Sept. 16, 1857, age 43.
Forbes, Joseph D., late of Perth Amboy, NJ, Oct. 19, 1867, age 49.
Forbes, Mary McKinney, wife of Capt. C., Jan. 16, 1857, age 42.
Forbes, Reginald Heber, Oct. 30, 1880, age 30; d. in Peabody, KS.
Forbes, Silas A., Dec. 1851.
Forbes, Thomas A., May 19, 1880, age 34.
Forbush, Eliakim, Dec. 18, 1867, age 55.
Forbush, Louisa M., wife of Dr. B. G., late of Buffalo, April 29, 1866, age 40, in Smellser Grove, Grant Co., WI.
Forbush, Lydia D., wife of Amos B., Nov. 13, 1870, age 42.
Forbush, Sophronia B., wife of Dr. B. G., dau. of Nathan M. Mann of Aurora, Sept. 8, 1850; taken to Aurora, NY.
Forbush, Walter H., Feb. 6, 1871, age 29; killed on the Hudson River Railroad at New Hamburg.
Ford, Andrew, formerly of Buffalo, Feb. 10, 1860, age 28, in Huntingdon, Canada East.
Ford, Catherine, May 14, 1871, age 56.
Ford, Daniel H., May 25, 1880, age 79; d. at Clifton, Can., formerly of Albany & Buffalo.
Ford, Hon. Elijah, March 9, 1879, age 74.
Ford, Mrs. Fanny Davis, widow of E., Feb. 16, 1880, age 86.
Ford, George, Dec. 11, 1872, age 26.
Ford, Henry John, printer, April 30, 1852, age 26.
Ford, John, June 22, 1866, age 27 y, 4 m; d. in Rochester, bur. in Buffalo.
Ford, Louisa J., wife of Elijah, Feb. 3, 1866, age 56.
Ford, Mrs. Mary, dau. of Mrs. B. Halloran, Sept. 3, 1877, age 28 y, 2 m.
Ford, Nelson, April 11, 1846, age 33.
Forde, Edwin J., bookkeeper, June 24, 1879, age 28.
Forde, Jessie, wife of Matthew, Nov. 19, 1866, age 44 y, 7 m, 16 d.
Forester, Margaret, wife of O., Fort Erie, Oct. 14, 1875, age 43.
Forlong, Ann, Feb. 13, 1871, age 58.
Forlong, Eliza A., July 11, 1865.

Forlong, Ellen D., April 10, 1865, age 21.
Forrest, Mrs. William, Jan. 1852.
Forrestell, Peter, Nov. 18, 1876, age 62.
Forristall, James A., formerly of Buffalo, March 30, 1849, age 58; d. in New Orleans.
Forrister, W. H., Nov. 9, 1862, age 48.
Forst, Mrs. R., mother of Mrs. M. Pinner, Oct. 23, 1861, age 78; taken to Cincinnati.
Forster, Andrew, June 22, 1880, age 29 y, 5 m, 16 d.
Forsyth, Mrs. Ann, Aug. 9, 1873, age 78.
Forsyth, Gilbert S., Oct. 7, 1832, age 33.
Forsyth, Mrs. Games G., May 1876.
Forsyth, Jane A., wife of Joseph, July 17, 1859, age 33.
Forsyth, Jenny E., wife of James G., May 13, 1876, age 44.
Forsyth, Joseph, native of Scotland, Oct. 5, 1867, age 49.
Forsyth, Miss Maria, Aug. 12, 1868, age 30.
Forsyth, Thomas, native of Scotland, formerly of Buffalo, Nov. 7, 1880, age 65; d. at
    Aurora, Erie Co.
Forsythe, Anne, Feb. 27, 1869, age 33.
Fortheringham, Mary, wife of Alexander, Sept. 13, 1862.
Fortier, Ann, wife of James, May 22, 1862, formerly of Port Colborne, Canada West.
Fortier, Mrs. Fannie, widow of P. J., March 11, 1880, age 44.
Fortier, James, Sr., Jan. 11, 1865, age 79, in Port Colborne, bur. in Buffalo.
Fortier, Jeannette R., formerly of Buffalo, wife of David H. A., March 26, 1874, age 33;
    d. in Port Colborne, Ontario, bur. in Buffalo.
Fortier, Peter J., Aug. 15, 1865, age 27.
Forward, Oliver, April 27, 1834.
Forward, Sally, wife of Oliver, Dec. 13, 1831, age 53; in N. Y. City. Interred in
    Presbyterian Burying Ground, Haerlem, NY.
Fosdick, Anna, widow of Soloman, Springville, NY, Aug. 8, 1858, age 81 y, 5 m, 6 d.
Fosdick, Clement, Sept. 16, 1861, age 42.
Fosdick, Morris, Springville, Feb. 3, 1872, age 67 y, 1 m, 25 d.
Fossett, Mary, Jan. 1, 1876, age 64.
Foster, Belinda, widow of Joseph, Hamburgh, July 23, 1872.
Foster, Charles H., formerly of Buffalo, April 10, 1871, age 21; d. in Washington, DC.
Foster, Clarrissa, May 24, 1873, age 74.
Foster, Edwin, late of NH, Dec. 14, 1834, age 22.
Foster, Miss Frances Caroline, dau. of Joseph, Hamburg, April 6, 1846, age 21; d. in
    Pieatonic, Winnebago Co., IL.
Foster, Frank B., son of Joseph, July 13, 1864, age 36; d. in CA.
Foster, Hannah, wife of Manning, Dec. 8, 1849, age 67.
Foster, Mrs. Harriet S., Nov. 1, 1878, age 73.
Foster, Harry, late of Buffalo, July 15, 1866, in Washington, DC.
Foster, Hiram, recently from Rochester, Oct. 29, 1830, age 28.
Foster, Mrs. Jane, Tonawanda, July 15, 1880, age 60 ?; sudden.
Foster, John B., May 31, 1874, age 24.
Foster, Deacon Joseph, West Hamburgh, March 14, 1865, age 69.
Foster (or Forster), Julia, Oct. 28, 1880, age 26 y, 7 m, 8 d.
Foster, Mrs. Levin, sister of Mrs. Abram and Mrs. Samuel Twichell, Nov. 28, 1870, age 64.
Foster, Lois, widow of Stephen, mother of Mrs. Samuel and Mrs. Abraham Twichel, Aug. 16,
    1859, age 77.
Foster, Lucy, niece of Aaron Parker, Hamburgh, NY, April 5, 1849, age 44.
Foster, Milton D., brother of Dr. H. A., July 1, 1875, age 31; taken to Clifton Springs,
    NY.
Foster, Ruth, wife of E., Oct. 25, 1812, age 28.
Foster, Sophronia H., wife of Edward J., Collins, NY, June 1, 1874, age 46.
Foster, Thomas, Sept. 12, 1865, age 42.
Foster, William C., Nov. 25, 1880, age 69 y, 24 d.
Foster, William F., veteran of the late war, Sept. 21, 1875, age 68.
Fouche, Francis, formerly of Buffalo, printer, Sept. 1, 1840; d. in Rochester, NY, age 25.
Fougeron, Frank, March 29, 1859, age 28 y, 4 m, 21 d.
Fougeron, Joseph S., April 12, 1858, age 72 y, 5 m, 11 d.

Fougeron, Mary Ann, wife of Simon, Dec. 14, 1865, age 70.
Fourby, Richard, July 19, 1878, age 72.
Fouse, Frank, June 13, 1878, age 33; drowned.
Fowler, Benjamin, July 9, 1858, age 69.
Fowler, Clark, Black Rock, NY, Sept. 29, 1821, age 35, bur. in Buffalo.
Fowler, E. Otis Hale, adopted son of Benjamin Fowler, Feb. 28, 1853, age 36; d. in Brooklyn.
Fowler, George A., son of Henry, May 18, 1870, age 22 y, 3 m, 17 d.
Fowler, George B., May 25, 1874, age 20.
Fowler, George L., Nov. 3, 1861, age 46.
Fowler, Henrietta M., wife of James S., May 20, 1878, age 26.
Fowler, Lucy, formerly of Buffalo, widow of Benjamin, Oct. 28, 1875, age 68; d. at Albion, Orleans Co., NY, bur. in Buffalo.
Fowler, Peter, late of Memphis, TN, Dec. 23, 1877.
Fowler, Mrs. Susan, formerly of Hopkinton, NY, Aug. 28, 1838, age 80.
Fowler, Thomas W., Concord, Aug. 14, 1864, age 38.
Fowler, Trueworthy, April 20, 1844, age 49.
Fox, Arthur W., Aug. 29, 1874, age 58.
Fox, Augustus Carlton, March 5, 1848, age 55. Lieut. in War of 1812. Formerly of Erie Co., d. in Bloomingdale Asylum, NY.
Fox, Mr. C. R., July 14, 1862, age 50; d. in Lockport, NY, bur. in Buffalo.
Fox, Mrs. Catharine D., March 1, 1873, age 58.
Fox, Charles, April 1876, age 64; advertised as missing 23 Feb.
Fox, Charles J., Oct. 11, 1859, age 33.
Fox, Charles J., May 12, 1872, age 23.
Fox, Charlotte M. Hayward, widow of Charles J., May 23, 1869, age 42.
Fox, George W., Jan. 10, 1827.
Fox, Capt. Henry, Lancaster, NY, Feb. 10, 1875, age 84.
Fox, Joseph, cabinet maker, June 18, 1880, age 50; suicide.
Fox, Leonard, Feb. 3, 1880, age 69.
Fox, Lillian C., Oct. 18, 1878, age 20; d. at Northville, PA, bur. in Buffalo.
Fox, Maria Monica, wife of A. R., Aug. 17, 1857, age 27. Taken to Rochester, NY.
Fox, Mary, widow of Capt. Simeon, Sept. 20, 1851, age 63.
Fox, Matilda, wife of Henry, May 4, 1870, age 27 y, 7 m, 4 d.
Fox, Olivia M., wife of J. H., Alden, May 25, 1860, age 25; taken to Geneseo, NY.
Fox, Oshea G., March 18, 1857, age 56.
Fox, Rhoda, wife of Christopher G., May 2, 1861, age 28.
Fox, Sally, wife of Capt. Henry, Jan. 15, 1857, age 57.
Fox, Capt. Simeon, Sept. 10, 1842, age 54.
Fox, Thomas, Nov. 18, 1877, age 32.
Fox, William, principal of the Angola Union School, Angola, April 8, 1874, age 25.
Foxlonger, Joseph, Tonawanda, NY, March 24, 1857, age 28.
Foy, John, Dec. 30, 1872, age 80.
Fradenburg, Mrs. Ann P., sister of Mrs. John T. Lacey, Dec. 22, 1872, age 74; d. in Jersey City, NJ, bur. Buffalo.
Frame, Helen E., wife of Alexander N., Oct. 25, 1861, age 43.
Frampton, Margaret Frances, wife of Edward, March 26, 1879, age 36.
Frances, James H. or Francis, Sept. 22, 1880, age 21; killed while switching cars.
Francis, Abigail D., wife of Calvin, Oct. 23, 1865, in Chatham, Sangamon Co., IL; formerly of Buffalo.
Francis, Alpheus, son of Lysander, Colden, NY, March 5, 1852, age 21.
Francis, Elizur G., brother of Daniel and Julius E., formerly of Buffalo, July 31, 1874, age 64; d. at Alexandria, LA.
Francis, Capt. Henry W., formerly of Buffalo, Dec. 1, 1874, age 45; d. at Burlington, VT.
Francis, Lovina, wife of Peter B., East Hamburgh, NY, Oct. 11, 1844, age 26.
Francis, Lysander, Colden, NY, Jan. 22, 1860, age 63.
Frank, Elizabeth, wife of Abraham I., Aug. 7, 1880, age 35 y, 11 m.
Frank, Elizabeth Graef, wife of Martin, Aug. 1877, age 40 y, 3 m, 13 d.
Frank, Henry J., Elma, Jan. 13, 1878.
Frank, Jacob, Oct. 28, 1878, age 78.
Frank, Martin, Sept. 17, 1877, age 48.

Frank, Miss Orvie, June 18, 1872, age 20.
Frank, Peter, German, Oct. 5, 1870, age 49; suicide by shooting.
Frank, Tony, son of John, May 5, 1878. D. in Virginia City, NV; taken to Bath, ME.
Franke, Mathilda, dau. of L. A., May 12, 1876, age 21 y, 7 m.
Franklin, Mrs. Anna, Dec. 15, 1879, age 96 y, 2 m.
Franklin, Ellen, wife of James, May 31, 1874, age 58 y, 2 m.
Franklin, Joseph, eldest son of James, Dec. 16, 1870, age 26 y, 3 m.
Franklin, Mary F., wife of James Jr., July 27, 1873, age 23 y, 5 m.
Franklin, Robert, colored man, Dec. 30, 1813; killed at the battle of Black Rock.
Franklin, Sylvester, Marilla, NY, March 17, 1873, age 55.
Franklin, William, June 15, 1849, age 66, at the Hydraulics.
Frary, Ann, formerly of Syracuse, NY, wife of R. A., mother-in-law of E. J. Clarke, July 22, 1859; taken to Syracuse.
Fraser, Mrs., March 1863, she and children bur. March 13.
Fraser, Catherine, wife of John, Nov. 8, 1878, age 37.
Fraser, Mrs. James, formerly of Buffalo, Aug. 21, 1878, age 80.
Fraser, James, Jan. 5, 1858 at Kelvin Grove Farm, IL, age 89.
Fraser, Donald, Keeper of Rob Roy House on Elk St., Jan. 17, 1854, age 50.
Frasier, John, formerly of Buffalo, 1846, age 35; d. in MI.
Frawley, Daniel, Sept. 13, 1870, age 35 y, 4 m, 5 d.
Frawley, William, Dec. 19, 1876, age 84.
Frazer, Maj. Donald, March 1860.
Fraser, John, Jan. 18, 1854, age 52.
Fraser, Miss Margaret, Oct. 9, 1843, age 26.
Frazer, Capt. William T., Oct. 9, 1876, age c. 45.
Frear, Simeon J., July 6, 1878, age 90.
Fredenberg, Isabella, wife of Mitchell W., April 5, 1859, age 24.
Frederick, Della M., dau. of Peter C., March 21, 1879, age 20.
Fredericks, Frederick, Jan. 20, 1877, age 54.
Frederickson, Charlotte Louisa, wife of Christian, May 10, 1866, age 67 y, 4 m.
Freeland, David, father of Mrs. Edward Curtis, Feb. 20, 1862, age 79.
Freeman, E. Henry, Jan. 20, 1879, age 38.
Freeman, Edwin P., Colden, March 1872, age 20; killed accidently at Big Rapids, MI.
Freeman, Elisha, East Hamburgh, NY, Aug. 30, 1865, age 71.
Freeman, Emily, wife of James, Dec. 9, 1836, age 30.
Freeman, Frances A., wife of James M., dau. of James Van Buren, Oct. 7, 1864, age 26.
Freeman, Hannah, wife of Noah, Aug. 24, 1858, age 76 y, 6 m, 9 d.
Freeman, Horace, April 9, 1878, age 34.
Freeman, Joseph, Alden, Nov. 3, 1867, age 80 y, 5 m.
Freeman, Miss Louisa E., formerly of Providence, RI, June 1847 at Dr. Austin Flint's.
Freeman, Melinda K., wife of Elias, East Hamburgh, NY, Sept. 25, 1862; d. at Great Valley, Cattaraugus Co., bur. in East Hamburgh.
Freeman, Nancy, wife of Joseph, Alden, NY, Feb. 6, 1831, age 50.
Freeman, Noah, Jan. 26, 1862, age 81.
Freeman, Orra, wife of Lansing, July 30, 1851, age 22; taken to Darien, NY.
Freeman, S. S. H., wife of Judge Joseph, Alden, May 30, 1856, age 65.
Freer, Mrs. Elizabeth, sister of John and George F. Allman, Dec. 24, 1867, age 47.
French, Chauncey, Newstead, NY, Dec. 13, 1842, age 40.
French, Mrs. Cordelia, at insane asylum, Feb. 2, 1880.
French, Mrs. Dell, Black Rock, NY, May 18, 1871.
French, Dorcas, widow of Harlow, Nov. 14, 1862, age 59.
French, Mrs. Esther, Aug. 22, 1839, age 80.
French, Fisher C., Nov. 3, 1878, age 67.
French, George P., Lancaster, NY, March 24, 1880, age 42.
French, Hovey, J., Black Rock, NY, Nov. 15, 1863, age 27 y, 5 m, 5 d. Taken to Albion, NY.
French, Ichabod, Concord, NY, Jan. 12, 1862, age 84.
French, Jerusha A., wife of Wallace W., March 31, 1856, age 24 y, 7 m, 24 d.
French, Mr. Prosper, Nov. 24, 1856, age 59.
Frentz, August, July 1871.

Freshour, Capt. George W., formerly of Buffalo, April 26, 1862 in Louisville, KY; bur. in Buffalo.
Frey, John, Amherst, Oct. 20, 1872, age 22; accidently shot.
Friar, Mrs. Nancy, April 20, 1848, age 70.
Frick, Anna Riest, wife of C. Z., Williamsville, NY, June 1, 1853, age 26 y, 10 m, 22 d.
Frick, Christian, formerly of Lancaster, PA, Nov. 18, 1815, age 60.
Frick, Mrs. Elizabeth, May 17, 1832, age 64.
Frick, Jacob, Clarence, March 4, 1871, age 69; suicide.
Frick, Jacob, Williamsville, NY, April 25, 1874, age 88.
Frick, John, Jan. 1, 1813, age 50.
Fridag, Mrs. Elizabeth, Aug. 15, 1858, age 41 y, 15 d.
Friday, Michael, Nov. 2, 1870, age 56.
Friedel, Augusta, Nov. 8, 1876, age 21 y, 7 m.
Friederich, Valentin, May 1875, age 55; d. in Rochester, NY, bur. in Buffalo.
Friedlander, Esther, wife of Samuel, Oct. 1, 1878, age 24 y, 2 m, 26 d.
Friedly, John, July 4, 1878, age 46.
Friedman, Anna, wife of Charles B., Titusville, April 9, 1878, bur. in Buffalo.
Friedman, Joseph, Aug. 10, 1879, age 54 y, 9 m.
Friend, Frederick, laborer, Jun 16, 1880, age 50 y, 2 m; killed by cave in of sand in Bird Ave. sewer.
Fries, Jacob, April 3, 1871, age 50.
Frink, J. Preston, M.D., late of Buffalo, March 12, 1876, age 24. D. and bur. at Aiken, SC.
Friseoff, Frank, May 1874; suicide.
Fritzsche, August H., Nov. 18, 1880, age 63; accidental death.
Fromreiter, Anton, Oct. 1878, age 68.
Frost, Angenett, wife of Frederick J., July 9, 1859, age 38.
Frost, Charles, Nov. 11, 1876.
Frost, Cloys, June 23, 1865, age 80 y, 2 m; taken to Evans Center, NY.
Frost, Mrs. Eleanor, Nov. 3, 1870, age 56.
Frost, Harriet M., wife of Ransom M., Sept. 6, 1872, age 41 y, 1 m, 1 d; taken to Fayetteville, NY.
Frost, John, b. Dec. 22, 1759, d. Oct. 16, 1853, bur. Evans Center, NY; Soldier of the Revolution.
Frost, Miss Prudence Ann, Dec. 13, 1837.
Fryer, Hester, Nov. 6, 1876, age 74 y, 1 m, 24 d.
Fryer, Mrs. Margaret Harriet, Oct. 30, 1872.
Fuchs, Edward, firm of Fuchs Brothers, May 29, 1870, age 44.
Fuenfgeld (or Funfgeld), Edward J., Dec. 16, 1878, age 22 y, 17 d.
Fulford, Mrs. Maria, dau. of Deacon Platt Wakely, Lancaster, NY, Feb. 19, 1840, age 34.
Fullem, James, brakeman, May 11, 1879, age 50; sudden death.
Fuller, Abel, Jan., 1813, age 30.
Fuller, Almira, Sept. 19, 1870, age 20; funeral from Buffalo General Hospital.
Fuller, Anna C., wife of William O., May 21, 1872, age 35; of Bay City, MI.
Fuller, Cyrenus, East Concord, June 17, 1873, age 20.
Fuller, Emma B., wife of James E., Oct. 13, 1877, age 32.
Fuller, Gustavus L., Feb. 8, 1861, age 20.
Fuller, Harvey, Oct. 11, 1874, age 65 y, 4 m.
Fuller, Henry, Clarence, NY, March 30, 1873, age 73.
Fuller, Henry W., Co. B, 116 Reg. N.Y.V., formerly of Clarence, NY, Jan. 28, 1864, age 25, at Franklin, LA, bur. at Harris Hill, NY.
Fuller, Mrs. Mahala, Eden Centre, NY, wife of Hosea, June 9, 1875, age 64 y, 9 m. Taken to Hamburgh, NY.
Fuller, Mrs. Margaret Ann, Oct. 19, 1873, age 55.
Fuller, Mary J., wife of Samuel, Aug. 8, 1842, age 42; formerly of Albany, NY.
Fuller, Nancy A., wife of Jerome, Aug. 2, 1852, age 36.
Fuller, Sergt. William, Co. H, 85 Reg. N.Y.S.V., Jan. 30, 1865. D. of cold and starvation in Rebel Prison, Salisbury, NC.
Fuller, Zacheus W., Sardinia, July 30, 1843, age 37.

Fullerton, David, father of J. C., John and George; Alden, NY, Sept. 12, 1874, age 59 y, 2 m.
Fullerton, Mrs. Sarah, mother of George, John and James C., June 3, 1878, age 69.
Fulmer, Jacob, Feb. 16, 1879, age 65.
Fulton, James T. Jr., Sept. 1879.
Fulton, Jane, formerly from north of Ireland, Feb. 15, 1844, age 21, at home of L. F. Allen, Black Rock, NY.
Furleck, Allice, mother of T. W., March 13, 1866, age 67; taken to Rochester, NY.
Furlong, Eliza, widow of Dr. Joseph, Dec. 16, 1863, age 65.
Furlong, John, May 10, 1879, age 83.
Furlong, Dr. Joseph, formerly of Ringwood, Newcastle, County Limerick, Ireland, March 7, 1862, age 60.
Furmston, Elizabeth, Aug. 19, 1863, age 79; d. Fort Erie, Canada West, bur. Buffalo.
Fursman, E. L., Treas. of Western Transfer Co., July 14, 1860, age 34 y, 6 m.
Fursman, Mary A., wife of Samuel, March 29, 1849, age 44.
Fursman, Samuel, formerly of Buffalo, Oct. 30, 1873, age 73; d. in Brooklyn, NY, bur. in Buffalo.
Fusnish, Marie Francaise Adelaide, late of Arnouville, France, April 16, 1840.
Fysh, Mrs. E. E., June 17, 1872, age 59 y, 10 m.

Gaenssleu, Harmon, Gowanda, Dec. 1879, age 21.
Gaetz, Daniel, Aug. 18, 1878, age 55 y, 8 m.
Gaetz, George, Dec. 19, 1875, age 51 y, 2 m, 21 d.
Gaetz, Michael, May 5, 1866, age 71 y, 5 m, 13 d.
Gaetz, Michael, Oct. 24, 1877, age 51 y, 2 m.
Gaffney, Ann, wife of Anthony, Nov. 27, 1868, age 35.
Gaffney, Matthew, printer, late of Kilkenney, Ireland, July 2, 1867, age 22 y, 1 m, 20 d.
Gaffney, Thomas, June 21, 1857, age 30.
Gage, Aaron, May 1, 1823, age 30.
Gage, George, May 30, 1851, age 80.
Gage, George, March 18, 1876, age 55.
Gage, Mrs. Jane, Oct. 2, 1849, age 65.
Gage, Lucy W., youngest dau. of George, Aug. 1, 1867 at Houghton, MI; bur. in Buffalo.
Gager, Mrs. E., March 20, 1879, age 43.
Gager or Gayer, Frederick A., April 15, 1876, age 20; taken to Iavonia, NY.
Gager, Jane Ann, wife of Capt. Charles L., March 27, 1854, age 46 y, 11 m, 9 d.
Gaige, Minnie, wife of S. P., June 23, 1876, age 36.
Gail, Betsy, wife of Lockwood, West Falls, May 28, 1869, age 57.
Gail, Mrs. Rufus, Aurora, NY, March 28, 1871, age 60; suicide.
Galbraith, James H., formerly of Glasgow, Scotland, Oct. 10, 1865.
Gale, Anthony, Nov. 9, 1873, age 78 y, 8 m.
Gale, Gilman, late of Lowell, NY, Sept. 6, 1849, age 45.
Gale, Dr. Henry M., formerly of Salamanca, Cattaraugus Co., NY, Dec. 11, 1867, age 36. Taken to Ashville, Chautaqua Co.
Gallagher, Edward M., Feb. 1879.
Gallagher, Francis Bernard, July 19, 1870, age 50.
Gallagher, Harriet, wife of Edward, Dec. 13, 1860, age 29 y, 7 m, 27 d.
Gallagher, Hugh, Almshouse, June 7, 1880, age 40.
Gallagher, James, Dec. 16, 1870, age 40.
Gallagher, John, Aug. 19, 1870, age 77.
Gallagher, M. J., June 7, 1876, age 42.
Gallagher, Margaret, wife of F.B., Oct. 16, 1867, age 49.
Gallagher, Margaret, wife of M. J., April 1, 1872, age 32.
Gallagher, Mary, Dec. 9, 1879, age 60.
Gallagher, Patrick, Dec. 15, 1871.
Gallagher, Patrick, Aug. 23, 1880, age 54.
Gallagher, Thomas, July 16, 1877, age 34; d. at Port Colborne, Ontario, bur. Buffalo.
Galley, Ann, April 15, 1876, age 67.
Galligan, John, Dec. 3, 1854. Lost in wreck of Schooner *R. A. Johnson*, body recovered, and bur. in Buffalo, Dec. 9.

Galligan, John H., son of William, Co. F, 21st Reg., April 28, 1862, age 19 y, 11 m, 28 d.
Galligan, Nancy, wife of William, March 2, 1858, age 47 y, 5 m, 20 d.
Galligan, William, May 1875, age 67.
Gallivan, Anne, wife of Martin, Feb. 14, 1868.
Gallivan, John, Aug. 1873.
Gallop, Mrs. Anne, May 9, 1876, age 60.
Galloway, Alexander R., Dec. 22, 1856, age 67.
Galloway, Phebe Means, wife of Alexander R., Dec. 24, 1861, age 70.
Galoska (Kalunski), Martin, Feb. 18, 1880, age 26, tannery worker. Accidental?
Galt, Eliza J., March 17, 1878, age 33.
Galvin, Edmund, Sisters of Charity Hospital, May 24, 1880, age 55.
Galvin, Martin, July 13, 1871, age 30.
Galvin, Mary, wife of Patrick, July 28, 1878, age 45.
Galvin, Mrs. Mary J., June 17, 1869, age 52 y, 4 m, 17 d.
Gamberle, Hencl., father of Mrs. F. Feyl and Mrs. J. H. Leech, July 28, 1869, age 69.
Gann, Mrs. Mary, Feb. 14, 1871, age 75.
Gangloff, Katharina, wife of Peter, Jan. 26, 1844, age 62 y, 9 m.
Ganson, Amanda L., wife of Holton, dau. of Rev. Lucius Smith, Feb. 14, 1867.
Ganson, C. R., Dec. 25, 1864, age 48; taken to Batavia, NY.
Ganson, Corneal B., March 25, 1871, age 17 y, 5 m. Son of the late Cornelius B., taken to Batavia. [One obituary gives name as Cornelius B. and d. date as March 24.]
Ganson, J. Edward, son of Joseph, formerly of Buffalo, March 18, 1871; d. in Jersey City.
Ganson, Mrs. James, widow of Maj. James of LeRoy, Genesee Co., April 18, 1866, age 85.
Ganson, Hon. John, Sept. 28, 1874, age 56.
Ganson, John S., Aug. 30, 1875, age 73; taken to Batavia, NY.
Ganson, Joseph, April 20, 1863, age 58.
Gantrer, J. M., Oct. 28, 1878, age 72; d. in Indianapolis, bur. at the Pine Hill Cemetery. His wife d. here in 1871.
Gantz, Esther, wife of A. B., Feb. 3, 1865, age 32; taken to Williamsville, NY.
Ganz, George, Abbott Road near Buffalo, July 7, 1880, age 79; suicide.
Garby or Garly, Peter, Elma, NY, May 24, 1875; suicide.
Gardiner, Benjamin, Springville, NY, July 1820, age 40.
Gardiner, Isaac L., son of Henry, March 18, 1874, age 26.
Gardiner, Laura M., July 22, 1879, age 24.
Gardiner, Lovisa, Dec. 5, 1856, age 66.
Gardiner, Joseph Y., son of Abraham, Feb. 1, 1862, age 29 y, 3 m, 18 d. Formerly of Springville, NY, d. in St. Louis, MO.
Gardner, Abel, Oct. 11, 1855, age 65.
Gardner, Alcy Marana, wife of N. H., Oct. 2, 1833, age 21.
Gardner, Ann S., widow of Joseph B., Dec. 5, 1863, age 46.
Gardner, Mrs. Catherine, June 30, 1878, age 73.
Gardner, Charles, Aug. 12, 1873, age 72.
Gardner, Edward Gager, Dec. 26, 1859, age 31.
Gardner, Eleanor, wife of E. C., Jr., April 12, 1838, age 24.
Gardner, Elizabeth, wife of D. W., Sept. 5, 1870, age 28.
Gardner, Fanny, wife of Noah H., May 21, 1868, age 57.
Gardner, Francis B., formerly of Nantucket, MA, Nov. 5, 1867, age 56.
Gardner, Mr. G., Hamburgh, Aug. 19, 1849, age 72.
Gardner, Miss Hannah Maria, Oct. 3, 1866.
Gardner, Jane M. McDermot, wife of John T., Oct. 13, 1874, age 35 y, 9 m.
Gardner, Jane Matilda, wife of Charles, Jan. 22, 1857, age 51 y, 3 m, 22 d.
Gardner, Joseph B., Hamburgh, Nov. 15, 1852, age 42; bur. in Buffalo.
Gardner, Martha, widow of John of Hamilton, Ontario, March 1873.
Gardner, Mary J., eldest dau. of Noah H., April 7, 1872, age 36.
Gardner, Noah H., Dec. 15, 1872, age 71.
Gardner, Peter, March 21, 1877, age 42.
Gardner, Capt. William, May 5, 1875, age 56; taken to Ogdensburgh.
Gardner, William G., Nov. 3, 1866, age 61.
Garland, Eliza, wife of J.G., formerly of Buffalo, Feb. 9, 1853 at Kalamazoo, MI.
Garland, Mary Martha, wife of Samuel, Aug. 25, 1853, age 39.

Garner, Martha, wife of George, Aug. 9, 1875, age 48.
Garretson, Anna S. Graham, wife of O.S., April 8, 1874, age 27.
Garrett, Cuyler, only son of Cuyler, Oct. 26, 1871, age 26.
Garrett, Henry, Feb. 9, 1849, age 36.
Garrett, Julia, wife of Cuyler, dau. of Martin Daley, Feb. 9, 1852, age 33; d. in Maumee City.
Garrigan, Maria Agnes, wife of Matthew, Aug. 8, 1872, age 43.
Garrison, Ella, wife of Eugene H., March 26, 1878, age 27 y, 3 m, 19 d.
Garrity, Bridget, June 22, 1875, age 48; found dead.
Garson, George, Nov. 25, 1870.
Garson, Moses J., formerly of Buffalo, March 5, 1878, age 35.
Garvin, Rev. Isaac of the Episcopal Church, June 29, 1848, age 75.
Garvin, Lucy Bostwick, widow of Rev. Isaac, Dec. 13, 1868, age 78.
Gash, Richard, Oct. 16, 1875, age 21 y, 10 m; taken to Lockport.
Gaskin, Winnifred, May 31, 1877, age 22.
Gastel, George, Nov. 20, 1879, age 95.
Gastel, Miss Lena, dau. of the late Magdalena, May 2, 1874, age 21.
Gastell, Mary, dau. of the late George, Sept. 2, 1869, age 20 y, 14 d.
Gastinel, Jenny Mark, wife of Arthur, formerly of Buffalo, July 14, 1880, age 33; d. at New Orleans.
Gates, Caroline Mathilda, eldest dau. of Horatio, Oct. 26, 1841, age 20.
Gates, Darius F., Sept. 28, 1872, age 35.
Gates, George B., June 27, 1880, age 67.
Gates, Grace, widow of J. H., Oct. 19, 1880, age 53.
Gates, Horatio, Principal of School No. 12, Feb. 14, 1852.
Gates, Jacob H., Jan. 18, 1857, age 40.
Gates, Jennette E., wife of Sigismund J., Sept. 25, 1854; d. in Chicago.
Gates, John L., son of George B., Sept. 16, 1875, age 29; d. at Eaton Rapids, MI, bur. in Buffalo.
Gates, Mary E., wife of Levi S., April 4, 1877.
Gates, Nicholas R., April 19, 1872, age 38.
Gates, Mrs. Rachel S., March 16, 1879, age 71; taken to East Haddam.
Gates, Sarah, wife of Capt. Daniel, Aug. 24, 1835, age 30.
Gates, Mrs. Spencer S., June 14, 1830, age 21.
Gates, Dr. Stephen, Evans Center, dentist, March 12, 1859, age 52.
Gates, Wesley, Dec. 30, 1872, suffocated by gas.
Gattie, Adam, German, Oct. 15, 1871; drowned.
Gault, H. Rebecca, Feb. 7, 1873, age 22.
Gault, Henrietta O., wife of Thomas, March 6, 1873, age 19.
Gault, Mary, wife of James, Dec. 3, 1872, age 55.
Gavin, James, Feb. 10, 1875, age 60.
Gavin, John, April 21, 1875, age 51.
Gavin, Patrick, Feb. 8, 1876, age 45.
Gaw-yeh-gwa-doh, or "Young King," head chief of the Senecas, Reservation, May 3, 1835; bur. by the side of Red Jacket.
Gay, Rachel Culbertson, Oct. 17, 1879, age 32.
Gaylor, Hiram, Oct. 7, 1856, age 51.
Gazlay, John F., Evans, Dec. 1875, age 88.
Gazley, Polly, wife of John F., Evans, Aug. 16, 1862, age 54.
Geary, Patrick, Oct. 8, 1877, age 54.
Gebhard, Laurens or Gebhardt, Lorenz, Feb. 8, 1871, age 73.
Gebhardt, Jacob F., July 31, 1878.
Geckler, Barbara, Oct. 26, 1877, age 47 y, 6 m, 2 d.
Geckler, William, Sept. 4, 1877, age 24 y, 10 m, 10 d; accidental death.
Gee, Mrs. John, Aug. 11, 1875, age 19; accidental death.
Geer, Jane, sister-in-law of E.L. Stevenson, Oct. 4, 1860.
Geer, Jefferson, Holland, railroad trackman, Nov. 28, 1880; d. of injuries received in a railroad accident.
Gehring, Frederick, Feb. 23, 1871, age 30 y, 6 m.
Geimer, Christian, May 13, 1878, age 80.

Geis, Mrs. Fronika, March 16, 1880, age 54.
Geiss, Frederick, Cheektowaga, NY, Dec. 2, 1872, age 50; killed on railroad in Buffalo.
Gellan, Paul R., Sept. 19, 1871, age 54.
Gelston, Charlotte, widow of Samuel F., formerly of Buffalo, April 1, 1880, age 90; d. at Roslyn, Long Island.
Gelston, Samuel F., Feb. 8, 1861, age 73.
Gennett or Jannett, Mrs. Mary Ann, from Canada, April 7, 1874, age 52.
Genor, Augustus, Dec. 22, 1868, age 61.
Genor, Henry A., July 6, 1879, age 41; d. at Utica, NY.
Gensler, John, April 4, 1878, age 82.
Gentle, Walter G., Sept. 7, 1879, age 25.
George, John, brother of J.C., formerly of Buffalo, April 25, 1850, age 42; in Franciscoville, MI.
George, John, May 21, 1877, age 58.
George, Nellie Georgiana, Dec. 1868; bur. Dec. 8.
Georger, Edward L., son of Charles, Aug. 15, 1872, age 21 y, 4 m, 8 d.
Georger, J. M., Jan. 27, 1859, age 63.
Gerardy, Peter, Tonawanda, Feb. 7, 1871, age 33; accidently killed.
Gerber, A. W., East Aurora, Dec. 4, 1879, age 69.
Gerber, Amilia, wife of Charles, Feb. 2, 1877, age 55 y, 6 m.
Gerber, Amelia, March 27, 1873, age 70 y, 6 m.
Gerber, Frank G., Oct. 16, 1876, age 47; accidental death.
Gerber, Jacob, laborer, Aug. 22, 1879; fell dead.
Gerber, Julius R., East Aurora, NY, Oct. 10, 1875, age 36.
Gerber, Sigmund, Nov. 16, 1877, age 72.
Gercken, Casper, May 9, 1874, age 34.
Gerhardt, Wolfgana, Sept. 20, 1876, age 58; accidental death.
Gerhartt or Gerhardt, John, Dec. 4, 1874, age 60.
Gering, Bartholomew, father of George J., May 26, 1872, age 72.
Germain, Charles, Aug. 21, 1877, age 48; suicide.
Germain, Charles C., Jan. 20, 1871, age 52.
Germain, Christine, wife of John C., Aug. 15, 1878, age 74.
Germain, E., widow of Col. C. C., Feb. 9, 1875, age 67.
Germain, Eliza, wife of Ira V., Nov. 9, 1844, age 26.
Germain, Ira V., formerly of Buffalo, Aug. 5, 1850; d. in Chicago.
Germain, James, North Buffalo, Oct. 2, 1865, age 83.
Germain, James Wallace, June 1863.
Germain, John C., Feb. 3, 1880, age 78.
Germain, Mary H., widow of Rollin, June 11, 1879.
Germain, Mary Hellen Willis, wife of Charles Jr., July 13, 1873, age 37.
Germain, Rollin, Feb. 6, 1871, age 60; killed on the Hudson River Railroad at New Hamburgh.
Germain, Sally Parks, widow of James, Feb. 16, 1873, age 94.
Germain, Lewis, Chenango, May 1819.
Gerring, Anna Christine, wife of George B., Feb. 20, 1870, age 65 y, 2 m.
Gesender or Geisner, Andrew, June 18, 1874, age c. 78.
Gessel, John, of Battery A., Buffalo Light Artillery, Nov 1875; funeral Nov. 14.
Getman, Joel Ervin, Dec. 31, 1879, age 45 y, 3 m, 22 d.
Getsinger, J. G., March 22, 1864, age 32.
Getsinger, M. Joseph, June 13, 1870, age 74.
Getting, Michael, July 7, 1873, age 27.
Getty, James, late of Hamburg, March 6, 1853, age 76; d. in Sharon, Whiteside Co., IL.
Getty, Lavant W., formerly of Hamburgh, Aug. 24, 1878, age 41; d. at Jackson, TN.
Getz, Jacob, Gowanda, NY, Feb. 1, 1880, age 53.
Getz, Joseph, Jan. 19, 1852, age 22.
Getz, Joseph, Williamsville, NY, May 6, 1878, age 75.
Getz, Susan, wife of Joseph, Williamsville, NY, April 1, 1857, age 56 y, 1 m, 24 d.
Geyer, Henry, Feb. 9, 1877, age 73.
Geyer, Winfield, Dec. 16, 1880, age 28 y, 1 m; d. in Detroit.
Geyser, F. C. W., June 28, 1880, age 72.
Gibbons, Abbey. L., wife of John J., Jan. 24, 1873; d. at Enterprise, MS, bur. in Buffalo.

Gibbons, Charles, May 11, 1873, age 45 y, 5 m., 22 d.
Gibbons, Mrs. Christine, Carolina or Caroline, widow of Patrick, accidently drowned, April 21, 1880, age 68.
Gibbons, Edward, May 7, 1871, age 24.
Gibbons, Mrs. Joanna M., Dec. 3, 1877, age 47.
Gibbons, Mary A., wife of Charles, Oct. 17, 1872, age 41 y, 6 m.
Gibbons, Philip, drowned, July 5, 1876, age 21.
Gibbons, William, formerly of Buffalo, Oct. 2, 1879, age 23; d. at Atlanta, GA.
Gibbs, James P., Feb. 25, 1876, age 21 y, 5 m., 15 d.
Gibbs, Mrs. Letitia M., March 27, 1866, age 53.
Gibbs, Rachel P., wife of Artemas, Sept. 1, 1873, age 50.
Gibbs, Sarah, wife of Asgill, Nov. 18, 1849, age 57; taken to Marshall, MI.
Gibney, Mrs. Bridget, Nov. 17, 1874, age 67.
Gibney, Christopher, Dec. 15, 1871, age 25.
Gibney, James, Jan. 17, 1876, age 76.
Gibson, Adeline, wife of Capt. A.B., Oct. 6, 1875, age 44.
Gibson, Benjamin, Nov. 5, 1869, age 58.
Gibson, E. W., telegraph operator, Sept. 16, 1878; d. at Memphis, TN.
Gibson, Fanny, May 27, 1879, age 50.
Gibson, James F., Jan. 4, 1873, age 26 y, 8 m, 2 d.
Gibson, John, Sept. 24, 1847, age 55, at Medina, NY.
Gibson, John G., Feb. 9, 1873; d. at Santa Barbara, CA.
Gibson, John R., March 21, 1854, age 46.
Gibson, Mary M., Feb. 24, 1880, age 46.
Gibson, Robert P., July 5, 1868, age 48 y, 8 m, 25 d.
Gibson, Robert W., Sept. 21, 1869, age 36.
Gibson, Samuel, Sr., July 24, 1879, age 83.
Gibson, William L., Nov. 20, 1866, age 46.
Gidding, Caroline, wife of A. H., May 1879, age 69 y, 1 m, 16 d.
Giddings, Niles, b. 1765, d. 1842, bur. Warsaw (Wyoming Co.); Soldier of the Revolution.
Gielsdorf, Mrs. M.F., dau. of John Deters, June 27, 1867, age 21 y, 9 m.
Giffing, Dr. Isaac H., Feb. 3, 1872, age 50.
Giffing, Margaret Van Ransselaer Keating, Oct. 29, 1879, age 83.
Giffing, William from N.Y. City, Aug. 3, 1854, age 68.
Giffing, William H., July 8, 1863, age 47.
Gifford, Mrs. Eliza, widow of Lewis, Eden, NY, April 21, 1879, age 69.
Gifford, Lewis, Eden, Jan. 12, 1876, age 75.
Gigley, William, Railroad accident, Jan. 15, 1877, agec. 45.
Gilbert, Colgate. D. in London, England, May 1, 1875.
Gilbert, Elmira, dau. of David, Jan. 15, 1860, age 25 y, 1 m.
Gilbert, Capt. Ephraim F., East Aurora, NY, Nov. 30, 1863, age 84.
Gilbert, Erastus, Sept. 26, 1847, age 52.
Gilbert, Henry S., May 1, 1868, age 54. Engineer of the propeller *Governor Cushman*.
Gilbert, Herman C., Obituary, BCA (July 10, 1858).
Gilbert, Ithamar P., Aug. 1822, age 35.
Gilbert, Miss J. J., Oct. 4, 1873, age 45.
Gilbert, John M., Jan. 2, 1878, age 62.
Gilbert, Maria, wife of Capt. E. F., Nov. 18, 1828, age 39.
Gilbert, Mary M., wife of Luzerne, Feb. 18, 1864, age 63.
Gilbert, Mrs. Sarah, widow of Erastus, Nov. 30, 1880, age 78.
Gilbert, William A., Sept. 26, 1851, age 30 y, 7 m.
Gilchrist, Mary, wife of John, July 8, 1879, age 45.
Gilder, Henry, Almshouse, Jan. 9, 1880, age 46.
Gildersleeve, George Latrop, formerly of Buffalo, March 8, 1879, age 26.
Gilfoy, Catherine, County Almshouse, March 25, 1879, age 28.
Gilgallon, Patrick, Dec. 20, 1872.
Gilgar, Edward, Aug. 18, 1876, age 30.
Gill, Patrick, July 6, 1869, age 53.
Gill, Thomas A., Oct. 7, 1832, age c. 43; in Painesville, OH.
Gilles, Matthias P., May 27, 1877, age 39.

Gillespie, Anthony, Sept. 13, 1864, age 75.
Gillespie, James G., June 19, 1864, age 75; in N.Y. City.
Gillespie, Janet Richmond, Sept. 23, 1877.
Gillespie, Martin, Nov. 9, 1873, age 41.
Gillespie, Roxella, formerly of Buffalo, widow of Anthony. D. at Lapeer, MI, Jan. 10, 1873, age 75; bur. at Buffalo.
Gillet, Albert A., Feb. 6, 1871, age 31 y, 2 m, 24 days; killed on the Hudson River Railroad at New Hamburgh.
Gillet, Caleb, April 9, 1848, age 61.
Gillet, Charlotte Augusta, wife of Henry T., Jan. 20, 1874, age 74.
Gillet, Dan Marvin, Oct. 1, 1849, age 32; in Niles, MI.
Gillet, Emily, wife of Caleb, Oct. 26, 1847, age 55.
Gillet, Frances A., wife of Caleb G., July 15, 1837, age 18.
Gillet, Harry, youngest son of Henry T., Jan. 25, 1865, age 20 y, 7 m. Killed at American Hotel fire.
Gillet, Henry Thomas, Nov. 23, 1874, age 80 y, 8 m.
Gillet, Jane, wife of Israel, April 18, 1851, age 28.
Gillet, Dr. Nathaniel from Newfield, Tompkins Co., Clarence, NY, April 19, 1832, age 23.
Gillet, Noel, son of Noel, nephew of Henry T., March 1, 1865; in Castle Rushan, Isle of Man.
Gillet, William Henry, (Obit. Jan. 26, 1865 & Feb. 1)
Gillett, Julia A., wife of Israel T., July 12, 1873; d. in NY City, bur. Buffalo.
Gillig, Frank L., formerly of Buffalo, March 6, 1878.
Gillig, Mrs. Franz, accidental death, Feb. 6, 1875; age 54 y, 7 m.
Gillig, Henry, son of Lorenz, Oct. 28, 1871, age 24. D. at Ft. Wayne, IN, bur. in Buffalo.
Gillig, Lorenz, Oct. 8, 1878, age 61 y, 1 m, 7 d.
Gillig, Mary Helen Magdalen, wife of Charles, June 14, 1869, age 20 y, 10 m.
Gillis, John, April 28, 1836, age c. 21.
Gillott, John, Jan. 5, 1876, age 43.
Gilman, Alfred W., Almshouse, July 8, 1880, age 52.
Gilman, H. J., Feb. 4, 1874, age 57.
Gilman, James W., Sr., May 29, 1867, age 57.
Gilman, Louisa M., d/o James W., March 23, 1869, age 23 y, 7 m.
Gilman, Maggie Calahan, wife of Oscar F., April 26, 1872, age 21 y, 8 m.
Gilman, Oliver H. Perry, Feb. 27, 1868, age 22 y, 27 d.
Gilmer, Mr., July 19, 1829, age 25.
Gilmore, Andrew, May 25, 1854, age 51; at Toledo, OH.
Gilmore, Thomas, July 19, 1829, age 22.
Gimp, William, almshouse, July 13, 1880, age 63.
Ginther, Frederick W., ship-carpenter, Sept. 2, 1878, age 43. Railroad accident.
Gipple, Conrad, Cayuga Creek, June 8, 1832, age 29.
Giraux, Joseph, drowned, Tonawanda, Jan. 23, 1874.
Gire, Josephine Havens, wife of Austin, formerly of Buffalo, Feb. 1873, age 22. D. at Grand Rapids, MI, bur. in Burralo.
Giskre, Frank, b. Bohemia, tailor, May 18, 1874, age 30.
Gisman, John, June 29, 1879, age 34.
Gittere, Charles Louis, d. at Provincial Hospital, Kimberly Diamond Fields, South Africa, formerly of Buffalo. July 4, 1880, age 22.
Gittere, Jacob, Jan. 16, 1875, age 63.
Gittere, John Jr., March 1878, age 20.
Given, Margaret, June 15, 1880, age 72.
Given, Miss Nancy, Feb. 21, 1868, age 23.
Glanz, Frederick A., Dec. 21, 1876, 47 y, 4 d.
Glass, John, April 1, 1874, age 31 y, 5 m, 25 d.
Glass, Lizzie, drowned with 3 others, July 4, 1874, aged 22.
Glass, William, March 12, 1879, age 47 y, 3 m.
Glasser (or Gloser), Christian, suicide, Sept. 4, 1875, age 21.
Glassford, Timothy H., Jan. 28, 1871, age 55.
Glaze, Mrs. Alta C. (formerly Salisbury), formerly of Buffalo, Oct. 9, 1875, age 58. D. at San Jose, CA, bur. in Buffalo.
Gleason, Flavia Hale, wife of G.B., May 7, 1844, age 27.

Gleason, George B., June 16, 1866, age 71; in East Haddam, CT.
Gleason, Henry E., late of US Navy, Nov. 9, 1870, age 23 y, 2 m, 4 days.
Gleason, Hugh, Feb. 16, 1878, age 70.
Gleason, John at General Hospital, Dec. 28, 1878, age 28.
Gleason, John, Sept. 19, 1880, age 58.
Gleason, John Ely, eldest son of Cyrenius of Buffalo, Sardinia, NY, Jan. 5, 1864, age 23.
Gleason, Julia, wife of W.H., Feb. 20, 1866, age 41.
Gleason, Mary Jane, May 23, 1880, age 22 y, 18 d.
Gleason, Michael, Jan. 23, 1870, age 21 y, 2 m, 10 days.
Gleason, P. W., March 4, 1878, age 52.
Gleed, Thomas, Jan. 7, 1859, age 55.
Glen, John, suicide, Dec. 25, 1872, d. at Marshall, Saline Co., MO.
Glennan, Mrs. Ellen, wife of James, June 7, 1879, age 41.
Glidden, Ruth M., Aug. 7, 1874, age 77.
Glynn, Hamilton, Jan. 19, 1878, age 82 y, 2 m, 9 d.
Glynn, Mary, wife of E.B., Grand Island, March 24, 1847, age 27 y, 8 m.
Glynn, Owen, Aug. 4, 1871.
Gobeil, Moses S., March 26, 1875, age 61 y, 2 m, 16 d.
Gockel, Elizabeth, wife of Michael, Dec. 6, 1864, age 36 y, 6 m.
Godard, Betsey W., wife of Alvan, Springville, NY, Nov. 24, 1845, age 32.
Godfrey, Catharine, wife of James J., April 3, 1871, age 27 y, 2 m.
Godfrey, Elizabeth, North Collins, NY, May 8, 1869, age 86. Mother of E.W. and Charles E.
    Godfrey of Oshkosh, WI.
Godfrey, Mary, wife of R. T. Williamsville, NY, March 9, 1843, age 23.
Goehrung, Christian, b. Baden, April 13, 1872, age 48.
Goesswein, Christian F., suicide, saloon keeper, Sept. 3, 1879, age 27.
Goettle, Jacob F., June 30, 1878, age 68.
Goettleman, Charles, suicide, June 1, 1872.
Goetz, John F. (or Wm.), July 4, 1880, age 29 y, 2 m.
Goetz, Susan, wife of Joseph, Oct. 9, 1879, age 22 y, 22 d.
Goffe, Louisa M., wife of William, Dec. 16, 1880, age 34.
Goggin, Mrs. Mary, Feb. 9, 1872, age 33.
Going, Capt. Jonathan, Revolutionary soldier, Aurora, NY, Aug. 25, 1848, age 87.
Gold, Catherine T., June 5, 1875, widow of Charles R.
Gold, Mary Ann, wife of William B., Lancaster, NY, Dec. 25, 1871, age 36.
Golden, Mrs. Ann, Oct. 7, 1877, age 49.
Golden, Mrs. M., formerly of Buffalo, Oct. 29, 1880, age 30 y, 4 m, 29 d.
Golden, William, alias William Harris, drowned, Oct. 24, 1872, age 24.
Goldfuz, Conrad, Clarence, Oct. 10, 187???, age c. 57.
Goldie, John, March 23, 1872, age 58.
Goldsmith, Abraham B., formerly of Buffalo, printer, May, 1874, age 43; d. in Chicago.
Goldsmith, Edward of US Rev. Cutter, *Commodore Perry* sailor, July 27, 1872.
Gollan, John, Oct. 30, 1874, age 63.
Goldwitzer, Christopher F., Oct. 7, 1876, age 24 y, 9 m, 3 d.
Golnor (or Gulnor), Joseph, drowned, Aug. 20, 1874, age 45.
Gonke (or Yonke), Henry, suicide, Oct. 18, 1876, age 46.
Good, Adam, formerly of Buffalo, Oct. 3, 1877, d. at Titusville.
Good, Julia, wife of John, dau. of Frederick Krefe, Jan. 28, 1864, age 22.
Good, Peter, Clarence, NY, April 30, 1878, age 85 y, 6 m, 8 d.
Goodale, Daniel, father of Mrs. F. S. Pease, March 25, 1858, age 69.
Goodale, Lucretia Porter, wife of Daniel, Feb. 10, 1858, age 59.
Goodall, Amelia, wife of William N., dau. of Rev. William Bishop of Bradford, England, Dec.
    11, 1847, age 41.
Goodall, Eliza, wife of W.A., Nov. 14, 1850, age 44.
Goodall, W.N., Jan. 4, 1855, age 48.
Goodel, James, Collins, March 16, 1844, age 85.
Goodell, David, July, 1827, age 30.
Goodell, Dianna, widow of Jabez, March 10, 1854, age 63; in Wellsburg, PA, bur. in Buffalo.
Goodell, Jabez, Sept. 26, 1851, age 75.
Goodell, Martha, mother of Deacon Jabez, May 28, 1830, age 82.

Goodhue, Desiah, wife of William H., March 30, 1852; at Michigan City, IN.
Gooding, Rodney, Jan. 15, 1874, age 62.
Gooding, Wealthy, wife of Rodney, Sept. 15, 1865, age 48 y, 5 m, 17 d.
Goodrich, Capt. Augustus M., formerly of Buffalo, Aug. 28, 1866 in New Orleans, LA, age 31 y, 9 m.; youngest son of Guy H.
Goodrich, Guy H., March 24, 1867, age 77.
Goodrich, James A., April 10, 1867, age 61.
Goodrich, Joseph Herrick, s/o the late Guy H., formerly of Buffalo, Sept. 9, 1875. D. at Gresco, IA.
Goodrich, Nancy, formerly of Buffalo, Feb. 2, 1873, age 69; widow of Guy H., d. at Attica.
Goodrich, Roswell, Revolutionary soldier, Sardinia, NY, Jan. 23, 1847, age 91.
Goodrich, Abby, wife of Chauncey A., Feb. 27, 1824, age 23.
Goodrich, Capt. Augustus M., youngest son of Guy H., Aug. 28, 1866, age 31 years, 9 months; in New Orleans, LA.
Goodrich, Eunice, wife of Levi, Clarence, NY, June 1, 1855, age 81; at Goodrich, MI.
Goodrich, Guy H., March 24, 1867, age 77.
Goodrich, James A., April 10, 1867, age 61.
Goodrich, Hon. John S., Clarence, NY, Oct. 15, 1851, age 36; in Detroit, Mich.
Goodrich, Margaret L., wife of E.H., June 4, 1865, age 49; in Chicago.
Goodrich, Nathaniel B., June 25, 1843, age 57.
Goodrich, Sarah A., wife of Guy H., May 5, 1822, age 20.
Goodwin, Mrs. Ann, June, 1830, age 74.
Goodwin, Charles A., Jan. 24, 1852, age 28.
Goodwin, Charles L. or J., Aug. 16, 1873, age 26 y, 1 m, 4 d.
Goodwin, David, Jan. 29, 1851, age 53.
Goodwin, Norman, March 22, 1832, age c. 60.
Goodwin, Patrick, formerly of Buffalo, June 13, 1874, Titusville.
Goodwin, Mrs. Sophronia, March 16, 1861, age 61.
Goodwin, Thomas S., July 25, 1849.
Gordinier, Maj. Jacob, Aug. 20, 1838, age 50.
Gordon, Caroline, wife of Charles A., April 30, 1876.
Gordon, Mary Ann of Ayshire, Scotland, June 30, 1863, age 40.
Gorges, John M., March 18, 1880, age 21 y, 5 m, 19 d.
Gorham, Mrs. Catharine, Sept. 6, 1880.
Gorham, Emily H., wife of George, dau. of Hon. N.K. Hall, May 29, 1863, age 24.
Gorham, Rawson L., May 1, 1846, age 36.
Gorham, Susan, wife of Benjamin L., Lancaster, NY, Sept. 15, 1865, age 58.
Gorman, Mrs. Mary, Aug. 10, 1856, age 52.
Gorman, Michael, Nov. 22, 1871.
Gorman, Michael, Erie Co. Almshouse, Aug 7, 1879, age 76, age 76.
Gorman, Patrick, formerly of Buffalo, March 10, 1873, bur. in Buffalo.
Gorman, Patrick, Nov. 29, 1874, age 48.
Gorton, Cyrus L., Aug. 14, 1876, age 41.
Goslin, Hon. Ezra P., Newstead, Jan. 16, 1870, age 59 y, 6 m.
Goslin, LeGrand, Akron, Dec. 14, 1877, age 32 y, 1 m.
Gosrow, H. C., Aug. 8, 1872, age 64 y, 4 m.
Gott, Dr. Nathaniel, Clarence, NY, Sept. 14, 1828, age 73.
Gotwalt, Anna C., Williamsville, NY, March 26, 1866, age 25.
Gotwalt, Mrs. Catharine, Williamsville, Sept. 5, 1877, age 85.
Gould, Aaron, East Hamburgh, Nov. 2, 1874, age 71.
Gould, Anna, wife of Asa, Hamburgh, NY, July 2, 1830, age 46.
Gould, Antoinette, only dau. of Benjamin, East Hamburg, NY, Jan. 27, 1865, age 22.
Gould, Asa, Revolutionary soldier, Colden, NY, Sept. 11, 1849, age 97 y, 6 d.
Gould, Charles R. (Gold), Police Justice, May 26, 1853, age 41.
Gould, Emmons S., March 16, 1871, age 51.
Gould, Eugene, suicide, Holland, Aug. 24, 1877, age 33.
Gould, Edward O., July 31, 1858; taken to Syracuse, NY.
Gould, Emily, wife of George L., March 21, 1860, age 26.
Gould, Dr. Emmons S., Hamburgh, NY, March 1, 1829, age 40.
Gould, Helen J., wife of William C., Aug. 29, 1880; bur. at East Aurora.

Gould, Isaac, Revolutionary soldier, Evans, NY, Feb. 18, 1844, age 85.
Gould, Jacob, Oct. 28, 1879, age 75.
Gould, Kate Blossom, wife of Frank J., June 13, 1870; d. in Cleveland, bur. Buffalo.
Gould, Lois, wife of Asa, Colden, NY, Nov. 2, 1847, age 77 y, 7 m, 2 d.
Gould, Lucinda, wife of E. S., March 14, 1855, age 32; taken to Mexico, Oswego Co.
Gould, Lucinda, widow of Dr. E.S., Hamburgh, NY, July 30, 1829, age 32.
Gould, Lucius, Aug. 5, 1832, age 44.
Gould, Phares, Aug. 24, 1862, age 76; in N.Y. City.
Gould, Susan M. Osborn, only dau. of Aaron, Hamburgh, NY, Jan. 23, 1865, age 25.
Gould, Susan M., wife of Royal A., West Seneca, June 8, 1874.
Gould, Truman, East Hamburgh, April 18, 1873, age 68.
Gould, William, July 30, 1832, age 32.
Goulding, D.S., Aug. 9, 1864, age 41; in Waterloo, C.E.
Goulding, Mary Ann, Nov. 22, 1875, age 53.
Gowans, Andrew, Dec. 21, 1870, age 66.
Gowans, James S., Feb. 18, 1874, age 35 y, 9 m, 15 d; d. at Elmira, bur. Buffalo.
Gowans, May, wife of Peter, Nov. 17, 1862, age 57.
Gowans, Peter, March 23, 1880, age 78.
Gowdy, Theodore, July 23, 1850; in Cincinnati, OH.
Grabau, Rev. J. A. A., June 2, 1879, age 75.
Grabenstatter, Frank, June 4, 1878, age 79.
Grace, Byron H., East Hamburgh, Dec. 25, 1875, age 23.
Grace, Mrs. Catherine, Feb. 8, 1872, age 50.
Grace, Oliver, d. at Co. Almshouse, Jan. 31, 1876, age 21.
Grady, John, accidentally killed, May 1, 1874, age 45.
Grady, Michael, accidental death, Aug. 1, 1873.
Graeber, Catharine, mother of Capt. John Yox, Buffalo Police Dept., Oct. 3, 1880, age 69.
Graeber, Charles H., March 1872, age 30 y, 7 m.
Graff, Hannah, mother of Mrs. Sarah Streiber, April 24, 1861, age 74 y, 6 m.
Graham, Amasa, July 13, 1874, age 64.
Graham, Betsey L., wife of Amasa, March 4, 1854, age 46.
Graham, Elizabeth, wife of John A., formerly of Buffalo, April 25, 1880, age 37; d. in New York.
Graham, George, Dec. 10, 1875, age 73.
Graham, George, Dec. 12, 1877, age 85.
Graham, James H., counsellor at law, April 98, 1854, age 44.
Graham, Lizzie, at Co. Almshouse, May 31, 1878, age 24.
Graham, Mrs. Margaret, widow of Samuel, April 27, 1879, age 78.
Graham, Matilda, Oct. 16, 1873, age 22.
Graham, Michael, Oct. 14, 1871, age 40 y, 8 m.
Graham, Nancy, widow of Philip, Feb. 2, 1870, age 64.
Graham, William C. or M., Jan. 4, 1876, age c. 50.
Grahamsley, George H., Jan. 11, 1873.
Grahling, Frederick, Jan. 19, 1871, age 24.
Grahling, Philip J., Dec. 18, 1869, age 81 y, 6 m.
Granby, Emeline McQuann, wife of John, Nov. 15, 1876, age 54.
Grandison, James, March 10, 1873, age 63.
Granger, Capt. Abner from Suffield, CT, Oct. 15, 1816.
Granger, Elizabeth S., widow of Judge Erastus, July 29, 1853, age 69.
Granger, Erastus, Dec. 21, 1826, age 62. [Another card: Granger, Erastus, b. 1765, d. Dec. 21, 1826, age 62, bur. Buffalo; Soldier of the Revolution.]
Granger, Rev. James N., Jan. 8, 1857.
Granger, James W., Sept. 25, 1813, age 17.
Granger, Polly, Sept. 27, 1860, age 89.
Granger, Sarah, wife of Seth, June 3, 1832, age 50.
Granger, Seth, Oct. 18, 1848, age 74.
Granger, Sophia Elizabeth, dau. of Warren, March 24, 1875, age 25.
Grannis, David from Wallingford, CT, Gowanda, NY, Oct. 12, 1867, age 77.
Grant, Angus, Nov. 5, 1873.

Grant, Serg. Charles H., 116th Reg. N.Y.V., Brant, NY, June 29, 1864, age 25. D. at Soldiers Rest in Buffalo.
Grant, David M., July 1867, age 54; in Brooklyn, NY.
Grant, Elizabeth M., wife of Hon. A.P., of Oswego, dau. of late Gen. Heman B. Potter, Oct. 24, 1854, age 34; taken to Oswego, NY.
Grant, Mrs. Jane, March 3, 1868, age 84.
Grant, Joseph, b. 1764, d. 1838, bur. Holland; Soldier of the Revolution.
Grant, Mrs. Nancy, Brant Center, Nov. 30, 1874, age 73 y, 2 m, 13 d.
Grant, Samuel P., Co. Almshouse, April 12, 1877, age 69.
Grant, William, July 24, 1824, age 39.
Grant, William, Aug. 12, 1880, age 27.
Grass, Ph., April 24, 1872, age 47 y, 2 m, 24 d.
Grasser, Christian, railroad accident, Oct. 1877; baker.
Grau, Maria Anna, wife of F. W., June 24, 1870, age 54; native of Germany.
Graumachin, Joseph, drowned, May 21, 1874, age 47.
Grave, Mrs. Hannah, Evans Centre, Feb. 22, 1870, age 77.
Graves, Charles, son of S.V.R., Aug. 6, 1877, age 31; funeral at East Hamburgh.
Graves, Delana, wife of S.V.R., East Hamburgh, March 17, 1869, age 61 y, 8 m, 20 d.
Graves, Eunice, wife of Constant, Springville, NY, July 10, 1844, age 51.
Graves, George E., Jan. 21, 1877, age 31 y, 7 m, 6 d.
Graves, Russell, June, 1826, age 55.
Graves, William B., Feb. 7, 1855; in Auburn, NY.
Gray, Catharine E., wife of William, March 12, 1850, age 20.
Gray, Dr. E. P., formerly of Buffalo, Aug. 9, 1872, age 49; d. at St. Joseph, MO.
Gray, Elizabeth, wife of Joseph, July 15, 1861, age 62.
Gray, James from Edinburgh, Scotland, June 30, 1866, age 64.
Gray, John, Willink, NY, Oct. 15, 1860, age 58.
Gray, Jabesh, Revolutionary soldier, from Saratoga Springs, NY, Jan. 29, 1836, age 76.
Gray, Margaret, widow of David, Oct. 18, 1854, age 74. From Cramond, near Edinburgh, Scotland.
Gray, Mary, wife of John, Aurora, NY, Aug. 29, 1848, age 42.
Gray, Oscar P., March 17, 1875, age 28.
Gray, William. Obituary Nov. 26, 1825.
Graybiel, David, Williamsville, May 7, 1877, age 92.
Greek, Dorothy, South Newstead, wife of Nicholas, Dec. 10, 1874, age 77 y, 8 m, 10 d.
Greek, Olive Ann, wife of George, Newstead, NY, Aug. 14, 1860, age 24 y, 7 m, 6 d.
Green, Mr., father of G. B., Hamburgh, NY, Feb. 24, 1826, age 75.
Green, Allen, Sardinia, NY, Sept. 13, 1859, age 81.
Green, Ann, wife of Capt. Thomas, Jan. 10, 1853, age 50.
Green, Mrs. Anna, March 18, 1873, age 67 y, 5 d.
Green, Ebenezer, canaler, Sept. 21, 1874, age c. 50; d. suddenly at the General Hospital.
Green, Ellen, wife of Capt. John, May 4, 1877, age 42.
Green, Finley F., formerly of Buffalo, Feb. 7, 1873, age 47; d. in Hamilton, Ontario.
Green, Frances B., wife of William S., March 13, 1874, age 35; taken to Rochester.
Green, J. B., diver, Oct. 16, 1868, age 45.
Green, Juliett, wife of Hiram T., West Falls, Aug. 25, 1856, age 28 y, 11 m.
Green, Laura, wife of Hiram T., Aurora, NY, Aug. 23, 1854, age 27.
Green, Lydia Ann, wife of Elias, Oct. 1, 1844, age 39.
Green, Mariin,?? dau. of George Vine & wife of Samuel, Oct. 17, 1874, age 23 y, 2 m.
Green, Martha H. Swallow, wife of J.C., Jan. 28, (or 8) 1873, age 38.
Green, Mrs. Mary, Jan. 5, 1873, age 92.
Green, Nathan, Co. Almshouse, April 18, 1877, age 39.
Green, Capt. Nathaniel S. and wife, brother of S. H., Oct. 1, 1878; d. near Memphis, TN.
Green, Paris, Bowmansville, Aug. 5, 1876, age 66 y, 6 m.
Green, Philinda, widow of George B., Hamburgh, Dec. 28, 1871, age 76.
Green, William A., M.D., Surgeon, U.S.N., Oct. 26, 1839 at Pensacola, FL.
Greene, George B., Hamburg, NY, July 7, 1854, age 59 y, 6 m.
Greene, George E., June 22, 1867, age 48.
Greene, Loring A., Lancaster, Oct. 22, 1860, age 31; in Clinton, IN.
Greene, Mary, wife of Charles, Feb. 11, 1878, age 51.

Greene, Dr. Stephen B., April 12, 1836, age 35.
Greenleaf, Ann Eliza, wife of W.R., April 8, 1865, age 44.
Greenleaf, William R., June 15, 1865, age 46.
Greenlees, William, Aug. 22, 1820, age 28.
Greenman, Mrs., Sept. 17, 1872, age 67; d. at the "Church Home."
Greenman, Edward M., durggist, Aug. 30, 1870, age 27 y, 6 m.
Greenman, Helen Mar? Burnet, wife of James L., Jan. 16, 1874, age 47; d. at Syracuse.
Greenman, J. Browne, Dec. 4, 1873, age 34 y, 2 m, 10 d.
Greenman, James L., formerly of Buffalo, April 22, 1880, age 57; d. in New York.
Greeno, Amos H., March 7, 1873, age 45; taken to Newark, Wayne Co.
Greenshield, John, Jan. 18, 1862, age 43 y, 6 m.
Greenshields, Mary, wife of John, Nov. 30, 1854, age 36 y, 6 m.
Greenslit, Nathaniel C. from Franklin, CT, June 3, 1854, age 52.
Greenwold (Gruenwald), Frederick, Aug. 31, 1873, age 66.
Greenwood, Simon L., July 22, 1875, age 59; d. at Hinckley, OH.
Greer, Mrs. Frankie, wife of J.F., formerly of Buffalo, May 5, 1879, age 22; d. in Chicago.
Greer, George, Aug. 3, 1869; d. at Lunatic Asylum, Utica, NY.
Gregg, Eleanor, wife of Charles, June 12, 1874, age 32 y, 9 m.
Gregg, John C., June 12, 1870, age 31 y, 6 m, 8d.
Gregg, Mrs. Mary Ann, March 10, 1870.
Gregg, Pamelia, wife of Benjamin, Aug. 2, 1814, age 37.
Gregg, Sarah A., wife of George H., Sept. 28, 1875, age 31.
Gregory, Calista, Feb. 20, 1877, age 67.
Gregory, Mrs. Mary, Sept. 5, 1873, age 49.
Gregory, Mary A., wife of Amos S., Feb. 15, 1869, dau. of the late Stephen Albro.
Gregory, Louisa, wife of A. W., March 9, 1876, age 27.
Gregory, William, Jan. 27, 1876.
Greiner, John Sr., March 29, 1876, age 79 y, 2 m, 13 d.
Greiner, John F., accident, laborer, May 31, 1879.
Greiner, Mary, wife of Frederick, suicide, Aug. 11, 1875, age 51.
Greiner, Michael, brother of John, formerly of Buffalo, Sept. 1878.
Greisen, Anna L., eld. dau. of the late John P., formerly of Buffalo, June 8, 1878, age 23; d. in Philadelphia.
Greisen, John P., lawyer, Dec. 25, 1868, age 39.
Grenan, Margaret, Nov. 8, 1860, age 20.
Grender, Edward, Co. Almshouse, Dec. 20, 1878, age 71.
Grey, Ann F., wife of Robert, Dec. 29, 1847, age 28.
Grey, Charles, Aug. 16, 1871, age 46; taken to Syracuse.
Grey, Charles, Feb. 11, 1871, age 55 y, 10 m.
Grey, Nathaniel, April 10, 1845, age 72; in Savana, IL.
Grey, William, March 22, 1853, age 50.
Grider, Nancy Ann, widow of Daniel, June 13, 1866, age 77 y, 11 m.
Gridley, Celement, Jan. 11, 1870, age 69; taken to Rochester.
Gridley, Frederick, Dec. 8, 1876, age 55.
Gridley, George Hollister, only son of Clement, Feb. 15, 1864, age 21.
Gridley, Harmony, widow of Frederick, Jan. 4, 1879, age 59.
Gridley, Thomas, Co. Almshouse, June 12, 1876, age 47.
Grierson, Clara C., wife of John P., March 24, 1862, age 25.
Griesman, Cornelia C., wife of Jacob, May 3, 1872, age 39.
Griffeth, Cynthia, wife of Jonathan, West Seneca, April 24, 1871, age 43.
Griffin, Ann, May 20, 1878, age 94.
Griffin, Charles N., July 9, 1875, age 69; taken to Detroit.
Griffin, Hannah, dau. of Henry of East Hamburgh, NY, March 15, 1846, age 33.
Griffin, Harmon, Nov. 28, 1870, age 65.
Griffin, Henry, from Carlyle, Schoharie Co., Jan. 9, 1852, age 23.
Griffin, Henry, East Hamburgh, NY, Jan. 31, 1860, age 85.
Griffin, Henry A., East Hamburgh, NY, Aug. 29, 1860, age 43.
Griffin, Horace, Oct. 12, 1837, age 45.
Griffin, Hugh, almshouse, Oct. 22, 1880, age 35.
Griffin, Isaiah, Feb. 17, 1868, age 39.

Griffin, Jacob, East Hamburgh, NY, Sept. 5, 1860, age 88.
Griffin, James, Hamburgh, April 13, 1868, age 62.
Griffin, James, East Hamburgh, Nov. 2, 1875, age 95 y, 2 m.
Griffin, Jennie, accidentally killed Dec. 25, 1873, age 42.
Griffin, Jonathan, East Hamburgh, NY April 30, 1850, age 48.
Griffin, Joseph C., East Hamburgh, NY, Nov. 17, 1875, age 66.
Griffin, Mary Jane, wife of Alanson C., East Hamburgh, NY, Aug. 8, 1863, age 27 y, 6 m.
Griffin, Maurice, June 18, 1871, age c. 35.
Griffin, Michael, March 19, 1874, age 40.
Griffin, Capt. Michael, of canal boat *Wheelock*, May 1874, age c. 35 or 23; accidently killed in New York.
Griffin, Mrs. Parnel, from Clinton, Oneida Co., Jan. 10, 1852, age 90.
Griffin, Midshipman Robert N., eldest son of John, formerly of Buffalo, living in Philadelphia at time of death, Sept. 7, 1867, age 23, on *U.S. Tacony*.
Griffin, Samuel, Black Rock, NY, 1841.
Griffin, Sarah, Aug. 5, 1841, age 47.
Griffin, Semira, wife of Hiram, Williamsville, May 26, 1873, age 53.
Griffin, T. Harley, March 6, 1876.
Griffin, Zachariah, June 12, 1850, age 83.
Griffith, Catalina W., wife of John M., Aug. 28, 1855, age 38.
Griffith, George, Tonawanda, Aug. 14, 1878, age 47.
Griffith, Huldah, wife of Henry L., Boston, July 29, 1876.
Griffith, John, Oct. 3, 1852, age 50, at Sheboygan, WI.
Griffith, John M., Feb. 1, 1864, age 53; at College Hill, Hamilton Co., OH.
Griffith, Mary W., Boston, May 28, 1874, age 69 y, 11 m, 6 d.
Griffith, Phebe S., dau. of John M., Jan. 22, 1863, age 21; in Chicago, IL.
Griffiths, John, Nov. 30, 1872, age 55 y, 6 m.
Grill, Jacob, formerly of Buffalo, March 21, 1878, age 75 y, 7 m, 24 d. D. at Lancaster.
Grimard, Gustavus, April 26, 1879, age 64.
Grimes, Helen M., wife of William H., Lancaster, NY, March 27, 1841, age 28.
Grimes, Henry M., Co. C, 116th Reg. NY Vol., Alden, NY, Aug. 14, 1863, age 25; in hospital in New Orleans.
Grimes, Mary A. Safford, wife of William H., Lancaster, NY, March 27, 1879, age 59.
Grimm, John or Felix, killed on railroad, Aug. 31, 1879.
Grimmell, Catharine E., wife of Jeremiah P., May 3, 1876, age 21 y, 6 m, 15 y.
Grimsby, John, of English birth, sailor, accidently killed, July 13, 1872, age c 30.
Grinnell, Mrs. Diadamia Brown, Cheektowaga, March 6, 1872, age 88.
Grinnell, William, Lancaster, NY, Jan. 14, 1864, age 85.
Grissim, Charles F., Oct. 26, 1877, age 31.
Grissim, John, Sept. 29, 1853, age 45.
Griswold, Alfred B., son of E.A., Aug. 21, 1876, age 21.
Griswold, Mrs. Caleb (Betsey), Aug. 12, 1879, age 69.
Griswold, Joab, late of Herkimer, NY, Sept. 7, 1835, age 24.
Griswold, Mrs. Lovina, July 22, 1862, age 80; bur. in Lyons, NY.
Griswold, Lucy Jane, dau. of Isaac, from Rouses Point, NY, July 22, 1862, age 80.
Grodrish, Rosa, d. at Co. Almshouse, Feb. 24, 1876, age c 40.
Groening, C.A., supposed suicide, Aug. 23, 1877, age 54.
Groesbeck, Addie M., dau. of J. L., Aug. 27, 1864.
Groesbeck, Jacob L., Feb. 20, 1864, age 60.
Groesbeck, Walter P., Jan. 1826, age 40.
Grome, Edwin, accident, laborer, May 31, 1879, age 40.
Grommon, Mrs. Sarah Ann, formerly of Buffalo, Dec. 15, 1876; d. at Coldwater, MI.
Groning, Albertine, wife of C.A., Feb. 1, 1873, age 44 y, 3 m.
Gronmeyer, Maria, July 12, 1878, age 57 y, 2 m, 9 d.
Groscurth, William, formerly of Buffalo, Jan. 1873; d. in Chicago.
Gross, Daniel, formerly of Buffalo, June 14, 1877; d. in Darien, Genesee Co., NY.
Gross, Henry, Dec. 1878, age 86 y, 2 m, 14 d.
Gross, John, Jan. 1873, age 51.
Gross, Peter, Wales, March 9, 1871, age 71 y, 7 m, 8 d.
Gross, Phebe, wife of Thomas, Clarence, NY, Dec. 8, 1826, age 55.

Gross, Rebecca, wife of Rev. Thomas, Williamsville, Aug. 14, 1820.
Gross, Susan, youngest dau. of Rev. Thomas, Williamsville, NY, Oct. 14, 1820.
Gross, Rev. Thomas, Lancaster, NY, c. April, 1842, age 85.
Grosvenor, Abel M., Sept. 6, 1849, age 39.
Grosvenor, Lucien, Oct. 20, 1862, age 45.
Grosvenor, Dr. S. L., March 20, 1865; bur. in Auburn, NY.
Grosvenor, Seth C., M.D., from Minot, ME, Jan. 27, 1850, age 35; in Sacramento, CA.
Grosvenor, Seth H., May 13, 1864, age 52.
Grosvenor, Col. Stephen K., Nov. 1, 1839, age 46 y, 7 m.
Grosvenor, William A., son of Lucien, May 6, 1862, age 20 y, 8 m, 6 d.
Groundwater, Margaret L., wife of James, March 18, 1874, age 40 y, 3 m.
Grove, Betsy, widow of John, Williamsville, June 3, 1862, age 71.
Grove, Mrs. Eliza, Williamsville, Jan. 12, 1871, age 55; d. in Buffalo.
Grove, John, Williamsville, Feb. 23, 1851, age 68.
Grove, Peter, Williamsville, July 13, 1877, age 66.
Gruber, Jacob, Jan. 1, 1871, age 53.
Grunwold, Bertha, mother of Siegmund Levyn, Sept. 11, 1880, age 80.
Guenther, Andrew, Jan. 21, 1878, age 68.
Guenther, Elvira Jane, wife of John G., April 11, 1853, age 25.
Guenther, Rev. Francis H., June 2, 1863, age 69 y, 29 d.
Guenther, Katharine, wife of Rev. Francis H., June 10, 1856, age 53.
Guernsey, Miss Sarah A., dau. of E. B., of Irving, Chautauqua Co., Aug. 31, 1851.
Guerre, Catharine, Boston Corners, NY, April 12, 1866, age 88.
Guetal, Catharine, c. Jan. 10, 1856, age 72.
Guild, Harry, Jr. (Harrison), July 24, 1880, age 40 y, 9 m, 2 d.
Guild, Herman, Cheektowaga, April 9, 1872, age 84; taken to Hornellsville.
Guild, Joseph Henry, eldest son of the late Joseph, formerly of Buffalo, Sept. 20, 1876.
Guild, Kate Ella, wife of Charles W., March 21, 1877, age 25.
Guinn, Mary, dau. of Capt. Obed, Hamburgh, Sept. 3, 1833, age 20.
Guiteau, John L., June 29, 1877, age 64.
Guiteau, Julius, formerly postmaster of Buffalo, Aug. 25, 1842, at Freeport, IL.
Guiteau, Ruby A. Marsh, widow of John L., Oct. 12, 1877, age 60.
Gungey, John, Oct. 17, 1876, age 68.
Gunn, Emeline, wife of Jefferson S., March 23, 1876, age 54 y, 9 m, 28 d.
Gunne, Mrs. Elizabeth, March 11, 1856, age 26.
Gunnison, William W., Aug. 12, 1880, age 40.
Gunther, John, accidently killed, Holland, April 9, 1873.
Gurney, Henry B., July 27, 1879, age 74 y, 9 m, 21 d.
Gurr, Rosalie, Jan. 1875, age 29 y, 11 m, 29 d.
Guthrie, Harriet S., wife of E. B., Sept. 22, 1873.
Guthrie, Mrs. S. S., May 26, 1880, age 56.
Guthrie (or Guttray), Mrs. Sarah, April 13, 1872, age 25.
Gwin, Mrs. Jane, widow of Thomas, Eden, Nov. 18, 1879, age 75.
Gwin, Jerome B., Oct. 15, 1877, age 57.
Gwin, Thomas, East Hamburgh, Sept. 21, 1871, age 84.
Gwinn, Emily A., wife of William R., eldest dau. of William H. Wells of Batavia, NY, July 18, 1860, age 34.
Gwinn, William R., July 1, 1861.
Gwyn, Obed, East Hamburgh, NY, Sept. 22, 1863, age 73.
Gwynne, Sidney George, Jan. 16, 1876, age 45; taken to Rochester.
Gygil, Francis, March 23, 1874, age 83 y, 7 m.
Gygli, Frederick, Feb. 27, 1864, age 45 y, 5 m.

Haack, Dorothea, widow of Christian, Dec. 13, 1875, age 52 y, 1 m, 3 d.
Haack, George, suicide, July 22, 1873.
Haag, J. W., killed on railroad near Town Line, May 30, 1878.
Haas, Abraham, Jan. 25, 1877, age 73.
Haas, August, Aug. 1874.
Haas, Charles, Oct. 17, 1870, age 25 y, 8 m, 12 d.
Haas, Gustavus, accident, Jan. 23, 1877, age 20.

Haas, Jacob, Jan. 9, 1870, age 46.
Haber, Christian, May 1, 1855.
Haberkorn, John, July 31, 1876, age 35.
Haberly, Caroline, wife of Martin, Brant, NY, March 13, 1872, age 24 y, 14d.
Haberman, Arhard (or Erhard), killed by the cars, Aug. 17, 1874, age 64 or 75.
Haberstro, Catharine, widow of Joseph, April 15, 1874, age 67 y, 2 m, 15 d.
Haberstro, Joseph, March 29, 1862, age 63.
Hachmann, Lizzie, wife of Frederick William, Feb. 23, 1878, age 64.
Hackemer, Catharine, Oct. 22, 1880, age 56.
Hackemere, Adam, fell dead, April 18, 1877, age 74.
Hackett, John, Feb. 15, 1876, age 40 y, 10 m.
Hackett, William Jr., March 6, 1873, age 36.
Hackett, William, Oct. 28, 1880, age 78 y, 2 m.
Hackford, Mrs. Mary Ann, widow, July 19, 1880, age 43; found dead in bed.
Hackley, Helen J., wife of C. of Saginaw City, MI, Feb. 27, 1865, age 23.
Hackmeyer, William, drowned while bathing, June 22, 1880, age 23.
Hacksteen, Dr. John E., July 8, 1861, at Brigham Hall, Canadanigua, NY.
Haddock, Benjamin F., formerly of Buffalo, Dec. 22, 1871, age 63; d. in Chicago, IL.
Haddock, Caroline M., wife of Joseph E., May 7, 1851, age 30.
Haddock, Mrs. Catharine, Feb. 12, 1875, age 72; taken to East Aurora.
Haddock, Dr. Charles C., July 12, 1849, age 44.
Haddock, Jane Ann, wife of Joseph E., April 24, 1845, age 28.
Haddock, John, formerly of Bath, NH, Sept. 30, 1818, age 41.
Haddock, Lorenzo E., April 20, 1871, age 55.
Haddock, Sarah Elizabeth Bigelow, wife of L. K., July 21, 1851.
Hadley, Miss Ann, dau. of the late Dr. James, Sept. 13, 1873.
Hadley, Daniel R., Aug. 31, 1853, age 21; at Sandy Creek, NY.
Hadley, Dr. George, Oct. 16, 1877, age 64.
Hadley, James, M.D., Oct. 17, 1869, age 84.
Hadley, Maria, widow of Dr. James, Sept. 22, 1875, age 80.
Hadley, Resign, mother of Mrs. John Bush, July 29, 1852, age 94.
Haefner, Johannah, May 11, 1879, age 25.
Hagan, Frank A., July 15, 1880, age 32.
Hagan, John, accidently killed, Tonawanda, Oct. 16, 1873, age 58.
Hagan, Mary, wife of Michael, May 9, 1870, d. at Wyoming, Canada West.
Hageman, Mortimer V., Nov. 30, 1880, age 20 y, 8 m.
Hagen, Christine, July 11, 1878, age 42 y, 8 m, 11d.
Hager, Barbara, Jan. 28, 1878, age 76 y, 5 m, 12d.
Hager, Christine G., wife of Raymond, May 17, 1878, age 67.
Hager, Raymond, March 23, 1880, age 71.
Hager, William L., Oct. 16, 1868, age 20 y, 7 m.
Hagerman, Norman, Nov. 20, 1877, age 53; d. at Kendall, PA, bur. Buffalo.
Haggart, Christeann, July 27, 1872, age 77.
Haggart, James, Black Rock, NY, March 23, 1861, age 67.
Haggerty, Capt. John C., Oct. 2, 1842, age 33.
Hagle, Catherine, wife of Michael, Sept. 30, 1871, age 46.
Haight, Edgar, formerly of Buffalo, Oct. 21, 1879.
Haight, Emily E., wife of C., Jan. 24, 1855; bur. in Rochester.
Haight, Helena, wife of Irving, May 28, 1874, age 31 y, 4 m, 27 d; taken to Irving, NY.
Haight, William D., April 11, 1180, age 86.
Haines, Mrs. Ann, wife of Samuel, Sept. 7, 1860, age 57.
Haines, Anna H., Jan. 18, 1863, aged 10 y, 6 m; dau. of Emmor and Ann M., bur. Forest Lawn.
Haines, Helen M. Jackson, May 25, 1870, age 22 y, 4 m, 17d, wife of Alfred, dau. of P.B. Jackson of Orleans Co. Bur. Forest Lawn.
Haines, John L., eldest son of Samuel, Sept. 11, 1860, age 34 y, 9 m.
Haines, Lindley Murray, April 2, 1865, age 5 y, 6 m, child of Emmor and Ann M.: bur. Forest Lawn.
Haines, Mary M., Feb. 1, 1845, aged 6 m; bur. at Millville, NY.
Haines, Moses, West Aurora, NY, Feb. 6, 1846, age 56.
Haines, Nancy, wife of Benjamin, July 2, 1814, age 34.

Haines, William, Co. Almshouse, Feb. 27, 1879, age 97.
Haiser, Mrs. Christianna, March 26, 1871, age 62.
Halbart, Caroline A., wife of Norman A., formerly of Buffalo, Feb. 25, 1880; d. near Patterson, NJ.
Hainning, James, Black Rock, NY, native of Dumfries, Scotland, July 23, 1822, age 42; merchant.
Haldane, Elizabeth G. Dalzell, wife of James, March 20, 1855, age 27.
Haldane, Margaret, wife of James, Sept. 26, 1876, age 52.
Hale, Miss, Nov. 2, 1880, age 84.
Hale, Benjamin, father of Henry H., Sept. 22, 1859, age 69.
Hale, Emily A., widow of Ebenezer, April 13, 1873.
Hale, J. Wilson, formerly of Buffalo, Oct. 24, 1865; in Cleveland, OH, age 26. Taken to CT.
Hale, Mrs. Knowles, mother of Mrs. B. C. Rumsey, Sept. 30, 1875, age 74.
Hale, Mrs. Louise Weed, wife of Rev. C. S., formerly of Buffalo, July 25, 1880; d. at Asheville, NC.
Hale, Mary Rightenburg, wife of Nathan, July 18, 1877.
Hale, Mrs. Sarah, formerly of Collins, NY, Dec. 19, 1849, age 49.
Hale, J. Wilson, Oct. 24, 1865, age 26; in Cleveland, OH; bur. CT.
Hale, Winslow S., formerly of Coldwater, MI, merchant, Oct. 12, 1847.
Haley, Ann, wife of John, March 30, 1876, age 54.
Haley, Catharine, widow of James, June 2, 1873, age 38.
Haley, Florence, drowned, June 7, 1874, age 26.
Haley, John, Oct. 27, 1873, age 67.
Haley, Mary, Nov. 4, 1879, age 82.
Haley, Norah, Co. Almshouse, April 3, 1878, age 25.
Haley, Owen, Aug. 13, 1877, age 77.
Haley, Mrs. Patrick, Feb. 10, 1872.
Haley, Patrick, accident, Sept. 6, 1874.
Haley, Thomas, Oct. 5, 1878, age 58.
Haley, Thomas E., Jan. 28, 1874, age 55; d. in NY City, bur. Buffalo.
Halks, Anthony, drowned, Jan. 3 or 4, 1872.
Hall, Albert G., Sept. 14, 1861, age 30.
Hall, Rev. Albina, Oct. 2, 1878, age 68; d. at North East, PA, firm of R. H. Hall & Co.
Hall, Anna Barker, only dau. of A. A., Sept. 20, 1864, age 21.
Hall, Asa, formerly of Buffalo, machinist of the National Theater, June, 1825, age 25; in Detroit, MI.
Hall, Charles J., brother of Andrew A., March 20, 1861; Medford, MA.
Hall, Daniel (Colored), Feb. 29, 1876, age c. 50.
Hall, Eli, Alden, NY, June 7, 1872, age 86.
Hall, Elizabeth, formerly of Buffalo, Sept. 1879; d. at Elizabeth, NJ.
Hall, Frederick F., Feb. 6, 1875, age over 50.
Hall, Mrs. Hannah, March 8, 1858, age 76.
Hall, Harriet A., wife of Joseph B., July 10, 1876, age 61; taken to Dunkirk, NY.
Hall, Henry, Collins, June 19, 1836, age 80 years.
Hall, Dr. Herman L., physician, d. in Pompey Hill June 13, 1879, age 56; bur. Buffalo.
Hall, Huldah K., wife of Capt. S. M., Oct. 10, 1859.
Hall, Ira, father of Hon. N.K. of Buffalo, Wales Center, NY, Jan. 19, 1860, age 72.
Hall, Ira, Jr., brother of N. K., Sept. 13, 1849, age 35.
Hall, Irving, d. from injuries by accident, July 20, 1879, age 35 y 2 m 25 d.
Hall, Jacob, carpenter, drowned, March 20, 1874, age 67.
Hall, James Q., April 12, 1875, age 58; taken to Batavia.
Hall, John (Rev. Dr.), Jan. 1869.
Hall, John, drowned, Cot. 6, 1871, age 24.
Hall, Mrs. Louisa, Aug. 25, 1873, age 63.
Hall, Lydia, widow, Revolutionary pensioner, Sept. 18, 1847, age 97.
Hall, Maria A., widow of Johnson, Jan. 26, 1871, sister of Thomas Farnham.
Hall, Martha, Oct. 14, 1871, age 72.
Hall, Mary K., wife of Jacob, Sept. 26, 1875, age 58 y, 7 m, 11 d.
Hall, Mason W., Oct. 12, 1880, found dead in bed.

Hall, Morris, Jan. 27, 1860, age 43.
Hall, Robert Wharton, Nov. 5, 1864, age 26; bur. in Hamilton, Canada West.
Hall, Hon. Nathan K., US Dist. Judge, March 2, 1874, age 63 y, 11 m, 2 d.
Hall, Richard H., formerly of Buffalo, Aug. 8, 1868, brother of A. A. Hall; d. at Ipswich, MA.
Hall, Samuel H. M., only son of Andrew A., Oct. 19, 1874, age 38 y, 10 m.
Hall, Sarah, wife of Rowland, Hamburg, April 20, 1841.
Hall, Sarah A., wife of Joel, formerly of Buffalo, Feb. 4, 1877, age 72 y, 10 m, 14 d.; d. Santa Cruz, CA.
Hall, Sarah E., wife of James H. and dau. of F. Gager, Aug. 23, 1872; d. at Seattle, Washington Territory.
Hall, Willard J., May 29, 1869, age 65.
Hall, William, Dec. 5, 1873, age 40; d. in NY City.
Hall, William Shelton, youngest son of Andrew A., June 12, 1870.
Hallack, Sally, wife of Joshua, formerly of West Falls, Dec. 23, 1872, age 58; d. in Lemont, IL.
Hallaway, William H., May 1876.
Hallenbeck, Amanda, youngest dau. of G.S., Sept. 22, 1859, age 25.
Hallenbeck, Edward, son of G.S., Oct. 21, 1854, age c. 34.
Hallenbeck, Gerritt S., April 14, 1860, age 70.
Hallenbeck, Susannah, wife of G.S., July 3, 1848, age 58.
Haller, Christoph F., Jan. 3, 1871, age 68 y, 3 m.
Haller, George J., Feb. 9, 1872, age 27 y, 18 d.
Hallock, Benajah, Collins, NY, April 30, 1836, age 80.
Hallock, Catharine, Collins, NY, wife of Benjah, June 22, 1835, age 70.
Halpin, Thomas, July 26, 1880, age 30.
Halsey, Cyrian, Black Rock, Jan. 1828, age 44.
Halsey, Henry S., Nov. 22, 1845, age 46.
Halsey, Melville, d. at Salina, bur. Batavia, brakeman(?), April 9, 1879, age 21.
Halter, Andrew, Clarence, NY, May 5, 1873, age 64.
Halty, Elizabeth, Aug. 31, 1863, age 72.
Hambleton, Ava, wife of Samuel A., Hamburgh, NY, March 24, 1838.
Hambleton, Erastus B., July 9, 1876; taken to East Hamburgh.
Hambleton, Hannah, wife of Samuel, East Hamburgh, NY, Aug. 4, 1854.
Hambleton, John D., East Hamburgh, July 26, 1877, age 52 y, 11 m.
Hambleton, Perry C., formerly of East Hamburgh, Sept. 15, 1868, age 40.
Hambleton, Samuel A., East Hamburgh, NY, March 25, 1859, age 56.
Hambleton, Sarah, East Hamburgh, NY, Oct. 1, 1855, age 50.
Hambleton, Sarah, wife of Orlando, East Aurora, April 20, 1873, age 42.
Hambleton, Mrs. Sophia, East Hamburgh, NY, mother of Mrs. Isaac Baker, May 14, 1859, age 57.
Hambleton, William D., East Aurora, Oct. 7, 1879, age 23.
Hamblin, David, b. 1752, d. 1839, bur. Clarence; Soldier of the Revolution.
Hamblin, John, b. 1753, d. 1836, bur. Wilson; Soldier of the Revolution.
Hambujer, Rebecca, wife of E., Dec. 25, 1862, age 22.
Hamet, Caleb, b. 1749, d. no date, bur. Sardinia, NY; Soldier of the Revolution.
Hamill, Alexander K., Sept. 25, 1878, age 28.
Hamill, Archibald, April 24, 1859, age 69.
Hamilton, Dallas, Nov. 13, 1877, age 43 y, 10 m, 5 d.
Hamilton, Emma, wife of William, Sept. 25, 1872, age 24.
Hamilton, Helen M., formerly of Buffalo, Feb. 14, 1876, age 37; wife of Col. Theodore B.; d. at Plainfield, NJ.
Hamilton, Henry, Sept. 5, 1852, age 55.
Hamilton, James Murray, late of Abbey, Dumfries, Scotland, May 20, 1862, age 42.
Hamilton, Louis W. Olds, son of L.H.F., July 27, 1875, age 27.
Hamilton, Lucinda, wife of C.N., mother of Dr. Frank H., April 13, 1856, age 71; bur. in Rochester, NY.
Hamilton, Maria A., June 10, 1874, age 62; wife of W.S., d. in Wilmington, NC, bur. Buffalo.
Hamilton, Mrs. Mary, March 9, 1877, age 80 y, 2 m.
Hamilton, Thomas (known as "Dublin"), near Buffalo, May 23, 1872; killed on the railroad.

Hamilton, Thomas H., d. at Anamosa, IA, formerly of Buffalo, May 2, 1879, age 48.
Hamilton, William Henry, eldest son of the late Henry, Jan. 2, 1870, age 32; d. at Bangkok, Siam.
Hamilton, Zane A., East Aurora, Dec. 5, 1863, age 79.
Hamlin, Caroline M. H., wife of Daniel R., March 6, 1878, age 68.
Hamlin, Charlotte, wife of D.R., Feb. 16, 1830, age 24.
Hamlin, David, Revolutionary soldier, Clarence, NY, Jan. 9, 1839, age 80.
Hamlin, Eliza C., wife of J.W., West Aurora, NY, Sept. 27, 1854, age 45.
Hamlin, Miss Eliza C., Clarence, NY, Oct. 29, 1860, age 20.
Hamlin, Helen M. Pratt, wife of Frank, Jan. 17, 1873; d. in Paris, France, bur. in Buffalo.
Hamlin, John S., late of Buffalo, Sept. 30, 1862; at home of brother in Canada.
Hamlin, John W., East Aurora, Dec. 12, 1880, age 74 y, 5 d.
Hamlin, Laura, Oct. 4, 1850, age 63.
Hamlin, Mary A., wife of John W., Aurora, NY, sister of Elijah Ford, May 22, 1862, age 51.
Hamm, Paul, Nov. 1878, age 48.
Hammellman, Sophia Hahn, wife of Paul, Oct. 22, 1878, age 30 y, 10 m.
Hammer, Mrs. George, Sept. 3, 1873, age 40.
Hammersly, Philomena, Feb. 8, 1872, age 80.
Hammond, E. D., Oct. 21, 1880, age 38.
Hammond, Eleanor, wife of Robert, Boston, NY, June 3, 1863, age 57 y, 8 m, 15 d.
Hammond, Mrs. Elizabeth, March 29, 1862, age 72.
Hammond, Frederick K., North Boston, July 19, 1868, age 33 y, 6 m.
Hammond, George W., Oct. 16, 1871, age 34.
Hammond, Helen M., wife of Edwin F., March 5, 1865, age 27.
Hammond, Miss Jane, Feb. 24, 1872.
Hammond, Jonathan, Nov. 15, 1853, age 29.
Hammond, Lizzie R., eldest dau. of Mrs. Ellen J., June 1864, age 20 y, 5 m.
Hammond, Mary, Nov. 20, 1877.
Hammond, Michael, Akron, Sept. 4, 1875, age 67.
Hammond, Mrs. Phebe, mother of Mrs. W.F. Ketchum, March 15, 1862, age 83.
Hammond, Robert, March 18, 1862; in Los Angeles, CA.
Hammond, Mrs. Robert, Boston, Feb. 22, 1878, age 70.
Hammond, Mrs. Sarah, Feb. 12, 1880, age 67.
Hammond, Werden, March 27, 1840, age 33.
Hammond, William S., Aug. 15, 1851, age 37.
Hampton, Minnie E., wife of Ellis C., East Hamburgh, March 9, 1877, age 27.
Hampton, Slater, North Boston, March 20, 1877, age 65.
Hampton, Thomas S., Sept. 27, 1860, age 41 y, 6 m, 24 d.
Hampton, William, drowned in Nooksack River, Washington Territory, formerly of Erie Co., Feb. 1878, age c. 55.
Hanbach, John Sr., June 9, 1877, age 67 y, 11 m, 20 d.
Hancit, Douglas, Co. Almshouse, Aug. 26, 1878, age 36.
Hancock, Levi from Winchinton, NH, May 7, 1843, age 37.
Hand, Capt. James H., tug-captain, killed by the explosion of the tug *R. R. Hefford*, taken to Bowmansville, June 10, 1876, age 27 y, 6 m, 21 d.
Handel, Christian Ludwig, Reserve, March 9, 1877, age 58 y, 9 m.
Handel, Francis J., May 5, 1861, age 65 y, 1 m, 5 d.
Handel, Miss Mary, dau. of the late Francis J., April 19, 1873, age 35 y, 8 m.
Handell, Catharine, wife of Francis J., April 12, 1854, age 45.
Handicourt, Elizabeth, March 31, 1865, age 41. [not in card file]
Handy, Eunice D., East Hamburgh, June 10, 1878, age 58 y, 11 m.
Hanford, Leander, Tonawanda, NY, Nov. 28, 1827, age 36.
Hankins, Beekman Van Buren, July 8, 1876, age 53.
Hankins, Henry, policeman, June 15, 1879, age 29 y, 9 m, 2 d.
Hanks, Ambrose S., March 13, 1871, age 44 y, 6 m.
Hanks, Henry, suicide, Tonawanda, Nov. 12, 1878.
Hanley, Julia, April 8, 1880, age 85.
Hanley, Mrs. Mary, Nov. 3, 1872, age 74.
Hanley, Mrs. Sarah, Grand Island, March 23, 1874, age 35.

Hann, Thomas R., formerly of Buffalo, Oct. 7, 1878, age 58; d. in Philadelphia, bur. in Buffalo.
Hanna, Mary M., widow of Samuel, Jan. 22, 1880, age 54 y, 7 m, 3 d.
Hanna, Nellie S., Aurora, Dec. 30, 1867; d. at Aurora, IL.
Hanna, Samuel, Sept. 25, 1877, age 44 y, 3 m, 12 d.
Hannah, John, Scotchman, May 18, 1851, age 49; d. in County Workhouse.
Hannah, Mary, Co. Almshouse, March 20, 1876, age 33.
Hannck, Charlotte, suddenly, coroner's case, April 15, 1879, age 83.
Hannegan, Mrs. Mary, mother of Rev. F. B., Jan 12, 1879, age 69 y, 8 m, 12 d.
Hannengraff, Michael, April 24, 1874, age 54.
Hannon, Judson, Jan. 28, 1857, age 45.
Hannon, Patrick, Co. Almshouse, Sept. 4, 1876, age 63.
Hanny, Carrie, dau. of Mrs. John, July 1, 1877, age 25 y, 7 m, 11 d.
Hanny, John, Oct., 1871, bur. Nov. 6.
Hanrahan, Elizabeth L., widow of Hon. Patrick, Nov. 7, 1880, age 32.
Hanrahan, Mary Jane, wife of James, March 14, 1876, age 30.
Hanrahan, Patrick, June 9, 1879, age 38.
Hans, George J. Sr., Mill Grove, NY, Oct. 29, 1866, age 49.
Hansen, Peter, Co. Almshouse, Jan. 11, 1876, age 60.
Hanson, Deacon Abraham, Nov. 16, 1863, age 65.
Hanson, Benjamin, April 4, 1871, age 40.
Hanson, Mrs. Elizabeth, mother of Mrs. S.L. Meech, Sept. 5, 1852, age 83.
Hanson, Hattie M., wife of A.T., Feb. 22, 1880, age 20.
Hanson, Joseph Lawrence, formerly of Bufalo, July 23, 1870, age 62; d. at his residence in Adelaide, South Australia.
Hanson, Nancy, wife of John, Feb. 1, 1862, age 44.
Hanson, Susan, Black Rock, NY, wife of Henry H., Feb. 12, 1831, age 34.
Hanvey, Jessie A., only dau. of Jesse H. A. Field, Lancaster, Nov. 11, 1875, age 31 y, 11 m.
Hard, Samuel, formerly of MD, April 11, 1847, age 41; in Utica, NY.
Hardiker, Mrs. Ann, Oct. 2, 1852, age 63.
Harding, Caroline H., wife of Leonard, May 7, 1875, age 65.
Harding, Frederick, Oct. 21, 1876, age 49; d. Chicago, bur. in Buffalo.
Harding, Rosabella N., formerly of Buffalo, Jan. 26, 1873, age 27 y, 8 m, 19 d. Wife of William T., dau. of the late Henry S. Fitch; d. in Strongville, OH.
Hardings, Edward B., eldest son of Mrs. S. L., drowned, Aug. 2, 182, age 20 y, 13 d.
Hardy, Mrs. Rose, wife of Thomas L., July 26, 1878, age 58.
Hardy, Timothy, May 16, 1873, age 60.
Harkness, O. P., Lawton's Station, Nov. 26, 1878, age 61 y, 11 m., 14 d.
Harle, Henry, Jan. 18, 1875, age 38.
Harlow, Mrs. Mary, March 11, 1873.
Harlow, Sally, widow of Augustus, Lancaster, Dec. 27, 1872, age 71.
Harman, Elder Elias, Aurora, NY, Aug. 7, 1844, age 70.
Harmer, Mrs. Elizabeth, April 20, 1868, age 81.
Harmer, Thomas, Sexton at St. John's Church, Oct. 19, 1880, age 53.
Harmon, Frank P., formerly of Buffalo, Jan. 19, 1876, age 60. D. at Canal Dover, OH.
Harmon, Harriet W., wife of E.F., May 17, 1858, age 32.
Harmon, Helen Gipsie, c. Jan. 15, 1865; bur. Jan. 18.
Harmon, Jenny, June 18, 1874, age 40.
Harmon, Judson, Jan. 28, 1857, age 45.
Harney, Edward, railroad accident, June 24, 1878, age 22.
Haron, Mrs. Marian, dau. of Jacob Wolf, Jan. 18, 1860, age 25.
Harper, Comer, March 19, 1879, age 51.
Harper, Mary Ann, wife of Joseph, July 14, 1858, age 32.
Harper, Sabrins, widow of Comer, May 9, 1879, age 48.
Harradan, James, Dec. 25, 1864, age 62.
Harraden, George C., son of James, May 18, 1866, age 20; at Nashville, TN.
Harries, Mrs. Anne, Dec. 11, 1874, age 86 y, 8 mo.
Harries, Charles, Oct. 26, 1866, age 38; at Jamestown, NY.
Harries, Edward, April 19, 1870, age 49.

Harries, Thomas, April 14, 1855, age 73; from Haverford West, Pembrokeshire, South Wales.
Harrington, Amanda, widow of Hon. Isaac R., Jan. 1, 1874, age 83.
Harrington, Celestia M., wife of Whitford, July 6, 1876, age 35 y, 8 m, 2 d; taken to Marilla, Erie Co.
Harrington, Charles L., eldest son of Hon. I.R., April 10, 1866, age 53.
Harrington, Daniel, farmer, June 28, 1879, age 66.
Harrington, Donald U., 2nd son of Hon. I.R., Nov. 7, 1851, age 31; in Sheboygan, WI, bur. in Buffalo.
Harrington, Henry V., Jan. 19, 1851, age 44; in Utica, NY, bur. in Buffalo.
Harrington, Isaac R., late mayor, also postmaster of Buffalo, Aug. 20, 1851.
Harrington, James, May 4, 1878, age 83.
Harrington, Marion, dau. of Capt. I.R., Nov. 6, 1843, age 20; in Detroit, MI.
Harrington, Rosannah, wife of Seth, Collins, NY, April 25, 1861, age 21.
Harrington, William, July 7, 1878, age 23.
Harrington, Capt. William L. formerly of Burlington, VT, Sept. 9, 1835, age 35.
Harris, Alfred, formerly of Buffalo, March 13, 1856, age 37; at Mascoda, WI.
Harris, Alla, wife of Peyton, Oct. 12, 1854, age 55 y, 4 m and 29 d; native of VA.
Harris, Ariel C., brother-in-law of Ex-President Fillmore, April 14, 1864, age 51; in Toledo, OH.
Harris, Asa, Clarence, NY, Dec. 15, 1812, age 50. [Another card: Harris, Asa, b. 1755 (1762?), d. 1812, bur. Harris Hill; Soldier of the Revolution.
Harris, Asa P., Dec. 9, 1870, age 47.
Harris, Betsey, wife of Capt. Asa P., Clarence, NY, Aug. 4, 1812, age 25.
Harris, Charles D., April 26, 1873, age 24 (or 34).
Harris, Chauncey L., brother of S.W. and L.E., Sept. 16, 1863, age 47.
Harris, Daniel P., April 25, 1871, age 54 y, 1 m, 12 d.
Harris, Mrs. Elizabeth, Hamburgh, Dec. 4, 1877, age 86.
Harris, Emily, wife of William H., June 15, 1849, age 27.
Harris, Emma Lett, dau. of Mrs. P. Harris, Sept. 15, 1875, age 36.
Harris, Fannie V., dau. of Peyton, Oct. 29, 1866, age 28 y, 2 m, 25 d.
Harris, George J., son of Joseph, May 21, 1877, age 48; d. in Brooklyn.
Harris, Dr. J. P., March 22, 1873, age 64; taken to Smithville, Ontario.
Harris, James, from Bristol, Ontario Co., Jan. 14, 1822, age 50.
Harris, James W., Aug. 3, 1872, age 88.
Harris, Jane, wife of Linus E., July 11, 1861, age 45; taken to Rochester, NY.
Harris, John, son of Joseph, July 15, 1850, age 27.
Harris, John Thomas, son of Peyton, Feb. 16, 1841, age 21.
Harris, Joseph, Hamburgh, NY, Dec. 7, 1812, age 50.
Harris, Linus E., April 10, 1874, age 56; taken to Rochester.
Harris, Mrs. Linus E., July 4, 1875, age 49. Taken with the remains of her dau. Miss Young, to Batavia, NY.
Harris, Maria, wife of Jesse, May 19, 1858, age 52.
Harris, Mary, Sept. 29, 1873.
Harris, Mary Ann, wife of Dr. F.L., Oct. 25, 1846, age 30.
Harris, Mary Ann, insane, at Co. Almshouse, July 20, 1879, age 52.
Harris, Mrs. Mary Belle, formerly of Buffalo, April 6, 1872, age 24 y, 7 m. d. at Canaseraga, NY.
Harris, Mary W., wife of S.W., March 31, 1860, age 56; taken to Rochester, NY.
Harris, Mrs. Selah, March 1, 1873, age 74.
Harris, Mrs. Sophia, Hamburg, Aug. 25, 1880, age 75.
Harris, Thomas, Englishman, Sept. 27, 1833, age 26.
Harris, William, son of Mrs. R. Harris of Rochester, Feb. 3, 1861, age 26; taken to Rochester, NY.
Harris, William alias William Golden, drowned, Oct. 24, 1872, age 24.
Harrison, Emeline Wilcox, wife of Joseph, June 25, 1868, age 51.
Harrison, Mary J., wife of Alfred, April 21, 1874, age 22.
Harrison, Melinda, wife of Richard B., Jan. 22, 1878, age 59.
Harrison, Richard Henry, only son of R. B., March 28, 1870, age 22 y, 6 m, 6 d.
Harrison, Robert B., Nov. 17, 1842, age 21.
Harrison, Seth, Oct. 24, 1862, age 83 y, 8 m, 15 d.

Harrison, Tunis, May 2, 1841, age 77.
Harrison, William or Frank, railroad accident, brakeman, April 27, 1878.
Harron, Robert, formerly of Buffalo, March 18, 1863, age 46; at Caledonia, NY.
Hart, Ansel, Black Rock, NY, Capt. Clark's Co. of U.S. Vol., Aug. 1812, age 28.
Hart, Capt. Asa E., Oct. 15, 1873, age 70.
Hart, Austin S., Jan. 8, 1874, age 47; d. in St. Augustine, FL, bur Buffalo.
Hart, Charles, May 2, 1878, age 52 y, 9 d.
Hart, Ellen Douglas, dau. of William A., Oct. 24, 1868.
Hart, Henry S., April 4, 1868, age 33 y, 8 m.
Hart, James W., June 4, 1879, age 37 y, 2 m, 21 d.
Hart, John, Feb. 17, 1871, age 47; taken to Northeast, PA.
Hart, Joseph, formerly of Fredonia, NY, tailor, Feb. 16, 1840.
Hart, Mary, widow of Osias, May 2, 1858, age 63 y, 8 m, 19 d.
Hart, Mary Ann Summerton, widow of William A., May 3, 1871, age 70.
Hart, Capt. Robert, Sept. 17, 1861, age 61.
Hart, Walter J., brother of Henry S. of Buffalo, Oct. 28, 1864, age 22. D. before Richmond from wounds in battle.
Hart, William ("B. William"), Jan. 26, 1876, age 26 or 34; taken to Philadelphia, NY.
Hart, William, Dec. 3, 1880, age 61.
Hart, William A., Aug. 9, 1865, age 68.
Hartman, David, Feb. 15, 1817, age 45.
Hartigan, Martin, Oct. 29, 1871, age 68.
Hartman, Mrs. Barbara, widow of Joseph, Jan. 14, 1875, age 61 y, 2 m, 3 d.
Hartnett (or Harness), Edward, June 23, 1878, age 22 y, 3 m.
Harty, John D., March 17, 1842, age 51.
Harty, Mrs. L., widow of John D., Aug. 8, 1857, age 58.
Harvey, Alexander W., formerly of Buffalo; d. in City of NY, bur. Buffalo.
Harvey, Alice B., wife of Benjamin F., Feb. 11, 1871, age 22.
Harvey, Mrs. Almira Powell, Aug. 9, 1876, age 78.
Harvey, Amos, suicide, Clarence, NY, Aug. 16, 1873, age 48.
Harvey, Benjamin F., Feb. 10, 1871, age 28.
Harvey, Catherine, Co. Almshouse, Sept. 29, 1878, age 40.
Harvey, Christopher, Clarence, NY, Dec. 23, 1836, age 45.
Harvey, Egbert, April 5, 1870, age 52.
Harvey, Franklin B., Feb. 6, 1871, age 26.
Harvey, James, Clarence, NY, Jan. 1813, age 50.
Harvey, ---, Clarence, NY, wife of James, Jan. 1813.
Harvey, James, Dec. 16, 1868, age 30; taken to Niagara, Canada West.
Harvey, Mrs. James, formerly of Buffalo, Nov. 5, 1879, age 65; d. at Niagara, Ontario.
Harvey, John, late of Buffalo, 50th NY Eng., July 5, 1864, age 42; in Hospital at Washington.
Harvey, Louisa, wife of John C., Jan. 6, 1860, age 32.
Harvey, Mary Eliza, Springbrook, Jan. 21, 1868, age 27; wife of S.D., d. at Springbrook, Erie Co., NY.
Harvey, Mary R. S., wife of F.B., Dec. 13, 1873, age 43; taken to Mohawk, Herkimer Co.
Harvey, Minerva P., Sept. 30, 1879, age 63.
Harvey, Phebe, mother of Mrs. Zenas Higgins, Aug. 28, 1861, age 74 y, 7 m.
Harvey, Samuel, Black Rock, NY, Jan. 1817, age 50.
Harvey, William Rufus, April 18, 1857, age 26; in Lockport, NY, bur. in Buffalo.
Hasafratz, Xavier, drowned, carpenter, July 18, 1874, age 25.
Hascal, Jonathan, Hamburgh, April 8, 1872, age c. 70.
Hascall, Maria, wife of George, Lancaster, NY, March 1, 1852, age 24.
Hasenzahl, Christian, July 27, 1879, age 37 y, 5 m.
Hasensal, Christopher, July 1879.
Haskell, Cornelius, North Evans, Jan. 9, 1879, age 37 y, 11 m.
Haskell, Julia A., wife of Norman F., dau. of William Crawford of Nevada, CA, May 16, 1863; at Toledo, OH; formerly of Buffalo.
Haskins, Eliza S., wife of R. W., June 21, 1836, age 36.
Haskins, George W., Associate Editor of *Buffalo Express*, March 7, 1857, age 32.

Haskins, Helen P., wife of John F., formerly of Buffalo, Dec. 1, 1877, d. in Philadelphia, PA.
Haskins, Leovid, June 24, 1852, age 46; in Fairfield, Herkimer Co., formerly of Buffalo.
Haskins, Roswell W. A. M., Jan. 15, 1870, age 74.
Haskins, Ruth J., wife of Capt. William P., Oct. 24, 1862, age 65.
Haskins, William P., Feb. 1, 1872, age 75.
Hassinger, William, 1875.
Hass, Eloise, wife of Louis F., Aug. 14, 1876.
Hassett, John G., Lancaster, Jan. 13, 1873, age 75.
Hassinger, William, March 1875, age 35 y, 9 m, 23 d.
Hastings, Anna Garrett, wife of William, formerly of Buffalo, Feb. 11, 1874, age 31; d. at Park Hill, Ontario.
Hastings, Barnard, Aug. 1, 1856, age 70.
Hastings, Chauncey, father of C.J. of Buffalo, Sardinia, NY, Aug. 24, 1864, age 72 y, 6 m.
Hastings, Eroe A., wife of E., mother of Mrs. C. C. Wyckoff of Buffalo, Nov. 24, 1863, age 60; in Louisville, KY.
Hastings, Eurotas, father of Mrs. C. C. Wyckoff, May 22, 1858, age 68.
Hastings, Jeremiah, suicide, Aug. 9, 1877, age 58.
Hastings, Luther S. or Lucius, accident, June 19, 1876, age 28.
Hastings, Maria Louisa, April 18, 1846, age 27.
Hastings, Thomas B., suicide, May 23, 1879, age 67.
Hasy, Michael, hod-carrier, Aug. 17, 1880, age 48; accident.
Haszel, Mary, June 5, 1880, age 30.
Hatch, Catherine, Black Rock, NY, wife of Junius H., Nov. 16, 1851.
Hatch, Clarence B., Sept. 30, 1880, age 32; bur. in Alleghany Co.
Hatch, Hon. Edward N., Boston, Oct. 7, 1868, age 51.
Hatch, Eliza C., dau. of the late Israel T., Jan. 28, 1879.
Hatch, Franklin C., late of Buffalo, Feb. 16, 1854, age 45; at "Prairie House," 22 miles from Sacramento.
Hatch, Frederick W., son of E. P. of Buffalo, March 14, 1870, age 20 y, 11 m; d. at Suspension Bridge.
Hatch, Henry D., April 16, 1877; d. at Kirkwood, MO, bur. in Buffalo.
Hatch, Israel T., Sept. 24, 1875.
Hatch, Jane P. Storrs, wife of William B., formerly of Buffalo, Jan. 6, 1876; d. in New York, bur. at Tarrytown.
Hatch, Junius H., April 20, 1869, age 78.
Hatch, Mrs. Lydia, June 8, 1852, age 69.
Hatch, Lydia A., wife of Israel, Feb. 20, 1862, age 48.
Hatch, Margaret, wife of Edward, Boston, NY, Aug. 19, 1866, age 75.
Hatch, Martha C., wife of Albert G., May 28, 1877, age 29.
Hatch, Mrs. Mary, formerly of Buffalo, April 10, 1870, age 70; d. at Peninsula, Summit Co., Ohio.
Hatch, Olive, wife of Ephraim, Aurora, NY, May 12, 1865, age 78.
Hatch, Olive Pringle, wife of E. P., formerly of Buffalo, Sept. 3, 1872, age 62; d. in Westfield (?).
Hatch, William B., youngest son of Junius H., Nov. 19, 1866, at Olney, IL; bur. in Buffalo.
Hathaway, Abraham, Sept. 3, 1843, age 25.
Hathaway, Amy W., wife of Obed, Evans Center, NY, April 11, 1859, age 70.
Hathaway, Daniel, of Taunton, MA, Dec. 12, 1829, age 34.
Hathaway, Isaac T., Feb. 7, 1880, age 84.
Hathaway, Capt. James, June 21, 1877, age 62; d. at East Saginaw, MI.
Hathaway, Susan Hoxie, wife of Arthur S., non-resident, March 10, 1880, age 32.
Hatton, Priscilla, wife of John, Feb. 27, 1870, age 55.
Hatwell, Charles, Sept. 13, 1875, age 26.
Hauck, Conrad, Oct.7, 1877, age 58 y, 19d.
Haudricourt, Elizabeth, March 31, 1865, age 41.
Hauenstein, George, suicide, Feb. 4, 1874, age 50.
Hausauer, Margaret, wife of Michael, Wales Center, April 6, 1880, age 77.
Hausle, John, Feb. 10, 1874, aged 36 y, 9 m; d. at Denver, CO, bur. in Buffalo.
Hauslholder, Henry, Lancaster, Sept. 13, 1871, age 42.

Haven, Charles Linneus, M.D., Boston, MA, Dec. 2, 1868, son of Dr. S. Z., age 35.
Haven, Solomon George, Dec. 24, 1861, age 51.
Havens, Ephraim S., April 17, 1877, age 72.
Havens, Hannah E., wife of Selah W., May 21, 1867.
Havens, Hiram, formerly of Buffalo, brother of E.S. of Buffalo, merchant, Dec. 27, 1847, age 43; in Michigan City, MI.
Havens, James M., law student, April 6, 1844, age 24.
Havens, Louisa, wife of Hiram, March 10, 1833, age 33.
Havens, Selah W., April 8, 1863, age 41; in Brantford, Canada West; bur. in Buffalo.
Hawkes, Mrs. Priscilla, late of Island of Bermuda, Nov. 10, 1827, age 46.
Hawkins, Mrs., Aug. 18, 1854.
Hawkins, Alida Maria, Sept. 14, 1854, age 22 y, 11 m.
Hawkins, Angeline G., wife of William, July 19, 1863.
Hawkins, Edgar E., formerly of Buffalo, April 8, 1872, d. in Cleveland, Ohio.
Hawkins, Esther, wife of David Henry, Feb. 14, 1857, age 53 y, 1 m, 20 d.
Hawkins, Gerrit G., brother-in-law of Thomas R. Conlon, April 25, 1846, age 27.
Hawkins, Mr. J. S., formerly of Lockport, Sept. 1857; in New York City, bur. in Buffalo Sept. 12.
Hawkins, John (colored), May 30, 1873, age 40.
Hawkins, Martha, sister of Mrs. Orson Swift, East Hamburgh, NY, March 14, 1865, age 62.
Hawkins, Mary, wife of Theodore A., Hamburgh, NY, May 18, 1823, age 19.
Hawkins, Morrison, July 9, 1850, age 51.
Hawkins, Philip, Co. Almshouse, May 4, 1876, age 32.
Hawkins, Samuel, East Hamburgh, NY, July 9, 1843, age 73.
Hawkins, Susanna, East Hamburgh, NY, wife of Samuel, March 16, 1841, age 66.
Hawkins, William, July 20, 1878, age 69 y, 9 m, 29 d.
Hawks, Mr., Aug. --, 1828, age 30.
Hawks, Ann, wife of Rev. C. S., Bishop of MO, formerly of Buffalo, July 9, 1855; in St. Louis.
Hawks, B. B., formerly of Buffalo, Dec. 1879; d. at Kearney, NE.
Hawks, George H., only son of Z., Co. K, 116th N.Y. Vol., Evans, NY, July 10, 1863, age 26 y, 11 m, 20 d; in Hospital at Baton Rouge, LA. Over exertion in seige of Port Hudson.
Hawks, Helen A., wife of A. Y., Jan. 3, 1878; d. at Collingwood, OH.
Hawks, Hester Ann, wife of T. S., April 26, 1872.
Hawks, James, formerly of Buffalo, Dec. 20, 1847; in Milwaukee, WI, age 26.
Hawks, Lovell O., freight conductor, run over by train, Nov. 4, 1880, age 31.
Hawks, Lydia W., wife of J. D. of San Francisco, CA, Dec. 30, 1853; taken to Auburn, NY.
Hawks, Selina A., dau. of Zadock, Evans Center, NY, Aug. 15, 1863, age 24 y, 10 m.
Hawley, Elijah J., formerly of Buffalo, brother of M.S., Dec. 9, 1872, age 52; d. in MI.
Hawley, Florence Butler, April 23, 1874, age 25 y, 3 m; wife of Edward S., d/o Morris Butler. Res. 1465 Niagara St., d. of typhoid fever, bur. Forest Lawn.
Hawley, Helen Goodrich, wife of Lucien, May 31, 1874; d. in NY City, bur. Buffalo.
Hawley, Irene B., wife of Lucian, Dec. 24, 1854, age 30.
Hawley, James, b. 1758, d. 1842, bur. E. Aurora; Soldier of the Revolution.
Hawley, Mrs. Marcia A., June 28, 1867, age 39.
Hawley, Joel E., Aug. 1859.
Hawley, Mary, Aug. 27, 1856, wife of Col. Alonzo; late of Hinsdale, Cattaraugus Co., NY; at Middle Haddam, CT.
Hawley, Myron, May 12, 1872, age 92.
Hawley, Myron G., Oct. 14, 1853, age 28.
Hawley, Salma, Brant, NY, Jan. 25, 1862, age 65.
Hawley, Sarah Donette, wife of J. H., Collins, NY, April, 1865, age 26 y, 10 m; in Grand Rapids, MI.
Hay, John, June 12, 1848, age 38.
Hayden, Cotton Mather, Sept. 16, 1840, age 45.
Hayden, Henry C., Jan. 4, 1848, age 24.
Hayden, Frederick, May 2, 1876, age 42.
Hayden, Seville Brace, widow of Albert, July 20, 1870, age 55.
Hayes, Abner, April 10, 1844, age 74.
Hayes, Mrs. Betsey, mother of Dr. George E., June 14, 1870, age 89.

Hayes, Eliza F., formerly of Buffalo, wife of J.L.H., Aug. 30, 1853; in St. Louis, MO.
Hayes, Emily M., wife of Dr. J. E., Dec. 12, 1856, age 48.
Hayes, Harriet Sophronia, dau. of William H., Colden, Nov. 4, 1870, age 23 y, 3 m, 11 d.
Hayes, Henry, son of Dr. George E., Jan. 27, 1859, age 21; in Aiken, GA, bur. in Buffalo.
Hayes, John, May 7, 1868, age 27.
Hayes, Mrs. Julia, widow, janitress, Sept. 30, 1880; burned to death in house.
Hayes, Maria, almshouse, March 17, 1880, age 66.
Hayes, Michael, Sept. 1, 1878, age 31 y, 8 m.
Hayes, Orange, May 22, 1848, age 49.
Hayes, Sarah S., Sept. 16, 1868, wife of Robert P.
Hayes, Timothy, Dec. 15, 1874, age 39 y, 9 m.
Hayner, Julia E., wife of Warren S., May 14, 1873, age 23 y, 9 m, 14 d.
Hayner, Kattie W., wife of W. S., Nov. 3, 1877, age 24 y, 6 m.
Haynes, Richard, Feb. 28, 1880, age 38; drowned in Buffalo River.
Haynes, William, suicide, Feb. 18, 1875, age 55.
Hayward, Abbie, wife of S. H., June 18, 1873, age 47 y, 3 m, 26 d.
Hayward, Deacon Elisha, June 12, 1846, age 44.
Hayward, Capt. Elisha L., Sept. 9, 1862, age 24; in Washington, DC.
Hayward, Jane A. C., wife of Plato B., Oct. 6, 1844, age 28 y, 2 m.
Hayward, John C., Oct. 7, 1859, age 35.
Haywood, Mrs. Elizabeth, April 27, 1880, age 38?; found drowned (suicide?).
Haywood, Hannah King, wife of Russell H., Nov. 5, 1880; d. at Andover, Mass.
Hazard, Frank L. Allen, wife of John H., Sept. 1, 1863, age 22.
Hazard, Margaret Dashler, wife of Edward E., Jan. 15, 1876.
Hazard, Maria B., widow of Morris, Nov. 3, 1873, age 65.
Hazard, Capt. Morris, Aug. 28, 1870, age 70.
Hazard, Morris, Jr., son of Morris & Maria B., Oct. 3, 1868, age 30.
Hazel, Catherine, June 11, 1878, age 49.
Hazell, Thomas, Nov. 14, 1878, age 65 y, 9 m.
Hazen, Mrs. Mary Ann, Aug. 29, 1876, age 78.
Hazanzab, Christopher, painter, July 27, 1879.
Heacock, Abby P., widow of R., Dec. 4, 1868, age 79.
Heacock, Abel M., son of Reuben B., July 9, 1843, age 28.
Heacock, Edna S., widow of Seth G., East Hamburgh, NY, Aug. 20, 1864; bur. in Buffalo.
Heacock, Eliza C., widow of Capt. Reuben B., Feb. 24, 1871; d. at Annapolis, MD.
Heacock, Eunice, b. Washington, CT, Sept. 25, 1839, age 84.
Heacock, Rev. Grosvenor W., D.D., May 6, 1877, age 55.
Heacock, Jesse Stone, son of the late Rev. Grosvenor R., April 7, 1862, age 26.
Heacock, Manson B., Wales, NY, formerly of Buffalo, May 13, 1854, age 49.
Heacock, R. B. (Capt.), May 19, 1864.
Heacock, Reuben B., April 7, 1854, age 65.
Heacock, Seth F., formerly of Buffalo, April 1, 1844, in Marion, Linn Co., IA.
Heacock, Seth G., late of Buffalo, April 1, 1844 in Marion, Linn Co., Ia., age 32.
Head, Ann M., Black Rock, NY, wife of James, dau. of Henry Streeter, April 4, 1863, age 28.
Head, Mrs. Catharine, mother of Joseph A. of Buffalo, Aug. 21, 1863 in Stanford, Canada West, age 74; bur. Buffalo.
Heafford, Richard, formerly of Buffalo, April 10, 1875, age 43; d. at Hamilton, Ontario.
Heahin (or Heabin), John, laborer, Aug. 26, 1874, age 35.
Healey, James, July 28, 1871, age 38.
Healt, Nelson, Aug. 10, 1871, age 53.
Healy, Ann T., wife of Samuel, Collins, Feb. 9, 1872, age 57.
Healy, George William, March 7, 1857, age 22.
Healy, Laura, widow of George W. of PA, Nov. 5, 1844, age 55.
Healy (Haley), Mrs. Mary, Sept. 9, 1879, age 55.
Heath, Charles, formerly of Buffalo, June 11, 1838, age 23; at Niles, MI.
Heath, John, formerly of Colden, March 4, 1872, age 67 y, 4 m, 27 d; d. near Fredonia, Ks.
Heath, Mrs. P., Clarence, March 18, 1874, age 74.
Heather, William, killed, Sept. 9, 1862, age 38.
Heaton, Luther, Eden, NY, March 15, 1842, age 46.
Heaton, Roxey, wife of Luther, April 28, 1832, age 33.

Hebard, Andrew, Chief Engineer U.S.N., Aug. 4, 1846, age 48.
Hebard, Capt. John, formerly of Buffalo, Jan. 24, 1879, age 79; d. at Norwich, Ct.
Hebard, Deacon Moses, native of Windham, CT, formerly of Lebanon, NH, Clarence, NY, March
    21, 1823, age 78.
Hebard, Sarah, widow of Andrew of US Navy, June 17, 1867, age 62.
Hebron, Mrs. Elizabeth, March 6, 1870, age 79.
Heckel, Adam J. or G., March 29, 1878, age 55.
Hecox, Emily Louise, Black Rock, NY, wife of William H., Aug. 23, 1847, age 23.
Hecox, Mary C., wife of William H., April 27, 1842, age 24; in Van Deusenville, MA.
Hecox, Susan, wife of Samuel, Jan. 6, 1868, age 74; d. at Lyons, NY.
Hecox, Louise, dau. of William H., formerly of Buffalo, Feb. 23, 1879, age 21; d. in
    Binghamton, NY.
Heddrich, Charles, wheelwright, accidentally killed June 25, 1874, age c. 60 or 70.
Hedge, George, Oct. 13, 1859, age 60 y, 6 m.
Hedge, Henrietta Ewing, Dec. 17, 1868, age 28, wife of George F.
Hedge, Kate S., wife of Charles L., dau. of James H. Mills, Aug. 27, 1866, age 23.
Hedstrom, Charlotte C., wife of E., Dec. 19, 1877, age 72.
Heeb, Charles H., April 22, 1876, age 33 y, 8 m, 11 d.
Heeb, Louisa, wife of Charles H., June 4, 1870, age 27.
Heellriegel, Apolonia, wife of Conrad, July 5, 1864, age 72.
Heellriegel, Capt. Jacob, May 4, 1845, age 29.
Heellriegel, John, Sept. 16, 1867, age 59 y, 1 m, 1 d.
Heellriegel, Nicholas, Aug. 28, 1848, age 36.
Heellriegel, Philip, Jan. 12, 1860, age 49.
Heerdt, Rosa, wife of August, Dec. 27, 1877, age 48 y, 4 m.
Hees, Charles, plumber, Feb. 13, 1872, age 22.
Hefferman, Mrs. Catharine, May 30, 1859, age 53.
Hefferman, John, patrolman, Oct. 7, 1875, age c. 30.
Hefferman, William, accident, Nov. 10, 1877, age 39.
Heffernan, William, Aug. 22, 1876, age 75.
Hefford, E. Sherman, Feb. 10, 1870, age 22.
Hefford, John, bur. May 16, 1853.
Hefford, Thomas, bur. May 17, 1865.
Heider, Philip, June 27, 1875, age 51; found in the water on Sunday, 27th inst.
Heidledich, George, formerly of Buffalo, Sept. 3, 1870; in Louisville, Ky.
Heilbeck, Cornelia, wife of Louis, Nov. 6, 1876, age 28 or 20 y, 4 m.
Heim, Laura J., Dec. 2, 1880, age 24.
Heimlich, Frederick, May 27, 1868, age 51.
Heimlich, P. J., formerly of Buffalo, Sept. 7, 1878, age 65; d. at Hiawatha, KS.
Heimlich, Philip J., April 5, 1863, age 78 y, 2 m, 19 d.
Heinicke, Mary, wife of John, May 4, 1880, age 44.
Heinold, Catherine, wife of Michael, March 31, 1880, age 66 y, 2 m.
Heinrich, Bernhard, Dec. 9, 1874, age 44.
Heins (or Heinz or Hines), Mrs. Barbara, wid. of Bernhard, shot by husband near Crittenden,
    July 5, 1879, age 61.
Heintz, Mrs. Charles, Sept. 5, 1876, age 23 y, 10 m.
Heintz, George John, Sept. 1863.
Heintzelman, Maj. Gen. S. P., formerly of Buffalo, May 2, 1880, age 73; d. at Washington,
    D.C.
Heinz, Charles, Dec. 24, 1875, age 44 y, 2 m, 4 d.
Heinze, Charles G., March 28, 1880, age 51.
Heinze, Susan M. Warner, wife of Charles G., Feb. 11, 1876, age 35 y, 7 m, 18 d; taken to
    Batavia.
Heiser, Elizabeth, wife of Godfrey, Dec. 1, 1864.
Heiser, Godfrey C. P., of firm of Heiser & Heiser, brewers, Nov. 9, 1869, age 27 y, 3 m,
    16 d.
Heiser, Henry, farmer, near Buffalo (5 mi.), July 24, 1879, age 85.
Heiser, Jacob M., Sept. 18, 1865, age 63 y, 3 m, 7 d.
Heiser, John, April 13, 1856.
Heiser, W., June 1872.

Heisser, Henry, eldest son of Godfried, May 19, 1866, age 26.
Heist, Frederick, railroad accident, Feb. 3, 1877, age 40.
Heitzel, John, June 14, 1879, age 28.
Heizenhout, Louis, Potters Corners, laborer, Nov. 22, 1871, age 52.
Held, Christian, Cheektowaga, Sept. 11, 1880, age 78.
Heller, Charles, accident, Gardenville, Dec. 29, 1877.
Hellriegel, Catharina, wife of Henry, Oct. 26, 1873, age 53 y, 9 m, 24 d.
Hellriegel, Conrad, May 20, 1871, age 84.
Hellriegel, Conrad, Nov. 27, 1877, age 37 y, 21 d; d. in San Francisco, bur. Buffalo.
Hellriegel, John, Dec. 21, 1877, age 35 y, 6 m, 21 d.
Helm, Jacob, Gordonville, May 15, 1877, age 20.
Helmer, Frederick, Co. Almshouse, Nov. 6, 1878, age 45.
Helms, Mrs., Hamburgh, NY, Dec. 1812, age 70.
Helms, Samuel, Dec. 30, 1813; at battle Black Rock.
Hely, James, April 18, 1869, age 32.
Hemans, Henry W., July 1871.
Hemenway, Anna C., wife of Edwin C., Oct. 2, 1876, age 34.
Hemenway, Edward S., son of Silas, May 1858; in KS; bur. in Buffalo.
Hemenway, Henry, H., Lancaster, Aug. 24, 1886, interred at Forest Lawn.
Hemenway, Nellie, wife of Henry B., Oct. 12, 1868, age 25.
Hemenway, Maj. Rufus, Revolutionary soldier, Fife-major with Lafayette, Dec. 22, 1839, age 77.
Hemenway, Rufus, Aurora, NY, Feb. 1, 1853, age 46.
Hemenway, Sarah Eleanor, wife of Henry B., Nov. 13, 1877, age 33 y, 6 m.
Hemerle, Joseph, suicide, March 11, 1878, age 32.
Heminway, Harvey, Dec. 20, 1840, age 36.
Hemming, Richard, July 9, 1862, age 47.
Hemmingway, Polly, widow of Major Rufus, Sept. 12, 1840, age 69.
Hemphill, Lt., killed in battle of Niagara, Aug. 1814.
Hemstreet, Sarah A., Alden, formerly of Buffalo, April 9, 1869, wife of Abram.
Hendershot, Mrs. Matilda, March 21, 1863, age 75.
Hendershot, William J., an invalid pensioner, May 17, 1833, age 56.
Henderson, Amorette, wife of Albert N., Jan. 6, 1862, age 32 y, 25 d.
Henderson, Charles H., youngest son of Edward, Jan. 12, 1873, age 26.
Henderson, Mrs. Chloe, Feb. 21, 1855, age 73 y 10 m.
Henderson, Daniel, Aug. 19, 1861, age 48.
Henderson, Duncan, blacksmith, late of Eldon, Victoria Co., Canada West, Sept. 20, 1863.
Henderson, Mrs. Elizabeth, March 16, 1871, age 46.
Henderson, Issa A., eldest dau. of Edward, June 2, 1877.
Henderson, Sophia, wife of John J., formerly of Buffalo, Oct. 26, 1867; in Cinncinati, OH.
Henderson, William, recently of Genesee Co., Dec. 1, 1847, age 73.
Henderson, William A., s/o Dr. Albert N., Oct. 29, 1878, age 32.
Hendery, Mrs. Mary, travelling from England to Portage, Wyoming Co., NY, Oct. 3, 1872.
Hendlen, Miss Jennie A., Oct. 25, 1868.
Hendrick, Mary Kimmit, wife of James, April 7, 1879, age 30 y, 7 m, 18 d.
Hendricks, Henry, Jan. 15, 1874, age 61.
Hendricks, Mary, Sept. 29, 1873, age 24 y, 1 m, 12 d.
Heneage, Robert, Oct. 20, 1879, age 55.
Hennesey, Patrick, Dec. 14, 1880, age 48 y, 11 m, 15 d.
Hennessey, Michael, Dec. 2, 1868, age 76.
Hennesy, Ann, April 5, 1873, age 45.
Hennington, John, Angola, NY, Oct. 15, 1867, age 45.
Henrich, Christian, formerly Quarter-Master Sergeant, 2nd U.S. Art., Sept. 25, 1842, age 31.
Henrich, Eva M., wife of John, May 14, 1876, age 36 y, 11 m, 4 d.
Henry, August, Oct. 23, 1880, age 27 y, 2 m, 23 d.
Henry, Charles, 1834; bur. on Harry H. Bissell lot in Forest Lawn Cemetery.
Henry, Robert, formerly of Buffalo, Aug. 21, 1875; d. at Chapinvillle, NY.
Henry, William, son of James (Louis W.?), Jan. 17, 1876, age 25 y, 2 m, 9 d.
Henshaw, Amy, wife of James S., Aurora, Feb. 21, 1868, age 83 y, 6 m, 3 d.

Henshaw, Calvin Lafayette, son of Manuel, Hamburgh, NY, June 3, 1857, age 31 y, 11 m.
Henshaw, Caroline C. Kittinger, dau. of Manuel, Dec. 22, 1851, age 27.
Henshaw, Elizabeth, mother of N., Aurora, NY, March 7, 1826, age 79.
Henshaw, Eunice Scott, wife of Isaac, Aurora, July 25, 1875.
Henshaw, Eveline, Aurora, July 26, 1876, age 25.
Henshaw, Hitty, wife of Nathaniel, Jan. 9, 1814, age 43; in Batavia.
Henshaw, Isaac, Augora, May 27, 1878, age 68 y, 10 m, 6 d.
Henshaw, J.H., Westfalls, NY, Feb. 14, 1867, age 39.
Henshaw, James Steuben, Aurora, Jan. 25, 1872, age 94.
Henshaw, Jefferson, Aurora, NY, Feb. 28, 1855, age 52.
Henshaw, Joseph M., West Falls, May 31, 1869, age 74.
Henshaw, Mary, widow of Jefferson, Aurora, NY, April 23, 1855, age 49.
Henshaw, Matilda, wife of Manuel, Hamburgh, March 18, 1844, age 39.
Henshaw, Nathaniel, Revolutionary soldier in prison 14 months in Bermuda, Aurora, NY, Aug. 22, 1838, age 70.
Henshaw, Miss Rusha, Elma, Feb. 6, 1874, age 72 y, 8 m, 7 d.
Henshaw, Miss Sally, March 1827, age 29.
Henshaw, Seymour, son of James S., Oct. 15, 1850, age 31 y, 4 m.
Henshel, Francisco (German), accidental death, Oct. 1, 1870, age 61.
Hensler, Emanuel Jr., Tonawanda, Feb. 3, 1879, age 83 y, 9 m, 18 d.
Hensler, Emanuel H., suicide, Tonawanda, Aug. 15, 1873, age 49.
Hensler, Michael, suicide, Clarence, April 18, 1874, age 55.
Hepworth, Anna Mary, wife of William H., Oct. 1, 1865, age 36.
Hepworth, Joseph C., Feb. 16, 1873, age 58.
Hepworth, Mary A., wife of Joseph, Jan. 11, 1872, age 62.
Hergott, Ludwig, found dead, July 28, 1879, age 54.
Herman, Mrs. Delia, Feb. 15, 1879.
Herman, John G., Oct. 1862.
Herman, Lenhardt, accidently killed, Aug. 17, 1874, age 64 y, 9 d.
Herrmann, Mary Ann, wife of Charles E., June 10, 1871, age 24 y, 9 m.
Hermon, Elizabeth, Jan. 20, 1865, age 20.
Herold, Mary, wife of Nicholas, Aug. 14, 1875, age 20 y, 1 m.
Herold, Nicholas, Feb. 22, 1876, age 26 y, 7 m, 18 d.
Heron, Peter R., April 4, 1863, age 33.
Herr, Annie E., dau. of Emanuel, Williamsville, NY, Feb. 21, 1863, age 22.
Herr, Emanuel, July 14, 1877, age 84.
Herr, Nancy, wife of Emanuel, Feb. 2, 1871, age 59.
Herr, Vitus, April 7, 1876, age 63.
Herrick, James, Feb. 6, 1875, age 56.
Herring, Asneath B., wife of John H., March 21, 1863, age 32.
Herring, Mrs. Eliza, April 15, 1866, age 84.
Herring, Henry, Co. Almshouse, Feb. 28, 1878, age 60.
Herrington, Benjamin, April 7, 1812, age 29.
Herrman, Christopher, Nov. 3, 1879.
Herrman, John G., 21st Reg., Sept. 29, 1862, age 19 y, 2 m, 23 d. D. in New York City, Bellevue Hospital, from wounds received in Battle of Bull Run; bur. Oct. 5.
Herron, Mrs. Jane L., Lancaster, Jan. 20, 1873, age 25 y, 6 m, 25 d.
Herron, Jeannette McLeish, wife of John, Aug. 25, 1870.
Hersee, Martha Waller, Sept. 4, 1863, age 74 y, 14 d; of Redgewick, Sussex Co., England.
Hersee, Thompson Jr., Nov. 15, 1875, age 30.
Hersee, William or James William, June 26, 1876, age 47.
Hersey, Gideon, Feb. 12, 1846, age 59.
Hersey, Solomon, May 8, 1863, age 84.
Hershey, Mrs. Fanny, Amherst, NY, eldest dau. of Benjamin Long, Feb. 25, 1852, age 20.
Hershey, Jacob, Williamsville, NY, July 7, 1840, age 41.
Hershey, Miss Mary A., Clarence, NY, March 14, 1864, age 40 y, 2 m, 23 d.
Hershey, Dr. Peter, Clarence, NY, Dec. 13, 1831, age 35.
Hersley, Miss Anna C., Williamsville, NY, Feb. 12, 1852, age 20; at Hiram Seminary, OH.
Hertel, Theresa, wife of John, Dec. 20, 1878, age 31.
Herter, Catharine, Eggertsville, wife of John, June 18, 1875, age 72.

Hertkorn, John, April 8, 1877, age 26 y, 1 m, 21 d.
Herttell, John C., Feb. 12, 1880.
Hervey, Mrs. Lucy, wife of R. G., formerly of Buffalo, June 25, 1880, age 33; d. at Niagara, Ontario, Canada.
Hesket, Bridget, wife of Samuel, July 23, 1880, age 54.
Hess, Sophane, North Buffalo, May 20, 1871, age 21.
Hester, Mary, Feb. 29, 1880, age 23.
Hester, Thomas, April 17, 1879, age 65.
Heth, Clarissa, wife of Franklin, New York, June 17, 1850. She with four of her children was lost on Steamer *G. P. Griffith*, buried in Buffalo.
Heth, Moddy, March 13, 1849, age 68.
Heth, Nelson, Aug. 10, 1871, age 50.
Hettel, John, night watchman, Feb. 3, 1880, age 76; found dead.
Hetz, Emma, wife of David, June 26, 1852, age 22.
Hetzer, John L., June 14, 1879, age 29 y, 4 m, 28 d.
Heussy, Harriet, formerly of Buffalo, wife of Casper E., d. in NY, bur. Buffalo.
Hewett, Mrs. Harriet Hall, June 24, 1879, age 70 y, 3 m, 18 d.
Hewitt, Amos, Jan. 1813, age 35.
Hewson, William, Buffalo, Abbott Rd., Dec. 13, 1880, age 73 y, 7 m.
Heyl, John, Amherst, NY, April 17, 1844, age 73.
Heywood, Charles R., youngest son of R., May 21, 1862, age 31.
Heywood, Daniel W., formerly of Buffalo, eldest son of R. H., April 19, 1863, age 36; in Milwaukee.
Heywood, Dr. John Wicks, May 17, 1854, age 25.
Heywood, Sarah, wife of R. H., July 18, 1843, age 39; at Clinton, Oneida Co.
Hibbard, Daniel, Black Rock, NY, April 21, 1871, age 80.
Hibbard, Daniel J.G., Nov. 16, 1866, age 41.
Hibbard, Eunice, wid. of Daniel, March 2, 1878, age 77.
Hibbard, Frances Eliza, wife of Capt. John, June 14, 1838, age 35.
Hibbard, Joseph, sailor, March 23, 1878, age 27; d. at the Penitentiary.
Hibbard, Mrs. Mary, Nov. 28, 1848, age 70.
Hibbard, Mrs. Polly, Collins, April 6, 1868, age 79.
Hibbard, Sally, wife of Luther, Eden, NY, Nov. 8, 1818, age 30.
Hibbard, Sarah, April 10, 1875, age 58.
Hibbard, Sovalla, wife of Lester D., Aug. 2, 1868, age 53.
Hibbard, William, Feb. 17, 1863, age 81; taken to Evans, NY.
Hibsch, Eliza, dau. of Michael, July 9, 1862, age 21 y, 11 m.
Hibsch, Michael, May 14, 1879, age 62 y, 11 m, 29 d.
Hichcock, Marcus, May 22, 1852, age 70; d. in Sisters' Hospital, Buffalo, supposed resident of Burton, OH.
Hickcox, Edward Y., Sept. 11, 1866; at San Jose, CA.
Hickey, Mrs. Ellen, Oct. 6, 1875, age 83.
Hickey, Dr. Eugene H., Aug. 6, 1878, age 33.
Hickey, Jeremiah E., son of Patrick, April 29, 1665, age 24 y, 4 m. Formerly of Glanmire, Co. Cork, Ireland.
Hickey, John, Dec. 26, 1875, age 31.
Hickey, John L., Nov. 21, 1879, age 40.
Hickey, Julia, wife of Hugh, March 19, 1878, age 59.
Hickey, Margaret L., wife of Patrick, Nov. 12, 1864, age 55.
Hickey, Patrick, April 17, 1871, age 64.
Hickley, George, March 25, 1862, age 37.
Hickman, Ann, wife of Arthur, Oct. 29, 1868, age 44.
Hickman, Emily Gregory, wife of Arthur W., July 12, 1880, age 29.
Hickock, Elisha C., June 11, 1852, age 60; in Madison, WI.
Hickox, John W., Hamburgh, NY, April 10, 1863, age 63.
Hicks, Mrs. Adaline R., Nov. 1, 1847, age 24.
Hicks, Christina, wife of John B., Nov. 23, 1853, age 18 y, 17 m, 19 d.
Hicks, Mrs. Corintha, Feb. 22, 1848, age 56.
Hicks, Daniel, Revolutionary soldier, March 18, 1853, age 101, bur. Buffalo.
Hicks, Harry, Marilla, NY, Nov. 29, 1862, age 58.

Hicks, Isaac B., Aug. 4, 1874, taken to Drummondville.
Hicks, John B., Dec. 22, 1829, age 38.
Hicks, John B., brother of Mrs. George W. Smith, June 13, 1870, age 39 y, 11 m.
Hicks, Mary, A., Jan. 12, 1866, wife of John, age 55 y, 14 d.
Hiestand, Christian, Oct. 3, 1865, age 67.
Higgens, Thomas G., Aug. 30, 1849, age 25.
Higgens, Walter, member of firm of R. Bullymore & Co., formerly of Horsham, Sussex, England, April 21, 1849, age 36.
Higgins, Alfred Winslow, Feb. 13, 1870, age 23; taken to Middle Haddam, CT.
Higgins, Caleb D., Feb. 28, 1873, age 65.
Higgins, Charles S., March 2, 1871, age 50.
Higgins, Mrs. E., mother of W. J. Mack, Dec. 1, 1856, age 80; taken to Fredonia.
Higgins, E. E., canal boatman, Sept. 11, 1876.
Higgins, Elizabeth, Sept. 2, 1852, age 65.
Higgins, Elizabeth, wife of Frincie Higgins, Dec. 11, 1855, age 66.
Higgins, Emma, wife of Edward, Jan. 14, 1848, age 28; d. at the Hydraulics.
Higgins, Henry, April 11, 1880, age 25 y, 9 m, 11 d.
Higgins, Honora, wid. of Matthew, Oct. 11, 1874, age 85.
Higgins, James, formerly of Buffalo, Oct. 31, 1842 in Fredonia, NY, age 76 y, 4 m.
Higgins, James W., April 27, 1835, age 32.
Higgins, John, Aug. 22, 1879, age 45.
Higgins, Mrs. Keturah, formerly of East Haddam, CT, Aug. 13, 1845, age 44.
Higgins, Mrs. Margaret, July 10, 1877, age 57.
Higgins, Matthew, March 27, 1873, age 78.
Higgins, Michael, July 11?, 1870, age 48 y, 6 m.
Higgins, Nancy, wife of James H., Aug. 9, 1825, age 50.
Higgins, Zenas, June 25, 1866, age 54 y, 8 m.
Higham, Anna F. Irton, wife of John B., Aug. 28, 1874, age 36 y, 1m, 28 d.
Higham, Thomas, formerly of Manchester, England; recently of Buffalo, May 18, 1854 in Rochester, NY, age 42.
Highland, Mrs. Bridget, Nov. 24, 1879, age 62.
Highland, Elizabeth, April 9, 1873, age 72.
Higinbotham, Anne Eliza, eldest dau. of Thomas, Feb. 9, 1856.
Higinbotham, Thomas, formerly of Buffalo, June 25, 1858 in Crummondsville, Niagara Falls, Canada West, age 71; bur. Buffalo.
Hildebrand, Charles, Feb. 23, 1873, age 35.
Hildreth, Eugenie, eldest dau. of Thomas, Willink, NY, Aug. 22, 1867, age 20.
Hildreth, Phebe A., wife of Thomas H., Willink, NY, Feb. 25, 1863, age 37.
Hildreth, Samuel, Aurora, suicide, April 1, 1880, age 25.
Hill, Mrs. Abigail Margaret, dau. of Judge Saunders of New Brunswick, NY, May 21, 1864, age 62.
Hill, Alma, wife of Henry, June 24, 1831, age 24.
Hill, Ann S., wife of Frederick C., Aug. 5, 1873, age 55.
Hill, Anthony, Cheektowaga, May 22, 1876, age c. 55.
Hill, Caroline, wife of James B., sister of Mrs. E. K. Bruce, April 28, 1866 in Chicago, IL; bur. Buffalo.
Hill, Catherine T., East Aurora, wid. of Dr. Eli, Jan. 23, 1877, age 76 y, 3 m, 24 d.
Hill, Charles, Aug. 7, 1849, age 52; b. Halifax, Nova Scotia.
Hill, Charles, b. Halifax, Nova Scotia, Aug. 7, 1849, age 52.
Hill, Cynthia, almshouse, Oct. 15, 1880, age 93.
Hill, Elisha, b. 1760, d. 1828, bur. Holland; Soldier of the Revolution.
Hill, Emeline C., Holland, NY, wife of H. M., formerly of Buffalo, Sept. 22, 1853, aged 29.
Hill, Hon. Henry, July 24, 1841, age 63.
Hill, Horace, brakeman, March 30, 1880, age 37.
Hill, J. Fellows, July 29, 1880, age 30.
Hill, James, Collins Centre, June 11, 1873, age 77.
Hill, Mrs. Lucy Munson, formerly of Buffalo, Nov. 23, 1860 in Homer, NY, age 74; bur. Buffalo.
Hill, Mrs. Martha, May 17, 1861, age 61.
Hill, Mary Sophia, wife of William, June 23, 1873, age 27.

Hill, Dr. Milo W., Feb. 25, 1877, age 72.
Hill, Nelson, Eden, NY, Feb. 20, 2867, age 57 y, 11 m.
Hill, Robert, Black Rock, NY, Dec. 30, 1813; killed at the battle of Black Rock, Jan. 25, 1814.
Hill, Ruth, wife of Dr. M. W., March 17, 1845, age 37.
Hill, Mrs. Sarah Jane, near Derby Station, Erie Co., March 2, 1880, age 23; killed by cars.
Hill Stephen G., formerly of Buffalo, June 19, 1873; d. in Meadville, PA.
Hill, William, b. 1746, d. 1837 (1828?), bur. Eden Center; Soldier of the Revolution.
Hill, William H., April 1, 1854, age 34.
Hill, William W., Akron, March 5, 1875.
Hillbridge, Henry, accidental death, Aug. 15, 1874, age 21.
Hillebrand, Peter, Dec. 16, 1838. Co. D, 2d Art.; d. at the barracks in this city, served in the Army 25 years.
Hiller, Michael, March 23, 1871, age 29.
Hilliard, Mrs. Jeannette C., June 1865; funeral June 7th.
Hillman, Minnie, Nov. 19, 1878, age 55.
Hills, Almira, Oct. 25, 1857, wife of Horace.
Hills, George B., April 12, 1874, age 37 y, 2 m, 11 d.
Hills, Horace, Sept. 18, 1873, age 86. Father of Rev. Horace Hills of MN, Rev. Geo. M. Hills of NJ & the Misses Hills, founders of the School for Young Ladies in Buffalo.
Hilton, John P., July 3, 1879, age 50.
Hilton, Mrs. Mary, April 9, 1869, age 29.
Hilton, Samuel, Amherst, NY, Dec. 7, 1822, age 24.
Himmelsbach, Philip J., Nov. 25, 1879, age 25 y, 11
Himmighofen, Charles P., Sept. 27, 1880, age 54.
Hinchman, Henry, Sept. 1827, age 20.
Hinde, Joseph G., formerly of Buffalo, Feb. 26, 1875; d. in Rochester.
Hindley, James A., formerly of Buffalo, Feb. 24, 1869; d. at Salamanca, NY.
Hindsley, (Livonia), fell during the War of 1812.
Hines (or Heins), Bernhard, farmer, near Crittenden, farmer, suicide, July 5, 1879, age 50.
Hines, Henry, July 31, 1844, age 21.
Hines, Henry L., East Aurora, Oct. 6, 1885, age 20 y, 4 m.
Hines, William T., Nov. 9, 1877, age 54.
Hingston, Catherine, March 11, 1876, age 85.
Hingston, Charlotte E. Cumming, wife of William, Jan. 13, 1877, age 51 y, 3 d.
Hingston, John T., drowned, Aug. 26, 1879, age 53.
Hingston, Samuel J., July 10, 1875, age 29.
Hinkley, Anna, wife of N.P., July 16, 1880, age 20 y, 5 m, 5 d.
Hinkley, Henry W., May 1, 1875, age 32 y, 8 m; d. at Atchison, KS, bur. in Buffalo.
Hinkson, Jane, April 16, 1868, age 64; d. at the Church Home.
Hinman, Mr. E. S., Oct. 12, 1859, age 42. Taken to Catherine, Schuyler Co., NY.
Hinman, Emily A., Evans, NY, March 1862, age 23; wife of Hiram.
Hinman, Eurotas, Aug. 24, 1833, age 29.
Hinman, Louisa L., wife of J. B., Oct. 14, 1876, age 49 y, 1 m, 2 d.
Hinman, Mary E., Aurora, NY, Oct. 1832, age 25. Wife of Capt. Hoel Hinman.
Hinsdale, John, formerly of Buffalo, March 13, 1851 in Brooklyn, Long Island, NY, age 75.
Hinsley, James, April 18, 1879, age 16.
Hinson, Elizabeth, Lancaster, NY, June 29, 1849, age 21; wife of William A. of Buffalo.
Hinson, George, July 30, 1873, age 55.
Hinson, Mrs. Mary J., Sept. 13, 1861, age 70.
Hinson, Robert, March 13, 1845, age 64; formerly of Warwickshire, England.
Hinson, William Adolphus, May 5, 1860, age 45 y, 3 m.
Hinterberger, Joseph, Jan. 23, 1878, age 28 y, 7 m, 23 d.
Hipelius, Joseph E., May 7, 1854; director of the Union Cornet Band of this city.
Hirn, Joseph, Nov. 6, 1880, age 26 y, 4 m.
Hirsch, Andrew, suicide, June 26, 1874, age 45.
Hirsch, John G., suicide, Dec. 3, 1878, age 32.
Hirsch, Xavier, Dec. 15, 1878, age 84.
Hirschbeck, Xavier, Nov. 30, 1872, age 45.
Hirschfield, Mrs. E., March 10, 1876, age 37.

Hirth, Gasper, native of Bavaria, Boston, NY, Sept. 23, 1871, age 62; accidental death.
Hitchcock, Alexander, drowned, Lancaster, NY, March 17, 1876, age 86.
Hitchcock, Apollos, Cheektowaga, NY, Aug. 24, 1870, age 73; accidently killed.
Hitchcock, James M., formerly of Cheektowaga, NY, June 6, 1866 in Chinandega, Nicaragua, Central America; age 27 y, 4 m.
Hitchcock, Jeremiah, Aug. 30, 1852 in Toledo, OH; firm of J. & C. Hitchcock of Buffalo.
Hitchcock, John, Cheektowaga, NY, May 14, 1851, age 63.
Hitchcock, Patience B., Cheektowaga, NY, April 4, 1859, age 41. Wife of James; formerly of Great Barrington, MA.
Hitchcock, Roxana, Amherst, NY, Sept. 14, 1830, age 68. Widow of Capt. Apollos; formerly of Suffield, CT.
Hitchcox, Hiram, Elma, NY, Jan. 10, 1866, age 68.
Hitchcox, Rachel Amaranth, Aurora, NY, March 22, 1850, age 40. Wife of Hiram.
Hitzel, Maggie, wife of Albert T., Sept. 19, 1878, age 37 y, 8 m, 16 d.
Hives, Mary L. G., March 16, 1852. Wife of Timothy; late of Rochester, NY & taken there.
Hoag, Caleb S., formerly of Buffalo, Oct. 8, 1876, age 50; d. at Hesper, KS.
Hoag, DeWitt C., May 29, 1858, age 35; taken to Hamburgh, NY.
Hoag, Joseph, July 4, 1863, age 66.
Hoag, Lucretia, Aug. 22, 1866, age 69; taken to Hamburgh, NY.
Hoag, Perses, Hamburgh, NY, Dec. 15, 1855, age 36, wife of Hiram; d. in Rockford, IL.
Hoarn (or Horan), Mrs. Mary, May 31, 1880, age 68.
Hoban, Edward, accident, carpenter, April 25, 1878, age 30.
Hobert, Miss Mehitable, formerly of Buffalo, Jan. 31, 1845 in Abington, MA, age 35.
Hobrook, Matthew, June 1869, age 24.
Hobson, Elizabeth, widow of James H., Jan. 21, 1879, age 78 y, 10 m, 21 d.
Hockstrasser, Mrs. Olivia, Jan. 26, 1861, age 82.
Hodge, Alfred, July 11, 1832, age 27.
Hodge, Amanda, Aug. 1825 in Salem, OH, age 19; wife of Loring.
Hodge, Benjamin Sr., Buffalo Town, NY, Feb. 23, 1837, age 84; Revolutionary Soldier.
Hodge, Col. Benjamin, June 8, 1868, age 71.
Hodge, Charles H., April 15, 1846, age 33.
Hodge, Eliza, Dec. 6, 1867, age 70; wife of Col. Benjamin.
Hodge, Jasper, Aug. 23, 1874, age 49.
Hodge, Lizzie, March 16, 1878, age 35; wife of Dwight W.
Hodge, Lorin, brother of the late Benjamin, formerly of Buffalo, Jan. 13, 1870, age 80 y, 9 m; d. in Saybrook, Ashtabula Co., OH.
Hodge, Maria, Oct. 15, 1826, age 24; wife of Col. Benjamin.
Hodge, Mary J., wife of Robert, Nov. 10, 1874, age 25 y, 15 d.
Hodge, Philander, Oct. 22, 1866, age 57.
Hodge, Philander Augustus, March 13, 1866, age 30; only son of Philander.
Hodge, Sally, May 20, 1835, age 79; wife of Benjamin Sr.
Hodge, Sally, widow of the late William, March 9, 1868, age 80.
Hodge, Miss Sarah, dau. of the late William, March 30, 1871, age 68.
Hodge, Susan Maria, Aug. 14, 1847, age 21; dau. of William.
Hodge, William, Black Rock, NY, Sept. 18, 1848, age 67.
Hodges, Charles Augustus, 1847, age 21. D. at sea on Merchant-Ship *Cohota*, returning from Canton.
Hodges, Lucy A., formerly of Buffalo, Aug. 29, 1866 in Adrian, MI, age 32. Wife of Corydon A. Hodges, dau. of William Cook, formerly of Buffalo.
Hodgkins, Jeanette Stanbridge, July 26, 1876, age 35 y, 9 m, wife of James.
Hodgkins, Rachel, Dec. 1, 1873, age 23 y, 7 m; wife of George.
Hodgkins, Lt. Thomas, Jan. 1863. Cothran's Lockport, NY Battery; d. at Stafford Court House [VA].
Hodgkins, William B., Black Rock, NY, July 5, 1855; firm of Hodgkins & Co.
Hodgson, Amy, wife of George, May 10, 1880, age 27 y, 10 m, 26 d.
Hodgson, Margaret, wife of George, Oct. 12, 1880, age 52.
Hodgson, Robert, April 6, 1873, age 38 y, 5 m, 10 d.
Hoefler, Catherine, Oct. 11, 1878, age 49.
Hoeg, Mary E., West Seneca, NY, June 19, 1877, age 44.
Hoenes, Jacob, accident, Nov. 1876, age 23.

Hoepfner, Anna, wife of Henry A., May 15, 1876, age 49.
Hofeller, Libbie, wife of Lehman, March 23, 1873, age 29.
Hofeller, Lillie, Dec. 6, 1877, age 19 y, 8 m, 6 d.
Hofeller, Sigmund, Jan. 29, 1875, age 46 y, 7 m.
Hofer, John S., Oct. 19, 1874.
Hoff, Widow Catharine, June 15, 1853. Mother-in-law of R. Fero. Formerly of Glen, Montgomery Co., NY.
Hoff, Richard, collector, d. in Station house, May 16, 1879, age 34.
Hoff (or Huff), Stephen, father of David, Tonawanda, May 18, 1876, age 84.
Hoffeler, George, June 21, 1877, age 50.
Hoffer, Henry, Aug. 4, 1878, age c. 45.
Hoffer, John George, Feb. 13, 1878, age 69.
Hoffman, Lt. Alexander, Jan. 27, 1844 in St. Augustine, FL; 2d Regt. US Infantry.
Hoffman, John, Aug. 28, 1876.
Hoffman, Leonard, Nov. 25, 1880, age 62 y, 9 d.
Hoffman, Peter, Eden, NY, Dec. 30, 1813. Killed at battle of Black Rock.
Hoffman, Peter, April 26, 1871, age 34.
Hoffman, Peter, accidently killed, Jan. 3, 1873.
Hoffman, Phocion, formerly of Buffalo, May 25, 1874; d. in Albany.
Hoffman, Samuel, Feb. 10, 1874, age 62.
Hoffman, Mrs. W.V.B., April 25, 1880, age 38.
Hoffmeyer, Lewis, Feb. 10, 1877, age 60.
Hoffner, Michael G., Nov. 1861, bur. Nov. 8.
Hofheins, Mrs. Wilhelmina, Dec. 28, 1873, age 73 y, 10 m, 28 d; mother of George F.
Hogaboom, Ann Eliza, formerly of Buffalo, March 18, 1841 in Nassau, Columbia Co., NY. Age 26, wife of John T.
Hogan, James, May 16, 1876, age 21.
Hogan, Mrs. Margaret, Dec. 17, 1872, age 57.
Hogan, Patrick, March 10, 1874, age 70.
Hohn, Ludwig, Sept. 29, 1877.
Hoile, John, Amherst, NY, Feb. 15, 1853, age 53.
Hoisington, Job, Dec. 30, 1813; killed at battle of Black Rock.
Holbrook, Anthony, Dec. 14, 1876, age 74.
Holbrook, Elizabeth, East Hamburgh, NY, March 18, 1857, age 21; only dau. of Marston Holbrook.
Holbrook, Miss Emily C., April 9, 1865, age 36 y, 6 m, 17 d; taken to Jamesville, Onondaga Co., NY.
Holbrook, Eugene E., son of the late Ora L., formerly of Buffalo, Aug. 10, 1871, age 23 y, 11 m; d. in Potter Valley, CA.
Holbrook, Marston, formerly of East Hamburgh, Oct. 18, 1874, age 74; d. in West Union, IA.
Holbrook, Mary A., widow of D. O., Oct. 3, 1871, age 72; taken to Attica.
Holbrook, Ora L., Oct. 25, 1850, age 31; merchant.
Holcomb, Margaret, wife of Charles G., Oct. 19, 1870, age 45; d. in Lockport, bur. in Buffalo.
Holerith, George, March 9, 1869, age 60 y, 6 m.
Holfelner, Joseph, suicide, May 31, 1878, age 24.
Holigan, Mrs. Mary, Lancaster, Aug. 18, 1876, age 60.
Holive (or Holwig), Charles, East Hamburg, April 11, 1879, age 45; d. at West Seneca.
Holland, Mrs. Bridget D., Nov. 1, 1878, age 62.
Holland, Miss Elizabeth, Springville, NY, Sept. 28, 1850, age 19; d. in Buffalo, taken to Springville.
Holland, Mrs. Julia, Aug. 9, 1871, age 41 y, 8 m.
Holland, Mrs. Maria, Jan. 19, 1858, age 47.
Holland, Robert, July 28, 1874, age 79.
Holland, Stephen, Dec. 2, 1812, age 40.
Holland, William C., formerly of Buffalo, Sept. 3, 1863 in Dunnville, Canada West, age 48; bur. in Buffalo.
Hollerith, Matthias, March 2, 1874, age 58.
Holley, Mrs., widow of Myron, Black Rock, June 6, 1868, age 82.
Hollidge, Eli, formerly of Buffalo, July 20, 1873; d. in St. Louis, MO, bur. in Buffalo.

Hollingshead, Laura, Dec. 7, 1851, wife of John.
Hollingshead, Martha A., wife of John, formerly of Buffalo, May 2, 1875; d. in Chicago.
Hollister, Abby, Nov. 19, 1834, age 35; wife of William, firm of Hollister & Curtiss.
Hollister, Belinda R., wife of Robert, Aug. 25, 1874, age 63.
Hollister, John, July 13, 1865, age 70.
Hollister, John Jay, formerly of Buffalo, Jan. 25, 1880, age 57; d. at New Rochelle, NY.
Hollister, Lutheria, formerly of Buffalo, Sept. 25, 1846; d. in Monroeville, OH, wife of John J.
Hollister, Miles B., Aug. 12, 1858, age 37.
Hollister, Orra, Aug. 12, 1853, age 82. Widow of William of OH; mother of John, James & Robert of Buffalo.
Hollister, Robert, Sept. 23, 1877, age 70.
Hollister, William, May 23, 1848, age 56.
Hollister, William, Oct. 27, 1855, age 28, son of William.
Holloway, Benjamin A., Aug. 1, 1877, age 30.
Holloway, Mrs. Elizabeth, mother of Isaac, Dec. 21, 1876, age 83.
Holloway, John, Dec. 27, 1853, age 34 y, 2 m, 16 d; firm of Holloway & Co.
Holloway, William Henry, son of Isaac, May 3, 1876, age 24 y, 5 m, 19 d.
Holman, Amelia, May 27, 1880, age 73.
Holman, Charles E., Nov. 8, 1880, age 41 y, 6 m.
Holman, Frances A., Aug. 25, 1854, age 22; wife of Edward D.
Holman, Frank R., East Hamburgh, NY, May 13, 1865, age 30.
Holman, Henry, accidental fall, carpenter, Sept. 1, 1874, age c. 25.
Holman, Lottie, Springville, NY, May 2, 1866, age 21 y, 10 m.
Holman, William, Aug. 27, 1876, age 76.
Holmes, Anna, wife of Seth, Wales, March 25, 1874, age 71.
Holmes, Dr. Augustine, Pine Grove, Erie Co., NY; Oct. 18, 1849 near Lebanon, PA, age 46 y, 4 m.
Holmes, Catherine, Aug. 31, 1875, age 44; wife of Isaac.
Holmes, Charles D., Nov. 8, 1850; taken to New York.
Holmes, Ebenezer, Wales, NY, April 10, 1839, age 75.
Holmes, Elizabeth, Wales, NY, Sept. 1, 1847, age 80; widow of Ebenezer.
Holmes, Emily J., wife of J.B., Sept. 9, 1873, age 40.
Holmes, George W., Wales, NY, June 10, 1837.
Holmes, Gilbert, Wales, NY, June 1, 1849, age 58 y, 1 m., 11 d.
Holmes, Henry, Aurora, NY, March 22, 1838, age 53; formerly of Herkimer Co., NY.
Holmes, James, June 30, 1859, in Alden NY, age 27.
Holmes, Jemima, Aug. 1, 1879.
Holmes, John, Wales, NY, Oct. 1, 1857, age 68 y, 2 m, 17 d.
Holmes, Nancy, Jan. 1827, age 25; wife of W. Holmes. Formerly of Avon, Livingston Co., NY.
Holmes, Philip M., East Evans, Oct. 8, 1877, age 78.
Holmes, Philip Miller, Dec. 24, 1814 in Geneva, NY, age 24. Son of Rev. Elkanah Holmes and son-in-law of Dr. Cyrenius Chapin. Bur. in Forest Lawn.
Holmes, Susan C., wife of J.B., July 10, 1878, age 61.
Holmes, Susannah B., June 18, 1874, age 91; widow of Rev. Benjamin.
Holmes, Thomas, Sardinia, NY, Feb. 2, 1865, age 79.
Holser, John J., May 10, 1876, age 41 y, 5 m, 6 d.
Holser, Rosina, Oct. 12, 1867, age 52; widow of Jacob.
Holslag, Frank, June 4, 1874, age 30 y, 6 m.
Holslag, John, Oct. 7, 1872, age 38.
Holt, Abby G., formerly of Buffalo, Feb. 7, 1865 in Brooklyn, NY. Wife of H. N. Holt and dau. of Henry R. Seymour.
Holt, Arrabert F., Nov. 25, 1869, age 43.
Holt, Dibdell, Nov. 18, 1831; hanged for the murder of his wife.
Holt, Jane, Oct. 29, 1855, age 40; wife of Capt. John.
Holt, Mary, Jan. 3, 1820, age 48; wife of Gen. Elijah.
Holt, Walter Cleveland, formerly of Buffalo, April 1, 1880, age 22 y, 4 m.; d. at Leadville, CO.
Holtz, Delia, wife of William, Oct. 10, 1877, age 22.
Holzer, Jacob, Aug. 22, 1867, age 60.

Homan, Charles, March 12, 1880, age 42. Almshouse.
Homer, Margaret, Dec. 31, 1879, age 60; sudden death.
Honihan, Miss Mary, Oct. 16, 1872.
Honk, Rosine, July 3, 1849, age 20; wife of Philip.
Hood, Samuel, West Seneca, March 3, 1876, age 73 y, 6 m, 27 d.
Hooker, Azel, formerly of Buffalo, Feb. 2, 1861 in Woodbury, Hancock Co., IL, age 64 y, 10 m, 21 d.
Hooker, Eliza, wife of Charles M., May 13, 1838, age 20. [not in card file]
Hooker, Mrs. Eliza, March 2, 1875.
Hooker, James, Oct. 29, 1858, age 28 y, 2 d; formerly of Buffalo, d. at Indianapolis, IN.
Hooker, Capt. Francis G., Aug. 9, 1854, age 40.
Hooley, Martha, Feb. 1, 1873; taken to Toronto.
Hooper, Capt. Francis G., Aug. 9, 1854, age 40.
Hooper, Frank, drowned, June 12, 1879, age 40.
Hooper, Matilda, Oct. 31, 1851, age 33; wife of Capt. F.G.
Hooper (or Huber), Peter, drowned Oct. 28, 1873.
Hoople, Eliza, May 13, 1838, age 20; wife of Charles M.
Hoover, Charlotte Mety, wife of Silas, Harris Hill, Sept. 5, 1877, age 34.
Hoover, Jacob, formerly of Erie Co., June 21, 1874, age 84. Father of George H. D. at Nashville, MI.
Hoover, Marietta, wife of George H., Nov. 28, 1872, age 34.
Hoover, Michael, June 10, 1880, age 73.
Hope, Bridget, wife of Edward, March 24, 1875, age 58.
Hope, Mrs. Christina, May 8, 1864, age 65.
Hope, John, formerly of Buffalo, father of Mrs. Gilbert Hyatt, Sept. 6, 1858, age 62; at Howell, Livingston Co., MI.
Hopkins, Rev. Dr., Nov. 27, 1847, age 42.
Hopkins, Mrs. Abigail, mother of Rev. A. T., Nov. 28, 1857, age 91.
Hopkins, Almira, Lancaster, July 31, 1874, age 42 y, 4 m, 8 d.
Hopkins, Byron, formerly of Clarence, NY, Dec. 2, 1848, age 30; at St. Louis, MO.
Hopkins, Carrie, wife of R. H. M., March 9, 1880, age 21 y, 9 m, 15 d.
Hopkins, Catharine R., wife of Charles M., April 10, 1841, age 21.
Hopkins, Charles A., Sept. 28, 1864, age 62.
Hopkins, Charles M., July 16, 1851, age 46.
Hopkins, Charles W., eldest son of Charles M., 63rd Reg. IL Vol., July 20, 1862, age 21; in Military Hospital, Cairo, IL Bur. in Buffalo. [not in card file]
Hopkins, Daniel B., Nov. 26, 1836, age 33.
Hopkins, Edward, Dec. 17, 1864, age 64.
Hopkins, James, b. 1749, d. Oct. 22, 1831, bur. Sardinia, NY; Soldier of the Revolution.
Hopkins, John A., Oct. 25, 1857, age 47.
Hopkins, Prof. John C., Sept. 8, 1872, age 32. D. at Chepatchet, RI.
Hopkins, Miss Julia Anne, sister of Rev. A. T. Hopkins, Aug. 23, 1843; late of Hartford, CT.
Hopkins, Lavinia, widow of Otis R., Clarence, NY, Feb. 28, 1852.
Hopkins, Lucy A., wife of Nelson K., only dau. of Orlando Allen, Jan. 30, 1853, age 25.
Hopkins, Miss Mary, Lancaster, Aug. 3, 1875, age 72 y, 3 m, 9 d.
Hopkins, Mary, widow of Nelson, Aug. 11, 1878, age 35.
Hopkins, Nancy, only dau. of Robert and Submet, Sardinia, NY, Feb. 26, 1845, age 24.
Hopkins, Nancy, wife of Gen. T.S., Amherst, April 2, 1848, age 70.
Hopkins, Nelson, July 23, 1864, age 45.
Hopkins, Otis R., Clarence, NY, Jan. 11, 1846, age 68.
Hopkins, Sarah, widow of Ichabod of Great Barrington, MA, Aug. 10, 1831, age 87.
Hopkins, Sarah, wife of Thomas N., Sardinia, July 25, 1851, age 71.
Hopkins, Thomas, Sardinia, Jan. 26, 1870, age 93 y, 8 m.
Hopkins, Gen. Timothy S., Amherst, Jan. 23, 1853, age 76. Biog. BET gives death as Jan. 28, 1853.
Hopkins, William, suicide, Sardinia, Sept. 9, 1873, age 49.
Hopkins, William, Eggertsville, July 24, 1880, age 70.
Hopkins, William H., brother of John A. of Flint, MI, Sept. 1, 1853; taken to MI.
Hopson, Heman, Aug. 4, 1846, age 22.

Horan, Mrs. Elizabeth, July 7, 1875, age 67.
Horan, John, accident, Nov. 25, 1875.
Horan, William C., connected with the *Courier*, Feb. 7, 1869, age 36. Of the firm of Warren, Johnson & Co.
Hornbeck, Edgar, June 2, 1874, age 26.
Hornbeck, James, July 28, 1852, age 23.
Hornbuckle, Richard, July 13, 1875, age 54 y, 4 m, 13 d.
Horner, George, Clarence, NY, May 5, 1832, age 40.
Horner, George W., killed by accident in Erie, PA, Artizan, July 3, 1879.
Horner, Michael, West Seneca, Jan. 8, 1874, age 37.
Horner, Mrs. Rosanna, grandmother of Mrs. John Pease and Mrs. J. M. Chamberlain of Buffalo, Dec. 14, 1856, age 82.
Horner, Elder William T., A.M., Aug. 21, 1875; d. at Middeltown, NY, bur. at Clarence, NY.
Hornung, Lawrence, Oct. 12, 1880, age 59; suicide.
Horrigan, Mary, Co. Almshouse, June 12, 1878, age 78.
Horter, John, Sept. 4, 1877, age 82.
Horton, Allen W., Aug. 11, 1873, age 59 y, 10 m.
Horton, Rev. Carlton S., Dec. 8, 1864, age 32 y, 6 m; taken to Palmyra, N.Y.
Horton, David H., Jan. 31, 1878, age 60 y, 11 m.
Horton, James Jr., July 15, 1871, age 61.
Horton, Lucretia Huntington, widow of Joseph G., Feb. 10, 1876, age 93.
Horton, Rev. Truman, Boston, Oct. 20, 1869, age 74.
Hose, Lydia, wife of David, Dec. 6, 1875, age 49; taken to Rochester, NY.
Hosford, Boswell, Revolutionary soldier, formerly of Williamstown, VT, Feb. 3, 1839, age 76.
Hosford, Lucretia B., mother of Mrs. Elias Green, Oct. 27, 1852, age 80.
Hosford, Roswell, Aug. 22, 1841, age 32.
Hosley, Mrs. Caroline F., late of Rochester, NY, April 18, 1857, age 60.
Hosmer, Abbie Stanley, dau. of Silas, April 21, 1864.
Hosmer, Alfred, drowned July 30, 1873, age 62; taken to Youngstown, Ontario.
Hosmer, Edward Jarvis, 52nd Reg. Mass. Vol., Jan. 24, 1863, age 19; at Baton Rouge, LA.
Hosmer, Ellen A., wife of Theodore M., Oct. 23, 1873, age 17.
Hosmer, Mary D., wife of H. L., formerly of Buffalo, April 30, 1858, age 40; at Toledo, OH.
Hosmer, Mary Elizabeth, wife of Gustavus P., Aug. 23, 1858.
Hosmer, Park S., furniture dealer, Nov. 18, 1880.
Hosmer, Silas, Oct. 1871, age 71.
Hotchkiss, Amos H., Nov. 17, 1863, age 76.
Hotchkiss, Hawley C., only son of the late George C., Feb. 9, 1869, age 20; taken to Lewiston.
Hotchkiss, Jane Elizabeth, wife of Wheeler, Aug. 22, 1846.
Hotchkiss, Mary Jane, wife of Frederick A., Feb. 22, 1876, age 46 y, 4 m, 9 d.
Hottinger, Ferdinand G., Oct. 1879, age 29.
Hottinger, Joseph, May 14, 1861, age 58.
Houck, Charles A., son of V.W., Oct. 21, 1874, age 25 y, 1 m, 25 d.
Houck, Christopher, Jan. 18, 1876, age 30.
Houck, Margaret, wife of Michael, April 25, 1871, age 47 y, 2 m, 7 d.
Houck, Michael, formerly of Buffalo, Jan. 12, 1879, age 58 y, 4 m, 15 d.
Hough, Dr. David C., Hamburgh, NY, Sept. 29, 1857, age 65.
Hough, Edwin, printer, May 3, 1870, age 62; founder of the *Hornellsville Tribune*.
Hough, Elizabeth E., April 22, 1878, age 53.
Hough, Lucretia, widow of Dr. D. C., May 25, 1875, age 76.
Houghton, George W., Feb. 16, 1872, age 65; taken to Forest Hill Cemetery near Boston.
Houghton, Louisa E., wife of Emory H., sister of J. H. Perry, Nov. 2, 1835, age 24.
Houghton, Olive, wife of Alfred A., Nov. 19, 1873, age 21.
Houlgrave, John, insurance & collecting agent, July (c. 29), 1870; murdered in Hamilton, Ontario.
Hourt, Michael, suicide, Lancaster, NY, Aug. 18, 1877.
House, Ann W., widow of Hiram, April 26, 1880.
House, Anne, wife of Joseph, Oct. 17, 1820, age 25.
House, Eliza Sutton, wife of Hamilton, June 22, 1878, age 48 y, 8 m, 15 d.

House, Hiram, father of Charles A., March 20, 1871, age 66; taken to Troy.
House, Dr. John G., formerly of Buffalo, physician, Jan. 1, 1880, age 63 y, 8 m, 15 d.
House, Sarah A., wife of Garrett, Aug. 18, 1870, age 44.
Hovey, Amanda S., dau. of Gen. Josiah, March 17, 1876, age 68; taken to Warsaw, Wyoming Co.
Hovey, Annie Louisa, wife of Darius A., Oct. 22, 1879, age 37 y, 2 m, 13 d.
Hovey, Josiah, b. 1747, d. 1820, bur. Warsaw (Wyoming Co.); Soldier of the Revolution.
Hovey, Gen. Josiah, June 18, 1867, age 88; taken to Warsaw, N.Y.
How, Ellen Rebecca, wife of Gen. C. of Chicago, dau. of John P. Shaw, Aug. 23, 1862, age 30.
Howard, A. M., wife of Capt. E. A., formerly of Buffalo, Sept. 29, 1873; d. in Detroit.
Howard, Alma, wife of D. H., July 20, 1835, age 27.
Howard, Asa, Jan. 4, 1875, age 66 y, 3 m.
Howard, Austin A., lawyer, Sept. 1, 1879, age 63.
Howard, C., M.D., Feb. 25, 1878, age 30.
Howard, Clara, widow of Charles, Aug. 1871, age 70; taken to OH.
Howard, Eddy, at the Hydraulics, April 2, 1851, age 54.
Howard, Edward F., recently of New York, Sept. 14, 1845, age 35.
Howard, Ellen, wife of George, May 2, 1846, age 33.
Howard, Frances Ann, wife of Lloyd, Sept. 19, 1860, age 42.
Howard, George H., Dec. 21, 1876, age 33.
Howard, Gibson F. (Col.), April 12, 1875, age 31.
Howard, Harriet Cowles, wife of Austin A., dau. of Peter Curtiss, Sept. 20, 1853, age 29.
Howard, Hattie Cornelia, only dau. of Gen. R. L., May 13, 1874, age 20.
Howard, Henry, eldest son of Henry and Catherine, Dec. 12, 1855.
Howard, Henry, Aug. 28, 1857, age 39.
Howard, Henry, July 15, 1878, age 78.
Howard, Hiram E., Feb. 8, 1868, age 68.
Howard, Hungerford. Jan. 22, 1869. ["Funeral held at residence of his father, No. 251 Delaware st., on Sat. 23d inst."]
Howard, Mrs. Irena, Oct. 18, 1848, age 66.
Howard, John H., son of Henry & Catharine, Feb. 17, 1873, age 31 y, 2 m. ["Formerly of Buffalo?."]
Howard, Joseph, Jr., Aurora, NY, merchant, Sept. 16, 1836, age 41.
Howard, Mrs. Lucy B., Holland, Jan. 13, 1871, age 72.
Howard, Marcus A., Elma, July 10, 1871, age 62.
Howard, Martha, Hamburgh, NY, March 24, 1822, age 49; wife of Simeon.
Howard, Mrs. Mary, April 5, 1861, age 57 y, 8 m.
Howard, Mary Anne, wife of Hiram E., Feb. 14, 1863, age 49 y, 2 m.
Howard, Mary E., wife of E. H., Feb. 22, 1844, age 29.
Howard, Mary Elizabeth, dau. of E.H., Sept. 30, 1864, age 20.
Howard, Mary L., wife of Edward D., Dec. 16, 1872, age 32.
Howard, Mary Louisa, wife of George, March 31, 1851, age 29.
Howard, Nancy, widow of Rufus, Jan. 19, 1860, age 70.
Howard, Rufus, father-in-law of Gibson T. Williams, formerly of Herkimer Co., Oct. 10, 1848, age 62.
Howard, Tom M., formerly of Buffalo, Oct. 26, 1880, age 20 y, 10 m, 3 d.
Howard, William D., son of Eddy, July 3, 1863.
Howard, William Parker, Aug. 21, 1878, age 90.
Howarth, Henry, Feb. 18, 1865, age 39; taken to Rochester, NY.
Howden, Christina, Black Rock, NY, wife of Rev. William, Feb. 1, 1849, age 66.
Howden, Peter J., formerly of Buffalo, July 29, 1847; at Syracuse, NY, age 22. Printer.
Howden, Rev. William, Aurora, NY, Feb. 15, 1865, age 82.
Howe, Bvt. Capt. Albion, formerly of Buffalo, April 26, 1873, age 32. Killed by the Modocs; bur. in Buffalo.
Howe, Allen S., Dec. 29, 1867; d. at Battlecreek.
Howe, Anna L., widow of Hon. Estes, late Recorder of the City of Albany, Dec. 14, 1862, age 74.
Howe, Carrie W., wife of A. S., May 10, 1858, age 19 y, 11 m.
Howe, Miss Eveline, dau. of J. D., Alden, July 19, 1847, age 24.
Howe, Mrs. Mary, mother of Mrs. William Wells, Sept. 8, 1858, age 84.

Howe, Mary E., Dec. 18, 1871, age 53.
Howe, Otis B., Oct. 20, 1878, age 69.
Howe, Squire, Newstead, Feb. 26, 1872, age 69.
Howell, Mr., laborer, Sept. 1815.
Howell, Charles Gibson, son of Stephen W., July 8, 1872, age 20.
Howell, Edward S., May 22, 1869, age 24.
Howell, Isabella, wife of William W., Dec. 26, 1856, age 42; taken to Rochester, N.Y.
Howell, James, Oct. 10, 1872, age 30.
Howell, Mrs. Susan, formerly of Buffalo, July 27, 1877, age 79 y, 9 m; d. in Evans, Erie Co., NY.
Howell, Dr. William, U.S. Navy, son of Stephen W., July 26, 1862, in New York City, age 29.
Howells, Rhoda C., wife of William, Sept. 6, 1854, age 34.
Howells, Sarah, wife of Thomas, Sr., July 21, 1849, age 65.
Howells, Thomas, Sept. 2, 1854, age 71.
Howells, William, Sept. 6, 1854, age 32.
Howes, Ebenezer A., formerly of Buffalo, March 17, 1842; at Monroe, MI, age 29.
Howes, Elizabeth, wife of Capt. Abner, sister of late George Day, April 21, 1865, age 29 y, 10 m.
Howes, Mrs. Sabrina Abbott, formerly of Buffalo, Sept. 9, 1876, age 87; d. in Hamburgh.
Howiller, John, Sept. 28, 1863, age 47.
Howland, Charles, Nov. 7, 1863, age 63.
Howland, Holder, S., formerly of Buffalo, Nov. 4, 1875, age 42; d. in Chicago, bur. in Buffalo.
Howley, Edward, March 6, 1873, age 58.
Howley (Hawley), Julia, wife of Patrick, June 4, 1880, age 45.
Hoxie, F. Helmena, wife of David, Colden, Feb. 26, 1880, age 47 y, 8 m.
Hoxie, Lyman, Colden, Feb. 24, 1873, age 76.
Hoy, Capt. J. A., native of France, Oct. 2, 1855, age 40.
Hoyt, Asa, June 1, 1875, age 69 y, 2 m.
Hoyt, Betsey, widow of William, April 15, 1874, age 73.
Hoyt, Delia T., wife of P. W., dau. of Mrs. Wealthy Thomas, Oct. 8, 1848; in Brooklyn, N.Y., age 25.
Hoyt, Mrs. Eliza, Aug. 24, 1843, age 35.
Hoyt, Isaac, Alden, NY, March 11, 1864, age 70.
Hoyt, Hon. James G., Oct. 29, 1863, age 58.
Hoyt, Joseph D., June 21, 1854, age 30.
Hoyt, Lucia Caroline, widow of Joseph D., second dau. of Rev. T. F. Whitcomb, March 18, 1857, age 33.
Hoyt, Polly, widow of Joseph, May 29, 1863, age 68.
Hoyt, Prudence, wife of Hon. Jonathan, Aurora, NY, March 22, 1844, age 55.
Hoyt, Satie J., sister of Mrs. Charles G. Williams, April 19, 1875.
Hoyt, William, Revolutionary Soldier, Wales, June 11, 1847, age 82.
Hoyt, William, April 3, 1874, age 81.
Hubbard, Alexander F., M. D., eldest son of Dr. H. H., late of Springville, N.Y., Nov. 14, 1847; at Racine, WI, age 26.
Hubbard, Amy C., wife of C. J., Jan. 29, 1877, age 58.
Hubbard, Credulia, wife of Alonzo, dau. of Daniel Sumner, Hamburgh, NY, Aug. 10, 1850; in Fairport, IL, age 38.
Hubbard, Daniel, Aug. 31, 1871, age 77.
Hubbard, Elias, May 23, 1850, age 52.
Hubbard, Miss Eliza M., Springville, NY, July 17, 1846, age 60.
Hubbard, Mrs. Emma, mother-in-law of I. A. Blossom; formerly of Belfast, ME, Feb. 16, 1847, age 70.
Hubbard, George, Sept. 11, 1844, age 59.
Hubbard, Linus P., March 20, 1863, age 54.
Hubbard, Mrs. Lucy, widow of George, formerly of Buffalo, June 9, 1880, age 89; d. in Cromwell, CT.
Hubbard, Mrs. Matilda H., Dec. 17, 1837.
Hubbard, Seneca, Aug. 10, 1875, age 74 y, 5 d; bur. in Wales Hollow Cemetery.
Hubbard, Susan E. A., wife of Charles J., Dec. 27, 1861, age 38 y, 24 d.

Hubbard, Walter B., Nov. 2, 1866, age 43.
Hubbell, Caroline E., Aug. 8, 1867, age 45.
Hubbell, Catharine, wife of Thomas, May 12, 1847, age 19 y, 4 m.
Hubbell, Charles A., Aug. 13, 1878, age 23.
Hubbell, Mrs. Charlotte W., West Falls, NY, June 17, 1878, age 83 y, 9 m.
Hubbell, Francis, Black Rock, soldier in U.S. Volunteer Army, June, 1812.
Hubbell, John, lawyer, Jan. 27, 1880, age 61; bur. at Rochester, Mt. Hope Cemetery.
Hubbell, Lewis D., Sept. 21, 1848, age 24.
Hubbell, Sarah, wife of Elnathan, May 3, 1849, age 31.
Hubbell, Selim B., formerly of Buffalo, July 5, 1876, age 46; d. at Fredonia, KS.
Hubby, Katharine M., wife of Frank W., formerly of Buffalo, Dec. 13, 1880; d. at Colorado Springs, CO.
Huber, Barbara, wife of Peter, July 6, 1848, age 71.
Huber, Nicholas, May 7, 1874, age 22.
Huber, Peter, March 8, 1852, age 79.
Hubers, Magdalena, Co. Almshouse, Feb. 4, 1876, age 37.
Hubner, Mrs. Mary, July 22, 1874.
Hucker, Eliza, widow of N. Sr., July 12, 1878, age 73.
Hucker, Nathaniel, Sr., March 9, 1859, age 56.
Huckerby, George, Oct. 26, 1880, age 22 y, 4 m, 1 d.
Hudd, Richard, whitewasher, May 14, 1840.
Huddleston, Julia M., wife of Lt. T. R., only dau. of Lyman Dunbar of Buffalo, Jan. 23, 1863; in Hastings, MN, age 28.
Hudson, Archibald C., Feb. 11, 1876, age 34.
Hudson, Charles, son of Widow Sarah of Buffalo, Dec. 1, 1849; in San Francisco, CA, age 24.
Hudson, Charlotte Mary, wife of M., April 5, 1874, age 22 y, 2 m, 7 d.
Hudson, Clark, Aurora, May 21, 1875.
Hudson, Gertrude Craig, wife of John T., Sept. 1, 1851, in Schenectady, NY, age 31.
Hudson, Henry, Dec. 24, 1875, age 47 y, 10 m, 2 d.
Hudson, Lydia, widow of Rev. Clark, Wales, NY, June 5, 1873, age 80.
Hudson, Mary Ann, wife of N. L., Feb. 13, 1847, age 23; funeral at Whites Corners, NY.
Hudson, Polly, widow of Benoni, Sardinia, April 6, 1853, age 80.
Hudson, Mrs. Sarah, sister of A. Cutter of Buffalo, formerly of Buffalo, June 26, 1871, age 73; d. in Philadelphia, PA.
Huetter, Mrs., March 4, 1873, age 39.
Huff, Henry D., March 12, 1874, age 40 y, 5 m; bur. in Tonawanda.
Huff, Isaac, Alden, Sept. 3, 1875, age 71.
Huff, Mrs. Jane, May 20, 1845, age 64.
Huff, Louisa, wife of W. W., May 26, 1849, age 33.
Huff, Lydia P., East Hamburgh, June 13, 1876, age 71.
Huff, Maria, wife of Isaac, Alden, Dec. 14, 1873, age 75.
Huff, Ruth, wife of Silas, April 20, 1865, age 35.
Huftill, Emma J., dau. of William, Aug. 5, 1877, age 19 y, 2 m, 1 d.
Huftill, William, April 19, 1878, age 48.
Huges, William J., formerly of Troy, N.Y., Oct. 30, 1846, age 40.
Hughes, Bernard, formerly of Buffalo, April 13, 1871; d. in Brooklyn, NY.
Hughes, Edward, March 14, 1876, age 66.
Hughes, Harriet, wife of Peter, July 8, 1858, age 34.
Hughes, James, Oct. 29, 1870, age 63.
Hughes, Julia, wife of John, Dec. 6, 1864, age 60.
Hughes, Kate, wife of John, West Seneca, July 18, 1880, age 23.
Hughes, L. L., June 30, 1876.
Hughes, Margaret, wife of John E., Sept. 23, 1863, age 42.
Hughes, Mary, wife of John, West Seneca, Oct. 10, 1880, age 37 y, 7 m, 10 d.
Hughes, Mary L. Clapp, wife of Mathew D., Jan. 10, 1875.
Hughes, Maryan (Sister Symplicia), formerly of Baltimore, MD, Jan. 24, 1852; at Hospital of Sisters of Charity, Buffalo, age 27.
Hughes, Robert K., April 22, 1874, age 33; taken to Erie, PA.
Hughes, Sophia, wife of John S., late of Albany, June 20, 1852, age 39 y, 7 m.

Hughes, Mrs. Sophia, mother of J. H. of Buffalo, Aug. 12, 1869, age 87; d. at residence of the "Fakir of Ava."
Hughes, William, Feb. 3, 1837, age 38.
Hughson, A. P., Oct. 6, 1871, age 42 y, 3 m, 24 d.
Hughson, Miss Dency M., formerly of Buffalo, Jan. 7, 1860; in St. Paul, MN, age 22.
Hughson, Loraine L. Luce, formerly of Buffalo, wife of Egbert E., Aug. 13, 1870, age 35 y, 10 m; d. at St. Paul, MN.
Hugron, Alexander, Sept. 14, 1849, age 20.
Hugron, Mrs. Catharine, May 26, 1878, age 78 y, 21 d.
Hugron, Francis, April 4, 1855, age 60.
Hugron, Frank, Feb. 8, 1870, age 50 y, 1 m, 27 d.
Hugson, Mrs. Julia, wife of Frank, May 17, 1880, age 56 y, 10 m, 17 d.
Hulbert, Frances, Aug. 5, 1872.
Hulbert, Hannah M., wife of Milton A., North Buffalo, NY, Jan. 12, 1865, age 55.
Hulbert, Hart, March 7, 1849, age 36.
Hulbert, Milton A., Feb. 20, 1876, age 66.
Hull, Mrs. Aletha, April 9, 1857, age 64.
Hull, Dea. Andrew, Clarence, May 5, 1879, age 73.
Hull, Araville, wife of E., Clarence, late of Freedom, Cattaraugus Co., May 3, 1852, age 30.
Hull, Ashbell, Clarence, July 8, 1823, age 58.
Hull, Charles H., March 11, 1879, age 26; d. at Ogden, UT. Territory, bur. in Buffalo.
Hull, David Buell, Feb. 19, 1874, age 63 y, 1 m.
Hull, Deborah, child of Daniel Wilber's, Jan. 19, 1813, age 22.
Hull, Deborah, Jan. 25, 1813, age 22.
Hull, Edmund, formerly of Clarence, NY, Black Rock, NY, Sept. 16, 1852, age 58.
Hull, Edmund C., March 13, 1866, age 66.
Hull, Eliza Ann, wife of Edmund, Clarence, NY, Feb. 5, 1843, age 35.
Hull, Elizabeth Jane, wife of D. B., April 14, 1863, age 46 y, 4 m.
Hull, Emily L. Stockbridge, Nov. 3, 1878, age 29; wife of Joseph H.
Hull, Hallet, Jan. 19, 1813, age 19.
Hull, Hattie E., wife of Rev. Robert B., June 18, 1873; d. in Philadelphia.
Hull, Helen Louise, Oct. 10, 1877; dau. of the late D.B.
Hull, James, July, 1864.
Hull, Lucy Ann, wife of Willard J., June 26, 1867, age 54.
Hull, Martha A., wife of Edmund C., March 22, 1864, age 55 y, 3 m, 24 d.
Hull, Martin V.B., April 22, 1865, age 29.
Hull, Miss Minerva, dau. of Warren, Clarence, NY, Nov. 24, 1830, age 26.
Hull, Stephen or Samuel or William, Jan. 19, 1879, age 45 or 49.
Hull, Warren, Revolutionary Soldier, Lancaster, NY, Oct. 22, 1838, age 76. (Wilhelm, NY, b. 1762)
Hulsart, Mrs. Ann, Sept. 21, 1868, age 78 y, 7 m, 15 d.
Hultz, William, Eden, NY, Jan. 26, 1851, age 40.
Humason, Gamaliel, June 9, 1878, age 61.
Humberston, John, father of Mrs. C. L. Smith, Aug. 18, 1869, age 69.
Humberstone, Elizabeth, wife of John, Jan. 9, 1863, age 55.
Humberstone, John Edward, Nov. 10, 1860, age 27.
Humberstone, Martha Elizabeth, dau. of John, May 19, 1863, age 21 y, 10 m.
Hummel, Mrs. Barbara Ann, Oct. 23, 1871, age 89 y, 5 m.
Hummell, Amelia, wife of Frederick Jr., Lancaster, April 29, 1880, age 26 y, 4 m, 10 d.
Humphrey, Catherine, wife of Richard, Nov. 29, 1880, age 36 y, 8 m.
Humphrey, David, formerly of Buffalo, late of Chicago, Aug. 27, 1852, in Sacramento, CA.
Humphrey, Lois, sister of James M., June 17, 1875, age 67.
Humphreys, Lucia Williams, wife of George, March 7, 1877, age 55.
Humphries, George, Jan. 4, 1880, age 60.
Humsberger, George, Dec. 5, 1879, age 58.
Hunn, Edmund, Feb. 3, 1869.
Hunsche (or Hanche), Christina, Dec. 22, 1875, age 76.
Hunt, Mrs. Calvin, Holland, March 28, 1878.
Hunt, Catherine H., widow of Emory W., Feb. 27, 1864, age 53.

Hunt, D. W., June 8, 1878, age 27 y, 8 m.
Hunt, David, b. 1761, d. 1848, bur. Holland; Soldier of the Revolution.
Hunt, Edward, April 1813, age 59.
Hunt, Elisha W., formerly of 49th NYS Vols., May 25, 1875.
Hunt, Mrs. Elizabeth, Jan. 10, 1864, age 78.
Hunt, Flavel S., Hamburgh, Nov. 13, 1873.
Hunt, Horace, formerly of Buffalo, Dec. 5, 1864; at Woodstock, VT, age 48.
Hunt, Mrs., wife of John, Feb. 30, 1830, age 32.
Hunt, John, Sept. 27, 1864, age 67.
Hunt, Timothy, Black Rock, canal contractor, Aug. 19, 1825.
Hunter, Alice Mary, wife of George, Feb. 11, 1874, age 35 y, 10 m, 23 d.
Hunter, Elizabeth, wife of Dr. James of Lewiston, mother-in-law of Dr. F. W. Bartlett of Buffalo, Feb. 20, 1863, age 69; taken to Lewiston, NY.
Hunter, George, formerly of Buffalo, Dec. 7, 1874; d. in New York, reported murdered.
Hunter, Dr. James, April 20, 1875, age 81.
Hunter, Jane E. N., eldest dau. of John B. & Mary, Feb. 25, 1874, age 21 y, 8 m, 27 d.
Hunter, John H., fireman, July 30, 1880, age 44; d. at Hancock, Delaware Co., NY.
Hunter, Mary, April 20, 1875.
Hunter, William, son of John B. of Buffalo, April 10, 1866, age 28 y, 11 m, 4 d; in Louisville, KY, formerly of Buffalo.
Huntington, Abel M., Alden, NY, Oct. 1828, age 32.
Huntington, Anna A., dau. of J. G., Oct. 3, 1855, age 20.
Huntington, Prof. G. R., Jan., 7, 1872, age 72.
Huntington, Gurdon, May 1855, age 76; bur. May 14.
Huntington, John, West Falls, Nov. 26, 1879, age 88.
Huntington, Sylvina, wife of John, West Falls, NY, Oct. 3, 1865, age 69 y, 5 m, 3 d.
Huntington, Theophilus, Clarence, NY, July 11, 1830, age 77.
Huntley, Frank W., May 16, 1880, age 52 y, 5 m, 12 d.
Huntley, Deacon R., Hamburgh, NY, July 7, 1846, age 82.
Huntly, Mary, sister of Mrs. J. J. Culbertson, East Hamburgh, NY, Oct. 30, 1869; d. at residence of P. W. Powers.
Huntly, Walter L., Nov. 11, 1879, age 37.
Hunz, John, night watchman in Tannery, scalded to death, Oct. 30, 1880, age 32.
Huppuch, Julia, suicide, June 9, 1877, age 20.
Hurd, Abigail, wife of Russel, Lancaster, June 16, 1853, age 63.
Hurd, Cordelia, wife of Cyrus, Lancaster, June 30, 1853, age 25.
Hurd, Eleaser, b. Aug. 15, 1758, d. April 1, 1838, bur. Evans, NY; Soldier of the Revolution.
Hurd, J. C. (Rev.), Dec. 21, 1879, age 50; d. at Burlington, IA.
Hurd, Marian, wife of Rev. J.C., Feb. 25, 1873; d. at Brantford, Ontario.
Hurd, Norman, formerly of Buffalo, Sept. 20, 1863; at Elmira, NY, age 58.
Hurd, Robert, b. 1755, d. 1818, bur. Warsaw (Wyoming Co.); Soldier of the Revolution.
Hurlbart, Mrs., wife of Abijah, Feb. 12, 1813, age 45.
Hurlbert, Edwin, Jan. 20, 1877, age 66.
Hurlburt, Nathan A., Jan. 10, 1838; at Rochester, N.Y., age 23.
Hurlbut, Walter B., formerly of Buffalo, June 8, 1849; at Granville, NY, age 30.
Hurley, Mrs. Anastatia, formerly of Buffalo, Nov. 10, 1875, age 50; d. in Clinton, IA.
Hurley, Margaret, wife of Timothy, Feb. 6, 1873, age 56.
Hurley, Margaret, Sept. 8, 1880, age 70.
Hurley, Patrick, Sept. 16, 1873, age 35.
Hurst, John, Feb. 12, 1862, age 37.
Hurst (or Foley), Mary, Sept. 16, 1879, age 70, Co. Almshouse.
Hurt, John, Feb. 12, 1862, age 37. [not in card file]
Husk, Julia V., March 21, 1865, age 20.
Huson, Edward H., May 7, 1868, age 36.
Hussey, George, clerk in drug store, July 29, 1872, age 22.
Hussey, James G., formerly of Buffalo, March 1874; d. at Moorhead, Clay Co., MN.
Hussey, Mary, wife of John, June 8, 1871, age 38.
Hussey, Stephen, North Collins, NY, April 1, 1862, age 72.
Hussong, Christian, Feb. 12, 1863, age 39.

Hussy, Margaret, dau. of John, Dec. 19, 1872, age 27.
Husted, Addison G., son of Emeline T., April 22, 1871, age 20 y, 20 d.
Husted, Ezekiel, March 29, 1867, age 41.
Husted, Samuel, Jan. 8, 1867, age 75; taken to Franklinville, Cattaragus Co., NY.
Husted, Sarah Elizabeth, widow of Ezekiel, March 28, 1869, age 39.
Husted, Stephen St. John, formerly of New Canaan, CT, Jan. 30, 1860, age 59; b. Aug. 11, 1811.
Husted, William L., Dec. 8, 1868, age 26 y, 6 m, 8 d.
Hustler, Thomas, b. 1753, d. 1821, bur. Lewiston (Niagara Co.); Soldier of the Revolution.
Huston, Samuel C., seaman, June 6, 1879.
Hutchins, David, July 19, 1849, age 43.
Hutchins, William, formerly of New York, May 9, 1840, age 40.
Hutchins, William A., June 4, 1865, age 39; taken to Cleveland, OH.
Hutchinson, Ann Elizabeth, wife of Thomas M., Lancaster, April 4, 1880, age 40.
Hutchinson, Daniel, Black Rock, NY, March 21, 1853, age 47.
Hutchinson, Dr. Elisha, Aug. 20, 1862, age 62.
Hutchinson, Eunice Abzina, wife of John M., dau. of Rufus Howard, March 13, 1852.
Hutchinson, Harriot Martin, Williamsville, April 6, 1874, age 81; widow of John.
Hutchinson, John, Williamsville, Aug. 28, 1865, age 73.
Hutchinson, Capt. Joseph, Soldier of 1812, formerly of Williamsville, NY, Aug. 28, 1867, age 79.
Hutchinson, Marietta B., widow of Dr. Elisha, formerly of Buffalo, Feb. 27, 1877, age 73; d. in Brooklyn, bur. Buffalo.
Hutchinson, Mrs. Sarah, Lancaster, March 1878, age 86 y, 3 m, 8 d.
Hutchinson, Sarah Maxwell, widow of Joseph, formerly of Williamsville, NY, Nov. 24, 1873, age 83; d. near Nevada City, CA.
Hutchinson, Selenda, widow of David, Williamsville, NY, Feb. 14, 1875, age 64.
Hutchinson, Thomas, Harris Hill, April 10, 1878, age 75 y, 2 m, 15 d.
Hutchinson, William H., formerly of Williamsville, June 16, 1878, age 65; d. in Chicago, IL.
Hutton, George, Jan. 10, 1878, age 67.
Huwerth, Charles J., Jan. 11, 1878, age 28 y, 2 m, 26 d.
Huwerth, Frederick E., April 8, 1880, age 25 y, 8 m.
Huwerth, Ricca Blaylock, dau. of H. K., Dec. 30, 1879, age 27 y, 9 m, 3 d.
Huxford, Frederick W., formerly of Buffalo, Jan. 2, 1852; at Ablion, MI.
Hyatt, Charles, Nov. 19, 1850, age 49; formerly of Sherbrook, Lower Canada.
Hyatt, Gilbert, Aug. 25, 1869, age 58.
Hyatt, Jay, Jan. 1, 1876, age c. 40; d. at Pass Christian, MS, bur. Buffalo.
Hyatt, Thankful B., wife of George, late of Buffalo, Oct. 13, 1843; at Franklinville, Cattaraugus Co., NY.
Hyde, Mrs. Anna, Black Rock, NY, Aug. 26, 1841, age 87.
Hyde, Clarissa, widow of Col. James of Darien, Genesee Co., April 9, 1849, age 57.
Hyde, Ezekiel R., formerly of Suffold, CT, 1816, age 60. Record given by Guy H. Salisbury from memory.
Hyde, Flora J., dau. of J. W., Oct. 5, 1863, age 25.
Hyde, Harriet, wife of Paris P., Nov. 12, 1815, age 19.
Hyde, James, Dec. 23, 1876, age 86.
Hyde, Miss Lydia, d. in the Buffalo General Hospital, June 19, 1875, age 91.
Hyde, Nancy, widow of E. R. May 3, 1823, age 65.
Hyde, Paris P., Dec. 1, 1839, age 56.
Hyde, Samuel, drowned Sept. 5, 1874, age 24; at Cleveland, OH.
Hyde, Zerotus Daniel, only son of R.A.G., Aurora, Oct. 14, 1874, age 46.
Hyman, Bonney, May 18, 1875, age 65.
Hyman, Nancy J., wife of Ellis, March 29, 1873, age 31; taken to Middletown, NY.
Hynes, Mrs. Bridget, mother of Rev. Thomas, Pastor at West Seneca, July 26, 1867, age 68.
Hynes, Catherine, May 31, 1875, age 46; wife of Michael.
Hynes, Stephen, July 6, 1871, age 38.

Illig, Mary, wife of Peter J., Nov. 17, 1877, age 44 y, 2 m, 2 d.
Illingworth, Mary Ann, wife of Edwin, Lancaster, May 22, 1868, age 36.

Indicott, William, July 13, 1861, age 30.
Ingalls, Charles, Aug. 15, 1880, age 30; Almshouse.
Ingalls, Dr. Daniel, formerly of Springville, NY, late of Pittsburg, PA, Nov. 3, 1842, age 50.
Ingalls, George W., Jan. 7, 1864, age 41 y, 8 m.
Ingalls, Hannah, wife of Otis, Clarence, NY, March 8, 1815, age 30.
Ingalls, Dr. Varney, Springville, NY, Nov. 20, 1843, age 50.
Ingalls, Zimri, Springville, March 27, 1872, age 69 y, 10 m, 10 d.
Ingersoll, Albert Grellet, Dec. 29, 1876, age 25; bur. Forest Lawn, Lot 22, Section E. (Data from cemetery, 1962.)
Ingersoll, Catherine Frances, wife of Rev. Edward, July 6, 1866; bur. in Forest Lawn, Lot 22, Section E.
Ingersoll, Catherine Maria, Sept. 6, 1863; buried in Forest Lawn, Lot 22, Section E.
Ingersoll, Gidney S., Evans, Jan. 30, 1872, age 73.
Ingersoll, Harriet Tupper, wife of John, Evans, NY, Dec. 3, 1861, age 61.
Ingersoll, Jonathan, July 29, 1847; bur. Forest Lawn, Lot 22.
Ingersoll, Robert S., Evans, NY, Aug. 11, 1864, age 71.
Ingersoll, Sarah A., only dau. of John, East Evans, NY, June 2, 1852, age 21.
Ingersoll, Seymour, June 3, 1879, bur. Forest Lawn, Lot 22.
Ingersoll, Sophia, wife of William H., North Evans, NY, June 11, 1865, age 56.
Ingles, John, July 24, 1876, age 54.
Inglesant, Mary, Sept. 7, 1862, age 29.
Inglesant, Mrs. Mary, Hall's Corners, NY, Oct. 24, 1871; bur. Buffalo.
Inglesant, William Knight, May 4, 1867, age 32.
Inglis, Mrs. Eliza, widow of James, April 12, 1880, age 73.
Inglis, James, April 13, 1876, age 73 y, 5 m.
Ingols, Alvin, Willink, NY, Nov. 1, 1811, age 22.
Ingram, Agnes H. Barnes, wife of John C., Aug. 26, 1886, age 29 y, 9 m.
Ingram, Hannah, wife of Daniel, Dec. 19, 1876, age 57 y, 1 m, 1 d.
Inman, George, H., accident, May 24, 1876, age 35.
Inman, Henry, July 2, 1866, age 65.
Inman, Susan A., wife of George H., June 12, 1872, age 23.
Innes, Alexander, Aug. 9, 1853, age 22.
Ipson, George, Feb. 12, 1877, age 40.
Ipson, Hans I., Feb. 12, 1877, age 41 y, 9 m, 11 d.
Ireland, Caroline, wife of P. A., Buffalo?, March 21, 1880, age 29 y, 5 m; d. at Custer City, PA.
Ireson, Ann Elizabeth, widow of William, mother of John, March 20, 1849, age 57.
Ireson, Frances, wife of John, July 16, 1857, age 36.
Irish, Atwood T., April 3, 1871, age 40.
Irish, Benjamin G., March 15, 1875, age 61.
Irish, Charles G. Sr., July 12, 1869, age 79.
Irish, Francewild V., wife of Atwood T., Jan. 28, 1869, age 35.
Irish, Ira E., Aug. 19, 1876.
Irish, Ira E., East Evans, Aug. 20, 1876, age 74.
Irish, L. D., June 26, 1866, age 39.
Irish, Lottie, wife of Arthur, formerly of Colden, Dec. 1879?.
Irish, Louisa G., widow of Hon. Ira E., East Evans, Dec. 14, 1878, age 69.
Irish, Mary E., widow of Edward of Halifax, Nova Scotia, Feb. 1, 1837, age 77.
Irish, Mehetabel, wife of Charles G., Aug. 8, 1866, age 78?.
Irish, Theodore, Hamburgh, NY, Dec. 29, 1832, age 22.
Irish, Washburn, Marilla, Jan. 9, 1876, age 64.
Irons, Betsy, widow of J.B., Jan. 4, 1878, age 49.
Irons, Jane, Oct. 8, 1874, age 29.
Irving, John N., April 28, 1874, age 33.
Isaac, Captain, a distinguished Seneca brave, who perished of cold in the streets of Buffalo, a few evenings since Jan. 2, 1836.
Islet, Charles, painter, sudden death, July 7, 1880, age 31.
Islet, Elizabeth, wife of Charles, Feb. 24, 1880, age 26.
Isherwood, Eliza, wife of H., artist of Eagle Street Theatre, Oct. 10, 1836, age 26.

Israel, Susan, Dec. 28, 1879.
Itjen, Henry, Feb. 10, 1863, age 48.
Ittell, C. M., widow of John, Dec. 15, 1875, age 87.
Ives, Amasa, Supt. of the Work House in Buffalo, Aug. 24, 1839, age 64.
Ivo, Peter J., March 20, 1879, age 68.
Izzard, Ann, formerly of England, March 28, 1853, age 63.

Jackman, Capt. Carter, Aug. 22, 1835, age 35.
Jackman, James R., Marilla, NY, Nov. 23, 1864, age 71.
Jackson, Abraham H., April 15, 1850, age 35.
Jackson, Ann, wife of Thomas, M.D., May 4, 1873, age 33; d. at Whitehaven, England.
Jackson, Celestia, wife of Amansel D., Dec. 26, 1875, age 65 y, 1 m, 26 d.
Jackson, Darius D., formerly of Buffalo, April 2, 1876; d. at Williamantic, CT, taken to Oneida, NY.
Jackson, Mrs. Fanny M., formerly of Buffalo, June 18?, 1860 in Cincinnati, OH.
Jackson, Frank D., Akron, July 25, 1876, age 31.
Jackson, Mr. G.L.J., April 28, 1858, age 26.
Jackson, George, stone-cutter, July 26, 1871.
Jackson, Mrs. Hannah, Dec. 1, 1844, age 52.
Jackson, Hilanco D., Akron, NY, Feb. 7, 1862.
Jackson, Gen. James, March 29, 1867, age 62.
Jackson, Jane Paton, wife of T. J., March 4, 1868, age 22.
Jackson, John, Dec. 12, 1880, age 75.
Jackson, Julia, wife of R. & dau. of the late T. S. Cutting, formerly of Buffalo, Dec. 4, 1873; d. in Brooklyn, NY, bur. in Buffalo.
Jackson, Maggie, May 26, 1872, age 25.
Jackson, Mary Jane, wife of William L., Dec. 30, 1880, age 49 y, 9 m, 3 d.
Jackson, Polly, wife of William, Hamburgh, NY, June 24, 1844, age c. 35.
Jackson, Sarah M., wife of Joshua S., dau. of Timothy Topspot, June 29?, 1864, age 26 y, 6 m.
Jackson, Sarah S., wife of Charles P. of CA, dau. of Z. A. Hamilton, East Aurora, NY, June 17, 1862, age 41.
Jackson, William, March 18, 1855, age 46.
Jackson, William M., Angola, Oct. 1870.
Jacobi, L. A., formerly of Buffalo, March 1878, age 70; d. in Milwaukee.
Jacobi, Theodore, Aug. 14, 1872, age 55.
Jacobia, Moncrief, May 13, 1872, age 26 y, 8 m, 8 d.
Jacobs, Frank, Aug. 10, 1878, age 33.
Jacobs, John, Sept. 3, 1838, Royalton Center, NY; Soldier of the Revolution.
Jacobs, S.B., obituary March 8, 1867.
Jacobson, Harold, Feb. 17, 1877, age 29.
Jacobson, Matilda, June 18, 1871, age 23.
Jacus, Nettie Holmes, wife of W.C., Feb. 13, 1873, age 34; taken to Palmyra.
Jaeger, John, suicide, June 20, 1875, age 62.
James, Almira, wife of Aaron, Jan. 28, 1822.
James, Clarissa M., Oct. 23, 1879, age 23 y, 7 m, 3 d.
James, Emily, wife of Freeman, Dec. 12, 1836, age 30.
James, John, Aug. 8, 1858, age 28.
James, John, Feb. 7, 1880, age 34; almshouse.
James, Joseph, late of County Clare, Ireland, formerly of Gloucestershire, England, Aug. 7, 1857, age 76 y, 8 m.
James, Margaret, Cheektowaga, May 30, 1869, age 68; wife of Thomas, mother of Mrs. William Lewis of Buffalo; taken to Fredonia.
James, Mary, widow of Joseph, Feb. 19, 1870, age 78.
James, Thomas, March 5, 1852, age 41.
Jamison, Mrs. Elizabeth, mother of James of Buffalo, June 21, 1869, age 76; d. at Statebridge, funeral in Buffalo.
Jamison, Capt. Joseph, May 28, 1869.
Jamison, Mary Ann, wife of William, Jan. 10, 1862, age 33 y, 4 m.
Janett (Gennett), Mrs. Mary, of Lower Canada, April 7, 1874, age 52.

Jangraw, Mary J., wife of Nicholas, Feb. 18, 1862, age 28 y, 5 m, 22 d.
Jansen, Dr. August F. D., Feb. 9, 1880, age 60.
Jaqueman, Francis, May 25, 1871, age 54.
Jaques, Henry, of Guelph, Canada West, formerly of Buffalo, Nov. 17, 1869; d. at Cleveland, OH, taken to Toronto, Canada West.
Jaques, Miss Mary Battey, eldest dau. of Henry, formerly of Buffalo, April 19, 1862; in Toronto, Canada West.
Jardeson, John, May 11, 1877, age 55.
Jarrett, William, Dec. 14, 1867, age 64.
Jarvis, Ralph L., Jan. 28, 1874, age 50.
Jebb, Mary E., wife of Thomas A., Nov. 18, 1860, age 30.
Jehle, Frank, father of Edward, Charles & Louisa, July 24, 1874, age 59.
Jemison, Wilton Burwell, Brant, NY, 1864.
Jendevine, Sarah, formerly of Buffalo, Feb. 1876, age 76; widow of Henry. D. at Galena, IL, bur. in Buffalo.
Jenkins, Caroline H., dau. of Lewis, April 11, 1861, age 33 y, 11 m.
Jenkins, Eliza M., widow of Lewis, April 13, 1873, age 78.
Jenkins, Helen D., teacher in the Female Seminary, formerly of Boston, MA, June 17, 1854, age 19.
Jenkins, Lewis, May 22, 1873, age 84.
Jenkins, Matilda, wife of William H., Aug. 6, 1873, age 23.
Jenkins, Robert Jr., Feb. 18, 1879, age 58.
Jenkins, Mrs. Sophia, mother of W. and H. D. Huff, May 28, 1848, age 57.
Jenks, Julia Ann, widow of William, Evans, NY, Oct. 23, 1848.
Jenks, Miss Zidana J. J., June 5, 1858, age 25.
Jenner, Richard, formerly of Buffalo, druggist, July 7, 1880, age 52.
Jenner, Mrs. Ruth, from Harmony, Chautauqua Co., NY; Eden, NY, Feb. 1, 1860, age 69.
Jennings, Isaac, Black Rock, NY, Dec. 1837 at Vicksburg, MS, age 46.
Jennings, John, d. of injuries received in Lockport riot. BRB, Jan. 16, 1823.
Jennings, Marian H., Jan. 26, 1876, age 65; widow of Selden, M.D., taken to Richmond, MA.
Jennings, Orrin, Jan. 23, 1875, age 59; taken to Pompey, Onondaga Co.
Jennings, Sibel Everett, wife of Benjamin, Aug. 31, 1852; age 61.
Jennison, John A., bookkeeper at D. N. Barney & Co., Dec. 17, 1846, age 52.
Jenrich, John, accident, Nov. 1, 1875, age 23.
Jenzer, Carl, Aug. 1, 1878.
Jerard, Mrs. Jane, Black Rock, Jan. 22, 1870.
Jerge, Jacob, Lancaster, Nov. 6, 1880, age 71.
Jerger, Lena, Sept. 7, 1870; found dead in bed.
Jessemin, Charles, Feb. 19, 1878, age 42.
Jessemin, Hannah, wife of Charles, Nov. 21, 1875, age 36.
Jessemin, Margaret Maloney, dau. of James, March 26, 1878.
Jessemin, Mary, wife of James, Sept. 21, 1877, age 69.
Juendevine, Henry, Dec. 23, 1862, age 69.
Jewell, Darius, Feb. 1, 1863, age 50.
Jewett, Annie P., widow of George W., April 4, 1877, age 67; taken to Howell, MI.
Jewett, Delia M., wife of Edward M., Oct. 27, 1880, age 39.
Jewett, Martha M., sister of E. R. of Buffalo, late of New Haven, VT, Aug. 31, 1849, age 23.
Jewett, Mary Frances Colegrove, wife of James H., Aug. 6, 1880, age 44.
Jewett, Sophia Skinner, mother of Sherman S., May 8, 1873, age 76; taken to Moravia, Cayuga Co.
Jewitt, Frances A., wife of Caleb, only dau. of Col. Ithiel Hickox of Washington, Litchfield Co., CT, Nov. 2, 1856, age 33.
Jimeson, Mary, "The White Woman," captured in childhood by the Indians, and could never be induced to leave them; Seneca Village, Sept. 19, 1833, age 91.
Jinks, Elizabeth, Co. Almshouse, April 1876, age 31.
Johanny, Francis B., Jan. 15, 1878, age 57 y, 10 m, 17 d.
Johnson, Mrs., mother of Col. Chas., Boston, NY, Feb. 1826, age 73.
Johnson, Abraham, Sept. 17, 1871, age 79 y, 3 m.
Johnson, Akins, son of David, Feb. 21, 1854, age 22 y, 6 m.

Johnson, Amanda Melvina, wife of N. B., Jan. 29, 1860, age 49 y, 11 m.
Johnson, Capt. Andrew M., Nov. 8, 1877; lost from Schooner *Berlin*, on Lake Huron.
Johnson, Mrs. Ann, mother of Henry & Augustus, Oct. 14, 1873, age 76.
Johnson, Anna, widow of Robert B., Nov. 1, 1864, age 31.
Johnson, Beatta E. W., wife of Gilbert, Wales Center, NY, March 15, 1861, age 23.
Johnson, Calvert H., formerly of Buffalo, Dec. 1871, age 26; d. in Chicago.
Johnson, Carr, May 17, 1862, age 62.
Johnson, Col. Charles, Hamburgh, NY, June 17, 1832, age 56.
Johnson, Charles, served in War of 1812, clothes-cleaner, Dec. 28, 1867, age 69.
Johnson, Charles F., youngest son of Joseph, Aug. 13, 1854, age 22; d. at Jackson, MI.
Johnson, Charles H., March 22, 1867, age 38; taken to Kenosha, NY.
Johnson, Curtiss, Hamburgh, NY, Sept. 21, 1845, age 61.
Johnson, Mrs. David, Jan. 17, 1854, age 55.
Johnson, Capt. Ebenezer, father of Dr. E., Feb. 8, 1841, age 81.
Johnson, Dr. Ebenezer, formerly of Buffalo, Sept. 23, 1849, age 62; at Tellico Plains, East TN.
Johnson, Eliza A., wife of J. B., Nov. 22, 1869, age 30; taken to New Haven, OH.
Johnson, Elizabeth, Hamburgh, NY, April 10, 1860, age 60.
Johnson, Mrs. Elizabeth, Feb. 17, 1866, age 62 y, 2 m.
Johnson, Mrs. Elizabeth, Aug. 24, 1879, age 55.
Johnson, Mrs. Emma L., Oct. 1866; funeral Oct. 4., from residence of E. K. Bruce.
Johnson, Mrs. Evelina, May 3, 1880, age 81.
Johnson, Fannie E., wife of Dr. Thomas M., youngest dau. of Walter Porter, April 5, 1865, age 22 y, 5 m, 12 d.
Johnson, Fanny, wife of Capt. Samuel, Dec. 27, 1845, age 47 y, 5 m.
Johnson, George, Black Rock, NY, Nov. 19, 1863, age 73.
Johnson, George, Aug. 30, 1872, age 43.
Johnson, George N., May 13, 1853, age 38. Killed by the falling in of Mr. Glenny's building.
Johnson, Lt. Col. George Washington, July 29, 1864; wounded in action July 12, 1864 at Ft. Stevens, DC. Funeral Aug. 7.
Johnson Hattie, wife of Alexander, Jan. 26, 1873.
Johnson, Henry C., April 1, 1824, age 35.
Johnson, Capt. Henry, Lancaster, Aug. 14, 1835, age 73d year. (b. 1762); Soldier of the Revolution.
Johnson, J. H., husband of Julia Devereux of this city, formerly of Buffalo, Aug. 14, 1875; d. at Saco, ME.
Johnson, James, May 17, 1872, age 36.
Johnson, James, May 18, 1872, age 40.
Johnson, Jane, wife of A.M., Jan. 9, 1875, age 46.
Johnson, John, July 10, 1870, age 21 y, 9 m.
Johnson, John, Towanda, cabinet maker, Oct. 23, 1870, age 65.
Johnson, John, Feb. 3, 1871, age 39.
Johnson, John, Oct. 10, 1871, age 40.
Johnson, John, employee on railroad, killed by engine, July 25, 1879, age 43.
Johnson, John J., Oct. 4, 1859, age 60 y, 1 m, 18 d.
Johnson, John T., Sept. 22, 1864.
Johnson, John T. P., Aurora, Nov. 27, 1869, age 64 y, 5 m, 26 d.
Johnson, John W., Aug. 21, 1871, age 54 y, 3 m.
Johnson, Jonathan, Sept. 13, 1866, age 69.
Johnson, Joseph, Jan. 15, 1879, age 88 y, 8 m, 17 d.
Johnson, Miss Julia, dau. of Zerah, Newstead, NY, April 20, 1850, age 22.
Johnson, Mrs. Kate, wife of Henry, Jan. 24, 1880, age 48 y, 9 m.
Johnson, Mrs. Laura, wid. of Henry W., formerly of Buffalo, Nov. 24, 1879, age 72 y, 2 m, 17 d; d. Kidder, Caldwell Co., MO.
Johnson, Mrs. Lavinia, colored, July 11, 1877, age 75.
Johnson, Deacon Lemuel, Aug. 13, 1849, age 85.
Johnson, Levi Chauncey, Nov. 4, 1870, age 51 y, 9 m.
Johnson, Lorenzo D., East Hamburgh, May 5, 1874, age 44.
Johnson, Louisa, wife of Mortimer F., dau. of late Samuel Wilkeson, Dec. 23, 1869.

Johnson, Lucy, wife of Deacon Samuel, May 22, 1842, age 77.
Johnson, Lucy E., widow of Dr. E. of Buffalo, 2nd dau. of Rev. John Lord of Madison Co., N.Y., Nov. 30, 1859, age 35; d. in Geneseo, NY.
Johnson, Lucy P., wife of Burdette J., formerly of Buffalo, March 12, 1871.
Johnson, Lydia, wife of Capt. John J., Dec. 17, 1841, age 44.
Johnson, Mr. M. A., formerly of Buffalo, Nov. 13, 1847; d. in Brooklyn, NY.
Johnson, Mrs. Mary, Feb. 18, 1865, age 85.
Johnson, Mary, July 5, 1871, age c. 50.
Johnson, Mary, Dec. 24, 1871, age 37.
Johnson, Mary A., wife of Col. George W., Nov. 12, 1863, age 33.
Johnson, Mary A., wife of William H., July 29, 1874, age 18 y, 10 m, 4 d.
Johnson, Miss Mary Ann, Feb. 18, 1863, age 25 y, 4 m.
Johnson, Mary F., widow of John W., Nov. 3, 1872, age 48.
Johnson, Merriam, wife of William, Hamburgh, Oct. 7, 1830, age 79.
Johnson, Col. Mortimer F., formerly of Buffalo, May 30, 1876; d. in Madisonville, TN.
Johnson, Nehemiah, March 14, 1851, age 41 years; in Utica, NY.
Johnson, Nettie, Co. Almshouse, March 26, 1876, age 25.
Johnson, Rachel A., widow of George, Black Rock, Nov. 6, 1872, age 80. Dau. of Jonathan and Sybil Andrews, b. in West Stockbridge, MA, m. in 1820.
Johnson, Richard, wrecked, Nov. 8, 1877, age 22 y, 6 m; d. on Schooner *Berlin*, on Lake Michigan.
Johnson, Robert, April 9, 1874, age 62.
Johnson, Robert, Feb. 11, 1876, accident, age c. 50.
Johnson, Robert Bruce, Co. B, 51st Regt., N.Y. Vol., Oct. 19, 1864, age 37; in Rochester, bur. in Buffalo.
Johnson, Mrs. Roxana, mother of Wallace and J. B., June 11, 1862, age 69; taken to OH.
Johnson, Rufus R., formerly of Buffalo, May 25, 1866, age 41; in Centreville, MI.
Johnson, Samuel, Boston, NY, Feb. 20, 1827, age 73.
Johnson, Samuel, Holland, Sept. 30, 1851, age 86.
Johnson, Capt. Samuel, brother of Hon. Ebenezer, April 1, 1854, age 59; at Belvidere, Il. Mrs. C. B. Harrington states that Capt. Samuel d. April 11.
Johnson, Capt. Samuel A., in the Lake trade, late of Buffalo, Jan. 9, 1864, age 42; in Chicago.
Johnson, Samuel B., son of Samuel of Buffalo, Aug. 4, 1844, age 21; at Belvidere, IL.
Johnson, Spencer H., Jan. 17, 1856, age 27.
Johnson, Sophia Louisa Bailey, wife of E. T., May 17, 1870, age 26 y, 7 m, 13 d.
Johnson, Sprague, formerly of Buffalo, Co. I, 13th Reg. N.Y. Vol., April 7, 1862. A good and manly soldier; d. at Fortress Monroe, VA.
Johnson, Swanson, laborer, accident, May 25, 1880, age 60; a Swede, 3 weeks in this country.
Johnson, Wallace, March 28, 1880, age 55.
Johnson, Warner, late of Milwaukee, WI, June 29, 1858, age 31.
Johnson, William, Dec. 9, 1853, age 33.
Johnson, William C., East Aurora, March 6, 1880, age 76.
Johnson, William H., son of Dr. E., late of Buffalo, May 6, 1845, age 28; at Fredonia, NY.
Johnson, William H., June 17, 1879, age 32 y, 1 m, 25 d.
Johnson, Gerard, Sept. 20, 1880, age 81.
Johnson, Jane, wife of George, Jan. 30, 1874, age 39.
Johnson, Mrs. Jane, Feb. 27, 1880, age 76.
Johnston, John, Sept. 22, 1828, age 66.
Johnston, Lucia Mary, wife of William, May 19, 1857, age 32.
Johnston, Mary, Feb. 21, 1880, age 90; almshouse.
Johnston, Robert, Nov. 25, 1873, age 68.
Johnston, Windsor, b. 1761, d. Nov. 16, 1853, Youngstown, NY; Soldier of the Revolution.
Johnstone, Mary, Dec. 30, 1880, age 70; almshouse.
Jones, Mrs., wife of Frederick S., Boston, NY, Jan. 26, 1833.
Jones, Alexander, Nov. 15, 1879; found drowned.
Jones, Alice, Eden, Sept. 14, 1868, age 19 y, 11 m; youngest dau. of Thomas.
Jones, Amelia A., wife of Howard P., March 11, 1875, age 30 y, 7 m, 25 d.
Jones, Mrs. Ann, July 1877, age 68.
Jones, Anne B., wife of R. I., M.D., Hamburgh, NY, Feb. 16, 1835, age 21.

Jones, Benjamin B., formerly of Buffalo, Sept. 7, 1870; d. in Milwaukee, WI.
Jones, Caroline D., wife of H. P., Dec. 19, 1875, age 55.
Jones, Charles R., Aug. 12, 1877, age 35.
Jones, Charles William, only son of Isabella, March 3, 1870, age 23.
Jones, Damaris, Boston, wife of Smith, Dec. 18, 1872, age 55 y, 10 m.
Jones, Daniel, Grand Island, Oct. 25, 1878, age 77.
Jones, DeGarmo, firm of Palmer & Co., formerly of Detroit, MI, Aug. 13, 1864, age 28.
Jones, Eliphalet, Aurora, NY, Sept. 5, 1858, age 67.
Jones, Eliza A., wife of George B., Aug. 19, 1873, age 56 y, 3 m.
Jones, Elizabeth, wife of John, March 26, 1871, age 60.
Jones, Elizabeth, Feb. 5, 1872, age 61.
Jones, Elizabeth, widow of Miles, Jan. 11, 1878, age 68.
Jones, Ellis, Sept. 28, 1880, age 37 (or 39); Almshouse.
Jones, Emily C., eldest dau. of the late George, June 7, 1878.
Jones, Mrs. Evan, Clarence, June 22, 1870, age c. 50.
Jones, George, Feb. 25, 1873, age 71 y, 10 m, 13 d.
Jones, George Cary, March 23, 1874, age 29; taken to Boston Corners.
Jones, Helen M., July 8, 1863, age 21; taken to Forestville, N.Y.
Jones, Henry, West Aurora, NY, April 24, 1854, age 56.
Jones, Jeremiah, father of Mrs. J. Swain, Aug. 29, 1864, age 70?.
Jones, John, March 15, 1857, age 56.
Jones, John, July 7, 1875, age 40.
Jones, John, Englishman, Aug. 3, 1876, age 72.
Jones, John J., Aug. 27, 1849, age 25. D. at residence of brother Isaac A.; taken to Rome, Oneida Co., NY.
Jones, John J., Co. Almshouse, July 26, 1877, age 66; taken to Ft. Erie, Ontario.
Jones, Joseph R., M.D., Hamburgh, Aug. 24, 1836, age 25; d. in Penn Yan, NY.
Jones, Julia Antoinette, wife of Wakely, North Boston, NY, Feb. 27, 1866, age 21 y, 6 m.
Jones, Julia C., dau. of George H., April 17, 1876, age 23 y, 6 m, 24 d.
Jones, Lottie, Co. Almshouse, Aug. 1, 1878, age 20.
Jones, Lydia H., wife of deacon George, May 3, 1869, age 66.
Jones, Maggie Shields, wife of G. B., March 19, 1875, age 20 y, 10 m.
Jones, Mary Ann, wife of Arthur W., youngest dau. of Robert Patterson, May 20, 1847, age 32; d. in London, England.
Jones, Mrs. Mary, Aurora, Nov. 8, 1869, age 73.
Jones, Mary E., wife of William D., East Aurora, March 7, 1879, age 30.
Jones, Miles, Jan. 4, 1869, age 65.
Jones, Nathaniel, May 24, 1880, age 69.
Jones, Nathaniel M., Boston, NY, June 9, 1866, age 74.
Jones, Miss Nellie, Sept. 5, 1878, age 45.
Jones, Palmer, May 3, 1874, age 27; d. in the Penitentiary.
Jones, Porter, Black Rock, NY, Co. H, 2d N.Y. Mounted Rifles, Oct. 14, 1864, age 18; d. in Beverly Hospital, N.J.
Jones, Ransom, Potters Corners, Aug. 7, 1876, age 54.
Jones, Mrs. Rebecca, June 3, 1879, age 77.
Jones, Richard, drowned, Sept. 7, 1873, age 62.
Jones, Stephen, April 17, 1880, age 60; family lived at Ft. Erie. Drowned.
Jones, Stephen H., formerly of Norwich, CT, Nov. 24, 1842, age 28.
Jones, Tyro, formerly of Batavia, NY, Feb. 1827.
Jones, Mrs. Watson, Nov. 4, 1870, age 32 y, 7 m, 3 d.
Jones, William, b. Sept. 18, 1764, d. April 22, 1839, bur. Wales Center, NY; Soldier of the Revolution.
Jones, William, Aug. 20, 1866, age 64.
Jones, William, Lawton's Station, an Indian, Oct. 24, 1880, age 26, killed by a railroad train.
Jones, William W. (Obit.) Jan. 22, 1868.
Jonson, George W., formerly of Buffalo, Aug. 3, 1880 at Royalton, Niagara Co., NY, age 79. Bur. in Forest Lawn on Lot 134, Section 1, owned by Benjamin H. Williams.
Jordan, Samuel, June 2, 1843, age 45.
Jorden, Beverly, drowned, Aug. 31, 1873, age 20.

Jordon, Bridget, wife of Matthew, Dec. 6, 1880, age 57 y, 3 m.
Jordon, Mrs. David, mother of M. and P., Oct. 5, 1863, age 70.
Jordon, Mrs. Lydia E., May 11, 1896, age 52.
Jordon, Samuel, formerly of Gardner, ME, Oct. 4, 1824, age 24.
Josephs, Priscilla, wife of Joseph, Nov. 27, 1863, age 29.
Joset, Joseph, Sept. 18, 1879.
Joslin, Mrs. Caroline M., North Buffalo, NY, June 3, 1866, age 34 y, 9 m, 19 d.
Joslin, John N., Wales, NY, March 1, 1844, age 33.
Joslyn, Albert S., Dec. 7, 1875, age 38.
Joslyn, Alvin, Oct. 26, 1866, age 77 y, 7 m, 16 d.
Joslyn, Amasa, Oct. 21, 1855, age 23.
Joslyn, Ann Eliza, wife of D.M., March 1, 1880, age 64.
Joslyn, Simeon H., Elma, Dec. 19, 1879, age 65 y, 11 m, 14 d.
Joslyn, Truman B., Dec. 31, 1852, age 23.
Josselyn, Amasa, Eden, NY, Feb. 20, 1852, age 75.
Josselyn, Miss Clementina, Lancaster, NY, March 2, 1848, age 44.
Josselyn, Hiram B., son of Samuel of Buffalo, formerly of Buffalo, Oct. 12, 1861, age 25 y, 15 d; at Moanequa, Shelby Co., IL.
Josselyn, Rebecca, wife of Samuel, April 27, 1859, age 60 y, 9 m.
Jost, Francis Joseph, Jan. 12, 1879, age 71.
Jost, Joseph F., April 5, 1877, age 35 y, 6 m.
Joy, Emma Curtis, wife of Lewis B., dau. of Thomas Stephenson, March 26, 1869, age 28 y, 6 m.
Joy, Huldah, widow of Thaddeus, July 9, 1860, age 76.
Joy, Deacon Ira, formerly of Buffalo, 1873; d. at Galesburg, MI.
Joy, Kate Palmer, wife of Lewis B., July 23, 1861, age 26.
Joy, Lewis, formerly of Buffalo, Dec. 10, 1867, age 53; in Brooklyn, N.Y.
Joy, Miles, March 18, 1877, age 70.
Joy, Roxa Abby, wife of Lewis, Dec. 1863, age 47; at Hudson City, N.J.
Joy, Thaddeus, June 4, 1853, age 68.
Joy, Walter, Dec. 24, 1863, age 53.
Joyce, Edwin C., formerly of Buffalo, Nov. 17, 1867, age 38 y, 6 m, 5 d; at Newburgh, Warwick Co., IN.
Joyce, Mrs. Margaret, Oct. 9, 1878, age 60.
Judd, Mrs. Elizabeth, from Paris, Oneida Co., Feb. 27, 1830, age 72.
Judd, Emily Sweetland, dau. of Orvan K., Aug. 4, 1870, age 21; taken to Stafford, NY.
Judd, Jennie, dau. of Orvan K., June 13, 1874, age 20; taken to Stafford, NY.
Judd, Mrs. Lina, Alden, NY, Sept. 27, 1849, age 56.
Judd, Margaret, wife of William, formerly of Buffalo, Oct. 29, 1867; at Gold Run, CA.
Judd, Truman (or Freeman), b. 1755, d. 1840, bur. Lockport (Niagara Co.); Soldier of the Revolution.
Judge, Mary Ann, wife of Henry, May 9, 1875, age 35.
Judson, Lebbeus, Jan. 29, 1879, brother-in-law of the late Dr. C. C. Haddock, age 65 y, 9 m, 3 d.
Judson, Marcus, Black Rock, NY, U.S. Vols., from Livonia, Ontario Co., NY, July 1812.
Judson, Mary Ann, wife of Rev. L. P., late pastor of Bethel Church Buffalo, Nov. 28, 1841; d. at Warsaw, Genesee Co.
Judson, Mary Palmer, wife of B. M., dau. of Elias W. Palmer, formerly of Buffalo, July 19, 1871; d. at Brookville, KS, bur. in Buffalo.
Judson, William Henry, Jan. 30, 1869, age 43 y, 1 m.
Jueneman, Rosina, Dec. 21, 1880, age 65.
Julier, Charles W., April 29, 1877, age 33.
Julier, Rhoda M., wife of H. S., Feb. 16, 1866.
June, Drances, formerly Brandon, VT, April 7, 1847, age 41 y, 3 m, 26 d.
Jungherr, August, April 20, 1875, age 46 y, 2 m.
Jungken, Eliza J., widow of Frederick H., Aug. 23, 1875, age 50.
Jungkin (Jungken), Frederick H., Aug. 11, 1875, age 53.
Justin, Anna, widow of Reuben, Aug. 6, 1862, age 68.
Justin, George R., June 29, 1867, age 33.
Justin, Mrs. Lucy, Feb. 8, 1852, age 87.

Justin, Margaret Adde, wife of Thomas, Jan. 6, 1879, age 39 y, 6 m, 14 d.
Justin, Reuben, June 8, 1861, age 69.
Justin, Corp. William, Co. H., N.Y. Mounted Rifles, March 31, 1865. Killed before Peterburg, VA; bur. in Buffalo April 20.

Kaden, Mary, wife of John, April 8, 1880, age 50.
Kadow, Henry, drowned, Grand Island, Blacksmith, Nov. 19, 1872.
Kaene, Lucy L., widow of William, Feb. 2, 1874, age 77; d. at Lafayette, IN, bur. in Buffalo.
Kaene, Phebe, widow of Robert, mother of William, Sept. 15, 1844, age 74.
Kaene, Capt. Robert, under General Wayne in his campaign against the Indians; was among the first settlers in Buffalo, Aug. 16, 1835, age 65.
Kaene, William, Sept. 22, 1852, age 56.
Kaffert (Krafferd), Anna Rosa, wife of Jacob, suicide, Jan. 2, 1874.
Kairns (Karins/Kerins), John, Abbott Road, Aug. 16, 1880, age 35. Murdered.
Kaiser, Henry, July 4, 1880, age 40. Deaf-mute, killed by cars.
Kalbfleisch, Margaret, wife of Henry, March 8, 1878, age 27 y, 1 m, 14 d.
Kaleski, Barbara, Nov. 3, 1880, age 75.
Kaley, Peter H., Oct. 26, 1875, age 27.
Kalunski (Galoska), Martin, accident in tannery, Feb. 18, 1880, age 26.
Kamerling, John H., Oct. 6, 1878, age 41 y, 3 m; d. at St. Paul, MN, bur. Buffalo.
Kamerling, Melissa, wife of Dr. A., March 8, 1878, age 27 y, 14 d.
Kamman, John F., Aug. 18, 1879, age 50 y, 5 m, 11 d.
Kammerer, Frank J., killed by a boiler explosion, April 2, 1880.
Kamper, Caroline, wife of Charles, Jan. 13, 1871, age 33.
Kamper, Carrie, wife of Charles, Jan. 31, 1875, age 22.
Kanaley, Margaret, June 28, 1880, age 64.
Kane, Catherine, wife of Michael, Sept. 9, 1876, age 65.
Kane, Daniel, Sept. 4, 1880, age 80; almshouse.
Kane, J. F., East Hamburgh, Feb. 16, 1871, age 60.
Kane, James, Jan. 7, 1872, age 56.
Kane, John, killed on railroad near Churchville, Jan. 25, 1874, bur. in Buffalo.
Kane, Martha A. Byrne, wife of James, Dec. 18, 1877, age 40.
Kane, Mrs. Mary Jane Garrity, wife of James, April 27, 1879, age 28 y, 8 m.
Kane (Cain), Michael, June 22, 1872, age c. 60.
Kane, Michael, Dec. 13, 1876, age 67.
Kane, Patrick, Co. Almshouse, June 17, 1877, age 38.
Kane, Thomas, railroad accident, Jan. 14, 1877, age c. 23.
Kaneen, Annie M., wife of William, formerly of Buffalo, Aug. 11, 1865; d. Wilmington, DE.
Kaneen, Mary Ann, wife of William, Nov. 17, 1878, age 54 y, 10 m, 11 d.
Kankelwitz, Charles, July 30, 1873, age 40 y, 7 m, 4 d.
Karn, Adam, Dec. 17, 1864, age 53.
Karnes, James, May 9, 1873, age 53.
Karon (Karrow), John, accidental death, June 30, 1878, age 53.
Karr, John, May 21, 1865, age 36.
Karr, Martha Denham, wife of James N., April 30, 1873, age 41.
Karstaedt, Henry, April 8, 1880, age 52 y, 3 m, 3 d.
Kasprowitch, Adam, Sept. 6, 1878.
Kasson, Archy, father of W. M., May 25, 1854, age 74; taken to Syracuse, N.Y.
Kasson, Emeline L., wife of William M., Feb. 2, 1852, age 37; taken to Syracuse, N.Y.
Kasson, Louise DePeyster, dau. of William M., Aug. 18, 1860.
Kasson, Melinda M., mother of William M., Sept. 25, 1868, age 87.
Kast, Constanze, wife of Joseph, July 17, 1878, age 35 y, 11 m, 14 d.
Kast, George, suicide, Whites Corners, April 29, 1873, age c. 60.
Kates, Nellie, Dec. 8, 1880, age 28; Almshouse.
Katz, Christian, Co. Almshouse, Oct. 2, 1878, age 36.
Kauffman, John, Co. G, 100th Regt., July 16, 1862, age 24. D. in Hospital, New Haven, CT.
Kautz, Teresa, wife of Christian J., Jan. 12, 1880, age 57 y, 4 m, 13 d.
Kavanagh, Patrick, July 13, 1876, age 81.
Kavanah, Mrs. Mary, Nov. 5, 1877, age 77.

Kay, Henry D., Jan. 3, 1867, age 39.
Kay, Joseph, April 20, 1880, age 33.
Kearn, Catharine Mitchell, wife of Patrick, Feb. 29, 1876, age 43.
Kearney, Ann Cloak, wife of John, April 16, 1866, age 32.
Kearney, Mrs. Margaret, Sept. 4, 1867, age 61.
Kearns, John, laborer, Feb. 14, 1874, age 27.
Kearns, Patrick, drowned, foreman of the tug *Pierce*, July 19, 1875.
Keating, Caroline W., wife of Robert, June 12, 1866, age 27.
Keating, Mary Ann, Nov. 17, 1871, age 23.
Keating, Michael, blacksmith, accidental death, Sept. 17, 1875.
Keays, Isabella, wife of W. J., Jan. 24, 1862, age 24; taken to Canada.
Kech, Jacob, Sept. 7, 1879, age 48. Found dead.
Keech, George, formerly of Buffalo, 1877, age 77; d. at Centreville, St. Joseph Co., MI.

Keech, Mrs. Rhoda, April 28, 1873, age 90.
Keech, Thomas J., Sept. 16, 1839, age 23.
Keech, William H., son of George, formerly of Buffalo, April 12, 1860, age 30; at Sherman,
    St. Joseph Co., MI.
Keefe, Daniel, Nov. 14, 1878, age 47.
Keefe (Kief), Jane, accidental death, Oct. 27, 1874, age 75.
Keefe, Richard, drowned at Erie, PA, May 12, 1872.
Keefe, Thomas, Oct. 22, 1874, age 36.
Keefe, Timothy, accidental death, Feb. 24, 1875, age 28.
Keel, Elizabeth, wife of James O., Oct. 12, 1863, age 59.
Keel, James O., formerly of Buffalo, Feb. 18, 1879, age 73; d. at Fort Erie.
Keel, Minerva Ann, wife of Charles A., Dec. 24, 1865, age 35 y, 4 m, 16 d.
Keeler, Abijah, April 22, 1836, age 50.
Keeler, Elizabeth, wife of James, July 20, 1845, age 30.
Keeler, Miss Mary, Aug. 5, 1849, age 46.
Keeler, Michael, carpenter, Nov. 27, 1873, age 54.
Keeler, Minnie, wife of E. W., Lancaster, Oct. 17, 1868, age 37.
Keeley, John, railroad accident, March 4, 1879.
Keeling, Edmond, Dec. 9, 1874, age 32.
Keena, Mary, widow of Peter, Feb. 7, 1870, age 80.
Keenan, Charles, Jan. 5, 1876, age 70.
Keenan, Francis, Oct. 3, 1875, age 30.
Keenan, Mrs. Margaret Maria, July 13, 1878, age 67 y, 7 m.
Keenan, Mary, widow of John, Sept. 13, 1874, age 55.
Keenan, Michael, Dec. 9, 1878, age 38.
Keenan, Timothy, May 27, 1869, age 24.
Keene, Isabella P., dau. of G. B., Nov. 9, 1875, age 24.
Keeney, Elisha J., formerly of Erie Co., May 12, 1874, age 64.
Keep, N.D., killed at Black Rock in battle, Dec. 30, 1813.
Keese, Elizabeth, wife of George, Oct. 27, 1820, age 26.
Keese, George; d. at sea, May 1821.
Keesey, Mrs. Robert K., Sept. 1, 1820, age 26.
Kehl, Mrs. Katherine, March 16, 1878, age 81 y, 9 m.
Kehl, Peter, Aug. 28, 1870, age 37; accidentally killed.
Keifer (Kieffer), George, Dec. 26, 1875.
Keil, Adam, railroad accident, Sept. 6, 1878.
Keil, Mrs. Rosetta H., Oct. 24, 1871, age 46.
Keinbel, Sophia, May 28, 1871, age 40.
Keiser, Andrew, June 13, 1875, age 45 y, 7 m, 5 d.
Keith, George, Nov. 18, 1824, age 40.
Keitz, Mary L., Nov. 4, 1875, age 70.
Kelderhouse, Jeremia, Oct. 7, 1856, age 62.
Keller, Daniel, April 14, 1870, age 87.
Keller, Jacob (or George), Sept. 18, 1879, age 45 y, 5 m.
Keller, Jacob, April 23, 1880, age 57.
Keller, Nancy Ann, Nov. 1, 1873, age 28.

Keller, Wallace, formerly of Buffalo, Jan. 5, 1866, age 33 y, 10 m; d. Little Falls, N.Y.
Kelley, Catherine, Nov. 14, 1878, age 44.
Kelley, Sgt. Daniel G., Willink, March 13, 1868, age 23 y, 3 m.
Kelley, Edgar W., May 5, 1874, age 25 y, 6 m.
Kelley, Edward, killed on railroad, May 6, 1879, age 22.
Kelley, Elizabeth, widow of John, East Hamburgh, March 7, 1872, age 82; taken to Evansville, WI.
Kelly, Mrs. John, Black Rock, NY, Aug. 12, 1849.
Kelley, John, Jan. 28, 1871, age 35.
Kelley, John, Sept. 28, 1880, age 52.
Kelley, John M., firm of Haas & Kelley, Jan. 11, 1873, age 36 y, 9 m, 24 d.
Kelley, Mary, Jan. 20, 1869, age 25.
Kelley, Mary E., April 5, 1868, age 20.
Kelley, Murt, son of M., Sept. 5, 1862, age 20.
Kelley, Thomas J., formerly of Buffalo, Dec. 11, 1880, age 43 y, 12 d.
Kelley, William Scott, Bay City, MI, Nov. 27, 1869, age 75 y, 5 m; father of John M., Thomas J., and Richard D., all of Buffalo. Bur. in Buffalo.
Kellogg, Alexander, Alden, June 30, 1876, age 82.
Kellogg, Chester A., formerly of Buffalo, Jan. 23, 1877, age 57.
Kellogg, Converse Augusts, formerly of Buffalo, one of the editors of the *Daily Republic*, April 25, 1860, age 29; bur. in Buffalo.
Kellogg, Ellen E., or Hellen E. Todd, wife of William H., Jan. 24, 1876, age 29 y, 10 m, 23 d.
Kellogg, Enoch, b. 1761, d. 1842, bur. Wales; Soldier of the Revolution.
Kellogg, James, Wales, NY, April 18, 1850, age 46.
Kellogg, Julia E., Aurora, NY, wife of S.S., youngest dau. of Lemuel Spooner, Aurora, Aug. 18, 1853, age 19.
Kellogg, Mrs. M., May 9, 1879, age 36.
Kellogg, M. R. Jr., formerly of Buffalo, April 21, 1875, age 27; d. at St. Joseph, MO.
Kellogg, Mrs. Rubie, Springville, Jan. 7, 1862, age 83.
Kellogg, Y. Y., Nov. 20, 1873, age 60.
Kelly, Betsy, wife of Dennis, Boston, NY, March 2, 1851, age 24.
Kelly, Daniel, Black Rock, July 10, 1870, age 72.
Kelly, George, Sept. 9, 1875, age 35.
Kelly, Miss Hellen, sister of John P. of US Navy, Sept. 21, 1868, age 25.
Kelly, James, Sept. 1, 1878, age 20 y, 10 m.
Kelly, James, Nov. 9, 1880, accidently shot.
Kelly, John, Lancaster, NY, March 2, 1864, age 49.
Kelly, John, Co. Almshouse, June 17, 1876, age 21.
Kelly, Mary, July 10, 1874, age c. 40.
Kelly, Mary Anne, wife of John, Abbott Road, Feb. 26, 1879, age 72.
Kelly, Michael, Nov. 16, 1875, age 44.
Kelly, Nicholas, killed by locomotive, Dec. 17, 1875.
Kelly, (Kelley) Susanna, wife of Jesse, formerly of Aurora, NY, Sept. 22, 1860, age 70; Harmonsburgh, PA.
Kelly, Timothy, Aug. 29, 1880, age 33.
Kelsey, Eliza, wife of Daniel of New York, March 27, 1838, age 57.
Kelsey, Henry, March 2, 1880, age 42.
Kelsey, Jared, July 15, 1868, age 44; accidently killed at Oil Springs, Canada West.
Kelsey, Samuel, Jan., 1813, age 60.
Kelsey, Mrs. Samuel, Jan. 1813.
Kelso, Mrs. Elizabeth, Collins, Feb. 19, 1880, age 84.
Kelsy, James, Jan. 1813, age 35.
Kelty, Bridget, wife of Michael, June 16, 1878, age 56.
Kemberle, Mary Catherine, wife of Jacob, Dec. 8, 1865, age 30 y, 11 m.
Kemp, George, April 21, 1862, age 78.
Kemp, Isabel, April 10, 1873, age 56.
Kemp, Thomas, June 6, 1878, age 66.
Kemp, William J., eldest son of William, Sept. 1, 1878, age 28.
Kempff, Frederick, Jan. 17, 1877, age 36.

Kempke, George, Oct. 31, 1879, age 49 y, 7 m, 24 d.
Kempston, James, Marilla, Sept. 21, 1876, age 42.
Kemter, Catharine, July 23, 1870, age 59; wife of George.
Kenaga, Ada S., dau. of John, March 11, 1872, age 26 y, 6 m, 26 d.
Kenaga, John, March 9, 1877.
Kendall, J. Milton, Dec. 2, 1879, age 55.
Kendall, Jacob, Sept. 3, 1874, age 56.
Kendall, Luther F., formerly of Buffalo, Nov. 5, 1873; d. at Westfield, NY.
Kendall, Mary E., wife of J.M., July 19, 1849, age 19.
Kendall, Mrs. Rebecca S., Alden, NY, mother of Frederick of Buffalo, April 28, 1866, age 71.
Kendall, Sarah A., wife of Rev. C., Feb. 5, 1863.
Kendall, Warren, March 30, 1842, age 51.
Kenderlink, Patrick, killed on the railroad, Sept. 11, 1872, age 21.
Kendig, Mrs. Amelia, Oct. 8, 1870, age 80; taken to Lockport, NY.
Kendrick, Kate, wife of Rodney, formerly of Buffalo, Dec. 17, 1879, age 26; d. at Portland, OR, bur. in Sacramento, CA.
Kenedy, Bridget, wife of James, April 10, 1870, age 36.
Kenefick, Jane Martin, wife of John, Nov. 1, 1879, age 49.
Kenefick, Thomas, Sept. 11, 1870, age 43.
Kenington, Amos, Dec. 5, 1872, age 35.
Kennedy, Allen, Cheektowaga, Sept. 9, 1878, age 35.
Kennedy, Caroline, wife of Thomas, Nov. 17, 1866, age 47 y, 3 m, 6 d.
Kennedy, Edward, suicide, US soldier, Sept. 18, 1877, age c. 25.
Kennedy, Miss Elizabeth, dau. of Thomas, Sept. 16, 1843.
Kennedy, Helen Maria, wife of Lester E., Feb. 17, 1862, age 27 y, 8 m, 4 d; taken to Attica, NY.
Kennedy, Homer, Aug. 11, 1872, age 35; d. at Lockport, IL, bur. Buffalo.
Kennedy, James, June 21, 1843, age 26.
Kennedy, James, Aug. 28, 1870, age 29.
Kennedy, John R., June 30, 1871, age 52.
Kennedy, Kate, June 10, 1876, age 30.
Kennedy, Capt. Marcellus, Dec. 19, 1873, age 59. Accidently killed. Day watchman at Erie Freight Depot. Taken to Rochester.
Kennedy, Mary, April 11, 1879, age 78.
Kennedy, Michael, March 20, 1872.
Kennedy, Mrs. Ruth, March 31, 1878, age 57.
Kennedy, Thomas, formerly of Buffalo, Feb. 22, 1878, age 67; d. at Dunkirk, NY, bur. Buffalo.
Kennedy, William, Nov. 11, 1863, age 46 y, 7 m, 23 d.
Kennelly, James M., formerly of Buffalo, Nov. 4, 1877; d. in NY City.
Kenney, Bryan, March 15, 1874, age 83 y, 2 m, 9 d.
Kenney, Daniel, Dec. 6, 1857, age 69 y, 9 m.
Kenney, John W., Dec. 29, 1876, age 49.
Kenney, Mrs. Keron, Oct. 12, 1879, age 79 y, 9 m.
Kenney, Lydia, wife of Elijah, Nov. 22, 1847, age 56.
Kennington, John, Angola, NY, Oct. 15, 1867, age 45.
Kenny, Dr. William J. C., June 1, 1873, age 33; taken to Batavia.
Kencche, George B., Tonawanda, Aug. 1868, age 22.
Kenopatzke, Mrs. Ernestine, March 16, 1875, age 39; suicide.
Kent, Abbie Gustie, wife of Granger D., niece of Paul Roberts of Tonawanda, Dec. 18, 1867.
Kent, Albert, drowned, Sept. 11, 1873, age 23.
Kent, Charles, Evans, NY, June 9, 1866, age 87.
Kent, Charles Farnham, 2d son of Henry M., Oct. 7, 1878, age 22; d. at Denver, CO, bur. Buffalo.
Kent, Granger D., son of John, Grand Island, Dec. 18, 1867.
Kent, Isaac, Black Rock, NY, Oct. 29, 1834 at Huron, OH.
Kent, J. P., Evans, March 24, 1874, age 61.
Kent, Joseph, Willink, NY, March 1813, age 32.
Kent, Mary, Tonawanda, NY, wife of Warren, May 30, 1828.

Kent, Mary, Aug. 29, 1863, age 73.
Kent, Mary, wife of Arthur, formerly of Buffalo, May 10, 1870, age 33; d. at Marshall, Marshall Co., IA.
Kenton, Judith A., wife of N. W., Aug. 2, 1869, age 76.
Kenton, Nicholas W., June 19, 1877, age 78 y, 4 m, 11 d.
Kenyon, Harriet E., wife of Robert, Nov. 19, 1850, age 21; taken to Chicago, IL.
Kenyon, Henry K., Aurora, West Falls, July 12, 1879, age 40.
Kenyon, Mrs. L. M. Obituary April 1879.
Kenyon, Mercy A., wife of Dr. L.M., April 17, 1879, age 54; bur. April 19th at Westfield, NY.
Keogh, Capt. Francis Gethings, formerly of County Carlow, Ireland, 29th Regt. of Foot, British Army, Jan. 9, 1854, age 59; taken to Toronto, Canada.
Keogh, Mrs. Mary, Dec. 12, 1872, age 69.
Keogh, Rachel L., Aug. 28, 1789 [sic], age 48.
Keough, Thomas, April 10, 1876, age 44.
Keppel, Frederick, Jan. 9, 1863, age 22 y, 2 m.
Kerby, Col. James, June 20, 1854, age 69.
Kerdel, Margaret, wife of John, June 7, 1872, age 35.
Kernick, Mrs. Ann, formerly of Montreal, April 12, 1880, age 79.
Kernick, Rosa, wife of John, Aug. 25, 1877, age 44; d. at the General Hospital.
Kerr, Alexander, Collins, NY, Jan. 20, 1833, age 35.
Kerr, Eleanor, wife of Elijah, Collins, NY, March 17, 1832, age 21.
Kerr, Jane, wife of George, Dec. 30, 1845, age 33.
Kerr, John, Sept. 13, 1852, age 54; mason.
Kerr, Margaret Patterson, wife of John, May 23, 1874, age 46.
Kerr, Marion, widow of John, April 18, 1870, age 54.
Kerr, Ruth A., wife of Robert, Feb. 26, 1875, age 21.
Kerrigan, Charles, Oct. 28, 1872, age 21.
Kerrigan (Kirwin/Kerwin), Patrick, laborer, Sept. 10, 1879, age 48. Found drowned.
Kessel, Christian Emil, Aug. 16, 1879, age 36.
Kessler, Johanna, wife of John, July 12, 1879, age 43 y, 4 m, 7 d.
Kester, Deborah, wife of John, Boston, NY, Aug. 8, 1835, age 37.
Kester, Mrs. Elizabeth, Jan. 5, 1879, age 86 y, 2 m, 23 d.
Kester, Elma, wife of James, Eden, NY, Oct. 24, 1850, age 40 y, 5 m, 10 d.
Kester, Emma L., dau. of Irving, Nov. 25, 1873, age 21 y, 3 m, 23 d.
Kester, Harry, July 26, 1864, age 24 y, 5 m, 15 d.
Kester, Hugh B., son of Benjamin H., Boston, NY, March 6, 1850, age 20.
Kester, John, Boston, NY, Sept. 16, 1849, age 55 y, 1 m, 16 d.
Kester, Samuel, Hamburgh, NY, May 13, 1843, age 58.
Kester, William S., son of Stephen of North Manchester, IN, North Boston, NY, March 23, 1854.
Ketchum, Addie L., dau. of William F., Oct. 2, 1859, age 21.
Ketchum, Mrs. Catharine, widow of John, Harris Hill, May 24, 1879, age 83.
Ketchum, Hester, widow of Zebulon, March 14, 1854, age 33.
Ketchum, Jesse, Sept. 7, 1867, age 86.
Ketchum, John, Clarence, NY, Dec. 19, 1859, age 72.
Ketchum, Lamira Callender, wife of William, Dec. 23, 1866, age 62 y, 10 m.
Ketchum, Lewis, firm of Tweedy & Ketchum, Dec. 29, 1834, age 26; at the residence of his mother in Victor, Ontario Co., NY.
Ketchum, Mary Ann, widow of Jesse, March 11, 1869, age 68.
Ketchum, William, Oct. 1, 1876, age 79.
Ketchum, William F., Jan. 23, 1865, age 61.
Ketchum, Mrs. William F., Obituary Jan. 1867.
Ketchum, Zebulon, Dec. 20, 1853, age 73.
Ketter, Charles, puddler, accident, Feb. 19, 1880, age 38.
Keyes, Catharine, Sept. 26, 1853, age 63.
Keyes, Jerome C., Jan. 8, 1869, age 29.
Keyes, Milton, formerly of Buffalo, April 9, 1850, age 61; near Pontiac, MI.
Keyes, Richard G., Black Rock, NY, Oct. 20, 1827, age 25.
Keygan, William, Aug, 9, 1873, age 22.

Keys, Richard, formerly of Richmond, VA, March 23, 1860, age 63 y, 7 d.
Kezer, Harry A., Lancaster, NY, June 21, 1852, age 38 y, 2 m, 8 d; on Steamer *Crescent City*, on his return from two years in CA.
Kibbe, Elizabeth, formerly of Buffalo, Dec. 15, 1879, age 88; d. Monmouth, IL.
Kibbe, Gaius, July 19, 1821, age 56; in St. Mary's Parish, LA.
Kibbe, George R., July 18, 1878, age 59.
Kibbe, Isaac, formerly of Buffalo, June 14, 1845, age 81; in New York.
Kibbe, Isaac, 2d son of George R., Nov. 25, 1873, age 23.
Kibbe, Mrs. Serene, April 3, 1867, age 83.
Kibbey, Ella O., wife of Rev. F. M., Jan. 26, 1873, age 25; taken to Monterey, KY.
Kibler, George Sr., Tonawanda, Feb. 8, 1877, age 75 y, 10 m.
Kidder, B. H., formerly of Buffalo, June 1878; d. at Pekin, Niagara Co.
Kidder, Benjamin, Alden, Dec. 30, 1874, age 75.
Kidriher, George, Clarance, NY, suicide, April 30, 1880.
Kiefer, Mrs. Catharine, widow of Charles, June 7, 1880, age 56.
Kiefer, Maria A., Oct. 16, 1877, age 33; wife of Matthew.
Kiefer, Nicholas, Feb. 18, 1868, age 34.
Kieffer, Charles, suicide, Hamburgh, NY, Dec. 31, 1874.
Kieffer, Charles, May 13, 1877, age 58 y, 6 m.
Kiene, Sebastian C., Sept. 8, 1880, age 55.
Kienner, Emmeran, Jan. 11, 1874, age 41.
Kieth, Miss Nellie, Oct. 10, 1877, age 83.
Kilcott (Chilcott), William, July 20, 1873, age 43.
Kilderhouse, Elizabeth, wife of Thomas, April 26, 1850, age 26 y, 7 m.
Kilduf, Michael, railroad accident, Jan. 9, 1877.
Kilhenny, Mary, Jan. 22, 1880, age 82.
Kill, George, April 5, 1871, age 52 y, 7 m.
Killinger, Anthony, coachman, April 30, 1880, age 45 y, 6 m, 14 d; drowned.
Killinger, Matthias, Millgrove, July 1880, age 52 y, 5 m, 12 d.
Killrat (Killroe), Mary, Aug. 16, 1880, age 78; almshouse.
Kilmore, Mrs. Elizabeth, Evans, NY, May 4, 1853, age 100.
Kilpatrick, Susan, March 9, 1871, age c. 36.
Kilpeck, Alice, wife of Bartholomew, Oct. 29, 1860; taken to Rochester, NY.
Kimball, Caroline C., wife of L. M., May 26, 1878, age 38.
Kimball, Charlotte, wife of Daniel F., March 15, 1840.
Kimball, Daniel F., Aug. 19, 1845, age 52.
Kimball, Granville, formerly of Buffalo, Jan. 1873.
Kimball, Hannah, wife of Smith, Holland, NY, March 18, 1861, age 38 y, 11 m, 10 d.
Kimball, Lovell, March 11, 1849, age 48.
Kimball, Lucinda, wife of William, Aurora, NY, Jan. 13, 1844, age 39.
Kimball, Lyman W., telegraph operator, Jan. 7, 1866, age 22; taken to Bloods, Steuben Co., NY.
Kimball, Mary, Dec. 3, 1865, age 80; taken to Rochester, NY.
Kimball, Otis, formerly of Buffalo, Aug. 1, 1878, age 62; d. in Boston, MA.
Kimball, Mrs. P., mother of L. T. Kimball of Buffalo, Jan. 26, 1867, age 77 y, 8 m; taken to Plymouth, MA.
Kimberly, Mrs. Abigail, Clarence, NY, March 23, 1853, age 73.
Kimberly, Elisha, Sept. 18, 1865, age 76.
Kimberly, Eliza, March 19, 1877, age 86.
Kimberly, Eliza A., wife of John L., June 27, 1863, age 56.
Kimberly, Heman B., Clarence, NY, Dec. 30, 1864, age 28 y, 6 m.
Kimberly, Jacob, Dec. 29, 1861, age 67 y, 6 m.
Kimberly, Lucinda M., wife of Trumball C., dau. of Hon. Benjamin Maltby of Glenwood, NY, July 23, 1866; in New York; bur. at Glenwood.
Kimberly, Mary Ann, wife of Lucius, Clarence, NY, June 8, 1863, age 52 y, 8 m, 1 d.
Kimberly, Mrs. Polly, April 29, 1871, age 90.
Kimberly, Susan, Dec. 27, 1879, age 86.
Kimmich, Peter, Oct. 21, 1872, age 21.
Kimmit, Francis, Jan. 21, 1868, age 56.
Kimmit, Mrs. Mary, June 18, 1875, age 73.

Kimmit, Michael, April 22, 1873, age 76.
Kimmitt, Mrs. Francis, March 16, 1864, age 56.
Kimmitt, Patrick, Sept. 1, 1858, age 52.
Kincaid, H. E., Co. A., 140th N.Y.V., June 19, 1864; in Armory Square Hospital, Washington, D.C., of wounds received before Richmond.
King, Aaron A., of the firm of King & Harrington, July 3, 1855, age 23 y, 6 m.
King, Annie L., wife of William, Aug. 2, 1878, age 19 y, 11 m.
King, Byram, formerly of Buffalo, April 27, 1841, age 30; in Chicago., IL.
King, Calvin W., Crittenden, June 17, 1874, age 78.
King, Charles, July 30, 1873.
King, Charles T., July 10, 1848, age 21.
King, Clara B., widow of Francis C., formerly of Buffalo, July 24, 1877; d. Brooklyn, NY.
King, Clement, Griffins Mills, NY, June 18, 1835, age 80. [Another card: b. 1756; Soldier of the Revolution.]
King, Elisha, Oct. 21, 1831, age 24.
King, Eliza A., wife of Alexander, June 26, 1849, age 21 y, 4 m.
King, Elizabeth, wife of Calvin W., Alden, Nov. 24, 1869, age 65.
King, Miss Elizabeth P., dau. of the late Hon. Cyrus of Saco, ME, Oct. 30, 1869; d. at the residence of her sister, Mrs. R. H. Heywood.
King, Francis C., Nov. 10, 1874, age 51.
King, George, father of Charles M., July 15, 1872, age 66.
King, George B., brother of Capt. S.B. and of 12th Penna. Cav., Aug. 8, 1863.
King, Henry, accidental death, June 7, 1875, age 22.
King, Ida, suicide, May 24, 1875, age c. 25.
King, Jeannie Pratt, wife of William J. Jr., Sept. 24, 1872.
King, John, laborer, April 3, 1874, age 28; killed at Linden, NY
King, Hon. John S., formerly of Williamsville & Buffalo, Sept. 10, 1873, age 69 y, 3 m, 6 d. D. at Sterling, Whiteside Co., IL.
King, Julia, Sept. 26, 1844.
King, Margaret, May 4, 1878, age 40.
King, Martha D., wife of Calvin E., Alden, NY, June 15, 1855, age 19.
King, Mary A., wife of William, May 10, 1858, age 29; taken to Palmyra, NY.
King, Mary Ann, wife of John S., Williamsville, NY, March 16, 1851, age 38 y, 10 m.
King, Michael, May, 1864; bur. May 25.
King, Mrs. Myranda, Williamsville, NY, Sept. 27, 1848, age 77.
King, Naoma, Alden, NY, wife of George, formerly of Milwaukee, dau. of Jabez Otis of Westfield, MA, Feb. 1, 1857, age 56.
King, Naomi, wife of Elisha, Sept. 5, 1834.
King, Nicholas, Feb. 18, 1868, age 75.
King, Oscar H., formerly of Buffalo, Feb. 21, 1879; d. in Rochester, NY.
King, Pauline, Sept. 30, 1874, age 53.
King, Rachel, March 7, 1858, age 72.
King, Robert, son of James of Waterford, PA, Aug. 2, 1845, age 20 y, 3 m.
King, William, March 19, 1879, age 38.
King, William S., formerly of Buffalo, Sept. 28, 1866, age 57; in St. Louis, MO.
Kingman, Clara Elizabeth, dau. of Mrs. George Kingman, Jan. 25, 1853, age 22; in Salisbury, CT.
Kingman, Elizabeth Doris, widow of George G., June 17, 1876, age 63 y, 11 m, 26 d. Dau. of Hon. Myron Holley.
Kingman, George G., March 30, 1844, age 39.
Kingmin, Leonard, Jan. 5, 1879, age 73 y, 9 m, 7 d.
Kingsbury, Edwin S., firm of Shiels & Kingsbury, native of Danville, NY, Dec. 17, 1858, age 33.
Kingscott, Fanny, wife of William, March 28, 1866, age 52.
Kingscott, William, Hamburgh, April 25, 1875, age 70.
Kingsley, Alban S., Feb. 24, 1876, age 63.
Kingsley, Isabella, wife of A. F., Evans Center, NY, Aug. 18, 1862, age 49.
Kingsley, Jesse E., Aurora, NY, Sept. 12, 1828, age 39.
Kingsley, Parnel, wife of the late Phineas, Feb. 24, 1868, age 83.
Kingston, George C., Dec. 24, 1875.

Kinlay, Mary, Co. Almshouse, Dec. 6, 1877, age 79.
Kinnane, Mrs. Edward (Ida), June 4, 1878.
Kinnane, John, Aug. 7, 1870, age 27. In the employ of Messrs. Mack & Hickey, Grocers.
Kinnane, William, Dec. 22, 1874, age 27 y, 4 m, 11 d.
Kinnear, Sylvester, May 6, 1868, age 43.
Kinnear, William, Eden, NY, July 21, 1849, age 49.
Kinney, Mrs. Asenath, Sept. 22, 1877.
Kinney, Catharine, wife of D., July 19, 1849, age 57.
Kinney, Catherine, March 29, 1877, age 50.
Kinney, Daniel. Obituary Dec. 1857.
Kinney, Miss Eleanor, Sept. 20, 1869, age 24.
Kinney, George N., formerly of Buffalo, Sept. 21, 1842, in Winnebago Co., IL; merchant.
Kinney, James, late of 155th NY Vols., April 18, 1870, age 33.
Kinney, John, Jan. 13, 1870, age 66.
Kinney, Mary, wife of Richard C., Jan. 12, 1870, age 26.
Kinney, Patrick, Dec. 2, 1880, age 84.
Kinney, Rudolph J., Willink, Aug. 3, 1869, age 59; father of Mrs. E. A. Spencer of this city.
Kinney, Samuel N., Feb. 6, 1877, age 59; taken to Cortland, NY.
Kinnier, Mrs. Sarah, Oct. 1826, age 35.
Kinscott, Mrs. William, July 3, 1844, age 40.
Kinsky, George, March 25, 1865, age 30 y, 5 m, 8 d.
Kinsley, Caroline, wife of William, Nov. 27, 1840, age 29.
Kinsley, Charles E., Co. K, 116th Regt., N.Y.S.V., Evans Center, NY, Aug. 27, 1863, age 18 y, 3 m; in Baton Rouge, La.
Kinsley, Olive, mother of A.S., Evans, NY, formerly of Buffalo, March 18, 1853, age 83.
Kinsley, Henry H., Co. G, 21st Regt., N.Y.V., Jan. 6, 1864, age 20; d. of consumption caused by wounds received at battle of Antietam.
Kinyon, Ellen R., wife of George W. M., May 8, 1867, age 33; taken to Rochester, NY.
Kip, Catherine Van Dusen, wife of Gardner J., Cheektowaga, NY, Sept. 21, 1867, age 54.
Kip, Charlotte M., wife of Henry, Feb. 29, 1872.
Kip, Christina, widow of Henry, formerly of Buffalo and bur. there, March 15, 1862, age 77; d. in Brooklyn, N.Y.
Kip, Delia M., wife of Thomas, Jan. 22, 1847, age 31.
Kip, Miss Elizabeth, Lancaster, NY, Sept. 15, 1867, age 57.
Kip, Gardner J., Alden, April 12, 1878, age 66.
Kip, Henry, formerly of Buffalo, Oct. 16, 1849, in 65th year; in New York.
Kip, Maria Herring, widow of Elbert, Cheektowaga, Sept. 25, 1853, in 74th year.
Kip, Samuel D., Feb. 24, 1847, age 28.
Kippasthul (Kipfsthul), George, Sept. 19, 1875, age 44.
Kirby, Chapman C., Feb. 11, 1874.
Kirby, Mrs. Fanny, mother of William A., June 23, 1859, age 68.
Kirby, Silas, North Collins, NY, March 14, 1861, age 78.
Kirchberger, Joseph, found dead, May 13, 1878, age 57.
Kirchermeyer, Frank, suicide, March 12, 1876.
Kirk, Henry, laborer, Dec. 26, 1874, age 45.
Kirkover, Charlotte, widow of Oliver, Nov. 11, 1877, age 70.
Kirkover, Louisa, Sept. 9, 1873, age 31.
Kirkover, Oliver, July 6, 1874, age 77 y, 1 m, 14 d.
Kirkwood, Mrs. Eliza, March 28, 1869, age 35.
Kirsch, Mrs. Margaret, wife of Emanuel, Dec. 12, 1880.
Kissock, Mrs. Elizabeth, April 7, 1871, age 80; taken to Franklinville, Cattaraugus Co.
Kistner, Mrs. Elizabeth, formerly Mrs. Bautz, March 2, 1880, age 55 y, 3 m, 6 d.
Kitching, Alice, wife of Henry, Jan. 7, 1874, age 44.
Kitler, John, May 23, 1872, age 55.
Kittner, Gustave, Jan. 21, 1875.
Klaes, John, April 1, 1874, age 31 y, 5 m, 25 d.
Klapp, Edward M., nephew of P.A. Barker, formerly of Buffalo, Aug. 27, 1840; at Palmyra, NY.
Klas, John, March 14, 1870, age 46.

Klas, Mary, wife of John, May 6, 1878.
Klaus, John, March 5, 1871, age c. 50.
Kleber, Joseph W., June 29, 1868, age 23.
Klee, John Joseph, Dec. 5, 1878, age 63 y, 7 m, 12 d.
Klee, William, June 11, 1871, age 26.
Klees, Charles, suicide, July 26, 1880, age 37.
Kleibor, Charles W. F., Co. E, 78th Regt., N.Y.V., March 16, 1864, in 18th year; in Hospital at Stevenson, AL.
Klein, Mrs. Catherine F., Oct. 26, 1876, age 60.
Klein, Charles, May 2, 1878, age 33.
Klein, Daniel, Sept. 29, 1869, age 80.
Klein, George, Feb. 5, 1844, age 34 y, 4 m.
Klein, Mrs. M., April 3, 1879, age 46.
Klein (Keem), Mrs. Mary, Aug. 21 or 31, 1874, age 21.
Klein, Polly, widow of Mathew, April 30, 1860, age 66 y, 9 m.
Klein, William, Elma, drowned Aug. 21, 1880.
Kleindienst, Jacob, Sept. 5, 1879, age 27 y, 24 d.
Klenck, Mrs. Susanna, April 24, 1873, age 27.
Kless, Charles, suicide, July 26, 1880, age 37.
Klicker, Eva Catharina, wife of Jacob C., Clarence, age 48 y, 7 m, 13 d.
Klicker, Jacob, Aug. 20, 1874, age 74 y, 5 m, 15 d.
Kline, Ida C. Boalch, wife of Charles J., June 26, 1874, age 22 y, 10 m.
Kline, Philip G., April 17, 1869, age 41.
Kline, Philip Jacob, Nov. 4, 1863, age 62 y, 3 m.
Klingmeyer, John and Caroline, murder and suicide, Aug. 3, 1876. John age 42, Caroline 37.
Klinger, Johanna Julie Ehrlich, June 30, 1875, age 65; wife of Charles W.
Klotz, John, accidental death, Aug. 29, 1874, age 35.
Klughertz, Michael, Co. Almshouse, March 26, 1877, age c. 50.
Klump, Mrs., May 16, 1877, age 70.
Knapp, Mrs. Anna, formerly of Concord, Erie Co., March 21, 1869, age 79.
Knapp, Daniel, suicide, Hamburgh, July 7, 1874, age 67.
Knapp, Daniel A., Oct. 17, 1878, age 57 y, 4 m; taken to Warsaw.
Knapp, David P., soldier of War of 1812, April 14, 1870; d. in Co. Almshouse, apparently of old age.
Knapp, Hannah Elizabeth, wife of Stephen L., May 17, 1872.
Knapp, Henry, Boston, Erie Co., NY, Sept. 26, 1833, age 38.
Knapp, Jared, b. 1751, d. ---; Soldier of the Revolution.
Knauber, Amelia, wife of Michael, July 10, 1875, age 46 y, 9 m, 2 d.
Knecht, Aloyies, adopted son of John Yax, June 23, 1872, age c. 21; drowned.
Knecht, Barbara or Catherine, July 11, 1878, age 40 or 45.
Knecht, Fredricke, wife of Edward, formerly of Buffalo, Jan. 1873, age 31; d. at St. Louis, MO.
Kneck, Mrs. Catharine, May 23, 1877, age 85.
Kneeland, Charlotte B., wife of E. Y., May 21, 1875, age 63.
Kneeland, Cyrus Franklin, Sept. 14, 1856, age 45.
Kneeland, Sarah A., dau. of Elisha Y., Dec. 29, 1871, age 20.
Kneupelt (Kneufelt), Christian, July 23, 1875, age 56.
Knight, August, Co. Almshouse, March 11, 1877, age 33.
Knight, George C., March 7, 1878, age 29.
Knight, Jonathan, formerly of Eden, July 25, 1872, age 62; d. at Storm Lake, IA.
Knight, Mrs. Margaret A., Aug. 2, 1861, age 26.
Knight, Maria, wife of William M., Oct. 15, 1873, age 53.
Knight, Theodore C., Oct. 9, 1879, age 55.
Knippel (Kniffle), Mrs., wife of Frederick or Philip, Aug. 12, 1875.
Knoll, John A., Sept. 12, 1871.
Knopte, George, April 2, 1844.
Knorr, John, suicide, Sept. 20, 1878, age 24.
Knower, Samuel, Sept. 28, 1839, age 56.
Knowles, Susan, wife of T.C., Aug. 24, 1876, age 49.
Knowlton, Ephraim Herrick, formerly of Buffalo, Wales, NY, Jan. 10, 1853, age 22.

Knowlton, Flora A., wife of C.C., Jan. 24, 1870, age 18 or 48?
Knowlton, Henry, printer, formerly of Buffalo, Dec. 24, 1863, age 36; in Dubuque, IA.
Knowlton, James S., June 30, 1849, age 26.
Knowlton, Laura E., wife of Henry, March 6, 1854, age 26.
Knowlton, Mrs. S. B., Sept. 21, 1871; taken to Albany.
Knox, Henry, Springville, NY, June 29, 1828, age 20.
Knox, Miss Nancy, Jan. 3, 1874, age 83; taken to Waterloo, NY.
Knox, Warren L., April 22, 1877.
Koboch, Margaret, Feb. 22, 1855, age 62.
Koch, Anthony, Aug. 9, 1880, age 27 y, 11 m, 5 d.
Koch, Elizabeth, wife of John, Williamsville, Sept. 11, 1872, age 54 y, 7 m, 20 d.
Koch, John, March 3, 1871, age 57.
Koch, John, Williamsville, Nov. 22, 1879, age 68 y, 3 m, 10 d.
Koch, Lucinda, wife of Jacob, Williamsville, Aug. 8, 1877, age 56 y, 3 m, 2 d.
Koch, Mrs. Sarah, mother of John, Williamsville, NY, Nov. 6, 1862, age 74.
Koehler, Caroline, Dec. 27, 1876, age 52; wife of John.
Koehler, Frederick R., Feb. 19, 1873, age 20 y, 10 d.
Koester, John, suicide, May 2, 1872, age c. 22.
Koester, Peter, Cheektowaga, Jan. 5, 1874, age 67.
Kohl, Mrs. Adam, suicide, Jan. 26, 1873, age 38.
Kohlbrenner, Jacob, Jan. 22, 1873, age 50.
Kohlbrenner, Mrs. Magdalena, Nov. 6, 1879.
Kokaski (Koloski), Lorenzo, accidental death, Aug. 28, 1877.
Kolb, Charles, son of the late Jacob, April 23, 1874, age 20 y, 8 m, 26 d.
Kolb, George Michael, Sept. 17, 1876, age 59 y, 7 m, 7 d.
Kolb, Jacob, Sept. 13, 1866, age 47 y, 4 m.
Kolb, Jacob, Feb. 6, 1872, age 20 y, 5 m, 6 d.
Kolb, Maria Eva, widow of Frank Anthony, Feb. 2, 1874, age 62 y, 2 m, 14 d.
Koll, Henry, Sept. 1871.
Kompf (Kumpf), J. Philip, suicide, March 27, 1876, age 38.
Koon, Mrs. Elenor, July 29, 1869, age 69.
Koon, Joseph, Alden, March 20, 1871, age 36 y, 10 d.
Koons, Alban, May 24, 1871, age 23; taken to Canton, OH.
Koons, Frederick, Nov. 4, 1873, age 53.
Koopmans, Mrs. T., Lancaster, May 2, 1880, age 68.
Kopf, John Philip, Sept. 14, 1876, age 40 y, 4 m, 14 d.
Kopka, Julius, railroad accident, May 5, 1876.
Kortz, Mary, drowned with 3 others, July 4, 1874, age 23.
Kortz, William, merchant, Dec. 6, 1841, age 33.
Korzelius, Jacob, March 6, 1878, age 37.
Korzelius, John Jr., March 28, 1878, age 50.
Koster, John F., Oct. 6, 1852, age 43.
Kraatz, Charles J., grocer, Oct. 1879, age 30. Found dead Oct. 5; last seen Sept. 30.
Kraft (Kroft), Francis, June 27, 1873, age 38; taken to Stevensville, Ontario.
Kraft, Kate, April 26, 1876, age 23.
Kranichfeld, Andrew, July 13, 1875, age 78 y, 3 m.
Kranichfeld, Mary, May 3, 1874, age 30 y, 1 m, 25 d.
Krannichfeld, Caroline, Sept. 5, 1870, age 35 y, 3 m, 5 d.
Kraus (Knautz), Gottleib, May 7, 1878, age 34.
Krauser, Louis, railroad accident, Feb. 1, 1876, age 45.
Krauslig, John, West Seneca, Sept. 7, 1872, age 25.
Krauss, Magdalena, wife of Godfrey, Aug. 30, 1873, age 39 y, 7 m, 10 d.
Krausskopf, Prof. William, Jan. 26, 1870, age 56.
Krauthaus, Annie, Aug. 31, 1875, age 24; d. at Hornellsville, NY, bur. in Buffalo.
Kregloh, John, Amherst, NY, Jan. 14, 1856, age 33 y, 10 m, 27 d.
Kreiner, Charles, Jan. 20, 1876, age 20 y, 10 m.
Kreiner, Frederick, laborer, May 31, 1879, age 30 or 35; buried alive, digging sewer.
Kreiner, Mary B., wife of George, Sept. 10, 1878, age 48 y, 6 m, 18 d.
Krengel, John, accidental death, Oct. 12, 1870.
Kress, Anna M., wife of Frederick, Aug. 9, 1876, age 58.

Kress, Frederick, Oct. 2, 1878, age 63.
Krettner, Jacob, eldest son of Col. Jacob, July 23, 1866, age 28; in New York.
Krettner, Col. Jacob, April 13, 1870, age 60.
Kretz, M., Oct. 24, 1870, age 48 y, 10 m; widow of Michael.
Kretz, Mary Ann, wife of Edward, April 19, 1873, age 22 y, 11 m, 7 d.
Kretz, Michael, March 24, 1867, age 44.
Kritzler, Conrad, accidental death, June 17, 1877.
Kroetch, Leonard, West Seneca, July 1871.
Krofmann, Louis, Jan. 30, 1873, age 22.
Kroll, Ernst G., Sept. 28, 1880, age 31 y 6 m.
Kroll, John, July 26, 1879, age 53 y, 9 m, 20 d.
Kromer, Frederick, suicide, Cheektowaga, June 1877, age c. 50.
Kron, John, Jan. 12, 1877, age 56.
Kronfeld, Julius William, March 13, 1871, age 52.
Kruegelstein, John S., formerly of Buffalo, June 5, 1878, age 85; d. at Attica, Wyoming Co.
Krueger, Herman, April 24, 1874, age 34.
Krumer, Christopher, accidental death, Boston, Feb. 22, 1874, age 66.
Krutzelmann, Charlotte, widow of Frederick, July 9, 1872, age 46 y, 7 m.
Kucherson, John, Oct. 1876, age 82.
Kuhn, George, Feb. 21, 1873, age 38.
Kuhn, Henry, July 24, 1871, age 51 y, 10 m.
Kuhn, John, Oct. 4, 1879, age 29 y, 2 m.
Kuhn, Mary Mayd., March 22, 1868, age 61.
Kull, Frederick, May 25, 1864, age 40.
Kumro, Frank, Nov. 16, 1880, age 32; d. at General Hospital.
Kuntzman, Andrew A., Martin's Corners, March 23, 1878, age 89 y, 3 m, 5 d.
Kuornick, Mary, March 28, 1872, age 44; suicide at the Poor House.
Kurc, Mrs. Catharine, d. suddenly, June 30, 1880, age 68.
Kurtz, Barbara, wife of Charles, Lancaster, Jan. 22, 1872, age 43.
Kurtz, Charles, brewer, May 9, 1873, age 33.
Kurtz, Sarah, wife of Joseph, Newstead, March 5, 1869, age 72.
Kurtzwarth, Frank X., Feb. 9, 1877, age 23.
Kurz, Mrs. Elizabeth, April 28, 1870, age 62.
Kyle, Alice, dau. of William, Sept. 1, 1852, age 23 y, 3 m, 14 d.
Kyle, Capt. William C., formerly of Buffalo, May 18, 1880, age 84; d. at Chicago.
Kynoch, William, late of Buffalo, Jan. 27, 1861, age 28 y, 6 m; in New York.

Lace, Mary, wife of Jacob, dau. of David Chadduck, Feb. 7, 1858, age 20.
Lacer, John G., June 3, 1848, age 24.
Lacke, Ladoiska M., wife of Warren of Logan, OH, dau. of Dr. G. C. Gage, of Lancaster, NY, July 5, 1856; taken to Alden, NY.
Lackie, Mrs. Catharine, Jan. 28, 1869, age 66; taken to Toronto, Canada West.
Lacy, Clark B., Aug. 30, 1869, age 33.
Lacy, Helen, wife of John T., March 11, 1873, age 63.
Lacy, Henry C., Oct. 26, 1876, age 32; taken to Detroit, MI.
Lacy, Jennie Emeline, wife of Edgar D., Dec. 26, 1871.
Lacy, John S., Black Rock, NY, July 20, 1834, age 70.
Lacy, John T., Aug. 7, 1879, age 75.
Lacy, William, son of John T., Jan. 2, 1869, age 22.
Lacy, William H., July 5, 1840, age 32.
Ladd, Charles W., Dec. 13, 1858; at Aurelius, Cayuga Co., NY.
Ladd, Grant, Williamsville, NY, May 31, 1867, age 65 y, 11 m.
Laemmbe, John Christoph, March 2, 1878, age 54 y, 2 m, 14 d.
Lafferty, Elizabeth, wife of Dewitt C., Nov. 27, 1872, age 41.
Laflam, Joseph, March 7, 1862, age 57.
Laforce, Charles, plasterer, Dec. 7, 1870.
LaForce, Eleanor E., widow of Charles, Feb. 20, 1879, age 53 y, 8 m, 6 d.
Laible, Regina, widow of Christopher Sr., North Buffalo, March 11, 1870, age 80 y, 5 m.
Laing, Abram, Feb. 29, 1868, age 51; d. at Volcano, WV.
Laing, David, Jan. 3, 1824, age 44.

Lake, Daniel, Boston, NY, Dec. 15, 1832, age 47.
Lake, Hiram M., recently of New York, Nov. 13, 1858, age 38.
Lake, Maria, wife of Cortland, July 8, 1871, age 52.
Lake, Sarah, wife of Cortland, April 14, 1849, age 27.
Lake, William F. G., Springville, NY, Aug. 1829, age 38.
LaMassh, Eleanor, wife of Edward, Feb. 5, 1880; d. at Grand Island.
Lamb, Eliza, wife of Thomas, Jan. 8, 1845, age 29 y, 7 m, 27 d.
Lamb, Frederick, May 27, 1873, age 60.
Lamb, Margaret Petree, wife of William, April 12, 1855, age 76.
Lamb, Thomas, formerly of Buffalo, May 26, 1877, age c. 65; d. at St. Paul, MN.
Lamb, William, father of John, Henry, and Thomas, Feb. 7, 1857, age 79.
Lambeck, Mrs. Helen, Jan. 23, 1872, age 40 y, 6 m.
Lambert, Amert E., wife of J. G., Sept. 15, 1865, age 19.
Lamberton, Mrs. W. B., Dec. 18, 1863, age 32.
Lamey, William, drowned, Sept. 2, 1878, age 25.
Lamoreaux, Mrs. Helen, mother of Mrs. C. C. Bogert, Feb. 22, 1861, age 64. Formerly of Rochester, and taken there.
Lamphear, Mary, wife of H. H., June 10, 1853, in 38th year.
Lamphear, Solomon, Williamsville, NY, Nov. 26, 1865, age 71.
Lamphear, Solomon, July 1, 1874, age 29.
Lamphier, Minnie, wife of Edward A., Oct. 15, 1875, age 23.
Lamphier, Mrs. Thomas, Oct. 5, 1879, age 57.
Lamphier, Thomas P., July 20, 1879, age 31.
Lampman, Warren, Dec. 1, 1878, age 62 y, 5 m.
Lamprie, Mary, wife of Michael, July 25, 1880, age 32.
Lander, Grace, widow of James, June 24, 1863, age 49.
Lander, James, Oct. 17, 1862, age 48.
Lander, Mary H., wife of William P., formerly of Buffalo, Sept. 5, 1870, age 64 y, 6 m; d. in Brooklyn.
Lander, William F., son of William P., Jan. 9, 1846, age 21.
Lander, William P., formerly of Buffalo, Aug. 4, 1877; d. at Brooklyn.
Landis, John, formerly of Dauphin Co., PA, Clarence, NY, Dec. 31, 1817, age 61.
Landon, Bethia, widow of Horace, Eden, April 28, 1877, age 80.
Landon, Cynthia, wife of Luther B., Boston Center, NY, Dec. 2, 1854, age 31.
Landon, J. Munson, Oct. 27, 1858, in 58th year.
Landon, Joseph, Black Rock, NY, April 27, 1847, age 78.
Landon, Milton, North Boston, NY, Feb. 25, 1851, age 26.
Landsittel, Anthony, Aug. 15, 1867, age 58.
Landsittel, William, accidental death, Aug. 10, 1874, age 36 y, 11 m.
Lane, Annie, wife of Alexander, July 30, 1877.
Lane, Elijah, Hamburgh, NY, Oct. 10, 1819, age 40.
Lane, Ezekiel, April 6, 1848, age 102.
Lane, George C., late of Buffalo, May 1, 1863, age 36; in Madison, NY.
Lane, J. Edwin, Jan. 1872; bur. Jan. 29.
Lane, Jeremiah, murdered by his son John, June 28, 1878.
Lane (Lone), John, drowned, Sept. 1, 1878.
Lane, Margaret A. Forrester, wife of George A., Feb. 1, 1865, age 43 y, 9 m, 4 d.
Lane, Mary, wife of John, Oct. 8, 1870, age 45.
Lanesterer, Henry W. F., drowned, July 23, 1874.
Lang, Abeloni, wife of Abram, April 17, 1872, age 57 y, 10 m.
Lang, Adam, Dec. 6, 1880, age 40; Poor House.
Lang, Michael, March 1, 1873, age 52 y, 4 m.
Lang, William, Cadet Engineer, Nov. 15, 1880.
Langanhadir, Herman H., May 29, 1869, age 62.
Langanhadir, Katie Holbrook, wife of John F., June 11, 1873, age 27.
Langanhadir, Louise, widow of Herman H., July 23, 1877, age 70.
Langdon, Barnabas, father of George W., Feb. 28, 1853.
Langdon, Charles Henry, formerly of Buffalo, Dec. 27, 1866, age 26; in Bethany, Western VA.
Langdon, Mrs. Charlotte, Jan. 2, 1859, in 74th year.
Langdon, James, Feb. 20, 1867, age 56.

Langdon, Jervis, Elmira, NY, Aug. 6, 1870.
Langdon, Hon. John, native of Portsmouth, N.H., May 26, 1852, age 72; in Rochester, N.Y.
Lange, Carl F., May 13, 1868, age 51.
Langenhadir, John F., Aug. 11, 1880, age 42; General Hospital.
Langing, Ida, Co. Almshouse, Nov. 22, 1878, age 28.
Langley, Thomas J., Feb. 2, 1863, age 32; in New York, bur. in Buffalo.
Langmeier, John, formerly of Buffalo, June 17, 1880; murdered at Leadville, CO.
Langner, Christina, wife of J. G., Nov. 8, 1868, age 42 y, 9 m.
Laning, Hon. Albert Pierce, Sept. 4, 1880, age 63; lawyer.
Laninger, Henry C., Nov. 1, 1878, age 21 y, 2 m, 6 d.
Lanior, Catharine, wife of Peter, May 20, 1844, age 48.
Lannan, Hugh, June 21, 1871, age 30.
Lannen, Thomas, Oct. 20, 1877, age 50.
Lannon, Patrick, d. at Insane Asylum, July 9, 1878, age 61.
Lansing, Henry Gibson, son of Gen. Henry L., May 30, 1870, age 31; d. at Montevideo, South America.
Lansing, Minney Frances, dau. of Garrett, Aug. 21, 1862.
Lansing, Phoenix, June 21, 1858, age 38.
Lansing, Rebecca, wife of Stephen, Oct. 3, 1879, age 59; d. at Brunswick, NY.
Lanson, Mrs. Mary, Sept. 20, 1853, age 25.
Lapey, Artie W., wife of John, Aug. 29, 1880, age 35.
Lapham, Abraham, Collins, NY, July 22, 1836, age 80.
Lapham, Catharine White, wife of Dr. G.H., East Aurora, Dec. 20, 1879, age 64.
Lapham, Hannah, Collins, NY, May, 1832, age 68.
Lapham, Otis, formerly of Buffalo, brother of Mrs. B. H. Austin, Oct. 17, 1858, age 57; at Erie, PA.
Lapham, Miss Sarah, March 18, 1877, age 79 y, 10 m.
LaPlant, John Baptist, Feb. 24, 1875, age 70 y, 10 m.
LaPlant, Joseph, Sept. 21, 1875, age 31 y, 8 m.
LaPlant, Louis, July 10, 1872, age 41; drowned in Bell River, Cayuga, Ontario, bur. in Buffalo.
Lapp, Barbara Kindig, wife of Christian, July 28, 1864, age 72 y, 18 d.
Lapp, Christian, b. in Berks Co., PA, [d.] June 13, 1866, age 74 y, 3 m, 14 d.
Lapp, Rev. Jacob, b. in Berks County, PA, Clarence, NY, June 24, 1854, age 87 y, 7 m, 29 d.
Lapp, Jacob, April 3, 1875, age 56 y, 5 m.
Lapp, Rev. John, Williamsville, Aug. 4, 1878, age 80.
Lapp, Margaret, wife of Jacob, Clarence, NY, Feb. 16, 1854, age 88 y, 6 m, 2 d.
Lapp, Martha J., Black Rock, NY, Dec. 13, 1864, age 20 y, 11 m, 7 d.
Lapp, Sarah Hayden, wife of Isaac S., July 11, 1875, age 57.
Lappin, Mrs. Jane, Sept. 22, 1864, age 73.
Lappin, Robert Sr., June 6, 1877, age 58 y, 8 d.
Lapsley, George W., Feb. 26, 1862, age 40; printer.
LeReau, Josephine, Tonawanda, Nov. 2, 1877.
Large, George, June 28, 1880, age 48.
Larish, Mary F. Bonney, wife of J. W., Nov. 29, 1873, age 22 y, 2 m, 7 d.
Larkin, Alvin J., son of the late Levi H., East Hamburgh, June 28, 1874, age 26.
Larkin, John, brother-in-law of Henry Hopkins, May 3, 1851, age 45.
Larkin, Thomas, Jan. 27, 1874.
Larned, Mary Ann, wife of H. S., Spring Brook, NY, Dec. 19, 1852, age 40.
Larraux, Miss Cecile, dau. of Noel, Feb. 26, 1875, age 25.
Larreau, Andrew N., May 8, 1865, age 48.
Larreau, Neal, Tonawanda, Sept. 16, 1875, age 73.
Larsson, John, Aug. 16, 1876.
LaRue (Larreau), Mrs., formerly of Buffalo, Aug. 15, 1876; d. in NY City, bur. in Buffalo. Said to have been poisoned.
Larzelere, A., March 24, 1841, age 54; at Ypsilanti, MI.
LaSalle, Thomas, June 21, 1871, age 32.
Lasell, Chancey, late of Dansville, Livingston Co., NY, July 10, 1852, age 50.

Laselle, Electa, widow of Chauncey of Dansville, mother of Mrs. S. P. Kittle, June 9, 1856, age 52.
Lasher, Rebecca, widow of John E., April 25, 1869, age 68; d. at the Church Home, taken to Lewiston.
Lasner, Nathan H., formerly of Amherst, NY, Aug. 26, 1857, age 81; in Green Oak, MI.
Lasson, Gustin, Black Rock Dam, NY, Co. J, 21st Regt., June 1863; bur. June 4.
Latham, Lt. Killed in Battle of Niagara. Obituary Aug. 1814.
Latham, Thankful Bushnell, wife of Obadiah B., Dec. 10, 1857, age 32.
Lathrop, Mrs., April 1829, age 45.
Lathrop, Anna, Oct. 1815, age 40, wife of Denison.
Lathrop, Belinda, June 30, 1829, age 47; wife of Denison.
Lathrop, Betsey, widow of Rufus, Eden, NY, July 10, 1848, age 63.
Lathrop, Betsey Farnsworth, Hamburgh, NY, Dec. 7, 1845, wife of Rev. John, late of Woodstock, VT.
Lathrop, Charlotte, wife of Joseph B., Aug. 29, 1840, age 46.
Lathrop, Mrs. Charlotte A., Nov. 11, 1875, age 56.
Lathrop, Deloss, May 29, 1835, in Albany, NY, age 31.
Lathrop, Denison, Dec. 19, 1846, age 73.
Lathrop, Mrs. E. L., Jan. 1856, age 66; in Stamford, CT.
Lathrop, Elderkin, April 19, 1875, age 74 y, 11 m, 8 d.
Lathrop, Ferdinand A., son of Mrs. L. L., June 11, 1874, age 29.
Lathrop, Heman F., Oct. 22, 1857, age 35.
Lathrop, Horace, Feb. 2, 1835, age 24.
Lathrop, John, May 16, 1870, age 61.
Lathrop, Laura Chase, wife of Paul B., Elma, April 2, 1872, age 58 y, 3 m, 21 d.
Lathrop, Louise Keyes, wife of Septimius, Oct. 16, 1865.
Lathrop, Miss Mary A., dau. of Denison, Nov. 20, 1841; in Jackson, MI.
Lathrop, Rufus, Eden, NY, Nov. 5, 1846, age 66; in Cheektowago, N.Y.
Lathrop, Sarah E., July 5, 1878.
Lathrop, Septimus, formerly of Buffalo, Jan. 30, 1874, age 67; d. at North Creek, NY, brought to Buffalo.
Lathrop, Maj. Solon H. Obituary Oct. 1867.
Lathrop, William Bryant, Co. H., 116th Regt., formerly of Eden, NY, Aug. 2, 1863, age 22 y, 6 m; at Baton Rouge, LA of wounds received at Donaldsonville, July 13.
Lathrope, Emilie E. H., dau. of Mrs. Charlotte, April 13, 1872, age 24.
Latimor, John, Oct. 8, 1872, age 55.
Latta, Elizabeth, wife of Robert, March 14, 1855, age 36.
Latta, Mary Jane, wife of Robert, May 6, 1863, age 42.
Latta, Robert, April 1, 1878, age 57 y, 6 m, 10 d.
Laubrick (Laubisch), Frederick, accidentally killed, May 29, 1874, age 44.
Lauer, Margaret, July 14, 1872, age 21.
Laughlin, Bridget, widow of Martin, Feb. 6, 1874.
Laughlin, Maggie E., dau. of Martin, Jan. 21, 1872, age 21.
Lauraen, Nicholas, suicide, Gardenville, Sept. 11, 1877, age 87.
Laury, Benjamin, son of John, Glenwood, Feb. 9, 1875, age 30.
Lautenschlaeger, Frederick, May 5, 1866, age 36 y, 10 m, 19 d.
Lauterman, Sophia C., widow of David of Binghamton, NY, Sept. 16, 1854, age 56.
Lauth, Michael, accidentally scalded, Nov. 28, 1874, age 21.
Lautz, M. Margaret, wife of F.C.M., Sept. 15, 1872, age 25 y, 11 m, 24 d.
Lautz, William Sr., Dec. 20, 1866, age 51 y, 7 m.
Laux, Catherine, wife of Martin, Oct. 31, 1879, age 48 y, 5 m, 2 d.
Laux, Martin, May 20, 1880, age 54 y, 9 m, 10 d.
Lavake, Elizabeth, wife of Thomas, Nov. 5, 1851, age 62.
Lavayea, Miss Mary, Jan. 28, 1856, age 22.
Laverack, Belle A., eldest dau. of William, Dec. 1, 1865, age 22.
Laverack, William A., Jan. 19, 1878, age 33 y, 7 m; eldest son of William.
Lavin, Mary E., April 18, 1876, age 20 y, 6 m, 15 d.
Lavin, Thomas, Oct. 23, 1868, age 38.
Law, Chauncey W., formerly of Aurora, NY, Dec. 11, 1862, age 53; d. in PA.
Law, Elizabeth, wife of James, Dec. 6, 1866, age 31.

Law, Irene, wife of Prentiss, May 22, 1843, age 28.
Law, John, Nov. 19, 1841, age 83.
Lawacatach, John, Jan. 2, 1880, age 42; drowned.
Lawfer, Adam, killed at battle of Black Rock, Dec. 30, 1813.
Lawhead, Thomas, Dec. 1812, age 47.
Lawken, William Gustav, Dec. 1, 1878, age 56 y, 7 m, 27 d.
Lawlass, Thomas, railroad accident, Jan. 6, 1879, age 27.
Lawler, John, April 15, 1871, age 28.
Lawler, Peter, June 9, 1873.
Lawless, John L., May 7, 1873, age 21 y, 4 m, 14 d.
Lawless, Lawrence W., May 8, 1873, age 38.
Lawless, Thomas, April 14, 1878, age 98.
Lawrence, Charles Mitchell, April 13, 1878, age 32 y, 2 m.
Lawrence, Daniel, formerly of Cooperstown, Otsego Co., Hamburgh, NY, July 27, 1838, age 49.
Lawrence, Emily, wife of Richard T., June 10, 1865, age 33.
Lawrence, John, June 17, 1874.
Lawrence, Mrs. Sarah, widow of Capt. John, Nov. 27, 1880, age 57.
Lawrence, William H., Oct. 21, 1853, age 37.
Lawson, Alexander, Feb. 24, 1846, age 29.
Lawson, Elizabeth, wife of Richard, June 8, 1849, age 37.
Lawson, Peter F., Sept. 28, 1876, age 36 y, 11 m, 21 d.
Lawson, Peter F., April 24, 1878, age 77 y, 8 m.
Lawson, Richard, June 22, 1867, age 57.
Lawton, Miss Emily, April 12, 1849, age 26.
Laxton, Robert, Boston, Lincolnsire, England, April 28, 1832, age 30.
Lay, Charles, March 11, 1868.
Lay, Emily Sophia, eldest dau. of Charles, Nov. 12, 1866.
Lay, Harry Macy, youngest son of the late John, formerly of Buffalo, July 3, 1876; d. in Calcutta, India.
Lay, John, Feb. 5, 1845, age 85.
Lay, John, July 10, 1850, age 60.
Lay, Nathaniel, father of Mrs. Martin Daley of Buffalo, East Evans, NY, July 27, 1844, age 79.
Lay, Phebe, wife of Nathaniel, East Evans, NY April 18, 1853, age 82; mother of Mrs. Martin Daley of Buffalo.
Lay, Miss Phebe C., Evans, NY, Feb. 6, 1844, age 20.
Laycock, Edward, Oct. 6, 1863, age 24.
Laycock, Elizabeth, widow of Thomas, Feb. 10, 1878, age 74.
Laycock, Hartley, Oct. 31, 1879, age 55; killed by the cars.
Laycock, Thomas, Jan. 14, 1865, age 61.
Layton, Miss Adelia M., dau. of Deacon John, Oct. 30, 1854, age 21 y, 10 m.
Layton, Anna, wife of John, Hamburgh, NY, Feb. 25, 1820.
Lazelle, Elias, Oct. 6, 1876, age 51. D. at Madison, WI, funeral from Woodside Church on the Abbott Rd., Oct. 9.
Leach, Cecilia Rosetta, wife of George, Jan. 21, 1875, age 20 y, 10 m.
Leach, Mrs. Lucy, Sept. 27, 1864, age 78.
Leach, Permilla, wife of Elijah, Dec. 23, 1827, age 35.
Leader, Mary A., March 20, 1868, age 48.
Leahey, Timothy, policeman, Feb. 28, 1878, age 35.
Lear, Jacob, Sept. 15, 1879, age 46.
Learmouth, M. A., wife of Hugh, Dec. 23, 1856, age 38.
Leary, Patrick H., Feb. 15, 1876, age 26.
Lec, Charles G., Oct. 25, 1861, age 46.
Lechrist, Catherine, mother of A. B. Gantz of Buffalo, April 13, 1865, age 58 y, 10 m, 20 d; funeral from Williamsville, NY.
Leck, William, April 28, 1874, age 45.
LeClear, Aaron, Boston, NY, Jan. 28, 1858, age 60.
LeClear, Bethia, wife of Hiram, West Falls, NY, May 16, 1867, age 62.
LeClear, Eli, Boston, Erie Co., Feb. 16, 1880, age 56 y, 6 m, 6 d.
LeCouteulx, Jane Eliza, wife of Louis Stephen, Feb. 11, 1838, age 72.

LeCouteulx, Louis, Nov. 17, 1840, age 84, philanthropist, News July 9, 1899. (Mounted Clipping) [B. at Rouen, France, Aug. 24, 1756.]
LeCouteulx De Caumont, William B., July 18, 1859, age 72.
Lederer, Charles, Feb. 9, 1876, age 64 y, 9 m.
Lee, Bartholomew, Jan. 6, 1880, age 51; d. at Batavia.
Lee, Prof. Charles A., M.D., Peekskill, NY, Feb. 14, 1872, age 72.
Lee, Cyrus H., son of James H., Aug. 25, 1871, age 21.
Lee, Daniel P., formerly of Buffalo, May 11, 1877; d. in NY City, bur. at Nyack, Rockland Co., NY.
Lee, Edward H., Eden Corners, NY, Aug. 28, 1852, age 30.
Lee, Fanny G., wife of William G., Williamsville, Aug. 17, 1864, age 40; bur. at Clarence, NY.
Lee, George F., lawyer, suicide, Feb. 10, 1874, age 36; d. in Savanah, GA, bur. Buffalo.
Lee, George W., son of Samuel W. of Rochester, May 28, 1865, age 22 y, 2 m, 13 d.
Lee, Harriet L., only dau. of Mary Ann Small, March 13, 1866, age 28 y, 4 m.
Lee, Harvey W., Nov. 23, 1879, age 70.
Lee, Helen, widow of Richard Hargrave, Feb. 15, 1876, age 73.
Lee, Horatio N. Capron, wife of Royal Lee, Nov. 13, 1839, age 28.
Lee, Janett, wife of R. Hargrave Lee, July 26, 1844, age 57.
Lee, Jonathan, father of Elisha and John R. of Buffalo, Clarence, NY, Feb. 15, 1852, age 70.
Lee, Julia Ann, wife of Daniel P., Aug. 4, 1847, age 30.
Lee, Mrs. Margaret, March 27, 1865, age 84.
Lee, Martha, June 30, 1867.
Lee, Mary, wife of Edward, drowned May 1873, age 55.
Lee, Mrs. Mary, Oct. 4, 1874, age 75.
Lee, Mrs. Mary R., mother of D.P. of Buffalo, Aurora, NY, March 5, 1844, age 52.
Lee, Oliver, July 28, 1846.
Lee, Paritta, widow of Samuel, Aug. 21, 1849, age 27.
Lee, Richard Hargrave, Sept. 5, 1856, age 75.
Lee, Robert, son of Richard Hargreave Lee, Nov. 11, 1849, age 30 y, 9 m.
Lee, Robert, Corp., Co. D, 49th Regt., N.Y.S.V., Feb. 10, 1863, age 40; at Point Lookout, MD.
Lee, Roderick, father of D. P. of Buffalo, Aurora, NY, Oct. 24, 1843, age 56.
Lee, Samuel A., connected with Wells & Co's. Express, Oct. 4, 1848, age 34.
Lee, Samuel W., brother of P.A., formerly of Buffalo; d. at Warsaw, NY, Dec. 9, 1866, age 37 y, 6 m, 19 d. Funeral from residence of William Stimpson.
Lee, Sarah A., Jan. 1, 1865, age 45.
Lee, Mrs. Sarah Jane Hill, near Derby Station, Erie Co., March 2, 1880, age 23; killed by cars.
Lee, Thomas, July 12, 1879.
Lee, William, native of Youghal, Co. Cork, Ireland, Dec. 18, 1873.
Leech, Elijah, Clarence, NY, June 11, 1841, age 56; formerly of Buffalo.
Leech, George B., son of Elijah, Springville, NY, May 14, 1851, age 23.
Leech, Miss Irene, Aug. 28, 1856; at Camden, Oneida Co., NY.
Leech, Jaruis H., Feb. 16, 1868, age 33.
Leech, Mrs. Maria, Whites Corners, NY, Nov. 28, 1857, age 36. Funeral from residence of Benjamin Dickey at the Hydraulics.
Leech, Richard, Asst. Justice, Court of Common Pleas, Nov. 2, 1812, age 40.
Leehan, Cornelius, railroad accident, May 10, 1876, age 24; taken to Driftwood, PA.
Lees, Andrew D., Nov. 21, 1875, age 25; d. at South Bend, IN.
Leese, Frank, accidental death, Nov. 26, 1870, age 25; foreman of the Distillery of H. F. Briggs & Co.
Leete, Thomas, late of Steamer *Chesapeake*, Sept. 1845, age 30.
Legge, Charles, Nov. 4, 1871, age 87; taken to Lockport.
Leggett, Mrs. John, fire accident, Nov. 17, 1878, age 45.
Lehman, Philip, Feb. 7, 1875, age 31.
Lehman, William, Oct. 16, 1879, age 36.
Lehmann, Amelia, June 3, 1877, age 19 y, 8 m.
Lehmann, Rosanna, May 31, 1879, age 61 y, 10 m, 4 d.

Leiblee, Elizabeth, Sept. 6, 1878, age 62 y, 1 m, 26 d.
Leiblee, Ernst Sr., Dec. 1876, age 70.
Leichtnam, Christina, wife of Joseph, Buffalo Plains, Sept. 25, 1874, age 81 y, 1 m.
Leigh, Richard, son of James, 16th WI S.V., Wales, NY, May 27, 1862, age 32; in Cincinnati, OH, from wounds in battle at Pittsburg Landing.
Leighton, Edward, Sept. 28, 1862, age 39.
Leighton, Robert, Aug. 16, 1880, age 70.
Leighton, Sophia T. Deuel, April 27, 1872, age 29 y, 6 m, 21 d. Wife of Walter H., d. in Marlboro, MA, bur. in Buffalo.
Leiser, Jacob, Co. Almshouse, July 9, 1876, age 75.
Leister, Joachim, suicide, Gardenville, July 8, 1875, age 71.
Leitch, Olive E., wife of John, Aug. 19, 1872, age 28.
Leitz, Joseph, formerly of Buffalo, June 6, 1878, age 59; d. at Williamsville.
Leland, Bainbridge P., formerly of Buffalo, July 4, 1854, age 39; in Hamilton, Canada West.
Lelsle (Leslie), John, accidental death, Nov. 23, 1875, age 25.
LeMay, Stephen, laborer, Sept. 27, 1880, age 35; accident.
Lembeck, Christopher, Feb. 15, 1877, age 54.
Lemmon, Col. J. C., father of Mrs. E. K. Bruce, formerly of Buffalo, Feb. 12, 1875; d. at Washington, DC, bur. Buffalo.
Lemon, Charles B., brother of Mrs. E. K. Bruce, formerly of Buffalo, Sept. 14, 1871; d. in New Orleans.
Lemott, Mr., a Canadian Frenchman, Jan. 22, 1817, age 45.
Lempert, Joseph, son-in-law of L. Collette, Band-master of the Eighth Regt. of Inf., Dec. 24, 1848; at Lavaca, TX.
Leng, William, Feb. 5, 1868, age 91.
Lenhard, Adam, Jan. 19, 1874, age 69.
Lenhard, Andrew, Nov. 12, 1872, age 26 y, 8 m, 21 d.
Lenhard, Andrew, Oct. 11, 1877, age 66 y, 8 m, 5 d.
Lenhard, Edward J., son of the late Jacob, June 3, 1875, age 23 y, 11 m, 16 d.
Lenhard, George F., Jan. 23, 1876, age 24 y, 5 m, 24 d.
Lenhard, Mary A., Dec. 2, 1879, age 60 y, 9 m.
Lenhart, Rebecca C., wife of John W., May 17, 1833, age 24.
Lenington, Mrs., Oct. 1824, age 50.
Leonard, Charles of 100th Regt., Black Rock, NY, Feb. 20, 1865, age 33.
Leonard, Delina C., wife of John J., Oct. 5, 1836, age 31.
Leonard, Edward P., Concord, Erie Co., Aug. 27, 1856, age 27.
Leonard, George, Oct. 19, 1867; at Hornellsville, NY, bur. in Buffalo.
Leonard, Gurdeon (Gurner) F., May 14, 1879, age 40.
Leonard, Mary, dau. of Patrick B., Sept. 3, 1874, age 23.
Leonard, Norman, May 28, 1863, age 56; taken to Lockport.
Leonard, Rebecca, wife of Dr. B., East Evans, NY, May 23, 1841, age 34.
Leonard, Rev. Samuel, formerly of Evans, April 19, 1862, age 85; at Chesterfield, MI.
Leonard, Thomas H., April 26, 1870.
LePage, Anna, Aug. 19, 1871, age 35 y, 4 m; wife of Remie, dau. of the late Joseph LaFlam; d. at Shamburg, PA, bur. Buffalo.
Lepper, James F., Oct. 2, 1875, age 39.
Lerock, Ellen Jones, wife of James, Dec. 1, 1876, age 37.
Leser, Catharine A., June 1, 1844, age 48.
Leslie, Daniel, April 30, 1867, age 31.
Leslie, Mrs. Mary, Jan. 25, 1872, age 39.
Leslies, James F., Aug. 6, 1858, age 27.
Lester, Orville J., Newstead, NY, Jan. 23, 1859, age 26.
Lester, Philip, Feb. 11, 1880, age 30 y, 3 m, 21 d; bur. at Utica.
Lester, Mrs. Sarah, Aug. 4, 1868, age 68; taken to Lyons.
Lesuer, Polly, wife of Nathan, March 29, 1813, age 30.
Letchworth, Mary R. Skinner, wife of Josiah & dau. of Hon. John B. Skinner, Sept. 23, 1868, age 29 y, 17 d; d. at Clarens, on Lake Geneva, Switzerland.
Lether, John, suicide, June 14, 1877, age 58.
Letson, Isaiah, Aurora, Feb. 2, 1880, age 83 y, 4 m, 22 d.
Letson, Sophia Smith, wife of Isaiah, Aurora, Nov. 24, 1872, age 73.

Letson, William, Aurora, NY, April, 1836 age 43. [Another card: Letson, William, b. 1761, d. 1835, bur. East Aurora; Soldier of the Revolution.]
Lett, Emma, dau. of Mrs. Peyton Harris, Sept. 15, 1875, age 56.
Lett, Urias, May 14, 1871, age 56.
Leutz, William, Nov. 27, 1877, age 25 y, 7 m.
Levake, Thomas, Sept. 9, 1859, age 63 y, 3 m, 5 d.
Levandesski (Travandusskie), John, March 5, 1874, age 50.
Levi, Clara, wife of Emanuel, Oct. 7, 1872, age 33.
Levings, Selah J., Dec. 29, 1866, age 32 y, 2 m, 12 d.
Levins, Pennel, April 1816, age 45.
Levy, Isadore, March 8, 1880, age 22, sudden death.
Levy, Mary Emilie, wife of S. N., Nov. 5, 1869, age 32; dau. of O. F. Haehn.
Lewin, William, July 22, 1878, age 75.
Lewin, William H., eldest son of William of Buffalo, Jan. 20, 1853; at Mobile, AL; age 24.
Lewis, Mrs., Union Town, Dec. 4, 1871.
Lewis, Amy, wife of Lovell, Sept. 12, 1859, age 64; at Cedar Rapids, IA.
Lewis, Mrs. Ann, Sept. 14, 1876, age 49.
Lewis, Annie, April 27, 1871, age 27.
Lewis, Charles H., son of Hiram A., June 24, 1878, age 22 y, 6 m.
Lewis, Daniel, Clarence, NY, May 5, 1831, age 59.
Lewis, Daniel W., Counsellor at Law, late of Geneva, NY, June 17, 1837, age 75.
Lewis, Dennis, Feb. 10, 1872, age 59; taken to Little Falls.
Lewis, Drayton, Concord, NY, April 14, 1861, age 52.
Lewis, Edwin J., barber, Jan. 16, 1871, age 70.
Lewis, Elias A., Sept. 28, 1874, age 69.
Lewis, Eliza, wife of Franklin, formerly of Buffalo, Nov. 8, 1870; d. at Chesaning, Saginaw Co., MI.
Lewis, Esther A., dau. of Dr. John, Bowmansville, June 9, 1869, age 37.
Lewis, Helen Sophia, wife of Irving H., dau. of Isaac Pomeroy of Colden, NY, Oct. 31, 1865, age 28; taken to East Hamburgh, NY.
Lewis, John, Oct. 23, 1847, age 30.
Lewis, John C., father of Drs. Dio and George W. & of L.L., June 2, 1867; in Auburn, NY, bur. in Buffalo.
Lewis, Lorenzo, Dec. 22, 1863, age 78 y, 3 m, 29 d.
Lewis, Mrs. Lucinda, Aurora, May 28, 1872, age 74.
Lewis, Mary, Co. Almshouse, June 1876, age 52.
Lewis, Mary Ann, dau. of John, Aug. 23, 1850, age 20; in Bertie, Canada West.
Lewis, Mary C., wife of Irving H., June 7, 1867, age 19 y, 9 m; taken to Wales, NY.
Lewis, Minerva, wife of Richard H., formerly of Buffalo, Aug. 3, 1869, age 18; d. at Vernon, MI.
Lewis, Morgan G., M.D., Black Rock, NY, Feb. 8, 1858.
Lewis, Peter, March 28, 1878, age 68.
Lewis, Thomas E., Aug. 14, 1863, age 34.
Lewis, William D., Colden, June 13, 1872, age 33 y, 8 m, 16 d.
Lewis, William J., July 12, 1876, age 34.
Leyon, Kate, July 12, 1878, age 28; d. at Sisters of Charity Hospital.
Liable (Laible), Christian, Feb. 6, 1877, age 60.
Libby, Mrs. Adaline King, wife of John, March 11, 1880, age 42.
Libby, Dorothy, wife of James, Sept. 14, 1856, age 32.
Lichtenstein, Eliza, wife of Barnett, Aug. 13, 1864, age 50.
Lichtenstein, Barnett, March 15, 1877, age 77; d. in Chicago, IL, bur. Buffalo.
Liebbetrut, Julius, Feb. 2, 1859, age 38.
Liger, Edmund, formerly of Buffalo, Springville, Nov. 14, 1827, age 28.
Liger, Gatien, Springville, NY, native of France, Nov. 7, 1828, age 68.
Linahan, Mrs. Bridget, April 7, 1874, age 67.
Lincoln, Maria, Feb. 6, 1872, age 75; taken to Webster, Monroe Co., NY.
Linder, Isabella M., wife of Capt. William, Dec. 23, 1851, age 39.
Linder, Mary, widow of Capt. William, April 17, 1864, age 28.
Linder, Capt. William, July 15, 1863, age 57.
Lindley, Mrs. L. M., wife of Nathaniel, Sept. 5, 1879, age 62.

Lindley, Samuel, father of Mrs. Silas Sawin, Aug. 6, 1851, age 70.
Lindsay, Mary E. Richards, wife of Oscar A., Jan. 9, 1869.
Lindsey, Matilda, May 14, 1853, age 54.
Lindsley, Matthew, b. May 12, 1763, d. April 5, 1839, bur. Alden, NY; Soldier of the
    Revolution.
Linibetz (Linnabitz), Carl (Charles), West Seneca, March 14, 1876, age 76.
Linman, William P., Sgt. Co. B., 16th NY Cavalry, killed on picket duty near Annandale, VA,
    Aug. 13, 1864.
Linnemann, Josephine, March 10, 1880, age 27; Almshouse (insane).
Linnenkohl, Frances A. M., Aug. 6, 1880, age 20.
Lindsey, Aaron, Collins, NY, May 5, 1832, age 55.
Linton, Miss Martha, April 27, 1848, age 22.
Lippert, Lewis E., July 6, 1878.
Liska, Frank, fisherman, drowned Dec. 6, 1877, age 29.
Little, Direxa, wife of Guy, Lancaster, April 1, 1875, age 63.
Little, George, Jan. 1875, age 44.
Little, Guy, Lancaster, NY, May 22, 1875, age 70.
Little, Henry, b. 1758, d. 1840, bur. E. Aurora; Soldier of the Revolution.
Little, James P., Feb. 14, 1880, age 25.
Little, Nelson, Aug. 30, 1859, age 50.
Little, Samuel C., firm of Little & Arnold, Aug. 7, 1862, age 48.
Littlefield, Mrs. Celia, mother of the late Wray S., Hamburgh, NY, Sept. 12, 1859, age 85.
Littlefield, Horace, June 21, 1851, age 25; en route to CA.
Littlefield, Louise C., wife of Lansing B., Oct. 3, 1877, age 47.
Littlefield, Mary L., wife of Leason C., East Hamburgh, NY, Dec. 31, 1852, age 29.
Littlefield, Nancy, widow of Wray S., March 5, 1873, age 79; taken to Hamburgh.
Littlefield, Sophia L., wife of L. B., Feb. 13, 1853, age 32.
Littlefield, Wray S., formerly sheriff of the County, Hamburgh, NY, Oct. 5, 1835, age 46.
Littlejohn, Mrs. Dewitt C., formerly of Buffalo, April 28, 1872.
Livingston, George W., April 7, 1852, age 32; in Sisters-of-Charity Hospital.
Livingston, James of Bath, N.Y., July 30, 1852, age 73.
Livingston, Miss Margaret, Feb. 24, 1853, age 56.
Livingston, Mrs. Nancy, Dec. 9, 1862, age 64; mother of Mrs. C. S. Macomber.
Livingston, Thomas, March 24, 1851, age 58.
Livingstone, Flora, Feb. 1880, age 60.
Lloyd, Elizabeth, widow of Henry, Dec. 8, 1880, age 68.
Lloyd, Henry, May 30, 1878, age 75.
Lloyd, John C., March 16, 1877, age 57; d. at the Buffalo General Hospital.
Loban, Alexander, May 4, 1851, age 29.
Lobdel, Mrs., Hamburgh, NY, Sept. 1819, age 60.
Lobon, Mary, wife of A., Aug. 1, 1849, age 24.
Lobstein, Edward, Aug. 14, 1880, age 34 y, 3 m, 13 d.
Lobstein, Mrs. Margarette, Jan. 14, 1880, age 58 y, 3 m, 16 d.
Locellie, Joseph, Dec. 23, 1878.
Locke, Annie, wife of Charles H., March 27, 1861, age 25.
Locke, Mrs. Harriet, wife of John, Feb. 22, 1880, age 71 (or 78).
Locke, James, father of Franklin D., Gowanda, Aug. 27, 1872, age 70.
Locke, Lydia Huntley, wife of W.C., Dec. 22, 1858, age 32.
Locke, Maggie, wife of E. A. & dau. of Benjamin Cook, formerly of Buffalo, April 8, 1873,
    age 32; d. at Erie, PA, bur. Buffalo.
Locke, Capt. Philander B., Jan. 25, 1879, age 48.
Locken, Charles, Jan. 11, 1870, age 42.
Lockrow, Mrs. Elsie, Feb. 16, 1872, age 74.
Lockrow, Peter V.B., Nov. 7, 1852, age 45; taken to Troy, NY.
Lockwood, Betsey, wife of Ebenezer, Hamburgh, NY, mother of Dr. T.T. Lockwood, Nov. 11,
    1847, age 71.
Lockwood, Charlotte, wife of T.T., Hamburgh, NY, Sept. 5, 1843, age 29.
Lockwood, Mrs. Clara, Jan. 12, 1877, age 24.
Lockwood, Daniel, April 3, 1858, age 60.
Lockwood, Ebenezer, Boston, NY, Aug. 19, 1856, age 82.

Lockwood, Esther Antoinette, widow of Ralph, dau. of Capt. Moses Gregory of Norwalk, CT, and sister of Com. F. H. Gregory, Jan. 3, 1856, age 60; taken to Milan.
Lockwood, Garrett B., Co. B, 21st Regt., May 9, 1862, age 22; at Fredericksburgh.
Lockwood, Harrison, brother of Dr. T. T., Hamburgh, NY, April 10, 1849, age 33.
Lockwood, Mrs. Helen M., Nov. 29, 1862, age 47 y, 9 m.
Lockwood, Imogene M., dau. of Dr. T. T., May 7, 1865, age 26.
Lockwood, Miss Jennie, dau. of Philo, East Hamburgh, Sept. 27, 1875, age 23.
Lockwood, Jesse, Boston, NY, June 3, 1857, age 51.
Lockwood, John F. Obituary July 1868.
Lockwood, Kate S., dau. of the late Dr. T. T., May 11, 1874, age 20.
Lockwood, Louisa C., wife of Hon. T. T., M.D., Oct. 25, 1869.
Lockwood, Lydia Ann, dau. of Philo D., East Hamburgh, NY, Aug. 28, 1857, age 19.
Lockwood, Maria, wife of William, Sept. 28, 1852, age 38.
Lockwood, Millington, May 19, 1860, age 83 y, 8 m.
Lockwood, Dr. N.S., July 8, 1863, age 28.
Lockwood, Oriel Wood, wife of Stephen, June 23, 1875, age 44; taken to East Hamburgh.
Lockwood, Orin, Sept. 11, 1865, age 58; bur. in East Hamburgh.
Lockwood, Philo D., brother of Dr. T. T., East Hamburgh, NY, Jan. 15, 1859, age 61.
Lockwood, Polly, widow of Philo D., East Hamburgh, May 21, 1869, age 63.
Lockwood, Sarah, widow, formerly of Onondaga Co., NY, July 21, 1832, age 70.
Lockwood, Susan Maria, dau. of Philo D., East Hamburgh, NY, Sept. 17, 1857, age 23.
Lockwood, T. T., M.D., Dec. 23, 1870, age 60; d. in Utica, bur. Buffalo.
Lockwood, Walter C., Aug. 4, 1849, age 27.
Lodge, Catharine, widow of Thomas, Aug. 16, 1832, age 20.
Lodge, Thomas, Aug. 15, 1832, age 37.
Loebrich, George, May 26, 1878, age 71 y, 8 m, 2 d.
Loegler, Frederick, July 3, 1875, age 55 y, 22 d.
Loegler, George, Jan. 5, 1859, age 22 y, 8 m, 20 d.
Loegler, Peter, April 4, 1869, age 21 y, 10 m.
Loersch, Dorothea, wife of Dr. J. Philip, July 18, 1871, age 73.
Loersch, John Philip, M.D., May 13, 1876, age 79.
Loesch, Nicholas, April 19, 1877, age 48 y, 4 m, 18 d.
Loew, Rev. Jacob, Pastor of German Baptist Church in Wales, NY, April 23, 1867, age 39 y, 11 m.
Loeweriberg, Joseph, Oct. 10, 1875, age 44.
Loft, Mrs. William, July 16, 1856, age 37.
Loftus, Daniel, June 10, 1880, age 49.
Loftus, Michael, policeman, Feb. 26, 1877, age c. 54.
Loftus, Michael, Oct. 27, 1879, age 28 y, 11 m.
Logan, David, Aug. 6, 1880, age 31.
Logan, Miss Mary A., formerly of Greece, Monroe Co., NY, March 18, 1867, age 25; taken to Rochester.
Lonergan, Lt. Edward K., June 2, 1866 at Ridgeway, Ontario, age 21.
Lonergan, John D., Aug. 5, 1872, age 31.
Lonergan, Joseph, May 7, 1873, age 75 y, 6 m.
Lonergan, Thomas K., May 29, 1857, age 21.
Long, Abbie Louise, wife of Alfred H., Sept. 14, 1870; d. in NY City.
Long, Abram, Cheektowaga, April 27, 1872, age 74.
Long, Abram B., Williamsville, April 27, 1872, age 26 y, 2 m, 19 d.
Long, Addie Crittenden, May 23, 1874, age 19 y, 9 m, 23 d; wife of Lucius S., taken to Williamsville.
Long, Ann, wife of Isaac, White's Corners, NY, Oct. 23, 1865, age 36 y, 1 m, 29 d.
Long, Anna Barbara (Huettenmeyer), Sept. 14, 1871, age 34 y, 7 m, 8 d.
Long, Benjamin, Tonawanda, NY, Sept. 29, 1859, age 74.
Long, Benjamin H., Tonawanda, Dec. 10, 1878, age 46.
Long, Daniel, Amherst, NY, March 24, 1852, age 31.
Long, Daniel, Dec. 11, 1870, age 27 y, 4 m.
Long, Daniel, railroad accident, June 12, 1876, age 22.
Long, Dorothea, widow of George, March 7, 1873, age 73 y, 7 m, 23 d.

Long, Edward O., Co. B., 51st Regt. N.Y.S.V., son of Macall, Clarence, May 18, 1864, age 29 y, 1 m, 18 d. Killed at Battle of Spottsylvania Court House.
Long, Eliza Tozard, wife of Lucius, May 30, 1857, age 52; taken to Lockport, N.Y.
Long, Mrs. Elizabeth, Clarence, NY, May 2, 1842, age 79.
Long, Elizabeth Huntington, wife of Rev. Walter R., March 31, 1874, age 55.
Long, Capt. George, Aug. 17, 1862, age 38 y, 4 m.
Long, Henry, March 26, 1845, age 21.
Long, Henry Clay, son of the late M., Williamsville, May 17, 1870, age 28.
Long, James, Lancaster, March 19, 1873, age 80 y, 11 m, 19 d.
Long, John, Feb. 5, 1845, age 85; taken to Batavia, NY.
Long, John, Clarence, NY, Dec. 23, 1845, age 60.
Long, John, Amherst, NY, Feb. 18, 1851, age 22.
Long, Lucius, Jan. 24, 1861, age 54; taken to Lockport, NY.
Long, Lyman, formerly of Colden, Jan. 16, 1878, age 20; d. in Derrick City, PA.
Long, Margaret, wife of Christian, Amherst, May 13, 1878, age 78 y, 2 m, 19 d.
Long, Mrs. Mary, Amherst, NY, Nov. 12, 1856, age 93 y, 9 m.
Long, Mary A., wife of Capt. George, Sept. 22, 1858.
Long, Mary E., widow of Macall, Clarence, Dec. 6, 1875.
Long, Mecall, Clarence Hollow, Dec. 5, 1868, age 61.
Long, Capt. Richard, April 20, 1852, age 52.
Longbone, Thomas, April 2, 1874, age 48.
Longford (Langford), Charles, drowned, laborer, July 31, 1872, age 27.
Longhurst, John, July 20, 1862, age 46.
Longnecker, Abram, Williamsville, Aug. 6, 1878, age 63; suicide.
Longnecker, Christian, Nov. 18, 1834, age 59.
Longnecker, Henry, March 14, 1873, age 71.
Longnecker, John, Williamsville, Dec. 23, 1876, age 67.
Longnecker, Martha, widow of Christian, April 30, 1841, age 67.
Longnecker, Michael, July 7, 1858, age 41.
Longnecker, Sarah, wife of John, Harris Hill, July 29, 1873, age 56.
Looby, John, railroad trackman, accidental death on railroad, Nov. 28, 1880.
Loomis, Mr., formerly from CT, Sept. 21, 1816, age 35.
Loomis, Caroline, wife of Harvey, mother of Dr. H. N., March 20, 1843, age 56.
Loomis, Elizabeth F., Jan. 26, 1879, age 54.
Loomis, Capt. Ezra, from Norwich, Chenango Co., NY, Nov. 8, 1860, age 92.
Loomis, Harvey, father of Dr. N.H., Oct. 27, 1862, age 80.
Loomis, Kate Maria, only dau. of Charles K., Jan. 27, 1863.
Loomis, Luther, Feb. 18, 1880, age 83.
Loomis, Mary Brockenbrough, widow of Charles K., Oct. 14, 1873.
Loomis, Mrs. Rachel, Dec. 6, 1845, age 66.
Loomis, William A., Jan. 21, 1869, age 42.
Loomis, William N., son of Dr. H. N., Nov. 4, 1862, age 26.
Looney, Robert, Looneyville, April 16, 1872, age 49.
Loop, Mrs. Harrietta, formerly of Hillsdale, NY, Amherst, NY, July 27, 1858, age 58.
Loos, Anna M., June 26, 1844, age 36.
Loosen, Frederick Sr., formerly of Buffalo, March 15, 1877, age c. 60; d. at Lockport.
Loosen, Salome, widow of Frederick, formerly of Buffalo, March 6, 1878; d. at Lockport.
Loper, Capt. B. E., Oct. 8, 1877, age 52; d. at Point au Pelee, Ontario.
Loper, Mrs., wife of Samuel, Newstead, NY, March 22, 1850.
Loper, Theresa P., Clarence, NY, wife of Samuel W., dau. of R. Oakley, Smithtown, Suffolk Co., NY, Sept. 15, 1850, age 27.
Lord, Mrs. Anne, Sept. 1862, age 55; bur. Sept. 11.
Lord, Rev. John C., D.D., Jan. 21, 1877, age 72.
Lord, Rev. John Way, Aug. 23, 1839, age 67.
Lord, Luke, July 29, 1866, age 49.
Lord, Rachel M., wife of T. D., Alden, NY, Jan. 18, 1852, age 30.
Lord, Salome, Black Rock, NY, widow of Capt. Andrew P., July 23, 1855, age 68.
Lord, Thomas, Jan. 1, 1876, age 65.
Lord, William, Alden, NY, June 13, 1862, age 83.

Lore, Rev. Dr. Dallas David, formerly of Buffalo, June 17, 1875, age 60; d. at his home near Auburn.
Lorenz, Catharine, relict of the late Frederick, May 19, 1868, age 65.
Lorenz, Elizabeth, wife of John, May 5, 1880, age 83 y, 4 m, 11 d.
Loring, James, July 19, 1849, age 46.
Loring, Marie S., widow of William N., Oct. 10, 1874, age 43 y, 3 m, 4 d. [William N. d. age 36, Hillsdale, MI; no date given.]
Lorquemain, John E., July 6, 1863, age 53.
Lortz, Peter, near Buffalo, June 8, 1871, age 47.
Losee, Maria, wife of Simeon, March 27, 1856, age 51.
Losee, Miss Susy, dau. of Simeon, formerly of Buffalo, May 17, 1863; in New York.
Losehand, Mary M., wife of B.C., Feb. 16, 1878, age 34 y, 1 m, 18 d.
Losson, Nicholas, Aug. 9, 1876, age 65 y, 8 m.
Lotcz, Malchoir, Nov. 5, 1879, age 43 y, 23 d.
Lothrop, Henry M., formerly of Buffalo, Dec. 7, 1868; d. in NY.
Lorthrop, Dr. Joshua R., July 22, 1869, age 46; d. at Plymouth, MA.
Loton, John, Eden, July 6, 1870, age 77.
Lotridge, Francis A., Nov. 30, 1864, age 35 y, 5 m, 6 d; in New York.
Lotz, Melchoir. Obituary Nov. 1879.
Loughlin, Mr., Nov. 1872.
Louttit, William H., Oct. 18, 1870, age 37 y, 9 m; d. in Batavia, bur. in Buffalo.
Love, Andrew A., Dec. 16, 1879, age 54.
Love, Annie E. Fox, wife of Rev. Robert J., Nov. 9, 1878, age 50.
Love, George C., formerly of Buffalo, Nov. 21, 1870; d. at Des Moines, IA.
Love, George M., Co. G, 52nd Reg. NY Vol., Jan. 9, 1865, age 22 y, 6 d; in Rebel prison pen, Salisbury, NC.
Love, Harlow S. Obituary March 1866.
Love, James, Dec. 24, 1876, age 41.
Love, John, July 10, 1876, age 74.
Love, Maria, widow of Judge Thomas C., Sept. 29, 1864, age 64.
Love, Mrs. Mary B., Sept. 21, 1875, age 76.
Love, Rhodie, widow of Solomon, formerly of Buffalo?, April 2, 1874, age 77; d. at Stirling, IL.
Love, Thomas, formerly of Washington Co., NY, Newstead, NY, March 29, 1839, age 70.
Love, Thomas C., Sept. 17, 1853, age 63.
Love, Thomas C., Jr., nephew of Hon. Thomas C. of Buffalo, Newstead, NY, Oct. 9, 1852, age 37.
Love, Thomas C., son of the late Maj. Levi of this city, formerly of Buffalo, April 23, 1870, age 31; d. at Des Moines, IA, bur. in Buffalo?
Lovecheck, Joseph, coachman, Jan. 2, 1880, age 35; suicide by drowning.
Loveday, Amelia E., wife of J. H., June 1, 1874, age 19 y, 10 d.
Lovejoy, Mrs. Catharine, March 25, 1872, age 89; taken to Newark, NY.
Lovejoy, Henry (J?), May 29, 1872, age 72 y, 2 m.
Lovejoy, Joshua, formerly of NH, Sept. 5, 1824, age 53; in New York.
Lovejoy, Sally, wife of Joshua, Jan. 1814, age 35; killed by British Indians at her home.
Lovejoy, Mrs. Sarah, Aug. 28, 1864, age 80.
Loveland, Lorinda, wife of M.R., Feb. 15, 1869, age 61; taken to Sardinia.
Loveland, Mitchell R., Jan. 27, 1870, age 62; taken to Sardinia.
Lovely, Edward, Collins, July 27, 1877, age 38.
Loveridge, Amasa, father of A.A. and E.D. of Buffalo, Concord, NY, May 17, 1855, age 67.
Loveridge, Amasa Austin, Dec. 19, 1868, age 53.
Loveridge, Mrs. Eunice, March 4, 1870; mother of E.D.
Loveridge, Orin, Springville, NY, Feb. 1845, age 53.
Lovering, Alice R., Aug. 1, 1873.
Lovering, Ann, wife of William Jr., Aug. 28, 1853, age 38.
Lovering, Mary S., wife of William, Sept. 21, 1865, age 76.
Lovering, William, April 27, 1869.
Lowe, Frederick C., Co. Almshouse, March 15, 1878.
Lowe, Louise E., wife of John C., June 2, 1870, age 20 y, 6 m.
Lowell, Catherine, wife of George, Oct. 6, 1874, age 45; suicide.

Lowry, George, May 17, 1863, age 57.
Lowery, George, Dec. 28, 1874, age 38; d. at the Sinclair House, New York.
Lowry, Warren, 21st Buffalo Regt., son of George, June 30, 1862, in hospital at Fredericksburg, VA; bur. in Buffalo.
Loyd, Mrs. Frances, sister of Miss Ann Clemons, Feb. 1, 1861, age 51.
Lucas, Calvin E., May 26, 1876, age 33 y, 4 m, 25 d.
Lucas, Emily E., March 25, 1872, age 62.
Lucas, Lavina A., wife of L. D., Sept. 16, 1862, age 21 y, 10 m.
Lucas, Lorenzo D., Faulkner, Jan. 26, 1878, age 50; bur. Buffalo.
Lucas, Mary J., wife of Lorenzo D., March 10, 1874, age 40.
Lucas, Nelson, drowned, Grand Island, April 19, 1873.
Lucassen, Florence, Aug. 1877, age 40; at Buffalo General Hospital.
Luce, Hon. Almond, Oct. 7, 1837, age 52.
Luce, Mrs. Anna, mother of Mrs. F. Gridley, March 28, 1866, age 70.
Luce, Esther, wife of Alfred, June 16, 1830, age 29.
Luce, Lauretta, widow of Truman, Williamsville, NY, May 28, 1865, age 73. Funeral in Lancaster, N.Y.
Luce, Mary, wife of Orlando, Lancaster, NY, Feb. 4, 1864, age 34; in New York. Bur. Greenwood Cemetery.
Luce, Truman, Dec. 30, 1863, age 76.
Ludi, James, Port Byron, II, Jan. 28, 1859, age 29.
Ludlow, Ann, Black Rock, NY, widow of Capt. Charles H., Aug. 30, 1865, age 53.
Ludlow, Catherine, wife of Ebenezer, April 25, 1866, age 34.
Ludlow, Capt. Charles H., Black Rock, Nov. 15, 1859, age 47; in Dunkirk, NY, bur. in Black Rock, NY.
Ludlow, Maj. Henry, Evans, NY, formerly of Lansing, Tompkins Co., NY, July 19, 1844, age 80.
Ludlow, Laura McIntosh, wife of Myron M., Dec. 7, 1876, age 24.
Ludwig, Anna Josephina, June 1880, age 22 y, 10 m, 11 d.
Ludwig, Conrad, June 18, 1878, age 75.
Ludwig, John A., March 21, 1879, age c. 60.
Luesenhop, Emma, wife of Adolph, Nov. 26, 1872, age 37 y, 10 m, 12 d.
Luh, Mrs. Margaret, Sept. 29, 1878, age 74 y, 10 m, 29 d.
Luik (Link), Simon, April 15, 1879, age 58; sudden (coroner's case), age 58.
Luippold, Mrs. Dorothy, April 12, 1878, age 70.
Luke, Kate, wife of Marvin S., Aug. 17, 1868.
Luscher, Mrs. Elizabeth, Black Rock, Jan. 25, 1874, age 49.
Lusk, Clarissa, 2nd dau. of William, Newstead, NY, Feb. 9, 1856, age 32.
Lusk, Julian Hamilton, March 24, 1876, age 66 y, 6 m; taken to St. Louis. D. at the Buffalo General Hospita.
Lusk, Stephen, Eden, NY, Jan. 1813, age 50.
Luther, Cromwell, b. Oct. 1762, d. March 1839, bur. Collins, NY; Soldier of the Revolution.
Lutted, Lizzie J., wife of James, Jan. 31, 1874, age 22 y, 3 m, 8 d.
Lutz, George, July 24, 1876.
Lutz, John M., March 27, 1873, age 30 y, 4 m, 18 d.
Lutz, Philip, Sept. 16, 1880, age 55 y, 7 m, 6 d.
Lutz, William, suicide, West Seneca, June 11, 1877.
Lyall, Maria, wife of Alexander, Oct. 6, 1850, age 62.
Lyman, David R., July 25, 1863, age 54.
Lyman, Jane, widow of Nathan, March 23, 1879, age 89 y, 7 m, 23 d.
Lyman, Jane Gardiner, wife of P. Stephen, Feb. 1, 1856, age 30.
Lyman, Lillie E., dau. of P. S., Feb. 27, 1879, age 24 y, 11 m, 17 d.
Lyman, Loomis, July 4, 1874.
Lyman, Mrs. Lucy Ann, wife of Loomis, July 13, 1879, age 67.
Lyman, Nathan, Feb. 16, 1873, age 83.
Lyman, Mrs. Philoxena, Nov. 22, 1856, age 83.
Lymburner, Harriet C., wife of Hamilton M., June 29, 1878, age 51.
Lymburner, Hattie M., dau. of Hamilton M., Dec. 22, 1875, age 21.
Lynch, Catharine, Oct. 18, 1878, age 71.
Lynch, Edward, May 30, 1875, age 44.

Lynch, Edward, railroad accident, April 11, 1876, age 40.
Lynch, James, April 23, 1872, age 43.
Lynch, James, Nov. 23, 1880, age 73.
Lynch, Sergt. John, Cincinnati, OH, July 1867, age 27; from a wound received at Battle of Ridgeway.
Lynch, John Joseph, son of late Edward, March 21, 1880.
Lynch, John L., July 21, 1879, age 40; at Co. Almshouse.
Lynch, Margaret, wife of Capt. Michael T., April 29, 1875, age 48.
Lynch, Mary Ann, wife of Patrick, Oct. 14, 1880, age 22 y, 6 m.
Lynch, Patrick, May 31, 1880, age 44.
Lynch, Sarah, May 10, 1880, age 43.
Lynde, Albertus L., May 21, 1865, age 49.
Lynde, Charles James, Aug. 21, 1876, age 28; d. at Dunkirk, bur. in Buffalo.
Lyng, Joseph Jr., Feb. 12, 1875, accidental death, age 25.
Lynn, Alice J., wife of John E., July 6, 1877, age 21 y, 10 m; of Port Hope, Ontario & taken there.
Lynn, Andrew, Sept. 22, 1867, age 32.
Lynn, Elizabeth, wife of Thomas, Aug. 30, 1876, age 39.
Lynn, Margaret, Dec. 2, 1868, age 75.
Lynn, Mary, Bowmansville, Oct. 1877, age 75.
Lynn, Thomas, June 30, 1879, age 40; found dead in bed.
Lynn, William, June 17, 1869, age 54.
Lyon, Agnes, May 6, 1870; d. at the General Hospital, taken to Hamilton, Canada West.
Lyon, Freeman, April 27, 1852, age 53.
Lyon, Jacob, Sept. 3, 1850, age 24.
Lyon, Martha Ann, wife of Jacob, formerly of Buffalo, Aug. 14, 1858; at Leavenworth City, KS.
Lyon, Mrs. Mary A., April 7, 1875, age 61.
Lyon, Sarah, wife of William, formerly of Buffalo, May 22, 1853, age 61 y, 4 m, 22 d; in Greenville, Greene Co., NY.
Lyons, Alice or Agnes, suicide, Nov. 7, 1871, age c. 20.
Lyons, Elizabeth, wife of Sergeant Cornelius, Nov. 22, 1879, age 34 y, 1 m, 8 d.
Lyons, George W., April 13, 1876, age 36.
Lyons, James, May 13, 1880, age 36 y, 4 m, 13 d.
Lyons, Johanna, wife of Freeman, Oct. 29, 1844, age 41.
Lyons, Lewis, Tonawanda(?), NY, March 7, 1846, age 45.
Lyons, Minnie, Feb. 16, 1877, age 33; Co. Almshouse.
Lyons, Rachel, mother of Stephen W., Feb. 15, 1854, age 79; taken to Troy, NY.
Lyons, Stephen W., June 4, 1872, age 64.
Lyport, David, April 17, 1873.
Lyport, Tobias, April 6, 1853, age 71.
Lytle, James, formerly of Buffalo, March 31, 1876, age 68; d. at Erie, PA.
Lytle, Joanna P., wife of Andrew, late of Williamsburg, VA, Jan. 11, 1863, age 40 y, 8 m.
Lytle, Martha J., July 30, 1857, age 43.

Mabey, Alfred, Jan. 30, 1879, age 45.
Mabon, Mrs. Candace, June 12, 1878, age 59 y, 11 m, 16 d.
Macbeth, Henry, Aug. 14, 1880, age 32.
MacCabe, Mary, widow of John, April 29, 1880.
Mace, Martha, Sept. 23, 1860, age 45.
Machlet, Philip, Jan. 15, 1861, in 25th year.
Machwirth, Adolph, Feb. 2, 1878, age 59 y, 7 m, 7 d.
Mack, David, Nov. 11, 1869, age 28; taken to Prescott, Canada West.
Mack, Elisha, formerly of Springville, NY, July 16, 1847, 49th year; at Nauvoo, IL.
Mack, James, Aug. 19, 1873, age 27.
Mackay, Dr. Edward, July 7, 1867, age 57.
Mackay, Lt. James E., Oct. 13, 1862, age 22 y, 8 m; 63rd Regt. NY State Vols. Aid-decamp to Gen. Meagher. D. of wounds received in battle of Antietam. Son of Dr. Edward.
Mackay, John, May 6, 1873, age 45.

Mackenroth, Rose, wife of J.C., formerly of Buffalo, Jan. 1876.
Mackey, James, Jan. 11, 1879, age 56.
Mackie, Adam Fordyce, March 27, 1869, age 26.
Mackintosh, Robert. Obituary Dec. 1863.
MacNamara, Patrick, J., Nov. 26, 1878, age 23.
MacNoe, Isabella, wife of George, July 9, 1871.
Macomber, Ellen, wife of E., Oct. 7, 1880, age 55 y, 1 m, 20 d; bur. at Erie, PA.
Macomber, Patience, widow of Luke, Colden, Jan. 12, 1878, age 85.
Macomber, Zebedee A., Sept. 21, 1868, age 79; father of Charles A.
Macconnell, John, Dec. 10, 1876, age 83; taken to Canandaigua.
Macy, Francis G., formerly of Buffalo, May 11, 1858, age 65; in New York.
Macy, Henry G., only son of Samuel H., formerly of Buffalo, Feb. 13, 1855, age 37; at Decatur, IL.
Macy, John B. Jr., only son of John B., formerly of Buffalo, Feb. 26, 1851, age 27; at Fond du Lac, WI.
Macy, Mary. Obituary Nov. 1872.
Macy, Mary, widow of John B., Nov. 4, 1877, age 79.
Macy, Samuel H., May 31, 1865, age 74.
Macy, Mrs. Sarah, Aug. 19, 1856, age 78 y, 16 d; taken to Geneva, NY.
Madden, Charles E., Dec. 15, 1877, age 32 y, 6 m.
Madden, Edward, late Alderman of Buffalo, Feb. 15, 1870, age 55 y, 9 m, 13 d.
Madison, Mrs., Sardinia, July 1873, age 84.
Madison, Albert B., son of William, formerly of Buffalo, Aug. 26, 1876, age 39; d. at Mackinac, MI.
Madison, Eliza A., wife of James H., March 26, 1862, age 25; taken to Silver Creek, NY.
Madison, Sergt. Joseph, youngest son of William, formerly of Buffalo, April 26, 1865, age 20; at Mackinac, MI.
Madison, Nellie M., formerly of Buffalo, Feb. 6, 1871; d. at Springfield, MO.
Madison, Otis, Nov. 16, 1872.
Madison, William Henry H., 2nd son of William, Dec. 14, 1855, in 21st year; lost at sea.
Magee, Adeline, wife of John H., May 30, 1880, age 47 y, 5 m, 22 d.
Mager (Mayer), Mrs. Elizabeth, mother of C. S., April 29, 1848, age 72 y, 4 m.
Manany, Dennis, Sept. 13, 1873, age 23.
Mahar, Peter, Aug. 15, 1877, age 25.
Maharg, Mrs. Elizabeth, Oct. 30, 1860, age 85.
Maharg, John, Sept. 14, 1863, age 55.
Maharg, Sarah, widow of John, Dec. 20, 1872, age 55.
Maher, Ann, wife of Martin, Oct. 7, 1875, age 30 y, 5 m.
Maher, John, Oct. 5, 1874, age 32 y, 2 m, 1 d.
Maher, John J., Jan. 10, 1880, age 22 y, 2 m, 20 d.
Maher, Mary, dau. of Patrick, Nov. 17, 1875, age 23 y, 8 m.
Maher, William, accidental death, Nov. 19, 1875.
Mahon, Dennis, Sept. 23, 1874, age 55.
Mahon, John, May 20, 1831, age 30.
Mahon, Martha Ann, wife of Samuel of Ira Harris' Cavalry, N.Y.V., May 21, 1863.
Mahoney, Mrs. Catharine, Oct. 20, 1876, age 78.
Mahoney, Catherine, July 7, 1878, age 30.
Mahoney, Cornelius, March 6, 1875, age 35.
Mahoney, Cornelius, April 4, 1877, age 65.
Mahoney, Mrs. D., suicide, Sept. 25, 1877, age c. 45.
Mahoney, Ellen, wife of Dennis, Aug. 21, 1873, age 33 y, 6 m.
Mahoney, Ellen, March 2, 1875.
Mahoney, Ellen, Jan. 1876, age 27 y, 2 m.
Mahoney, James, July 27, 1879, age 38; drowned.
Mahoney, Julia, May 12, 1879, age 73.
Mahoney, Kate, Sept. 12, 1874, age 24 y, 6 .
Mahoney, Mrs. Mary, Feb. 24, 1878.
Mahoney, Mary, Oct. 6, 1879, age 21.
Mahoney, William, Sept. 4, 1875, age 24.
Mahony, Lucy, wife of James, April 2, 1869, age 24; dau. of the late James Flynn of Buffalo.

Mahor, Mrs. Ann, July 15, 1856, age 45.
Mahor, John, July 16, 1856, age 45.
Maier, John, Oct. 3, 1876, age 51 y, 1 m, 25 d.
Main, Ann, West Seneca, Erie Co., July 3, 1862, age 85. Limestone Ridge.
Main, Jane Elizabeth, wife of Miles, Lancaster, NY, March 14, 1859, in 24th year.
Main, Mary, April 1, 1872, age 84.
Mallon, Mrs. Hugh, Feb. 25, 1844, age 28.
Mallon, James, Evans, Oct. 2, 1880, age 79.
Mallon, Mrs. Margaret, wife of Daniel, May 5, 1879, age 68 y, 8 m.
Mallon, Mary A. Christian, wife of Capt. Hugh, Dec. 6, 1874, age 47.
Mallory, Sterling, father of James A. of Buffalo, recently of Water Valley, NY, Aug. 15, 1850; Milwaukee, WI.
Malloy, Catharine, June 25, 1878, age 61.
Malloy, William S., Feb. 25, 1849, age 27.
Malone, David, April 8, 1873, age 68.
Malone, Mary, Aug. 20, 1880, age 80.
Malone, Mary Ann, eldest dau. of Patrick, May 13, 1863, age 21.
Malone, Patrick, Co. Almshouse, Oct. 29, 1876, age 54.
Maloney, Mrs. Elizabeth, Dec. 7, 1865, age 60.
Maloney, Mrs. Helen, Nov. 22, 1874, age 30.
Maloney, John, Co. Almshouse, Oct. 11, 1880, age 70.
Malony, Johanna, May 17, 1875, age 21 y, 17 d.
Maltbie, Miss Fanny, youngest dau. of Isaac F., Nov. 21, 1862.
Maltby, Hattie A., wife of F. A., Derby, Oct. 7, 1877, age 25 y, 11 m, 27 d.
Maltby, Isaac F., March 17, 1846, age 39.
Maltby, Lucinda, widow of Gen. Isaac of Waterloo, NY, June 9, 1844, age 73; taken to Waterloo.
Mampel, Ernest, Aug. 23, 1880, age 40 y, 1 d.
Managan, John, May 25, 1872, age 40.
Managan, Patrick, Jan. 4, 1872, age 67.
Manaher, Mary, June 14, 1880, age 76.
Manay, Hattie, wife of A., only dau. of John S. Wald, formerly of Hamburgh, NY, March 23, 1864, age 22; in Cherry Tree, Venango Co., PA.
Manchester, Bradford A., banker, May 3, 1862, age 47.
Manchester, Edward B., son of the late Bradford A., March 10, 1872, age 23.
Mandet, Charles, railroad employee, Oct. 15, 1880, age 40.
Mane, Rosa, wife of John, Aug. 13, 1849, age 23.
Maney (Meany), Mrs. Bridget, April 3, 1874, age 60.
Mang, August. Died 1860. Body transferred from North St. Cemetery to Forest Lawn, 1902.
Mang, Catherine. Died 1878. Bur. in North St. Cemetery, body transferred to Ridge Lawn Cemetery May 1901.
Mang, Clara. Died 1879. Bur. in North St. Cemetery, body transferred to Forest Lawn Cemetery, 1902.
Mang, Mrs. Elizabeth C., April 12, 1878, age 69.
Mang, Phineas, April 21, 1873, age 25 y, 9 m, 14 d.
Manghan, Louise C., wife of James Jr., Black Rock, March 14, 1870, age 22y, 7 m.
Mangold, Jacob, Sept. 28, 1873, age 47.
Mangs, Louis, July 17, 1875, age 37.
Mangus (Mange/Manges), William, suicide, Sept. 4, 1876, age 52.
Manhart, Leana, wife of Jacob, Jan. 13, 1880, age 40 y, 7 m.
Manke, Charles (Carl), Elma, Erie Co. farmer, May 14, 1880, age 50? 52. Executed at Erie Co. Jail for murder of John Atloff.
Manley, Minerva, wife of William R., dau. of Gen. Orville Clark, March 29, 1857, in 26th year; at Sandy Hill, NY.
Manley, R. S., formerly of Buffalo, July 30, 1865, age 29. Lost from Steamer *Brother Jonathan*, off coast of CA. Bur. at Upper Bluff, CA.
Manley, Will D., formerly of Buffalo, July 25, 1880, age 24; bur. at Jamestown.
Manly, George, July 19, 1852, age 35.
Manly, John, Sept. 1871; bur. Sept. 8.
Mann, Anna D., wife of William W., July 21, 1866, age 51 y, 7 m.

Mann, Charles, Elma, suicide, June 12, 1873.
Mann, Clara Eugenie, eldest dau. of C.J., March 20, 1877, age 33.
Mann, David, father of Mrs. Dr. Kenyon, formerly of Buffalo, Jan. 24, 1863, age 64; at Westfield, NY.
Mann, Mrs. Elijah, Darien Center, Jan. 8, 1875, age 76.
Mann, George, father of William B. and Charles J. of Buffalo, Sept. 29, 1863; at Yokohama, Japan. Age 74 y, 7 m, 8 d.
Mann, John, formerly of Buffalo, Wales, NY, April 18, 1828, age 38.
Mann, Mrs. Mary, March 16, 1880, age 63.
Mann, N. M., Willink, June 4, 1870, age 76.
Mann, Nancy, wife of David, Jr., Wales, NY, Oct. 21, 1823.
Mann, Owen, compositor, found drowned, Nov. 22, 1879, age 40.
Mann, Robert, Co. Almshouse, Jan. 9, 1878, age 45.
Mann, Thomas, Hamburgh, NY, Dec. 27, 1831, age 35.
Mann, William, engineer on the Lakes, Dec. 7, 1854, age 38.
Mann, William H. H., Oct. 31, 1880, age 44.
Mannin, Mrs. Patrick, April 1878.
Manning, Charles (or Thomas) April 4, 1873, age 33.
Manning, James, July 3, 1870, age 33; night watchman at the Buffalo Steam Forge.
Manning, John, Jan. 30, 1878, age 38; d. at Petrolia, PA, bur. in Buffalo.
Manning, Mary, Oct. 11, 1878, age 83.
Manning, Patrick, July 5, 1874, age 28 y, 7 m, 28 d.
Manning, William, May 30, 1874, age 64.
Manser, Mary, wife of Thomas, March 19, 1875, age 86 y, 9 m.
Manser, Thomas, May 8, 1875, age 87.
Mansfield, Emma Eleanor, Aug. 12, 1856, wife of Dr. W. Q.
Mansfield, Mrs., wife of Gen. Orange, Clarence, NY, Jan. 29, 1831.
Mansfield, Eleanor, wife of Dr. W. Q., Aug. 12, 1856.
Manville, Emily S., mother of Mrs. Dr. A. W. Brown, and Mrs. James H. Wilgus of New York, formerly of Buffalo, Sept. 18, 1860, age 65; in Westfield, NJ.
Mapelsden, Henry, Eden, NY, July 15, 1864, age 90.
Mapes, Sarah H., wife of Stephen, Aug. 9, 1867, age 29.
Mapes, Stephen, June 12, 1871, age 43.
Mapes, E., wife of Deacon Josiah, Aurora, formerly of Milo, Yates Co., NY, Sept. 27, 1831, age 50.
Maples, J. Lee, South Wales, NY, April 17, 1848, age 38.
Maples, Josiah, b. 1762, d. 1847, bur. E. Aurora; Soldier of the Revolution.
Marble, Danforth, May 13, 1849.
Marchand, Louis, Dec. 12, 1872, age 36.
Marcy, Betsey, Nov. 20, 1838, age 31, wife of D. G.
Marcy, Edward, June 25, 1854, age 32; d. in Detroit, MI.
Marcy, Oliver M., brother of D. G., formerly of Buffalo, Nov. 27, 1850, age 28; in San Francisco, CA.
Marcy, Mrs. Sarah, mother of D. G., formerly of Buffalo, June 6, 1848, age 60; at Webster, MA.
Mareus, Rosalie, July 9, 1879, age 86.
Marhover, Jacob, Nov. 14, 1875, age 37 y, 5 m, 14 d.
Markham, G. T., Oct. 24, 1877, age 34; bur. at Elma.
Markham, Lizzie, widow of G. T., July 8, 1878, age 34.
Markham, Miss Maggie C. of M., Nov. 13, 1872, age 20.
Markham, Stephen, Elma, April 1, 1879, age 70; d. in Wilmington, DE; bur. in Elma.
Marlin, George, formerly of Buffalo, Co. A, Porter Guards, 10th Regt., N.Y. Cavalry, July 29, 1862; killed by the cars.
Marlo (Marlow/Morlo), John, soldier, Feb. 1880?, disappeared in Nov. 1879, found dead in Canal Feb. 28, 1880.
Marnane, John, Jan. 8, 1878, age 65.
Marratt, Thomas, Sept. 1828, age 30.
Marsden (Mundson), Charles A., drowned, Sept. 19, 1878.
Marsden, Jonathan G., Buffalo?, May 8, 1879, age 50. Drowned, no relatives in this country.
Marsh, Amarillas, widow of L. W., Aug. 8, 1876, age 45; taken to Rochester.

Marsh, Charles Henry. (BDC Sept. 10, 1873)
Marsh, Joseph, June 7, 1876, age 68.
Marsh, Lucy Ann, wife of LeRoy W., dau. of Philander Wheeler, formerly of VT, Jan. 22, 1849, age 25.
Marsh, Mary, wife of George D., Jan. 26, 1877, age 22.
Marsh, Mrs. Mary Ann, Jan. 13, 1859, age 55.
Marsh, Phineas S., Aug. 28, 1876, Aug. 28, 1876, age 58, d. in NY City, bur. in Buffalo.
Marsh, Ray, proprietor of the Eastern Hotel, Jan. 30, 1849; taken to Rochester.
Marsh, Ray, April 10, 1849, age 80.
Marsh, Samuel, formerly of Clarence, May 16, 1874; d. at West LeRoy, MI.
Marshall, Anthony, Aug. 6, 1872, age 58 y, 6 m, 19 d.
Marshall, George W., Sept. 8, 1869, age 29 y, 6 m, 7 d.
Marshall, Charles B., April 2, 1866, age 62 y, 1 m.
Marshall, Capt. John, of Brig. *Iroquois* of Clayton, Jefferson Co., NY, Aug. 20, 1854, age 32.
Marshall, Dr. John Ellis, Dec. 27, 1838, age 53, father of Orsamus H. Marshall.
Marshall, Josiah T., Nov. 23, 1875, age 72.
Marshall, Mary Ann, June 11, 1879, age 40; by laudanum.
Marshall, Patrick, Nov. 21, 1880, age 22 y, 6 m.
Marshall, Rosalie Rontine, widow of John, Dec. 2, 1874, age 64 y, 1 m.
Marshall, Ruth Holmes, widow of Dr. John E., Sept. 29, 1878, age 88 y, 9 d.
Marshall, Thomas, railroad accident, Mill Grove, July 28, 1878.
Martel, Joseph, Dec. 8, 1864, age 26.
Martin, Aaron, supervisor of 13th Ward, Sept. 1, 1861, age 55.
Martin, Adelina M. W., Alden, Nov. 14, 1878, age 71; wife of Isaac H.
Martin, Alice Elizabeth, wife of George A., Aug. 2, 1871, age 38; taken to Lockport.
Martin, Mrs. Barbara, June 14, 1875, age 75.
Martin, Bethel, fell during the War of 1812 (Jan. 1814)
Martin, Christian, wife of William, Jan. 4, 1872, age 50.
Martin, David, Feb. 5, 1872, age 54.
Martin, Delos Washington, Evans, May 5, 1867, age 23.
Martin, Mrs. Ellen, March 16, 1879, age 87.
Martin, Frances Charlotte, wife of Lieut. Martin, 2nd Reg., U.S. Inf., Oct. 25, 1846, age 22.
Martin, Frederick, July 1, 1871, age 22.
Martin, Guy Carleton Jr., Sept. 15, 1878, age 26 y, 7 m, 5 d.
Martin, Helen J., wife of Frederick S., March 10, 1878.
Martin, Henry, railroad accident, Oct. 16, 1877, age 45.
Martin, Henry S., Dec. 16, 1857, age 30.
Martin, Rev. J. Sella, formerly of Buffalo, Aug. 11, 1876.
Martin, Jacob, at Wende Station on the Central Railroad, laborer, Aug. 13, 1872.
Martin, John, Aug. 18, 1868, age 46.
Martin, John, March 9, 1870, age 32 y, 8 m.
Martin, John, Jan. 13, 1876, age 28.
Martin, Malinda, widow of John, of Stronach, MI, Aug. 19, 1874.
Martin, Maria E., Wales Centre, NY, Jan. 25, 1864, age 27 y, 14 d. Wife of William N. Martin; only dau. of S. J. Searls.
Martin, Martha O., wife of John M., sister of Noah P. and Dr. A. S. Sprague, formerly of Buffalo, July 3, 1852, age 44; in Peacham, VT.
Martin, Mrs. Mary, May 27, 1866, age 59 y, 9 m.
Martin, Mary, Aptil 8, 1876, age 65.
Martin, Mary, Dec. 26, 1880, age 45; Almshouse.
Martin, Mary Louisa, wife of E. M., dau. of George W. Allen, July 18, 1860, age 31.
Martin, Pernina, wife of Jesse, March 6, 1855, age 33.
Martin, Capt. Robert, May 21, 1867, age 45.
Martin, Mrs. Sarah, Dec. 21, 1876, age 79.
Martin, William, March 30, 1863.
Martin, William A., Dec. 26, 1878, age 23.
Martindale, L. K., Sept. 7, 1870, suicide during temporary insanity.
Martine, Catharine, wife of Joseph Z., Feb. 12, 1869, age 58.

Martine, Joseph T., formerly of Buffalo, Sept. 28, 1879, age 73; d. at Niagara Falls.
Martyn, Margaret Jefford, wife of William T., late of Quebec, Canada, Feb. 29, 1844.
Marvel, Mrs., mother of Charles, June 3, 1860, age 80.
Marvel (Marble), Charles, April 27, 1876, age 62.
Marvel, Mrs. Mary A., Dec. 20, 1874, age 56.
Marvin, Ann Eliza, wife of Z. H., Nov. 6, 1872, age 38.
Marvin, Asa, father of Le Grand and George L., late of Norwalk, CT, Dec. 12, 1849, age 71.
Marvin, Mrs. Charles A., Aug. 1871, age 27; taken to Laporte, IN.
Marvin, Charles A., formerly of Buffalo, June 21, 1875, age 33; d. in Utica, bur. in Buffalo.
Marvin, Emma Maria, May 23, 1879, age 22.
Marvin, Frederick W., railroad accident, Dec. 29, 1876.
Marvin, James, April 26, 1880, age 78.
Marvin, Lucy, wife of Sylvanus, May 1825, age 25.
Marvin, Mrs. Sarah L., widow of Asa, mother of Le Grand and George L., Dec. 29, 1863, age 82.
Marvin, Sylvanus, Sept. 5, 1831, age 35.
Marvin, Theresa C., wife of Henry, formerly of Buffalo, March 11, 1872; d. at Niagara Falls.
Marvine, Edward C., Nov. 26, 1878, age 39; taken to Auburn.
Mary, Mrs. Theresa, mother of Charles, Oct. 17, 1873, age 67; taken to Geneva.
Mary Ursula, "Sister," Sister of Charity, formerly of Buffalo, April 10, 1874, age 71; d. in Baltimore, MD.
Maske, J. F., drowned, Aug. 13, 1876, age 27.
Mason, Mrs. Altana, Nov. 8, 1861, age 65.
Mason, Andrew S. (or G.), formerly of Buffalo, Dec. 24, 1870, in East Aurora, NY, age 51; bur. in Buffalo.
Mason, Arnold W., Marilla, NY, Feb. 26, 1858, age 29.
Mason, Eliza P., wife of David H., dau. of E.B. Cobb, Dec. 2, 1868, age 44.
Mason, Elizabeth, wife of Capt. Robert, Feb. 11, 1878, age 33.
Mason, George Dove, formerly from Melbourne near Pocklington, Yorkshire, England, Aug. 17, 1853, age 30.
Mason, Harriet A., wife of Frank B., Aug. 29, 1874, age 28.
Mason, James, Sept. 1832, 45.
Mason, John, April 18, 1874, age 70.
Mason, Joseph, April 8, 1851, age 71.
Mason, Joseph B., letter-carrier, Oct. 27, 1875, age 39 y, 1 m.
Mason, Marion, wife of Charles R., Sept. 10, 1871, age 18 y, 10 m.
Mason, Mary A., wife of Amasa, Sept. 4, 1859, age 27 y, 9 m.
Mason, Mary M., widow of Andrew S., Aurora, Jan. 15, 1874, age 49 y, 4 m, 6 d; bur. in Buffalo.
Mason, Sarah Jane, dau. of Daniel, Jan. 11, 1877, age 31.
Mason, William G., son of Joseph, June 4, 1849, age 21.
Mason, William H., son of John, Dec. 26, 1872, age 35.
Mason, WIlliam H., April 24, 1873, age 36.
Mason, William W., Oct. 26, 1860, age 48.
Mass (Moss), Frederick, railroad accident, April 2, 1878, age 21.
Massing, Louis, accidently killed, March 1, 1873, age 42.
Masten, Agnes, mother of Judge Masten, May 29, 1859, age 73.
Masten, Miss Ann, April 9, 1840, age 65.
Masten, Capt. Frederick H., Sept. 8, 1874, age 63.
Masten, Frederick H., Feb. 4, 1876, age 31.
Masten, John, April 18, 1871, age 55.
Masten, Judge Joseph G., April 14, 1871, age 62.
Masten, Seth F., Aug. 12, 1848, age 29 y, 3 m.
Masters, Eugene J., son of Capt. Robert, of Jefferson, WI, Dec. 7, 1841, age 23 y, 8 m.
Masters, Mrs. Orrin Abbott, Co. Almshouse, Aug. 10, 1876, age 67.
Masters, Samuel, May 25, 1867, age 23.
Masterson, Mrs. Catherine, Feb. 24, 1879, age 49 y, 8 m.
Masterson, Edward, April 9, 1874, age 52.
Masterson, Frank, July 25, 1866, age 31 y, 6 m, 25 d.

Mather, Mrs. Aschsah Seaver, Clarence, NY, Sept. 3, 1856, age 82.
Mather, Joseph, Clarence, NY, Sept. 14, 1862, age 96 y, 2 m, 10 d.
Matheson, Grace (Obituary May 1866)
Mathews, Mrs. Charlotte, North Evans, NY, Feb. 6, 1851, age 74.
Mathews, E. B., widow of Gen. Sylvester, formerly of Buffalo, Nov. 24, 1863, Columbus, OH.
Mathews, Miss Emily Maria, June 12, 1855, age 23.
Mathews, Jacob, Co. Almshouse, April 17, 1876, age 27.
Mathews, Lieut. John H., son of Gen. S. of Buffalo, c. Sept. 3, 1838, age 20. US Army.
Mathews, Kinyon, June 5, 1856, age 51 in Columbus, OH.
Mathews, Mrs. Kinyon, June 19, 1858, age 48.
Mathews, Morris S., March 31, 1855, age 19 y, 11 m.
Mattchet, Mrs. Almyra, April 24, 1854, age 22.
Matterson, William, Jan. 5, 1866, age 41.
Matteson, Carlos W., eldest son of H. H., March 22, 1879, age 41 y, 8 m, 18 d; d. in San
    Quentin, CA.
Matteson, Ellis M., "pedlar," Aug. 2, 1879, age 27.
Matteson, Harriet White, wife of Major Henry H., Aug. 27, 1849; d. and bur. at Gowanda, NY.
Matteson, Mary, Boston, NY, Sept. 11, 1871, age 60.
Matteson, Philip, b. 1759, d. 1827, bur. Buffalo; Soldier of the Revolution.
Matteson, Rhodes, Boston, NY, Aug. 30, 1871.
Matteson, Sarah, June 18, 1855, age 84.
Matthews, Mrs. Elizabeth, Aug. 1, 1871, age 78.
Matthews, Louisa Bliss, wife of Sylvester, June 9, 1823, age 23.
Matthews, Mary, Sept. 30, 1878, age 45.
Matthews, Mary A. Paxson, wife of L. B., East Hamburgh, July 6, 1874, age 68.
Matthews, Gen. Sylvester, Aug. 10, 1842.
Matthews, William, Andersonville, GA, Nov. 4, 1864, age 25 y, 4 m. Member Co. I, 155th NYS
    Vols., interred in Forest Lawn with military honors.
Mattice, F. M., Dec. 1876, age 64; d. in Cleveland, bur. Buffalo.
Mattison, Charlotte, widow of William, March 30, 1866, age 39.
Mattison, Ellen, wife of Charles T., Jan. 7, 1863, age 36.
Mattson, Susan, wife of John C., March 17, 1874, age 41.
Maugham, Alice, dau. of James & Elizabeth, Sept. 28, 1873, age 22.
Maurer, John F., Sept. 7, 1878.
Maurer, Louis P., March 19, 1874, age 38 y, 10 m, 5 d.
Maurer, Mary E., April 10, 1870, age 59, wife of John.
Maurice, Martin, March 2, 1874, age 33 y, 2 m, 7 d.
Maxon, Alanson, formerly of Buffalo, Sept. 26, 1873, age 53; d. at Jacksonville, FL.
Maxon, Clark, June 25, 1832, age 60.
Maxwell, Elizabeth H., wife of Joshua, Sept. 8, 1870, age 65.
Maxwell, Mrs. Eunice, mother-in-law of H. Slade, April 12, 1844, age 82.
Maxwell, Joseph (Joshua/Thomas), April 1, 1874.
Maxwell, Joshua, March 20, 1880, age 70.
Maxwell, Lydia Ann, wife of Joshua, Aug. 18, 1842, age 34.
May, Rev. Biram, Lancaster, Dec. 7, 1876, age 79.
May, Ellen M., wife of William J., late of Buffalo, Jan. 11, 1848; in Cleveland, OH.
May, Martha, wife of Patrick, July 1822; on Schooner *Hannah* bound for Detroit, MI.
May, William, Lancaster, NY, May 19, 1859, age 71.
May, Mrs. William, Bowmansville, March 13, 1870, age 73 y, 3 m, 7 d.
Mayberry, Catharine, wife of George, Oct. 4, 1851.
Maybury, George, June 1858; bur. the 28th.
Mayer, Joseph, accidental death, June 7, 1877, age 53.
Mayer, Tiney, wife of George C., formerly of Buffalo, May 15, 1875, age 32 y, 7 m, 18 d.
Mayer, William J., Feb. 5, 1880, age 32 y, 7 m, 17 d.
Mayhew, Frederick A., May 14, 1871, age 42.
Mayloth, Mrs. Magdalena, May 23, 1877, age 67.
Maynard, Elisha Allen, May 5, 1866, age 61 y, 2 m, 7 d.
Maynard, Emeline B., wife of Robert H., April 7, 1866.
Maynard, Mrs. Nancy, formerly of Greene Co., NY, Feb. 14, 1852, age 44.
Maynard, Robert H., Nov. 17, 1876, age 73.

Mayne, Louisa, wife of Richard T., Sept. 19, 1880, age 40.
Mayo, Nancy M., wife of E., Concord, NY, Feb. 15, 1852, age 42.
Mayo, Olive, wife of Charles P., Dec. 12, 1835, age 28.
Mayo, Mr. S.J.G., Griffins Mills, NY, Feb. 10, 1842, age 21.
Maytham, Capt. John, Oct. 1, 1878.
Maythan, George, formerly of Buffalo, Oct. 3, 1879, age 37; d. at Larned, Pawnee Co., KS.
McAdams, John, Oct. 3, 1867, age 59 in Sisters of Charity Hospital.
McAlester, Bvt. Brigade Gen. Miles D., Major of Engineers, USA, April 23, 1869, age 36.
McAllester, A. W., (Obituary Nov 1860)
McAllester, Miriam G., wife of Ebenezer, Aug. 19, 1858, age 72.
McAllister, Widow Anna, Aug. 6, 1832, age 49.
McAllister, Archibald W., Nov. 19, 1860, age 49.
McAllister, Ebenezer, June 1, 1868, age 87.
McAloon, James, Dec. 15, 1875, age 27.
McAloon, John, Dec. 30, 1874, age 65.
McAloon, John, April 27, 1879, age 28.
McAndrew, Patrick, Sept. 29, 1876.
McArthur, Arthur, Dec. 4, 1871, age 64.
McArthur, John, Dec. 25, 1875, age 86.
McArthur, Margaret, Feb. 20, 1868, age 81.
McArthur, Rachel, wife of Arthur, Jan. 4, 1869.
McAuliffe, Daniel, b. Ireland, d. June 11, 1872, age 66.
McAuliffe, Hannah, only dau. of Daniel, May 9, 1869, age 22.
McAuliffe, Jeremiah, Nov. 18, 1878, age 67.
McBean, Mrs. Margaret, May 21, 1870, age 53 y, 5 m, 6 d.
McBeth, Clara P. Taber, wife of Dr. John, Wales Center, Feb. 24, 1876.
McBridfe, Capt. D. H. (Obituary March 1871)
McBride, J. J., March 28, 1877; drowned at Boston, MA.
McBride, Marinda, wife of William, Sept. 2, 1854.
McBryer, Naomi, Dec. 3, 1876, age 47.
McBurney, Catherine E. Fortien, wife of John, Aug. 1, 1867, age 37.
McCabe, Barney, June 7, 1880, age 22 y, 5 m, 2 d.
McCabe, Bernard, April 18, 1851, age 31.
McCabe, Mrs. Bridget, mother of Hugh, July 31, 1878, age 80.
McCabe, Catherine, Nov. 30, 1880, age 79.
McCabe, Joanna, April 22, 1873, age 30.
McCabe, John, March 5, 1874, age 21.
McCabe, Joseph, accidently killed, April 20, 1872.
McCaber, Michael, Aug. 10, 1876, age 83.
McCabe, Michael, Aug. 20, 1880, age 85.
McCabe, Patrick, Aug. 31, 1874, age 69 y, 5 m, 14 d.
McCaffrey, Ann, Feb. 18, 1864, age 75.
McCall, Celicia, wife of Ira, formerly of South Wales, April 10, 1872; d. near Saratoga, Santa Clara Co., CA.
McCall, Ella, formerly of Buffalo, July 17, 1878, age 17; suicide, d. in New York City.
McCall, Thaddeus C., April 22, 1867, age 25.
McCann, Mr., Oct. 20, 1870.
McCarney, Capt. Niel, Aug. 12, 1865, age 32.
McCarney, Peter, May 5, 1865, age 58.
McCarrick, George F., May 10, 1877, age 36 y, 9 m, 6 d; taken to Grand Island.
McCarrick, Martin, accidental death, formerly of Buffalo, April 5, 1874, age 22.
McCarroll, William, Dec. 4, 1863, age 29.
McCarthy, Agnes, wife of John, March 8, 1876, age 46.
McCarthy, Alexander, Aug. 14, 1877.
McCarthy, Ann, Dec. 4, 1880, age 70.
McCarthy, Catherine, widow of John, Aug. 20, 1875, age 61.
McCarthy, Cornelius, Dec. 16, 1865, age 67.
McCarthy, Dennis, Aug. 7, 1870, age 22.
McCarthy, Ellen McIntyre, Jan. 11, 1880, age 28 y, 8 m.
McCarthy, Florence, May 16, 1871.

McCarthy, James, Sept. 6, 1870, age 22.
McCarthy, James, Co. Almshouse, April 3, 1878, age 49.
McCarthy, Mrs. Jane Burns, widow of Theodore Burns, Feb. 26, 1880, age 53.
McCarthy, Katy Ella, Dec. 6, 1879, age 25.
McCarthy, Louis, Oct. 5, 1870, age 25.
McCarthy, Maggie, wife of Cornelius, July 1872.
McCarthy, Margaret, Jan. 8, 1879, age 40.
McCarthy, Matilda, wife of Richard, Nov. 8, 1858.
McCarthy, Timothy, April 27, 1879, age 35.
McCarthy, William May 14, 1871, age c. 20.
McCarthy, William, Sept. 16, 1873, age 26.
McCarty, Hannorah, wife of John, March 17, 1847, age 40.
McCarty, John, Jan. 29, 1871, age 48.
McCarty, John, July 27, 1877, age 24.
McCarty, John J., May 2, 1871.
McCaul, John, printer, Feb. 1872; d. at Mumford, NY, bur. Buffalo.
McCay, Maria, Co. Almshouse, March 16, 1877, age 70.
McClanan, Mrs. Eleanor, Feb. 20, 1837, age 67.
McClanan, Miss Serena, Oct. 14, 1864.
McClannan, James, jeweler, Aug. 19, 1840.
McClary, John, East Hamburgh, NY, Oct. 27, 1867, age 71.
McClary, Mrs. Wealthy, East Hamburgh, Oct. 3, 1877, age 75 y, 3 m.
McClean, Miss Rachel formerly of Hartford, CT, Springville, NY, Oct. 10, 1859, age 85.
McCleary, Dr. Daniel, Clarence, NY, Jan. 2, 1816, age 32.
McClerg, George, Feb. 2, 1877, age 54.
McClevey, William, Sept. 24, 1847, age 33.
McCloskey, John, June 30, 1871.
McClroe(?), James, Nov. 28, 1841, age 24.
McCluer, Heman, Angola, NY, May 2, 1859, age 73 y, 10 m.
McClur, Henry C., formerly of Hamburgh, Jan. 18, 1871, age 59; d. at Decatur, MI.
McClure, Jane, lunatic, suicide, Feb. 24, 1875.
McClure, Julia, wife of A. B., formerly of Buffalo, Sept. 12, 1872; d. at Wilkesbarre, PA.
McClure, Maria, wife of Joseph, April 17, 1858, age 42.
McClure, Martha, wife of Heman, Angola, NY, Dec. 27, 1860, age 72.
McClure, Robert, found dead in bed, Colden, May 5, 1877; d. at Brown's Hotel, Buffalo.
McCollom, P. F., Nov. 24, 1861, age 61.
McCollum, Mrs. Catharine, Feb. 24, 1871, age 65.
McCollum, Laura A., wife of Otis, Oct. 12, 1876, age 50.
McComb, Mrs. Elizabeth, Seneca Road, July 4, 1872, age 81.
McComb, John, drowned June 8, 1873, age 27.
McComb, William, eldest son of Robert, Nov. 3, 1877, age 27 y, 11 m, 21 d.
McCombs, Thomas, Dec. 13, 1859, age 31.
McConnell, James, Dec. 25, 1876, age 47.
McConnell, Joseph Dow, March 7, 1874, age 69.
McConnell, Michael, West Seneca, Dec. 2, 1872, age 60 y, 10 m, 27 d.
McConville, John, formerly of Buffalo, March 11, 1880, age 41 y, 11 m, 24 d; d. at Soldiers' Home, Bath, NY.
McConville, Mrs. Mary, Sept. 28, 1871, age 58.
McConvy, John, March 28, 1869, age 28.
McCook, Mrs., native of Scotland, April 14, 1871, age 80.
McCool, Margaret, wife of James, Sept. 13, 1879.
McCoord (McCourt/McCord), Andrew, July 8, 1872, age 45.
McCoord, Mrs. Jane M., Sept. 13, 1861, age 22.
McCord, Daniel, son of Widow O'Brian, Feb. 24, 1845, age 20.
McCormic, Mrs. Margaret, Sept. 2, 1870, age 69; at the "church home."
McCormick, Mrs., Black Rock, NY, March 27, 1843.
McCormick, Edward P., Nov. 7, 1873, age 20.
McCormick, Peter, accidental death, Jan. 4, 1876, age 55.
McCourt, Catherine, Sept. 3, 1873, age 44; wife of John.
McCourt, Dehlia E., Feb. 8, 1870, age 21.

McCourt, James, June 26, 1847, age 33; in Troy, NY, bur. in Buffalo.
McCoy, Elizabeth, wife of J. A., Feb. 8, 1868, age 27; d. at Paris, Ontario.
McCoy, M. A., formerly of Buffalo, Sept. 2, 1877; d. at Omaha, NE.
McCray, Samuel, Oct. 22, 1880, age 56; Almshouse.
McCready, Andrew S., June 12, 1850, age 52; in St. Louis, MO.
McCready, Charlotte Stevens, wife of James, May 19, 1875, age 64.
McCready, Jeannie S., Sept. 20, 1861, age 26.
McCready, Richard R., April 9, 1860, age 23.
McCredie, Elizabeth Lorena, wife of W. B., July 14, 1853, age 22 y, 10 m.
McCredie, James A. Sr., of Savannah, GA, Nov. 6, 1846, age 56.
McCredie, William B., printer, April 27, 1855, age 35.
McCrogan, Thomas, May 19, 1871, age 75.
McCrowell, Rachel, dau. of Henry, Feb. 1878, age 21 y, 10 m.
McCue, P., Oct. 20, 1877, age 77.
McCuffery, James, alias Jimmy Papes, formerly of Buffalo, thief, July 1879, age 44?; d. at Toronto, Canada.
McCulloch, Alexander, Sept. 27, 1846, age 41.
McCulloch, Alexander, March 23, 1847, age 75.
McCullock, Mrs. Elmira, Dec. 13, 1880, age 63.
McCullor, Charles H., Evans, Nov. 15, 1876, age 57.
McCullor, Levi, Evans, May 4, 1874, age 91.
McCullough, John, formerly of Buffalo, Dec. 5, 1876, age 22; lost in the burning of Brooklyn theater.
McCumber, Martha Maria, wife of Orlando, April 8, 1860, age 34; taken to Colden, NY.
McCurrie, Absalom, Hamburgh, NY, Dec. 1812, age 30.
McDaie, Catharine, Aug. 28, 1870, age 24.
McDearbon, Charlotte, wife of Joseph, Aurora, NY, June 10, 1838, age 53.
McDermot, Anna, wife of William, Oct. 7, 1871, age 41.
McDermot, Ellen, Sept. 13, 1878, age 21 y, 3 m, 28 d.
McDermot, Mrs. Margaret, May 21, 1877, age 72.
McDermot, Mary A., Sept. 9, 1870, age 42.
McDermott, Daniel, Sept. 21, 1878, age c. 50.
McDermott, Francis C., April 24, 1872, age 35 y, 4 m.
McDermott, Hugh, Oct. 26, 1875, age 60.
McDermott, John, June 1, 1851, age 50.
McDermott, Michael, Sept. 19, 1879, age 52.
McDole, Isabella, April 10, 1859, age 31.
McDonald, Bernhard, July 21, 1880, age 87.
McDonald, Daniel, chairmaker, May 1, 1849, age 23.
McDonald, David B., Corp. of Co. H, 116th Regt., N.Y.V., brother of C. R. of Buffalo; killed at Battle of Cedar Creek, Oct. 19, 1864, age 21 y, 7 m.
McDonald, Donald, March 19, 1872, age 58.
McDonald, Elizabeth J., May 1, 1874, age 44.
McDonald, Capt. James, 14th U.S. Inf., Nov. 11, 1814.
McDonald, John, Aug. 26, 1857, age 65 y, 6 m.
McDonald, John G., March 17, 1876, age 27; taken to Batavia.
McDonald, Kate, Dec. 31, 1871.
McDonald, Margaret, June 20, 1878, age 20 y, 7 m.
McDonald, Martin, Dec. 25, 1879, age 72; Almshouse.
McDonald, Mary Ann, wife of William, Oct. 24, 1873, age 38.
McDonald, Michael, Hamburgh, NY, July 4, 1858, age 61.
McDonald, Patrick, March 18, 1871, age 60.
McDonald, Robert, Jan. 16, 1855, age 24.
McDonald, Simon, June 9, 1878; found drowned, missing since June 3.
McDonald, Thasa Maria, wife of William H., dau. of Daniel Finch, Jan. 8, 1865, age 20 y, 5 m, 2 d.
McDonald, Mrs. Thomas, Nov. 22, 1877.
McDonald, William T., July 3, 1866, age 28.
McDonell, James, formerly of Edenton, N.C., Nov. 6, 1867, age 41.
McDonnell, Mrs. M., Sept. 9, 1879, age 48; d. at Niagara Falls.

McDonnell, Mary Ann, dau. of Martin, Aug. 23, 1874, age 22 y, 4 m, 12 d.; d. at Lewiston, NY, bur. Buffalo.
McDonough, William, Co. Almshouse, June 11, 1878, age 45.
McDougal, Ronald, Sept. 16, 1867, age 63 y, 8 m, 16 d.
McDougall, Alexander, Aug. 6, 1878, age 55.
McDowell, Henry M., March 3, 1878, age 50.
McDowell, Rachel, dau. of Henry, Feb. 1878, age 21 y, 10 m.
McDuff, Capt. James, seaman and boat owner, May 16, 1880, age 43.
McElvany, Alta Palmer, wife of Charles T., March 11, 1834, age 42; taken to Hornellsville, Steuben Co., NY.
McElwain, Elizabeth, wife of W.D., Wales, Dec. 19, 1870, age 30 y, 7 m.
McEvoy, Mrs. Elizabeth, May 15, 1867, age 105 y, 11 m
McEvoy, Ellen, sister of Thomas and Elizabeth, Aug. 30, 1875, age 74.
McEwen, Abby, wife of William B., Oct. 21, 1861, age 44.
McEwen, Eliza Ann, wife of Hugh C., Jan. 1, 1879, age 45 y, 6 m, 6 d.
McEwen, Huldah, wife of Timothy, Feb. 2, 1822, age 34.
McEwen, Julian, wife of Stephen, Springville, NY, Nov. 8, 1845, age 30.
McEwen, Lalie, April 19, 1875, age 25; wife of Henry.
McEwen, Mary, wife of Timothy, East Evans, NY, May 3, 1851.
McEwen, Timothy, formerly of Buffalo, Evans, NY, July 27, 1858, age 71.
McEwen, William B., Sept. 2, 1864, age 50; taken to New London, CT.
McFarland, Eliza R., dau. of Levi, April 14, 1863, age 24.
McFarlane, Thomas, Grand Island gardener, Aug. 31, 1879, age 64; sudden death in Park.
McFaul, Laura, wife of Thomas, April 21, 1870, age 39.
McFee, John, July 14, 1876, age 85; taken to Spring Brook.
McFee, Mary, wife of Peter, Jan. 15, 1870, age 50.
McFeely, Edward, Feb. 5, 1879, age 80 y, 6 m.
McGarrey, Albert A., formerly of Buffalo, March 28, 1872, age 43; d. in St. Louis.
McGean, James, Jan. 29, 1865, age 50.
McGee, Jennie Dunn, Oct. 30, 1871, wife of P. H.
McGee, Patrick, Aug. 9, 1872, age 47.
McGetrick, Mrs. Margaret, West Seneca, March 20, 1871, age 33.
McGhie, David, May 2, 1876, age 38.
McGibbon, Joseph, Aug. 23, 1879, killed on railroad.
McGillivray, Mariana M., wife of William, Jan. 25, 1854, age 25.
McGilvray, Neal A., b. in Buffalo, d. Oct. 1880, age 32. Victim of the wreck of the Steamer *Alpena*. Home, St. Joseph, MI.
McGinnis, Mary Elizabeth, Jan. 26, 1860, age 36.
McGloin, Miss Ellen, March 21, 1879, age 40.
McGloin, Johanna Ryan, Aug. 15, 1873, age 32; wife of J.D.
McGloury, Thomas, Sept. 1827, age 38.
McGlynn, James, Jan. 8, 1868, age 58.
McGorry, Sarah, wife of Bernhard, Dec. 28, 1879, age 45.
McGowan (McGouland/McGowland), Andrew, June 3, 1852, age 67.
McGowan, Eliza, wife of Henry H., Nov. 27, 1858, age 36.
McGowan, Maggie, wife of John, Feb. 23, 1873, age 23; burned to death.
McGowan, Mrs. Margaret, mother of Mrs. R. R. Best, Jan. 27, 1855, age 78.
McGowan, Mary, formerly of Ireland, April 4, 1840.
McGowan, Mary S., widow of Andrew, Sept. 29, 1878, age 75.
McGowan, Robert H., son of Henry H., May 31, 1877, age 37 y, 10 m.
McGowan, Sarah, wife of John, Nov. 27, 1836, age 37.
McGowan, John, formerly a merchant in New York, Nov. 15, 1841, age 73.
McGrath, John H., Aug. 14, 1877, age 34.
McGrath, Mrs. Margaret, June 1873, age 60.
McGraw, Mary Frances, wife of Michael, dau. of James Farthing, Aug. 31, 1863, age 17 y, 7 m, 9 d.
McGuckian, Annie, Nov. 4, 1873, age 23 y, 1 m, 13 d.
McGuigan, Mrs. Rose, Jan. 26, 1880, age 58.
McGuigen, Patrick, March 24, 1868, age 59.
McGuire, Charles, Feb. 1880, age 74.

McGuire, Elizabeth, Irish, April 16, 1850, age 67.
McGuire, John, Co. Almshouse, Aug. 11, 1876, age 55.
McHenry, James, May 18, 1861, age 44.
McIlheron, Robert, accidental death, March 11, 1879.
McIlroy, Ann, Feb. 12, 1871, age 23 y, 5 m.
McIlvena, Henry J., Nov. 13, 1876, age 24.
McIlvina, Sarah, Oct. 27, 1879, age 50.
McIlwreth, Fanny Ann, Aug. 29, 1865, age 39; wife of Andrew.
McIndoe, Mr. J., formerly of Buffalo, Dec. 1874, age 25.
McIntosh, Mrs. Ann, Oct. 15, 1863, age 64.
McIntosh, George, Dec. 5, 1863, age 48.
McIntosh, William, April 13, 1872, age 50.
McIntyre, Mrs. Alice A., July 10, 1863, age 31.
McIntyre, Daniel, Jan. 4, 1876, age c. 36.
McIntyre, James, June 21, 1864, age 47.
McIntyre, Robert, railroad accident, May 17, 1876, age 30.
McIntyre, Rose G. Clark, wife of Robert J., July 4, 1880, age 25 y, 9 m, 27 d.
McIntyre, William, May 1880, age 25?; found drowned May 11. Last seen alive 3 weeks since, at midnight.
McIntyre, William J., July 25, 1880, age 26 y, 10 m.
McKarroll, Mrs. Mary, Dec. 26, 1871, age 23.
McKay, Agnes, April 2, 1875, age 56.
McKay, Anna Maria, wife of Alexander, July 3, 1877, age 56.
McKay, Eliza, wife of James, July 11, 1833, age 26.
McKay, Emily B., wife of Col. James, June 28, 1849, age 41.
McKay, Esther Sutherland, sister of Robert, formerly of Milwaukee, WI, June 19, 1863, age 40.
McKay, Garles, late Lt. 3d Cav., NYSV, April 12, 1870, age 28.
McKay, Lily Rose, wife of D. T., June 26, 1866, age 33.
McKay, Robert, formerly of Scotland, late of Milwaukee, WI, Aug. 28, 1862, age 60.
McKay, Sarah Ann, March 13, 1873, age 33; taken to Sultan, Ontario.
McKay, Seth, Aurora, NY, Feb. 23, 1826, age 48.
McKay, Seth, Aurora, NY, May 3, 1826, age 22.
McKean, Sally, wife of Capt. John, Nov. 26, 1823, age 35.
McKee, Mary Gager, wife of Thomas, Jan. 14, 1863, age 27; at Sandwich, Canada West.
McKee, Silence, wife of Joshua, Aug. 26, 1835, age 53.
McKeen, Almira, Aurora, NY, May 4, 1841 in Clintonville, NY; she and Robert (husband) d. at the same hour.
McKeen, Miss Annis, Wales, NY, May 5, 1836, age 29.
McKeen, Robert, Aurora, NY, age 45 y, and wife Almira, Clintonville, NY May 4, 1841. [See Almira above.]
McKeen, Sally, Aurora, NY, Feb. 17, 1845, age 24.
McKelip, Syche, wife of Robert, Clarence, NY, Aug. 12, 1832, age 36.
McKellip, Robert, Jan. 31, 1866, age 77.
McKendry, John, Co. Almshouse, June 9, 1878, age 41.
McKenna, Ellen, wife of James, Dec. 3, 1867, age 31.
McKenna, J., April 29, 1869, age 25.
McKenny, Daniel, accidental death, Nov. 4, 1875.
McKenzie, Daniel, July 24, 1872, age 21.
McKenzie, James, Dec. 26, 1859, age 67.
McKeon, Mary, wife of Michael, Black Rock, Jan. 23, 1874, age 28; murdered by her husband.
McKevitt, Francis, sailor, April 30, 1873, age 18.
McKibbin, Miss Eliza, sister of Robert H. & Hugh, July 22, 1874.
McKibbin, Hugh, Sept. 11, 1861, age 73.
McKim, Robert, July 5, 1873.
McKinley, Charles H., June 12, 1879, age 35.
McKinley, Lydia Jane Bothwell Lyon, wife of Edward, late of Buffalo, Jan. 4, 1853, age 25; d. on Steamship *Panama*, en route to San Francisco.
McKinney, David, son-in-law of J. Risley of Fredonia, Sardinia, NY, Feb. 21, 1849.

McKinney, David D., formerly manager of the Eagle St. Theater, Buffalo, Nov. 29, 1839; in New York.
McKinney, Harriet D., wife of O.W., April 21, 1848, age 26.
McKinnon, Ann, June 28, 1878, age 85.
McKinzie, Mary, June 19, 1874, age 545.
McKnight, George, March 4, 1845, age 41.
McKnight, James, Jan. 8, 1868, age 81.
McKnight, Sarah G., widow of James, Oct. 11, 1868, age 76.
McKurnan, Patrick, Feb. 21, 1879, age 78.
McLain, Caroline, wife of Andrew, Newstead, Feb. 11, 1877, age 55.
McLane, Flora, Feb. 13, 1872, age 28.
McLane, John, Sept. 11, 1854.
McLane, John Jr., April 30, 1874, age 25.
McLane, John, May 2, 1878, age 70.
McLane, Polly, Oct. 2, 1872, wife of Henry.
McLaren, Minnie, dau. of William, Sept. 7, 1874, age 19 y, 1 m, 11 d.
McLaren, William, formerly of Buffalo, May 27, 1873, age 69 y, 9 m; d. in Chicago.
McLarnan, Thomas, Jan. 25, 1871, age 31.
McLaughlin, James, Sept. 26, 1871.
McLaughlin, Josephine, wife of Dr. S. J., April 29, 1869, age 26 y, 6 m, 13 d; d. in NY City, bur. Buffalo. Dau. of the late Martin Rowan.
McLaughlin, Mrs. Margaret, June 11, 1873, age 63.
McLaughlin, Salome, Feb. 11, 1873, age 63.
McLean, Alexander, formerly of Albany, May 14, 1847, age 40.
McLean, Mrs. Alexander, Nov. 1873.
McLean, John, July 7, 1871.
McLean, Sophia C. Rowland, wife of Rev. Alexander, Nov. 4, 1873, age 34; taken to Fairfield, CT.
McLean, (Capt.) William, April 1863.
McLeish, Mrs. Charles, mother of Archibald, James & Charles G., Feb. 21, 1874.
McLeish, James, Sept. 13, 1860, age 56.
McLin, Daniel, July 7, 1872, age 27 y, 5 m; taken to Springville.
McMahon, "Father"--Catholic priest, well known in Buffalo, April 27, 1872; d. at Reynolds Station, IN.
McMahon, Mrs. Ellen, Oct. 28, 1878, age 33.
McMahon, Col. John E., 164th Regt., Corcoran Legion, March 1863, age 28; bur. 15th.
McMahon, Margaret, wife of James, April 13, 1870, age 27 y, 1 m, 19 d.
McMahon, Michael, Nov. 14, 1876, age 26; drowned.
McMahon, Thomas, June 5, 1879, age 70 y, 2 m; at St. Francis Hospital.
McManus, Frances M., March 20, 1880, age 74 y, 6 m.
McManus, Henry, June 14, 1870, age 35.
McManus, Mrs. Margaret, mother of John, Feb. 9, 1878, age 73.
McManus, Thomas A. Emmet, May 4, 1868, age 42.
McMartin, Ann J., wife of Peter, formerly of Black Rock, NY, Aug. 15, 1865, age 42; at Port Huron, MI.
McMaster, Mrs. Catharine, Feb. 1, 1865, age 65.
McMaster, James, June 5, 1847, age 49.
McMaster, Robert H., formerly of Strauraer, Wigtonshire, Scotland, formerly Buffalo, May 30, 1858, age 29; in San Francisco, CA.
McMasters, Hugh, formerly of Armagh, Ireland, Feb. 23, 1844, age 37.
McMasters, Mrs. Sarah, sept. 19, 1871, age 81.
McMichael, Frances E., wife of William J., July 24, 1868, age 22 y, 8 m.
McMichael, William H., Aug. 24, 1855, age 34.
McMillan, Daniel C., Aug. 14, 1852, age 51.
McMillan, James, Sept. 26, 1827, age 40.
McMillen, Betsey R., widow of Daniel H., Feb. 22, 1874, age 58.
McMillen, Esther, widow of Hugh, April 17, 1873, age 59.
McMillen, Hugh, Oct. 11, 1860, age 55.
McMillen, Capt. James, April 27, 1879, age 79.
McMillen, John, March 19, 1849, age 38.

McMillen, Mrs. Rachel, mother of Mrs. Wells Brooks, March 11, 1864, age 70.
McMullen, Alexander, Sept. 21, 1860, age 76.
McMullen, James, Jan. 20, 1866, age 36 y, 8 m.
McMullen, Mrs. Magdalene, Williamsville, April 15, 1878, age 94.
McMurray, Samuel J., July 4, 1870, age 33; d. at Salt Lake City, FL.
McMurray, Mr. T., June 10, 1849.
McMurtry, James A., Nov. 22, 1879, age 44.
McMurty, Charles (or Mack Murty), laborer, drowned, Sept. 5, 1873, age 35.
McNally, Mrs. Sarah, Jan. 19, 1872, age 86.
McNamara, Ann, Dec. 4, 1880, age 61.
McNamara, Honora, wife of Joseph, July 26, 1878, age 50.
McNamara, James, April 21(?), 1871, age 32.
McNamara, Mrs. Mary Techan, wife of James, June 19, 1880.
McNamary, Patrick John, Aug. 17, 1871, age 80.
McNaughton, Gilbert J., May 28, 1879, age 43 y, 6 m, 22 d.
McNaughton, Mrs. Rebecca, May 13, 1877, age 86 y, 6 m.
McNeal, Alice A. Church, wife of John W., Feb. 4, 1872, age 28.
McNeal, Catharine (McGuire), wife of William, formerly of Buffalo, murdered by her husband
    at Albany, May 21, 1880, age 28?
McNeal (or McNeau), Elias H., June 30, 1873, age 46.
McNeal, Mary, wife of Andrew, Aug. 21, 1880, age 58.
McNeal, Milton, Lancaster, June 25, 1871, age 71.
McNeff, Michael, Aug. 13, 1880, age 24.
McNiel, John, Black Rock, NY, April 27, 1828, age 54.
McNish, D. B., Feb. 25, 1880, age 38 y, 5 m.
McNish, Jane, wife of William, Sept. 30, 1876, age 67.
McPherson, Sarah Ann, wife of Samuel, Dec. 11, 1867, age 63.
McPike, John, County Almshouse, Dec. 19, 1877, age 71.
McQuade, Bernard, March 3, 1871, age 65.
McQuade, Thomas or John, accidentally killed, July 15, 1872, age 75.
McQueen, Mrs. Louisa, wife of Alexander, Nov. 13, 1879, age 32 y, 6 m.
McQuon, George W., April 9, 1872, age 44 y, 8 m.
McRobert, John, May 4, 1879, age 63 y, 10 m, 17 d.
McSharry, Patrick, Almshouse, Aug. 14, 1880, age 65.
McSourley (or McSoubley), Sarah, Oct. 15, 1877, age 27.
McTegart, Philip, Nov. 22, 1874, age 74.
McTigue, James, Sept. 11, 1880, age 41.
McTigue, Michael, April 19, 1871, age 25; killed (shot) near Berlin, OH, bur. in Buffalo.
McVey, Peter, killed on the railroad at Dewitt, May 16, 1877.
McVicar, Mrs. E. A., Dec. 22, 1880, age 64.
McWade, Mrs. Jennie, April 3, 1876, age 67.
McWhorter, J. N., East Aurora, June 28, 1877, age 53 y, 8 m, 28 d.
McWhorter, John, Sept. 29, 1867, age 67; taken to Westfield, Chautauqua Co., NY.
McWilliams, Frank, son of Francis, formerly of Buffalo, March 2, 1873; d. in IA.
McWilliams, Mrs. Mary, Dec. 23, 1862, age 85.
Meacham, Abraham, Oct. 26, 1854, age 35.
Meacham, Caroline H., wife of George, June 22, 1863, age 39.
Meacham, George, Hamburgh, NY, April 28, 1823, age 40.
Meacham, Capt. Henry M., Newstead, July 21, 1853, age 45 y, 7 m.
Mead, Edward A., telegrapher, March 20, 1880, age 33.
Mead, Eliza, wife of William, Dec. 24, 1854.
Mead, George R. E., only son of Mrs. G. W. Clark of Buffalo, July 24, 1866, age 24.
Mead, Joan, wife of William, Jan. 9, 1846, age 49.
Mead, Orlando, son of Alfred, Newstead, NY, Jan. 29, 1857, age 23 y, 11 m, 14 d.
Mead, Samantha, wife of Hiram, Aug. 15, 1852, age 34.
Mead, Silas, b. May 6, 1762, d. 1843, bur. Somerset, NY; Soldier of the Revolution.
Mead, William, Jan. 6, 1857, age 66.
Meads, Martha Rose, wife of Willis H., Dec. 3, 1876, age 28 y, 1 m.
Meagher, Laurence, Dec. 2, 1879, age 22; killed by the cars, parents in Livonia.
Meany, Ellen, sister of Mrs. Michael Corcoran, Aug. 1874, age 55.

Meany, Patrick, June 28, 1872, age 28 y, 3 m.
Meatyard, Charles, East Hamburgh, Feb. 14, 1872, age 74.
Medow, Martin, a soldier in the war of '56 and also in that of revolution, Feb. 5, 1822, age 94.
Meech, Adaline, wife of Henry T., Aug. 30, 1858, age 44 y, 4 m, 9 d; taken to Albany.
Meech, Agnes B. Ahern, wife of Samuel G., Nov. 26, 1875, age 38.
Meech, Col. Asa B., formerly of Buffalo, Jan. 4, 1869; d. in Schenectady.
Meech, Elizabeth A., May 21, 1859, age 74.
Meech, Henry T., Dec. 5, 1870, age 65; d. in Hartford, CT, bur. in Albany.
Meech, Horace, Dec. 29, 1852, age 63, in Freeport, IL; taken to Geneva.
Meech, Lt. Horace J., Dec. 30, 1855, age 34; taken to Schenectady.
Meech, Samuel L., Aug. 16, 1873, age 67 y, 7 m, 25 d.
Meech, Hon. William B., Dec. 31, 1858, age 38.
Meeham, John E., June 24, 1873, age 30.
Meehan, John, Aug. 1, 1878, age 35.
Meehan, John Francis, Oct. 16, 1878, age 54; of St. Johns, Newfoundland, and taken there.
Meehan, Patrick, April 18, 1880, age 57.
Meehan, Mrs. Sophia, Jan. 17, 1872, age 62.
Meeks, Sarah Ann, wife of James C., March 27, 1838; in New York.
Meeney, Michael, son of John and Bessie, March 8, 1877, age 32.
Mehan, John, drowned, June 14, 1876, age 60.
Mehan, John, railroad accident, April 9, 1878, age 22; belonged in Dunkirk.
Mehan, John, County Almshouse, July 3, 1879, age 26.
Mehl, Mary, d. at County Almshouse, Feb. 5, 1876, age 30.
Meidenbauer, J.G., Nov. 4, 1872, age 58.
Meigs, Charles P., June 6, 1849, age 20.
Meigs, Capt. Gideon, April 18, 1870, age 66.
Meissner, William E. G., bur. Aug. 24, 1864, age 43 y, 6 m, 21 d.
Meldrum, Eveline, wife of Robert O., Westfalls, NY, dau. of late James H. Henshaw, of Aurora, NY, Dec. 27, 1851, age 23.
Melican, John, seaman, washed overboard, Nov. 29, 1878.
Melling, John, Co. D, 116th Regt., N.Y.S.V., Dec. 19, 1862; at Chesapeake Gen. Hospital, Fort Monroe, VA; bur. in Buffalo.
Mellon, Mary, wife of Capt. N., of Schooner *Grant*, Feb. 25, 1844, age 27.
Mendel, Henry, Oct. 22, 1872, age 50 y, 6 m.
Mendell, Mrs. Louisa, Cheektowaga, April 5, 1865, age 85 y, 20 d.
Mendt, John Adam, Feb. 14, 1879, age 56.
Meng, Henry J., formerly of Buffalo, Aug. 15, 1878, age 28; d. at Erie, PA, see *Erie Dispatch* of Aug. 16.
Mensch, Charles, March 22, 1877, age 28.
Mensch, Miss Fannie Ellen, June 21, 1877.
Mensch, Frederick, Capt. of Canal Boat, April 30, 1871.
Mensch, John C., Sept. 30, 1872, age 39; d. in NY City, bur. in Buffalo.
Mensch, Margaret, widow of Valentine, Aug. 27, 1865, age 78.
Mensch, William, 12th N.Y. Cav., Jan. 13, 1865, at hosp. at Newberne, NC; bur. in Buffalo.
Mensch, William, Aug. 1, 1874, age 32.
Mensch, William L., Sept. 30, 1864, age 47 y, 4 m.
Mentzmer (or Mentzon), Henry, Feb. 22, 1848, age 29.
Mercer, Elizabeth, Almshouse, insane, Nov. 16, 1880, age 26.
Mercer, William, formerly of Buffalo, April 22, 1871, age 50 y, 1 m, 1 d; d. at Indianapolis, IN.
Mercier, Mrs. Louisa, July 1, 1869, age 57 y, 4 m.
Meredith, (Gen.) Sullivan A., Dec. 26, 1874, age 58.
Mergenhagen, Andrew, son of Joseph, Sept. 24, 1878, age 21 y, 9 m.
Mergenhagen, Charles, son of Joseph, Jan. 27, 1879, age 22.
Mergenhagen, John, Dec. 21, 1869, age 47.
Merhoff, Mrs. Eliza, Nov. 8, 1878, age 69.
Markel, Anthony, suicide, Sept. 14, 1877, age c. 35.
Markle, Valentine, Clarence, Aug. 25, 1871, age c. 40.
Merrick, Aaron C., April 9, 1858, age 39 y, 4 m.

Merrick, Abraham W., Jan. 17, 1866, age 30 y, 6 .
Merrill, Mrs. Bethsheba, mother of George W., Aug. 14, 1850, age 83.
Merrill, Charles Thompson, formerly of Buffalo, April 15, 1880, age 24; d. at Erie, PA.
Merrill, Frederick B., May 1866.
Merrill, George, father of George W., June 9, 1848, age 67.
Merrill, George W., formerly of Buffalo, May 2, 1866; in Erie, PA.
Merrill, Ira, Jan. 20, 1873, age 78.
Merrill, Lucy, wife of Ira, Sept. 30, 1868; d. in Rushville, Ontario Co., bur. in Buffalo.
Merrill, Mary Ann, wife of William H., dau. of late Chas. T. Rand of Buffalo, Dec. 18, 1861, age 24 y, 9 m; at Sommerville, MA.
Merrill, Sophia, formerly of Clarence, NY, wife of Col. Frederick B., dau. of Col. Ransom of Clarence, NY, 1850, age 52; d. Shawneetown, IL. First white female b. on the "Holland Purchase."
Merritt, George H., July 8, 1864, age 33; in Batavia, NY.
Merritt, Jesse, M.D., Dec. 27, 1849, age 58.
Merritt, Jesse A., youngest son of Dr. J., March 17, 1843.
Merritt, Peter, Oct. 14, 1867, age 79.
Merritt, Russell A., Aug. 13, 1861, in Milwaukee, WI; formerly of Buffalo.
Merritt, Rhoda M. Randall, wife of G. H. Jr., Colden, Nov. 23, 1874, age 19 y, 7 m.
Merritt, Sarah L., wife of Peter, March 18, 1867, age 62.
Merritt, Sylvia, wife of Peter, Jan. 15, 1852, age 61.
Mertz, Rev. Mr., first Catholic priest stationed in Buffalo, Eden, NY, Aug. 10, 1844, age 81.
Mesmer, Mrs. Frances, Sept. 8, 1867, age 90.
Mesmer, Mary N., dau. of Peter, Feb. 20, 1878, age 20 y, 2 m.
Messer, Carissa H., Black Rock, NY, wife of Christian, dau. of Amos Root, June 14, 1852, age 24.
Messing, Frederick, Dec. 11, 1876, age 28.
Messing, Peter, Nov. 26, 1874, age 72.
Messler, Mrs. Ellen, April 9, 1854, age 63.
Metcalf, Bela B., Sept. 15, 1858, age 27; in Charleston, SC, formerly of Buffalo.
Metcalf, David, March 13, 1877, age 25.
Metcalfe, James Harvey, Oct. 5, 1879, age 57.
Mettler, John, Jan. 1880.
Metz, Mrs. Barbara, mother of Mr. C. Metz of Buffalo, Clarence, NY, July 17, 1864, age 68.
Metz, Charles, Jan. 25, 1865, age 43 y, 5 m.
Metz, Christian, Clarence, NY, Aug. 12, 1855, age 63.
Metz, Edward, son of Abraham, Amherst, Oct. 12, 1869, age 27 y, 6 m, 6 d.
Metz, H., wife of John, Eden Center, July 5, 1874.
Metz, Jacob, Dec. 22, 1880, age 64 y, 3 m, 6 d.
Metz, John, Sept. 4, 1855, age 40.
Metz, Louis, formerly of Clarence Centre, Sept. 11, 1875, age c. 21; shot by George Ochs at Suspension Bridge.
Metzger, Daniel D., May 14, 1854, age 29; taken to Liverpool, Onondaga Co., N.Y.
Metzger, Margaret, wife of Nicholas, April 20, 1880, age 51.
Metzler, Henry, Dec. 16, 1872, age 34.
Meurret, Eugene, June 16, 1880, age 28 y, 8 m.
Meusch, Catharine, March 27, 1880, age 64.
Meyer, Adolphus Gustavus, son of J.W.A., Oct. 7, 1865, age 23 y, 8 m, 17 d.
Meyer, Andrew, Sept. 13, 1876, age 81 y, 6 m.
Meyer, Charles L., Middle Ebenezer, NY, Secy. and Gen. Agent of the "Ebenezer Society," March 13, 1862, age 56.
Meyer, Christopher, accidental death, Blossomville, Dec. 27, 1875.
Meyer, Daniel, suicide, July 21, 1872, age 53.
Meyer, Dora, wife of Frank X., Jan. 26, 1871, age 20.
Meyer, Edward Horatio, son of J.W.A., Jan. 18, 1866, age 20 y, 1 m, 25 d.
Meyer, Francis X., Jan. 22, 1874, age 29 y, 7 m.
Meyer, George, Boston, Erie Co., Sept. 13, 1879.
Meyer, H.C.A., Feb. 28, 1880, age 38 y, 8 m.
Meyer, Susan, March 4, 1874, age 31.

Meyers, Henry, April 24, 1879, age 22 y, 4 m, 19 d.
Meyers, Joseph or John, suicide, July 20, 1873, age 45.
Meyers, Louis, Almshouse, Feb. 27, 1880, age 36.
Meyers, Mary Kate, wife of F. A., formerly of Buffalo, March 21, 1875, age 25 y, 4 m; d. in Cleveland, OH, bur. Buffalo.
Miatt, William P., April 11, 1871, age 40.
Michael, Michael, peddler, suddenly, heart disease, Jan. 13, 1880, age 31.
Michels, Mrs. J., Feb. 8, 1873, age 37.
Middleditch, Alonzo, Boston, NY, Oct. 14, 1865, age 58 y, 11 m, 14 d.
Middleditch, Ruth, County Almshouse, Jan. 29, 1876, age 28.
Middleditch, Schinler, son of Alonzo, Boston, NY, May 9, 1859, age 21 y, 10 m, 14 d.
Milenbower, John, Buffalo?, Feb. 9, 1880, age 20.
Miles, Mrs., wife of Rev. Miles, Clarence, NY, Aug. 1838; formerly of Mayville, Chautauqua Co., NY.
Miles, John W., 1st Engineer of Steamer *Louisiana*, Aug. 18, 1850, age 35.
Miles, Peter E., Sept. 5, 1832, age 35.
Miles, Rebecca H., widow of Peter E., Jan. 31, 1859, age 63.
Miley, John, Nov. 11, 1876, age 37 y, 6 m, 14 d.
Milkes, Benjamin, Gowanda or West Seneca, June 1874, age 82.
Millar, Bettie M., wife of Allan P., Jan. 29, 1860.
Millar, Robert W., Dec. 4, 1865, age 33.
Millar, Ruth Ann, wife of Thomas, Marilla, NY, May 7, 1866, age 34.
Millard, Henry, Oct. 28, 1869.
Millard, Thomas, formerly of Black Rock, June 2, 1870; d. at Niagara, Ontario, bur. in Buffalo?
Miller, Abraham, Dec. 8, 1845, age 56.
Miller, Abraham, M.D., Nov. 15, 1879, age 75.
Miller, Alexander, June 15, 1872, age 22.
Miller (or Mueller), Allen (or Albert D.), drowned, Aug. 16, 1874, age 24 y, 7 m, 13 d.
Miller, Anna, wife of Philip, Dec. 26, 1872, age 27 y, 9 m.
Miller, Anne Neff, wife of Joseph, Eggertsville, Feb. 17, 1877, age 67 y, 8 m.
Miller, Archibald, July 29, 1834, age 35.
Miller, Mrs. Barbara, mother of Benjamin & Joseph, Amherst, March 22, 1873, age 83.
Miller, Mrs. Catharine, mother of Peter P., Dec. 6, 1868, age 69.
Miller, Charles, Aug. 28, 1874.
Miller, Charles, suicide, Aug. 27, 1875, age 36.
Miller, Clara Dolan, widow of W. F., March 25, 1877, age 27.
Miller, Dianna E., widow of Jacob S., July 19, 1879, age 69.
Miller, Edward, County Almshouse, Sept. 5, 1877, age 24.
Miller, Eliza J., wife of Myron H., dau. of John A. Burk, April 11, 1843, in Louisville, KY; formerly of Buffalo.
Miller, Eliza W., wife of Luman A., May 30, 1856, age 47.
Miller, Elizabeth, widow of Major F., May 6, 1848, age 80.
Miller, Elizabeth, widow of Daniel, Williamsville, Aug. 21, 1877, age 83.
Miller, Elizabeth, wife of Frank J., March 31, 1879, age 24 y, 6 m, 21 d.
Miller, Elizabeth G., widow of William T., Nov. 30, 1871, age 72.
Miller, Emily Bryan, wife of Charles G., formerly of Buffalo, Aug. 4, 1875; d. at Minneapolis, MN.
Miller, Fannie Curtis, wife of Robert W., June 29, 1861, age 28.
Miller, Festus A., son of the late Charles, Jan. 14, 1876, age 21 y, 5 m, 9 d; d. at Fort Reid, FL.
Miller, Major Frederick, Jan. 21, 1830, age 70. [Another card: Miller, Frederick, b. 1764, d. 1830, bur. Buffalo; Soldier of the Revolution.]
Miller, Frederick A., March 28, 1872.
Miller, George, Nov. 13, 1871, age 64 y, 7 m.
Miller, Harry, May 19, 1862, age 65 y, 7 m, 20 d.
Miller, Henry Hoyt, formerly of Buffalo, Dec. 15, 1879, age 44 y, 9 m; d. at Riverside, Chicago, IL.
Miller, Dr. Horace B., Aug. 1880.
Miller, Horatio B., M.D., Aug. 12, 1880, age 62.

Miller, J. S., bur. Oct. 3, 1855.
Miller, Jacob, June 6, 1872, age 51.
Miller, Jacob, Nov. 3, 1874, age c. 25.
Miller, Jacob, April 1876.
Miller, Jacob, Oct. 11, 1876, age 46.
Miller, James, Dec. 7, 1877, age 88.
Miller, James, June 16, 1880, age 66.
Miller, James Wilson, Aug. 1, 1875, age 25 y, 5 m, 7 d.
Miller, John, March 31, 1854, age 42.
Miller, John, drowned, April 17, 1874, age 47 y, 8 m.
Miller, John, drowned, May 20, 1876, age c. 50.
Miller, John, son of Richard, Feb. 17, 1878, age 23 y, 3 m, 20 d.
Miller, John, Nov. 23, 1878, age 58 y, 2 m, 15 d.
Miller, John A., father of A.D.A., May 5, 1855, age 70; in White Lake, Oneida Co., N.Y., bur. in Buffalo.
Miller, John G. C., Jan. 24, 1880, age 34.
Miller, Kate Burwell, dau. of the late Jacob S., July 19, 1877.
Miller, Lewis, accidental death, July 16, 1875, age 44.
Miller, Luman A., Jan. 2, 1873, age 64.
Miller, Martha, Aug. 17, 1838, age 26.
Miller, Mary, wife of Thomas C., March 30, 1852; in Detroit, MI, formerly of Buffalo.
Miller, Mary K. E., wife of C., Dec. 6, 1867, age 51 y, 1 m, 20 d.
Miller, Mathias, Nov. 18, 1873, age 52.
Miller, Merritt B., adjutant of 125th Regt., N.Y.S.V., June 26, 1864, age 20; d. of wounds at City Point.
Miller, Myron H., brother of Capt. Frederick S., formerly of Buffalo, July 30, 1875, age 69; d. at Memphis, TN.
Miller, Peter, July 19, 1874, age 64.
Miller, Philip, Aug. 12, 1859, age 51.
Miller, Philip or William, Nov. 1, 1878, age 41.
Miller, Richard, May 12, 1879, age 60.
Miller, Col. Samuel, Jan. 17, 1844, age 42.
Miller, Sarah, wife of John U., Williamsville, Aug. 1, 1856, age 76 y, 8 m.
Miller, Sarah Hobrow, wife of James, June 9, 1867, age 79.
Miller, Susannah, Williamsville, wife of Benjamin, Jan. 11, 1879, age 65.
Miller, Tabitha Ann, wife of W.G., Oct. 9, 1844, age 35.
Miller, William, June 1, 1878, age 34.
Miller, William John, son of Adam, June 5, 1875, age 21 y, 9 m, 5 d.
Miller, William S., brother of Jacob and Philip, June 1, 1874, age 24 y, 8 m.
Miller, William T., Cold Spring, NY, March 30, 1853, age 61.
Miller, William T., March 13, 1875, age 33.
Miller, William W., May 4, 1880, age 54, wife & family in Chicago.
Millet, Mrs. Mary P., Aug. 25, 1849, age 73.
Milley, Lizzie J., Oct. 15, 1879, age 20 y, 11 d.
Millican, Patrick, June 4, 1878.
Milligan, Mary, wife of Martin, July 17, 1878, age 38.
Milliken, Col. C. A., 1867 in Galveston, TX. Formerly of Buffalo. Late Lt.-Col. of 43d N.Y.S.V., organized in Albany in 1861.
Millington, Joseph, March 20, 1873, age 43.
Millington, Laura Stickney, wife of Joseph, Black Rock, NY, May 8, 1860, age 28 y, 9 m.
Mills, Alice, wife of George, Dec. 18, 1858, age 48.
Mills, Ann, wife of John, March 3, 1859, age 43.
Mills, Ansel, Lancaster, June 8, 1873, age 83.
Mills, Calvin, father of S.J. and C.J. of Buffalo, Alden, NY, March 17, 1850, age 56.
Mills, Catharine, wife of Ansel, Feb. 12, 1852, age 53.
Mills, Cephas, formerly of Montreal, Lower Canada, recently of NY, merchant, Feb. 9, 1842.
Mills, Edward M., April 8, 1849, age 21.
Mills, Eliza J., wife of M. C., Sept. 17, 1873, age 25.
Mills, George, Jan. 10, 1869, age 71.
Mills, George C., Jan. 28, 1869, age 42; d. at Palmyra, MO.

Mills, George Chandler, March 1, 1853, age 25.
Mills, Mary, wife of Cyrus, Hamburgh, NY, Dec. 6, 1845, age 26.
Mills, Mary, eldest dau. of Loring Danforth, Feb. 1, 1867, age 20.
Mills, Mary M., widow of Rev. James H., Oct. 7, 1863, age 74.
Mills, Rose McMaster, wife of Rev. Charles R., formerly of Buffalo, Feb. 3, 1874; d. at Tung Chow, China.
Mills, Samuel J., Sept. 24, 1853, age 38.
Mills, Sarah, dau. of Dr. William M., Feb. 16, 1877, age 35 y, 4 m, 3 d; d. at Petrolia, Butler Co., PA, bur. in Buffalo.
Mills, Sophia R., widow of Calvin, March 9, 1852, age 61.
Mills, Miss Susan E., Boston, N.Y., notice in paper April 15, 1848, age 23.
Mills, Thomas, Oct. 20, 1876, age 28 y, 2 m, 10 d.
Mills, Dr. W. Baxter, Aug. 29, 1845, age 23; late of Springfield, MA.
Mills, William, Aug. 15, 1867, age 74 y, 6 m.
Mills, William E., July 28, 1861, age 41; taken to Clarence, NY.
Milnor, Elizabeth D., wife of William, Nov. 6, 1867, age 41.
Milnor, George A., April 10, 1874, age 74.
Milnor, James, Oct. 1, 1849, age 55.
Milnor, John Redmond Coxe, son of Dr. Robert, Dec. 4, 1852, age 32.
Milnor, Robert, M.D., Dec. 24, 1855, age 47.
Milson, George Washington, Aug. 21, 1864, age 24.
Milson, Wilson, Lancaster, May 16, 1868, age 31 y, 11 m, 3 d.
Milton, Francis X. B., son of Patrick, April 22, 1849, age 20; at Montreal College, bur. in Buffalo.
Milton, Mary Jane, wife of Patrick, Jan. 18, 1830, age 21.
Milton, Patrick, Oct. 10, 1859, one of the oldest residents of the city.
Minar, Mrs. Sarah Crary, March 27, 1869, age 65; funeral at Bowmansville.
Minehan, Michael, Dec. 12, 1879, age 49.
Miner, Delia, alias Holmes, Sept. 4, 1871, age c. 30.
Miner, John, colored cook of Steamer *Henry Clay*, Dec. 1827, age 30.
Miner, Kittie, Dec. 22, 1877, age c. 30.
Miner, Robert J., accidental death, Nov. 4, 1875, age 24; d. in Philadelphia, bur. in Buffalo.
Minkler, Sarah, May 21, 1874, age 58.
Minor, David, Lancaster, June 15, 1868, age 77 y, 1 m.
Mintler, Elizabeth E., wife of Andrew, Tonawanda, Feb. 28, 1872, age 20 y, 4 m, 7 d.
Minton, Daniel, June 12, 1831, age 40.
Minton, Mrs. Rebecca, Wales Center, Sept. 22, 1869, age 80; mother of Jones Minton of Niagara Falls.
Mitchell, Catherine, Dec. 10, 1867, age 63.
Mitchell, Mrs. Catherine, June 14, 1875, age 65; mother of William, John and Thomas.
Mitchell, Edward, formerly of Buffalo, April 4, 1874, age 40 y, 5 m, 18 d; d. at Joliet, IL.
Mitchell, Henry, many years a resident of Buffalo, May 28, 1846, age 24; d. on steamship between Liverpool and Beaumoris, in North Wales.
Mitchell, Henry, May 2, 1876, age 35.
Mitchell, James, Jan. 14, 1864, age 54.
Mitchell, Jane, wife of George B., Jan. 1872; d. in Pittsburgh, PA, bur. in Buffalo.
Mitchell, John D., accidental death, July 18, 1878.
Mitchell, Maggie, County Almshouse, Dec. 22, 1877, age 30.
Mitchell, Mrs. Martha, Sept. 18, 1860, age 35.
Mitchell, Mary, widow of James, Sept. 28, 1869, age 51.
Mitchell, Mary M., Oct. 21, 1867, wife of Robert.
Mitchell, Nathaniel, Oct. 30, 1868, age 29.
Mitchell, Olivia, widow of Dr. J. R. of Northampton, Fulton Co., NY. Mother of Mrs. George Hodge, Feb. 10, 1858, age 71.
Mitchell, Rachel, widow of William H., June 28, 1874, age 71 y, 6 m.
Mitchell, Susan, wife of Joshua, Elma, April 21, 1862, age 25.
Mitchell, William, Oct. 2, 1868, age 73.
Mitchell, William, Almshouse, Sept. 28, 1880, age 76.

Mitchell, William J., Oct. 6, 1875, age 37.
Mittler, John, policeman, Jan. 11, 1880, age 44.
Mixer, Miss Minnie, railroad accident, Dec. 29, 1876, age 20 y, 6 m.
Mochel, William F., Feb. 19, 1879, age 30.
Mochle, Charles, Clarence Centre, Feb. 27, 1870, age 63.
Mock (or Moch), Joseph, May 13, 1880; killed when jumping from a car.
Moelecker, Margaretta, April 29, 1873, age 41.
Moershfelder, Nicholas Sr., Feb. 16, 1880, age 73.
Moes, George, Nov. 1880.
Moessinger, George, Nov. 18, 1880, age 56.
Moevius, Charles, formerly of Buffalo, Sept. 1878, age 92; d. in Erie.
Moffat, James, April 4, 1863, age 57.
Moffat, John, Scotchman, July 13, 1845, age 80.
Moffat, Mrs. Matilda, mother of James and William, May 22, 1860, age 84.
Moffat, Parley, of Hamburgh, NY; killed at Battle of Black Rock, Dec. 30, 1813.
Moffat, Amelia, widow of James, Aug. 23, 1864.
Moffatt, Mrs. John, Feb. 18, 1879, age 36.
Molder, Charles, March 2, 1866, age 24 y, 4 m, 16 d.
Moll, Widow Christina, June 9, 1844, age 48.
Mollin, Peter, Dec. 27, 1880, age 64 y, 10 m, 16 d.
Molloy, Mrs. Mary, June 16, 1868, age 73.
Moloney, David, March 11, 1872, age 60.
Molter, Catharine, Jan. 24, 1875, age 53 y, 8 m, 24 d; wife of Jacob.
Monaghan, George C., accidental death, Feb. 1, 1875, age 45.
Monard, John, suicide, Aug. 6, 1878.
Monforte, Martha, wife of Capt. Joseph C., Jan. 21, 1836, age 23.
Monghan, Mrs. Mary, formerly of Toronto, Canada West, July 23, 1867, age 73 y, 5 m.
Monk, Nels, formerly of Buffalo, Feb. 8, 1877; d. at Jamestown, NY.
Monnin, Charles, July 27, 1862, age 52.
Monroe, Dr. Rev., Feb. 1867.
Monroe, Charles H., July 17, 1850, age 36.
Monroe, George H., Co. B., 10th U.S. Inf., April 5, 1866, age 18.
Monroe, Jane, Sept. 14, 1844, age 63; at residence of her son-in-law, Mr. Sheppard, Perrysburg, Cattaraugus Co., N.Y.
Monroe, Jeremiah D., Sept. 1, 1857, age 43.
Monroe, N. Jennie, Town Line, April 18, 1871, age 31 y, 4 m.
Monteath, Emma, eldest dau. of William, Nov. 30, 1864; in NY, funeral in Albany.
Monteath, William, Dec. 12, 1870; d. in NY City.
Montgomery, Elizabeth, wife of Rev. G. W., eldest dau. of Moses Baker, March 11, 1847, age 33; in Rochester, bur. in Buffalo.
Montgomery, Laura Williams, wife of Capt. Robert, Dec. 2, 1865, age 38.
Montgomery, Mary A., wife of H. M., May 27, 1869.
Moodie, John W., Aug. 7, 1879, age 67 y, 8 m.
Moodie, Lucinda P., wife of John W., Oct. 18, 1869, age 53.
Moon, David, father of M.A. of Buffalo, Evans, Jan. 7, 1870, age 81.
Moon, Mrs. Nancy, Evans, NY, Aug. 31, 1866, age 77 y, 10 m.
Mooney, Bridget, wife of John, Feb. 3, 1870, age 59.
Mooney, Catharine, alias Tucker, April 1, 1880, age 29; County Almshouse.
Mooney, Charles, July 21, 1849, age 47.
Mooney, John, Jan. 12, 1873, age 47.
Mooney, John, Sept. 24, 1880, age 70.
Mooney, Lawrence, April 22, 1864, age 53.
Mooney, Mary Jane, Sept. 5, 1879, age 23.
Mooney, Patrick, County Almshouse, Feb. 19, 1877, age 77.
Mooney, Permelia, wife of John A., Nov. 7, 1859, age 43.
Moore, Augustus, March 9, 1874, age 31.
Moore, Rev. Daniel DeLacy, formerly of Buffalo, Jan. 10, 1871; d. at LeRoy, bur. in Buffalo.
Moore, Mrs. E. D., Brant, Sept. 1, 1878, age 66, mother of W. L. Darbee.
Moore, Mrs. Elizabeth, July 1, 1878, age 77.

Moore, George H., son of Col. John O., formerly of Buffalo, Oct. 16, 1872, age 29 y, 5 m; d. near Pontiac, IL.
Moore, Hugh, Oct. 29, 1872.
Moore, James, father of Capt. James, Lake View, April 15, 1871, age 78.
Moore, James, Aug. 1, 1874, age 76.
Moore, James, May 12, 1879, age 23; burned.
Moore, James H., Dec. 15, 1869, age 28 y, 3 m; taken to Red Creek, Wayne Co.
Moore, Jane, Aug. 7, 1880, age 68.
Moore, Jane Ann, wife of William H., dau. of Elihu Russell of Albany, June 7, 1863, age 45; in Lockport, NY, bur. in Buffalo.
Moore, Jane W., wife of Andrew B., Jan. 6, 1848, age 22; late of Newark, OH.
Moore, John, July 6, 1871, age 21.
Moore, Judson H., Bergen, NY, formerly of Buffalo, telegraph operator, Oct. 16, 1863, age 23.
Moore, Margaret, Oct. 10, 1873, age c. 56.
Moore, Mrs. Margaret, Dec. 31, 1874, age 74 y, 10 m.
Moore, Margaret, Oct. 7, 1877, age 84.
Moore, Mrs. Martha, Jan. 15, 1876.
Moore, Mary, wife of John, June 22, 1880, age 33.
Moore, Miss Matilda, May 22, 1867, age 25.
Moore, Minnie E., Dec. 7, 1877, age 19 y, 5 m, 18 d.
Moore, Reuben W., Cattaraugus Creek, NY, Jan. 1, 1842, age 46.
Moore, Thomas, drowned, Jan. 4, 1872; body recovered March 27.
Moore, Capt. William, May 9, 1861, age 37; in NY, bur. in Buffalo.
Moore, William H., Aug. 26, 1876, age 62.
Moores, Mrs. Helen M., wife of W.P., formerly of Buffalo, Oct. 29, 1880; d. in Kansas City.
Moores, Mrs. Loxanna, Dec. 2, 1848, age 53.
Moores, Mrs. William P., Nov. 1880.
Moorhead, Mrs. Margaret, Dec. 27, 1862, age 55.
Moorehead, Robinson, Oct. 28, 1849, age 48.
Moormann, Ferdinand, April 14, 1850, age 37.
Mora, Rachel, Hamburgh, NY, Feb. 12, 1837, age 76.
Moran, Henry, May 16, 1872, age 24.
Moran, John, Oct. 31, 1871, age 28.
Moran, Margaret, Jan. 20, 1877, age 89.
More, John, Hamburgh, NY, late of Yarmouth, Canada West, March 7, 1850, age 78.
Morehouse, Albert, June 11, 1873, age 46.
Morehouse, Anna, widow of Thaddeus of Danbury, CT, Feb. 12, 1860, age 91 y, 10 m.
Morehouse, Charles, Aug. 18, 1871.
Morey, Deborah, wife of Amzi, Holland, NY, March 24, 1853, age 73.
Morey, Nancy A., wife of Capt. H.G., April 4, 1874, age 35.
Morgan, ---, late of Albany, July 2, 1835, age 58.
Morgan, Abel, formerly of Buffalo, Jan. 7, 1844, age 24; Jamestown, Chautauqua Co., N.Y.
Morgan, Adelaide Phelps, wife of A.R. of Detroit, MI, April 1, 1856, age 26.
Morgan, Charlotte, wife of Richard, formerly of Buffalo, Sept. 4, 1877, age 68 y, 7 m.
Morgan, Mr. E. M., May 15, 1855, age 36.
Morgan, Elizabeth, widow of Edward, Jan. 17, 1859, age 64; taken to Rochester, NY.
Morgan, Mrs. Emily B., Jan. 11, 1858, age 22.
Morgan, Mrs. Hannah, mother of Amos, June 26, 1870, age 84.
Morgan, James, of Co. F, 15th Regt. H Art., NY State Volunteers, Sept. 30, 1878, Soldiers Home, Bath, age 54.
Morgan, James Gilbert, Oct. 2, 1872, age 33.
Morgan, James R., April 17, 1878, age 67 y, 1 m, 2 d.
Morgan, John J., Feb. 28, 1879, age 33 y, 8 m.
Morgan, Miss Mary, Nov. 12, 1874, age 65.
Morgan, Mrs. Mary Ann, March 4, 1880, age 72.
Morgan, Mrs. Orra, formerly of Rochester, NY, Feb. 2, 1870, age 78.
Morgan, Patrick, suicide, April 16, 1877, age 75.
Morgan, Miss Sarah, March 28, 1850, age 22.
Morgan, Sarah W., only dau. of A.G., March 9, 1871, age 22; d. at East Hamburgh.

Morgan, Walter, late of Randolph, NY, formerly of Buffalo, Oct. 8, 1855; in Columbus, OH.
Morgan, William E., Feb. 25, 1868, age 38 y, 9 m; d. at Newburgh, OH.
Morgenstern, Phillipina, June 5, 1880, age 75.
Moriarty, Bridget, wife of B. J., Jan. 18, 1878, age 28.
Moriarty, John, accidental death, Lancaster, brakeman on Erie Railway, Oct. 27, 1874.
Moriarty, Joseph, shoemaker, suicide, July 20, 1875, age c. 35.
Moriarity, Mary, County Almshouse, March 7, 1879, age 80.
Morin, Harriet, Feb. 2, 1852, wife of William.
Morley, James P., Feb. 14, 1880, age 57.
Morley, Thomas, Cold Springs, NY, June 25, 1861, age 42.
Morley, William, June 23, 1859, age 49; taken to Canada.
Morrasay, Catharine, April 25, 1853, age 35, wife of Michael.
Morris, Charlotte, wife of Warren, Alden, Feb. 19, 1876, age 48.
Morris, David J., Spring Brook, June 17, 1874.
Morris, Ellen, wife of Rees T., Eden, NY, Aug. 20, 1863, age 21.
Morris, Miss Fanny, late of South Wales in this country, Feb. 8, 1852, age 20.
Morris, George P. (Gen.), July 1864.
Morris, John B., Oct. 20, 1878, age 40.
Morris, John S., Nov. 5, 1867, age 67.
Morris, Michael, Sept. 8, 1871, age 41.
Morris, Natalie Mary, dau. of the late Henry, formerly of Buffalo, Nov. 6, 1870; d. at Glion, Switzerland.
Morris, Reese, July 14, 1876, age 83 y, 3 m, 8 d.
Morrison, Mrs. Amelia J., Dec. 30, 1873, age 29; taken to Mt. Hope, Rochester.
Morrison, Ann C., Feb. 23, 1850, age 30, wife of John.
Morrison, Catharine S., Sept. 1850, age 34, wife of William P.; bur. Sept. 11th.
Morrison, Eliza Morehead, wife of William P., March 30, 1867, age 45 y, 6 m.
Morrison, Horace W., March 6, 1849, age 37.
Morrison, James, March 28, 1848, age 63.
Morrison, James W., Sept. 6, 1852.
Morrison, Lt. John Whiteford, May 6, 1855, age 72; late of Her Majesty's 79th Regt. & 9th Royal Veteran Battallion; taken to Stamford, Canada West.
Morrison, Judson, formerly of Buffalo, accidentally drowned in Lake Ontario, Dec. 2, 1879, age 30.
Morrison, Sarah Emma, Dec. 23, 1848, age 24; dau. of J. W. Morrison, late of the British Army.
Morrison, Susannah, wife of William, Sept. 9, 1850, age 34.
Morrissey, Mrs. Ann, murdered by her son, June 23, 1872, age c. 55.
Morrissey, Patrick, executed for the murder of his mother, Ann, Sept. 6, 1872.
Morrow, Caspain R., M.D., Dec. 30, 1879, age 52.
Morrow, Mrs. Elizabeth, formerly of Buffalo, May 24, 1858; in Chicago, IL, age 75.
Morrow, Henry, father of Dr. Morrow Buffalo, Aurora, Oct. 30, 1868, age 67.
Morrow, Maria, formerly of Buffalo, wife of Elisha, youngest dau. of the late Asaph S. Bemis of Buffalo. March 24, 1852, age 29; in Green Bay, WI, bur. in Buffalo.
Morrow, Mary Ann, formerly of Buffalo, wife of Hugh, June 7, 1855, age 38.
Morrow, Mrs. Mary J., Sept. 5, 1873, age 30.
Morrow, William, accident, Oct. 7, 1879, age 21.
Morse, Caroline C., wife of Dr. C. W., Eden, NY, Feb. 1866, age 32.
Morse, Charles B., Nov. 3, 1877, age 68.
Morse, Charles H., Nov. 13, 1863, age 31.
Morse, Chauncey Franklin, May 1864, bur. May 8th.
Morse, Conelia Hawes, wife of Alanson, Jan. 14, 1864, age 22 y, 11 m, 27 d.
Morse, Henry P., Sept. 22, 1864, age 31.
Morse, Joel, Dec. 22, 1854.
Morse, Mary H., wife of Parker, April 28, 1859, age 50.
Morse, Murrey, formerly of Colden, NY, April 16, 1862 in Havre de Grace, MD, age 20. Eldest of 3 brothers who enlisted in Co. D, Porter Guards, 10th NY Cav. Regt. Sons of Alfred Morse of Colden, NY.
Morse, Parker, Aug. 18, 1860 in Rochester, VT, age 58; bur. in Buffalo.

Morse, Sophronia R., formerly of Colden, wife of Charles, March 17, 1876, age 27; d. in Pine Island, MN.
Morseman, W. W., Evans, NY, March 24, 1848, age 70.
Mortimer, George, Nov. 23, 1870, age 25 y, 1 m, 7 d.
Morton, Alanson P., Springville, March 4, 1872, age 58 y, 10 m, 18 d.
Morton, Miss Eliza S., Morton Corners, Dec. 28, 1877, age 73 y, 3 m, 13 d.
Morton, Isabella, wife of James, July 14, 1877, age 37.
Morton, John, Dec. 3, 1879, age 35.
Morton, John F., formerly of Buffalo, May 15, 1875; d. at Plymouth, NH.
Morton, Mary A., wife of O. C., sister of Mrs. E. H. Howard of Buffalo, Springville, NY, Dec. 12, 1841, age 26.
Morton, Orville, formerly of Adams, Jefferson Co., NY, July 27, 1832, age 22. Clerk of James L. Barton & Co., d. of cholera.
Morton, Pamilia, July 27, 1880, age 67.
Morton, Mrs. Sylvia, Nov. 2, 1872, age 85.
Moseley, Elizabeth W. DeAngelis, wife of Hon. William A., April 5, 1855.
Moseley, Hon. William A., Nov. 19, 1873; d. at Fifth Ave. Hotel, NY City, bur. in Buffalo.
Mosely, George T., April 14, 1868, age 41.
Mosely, Hon. William A., Nov. 1873.
Moser, George, suicide, Sept. 3, 1876, age 55.
Moser, Joseph, suicide, March 1, 1879.
Moses, Margaret P., wife of William, Feb. 11, 1873, age 38.
Moses, Mary Ann, late of Corinth, ME, wife of H., Dec. 8, 1843, age 25.
Mosher, David, Aug. 17, 1864, age 83; taken to Aurora, NY.
Mosher, Hannah, wife of David, Aurora, NY, Dec. 15, 1835, age 47.
Mosher, Hezekiah, East Aurora, June 4, 1872, age 74.
Mosher, Sylvia, widow of Hezekiah, East Aurora, July 2, 1873, age 73.
Mosier, Elzora L., wife of Louis, Jan. 18, 1878, age 28 y, 3 m, 3 d.
Mosier, James, Jan. 19, 1867; one of the oldest residents of Buffalo; Frenchman.
Mosier, Mary C., wife of John, Jan. 9, 1866, age 25.
Moss, Margaret, widow of Jacob, Dec. 22, 1880, age 79 y, 4 m.
Mott, Maj. John W., son of Mrs. Dr. Loomis, Lancaster, OH, July 16, 1871, age 44; bur. in Buffalo.
Mott, Vancleve, formerly of Buffalo, Dec. 28, 1873, age 27; d. at Newark, NJ.
Mott, Capt. William, May 29, 1877, age 48; taken to North Evans.
Motteler, Julia, wife of Frederick, April 4, 1879, age 30.
Motter (or Molter), Jacob, May 30, 1875, age 60.
Motz, W. A., Sept. 21, 1877, age 63.
Moulton, Abby, only dau. of A. H., Lancaster, Nov. 28, 1870, age 31 y, 11 m, 7 d.
Moulton, Edward, drowned, Tonawanda, Sept. 9, 1875, age c. 32.
Moulton, Joseph White, formerly of Buffalo, April 20, 1875, age 86; d. at Roslyn, Long Island.
Mount, Celeste, widow of Francis of St. Charles, Canada East, Sept. 21, 1866, age 64.
Mount, Eliza Jane, wife of George, dau. of James Donaldson of NY, Nov. 23, 1848. Taken to Greenwood Cemetery, Brooklyn, NY.
Mount, Ezekiel Jr., April 17, 1844, age 38.
Mount, Forman, Hamburgh, formerly of Buffalo, April 29, 1880, age 66 y, 3 m.
Mount, George, April 27, 1854, age 60.
Mount, Mrs. Hester, May 16, 1873.
Mount, Humphrey, father of Mrs. J. R. Fero, Jan. 7, 1869, age 61.
Movius, Julius, Oct. 14, 1871, age 59.
Movius, Mary Leonard Vibbard, wife of Julius, Feb. 9, 1870, age 58 y, 9 m.
Moxley, Eliza, wife of Henry, March 8, 1859, age 49.
Moxley, Henry, barber, Dec. 21, 1878, age 75.
Moyer, Jackson W., railroad accident, Nov. 16, 1878, age 24.
Moyer, Jonas William, Oct. 15, 1878, age 61 y, 3 m, 18 d.
Moyes, Samuel, June 13, 1873, age 32.
Moyland, James, Dec. 25, 1880, age 77.
Moynahan, Mrs. Honora, Dec. 11, 1871, age 70.
Moynihan, Rev. Patrick, formerly of Buffalo, Dec. 10, 1878.

Muckridge, Mrs. H. H., sister of Mrs. M. Hazard of Centreville, IN, Dec. 17, 1863.
Muehlhauser, Theresa Ruth, wife of George J., April 2, 1880, age 22 y, 5 m, 8 d.
Mueller, Christian, Feb. 27, 1880.
Muentzer, Sally C., June 30, 1870, age 79 y, 11 m, 18 d.
Mugler, Philip, late of Strasburgh, France, May 7, 1862, age 49 y, 7 d.
Mugridge, James, March 21, 1863, age 67.
Mugridge, Kate J., wife of Adrian E., March 31, 1879, age 29.
Mugridge, Laura, wife of George, Dec. 6, 1862, age 43.
Mulcahy, Annie, wife of William, March 1, 1875.
Mulcahy, John, suicide, Aug. 31, 1877, age 50.
Mulhall, Mary A., wid. of Stephen J., age 47.
Mulhall, Stephen J., Jan. 20, 1875, age 57.
Mulhern, Martin, March 26, 1878, age 52.
Mullen, Annie, wife of James, formerly of NY City, July 18, 1868, age 36.
Mullen, Hugh, railroad accident, Dec. 30, 1877, age 22.
Mullen, James, March 29, 1876, age 55.
Mullen, Kearn, railroad accident, Feb. 4, 1878, age 43.
Mullen, Mary, County Almshouse, July 3, 1877, age 33.
Muller, Rev. G. A., formerly of Buffalo, March 1878; d. at Westfield.
Mullett, Hervey, Dec. 11, 1820, age 25.
Mullett, Psyche, Darien, NY, wid. of Elnathan, March 30, 1865, age 69; bur. in Cheektowaga, NY.
Mulligan, Lt. Gregg, March 1864.
Mulligan, Harriet, wife of Eugene, dau. of G. B. Rich, May 16, 1854, age 29.
Mulligan, Lt. James S., June 10, 1863; d. at Buffalo of wounds received at Second Battle of Bull Run.
Mulligan (or Malligan or Malligar), Margaret, April 29, 1873, age 49.
Mulligan, Olivia, wife of Samuel, Dec. 2, 1872, age 34; taken to Evans Center.
Mumford, Catherine, Almshouse, Dec. 18, 1880, age 40.
Munce, Maria, wife of James, Oct. 12, 1876, age 68.
Munce, Robert, April 30, 1875, age 29 y, 6 m.
Munch, Peter, Buffalo Plains, June 27, 1872, age 72.
Munderbach, John S., Jan. 30, 1880, age 59; d. in NY City, remains to Buffalo.
Munger, Annie J. Milne, wid. of Rev. Orrin Munger, Alden, NY, Nov. 2, 1864, age 24.
Munger, Edwin H., Sept. 22, 1867, age 64.
Munger, Mary, wife of Edward H., July 12, 1845, age 39.
Munger, Samuel T., Gowanda, April 14, 1875, age 70.
Munn, Asa, Alden, NY, March 26, 1848, age 26; in Crosbyville, NY.
Munro, Sarah M., wife of Peter G., Dec. 22, 1878; d. in Boston, MA.
Munroe, Mary E., recently from Woburn, MA, wife of Charles H., June 17, 1848.
Munroe, William C., Feb. 5, 1873, age 66.
Munsch, Mrs. Nicholas, drowned, Tonawanda, Oct. 12, 1871.
Munschauer, George, Oct. 27, 1868, age 63 y, 6 m, 19 d.
Munzerter, Nicholas, Feb. 2, 1877, age 59.
Murbach, Caroline, wife of Casper, Jan. 23, 1875, age 49 y, 8 m.
Murdock, Julia, wife of Jasper, Nov. 9, 1846, age 36.
Murdock, Robert, drowned, Oct. 29, 1874.
Murphy, Ann, wife of Stephen, May 18, 1872.
Murphy, Mrs. Ellen, March 14, 1866, age 61.
Murphy, James, Nov. 22, 1873.
Murphy, John, musician, many years attached to menageries travelling in this country, Sept. 18, 1842.
Murphy, John, late of Bally Colane, County Kildare, Ireland, May 16, 1866, age 70 y, 2 m.
Murphy, John, County Almshouse, May 3, 1876, age 30.
Murphy, John, formerly of Buffalo, Dec. 14, 1880; d. in Chicago.
Murphy, Hon. John W., Aug. 27, 1878, age 48.
Murphy, Lawrence, April 7, 1879, age 61.
Murphy, Margaret, wife of Edward, July 15, 1880, age 32.
Murphy, Mary, wife of John, Limestone Hill, Aug. 31, 1876.
Murphy, Mary J., wife of Michael E., Dec. 21, 1880, age 66.

Murphy, Mary Jane, wid. of John Francis, Sept. 12, 1874, age 74.
Murphy, Michael, July 19, 1866.
Murphy, Michael, April 11, 1868, age 42.
Murphy, Michael, April 1872, age 32.
Murphy, Michael, Aug. 31, 1877.
Murphy, Patrick, Nov. 8, 1871, age 54.
Murphy, Patrick, July 26, 1878, age 68.
Murphy, Patrick, Oct. 10, 1879, age 46.
Murphy, Rosey, wife of James, June 1872.
Murphy, Thomas, July 19, 1876, age 40.
Murphy, Timothy, railroad accident, Lancaster, Nov. 7, 1873, age 20.
Murray, Alexander, native of Lairg, Sutherlandshire, Scotland, March 19, 1858, age 42.
Murray, Alexander, son of the late Hugh, formerly of Buffalo, Jan. 3, 1878, age 37; d. in Chicago.
Murray, Alexander, formerly of Buffalo, March 1878; d. in Chicago, bur. in Buffalo.
Murray, Alice, 3rd dau. of John, Dec. 9, 1866, age 20 y, 4 m, 2 d.
Murray, Bernard, sailor, July 8, 1872, age 38.
Murray, Catharine, wife of Thomas, July 8, 1868, age 29.
Murray, David S., July 5, 1877, age 58.
Murray, Edward J., brother of James A. and Francis P., May 20, 1875, age 25 y, 4 m, 21 d; d. in Brooklyn, taken to Mt. Read Greece, Monroe Co.
Murray, Elizabeth, Feb. 19, 1873, age 35.
Murray, Elsey Maria, wife of W. G., Nov. 9, 1843, age 28.
Murray, Hugh, Jan. 15, 1825, age 35.
Murray, Hugh, Aug. 16, 1870, age 55.
Murray, James, drowned, June 26, 1872, age 34.
Murray, John, May 20, 1867, age 50; taken to Mt. Read, Monroe Co., NY.
Murray, John A., eldest son of Hugh, Dec. 6, 1869, age 25 y, 9 m, 6 d; of firm of Murray, Sons and James.
Murray, John B., eldest son of John, late of Toronto, Canada West, July 26, 1864, age 24 y, 7 d.
Murray, John R. V., son of Samuel Anna E. [sic], March 9, 1874, age 22; d. at Petrolia, PA, bur. in Buffalo.
Murray, Jonathan, Springville, NY, May 11, 1846, age 66.
Murray, Joseph, Feb. 1, 1875, age 25; taken to Colden.
Murray, Mrs. Lucy J., formerly of Aurora, dau. of Dexter Brown, April 1870, age 34 y, 5 m, 25 d. Died at Shamburg, PA, bur. in Griffins Mills Cemetery.
Murray, Margaret, wid. of James C., Colden, NY, Sept. 9, 1864, age 73 y, 6 m.
Murray, Miss Margaret I., Sept. 29, 1880.
Murray, Michael, Jan. 31, 1872.
Murray, Patrick, drowned, Aug. 14, 1876.
Murray, Timothy, brother of Thomas & Hubert, Oct. 18, 1873, age 47.
MUrray, William, of the firm Murray & Lynde, Jan. 19, 1871.
Murry, Ellen, Almshouse, July 24, 1880, age 40.
Murster, John, Sept. 2, 1879, age 22 y, 10 m, 20 d.
Musier, Mrs. Sarah, mother of Mrs. H. P. Russell, April 24, 1842, age 69.
Musson, Ellen A., wife of Henry W., Aug. 24, 1864; at Boston, NY.
Musson, Mrs. Julia, Feb. 17, 1875, age c. 23.
Mutz, William, accidental death, Black Rock, April 17, 1875, age c. 50.
Muzzy, Charles E., Jan. 9, 1852, age 44; in Auburn, NY, bur. in Buffalo.
Myer, Brig. Gen. Albert J., Aug. 24, 1880, age 52. Chief signal officer, USA, formerly of Buffalo. [Will on file in Record Room, Surrogate's Court, Erie Co. Hall.]
Myer, Eleanor, wife of Henry, July 23, 1835, age 39.
Myer, Mrs. Eliza, Feb. 25, 1863, age 64; taken to Wilkesbarre, PA.
Myers, ---, killed at Black Rock, Dec. 30, 1813.
Myers, Catharine, wife of Eugene, Sept. 14, 1847, age 21.
Myers, Eugene, May 22, 1857, age 38.
Myers, Francis H., Sept. 20, 1878, age 77.
Myers, Frank, accidental death, mason, Sept. 24, 1874.
Myers, Frank G., Nov. 3, 1865, age 20 y, 4 m.

Myers, George, Sept. 14, 1875, age 58.
Myers, Joseph A., Aug. 3, 1870, age 28 y, 6 m.
Myers, Mary Angeline, wife of Francis H., Oct. 17, 1857, age 59.
Myers, Mrs. Nancy, Aug. 3, 1854, age 56.
Myers, Rebecca Ann, wife of O. T., Dec. 24, 1870, age 28 y, 10 m, 12 d; taken to Wainfleet, Ontario.
Myers, Sarah S., wife of Jacob, Sept. 24, 1843, age 28 y, 27 d.
Myles, Frances or Francis, Aug. 1, 1875, age 34.

Nachbar, Werner, Aug. 7, 1875, age 32 y, 7 m.
Nagel, Emma E., wife of John C., Sept. 6, 1870, age 26 y, 9 m, 5 d.
Nagel, John M., July 11, 1876, age 72.
Nagel, Magdalena Hoffman, wife of John M., May 16, 1874, age 66 y, 26 d.
Nagle, Robert, April 6, 1875, age 72.
Nakel, Christopher, Almshouse, Dec. 31, 1879, age 63.
Napier, Agnes, wife of Peter, Nov. 3, 1868, age 47; d. in NY City, bur. in Buffalo.
Nash, Aaron (Hanover), fell during war of 1812, Jan. 1814.
Nash, Arthur, Aug. 29, 1880, age 28 y, 5 m, 3 d.
Nash, Dr. Daniel, Springville, Oct. 23, 1874, age 78.
Nash, Hannah, wife of Richard, Oct. 20, 1872, age 45.
Nash, John, Aug. 7, 1877, age 45.
Nash, Mrs. Julia, July 31, 1873, age 57.
Nash, Thomas, son of Capt. Thomas of 16th WI, brother of Peter of 116th N.Y. Vol., killed at Port Hudson, age 28.
Natter, William, Nov. 22, 1863, age 72.
Nauert, John Jacob, May 4, 1870, age 78 y, 5 m, 28 d.
Naughton, James, Feb. 3, 1872, age 56.
Naughton, Margaret, wid. of James, Nov. 22, 1874, age 43.
Naughton, Mary, wife of William, Dec. 27, 1879, age 54.
Nayler, Capt. John, March 12, 1877, age 77.
Neal, John, Aug. 1, 1876, age 61.
Neale, Joseph, July 4, 1850, age 43.
Neanhoun, Mrs. Johanna, drowned, July 21, 1874, age 26.
Near, Anna M., wife of Peter, May 19, 1879, age 46 y, 3 m, 18 d.
Neason (or Neeson), Barry (or Bernard), Feb. 14, 1875, age 35.
Neber, Valentine, March 12, 1878, age 55.
Nechter, Mary A., dau. of James & M. A. Wechter [sic], June 9, 1879.
Needham, A. C., Sardinia, NY, July 1, 1846, age 35.
Needham, Daniel, April 1846, age 70.
Needham, Joann W., wid. of Joseph P., March 15, 1867, age 73.
Needham, Joseph P., June 5, 1865, age 78.
Needham, Joseph P., Jr., Dec. 1857; bur. Dec. 16.
Neeper, Sarah Ann, wife of James, dau. of Nathaniel Knight, March 20, 1859, age 36.
Neeve, Ellen R., wid. of John, Jan. 26, 1873, age 72; taken to Guelph, Ontario.
Neff, Mrs. Catherine, Tonawanda, Aug. 21, 1879, age 83.
Negus, Allen W., of Co. G, Hawkins Zouaves, killed in Battle of Antietam, Sept. 17, 1862, aged 30. Hero of many hard fought fields.
Negus, Ann, wife of John G., March 4, 1852, age 42.
Negus, Edward H., Jan. 23, 1875, age 23 y, 8 m.
Negus, George, son of J.G., Dec. 18, 1861, age 24 y, 2 m; at Upton Hill, VA in service of his country; bur. in Buffalo.
Negus, John G., May 12, 1872, age 71 y, 5 m.
Negus, Miss Libbie, dau. of the late John, Dec. 29, 1876, age 28.
Nehin, Mary, wife of John, Oct. 21, 1873, age 28.
Neiman, Charles, Tonawanda, Feb. 26, 1872, age 33.
Neilss, George Frank, Nov. 19, 1879, age 22.
Nellany, Minnie Crogan, wife of Michael, April 11, 1877, age 31.
Nellany, Owen, Aug. 26, 1876, age 84.
Nelson, Ann, wife of Charles, March 26, 1864, age 46.
Nelson, Daniel, Nov. 6, 1875, age 65.

Nelson, Mrs. Eliza, North Buffalo, NY, Feb. 16, 1865, age 74.
Nelson, Mrs. Mary A., Aug. 31, 1873, age 78.
Nelson, William, April 13, 1850, age 47.
Nerkday, Peter, Almshouse, Dec. 14, 1879, age 65.
Nesbit, James, killed at Battle of Black Rock, Dec. 30, 1813.
Nesen, Joseph, 2nd Asst. Engineer, U.S. Navy, Oct. 24, 1866, age 27; on a voyage from Hayti to NY; bur. in Buffalo.
Nesson, John, killed on railroad, June 5, 1879.
Netcher, Mary Louisa, wife of Louis, April 18, 1878, age 30 y, 5 m, 10 d.
Neuman, John R., formerly of Buffalo, Jan. 10, 1875, age 54 y, 8 m; d. at Detroit City, MN.
Neurehor, Joseph, Nov. 4, 1885, age 35.
Neuroth, George, County Almshouse, July 13, 1877, age 46.
Nevitt, Isabella, wife of C.R., Feb. 17, 1850, age 21; taken to Batavia, NY.
Nevitt, Lydia, April 20, 1869, age 61.
Nevitt, Robert, Jan. 25, 1856, age 54.
New, Edith C., widow of Thomas of Detroit, MI, April 5, 1867.
Newbould, John A., formerly of Buffalo, May 31, 1871, age 61; d. in Brooklyn.
Newcomb, John, railroad accident, July 21, 1876, age 26.
Newell, Miss Ada L., Dec. 20, 1868, age 23.
Newell, Aurelia W., wife of V.C., Nov. 8, 1856, age 33 y, 4 m.
Newell, Edward A., Jan. 1, 1879, age 21.
Newell, Emmett, suicide, Eden, May 19, 1876, age c. 40.
Newell, Guy C., Hamburgh, NY, Oct. 1818, age 28.
Newell, James, July 23, 1875, age 55 y, 2 m.
Newell, Miss Mandana, Black Rock, NY, July 1827.
Newell, Mary Ann, wife of V.C., Jan. 31, 1863, age 37 y, 6 m, 22 d; taken to East Hamburgh, NY.
Newell, Mrs. Matilda, Oct. 9, 1863, age 58.
Newell, Raphael, Oct. 4, 1854, age 78 y, 4 m.
Newell, Rosa Lina, wife of Raphael, May 27, 1862, age 83 y, 5 m, 17 d.
Newell, Sabina, Dec. 2, 1880, age 55.
Newell, Seth P., formerly of Buffalo, Sept. 6, 1878, d. at Sherman, TX.
Newkirk, Isaac W., March 28, 1849, age 54.
Newkirk, John, S., May 30, 1866, age 51.
Newkirk, Mrs. Mary B., July 10, 1854, age 51 y, 11 m, 3 d.
Newland, Austin, Marilla, June 4, 1877, age 48.
Newland, Hannah, wife of John, Oct. 7, 1858, age 58 y, 9 m.
Newland, John, Feb. 9, 1875, age 78.
Newland, Joseph, son of John of Buffalo, Aurora, NY, Aug. 1859, age 32 y, 4 m; bur. in Buffalo Aug. 27.
Newland, William, son of John & Hannah, Aug. 30, 1849, age 28.
Newman, Charles, Aurora, NY, Jan. 28, 1864, age 28 y, 10 m.
Newman, Elizabeth, wife of John, March 12, 1859, age 71.
Newman, Ellen S., wife of Dr. James M., dau. of Maynard Bragg of Lowell, MA, Oct. 7, 1860.
Newman, Emanuel, May 24, 1877, age 72.
Newman Capt. Eugene, Sept. 2, 1870, age 46.
Newman, George H., April 21, 1871, age 32.
Newman, James M., M.D., Jan. 7, 1861, age 37.
Newman, Mrs. Jane, May 4, 1868, age 88.
Newman, John, Aug. 28, 1867, age 71.
Newman, Miss Margaret, eldest dau. of Henry, formerly of Buffalo, Jan. 16, 1843; at Pontiac, MI.
Newman, Marianne Sophia, March 26, 1868.
Newman, Phebe L., wife of Sumner, June 24, 1880, age 33 y, 11 m, 17 d.
Newman, Thomas B., May 15, 1873, age 73.
Newman, William, native of Boston, MA, April 4, 1860, age 60.
Newton, Ann Rebecca Hopkins, dau. of James, April 26, 1871, age 34.
Newton, Daniel R., East Hamburgh, May 30, 1875, age 67.
Newton, Mrs. Eliza, July 12, 1874, age 61 y, 10 m, 9 d.
Newton, Emeline, Newstead, NY, April 14, 1841, age 22.

Newton, Isaac, May 5, 1876, age 57.
Newton, James (colored), Jan. 30, 1874, age 73.
Newton, Joshua, East Hamburgh, April 4, 1865, age 84.
Newton, Luther G., July 20, 1869.
Newton, Mary C. Stambach, wife of D. R. Jr., East Hamburgh, NY, Sept. 20, 1877, age 29.
Newton, Mrs. Nancy N., Jan. 12, 1867, age 67 y, 7 m.
Newton, Capt. Obediah, Hamburgh, Oct. 13, 1873, age 91.
Newton, Philo, Aug. 25, 1872, age 34; funeral in Hanover, Chautauqua Co.
Newton, Robert, Oct. 8, 1864, age 46.
Newton, Robert Sr., Dec. 4, 1858, age 76.
Newton, Samuel Jr., Aug. 11, 1871.
Neylan, John F., June 7, 1878, age 27.
Neylan, Patrick B., Dec. 21, 1876, age 21 y, 7 m.
Nial, Hugh B., Aug. 21, 1880, age 77.
Nibecker, Philip J., Jan. 23, 1879, age 60.
Nichols, Asher P., lawyer, May 30, 1880, age 65; d. at Clinton, NY.
Nichols, Benjamin W., March 27, 1880, age 60 y, 1 m.
Nichols, Charlotte, Evans, wife of David, March 16, 1880, age 66.
Nichols, Daniel, Aurora, NY, May 24, 1866, age 76.
Nichols, Elizabeth, mother of Merritt and Silas C., Jan. 29, 1866, age 77.
Nichols, Elizabeth, wife of Levi, Sept. 6, 1879, age 33.
Nichols, Mary, dau. of the late Daniel, Aurora, Nov. 17, 1871, age 42; d. in Cummng, GA.
Nichols, Mary J., East Hamburgh, Oct. 8, 1876, age 59 y, 25 d.
Nichols, Peleg, father of Merritt and Silas C., Nov. 24, 1860, age 72.
Nichols, Polly, widow of Daniel, Aurora, April 16, 1867, age 75.
Nichols, Reuben, b. Aug. 1752, d. July 20, 1840, bur. Sardinia, NY; Soldier of the Revolution.
Nichols, Richard Whelen, Sept. 7, 1846, age 32; in Northhampton, MA.
Nichols, Mrs. Sarah Ann, formerly of Buffalo, Feb. 18, 1878, age 74; d. in Dallas, TX.
Nicholson, Gavin Sr., July 19, 1876, age 61; taken to Chippewa, Ontario.
Nicholson, James, June 25, 1866, age 38.
Nickels, Samuel Smith, formerly of Buffalo, Nov. 14, 1857, age 41. Member of the House of Nickels, Loring & Co., Talcshuano, Chili.
Nickerson, Jane E., wife of Capt. Alfred, April 19, 1849, age 26.
Nickerson, Jeptha G., July 1, 1868, age 20.
Nickles, Bartholomew, Dec. 3, 1880, age 45; killed by the cars.
Nicklin, Harriet, July 27, 1863, age 55.
Nicklis, Ferdinand, April 3, 1872, age 26.
Nicklis, William, Sept. 11, 1874, age 65.
Niederlander, Henrietta Co., Bowmansville, wife of N.F., Jan. 30, 1871, age 27 y, 3 m; d. at Boonsboro, IA.
Niemann, Lottie Dunlap, wife of A.D., youngest dau. of the late Horace Dunlap of Buffalo, formerly of Buffalo, Feb. 1, 1877; d. at Mansfield, OH.
Niergarth, Elizabeth, wife of Frederick, formerly of Buffalo, dau. of Philip Miller, Dec. 14, 1855; at Kappa, IL.
Niess, George, Sept. 11, 1872, age 43.
Niles, Abagail, widow of Maj. Jeremiah of RI, July 31, 1844, age 86.
Niles, Hiram, formerly of Buffalo, Jan. 19, 1879; d. in Chicago.
Niles, William, Boston, NY, July 2, 1880, age 66 y, 22 d.
Nilsson, Andrew, Sept. 1, 1873.
Nimbs, A.B., May 21, 1866, age 39.
Niquet, Mr. E. C., Oct. 15, 1847, age 51.
Nisel (or Neisel or Nison), Edward, July 19, 1873, age 47.
Noah, Michael W., Nov. 19, 1853, age 50.
Noble, Alfred, accidental death, May 28, 1876, age 25.
Noble, Anne, widow of Capt. James, Dec. 28, 1877, age 63.
Noble, Charles E., formerly of Buffalo, Dec. 27, 1873, age c. 48; d. in NY City.
Noble, Cyrenus, March 16, 1857, age 31; taken to Detroit, MI.
Noble, Dewitt D., April 8, 1871, age 21.
Noble, Hezekiah, March 23, 1827, age 82.

Noble, John F., Feb. 11, 1872, age 24.
Noble, Major, Williamsville, NY, Jan. 8, 1860, aged 80 y, 7 m, 6 d. "Major" a first name, not military rank. Bur. in Christian or Schenck Family Cemetery, Town of Amherst. Bodies moved to Skinnerville Cemetery, same town, 1956.
Noble, Margaret, wife of Capt. W., Feb. 18, 1867, age 31 y, 3 m, 13 d.
Noble, Mrs. Mary, Sept. 16, 1879, age 60.
Noble, Robert P., formerly of Buffalo, June 30, 1872, age 40; d. at Rome, NY.
Noble, Usual S., printer, May 17, 1869, age 29.
Noble, William F., July 12, 1835, age 25.
Noethen, Rev. Theodore, Catholic priest, formerly of Buffalo, April 10, 1879, age 63. Born at Cologne, came to this country in 1845.
Nolan, Ann, wife of Bartholomew, Jan. 31, 1872, age 35.
Nolan, Annie F., dau. of Edward, Aug. 2, 1875, age 25.
Nolton, Kate Stover, wife of Hiram G., May 22, 1866; in Lockport, bur. in Buffalo.
Noon, Martin, Sept. 26, 1878, age 66.
Noonen, Thomas, Sept. 17, 1878, age 19 y, 11 m, 2 d.
Nork, Andrew, Aug. 31, 1875, age 20.
Norris, Abram, Jan. 26, 1880, age 71; bur. at Palmyra, NY.
Norris, Cynthia E., wife of Abram, April 9, 1877, age 59.
Norris, Major John, Nov. 6, 1876, age 45.
Norris, Lorenzo E., formerly of Buffalo, Jan. 1, 1873; d. at Tonawanda.
Norris, Luanna, wife of James, Aug. 25, 1849, age 24.
Norris, Thomas, Nov. 4, 1879, age 48.
Norris, Capt. William, suicide, Erie, PA, Aug. 19, 1878, age c. 45.
Norse, Frank G., sailor, drowned, Oct. 16, 1877, age 26.
North, Henry J., Nov. 30, 1854, age 40.
North, Mrs. Ruth, Black Rock, NY, mother of Captains Walter and James, Feb. 18, 1836, age 74.
Northort, Hopestile, Hamburgh, NY, 1850, age 93.
Northrup, Mrs. Avis, Dec. 8, 1876, age 78 y, 5 m.
Northrup, Joel, formerly of Oneida Co., April 7, 1841, age 67.
Northrup, John, Hamburgh, NY, March 2, 1847, age 78.
Northrup, Joseph, Hamburgh, NY, March 25, 1848, age 45.
Northrup, Lewis G., Springbrook, NY, Sept. 16, 1867, aged 39 y, 10 m, 23 d.
Norton, Abigail, Jan. 24, 1858, age 87.
Norton, Catharine Ann, wife of Enoch B.H., Willink, NY, April 27, 1850, age 38.
Norton, Charles, brother-in-law of the late Albert H. Tracy, March 12, 1870, age 66. Died at his residence, Farnham Station, town of Brant, Erie Co., NY, bur. in Buffalo.
Norton, Mrs. Charles, formerly of Buffalo, Dec. 12, 1873; d. in San Francisco, CA.
Norton, Charles Davis, April 11, 1867, age 47.
Norton, David, Wales Center, NY, March 8, 1863, age 77.
Norton, Ebenezer F., May 11, 1851, age 77.
Norton, Edward, May 1872, brother of Mrs. Albert H. Tracy.
Norton, Elizabeth Huntington, eldest dau. of Joseph G., May 18, 1848.
Norton, Frances R., sister of the late Charles D., April 13, 1876.
Norton, Frank L., Aug. 6, 1876, age 21 y, 4 m, 14 d; taken to East Concord.
Norton, Harry J., formerly of Buffalo, June 6, 1880, age 40; printer & journalist. Died at Leadville, CO.
Norton, James, Feb. 1861.
Norton, John, Sept. 14, 1850, age 37.
Norton, Joseph G., Sept. 4, 1844, age 63.
Norton, Lucretia Huntington, widow of Joseph G., Feb. 10, 1876, age 93.
Norton, Miss Mary, Black Rock, NY, Aug. 8, 1820, age 27.
Norton, Mary, wife of Dr. M.B., Black Rock, NY, June 16, 1852, age 28.
Norton, Mary, March 16, 1871, age 34.
Norton, Minnie C., wife of James M., Feb. 13, 1866, age 25.
Norton, Pamila, July 27, 1880, age 67.
Norton, Phoebe M., wife of J.S., March 2, 1875, age 48 y, 3 m, 23 d.
Norton, Samuel B., Aug. 1, 1853, age 42.
Norton, Seymour M., formerly of VT, April 4, 1869, age 68.

Norton, Sophia, widow of Capt. Walter, March 18, 1860, age 65.
Norton, Thomas J., Aug. 21, 1880, age 30 y, 9 m.
Norton, Capt. Walter, Feb. 21, 1849, age 62.
Norton, William, killed by a horse, Aug. 30, 1873, age 26.
Nothnagel, Philip, April 4, 1869.
Nott, Gen. Ezra, Sardinia, NY, Aug. 3, 1864, age 77 y, 2 m, 21 d.
Notter, Charles Edward, Co. A, 10th U.S. Infantry, Jan. 1865, age 17 y, 6 m. Died of disease contracted in the Rebel Pen at Salisbury, NC.
Notter, Richard, formerly of Buffalo, March 11, 1874; d. at Dunleith, IL, bur. Buffalo.
Notter, Thomas, formerly of Buffalo, Jan. 16, 1874, age 63; d. in Chicago.
Notterbruck, Mrs. County Almshouse, insane, Jan. 23, 1880, age 40.
Noye, Jane G., sister of John T., Sept. 13, 1870; d. in Chicago, bur. Buffalo.
Noye, Maria Kirby, wife of John T., March 18, 1876.
Noye, Mary, wife of Rev. R., mother of J.T., Oct. 27, 1845, age 50.
Noye, Rev. Richard, father of John T. of Buffalo, March 19, 1869, age 78; d. in Chicago, bur. Buffalo.
Noyes, Charles E., formerly of Buffalo, July 30, 1855, at Baton Rouge, LA.
Noyes, Cornelia, wife of Daniel, dau. of Harry Thompson of Buffalo, Feb. 15, 1862, age 31; in La Porte, IN, bur. in Buffalo.
Noyes, George Milton, lawyer, April 25, 1862, age 32.
Noyes, Mrs. M. A., April 3, 1859.
Noyes, Milton, Wales, NY, March 2, 1844, age 46.
Nugent, James, railroad accident, formerly of Buffalo, May 21, 1875; killed on Canada S. railroad near Detroit, MI.
Nugent, Nevin, Tonawanda, Feb. 12, 1868, age 45.
Nugent, Mrs. Sarah, Tonawanda, June 1, 1878.
Nuhn, Conrad, March 2, 1871, age 60.
Nuhn, Henry Frederick, son of J.A., butcher, July 29, 1875, age 23; murdered at Hillsdale, IL.
Nutting, Arthur F., Wales Center, Nov. 23, 1871, age 84 y, 10 m, 18 d.
Nutting, John F., East Wales, July 14, 1872, age 55 y, 6 m, 18 d.
Nutting, Mary, wife of Abner F., Wales, NY, May 7, 1850, age 62.
Nye, Charles W., April 16, 1880, age 21.
Nye, Edward J., postmaster, Aurora, NY, Oct. 4, 1832.
Nye, Emeline Hale, wife of Barton, East Aurora, March 21, 1877, age 43 y, 3 m, 4 d.
Nye, Miss Emma, Sept. 29, 1870, age 24 y, 8 m.
Nye, John, East Aurora, Nov. 10, 1874, age 80.
Nye, Monroe, Oct. 18, 1875, age 52.
Nystrom, Nicholas J., Feb. 28, 1876, age 32; taken to Quincy, MA.

Oades, Francis, son of James, of Egham, Surrey, England, Dec. 26, 1862; Buffalo General Hospital.
Oakes, Esther, widow of Samuel, East Hamburgh, July 4, 1868, age 69.
Oakes, John H., Jan. 4, 1876, age 23 y, 8 m, 10 d.
Oakley, Augustus, Clarence, May 19, 1876, age 77 y, 2 m, 8 d.
Oakley, Mrs. Augustus, Clarence, April 20, 1877; widow.
Oakley, James S., Jan. 3, 1874, age 47; taken to Clarence.
Oaks, George, East Hamburgh, March 16, 1872, age 45.
Oaks, Joanna, wife of Samuel F., East Hamburgh, Oct. 4, 1875, age 24.
Oaks, Lyman, father of Ira & Samuel, Hamburgh, Feb. 7, 1873, age 76.
Oaks, Mary, wife of Ira, Feb. 15, 1878, age 58 y, 1 m, 8 d; taken to Abbott's Corners, NY.
Oaks, Samuel, East Hamburgh, NY, May 28, 1850, age 54.
Oaks, Silas, Co. C, Scott's 900 Cavalry, Oct. 8, 1864, age 35. Funeral at Abbotts Corners.
Oaks, William, East Hamburgh, NY, Dec. 2, 1867, age 46.
Oatman, Lyman, Angola, Sept. 9, 1877, age 61.
Oatman, Orlin, March 23, 1852, age 29.
Oatman, Walter George, Sept. 28, 1869, age 67 y, 4 m.
Oberist, Alfred J., Dec. 24, 1879, age 26.
Oberist, Charles E., March 4, 1878, age 35 y, 4 m, 6 d.
Oberist, Samuel, Feb. 28, 1865, age 52 y, 5 m.

Oberist, Samuel J., son of Samuel, June 19, 1865, age 26 y, 8 m.
Oberst, Thomas, June 1874, age 75.
O'Brian, Bridget, dau. of Patrick, Sept. 10, 1852, age 26.
O'Brian, Bridget, Sept. 14, 1873, age 48.
O'Brian, Charles, County Almshouse, Aug. 27, 1876, age 75.
O'Brian, Daniel, missing since last Oct., March 23, 1877, age 22. Found under the ice, March 23.
O'Brian, Eliza, wife of John P., Dec. 18, 1875, age 40.
O'Brian, Mrs. Ellen, Feb. 22, 1875, age 86.
O'Brian, James, July 13, 1866, age 63.
O'Brian, James, Feb. 1875, age 41.
O'Brian, James, June 7, 1875, age 30.
O'Brian, James, Oct. 19, 1876, age 21 y, 9 m, 13 d.
O'Brian, John, keeper of the Great Western Hotel, May 19, 1842.
O'Brian, John, Sept. 6, 1872, age 70.
O'Brian, Patrick, Dec. 14, 1868, age 74.
O'Brian, Sarah E., wife of Matthew, West Seneca, Feb. 5, 1879, age 48.
O'Brian, Thomas, Sept. 24, 1874, age 65.
O'Brian, Timothy, July 18, 1865, age 58.
O'Brian, Violete, wife of John, May 5, 1858, age 39.
O'Brian, Winnifred Lloyd, dau. of the late Thomas, Jan. 21, 1880, age 33.
O'Brien, Anastasia, wife of Capt. Thomas James, formerly of Quebec, Canada East, Aug. 1, 1866, age 45.
O'Brien, Anson J., Collins, NY, Dec. 28, 1852 in Buffalo, age 21; taken to Collins.
O'Brien, Betsey Ann, widow of John, July 14, 1849, age 46.
O'Brien, Daniel, Shirley (formerly Collins), Erie Co., NY, Feb. 1853, age 23.
O'Brien, Frances Cecelia, wife of William Lloyd, late of Mount Francis, County Roscommon, Ireland, Sept. 18, 1848, age 53.
O'Brien, James, killed on the track, Oct. 25, 1872.
O'Brien, James, Sept. 23, 1877, age 46.
O'Brien, John, barber, May 25, 1843, age 35.
O'Brien, John, June 5, 1880, age 35.
O'Brien, Margaret, sister of Mrs. Nehemiah Case & Mrs. Hannah Blackwood, Dec. 8, 1869, age 84.
O'Brien, Mary, wife of Martin, Oct. 27, 1877, age 25.
O'Brien, Michael, Sept. 27, 1851, age 34.
O'Brien, Thomas E., formerly of Collins, NY, May 22, 1856, age 34.
O'Brien, William, Collins Centre, NY, Feb. 17, 1849, age 60.
O'Brien, Mrs. William, drowned, Aug. 22, 1873.
O'Brien, William Lloyd, Aug. 25, 1849, age 56.
O'Bryan, Bridget, dau. of Patrick, Sept. 10, 1852, age 26.
O'Bryan, Patrick, Dec. 11, 1858, age 64.
O'Connell, Daniel, Aug. 25, 1867, age 75.
O'Connell, David, accidently killed, June 19, 1874, age 66.
O'Connell, Patrick, Nov. 25, 1873, age 53 y, 10 m, 25 d.
O'Conner, Mrs. Bridget, Nov. 27, 1863, age 49.
O'Conner, Daniel M., Nov. 19, 1861, age 29.
O'Conner, Mrs. Eliza, May 18, 1863, age 37.
O'Conner, John, March 29, 1864, age 56.
O'Conner, Thomas, June 22, 1879, age 28; d. at Sisters Hospital.
O'Connor, Catharine F., wife of John, Jan. 9, 1878.
O'Connor, Hannah, wife of Daniel, April 26, 1858, age 24.
O'Connor, Johanna, mother of D.M., Dec. 15, 1859.
O'Connor, John, Nov. 4, 1878, age 38.
O'Connor, Margaret, wife of John, Feb. 21, 1873, age 50.
O'Connor, Rev. Martin, Dec. 12, 1870; d. at Suspension Bridge, bur. in Buffalo.
O'Connor, Mary, June 11, 1867, age 22.
O'Connor, William, June 12, 1878, age 35.
O'Connor, William, Feb. 6, 1880, age 64.
O'Day, Bridget, wife of Edward, June 11, 1874, age 32.

O'Day, Mary, Feb. 26, 1875, age 65.
O'Day, Susan, Black Rock, NY, Feb. 28, 1862, age 20.
Odell, Betsy A., wife of A., Hamburgh, Feb. 7, 1854, age 26.
Odell, Esther, wife of Daniel, Hamburgh, Jan. 21, 1845, age 51.
Odelum, John, son of James, March 20, 1850, age 31.
Odlum, James, Feb. 11, 1868, age 78.
Odlum, Margaret, Sept. 19, 1878, age 85.
O'Donnel, John, accidently killed, Jan. 29, 1875, age 74.
O'Donnell, Annie, Sept. 10, 1880, age 21 y, 2 m, 3 d.
O'Donnell, John, accidently killed, May 26, 1873.
O'Donnell, John, accidently killed on railroad, locomotive engineer, Sept. 18, 1873, age 26.
O'Donnell, Joseph, Aug. 6, 1873, age 20.
O'Donnell, Leander, June 23, 1875.
O'Donnell, Simon, June 9, 1879, found drowned after being missing for a week.
O'Donoghue, Rev. John, March 8, 1875, age 31.
O'Dwyer, Timothy, Aug. 19, 1857, age 67.
Oehmig, Augusta, wife of Frederick N., Feb. 2, 1879, age 55 y, 11 m, 26 d.
Oehmig, Mary Helen Kinner, wife of Charles, May 10, 1877, age 26 y, 5 m, 9 d.
O'Farrell, Bridget, County Almshouse, Dec. 31, 1878, age 50.
Offenbacher, Mary, wife of Valentine, Jan. 17, 1877, age 53.
Ogden, Catherine, wife of William Jones Ogden of Lancashire, England, Aug. 16, 1866, age 32.
O'Grady, Edward, suicide, July 11, 1871, age 38.
O'Grady, Joseph, Dec. 25, 1863.
O'Grady, Thomas, son of Thomas, July 23, 1866, age 23.
O'Grady, Thomas, ex-alderman, March 14, 1874, age 73.
O'Haggerty, Jeremiah, March 15, 1875, age 70.
O'Hanlon, Michael, laborer, accidently drowned, Sept. 14, 1871, age 49.
O'Hara, Bridget, Jan. 10, 1877, age 27 y, 6 m.
O'Hara, Dennis, suicide, fisherman, June 23, 1874, age 40.
O'Hara, Mary, Suspension Bridge. Employed as a servant in Buffalo. Drowned from railroad bridge over Hamburg canal, July 25, 1879, age c. 35.
Ohlmer, Henrietta Augusta, wife of Harmon, Jan. 8, 1869, age 40 y, 5 m, 10 d.
Oishei, Joseph, Aug. 11, 1878, age 48.
O'Keefe, John, April 15, 1869, age 33.
O'Keefe, Mrs. Margaret, Dec. 18, 1873, age 31 y, 2 m, 8 d.
O'Keefe, Mary Ann, wife of John, March 27, 1867.
O'Laughlin, Martin, May 22, 1873, age 53.
O'Laughlin, Michael, Oct. 11, 1879, age 63.
Olcott, William, formerly of Buffalo, April 1, 1851; in LA, age 42.
O'Leary, Mrs. J., formerly of Rochester, NY, July 14, 1880, age 75.
O'Leary, Mary Jane Rodgers, wife of Michael, March 10, 1880, age 31 y, 4 m, 10 d.
O'Leary, Patrick, Oct. 13, 1872, age 35.
Olin, Jeremiah M., Feb. 19, 1874, age 40.
Olin, John, March 15, 1877, age 45.
Olin, William, Boston, Oct. 6, 1876, age 74.
Oliver, Mrs. Elizabeth, April 11, 1865, age 73.
Oliver, Dr. Frederick, dentist, Oct. 8, 1874, age 55.
Oliver, James, formerly of Buffalo, Dec. 17, 1850; in Kilwinning, Scotland.
Oliver, Capt. Jeremiah C., Hamburgh on the Lake, NY, Sept. 10, 1854, age 51.
Oliver, John N. Jr., Aug. 16, 1878, age 46 y, 11 m, 21 d.
Oliver, Robert B., Feb. 14, 1877, age 24 y, 9 m.
Oliver, William G., Sept. 18, 1868, age 60; d. in Brooklyn, NY, bur. in Buffalo.
Olliver, Anna M., wife of W.W., Oct. 18, 1870, age 22.
Olmstead, Emily E., Newstead, NY, April 18, 1841, age 22.
Olmstead, Margaret, wife of John, Nov. 1812, age 24.
Olson, Peter, protection, railroad employee, Feb. 1, 1880, age 41; killed near Holland while attempting to board a coal train.
Olver, Miss, May 1867; funeral May 20.

Olver, Horatio C., formerly of Land's End, England, Dec. 20, 1863, age 38.
Olver, Susan S., wife of Nicholas, Sept. 4, 1874, age 49.
Olver, Thomas Orlando, Jan. 8, 1875, age 46.
O'Malley, Dolly, wife of Patrick, Nov. 1872.
O'Malley, Patrick, Feb. 22, 1865, age 23 y, 3 m, 21 d.
O'Mally, Parick, Oct. 15, 1880, age 45, drowned; body recovered Oct. 22; laborer.
O'Mara, John, March 22, 1880, age 46; Almshouse.
O'Melia, Peter, laborer, drowned, July 5, 1880, age 46.
O'Neil, Mrs. Arthur, Oct. 31, 1876, age 74; taken to Niagara, Ontario.
O'Neli, Ellen, June 6, 1871, age 32.
O'Neil, James, Oct. 1880, age 26. Laborer, killed by fall from an oil tank.
O'Nelil, Johanna, Jan. 17, 1875, age 72.
O'Neil, Mary Ann, Aug. 23, 1871, age 24.
O'Neil, Patrick, April 23, 1874, age 33.
O'Neill, Mrs. Ann, widow, Feb. 9, 1877, age 40.
Ongley, Mary, wife of William H., July 30, 1842, age 28.
Orcutt, Benjamin, Jan. 1825, age 36.
Ord, Annie, wife of Robert, Aug. 27, 1879, age 42.
Ordner, John, suicide, Feb. 21, 1875, age c. 60.
Ordner, Maria, April 20, 1869, age 45 y, 3 m, 20 d.
Ordway, Mrs. Abby B., Nov. 23, 1866, age 65.
O'Reilley, Michael, June 25, 1868; taken to Rochester for interment.
Organ, John, Oct. 1, 1875, age 34 y, 6 m.
Ormrod, William, sailor, accidentally drowned, Aug. 28, 1870, age 25.
O'Rourke, Patrick, Dec. 1825, age 50.
Orr, Alvin, father of Hon. C. A., Holland, April 27, 1877, age 72 y, 2 m, 18 d.
Orr, Amzi M., Holland, July 30, 1876, age 39.
Orr, Lewis, Holland, NY, Feb. 10, 1848, age 41.
Orr, Louise C., wife of George, July 17, 1857, age 31.
Orton, Rev. Samuel G., D.D., formerly of Buffalo, May 12, 1873; d. at Sandusky, OH.
O'Ryan, William, formerly of Buffalo, Aug. 6, 1871, age 39; d. at Bansha, Ireland.
Osborn, Asa, April 21, 1814, age 65.
Osborn, Elias, Aug. 20, 1830, age 67; Erie in this County.
Osborn, Elias, late of Albany, Oct. 19, 1862, age 54.
Osborn, Lemuel, Newstead, NY, July 29, 1850, age 73.
Osborn, Marietta, sister of Mrs. H. A. Salisbury, June 3, 1875, age 71.
Osborn, Ogden H., July 17, 1866, age 42.
Osborn, Phebe, widow of Elias of Newstead, March 16, 1845, age 76.
Osborn, Stephen, Jan., 1855; funeral Jan. 12.
Osborne, Mrs., formerly of Buffalo, March 1876.
Osborne, Elihu, Newstead, NY, Feb. 8, 1846, age 39.
Osborne, George H., Lancaster, NY, May 15, 1861, age 30 y, 5 m.
Osborne, James, Jan. 26, 1875, age 69.
Osborne, Miss Phebe, May 3, 1814, age 20.
Osborne, Robert, May 28, 1876, age 23.
Osborne, Samuel A., Tonawanda, NY, May 4, 1866, age 41.
Osgood, Sarah M., wife of David R., Aug. 20, 1875, age 63.
O'Shea, Daniel, Sept. 4, 1870, age 59.
O'Shea, Isabella M., youngest dau. of the late Daniel, Dec. 12, 1870, age 20.
O'Shea, James, June 3, 1872, age 46.
O'Shea, Mary Emma, widow of Daniel, Dec. 13, 1876, age 56.
O'Shea, Michael, Dec. 22, 1852; d. at Hospital of Sisters of Charity.
Osman, Emanuel, Feb. 27, 1877, age 48.
Osorman, Michael, County Almshouse, Aug. 7, 1879, age 76.
Ostertag, William R., Nov. 18, 1879, age 24 y, 10 m.
Ostheim, William, Aug. 1874, age 31.
Ostrade, Mrs. Mary P., July 2, 1863, age 34.
Ostrander, Amasa K., Jr., Hamburgh, March 6, 1878, age 28 y, 6 m, 21 d; d. at La Crosse, WI.
Ostrander, Charles, late of Auburn, Cayuga Co., N.Y., Sept. 9, 1841.

Ostrander, Jeanette, 2d dau. of Amasa K., Hamburgh, NY, Sept. 7, 1863, age 22.
Ostrander, John, East Hamburgh, NY, March 10, 1856, age 96.
Ostrander, John, West Falls, June 5, 1868, age 64; formerly of East Hamburgh.
Ostrander, Thomas, East Hamburgh, NY, June 21, 1866, age 58 y, 10 m, 19 d.
Ostrander, Mrs. Tirzah, Abbotts Corners, Dec. 25, 1879, age 67 y, 6 m, 19 d; wife of A.K.
Ostrom, Mrs. Anna M., dau. of Daniel Bowen, April 28, 1873, age 34.
O'Sullivan, Jeremiah, Oct. 25, 1872, age 26.
O'Sullivan, Owen, Sept. 24, 1871, age 70.
Oswald, Mrs., Sept. 11, 1870, age 36; accidental death by burning.
Oswald, Anthony, killed by John Peters, Jan. 3, 1874, age c. 24.
Otis, Mary, widow of Chandler of Troy, NY, June 12, 1876; taken to Troy.
Otis, Mary Jane, wife of Ceylon, Sept. 11, 1858, age 33.
Otis, N. E., July 26, 1854, age 51.
Otis, Nathaniel T., Jr., only son of Nathaniel T., medical student, Aug. 14, 1849, age 19 y, 6 m.
Ott, Conrad, May 18, 1871, age 38.
Ottenot, Augustus, Dec. 3, 1876, age 29 y, 3 m, 17 d.
Ottenot, Catherine, wife of Nicholas, Aug. 28, 1860, age 25 y, 1 m, 5 d.
Ottenot, Frances, wife of Nicholas, Feb. 25, 1859, age 38 y, 8 m, 25 d.
Ottenot, Josephine, June 15, 1877, widow of Louis J., age 31 y, 6 m.
Ottenot, Louis J., June 6, 1877, age 33 y, 4 m, 14 d.
Otto, Frederick, Jan. 1, 1873, age 27 y, 7 m, 7 d.
Otto, John S., formerly of Buffalo, Jan. 14, 1880, age 26; d. at Orange Grove, Clay Co., FL; son of the late William E.
Otto, Josiah, County Almshouse, Feb. 15, 1876, age 62.
Otto, Maria Louise, wife of James W., Aug. 15, 1855, age 34.
Otto, Phebe, widow of Jacob S. of Batavia, NY, June 1, 1867, age 75.
Otto, Valentine, April 2, 1877, age 45.
Otto, William Edmund, Feb. 28, 1869, age 45.
Otts, Frederick, Jan. 1, 1873, age 22.
Outmeyer, Frank, drowned, Dec. 6, 1877, age 35.
Ovens, Robert B., 2nd son of Robert, Jan. 4, 1864, age 28 y, 9 m, 12 d.
Ovens, Thomas J., Nov. 21, 1860, age 23 y, 9 m.
Overfield, F. J., May 1871, age 22 y, 1 m, 23 d.
Overland, James, sudden death Dec. 18, 1879; family in England.
Ovington, William H., formerly of Buffalo, May 11, 1880; d. at Chicago.
Ovitch, Casper, accidental death, Sept. 10, 1878.
Owen, E. A., April 29, 1879, age 62.
Owen, Elizabeth, wife of John, May 12, 1878, age 65.
Owen, Ellen J., dau. of Joseph, March 5, 1879, age 23 y, 19 d.
Pwem. Joseph, mill-wright & carpenter, Jan. 29, 1880, age 63 y, 9 m, 22 d.
Owen, Joshua, colored, Jan. 23, 1835, age 35. Esteemed a man of worth and integrity.
Owen, Mary Josephine, Oct. 13, 1859, age 65.
Owen, Samuel, Revolutionary soldier, Newstead, NY, Dec. 23, 1831, age 74.
Owens, Julia, wife of Joshua, Jan. 28, 1832, age 27.
Oyer, William, July 17, 1871, age 56.

Packard, Benjamin F., Aurora, July 21, 1873, age 54.
Packard, Elizabeth, wife of Capt. S., Oct. 30, 1873, age 56.
Packard, James, Aurora, NY, July 5, 1866, age 83 y, 1 m, 10 d.
Packard, Capt. Samuel, April 26, 1875, age 73.
Packard, Tillie E., April 15, 1868, age 28.
Paddock, Mrs. Hannah M., sister of Mrs. C. G. Brundige, Sept. 9, 1857, age 24.
Paddock, James Oscar, brother of Julia E., April 14, 1862, age 21; at Pittsburg Landing.
Paddon, William W., May 17, 1879, age 56.
Padgett, Mrs. Edith, Gowanda, mother of Mrs. Ann Butler of Buffalo, April 6, 1870, age 78.
Pagan, Thomas, June 28, 1854, age 35.
Page, David B., March 24, 1862, age 63; taken to Bennington, Wyoming Co., N.Y.
Page, Mrs. Hannah C., Aug. 13, 1849, age 63.
Page, Ida J., only dau. of David P., May 4, 1872, age 16 y, 11 m, 17 d.

Page, Jerusha, wife of Capt. Timothy, June 19, 1822, age 53.
Page, Lucius H., Oct. 14, 1880, age 46; bur. at Ashtabula, OH.
Page, Lyman A., May 4, 1860, age 40 y, 5 m.
Page, Capt. Timothy, 1839, age 73; in Dunville, Upper Canada.
Paige, Mrs. Abigail, Feb. 9, 1820, age 29.
Paige, Eliza W., wife of Timothy, Oct. 10, 1855, age 54.
Paine, Judge Edward, Aurora, Oct. 19, 1872, age 82.
Paine, Edwin, Aurora, NY, Oct. 20, 1856, age 62 y, 4 m, 21 d.
Paine, Maria, dau. of James M., Aurora, NY, Feb. 28, 1866, age 20; in East Hamburgh, NY.
Paine, Mary, Almshouse, Dec. 18, 1879, age 65.
Palflen, August, Oct. 29, 1871, age 50.
Pallusser, Rudolph, Almshouse, Feb. 10, 1880, age 62.
Palmer, Alanson, Dec. 18, 1875, formerly of Buffalo; d. in Ovid, NY, Insane Asylum.
Palmer, Archibald, Sept. 23, 1876.
Palmer, Asa, Springbrook, NY, Dec. 9, 1861, age 76 y, 9 m, 2 d.
Palmer, Charlotte, wife of Edward W., Oct. 15, 1863, age 34 y, 11 m.
Palmer, David, Hamburgh, NY, Jan. 1813, age 20.
Palmer, Mrs. Elenor, mother of J.H., March 7, 1866, age 88; taken to Rochester, NY.
Palmer, Elizabeth, mother of Mrs. A. Hosmer, Dec. 29, 1856, age 74; d. at Fort Porter.
Palmer, Emily A., Sept. 13, 1859, age 40 y, 6 m, 10 d.
Palmer, Excy Anna, wife of Everard, Aug. 15, 1853, age 22.
Palmer, Frances H. M., wife of Edward D., Jan. 9, 1850, age 19.
Palmer, George, Sept. 19, 1864, age 72 y, 5 m.
Palmer, George Le Grand, grandson of R. G. Buchanan, April 3, 1869, age 30; d. in Jersey City, bur. Buffalo.
Palmer, Hannah Jeannette, wife of Everard, Jan. 19, 1849, age 26.
Palmer, Harlow, Aug. 27, 1852, age 31.
Palmer, Harriet, widow of George, Aug. 15, 1874, age 76.
Palmer, Mrs. Hezekiah, July 12, 1866.
Palmer, Capt. Innis B., brother of Col. Alanson, formerly of Buffalo, July 2, 1843, age 56; d. in Rochester, NY.
Palmer, Jane, wife of Bartlett, formerly of Canandaigua, NY, March 10, 1835, age 25.
Palmer, Joseph, July 14, 1865, age 34.
Palmer, Mrs. Lydia, June 24, 1832, age 40.
Palmer, M. A., widow of N.B., Jan. 5, 1869; d. in Jersey City, bur. Buffalo.
Palmer, Martin, Aurora, NY, Jan. 23, 1857, age 51.
Palmer, Mrs. Mary, formerly of Simsbury, CT, June 13, 1845, age 64.
Palmer, Mrs. Mary E., formerly of Buffalo, dau. of Alpha Tyler of Buffalo, Oct. 29, 1861, age 24.
Palmer, Mary E., wife of J. H., Feb. 27, 1866, age 47; taken to Rochester, NY.
Palmer, Mary Hebron, wife of William J., Dec. 21, 1868, age 34 y, 11 m.
Palmer, Merret, Feb. 10, 1847, age 56.
Palmer, Mr. N. B., Aug. 16, 1852, age 35 y, 1 m.
Palmer, Nancy, wife of E. J., formerly of Watertown, Jefferson Co., NY, April 2, 1848, age 28.
Palmer, Oliver, formerly of Buffalo, Sept. 22, 1875, age 57; d. at Avondale near Cincinnati.
Palmer, Oscar, son of George, July 2, 1846, age 20.
Palmer, Patty, wife of Alanson, Sept. 11, 1821, age 25.
Palmer, Robert S., Sept. 18, 1880, age 64.
Palmer, Sally M., sister of Mrs. Grace B. Wilgus, Nov. 3, 1874, age 69 y, 10 m; taken to Stonington, CT.
Palmer, Samuel, Concord, NY, Aug. 22, 1852, age 72.
Palmer, Miss Sarah, Evans, NY, June 26, 1853, age 20.
Palmer, Sarah A., Dec. 18, 1849, age 21 y, 11 m; wife of Harlow.
Palmer, Sarah A., wife of Elias W., dau. of William Wells of Colchester, CT, April 4, 1850, age 41.
Palmer, Theodore, Black Rock, NY, April 30, 1853, age 37.
Palmerton, Hannah, Collins Center, Dec. 19, 1870, age 78.
Palmerton, Joshua, Collins Center, July 18, 1873, age 89.
Pandermeer, H. John, Jan. 30, 1876, age 70 y, 9 m.

Pannon, Thomas, March 11, 1871, age 40.
Pappino, Minerva S., Aug. 26, 1853.
Parish, Lydia G., wife of Joshua L., dau. of Charles G. Irish, July 29, 1849, age 22; at Java, Wyoming Co., NY.
Park, Adah, wife of Paul, Oct. 18, 1874, age 64.
Park, Frances, wife of Edgar of Chicago, IL, Oct. 8, 1863.
Park, James, Jan. 19, 1869, age 26.
Park, John P., Dec. 20, 1880, age 29.
Park, Miss Mary, formerly a teacher in Public School No. 7, Buffalo, Feb. 1867; in Fitchburg, MA.
Park, Paul, Dec. 1880.
Park, William H., April 7, 1862, age 24.
Parker, Mrs., mother of Aaron, Hamburgh, June 15, 1824, age 80.
Parker, Aaron, father of Perry G. of Buffalo, Oct. 16, 1860, age 75. D. at Fort Hill, IL, bur. at Abbotts Corners in Hamburgh, NY.
Parker, Alonzo E., East Aurora, Nov. 22, 1878, age 66.
Parker, Andrew, May 23, 1873, age 54.
Parker, Anna, widow of Capt. Joseph, Lancaster, NY, April 8, 1848, age 73.
Parker, Cleaveland, son of Judge P. of Cincinnati, OH, April 6, 1856, age 22; taken to Perth Amboy, NJ.
Parker, Cuthbert, April 28, 1872, age 56.
Parker, Edward H., formerly of Buffalo, Sept. 1, 1877, age 45.
Parker, Ellen, wife of T. L., Aug. 21, 1852, age 31.
Parker, Elvira Nash, wife of Andrew, Nov. 22, 1863, age 43.
Parker, Emeline, wife of Jason, July 30, 1852, age 38.
Parker, Eugenia C., wife of John P., Oct. 29, 1878, age 65 y, 10 m.
Parker, Francis B., Water Valley, May 11, 1873, age 68.
Parker, Frank H., April 1, 1872, age 31; taken to Boston Corners.
Parker, George H., Sept. 17, 1874, age 24.
Parker, Henry, son of Charles, drowned, Newstead, May 19, 1877, age c. 25.
Parker, Jacob A., June 2, 1859, age 66.
Parker, Jason, Sept. 19, 1876, age 62 y, 5 m, 25 d.
Parker, Mrs. Joanna, March 22, 1866, in 77th year; taken to Warsaw, NY.
Parker, Julia Frances, wife of John, Lancaster, NY, Dec. 23, 1851, age 38.
Parker, Julius W., son of John P., Sept. 20, 1868, age 31.
Parker, Margaret E., wife of Wing T., May 3, 1876, age 31 y, 8 m, 9 d.
Parker, Margaret E., East Aurora, wife of George W., June 5, 1879, age 24.
Parker, Mary, wife of John K., Evans, NY, April 29, 1866, age 43 y, 11 m, 7 d.
Parker, Mrs. Mary, Sept. 29, 1869, age 84.
Parker, Mary, May 16, 1874, age 50.
Parker, Mary C., May 21, 1874, age 55.
Parker, Mary Hamilton, wife of Perry G., June 21, 1870, age 52.
Parker, Nathan, March 7, 1868, age 78.
Parker, Nathan H., formerly of Lancaster, NY, Dec. 11, 1867 in Erie County Poor House.
Parker, Dr. Orlando K., Clarence, Nov. 16, 1872, age 47.
Parker, Perry G., Dec. 25, 1879, age 60.
Parker, Phoebe, wife of Francis B., Hamburgh, NY, Nov. 21, 1840, age 21.
Parker, Raymond J., Sept. 24, 1874, age 27 y, 3 m.
Parker, Rosana, widow of Raymond J., Oct. 1874, age 29 y, 1 m, 20 d.
Parker, Mrs. Sarah, mother of Thomas R., July 13, 1854, age 69.
Parker, Sarah, widow of Aaron, Hamburgh, Nov. 28, 1870, age 81 y, 6 m, 5 d.
Parker, Stephen, Alden, NY, Revolutionary soldier, Sept. 30, 1831, age 78.
Parker, Stephen, Holland, Nov. 17, 1876, age 90 y, 20 d.
Parker, Thomas R., formerly of Buffalo, Dec. 26, 1863; in Milwaukee, WI.
Parkhill, John, Evans, NY, March 2, 1840, in 49th year.
Parkhill, Capt. John, July 26, 1861, age 34.
Parkhurst, Albert Wilson, son of Abram W., Alden, NY, Sept. 11, 1855, age 21 y, 9 m, 22 d.
Parkhurst, Lemuel, Oct. 29, 1852, age 62.
Parkhurst, Mary Ann A., widow of Lemuel, Oct. 6, 1862, age 58 y, 9 m.
Parkinson, Hester Ann, wife of Reuben, Collins, NY, Dec. 4, 1840.

Parkinson, Jennett, wife of James, March 19, 1869, age 62; sister of J. B. Sackett.
Parks, James S., May 30, 1863, age 32 y, 9 m.
Parks, John, drowned, Grand Island, April 19, 1873.
Parks, Mrs. Sarah K., mother of Dr. Charles C. Haddock, July 16, 1850, in 69th year.
Parmalee, Mr. F. W., teacher, March 13, 1841, age 40.
Parmalee, Mary J., Sept. 16, 1880, age 26; bur. at Tonawanda.
Parmalee, Solomon, formerly of Buffalo, Jan. 10, 1876, age c. 75; d. in Toledo, OH, bur. in Lockport, NY.
Parmele, Elijah K., June 25, 1878, age 29.
Parmelee, Celina E., wife of Roswell, April 6, 1837, age 21.
Parmelee, Elizabeth Russell, wife of Edward F., formerly of Buffalo, April 18, 1877, age 21 y, 6 m; d. in New Haven, CT.
Parmelee, Philemon, East Hamburgh, NY, Sept. 8, 1859, age 34.
Parmelee, Sally, wife of Lemuel, Hamburgh, NY, May 20, 1827.
Parmelee, Theodore N., formerly of Buffalo, July 3, 1874, age 70; d. at Branford, CT.
Parr, Mrs. Ellen, Aug. 3, 1879, age 68.
Parr, George, Nov. 12, 1880, age 50; Edge Tool Manufacturing.
Parr, George H., Nov. 3, 1877, age 34.
Parsell, Mrs. Maria, Clarence, NY, Aug. 11, 1830, age 82.
Parshall, William Henry, formerly of Buffalo, March 17, 1871, age 32; d. in Lyons, NY.
Parson, Mrs. Lydia, Sept. 25, 1850, in 65th year.
Parson, Maria P., Oct. 13, 1866, age 28.
Parson, Mary, wife of Francis J., Cold Spring, NY, formerly of Lancaster, England, May 23, 1855, age 32.
Parsons, Comfort, father of Galusha, Marilla, Sept. 6, 1870, age 83 y, 5 m.
Parsons, Edward, found drowned May 1, 1878.
Parsons, Edward B., son of H. A. of Buffalo, Nov., 1849, age 19; in San Francisco, CA.
Parsons, Ethelbert H., formerly of Buffalo, Aug. 8, 1875, age 29; drowned at Niagara Falls.
Parsons, Ezra K., formerly of Buffalo, 1867, of the House of Smith and Parsons, Vicksburg, MS. Newspaper dated Nov. 25, 1867. D. in Vicksburg.
Parsons, George F., Jan. 24, 1876, age 52; taken to Ridgeway, Ontario.
Parsons, Rev. H. C., Tonawanda, NY, Oct. 26, 1864.
Parsons, Rev. Horatio A., formerly of Buffalo, Sept. 4, 1873, age 76 y, 5 m, 13 d; d. at Niagara Falls, bur. in Buffalo.
Parsons, James W., formerly of Buffalo, Jan. 5, 1873; d. in Erie, PA.
Parsons, Mrs. L., widow of the late G., April 8, 1879.
Parsons, Levi, son of Lewis B. of Buffalo, April 9, 1850; in St. Louis, MO.
Parsons, Lucy, wife of Silas, March 10, 1871.
Parsons, Mary Cornelia, wife of Charles W., Oct. 3, 1880, age 30; bur. at Warren, OH.
Parsons, Moses, Sept. 13, 1848, in 30th year.
Parsons, Miss Sarah Hannah, Oct. 7, 1863.
Parsons, Silas, b. 1761, d. 1839, bur. Lockport (Niagara Co.); Soldier of the Revolution.
Partridge, Anna, wife of Mason, Hamburgh, July 31, 1867, age 52.
Partridge, Asa, Colden, NY, Dec. 30, 1845, age 66.
Partridge, Frederick S., son of Joseph, Co. G, 100th Regt., N.Y.S.V., Sept. 1, 1863, age 24 y, 2 m, 3 d; at Morris Island, SC.
Partridge, Joseph, March 21, 1873, age 74.
Partridge, Mason, West Seneca, suicide, May 19, 1877, age 68.
Patch, Thompson, Wales, March 20, 1872, age 64.
Patchin, Aaron D., July 27, 1864, age 56.
Patchin, Clarissa, widow of Talcott, Abbotts Corners, Feb. 10, 1872, age 82.
Patchin, Hattie, dau. of A. T., Jan. 26, 1869, age 24.
Patchin, Isabella M., widow of Aaron D., Sept. 23, 1872.
Patchin, Richard J., Nov. 24, 1870, age 57 y, 5 m, 4 d.
Patchin, Thaddeus Darwin, April 8, 1874, age 38.
Patching, Luther T., Boston, NY, Feb. 6, 1836, in 20th year; in San Jacinto, TX.
Patching, Tallcut, formerly of Boston, NY, April 17, 1855, in 65th year; at Galveston Bay, TX.
Patrick, Lorinda, West Hamburg, Dec. 7, 1880, age 71 y, 11 m.
Patridge, Mrs. Adelia, March 31, 1872, age 22; taken to Darien.

Patridge, Frank W., June 17, 1874, age 23.
Pattee, E. F., June 20, 1871, age 52 y, 3 m.
Pattee, Rev. William M., formerly of Buffalo, July 20, 1862, age 29; Felt's Mills, NY.
Patten, James W., formerly of Buffalo, Sept. 20, 1861, age 67 y, 9 m, 28 d; d. at Patten's Mill, near Waco, TX.
Patten, Julius C., Oct. 16, 1861, age 42 y, 2 m, 13 d; Millbank, McLuman Co., TX or at Patten's Mill, near Waco.
Patten, Mrs. Louisa, Cold Spring, NY, sister of Mrs. Benjamin Hodge, April 20, 1846, age 39.
Patten, Mrs. Narcissa, formerly of Buffalo, Oct. 13, 1869, age 68 y, 5 m, 28 d; d. at Patten's Mill, near Waco, TX.
Pattengell, Allen O., Wales Center, Feb. 7, 1871, age 58.
Pattengill, George, Aurora, NY, Sept. 3, 1824, age 20.
Pattengill, Laura, wife of A. O., Wales Center, NY, March 22, 1866, age 43 y, 5 m, 23 d.
Pattengill, Oliver, b. 1752, d. 1818, bur. E. Aurora; Soldier of the Revolution.
Patterson, Rev. Albert Clarke, Oct. 21, 1874, age 65 y, 4 m, 8 d; taken to Boston.
Patterson, Capt. Alvin, of Schooner *Prince Eugene*, Oct. 26, 1834, age 26.
Patterson, Amy, wife of the late James, Jan. 5, 1868, age 62 y, 11 m.
Patterson, Betsey, March 13, 1857, age 26.
Patterson, David, Dec. 18, 1871, age 29.
Patterson, Ebenezer, b. 1760, d. 1846, bur. Griffins Mills. [in with Soldier of the Revolution cards.]
Patterson, Mrs. Eliza A., formerly of Buffalo, Nov. 25, 1874, age 63; d. in Chicago, IL, bur. in Buffalo.
Patterson, Elizabeth M., wife of C. H., July 1, 1875, age 31.
Patterson, George A. H., formerly from Hudson, NY, Sept. 23, 1843, in 33rd year.
Patterson, John, Jan. 1, 1852, age 30.
Patterson, John, April 21, 1863, age 26 y, 3 m.
Patterson, John, Alden, Feb. 13, 1872, age 63 y, 9 m, 24 d.
Patterson, John J., July 4, 1873, age 20; d. at Saratoga. Known as "Little Johnny Patterson."
Patterson, Mrs. Margaret A., April 26, 1878, age 63 y, 9 m, 23 d.
Patterson, Margaret Jane, wife of F. G., Nov. 27, 1856, age 36.
Patterson, Mrs. Martha, Jan. 12, 1873, age 66 y, 11 m.
Patterson, Mary, wife of John, June 22, 1880, age 70.
Patterson, Nancy, wife of William W., Dec. 21, 1843, age 54.
Patterson, Nettie L., dau. of James, Evans, NY, Oct. 30, 1864, age 28.
Patterson, Mrs. Rebecca, Aurora, NY, Aug. 1830, age 70.
Patterson, Rebecca, wife of Robert, Dec. 21, 1857, age 79.
Patterson, Robert, Jan. 3, 1851, age 73.
Patterson, Robert, May 12, 1869, age 80.
Patterson, Rowland J., Co. M, 24th NY Cav., Evans, NY, May 9, 1865, age 32.
Patterson, Susan, County Almshouse, April 26, 1876, age 38.
Patterson, Thomas, Marilla, Feb. 5, 1872, age 36 y, 1 m, 11 d.
Patterson, Thomas, May 16, 1879, age 47; found dead in creek.
Patterson, William, switchman of Erie Railroad, accidentally killed on railroad, July 24, 1870, age 21.
Patterson, William, Oct. 12, 1872, age 43.
Pattie, Mary, wife of D., Feb. 12, 1867, age 34.
Pattingill, Jacob, b. 1764, d. [none given], bur. East Aurora, NY; Soldier of the Revolution.
Pattison, Francis M., Aug. 12, 1870, age 21.
Pattison, Mrs. Sarah, Dec. 18, 1846, age 75.
Pattison, William W., Aug. 3, 1876, age 84.
Patton (or Patten), John, March 7, 1874, age 50.
Patton, Susan, Almshouse, May 24, 1880, age 32.
Paul, Alsemena, wife of James C., West Aurora, NY, Sept. 1, 1853, age 23.
Paul, Augustus, Nov. 27, 1873, age 46.
Paul, Mrs. Catharine, widow of Mathias, May 7, 1880, age 62 y, 8 m, 23 d.
Paul, Elizabeth, Sept. 26, 1878, age 35.

Paul, James A., Colden, NY, Jan. 10, 1872, age 59.
Paul, Jay I., Holland, NY, July 28, 1879.
Paul, Mrs. Lizzie Huntzinger, wife of Joseph, April 2, 1880.
Paul, Martin, Springville, NY, June 9, 1872.
Paul, Mary Ann A., wife of Adams, Aurora, Sept. 27, 1826, age 30.
Paul, Matthias, Nov. 1873, age 61 y, 5 m, 19 d.
Paul, Pliny, Colden, NY, May 8, 1839, age 37.
Paul, Roxanna, wife of Abijah, West Falls, NY, May 7, 1861, age 58.
Paul, William, of Sydenham, Townlake, Devonshire, England, Jan. 19, 1833, age 56.
Paulin, Mrs. Ann B., Aurora, formerly of Bridgeton, Cumberland Co., N.J., Feb. 26, 1848, age 58.
Paulsackel, Frederick, suicide by drowning, cattle dealer, June 5, 1870, age 23.
Pauly, Caroline, Feb. 8, 1880, age 28 y, 6 d; wife of Frederick.
Pautler, George, Sen., Alden, Jan. 22, 1878, age 69.
Pawling, Eunice, widow of Col. Pawling of Troy, NY, sister of Judge and General Porter of Niagara Falls, mother of W.A. Bird of Black Rock, NY, March 15, 1848, age 83.
Pax, Alexander, March 18, 1876, age 29 y, 3 m.
Paxon, Betsy, wife of William, Hamburg, NY, June 1, 1838.
Paxon, Ella M., Akron, NY, Sept. 28, 1879, age 26.
Paxon, Semantha L., wife of William L., Akron, Aug. 9, 1872, age 37.
Paxon, Mrs. Theodore, East Aurora, NY, Jan. 6, 1867, age 25.
Paxson, Abigail, widow of John, Sept. 5, 1878, age 82.
Paxson, James, East Hamburgh, April 30, 1871, age 80.
Paxson, John, Aug. 10, 1878, age 84 y, 2 m, 15 d.
Paxson, Sarah C., wife of James, West Aurora, April 28, 1869, age 75.
Paxson, Thomas G., Collins Center, Feb. 27, 1877, age 60.
Paxson, William, East Hamburgh, June 21, 1871, age 74.
Paxton, Calvin, formerly of Buffalo, Aug. 16, 1860, age 36; Rockford, IL.
Paxton, Lydia Jane, wife of Ahaz, Feb. 21, 1855, in 38th year.
Paxton, Mrs. Peminah, Eden, NY, Oct. 19, 1851, age 69 y, 3 m.
Paxton, Rebecca, wife of Thomas, May 10, 1857, age 39 y, 11 m, 23 d; dau. of L. S. Pound.
Payne, Betsey, wife of Truman B., Collins, NY, Feb. 28, 1860, age 65 y, 2 m, 14 d.
Payne, Caroline, wife of William, July 19, 1833, age 23.
Payne, Charles T., formerly of Buffalo, Dec. 25, 1868, age 65; bur. in Buffalo.
Payne, Eleanora, dau. of Col. L. S., Tonawanda, June 21, 1876, age 28.
Payne, Florence E., wife of F. A., April 19, 1875, age 31.
Payne, George, Aug. 24, 1851, in 44th year.
Payne, George, Feb. 17, 1863, age 49 y, 10 m.
Payne, Milton, Aurora, NY, Dec. 4, 1827, age 36; d. in Buffalo.
Payne, Narcissa, wife of George J., Feb. 25, 1849, age 51.
Payne, Sarah, wife of Judge C., West Seneca, March 6, 1866, age 57.
Payne, Simon, Sardinia, NY, Oct. 8, 1865, age 68 y, 6 m, 10 d.
Payne, Thomas, baker, June 11, 1853, age 55.
Payne, William A., suicide, East Elma, May 5, 1879, age 37.
Peabody, Eliza P. H., wife of John M., Dec. 28, 1877, age 75.
Peabody, Elizabeth, Alden, Nov. 16, 1872, age 80.
Peabody, John Mason Jr., July 24, 1850, age 20 y, 1 m.
Peabody, John N., Nov. 24, 1868, age 27; d. in San Francisco, CA.
Peabody, Dr. Joseph, June 18, 1853, age 58.
Peabody, Joseph W., March 3, 1874, age 36.
Peabody, Miss Juliette L., Aug. 10, 1849, age 32.
Peabody, Mrs. Mary, March 12, 1848, age 82.
Peabody, Mary, wife of Dr. Joseph, Aug. 12, 1849, age 40.
Peabody, Samuel, Alden, Feb. 7, 1870, age 84.
Peabody, Thomas, April 16, 1835, age 38.
Peace, Unice, dau. of William, Dec. 7, 1876, age 20 y, 8 m.
Peacock, Alice, wife of William, Jan. 29, 1833, age 71.
Peacock, James, Sr., April 19, 1876, age 77.
Peacock, James Gibson, Gowanda, Jan. 13, 1868, age 20; d. at Gowanda.
Peacock, Mary E., wife of Henry, Nov. 3, 1873, age 33 y, 2 m.

Peacock, Sarah, wife of James, Sept. 1, 1871, age 74.
Peacock, William, formerly of Buffalo, Feb. 21, 1877, age 97; d. at Mayville, Chautauqua Co., NY.
Peacock, William W., June 2, 1867, in 52nd year.
Peak, Ann, wife of George, mother of Mrs. A. A. Loveridge of this city, Aurora, NY, March 8, 1869, age 78.
Peapey, Francis, Jan. 1, 1880, age 34.
Pearson, Mrs. Christopher, formerly of Buffalo, Jan. 22, 1870, age 79; d. at Middletown, MO.
Pearson, Emma Matilda, wife of Christopher, Jr., Hamburg, NY, April 1, 1841, age 21.
Pearson, Abby F., widow of Joseph, June 6, 1864; at Cuyahoga Falls, Ohio.
Pearson, Frances Maria, wife of Thomas, dau. of Lyman Rathbun, Sept. 2, 1852, age 23.
Pearson, Thurston, youngest son of C., May 26, 1848, in 20th year; at Middletown, MO.
Pease, Arthur W., Feb. 6, 1871, age 26; killed by accident on Hudson River Railroad at New Hamburgh.
Pease, Charles H., Oct. 7, 1869, age 28.
Pease, Electa, wife of William, Oct. 27, 1845, age 48.
Pease, Gideon, Dec. 20, 1844, age 45.
Pease, Harriet, wife of Alvan, Aurora, NY, Nov. 23, 1829.
Pease, Julia T. Watson, (Mrs. Arthur W.), Feb. 6, 1871, age 26; killed by accident on Hudson River Railroad at New Hamburgh.
Pease, Mary, widow of Gideon, March 28, 1850, in 50th year; at Dunville, Canada West.
Pease, Mrs. Phebe, Jan. 10, 1857, age 60.
Pease, Sarah Eliza, wife of John, Oct. 22, 1873, age 55 y, 9 m.
Pease, William, March 29, 1850, age 60; at Geneva, N.Y.
Pease, Capt. William T., Feb. 18, 1876, age 73.
Peate, Mrs. Ann, mother of Rev. John, Oct. 19, 1863, age 68.
Peay, Charles W., formerly of Toronto, Canada West, Sept. 27, 1864.
Peck, ---, wife of John, Clarence, April 14, 1820, age 40.
Peck, Amanda L., wife of Hiram, Feb. 14, 1829, age 24.
Peck, Charles Egbert, May 5, 1869, age 49 y, 4 m, 27 d.
Peck, Charles H., son of Daniel, Newstead, NY, Jan. 18, 1865, in 28th year; taken to Boston Centre, NY.
Peck, Mrs. Clarissa, Sept. 24, 1853, age 22.
Peck, Daniel, formerly of Buffalo, Sept. 3, 1875, age 75, d. near Gurthrie, MO.
Peck, Mrs. Eliza D. S., mother of William B. and Charles E., sister of Oliver G. Steele, Feb. 21, 1861, age 65.
Peck, James, Jan. 24, 1877, age 88
Peck, Capt. Jesse S., formerly of CT, March 1, 1843, age 73.
Peck, Johanna C., Sept. 25, 1873, age 42.
Peck, Mary, wife of Jacob P., June 22, 1873, age 28 y, 1 m, 2 d.
Peck, Mrs. Mary A., widow of Jesse, Nov. 23, 1878, age 80.
Peck, Mary E., widow of Charles E., Feb. 27, 1875, age 47.
Peck, Nancy M., wife of Daniel, July 27, 1862, age 62; taken to Boston Center, NY.
Peck, Sarah, widow of Jesse S., July 20, 1851, age 83.
Peck, Sperry, father of Daniel, Boston, July 29, 1850, in 83rd year.
Peck, William B. Jr., Nov. 22, 1875, age 31; d. at sea.
Peck, William B., July 31, 1880, age 63.
Peckham, Guy C., Lancaster, NY, Aug. 4, 1854, age 28.
Peckham, Pardon, b. 1763, d. 1851, bur. Lancaster; Soldier of the Revolution.
Peckham, Philip, formerly of RI, Clarence, NY, April 3, 1818, age 93 y, 12 d. [Another card: Peckham, Phillip, b. 1725, d. 1818, bur. Lancaster, NY; Soldier of the Revolution.]
Peckham, Philip, father of Mrs. C. H. Needham, Lancaster, NY, Jan. 14, 1864, age 78 y, 2 m, 1 d.
Peckham, Mrs. Sarah, Aug. 28, 1878, age 42.
Peckham, Solomon C., oldest son of Philip, Lancaster, NY, Co. K, 12th Regt. WI Vol., Nov. 1863; in hospital at Vicksburg, MS. Age 49 y, 2 m, 24 d.
Peckham, Sophoronia A., Lancaster, Aug. 6, 1879, age 74; wife of T.N.
Pedilerie, John, Erie Co. Almshouse, Oct. 10, 1878, age 104.
Peek, Carrie, wife of John S., Eden, NY, March 16, 1871, age 33 y, 5 m.

Peek, George, father of Mrs. A. A. Loveridge of Buffalo, Aurora, NY, June 20, 1869, age 85.
Peek, Lydia, wife of Samuel, Eden, NY, Jan. 8, 1855, age 57.
Peek, Urial S., Aug. 7, 1849, in 34th year.
Peel, Alfred, Aug. 17, 1874, age c. 63.
Peels, Charles, accidental death, May 10, 1880, age 61.
Peer, Maria, Sept. 13, 1878, age 47 y, 11 m, 21 d.
Peet, Lieut. James, Aug. 28, 1849, in 25th year.
Peirce, Ann, wife of John, Sept. 7, 1842, age 36.
Peitch, Emma Taylor, Feb. 15, 1880, wife of Thomas.
Pellet, George H., July 14, 1862; taken to Rochester, N.Y.
Pells, Mary M., wife of George H., Aug. 20, 1878, age 37.
Pelo, Mary Ann, Sept. 15, 1867, age 103 y, 2 m.
Pelton, Dolphin S., Dec. 31, 1845, age 31.
Pelton, Mrs. Elizabeth B., Dec. 8, 1858, age 84; in Syracuse, bur. in Buffalo.
Peltoin, Ephraim T., Aug. 31, 1860, age 56.
Pembroke, Anastasia, wife of Kerin, Sept. 15, 1878, age 43.
Pendergast, Thomas, Erie Co. Almshouse, July 4, 1879, age 71.
Pendergast, Thomas, July 2, 1875, age 54.
Penfield, Daniel, March 20, 1879, age 54.
Penfield, George W., May 19, 1860, age 62 y, 6 m.
Penfield, Henry, Jan. 7, 1868, age 83.
Penfield, Huldah M., wife of William, Oct. 19, 1849, age 27.
Penfield, James, formerly of Buffalo, Sept. 1, 1874; d. at Saratoga Springs.
Penfield, Jane E., widow of George W., mother of Daniel and T. V. N. of Buffalo, March 4, 1863, age 64.
Penfield, Theron N., Feb. 21, 1872, age 40.
Penfold, William, father of Frank & Charles, Nov. 23, 1875, age 48 y, 4 m, 7 d.
Penn, Henry, formerly of Manchester, England, Sept. 13, 1854, age 56.
Pennell, Osceola H. S., youngest brother of Rev. G. C., Dec. 23, 1866; taken to Pennellville, Oswego Co.
Pennels, Thomas, kicked by a horse, Sept. 17, 1876, age 68.
Pentecost, John, Sept. 7, 1864, age 36.
Pepper, Susan P., wife of Calvin, formerly of Derry, N H, March 15, 1835, age 24.
Perault, Joseph, Jan. 5, 1877, age 34.
Perham, Louisa, wife of B., oldest dau. of Widow Polly Waterman, late of Buffalo, Nov. 26, 1861, age 51; in Brattleboro, VT.
Perine, Benjamin, Eden, Erie Co., NY, March 15, 1868.
Perine, Francis, Erie Co. Almshouse, Oct. 9, 1878, age 47.
Perine, Lucy, widow of Benjamin, Eden, NY, Jan. 26, 1869.
Perine, P. M., wife of R. B. G., Clarence Center, NY, June 23, 1861, age 35 y, 10 m, 8 d.
Perkins, Ellen S., wife of Thomas G., April 12, 1851.
Perkins, Frank P., brother of C.H.B. of this City, Nov. 23, 1878, age 24; resident of Wyoming, NY.
Perkins, George D., freight train conductor, Aug. 21, 1869, age 26 y, 9 m; accidentally killed at Morehead's Staion, PA, bur. Buffalo.
Perkins, Isaac B., April 3, 1848, age 29.
Perkins, Loman, Aug. 17, 1832, age 30. His widow d. on the 19th of Aug. 1832.
Perkins, Lucy M., sister of William, July 19, 1868; d. at Painesville, OH.
Perkins, Lydia, wife of Philetus, Aug. 20, 1853, age 68.
Perkins, Marcia, wife of Nelson, West Falls, March, 1869, age 50 y, 3 m, 5 d.
Perkins, Mary Lyon Sabin, wife of L.P., Oct. 14, 1880, age 55 y, 1 m, 18 d.
Perkins, Nathaniel T., Oct. 23, 1862, in Indianapolis, IN; bur. in Buffalo.
Perkins, Phineas, Black Rock, NY, Feb. 25, 1824, age 34.
Perkins, Thomas, Nov. 13, 1866, age 57.
Perkins, William F., March 22, 1864, age 27.
Perkinson, Charles E., Feb. 19, 1873, age 28.
Perrie, Eliza, wife of George, formerly of Buffalo, Nov. 20, 1876, age 35.
Perrin, Mr., Oct. 21, 1871, age 22.
Perrin, Agnes, May 28, 1873, age 21; bur. at Evans Center.
Perry, Almon, Alden, Nov. 22, 1876, age 86.

Perry, Amelia Jane, wife of Philip, Feb. 25, 1870, age 31; taken to Canada.
Perry, Andrew, Aurora, West Falls, NY, June 28, 1851, age 63.
Perry, Charlotte, widow of H. A., March 22, 1875, age 53; taken to East Rush, NY.
Perry, H.O., March 16, 1873, age 61.
Perry, Horatio, April 20, 1832, age 50.
Perry, Israel B., Dec. 28, 1873, age 79.
Perry, Col. James, Alden, NY, Nov. 29, 1860, age 64.
Perry, Jeremiah, Aurora, NY, Feb. 13, 1853, age 49.
Perry, John H., native of London, England, Jan. 27, 1874, age 23.
Perry, Mary, widow of Isaac of Le Roy, Genesee Co., Alden, NY, March 20, 1857, in 86th year.
Perry, Judge P. H., Collins Center, NY, Nov. 12, 1877, age 61.
Perry, Philip, Oct. 18, 1872, age 32.
Person, Alta, wife of Robert, East Aurora, March 25, 1863, age 62.
Person, Charles M., April 6, 1879, age 29 y, 2 m, 13 d.
Person, Robert, Aurora, Aug. 29, 1864, age 71 y, 5 m.
Persons, Charles P., Aurora, NY, Feb. 3, 1871, age 75.
Persons, James E., formerly of Buffalo, Dec. 2, 1878, age 43; d. at Petosky, MI, bur. in Buffalo.
Persons, Jane B., wife of Byron D., East Aurora, NY, July 18, 1877, age 44 y, 9 m, 6 d.
Persons, Mrs. Marion B., dau. of Erastus Wallace, East Aurora, Dec. 24, 1862, age 28 y, 9 m.
Petch, Dr. P. P., July 16, 1847, age 38.
Peter, Catharine B., wife of James F., Jan. 17, 1851, age 26.
Peter, James F., June 11, 1878, age 58.
Peter, Mary A., wife of John S., Dec. 13, 1873, age 42.
Peters, Elizabeth, wife of Samuel, June 4, 1872, age 68.
Peters, John, April 1872.
Peters, John Frederick, April 26, 1878, age 76 y, 7 m, 6 d.
Petera (or Petrusat), Joseph, July 4, 1875, age 58.
Peters, Theodore C., formerly of Buffalo, May 6, 1876, age 70; d. in Brooklyn, NY.
Peterson, Henry, Tonawanda, Oct. 30, 1871, age 30.
Petersen, John, Feb. 21, 1868, age 29 y, 7 m.
Peterson, Matilda Schlinger, Dec. 29, 1880, age 86.
Peterson, Peter, drowned between Jan. 16 & 18, 1871.
Peterson, Lieut. Pierson B., 78th N.Y.S. Vol., Oct. 27, 1862; from wounds received at Battle of Antietam. D. in Snaketown Hospital near Sharpsburg, MD, bur. in Buffalo.
Peto, Mary Ann (or Pelo), Sept. 15, 1867, age 103 y, 2 m.
Petrie, Alexander, West Seneca, Sept. 9, 1872, age 72.
Petrie, Alexander, brother of William, suicide, May 8, 1874; boatman.
Petrie, Desdemona, wife of Wililam, July 2, 1852, age 33.
Petrie, Electa, wife of Alexander, March 5, 1855, age 48.
Petrie, Ruth, wife of William, Oct. 22, 1861, age 33.
Petrie, Mrs. Ruth, Feb. 17, 1878, age 96 y, 1 m, 17 d.
Petrie, Theodore, Erie Co. Almshouse, May 30, 1876, age 23.
Petrie, Thomas F., son of Col. Petrie, March 21, 1852, age 20 y, 11 m, 3 d.
Pettes, Sophronia Ann, wife of William H., March 18, 1858, age 34.
Pettit, Joseph, Black Rock, Oct. 23, 1869, age 93.
Pettit, Ontario J., Sept. 5, 1875, age 35.
Pettit, William B., Dec. 6, 1876, age 51.
Peugeot, Frederick L., late of Chicago, Nov. 9, 1864, age 28.
Peugeot, George F., of Vermillion, KS, April 2, 1877, age 70.
Peugot, Peter, Nov. 20, 1875, age 74.
Peugot, Louis D., Cheektowaga, Feb. 15, 1875, age 35. Suicide.
Pfanner, Peter, Aug. 1, 1856, age 52.
Pfau, Gustavus, Dec. 28, 1869, age 40.
Pfeifer, Charles H., son of George F., Jan. 7, 1873, age 23 y, 1 m, 24 d.
Pfeifer, George, Dec. 16, 1848, age 24.
Pfeifer, Louis Philip, April 10, 1880, age 32 y, 8 m, 7 d.
Pfeiffer, Mrs. Elizabeth, suicide, Feb. 5, 1873, age 50.
Pfeiffer, George, Dec. 25, 1875, age 58.

Pfeiffer, George, April 24, 1877, age 90.
Pfeiffer, George F., Oct. 26, 1861, age 80 y, 7 m, 7 d.
Pfeiffer, Henry C., Nov. 9, 1880, age 51 y, 10 m, 9 d.
Pfeiffer, Magdalena, Cold Springs, NY, wife of George, Feb. 10, 1864, age 77.
Pfeiffer, Mrs. Mary, Jan. 31, 1871, age 44.
Pfeil, Mrs. Christina, wife of Philip, Nov. 26, 1879, age 51 y, 1 m, 22 d.
Pfeil, Louise, wife of Peter, April 2, 1880, age 35 y, 1 m, 30 d.
Pfeil, Philip, Feb. 11, 1876, age 40 y, 10 m.
Pfiefer, Henry, accidental death, Nov. 4, 1875.
Pfitzenmaier, Mrs. Marie, formerly of Buffalo, Jul 15, 1878, age 74; d. at Tellico Plains, E. TN.
Pfitzenmeyer, Anna Marie, March 8, 1879, age 86; bur. at Grand Island.
Pfizenmier, Frederick, Sept. 21, 1861, age 37.
Pfoetzer, David, Sept. 30, 1871, age 49 y, 8 m, 29 d.
Phelps, Mrs. Abigail St. John, widow of Oliver, May 4, 1871, age 88; taken to St. Catharines, Ontario.
Phelps, Mrs. Catherine, Dec. 8, 1880, age 65.
Phelps, Cornelius, b. 1761, d. 1844, bur. Evans Center; Soldier of the Revolution.
Phelps, Elihu, late of Troy, N.Y., June 23, 1855.
Phelps, Elisha B., March 21, 1880, age 75.
Phelps, James D., printer, formerly of Buffalo, Dec. 8, 1865, age 54; in Detroit, MI.
Phelps, Maria L., dau. of the late Orson, June 10, 1871, age 22.
Phelps, Martin H., Wales, NY, March 30, 1860, age 39.
Phelps, Nancy, March 22, 1866, age 75; taken to Griffin's Mills.
Phelps, Oliver, May 1851.
Phelps, Orson, March 15, 1870, age 65.
Phelps, Pauline E., wife of George E., East Aurora, Dec. 1876, age 28.
Phelps, Philander W., July 1, 1860, age 49 y, 11 m, 15 d.
Phelps, Rebecca L., wife of C. B., dentist, Aug. 6, 1859; taken to New York.
Phelps, Walter J., July 4, 1869, age 28 y, 8 m.
Phelps, William C., formerly of Buffalo, Dec. 28, 1869, age 33 y, 6 m; d. in St. Louis, MO, bur. in Buffalo.
Phillips, Mrs., Sept. 10, 1821, age 40.
Phillips, Anna, Erie Co. Almshouse, June 23, 1877, age 27.
Phillips, Ellen, Erie Co. Almshouse, June 28, 1878, age 35.
Phillips, Elizabeth, wife of Stephen, Dec. 19, 1849, age 34.
Phillips, Mary, dau. of Seneca, Oct. 28, 1862, age 22.
Phillips, Jane, June 16, 1874, age 40.
Philipps, John, Cheektowaga, Dec. 28 or 23, 1869, age 70.
Phillips, John, son of Mrs. Sophia, July 4, 1877, age 35.
Phillips, John, March 28, 1878, age 72.
Phillips, John N., Sept. 23, 1871, age 35 y, 26 d.
Phillips, Lucius H., son of P. H., Nov. 6, 1868, age 23; d. at St. Paul, MN.
Phillips, Margaret, wife of Edward B., eldest dau. of Samuel Nesbitt, May 31, 1870, age 25.
Phillips, Mary E. Duell, wife of J. H., Aug. 1876, age 40 y, 2 m.
Phillips, Samuel, Aug. 3, 1843, age 44.
Phillips, Sarah C., wife of Andrew W., Evans, July 12, 1873, age 62 y, 10 m.
Phillips, Stephen G., Feb. 2, 1870, age 50.
Phillips, Thomas Benton, son of Thomas of Buffalo, Jan. 6, 1861, age 19 y, 6 m; at Key West, FL.
Phillips, Thomas H., son of Richard, March 7, 1862, age 20 y, 8 m, 18 d.
Phillips, William, Nov. 5, 1824, age 38.
Phillips, William, Feb. 13, 1864, age 29.
Phillipson, George L., Dec. 11, 1871, age 29 y, 10 m.
Phillipson, Isabella, wife of Isaac, May 9, 1860, age 35.
Philpot, Caroline, wife of William S., March 28, 1877, age 73.
Philpot, Emma E. Harris, eldest dau. of James Harris, wife of J. N., Jan. 27, 1870, age 23 y, 2 m, 10 d.
Phinney, Elihu, Jan. 26, 1863, age 78; in Cooperstown, NY.
Phinney, Henry Frederick, formerly of Buffalo, Nov. 1875, age 59; d. in Cooperstown, NY.

Pickard, Nicholas, formerly of Tonawanda, June 2, 1876; d. at Leland, MI.
Pickering, Amelia A., wife of Thomas, July 1, 1848, age 22.
Pickering, Angeline, wife of Rev. D., Aurora, Nov. 3, 1851; bur. in Buffalo.
Pickering, Rev. David, formerly pastor of First Universalist Society of Buffalo, Jan. 6, 1859, in 71st year; in Ypsilanti, MI.
Pickering, John, railroad accident, Dc. 29, 1876, age 30.
Pickering, John D., Dec. 29, 1876, age 30.
Pickering, John F. I., formerly of Buffalo, March 2, 1880; d. at Peotone, IL.
Pierce, ---, wife of James, March 8, 1826.
Pierce, Aaron B., Hamburgh, NY, May 19, 1875, age 54.
Pierce, Allen, Hamburg, July 29, 1832, age 25.
Pierce, Amial, formerly of Wales, NY, Aug. 29, 1863, in 75th year; in Polo, IL.
Pierce, Belle, July 30, 1875, age c. 30.
Pierce, Calvin, formerly of Suffield, CT, Oct. 31, 1839, age 29; Hamburgh, NY.
Pierce, Charles S., Feb. 19, 1864, age 63; [son, Jerome, living in 1874.] [not on card.]
Pierce, Charles L., May 5, 1869, age 40.
Pierce, Clark, Jan. 9, 1872, age 78.
Pierce, Elizabeth, mother of Mrs. O. B. Titus, Feb. 4, 1865, age 77.
Pierce, Elizabeth, wife of Charles L., April 16, 1869, age 37.
Pierce, Mrs. Elizabeth, July 29, 1873, age 73.
Pierce, Esther, wife of John, Jan. 21, 1833, age 34.
Pierce, Esther, wife of Calvin, formerly of Suffield, CT, Brant, NY, Jan. 6, 1853, age 70.
Pierce, George L., accidental death, Nov. 124, 1877.
Pierce, Mrs. Hannah, mother of Alanson Palmer of Buffalo, Hamburgh, NY, Nov. 17, 1822, age 52.
Pierce, Hannah, Hamburgh, NY, May 15, 1820, age 56; wife of Giles P.
Pierce, Ida Jane, wife of Dr. F. D., June 5, 1877, age 32 y, 8 m, 23 d.
Pierce, Jerome, Jan. 3, 1878.
Pierce, James B., Dec. 5, 1862, age 38; taken to Lyons, Wayne Co.
Pierce, Jonathan, shoemaker, res. of Buffalo nearly half a century, Aug. 22, 1869, age 75.
Pierce, Joseph, East Elma, April 1879, age 86.
Pierce, Julia A., wife of Loring, July 4, 1860, age 55 y, 2 m.
Pierce, Mrs. Lafayette, Aurora, suicide, Arpil 21, 1871, age c. 40.
Pierce, Loring, undertaker, May 24, 1870, age 73.
Pierce, Lucius, formerly of Buffalo, Jan. 2, 1866, age 64; in Iowa City, IA.
Pierce, Maris B. ("Ha-dya-no-doh"), a Seneca, Cattaraugus Reservation, Aug. 9, 1874, age 65.
Pierce, Mary E. L., dau. of the late Charles L., Sept. 30, 1878.
Pierce, Nathan J., son of Charles S., Nov. 2, 1859, age 26 y, 11 m.
Pierce, Olive J., wife of Eugene, May 16, 1878, age 26 y, 8 m.
Pierce, Oliver, Hamburgh, July 22, 1874, age 83 y, 5 m, 11 d.
Pierce, Pardon, Boston, NY, June 8, 1848, age 68 y, 9 m; at Southpost, WI.
Pierce, Piania, wife of Sanford B., Hamburg, May 1, 1850, age 31.
Pierce, Polly, widow of Pardon, Boston Corners, NY, June 12, 1859, age 74.
Pierce, Mrs. Ruth M., widow of Clark, Black Rock, NY, June 27, 1874, age 77 y, 11 m, 7 d.
Pierce, Sophia, widow of Charles S., March 9, 1877, age 74.
Pierce, Susan S., wife of Cornelius H., formerly of Hamburgh, NY, dau. of Chauncey Abbott, March 17, 1853, age 24; bur. at White's Corners.
Pierce, Susanna, wife of Oliver, Hamburg, Sept. 21, 1866, age 71.
Pierce, Welington A., Oct. 20, 1871; d. at Sisters of Charity Hospital.
Pierce, William, father of Mrs. W. P. Mooses of Buffalo, Hamburgh, NY, Oct. 29, 1857, age 72 y, 10 d.
Pierson, Alanson, formerly of Cooperstown, NY, Feb. 13, 1848, age 48.
Pierson, Charles, formerly of Buffalo, March 1, 1874, age 51; d. at Canandaigus.
Pierson, Edward, formerly of Buffalo, April 22, 1878; d. at Fairfield, CT, taken to NY.
Pierson, Frederick A., Feb. 13, 1854, age 30; in Vernon, Oneida Co., NY.
Pierson, George E., Aurora, Sept. 15, 1862, age 23; in Chicago; bur. in Aurora, NY.
Pierson, Joseph, May 23, 1860, in 38th year.
Pierson, Maria, wife of Gurdon, Aurora, July 28, 1822, age 20.
Pierson, Nancy, wife of Gordon, Aurora, May 27, 1843, age c. 40.

Pierson, Mrs. Temperance, Sept. 12, 1847, age 71.
Pike, Lucy Ann, wife of Stafford, Wales, Feb. 10, 1844, age 26.
Pike, William, submarine diver, Jan. 18, 1866, age 33.
Pilliard, Maria, wife of Frederick, Aug. 30, 1878, age 59 y, 6 m.
Pinckney, Joseph, Sr., April 9, 1856, age 65.
Pine, Hiram S., formerly of Buffalo, Jan. 9, 1863, in 35th year; in San Francisco., CA.
Pine, Polly, wife of Samuel, Dec. 12, 1863, age 72 y, 9 m, 10 d.
Pingree, Lucy Cochrane, wife of John T., dau. of A. C. Cochrane, Jan. 2, 1870, age 35 y, 4 m.
Pinkney, Mrs. Jane, wife of John, Nov. 24, 1859, age 73.
Pinkney, Joseph, July 7, 1873, age 48.
Pinkney, Pamelia, wife of Joseph, Aug. 24, 1864, age 34 y, 8 m.
Pinkney, Mrs. Sarah, June 2, 1837, age c. 40.
Pinner, Helen, dau. of Michael and Debby, June 5, 1874, age 20.
Pinner, Henry, Sept. 25, 1856, age 64.
Pinner, Thomas, father of James N. of Buffalo, Nov. 23, 1850, age 50; late of Leon, Cattaraugus Co., NY.
Pinney, Harriet Eliza, wife of Austin, July 20, 1841, age 32.
Pinney, Joel, Sept. 11, 1848, age 80.
Pinney, Joel R., Aug. 26, 1847, age 42.
Pinton, Gustavus, Dec. 5, 1877, age 39.
Piregry, Cythria, Aurora, wife of Aquilla, July 31, 1879, age 74.
Pitken, Nicholas, July 25, 1875, age 36.
Pitkin, Miss Annie, Feb. 23, 1876, age 24 y, 8 m.
Pitkin, Maria Louisa, wife of J.F., March 27, 1858.
Pitkin, Michael, May 27, 1868, age 32.
Pitts, Horatio W., son of John A., Feb. 26, 1858, age 31; in Havanna, Cuba. Taken to Rochester, April 7, 1858.
Pitts, John A., July 1, 1859, age 59; taken to Rochester, NY.
Pitts, Mrs. Mary, Sept. 15, 1876, age 76.
Pitz, Jacob, April 11, 1878, age 34 y, 4 m, 14 d.
Pixley, Philander, July 10, 1878, age 66.
Planz, Jacob, Dec. 10, 1879, age 36 y, 10 m, 17 d.
Plato, Hiram, Willink, NY, Oct. 30, 1860 in Boonville, MO, age 21, son of J.D.
Platt, Anson B., Dec. 27, 1869, age 55.
Platt, Charles M., Alden Center, Jan. 23, 1875, age 50.
Platt, David, d. of cholera, Aug. 21, 1832, age 25.
Platt, Fannie H., Hamburgh, NY, Aug. 17, 1865, age 25.
Platt, James B., son of L. B., March 5, 1874; d. at Baltimore, MD.
Platt, John G., March 14, 1865, age 63.
Platt, Mrs. Mary A., Nov. 25, 1872, age 41.
Platt, Montague F., formerly of Buffalo, June 20, 1874, age 35; d. at Marquette, MI.
Playter, Charles G., Sept. 19, 1861, age 47.
Playter, Charlotte A., widow of Charles G., July 24, 1879.
Pledge, Mary, Almshouse, March 21, 1880, age 26.
Plenthner, John, Oct. 6, 1858, age 48.
Pleuthner, Caroline, widow of John, Oct. 10, 1874, age 30.
Pleuthner, Mrs. Johanna Christian, June 7, 1872, age 62.
Plduthner, John G., Jan. 20, 1870, age 27.
Plimpton, Luman K., Dec. 17, 1869, age 60.
Plimpton, Roxalana, widow of Deacon Daniel Plimpton of Sturbridge, MA, Feb. 5, 1860, age 79.
Plogsted, J. F. W., ("J. P. Howard"), Sept. 11, 1878, age 32.
Plumb, Joseph, formerly of Buffalo, May 25, 1870; d. at Cattaraugus.
Plumb, Miles D., formerly of Buffalo, May 1872, age 69; d. at Monroe MI.
Plumb, Parmelia, wife of Miles D., Sept. 28, 1826.
Plumer, Charlotte, March 22, 1879, age 21 y, 11 m.
Plumley, Benjamin F., Co. Almshouse, Dec. 2, 1878, age 70.
Plumley, George G., formerly of Buffalo, youngest son of Allen S., Nov. 29, 1864 in Kendall's Corners, Orleans Co., NY.

Plumley, Granville, May 8, 1863.
Poh, Catherine, wife of Louis, Nov. 15, 1875, age 39 y, 3 m, 23 d.
Pohl, John, Co. Almshouse, Feb. 28, 1878, age 50.
Polgreen, Mrs. James, Feb. 2, 1847, age 82.
Pollard, Mrs. Flora, smothered, accidentally, Nov. 24, 1879, age 72.
Pollard, J. J., May 24, 1864 in Chattanooga, TN, age 19; 124th OH Vols. Formerly of Sackett Zouaves of Buffalo. Son of John O. Pollard; youngest of 3 now in the Union Army. Bur. in Buffalo.
Pollard, Laura G. Grannis, wife of B. F., March 23, 1862, age 32 y, 1 m.
Pollard, Sarah Jane, 3d dau. of John, June 12, 1862, age 23.
Polley, Eunice S., wife of John H. of NY; dau. of Lester Day of Buffalo, March 6, 1867.
Pollock, Cornelia C., wife of Joseph M., Nov. 13, 1876, age 30 y, 2 m, 10 d.
Pomeroy, Ann, widow of Oliver, Oct. 24, 1851, age 75.
Pomeroy, Elizabeth C., widow of Robert, Lancaster, April 20, 1873, age 60.
Pomeroy, Miss Fanny, Aug. 10, 1830, age 34.
Pomeroy, Henry F., Williamsville, NY, May 30, 1816, age 25; formerly of Cheshire Co., NH.
Pomeroy, Jane E., wife of Emerson C., Jan. 31, 1880, age 54.
Pomeroy, Mrs. Lydia, Sept. 1, 1872, age 93 y, 8 m.
Pomeroy, Minnie S., wife of J. A., Feb. 24, 1875, age 31.
Pomeroy, Oliver, formerly of Northampton, MA, Jan. 9, 1843, age 76.
Pomeroy, Ralph M., formerly of Northampton, MA, Jan. 6, 1832, age 57.
Pomeroy, Syvil, wife of Oliver, Oct. 4, 1824, age 51.
Pond, Mrs. B., formerly of Buffalo, June 23, 1875, age 73; d. in Cleveland, OH.
Pond, Gertrude, wife of Lawrence, Williamsville, Jan. 19, 1875, age 70.
Pond, Miss Polly, Eden, NY, Oct. 1825, age 34.
Poole, Arthur A., July 10, 1878, age 28; accidental death.
Poole, Julia A., wife of C. O., March 19, 1864.
Pope, Henry J., Feb. 4, 1875, age 35 y, 11 m, 3 d.
Pope, Mrs. Joanna M. R., July 17, 1876, age 74 y, 2 m, 13 d.
Poppenberg, Gustavus, Feb. 8, 1880, age 62 y, 29 d.
Popple, A. W., formerly of Erie Co., March 24, 1877, age 45 y, 8 m; d. at Dunkirk.
Porcher, Kittie, wife of A. J., Jan. 24, 1875, age 20 y, 9 m, 1 d.
Porter, Almeda M. Newell, widow of James E., Nov. 27, 1865, age 41.
Porter, Annie, March 1, 1880, age 37.
Porter, Archa, Alden, NY, Feb. 6, 1853, age 42.
Porter, Judge Augustus, Niagara Falls, NY, June 10, 1849; first judge of Niagara Co.
Porter, Hon. Augustus S., Niagara Falls, Sept. 18, 1872, age 75.
Porter, Miss Elizabeth L. or S., Jan. 28, 1876, at Niagara Falls. Dau. of late Gen. Peter B.
Porter, Ellen D., wife of Stephen B., only dau. of John Swartz, July 9, 1860, age 27.
Porter, Rev. George P., formerly of Buffalo, June 11, 1877; d. at Cowlesville, Wyoming Co., NY.
Porter, James, Clarence, NY, Nov. 10, 1829, age 55.
Porter, Mrs. Jane, Niagara Falls, NY, wife of Judge Augustus, Jan. 31, 1841.
Porter, Lavinia E., dau. of Judge Augustus, Niagara Falls, April 13, 1863.
Porter, Letitia Breckinridge, July 27, 1831, age 45. Wife of Peter Buell Porter. Born June 22, 1786. (Data from Oakwood Cemetery, Niagara Falls, inscription, 1948)
Porter, Mrs. Letitia R., Aug. 1831.
Porter, Mary Breckenridge, wife of Peter A., dau. of Dr. John Breckenridge of NC; Aug. 4, 1854 at Niagara Falls, NY.
Porter, Mary C., Aug. 1854.
Porter, Gen. Peter B., formerly of Black Rock, March 20, 1844, age 71; at Niagara Falls, NY.
Porter, Hon. Peter Buell Jr., Niagara Falls, NY, June 15, 1871, son of Judge Agustus & nephew of Gen. Peter B. Porter.
Porter, Phebe, relict of James, Clarence, June 16, 1868, age 84; d. at Dixon, IL.
Porter, Capt. Richard, formerly of Buffalo, Feb. 1, 1856; in San Francisco, CA, age 37.
Porter, Samuel, brother of Rev. J. J., formerly of Buffalo, Feb. 22, 1874; d. at Albion, NY, bur. in Geneva.
Porter, Mrs. Sarah, June 13, 1867, age 87.

Porter, Sarah Augusta, Black Rock, NY, wife of Augustus S., May 27, 1824, age 23.
Porth, Sarah, widow of Henry, Sept. 24, 1876, age 54 y, 7 m, 3 d.
Poseiner, Jacob, May 26, 1878, age 38.
Poseiner, Marie, widow of Jacob, May 28, 1876.
Possee, Mrs. Mary, Dec. 17, 1878, age 40.
Posselyn, Amasa L., Oct. 21, 1855, age 23 y, 1 m, 16 d.
Post, Eliza M., North Buffalo, dau. of William, June 20, 1866, age 23.
Post, Frank, North Buffalo, July 14, 1867, age 21.
Post, Michael E., Oct. 24, 1883, age 38, painter.
Post, Mrs. William, Aug. 21, 1872.
Postal, Elizabeth, Oct. 22, 1865, age 37.
Postal (or Portal), Mrs. Fanny, mother of Mrs. S. Angeles, Sept. 22, 1864, age 63.
Poth, George H., March 8, 1876, age 57 y, 10 m, 15 d.
Poth, Sarah, wife of George H., March 20, 1859, age 33.
Potter, Abner G., East Hamburg, NY, Aug. 12, 1857, age 36 y, 11 m, 20 d.
Potter, Allen, accidental death, East Hamburgh, May 31, 1877, age 69 y, 11 m, 19 d.
Potter, Alme, wife of Jacob, East Hamburgh, Feb. 8, 1875.
Potter, Alpheus W., Dec. 3, 1871, age 38; d. at Titusville.
Potter, Amos K., May 26, 1862, age 45.
Potter, Mrs. Charlotte Bliss, July 26, 1880, age 71.
Potter, Diadamic, wife of Dr. Samuel, Lancaster, NY, Feb. 2, 1855, age 30.
Potter, Edward, accidentally killed, Oct. 2, 1872, age 30.
Potter, Electa, widow of Heman B., Oct. 13, 1854, age 64.
Potter, Eliza, widow of Allen, East Hamburgh, NY, March 20, 1878, age 68.
Potter, Esther, sister of H. B., Oct. 18, 1820; at Tioga, NY.
Potter, Eunice E. Hayward, wife of George R., Jan. 9, 1876, age 39.
Potter, Fanny M., wife of Dr. Samuel, Lancaster, NY, April 4, 1861.
Potter, Heman B., Oct. 7, 1854, age 68.
Potter, Heman B., late of Buffalo, late 1st officer of Ship *Gentoo*, July 30, 1859; in Calcutta.
Potter, Hosea E., Concord, NY, April 24, 1862, age 74 y, 8 m, 20 d.
Potter, Jacob, East Hamburg, NY, Nov. 9, 1880, age 84.
Potter, Judith, widow of Joshua, East Hamburgh, July 24, 1873; d. at Angola, NY, bur. in East Hamburgh, NY.
Potter, Hon. Levi, formerly of East Hamburgh, May 5, 1878, age 65; d. Chicago, IL.
Potter, Lydia, wife of Levi, Hamburgh, May 7, 1874; d. in Chicago, IL, bur. in Hamburgh, NY.
Potter, Martin, father of George S. of Buffalo, June 16, 1869 in Gowanda, NY, age 70.
Potter, Mary, County Almshouse, Feb. 20, 1878, age 41.
Potter, Mary Lobdell, wife of Dr. Milton, dau. of Godfrey Grosvenor of Buffalo, Sept. 17, 1847, age 29; bur. in Colesville, Wyoming Co., NY.
Potter, Milton Grosvenor, M.D., Jan. 28, 1878, age 35.
Potter, Noel, b. Aug. 13, 1758, d. Nov. 3, 1847, bur. Hartland, NY; Soldier of the Revolution.
Potter, Phoebe C., wife of Gilbert, EastHamburgh, Dec. 31, 1877, age 50 y, 10 m, 11 d.
Potter, Sarah, wife of Frederick A., Nov. 22, 1849, age 40.
Potter, Mrs. Thomas, Springville, NY, Nov. 26, 1861, age 48.
Potter, William, April 10, 1835, age 35.
Potter, Zenas S., Clarence, NY, June 16, 1824, age 60.
Pound, Joseph D., formerly of Collins, NY, Jan. 3, 1862, age 22; in California, MO.
Pound, Lydia, wife of J., Collins, NY, Sept. 28, 1841, age 36.
Powell, Mrs. Casendary, Feb. 19, 1865.
Powell, David, Sept. 16, 1864, age 53.
Powell, James, late of Colfort, Glostershire, England, Sept. 30, 1849, age 40.
Powell, Jane M., wife of Dr. Elisha, formerly of Buffalo, Oct. 19, 1849, age 44; in New York.
Powell, Jerusha S., widow of M. H., Cheektowaga, Dec. 5, 1878, age 78 y, 7 m, 7 d.
Powell, M. K., Ilion, NY, Dec. 19, 1875, age c. 35.
Powell, Mary A., wife of N.O., Feb. 2, 1873, age 43 y, 9 d.
Powell, Mary A., wife of John, Feb. 10, 1879, age 76.

Powell, Moses H., March 1, 1861, age 63.
Powell, Peter, son of John, June 26, 1857, age 21 y, 3 m.
Powell, Sarah, widow of David, Dec. 28, 1871, age 62.
Powell, Thomas, b. 1754, d. Sept. 20, 1843, bur. Sardinia, NY; Soldier of the Revolution.
Powell, William, Co. K, 16th N.Y. Cav., July 14, 1864, age 47; at Alexandria, VA.
Powellson, Catharine L., wife of B. F., July 20, 1849, age 20 y, 2 m.
Power, John, June 3, 1870, age 44; native of Parish of Butler's Town, County Waterford, Ireland.
Powers, Mrs., mother of Averill and William, Hamburgh, NY, Dec., 1812, age 55.
Powers, Averill, Hamburgh, NY, Dec. 4, 1812, age 28.
Powers, Cordelia S., wife of O. T., Lancaster, NY, April 23, 1849, age 24.
Powers, Jacob, Clarence, NY, Nov., 1812, age 46.
Powers, Julia, Dec. 1, 1879, age 24.
Powers, Patrick, Jan. 20, 1865, age 40.
Powers, Sarah, formerly of Buffalo, Aug. 5, 1880, age 27.
Powers, Talbot P., June 22, 1848; at the Utica Asylum.
Powers, William, Hamburg, NY, Dec. 5, 1812, age 21.
Pratt, A. Bartlett, son of Asabel of Gates, NY, son-in-law of Isaac W. Thompson of Buffalo, April 3, 1858, age 29.
Pratt, Almira, dau. of Luke M., Aurora, NY, Jan. 5, 1863, age 20.
Pratt, Capt. Ames, Jan. 27, 1862, age 56 y, 5 m, 6 d.
Pratt, Anna, widow of John C., Aurora, Feb. 13, 1838, in 71st year.
Pratt, Bartholomew, Aurora, Jan. 23, 1871, age 65; killed by accidental discharge of his gun.
Pratt, Cynthia, wife of Lucius H., March 3, 1843, age 27.
Pratt, Cynthia, Aurora, NY, formerly Mrs. Payne, mother of Mrs. N. K. Hall of Buffalo; March 1, 1864, in 72nd year.
Pratt, Ellen M., wife of Byron F., Aurora, Dec. 17, 1872, age 41.
Pratt, Elon G., formerly of Buffalo, Dec. 8, 1872, age 51; of the firm of Pratt & Fox of St. Louis, MO; d. in St. Louis.
Pratt, Esther, widow of Capt. Samuel, March 21, 1830, age 64.
Pratt, Fanny F., wife of Benjamin, North Collins, NY, Dec. 30, 1853, age 56.
Pratt, Dr. Gorham F., April 6, 1871, age 68.
Pratt (or Platt), Mrs. Harriet A. B., formerly of Buffalo, widow of Anson B., Oct. 10, 1880, age 66 or 67.
Pratt, Miss Hattie, East Aurora, Aug. 21, 1867, age 24.
Pratt, John, Dec. 12, 1872, age 40.
Pratt, John C., Sr., Aurora, NY, Sept. 19, 1836, age 73.
Pratt, John C., formerly of Aurora, NY, Dec. 28, 1843, 57th year; at Lyndon, IL.
Pratt, Julius H., son of Rachel, late of Buffalo, Nov. 8, 1845, age 25; in St. Louis, MO.
Pratt, Lucius H., West Seneca, NY, July 24, 1876, age 68.
Pratt, Luke M., Aurora, NY, July 24, 1863, age 74.
Pratt, Maria F., widow of the late Hiram, Feb. 5, 1868, age 69.
Pratt, Pascal P., Oct. 25, 1828, in 34th year.
Pratt, Peter, Collins, NY, Oct. 19, 1845, age 76.
Pratt, Rachel S., widow of Pascal P., mother of Elon G., sister of Smith H. and Hezekial A. Salisbury; March 23, 1870, age 75. D. at Tarrytown, NY, bur. Buffalo.
Pratt, Richard, an Englishman, age 50 years, June 20, 1843.
Pratt, Capt. Samuel, Aug. 31, 1812, age 48. [Another card: Pratt, Samuel, b. 1764, d. 1812, bur. Buffalo; Soldier of the Revolution.]
Pratt, Samuel, formerly Sheriff of Niagara Co., NY, Aug. 9, 1822, age 35.
Pratt, Samuel F., April 28, 1872, age 65.
Pratt, Silas, Newstead, NY, Nov. 4, 1851, age 75.
Pratt, Mrs. Sophia, March 19, 1862, age 74.
Pratt, Thomas, a Revolutionary soldier, Aurora, NY, Dec. 13, 1833, age 80.
Pratt, Thomas, son of Capt. Amos, March 26, 1857, age 23 years, 5 months, 13 days.
Pratt, Dr. W. H., Eden, Nov. 28, 1858.
Premo, Mary, March 7, 1878, age 86 y, 6 m.
Prenatt, Melissa D., wife of Augustus, Abbott Rd., Nov. 5, 1873, age 38.
Prentice, Robert H., East Aurora, June 10, 1873, age 26.

Presbrey, Elizabeth F., sister of O. F., Oct. 14, 1870, age 43.
Prescott, Alexander H., formerly Preceptor of Plattsburg Academy, Clinton Co., NY, Nov. 15, 1836.
Prescott, Asenath, wife of William, formerly of Buffalo, East Hamburg, June 6, 1867, age 62 y, 8 m, 14 d.
Prescott, Charles L., son of William, formerly of Buffalo, April 30, 1869, age 28 y, 3 m; d. at Bear Valley, MN.
Prescott, Juliette E., wife of William C., dau. of Austin Barnum, April 13, 1851, age 22.
Prescott, Mrs. Lucinda, March 18, 1846, in 43d year; in Eden, NY.
Prestidge, Susan, Aurora, NY, April 16, 1855, age 84; at residence of Thomas Codd.
Preston, Clara Ann, Sept. 4, 1879, age 20 y, 6 m, 7 d.
Preston, Emma Jane, dau. John R., Jan. 12, 1878, age 21.
Preston, Mr. G. A., Feb. 9, 1835, age 40.
Preston, Isabella, wife of John R., Dec. 30, 1871, age 44.
Preston, Joab, Springville, NY, Dec. 9, 1861, age 65.
Preston, Zaccheus, Concord, NY, April 7, 1863, age 84 y, 1 m, 16 d.
Price, Emma, wife of Charles, Oct. 13, 1873, age 40.
Price, William, March 10, 1863, age 53 years, 11 months.
Pride, Augusta T., wife of Dr. J. B., Alden, NY, March 18, 1843, in 32d year.
Pride, Mariette, Alden, NY, wife of Dr. John B., March 16, 1853.
Priest, Mrs. Eliza, July 17, 1878, age 89.
Priest, Eliza R., May 17, 1865.
Prim, Josephine (see Linnemann), March 10, 1880, almshouse (insane).
Prince, Hon. Alpheus, Newstead, April 22, 1870.
Prince, Amy M., wife of Alpheus, Clarence, NY, June 13, 1858, in 35th year.
Prince, Charles F., brother of George A., Aug. 25, 1878, age 41.
Prince, Charles S., Lancaster, NY, Aug. 3, 1866, age 31.
Prince, George J., father of George A., formerly shipmaster out of the port of Boston, Aug. 15, 1848, age 67.
Prince, Hattie L., dau. of the late Hon. Alpheus, Clarence, NY, June 28, 1880, age 22.
Prince, James O., son of John R. of Marilla, NY, June 3, 1864, age 33 y, 7 m.
Prince, John, Jan. 18, 1842, age 45.
Prince, John, Marilla, formerly of Buffalo, June 16, 1870, age 63. Bur. Buffalo.
Prince, Kate E., dau. of the late J. R. of Marilla, May 8, 1875.
Prince, Mrs. Mary Ann, widow of Capt. George I., May 12, 1879, age 83.
Prince (or Prine), Mary Frances, wife of Hamilton, Sept. 14, 1879, age 38 y, 6 m.
Pring, Mary Ann, wife of William J., March 12, 1880, age 30 y, 1 m, 2 d.
Pringle, Doctor, formerly of Hamburgh, Sept. 1873, age 80; d. at Fredonia.
Prior, Thomas B., West Seneca, April 17, 1876, age 58 y, 5 m.
Proctor, Sarah, Erie Co. Almshouse, Jan. 9, 1878, age 26.
Progranz, Stephen, July 6, 1873, age c. 50.
Proper, Elizabeth, wife of John, dau. of Reuben Redfield, Evans, NY, July 14, 1840, age 37.
Prossel, Lewis A. J., Dec. 23, 1864, age 55 years, 7 days.
Prosser, James, caneller, suicide, Nov. 20, 1880, age 52.
Prosser, Mrs. Kate M., sudden death by accident (suicide?), wife of E.S., May 12, 1880, age 26.
Prosser, Lucy Millen, wife of E. S., Dec. 27, 1874; d. at Avon, NY, bur. Buffalo.
Prothaes, Mrs. Elizabeth, Nov. 16, 1874, age 70 y, 1 m, 22 d.
Prothais, John F., May 18, 1861, age 58 y, 1 m, 23 d.
Prouse, Eliza, Jan. 8, 1867, age 28; at Yorktown, VA.
Prouty, Amelia Agnes, wife of Wallace, Nov. 2, 1862, age 22 y, 2 m, 10 d.
Prouty, George W., son of James, Dec. 6, 1863, age 22.
Prouty, James, Nov. 18, 1870; d. at St. Catharines, Ontario, bur. Buffalo.
Provoost, Ann, wife of David, Sept. 14, 1879.
Provoost, Charles M., Sept. 26, 1875, age 31.
Provoost, Mrs. E. W., May 18, 1879, age 34.
Provoost, James P., July 24, 1868, age 67 y, 7 m.
Provoost, Mary C., widow of James P., Nov. 21, 1871, age 61.
Provoost, Robert C., Oct. 1, 1880, age 39.
Provost, George, native of Port Chester, NY, and taken there, June 2, 1854, age 40.

Provost, Harriet S., wife of Samuel A., March 20, 1853, age 44.
Provost, Mary Carr, wife of William K., March 27, 1865, age 31 y, 7 m.
Provost, Robert, sail-maker, Aug. 19, 1840.
Prozeller, Mary, wife of Joseph M., Jan. 31, 1878.
Pucher, Charles F., formerly of Buffalo, Sept. 4, 1878, age 35; d. in New Orleans.
Puninton, Sarah J., wife of A. J., Aug. 1, 1876, age 32 y, 1 m.
Purdie, Hadwin L., son of John, May 22, 1871, age 29.
Purdey, Louisa J., wife of John, May 24, 1880.
Purdy, Mary J., wife of Samuel, dau. of Erastus Sparrow, March 23, 1846, age 25.
Purrington, George A., railroad accident, Dec. 29, 1876, age 57.
Purrington, Nancy, wife of George A., March 8, 1875, age 48.
Purrington, Sarah J., wife of A. J., Aug. 1, 1876, age 32 y, 1 m.
Pursel, Frank M., eldest son of J. N., Oct. 24, 1877, age 24.
Putnam, Mrs. Amanda M., May 8, 1856, in 35th year.
Putnam, Asa, Sept., 1813, age 35.
Putnam, Catharine V. V. Dubois, wife of John S., Aug. 3, 1840, age 20.
Putnam, Harriet, wife of James O., May 3, 1853, age 33.
Putnam, Lizzie R., formerly of Buffalo, wife of Henry E., April 9, 1873; d. at Worcester, MA.
Putnam, Martha, widow of Timothy, Aurora, Sept. 24, 1868, age 90.
Pye, Richard, Petroleum Center, Feb. 14, 1868, age 23.
Pye, William, May 10, 1863, in 23rd year; d. in Chicago, bur. in Buffalo.
Pynchon, Lucius K., Feb. 4, 1880, age 72.

Qualey, Patrick, July 31, 1879, age 22 y, 9 m.
Qualls, Mrs. Adelaide, dau. of Peyton Harris, July 9, 1871, age 48.
Qualls, Elizabeth, Feb. 19, 1862, age 30.
Qualls, William, formerly of Buffalo, Sept. 19, 1863, age 53; in Red Bluff, CA.
Queenan, Mary L., Feb. 1873, age 24 y, 6 m, 4 d.
Queenan, Patrick, Dec. 28, 1875, age 67.
Quick, Mary E., wife of William H., formerly of Buffalo, March 2, 1870, age 34; d. at DesMoines, IA, dau. of the late Maj. Levi Love of Buffalo.
Quigley, Kate Riley, wife of Patrick, Sept. 23, 1880, age 28.
Quigley, Michael, May 18, 1876, age 60; d. in Utica, bur. in Buffalo.
Quilty, Dennis J., Aug. 1876.
Quin, John, Jan. 17, 1856, age 45 y, 9 m, 25 d.
Quinby, Ephraim, late of Bellview, OH, Aug. 11, 1852, age 45.
Quinlan, James J., Feb. 19, 1878, age 31 y, 4 m.
Quinlan, Jane Cuyler Shepard, wife of Dr. John D., March 11, 1868, age 36; d. in Chicago, IL.
Quinlan, Morris, drowned, newspaper carrier, May 22, 1873, age 26.
Quinlin, Charles, Feb. 3, 1869, age 65.
Quinn, Mrs. Catherine, Newstead, July 24, 1872, age 50.
Quinn, Catharine, Erie Co. Almshouse, Aug. 25, 1877, age 23.
Quinn, Christopher, Co. Almshouse, Oct. 23, 1878, age 79.
Quinn, James, Aug. 12, 1873, age 60.
Quinn, John, suicide, March 21, 1880, age 53.
Quinn, Joseph, March 22, 1872, age 55.
Quinn, Joseph, son of the late Joseph, Feb. 10, 1873, age 21 y, 8 m.
Quinn, William, b. Oct. 1762, County Kerry, Ireland, d. Feb. 24, 1870, age 109.
Quinn, Mrs. Rosanna, formerly of Philadelphia, Jan. 3, 1854, age 64.
Quinton, Eliza, Jan. 7, 1880, age 75.
Quirk, Eliza, Dec. 22, 1868, age 56.

Rabbetoy, Mrs. Frances, July 4, 1878, age 67.
Rabel, John, Dec. 12, 1871, age 45.
Race, Mrs. C. W., Evans, March 12, 1877, age 75 y, 3 m.
Racey, Edward T., Dec. 10, 1872.
Radcliffe, Arianda Webster, widow of Jerry, mother-in-law of Walter Joy, Oct. 1, 1862, in 81st year.

Radcliffe, Jerry, March 21, 1856, age 79.
Raeling (or Ruding/Roeling), Herman, Nov. 22, 1873, age 41.
Raffeiner, Rev. Joseph, formerly of Buffalo, Aug. 31, 1872, age 58; d. in Meran, Lower Tyrol.
Rahlow, Henry, sailor, Aug. 21, 1873.
Raichle, Charles, Feb. 7, 1877, age 40.
Raichle, Mary, wife of Charles, March 18, 1866; taken to Cincinnati OH.
Rainey, Alexander, confectioner, Aug. 7, 1832, age 35.
Rainey, Hamilton, June 4, 1875, age 66.
Rainey, Samuel, Aug. 25, 1850, age 37.
Rainforth, Matthew, Jan. 6, 1866, age 61; taken to Lockport, NY.
Raleigh, Katie, May 23, 1878, age 22.
Raleigh, Mary, July 18, 1880, age 90.
Ralph, Almira, wife of Capt. Edward, Oct. 6, 1857, age 41.
Ralph, Christopher, Dec. 23, 1850, age 37; d. at the Asylum in Utica, NY.
Ralph, Mary Ann, wife of Reuben L., April 22, 1853, age 19.
Ralph, Melena, wife of Fesse, July 4, 1870, age 60 y, 4 m.
Ralph (or Rolph), Mrs. Margaret, April 16, 1878, age 46.
Ralph, Reuben L., Oct. 8, 1862, age 31 y, 11 m, 7 d.
Ramage, George A., only son of George, Nov. 29, 1867, age 22.
Ramage, Mrs. Mary, mother of Thomas Hampton, Oct. 14, 1850, in 70th year.
Ramsdell, A. G., eldest son of late Capt. Alexander, formerly of Buffalo, March 1, 1864, in 41st year; in San Francisco, CA.
Ramsdell, Albert N., eldest son of O.P., July 28, 1878, age 25.
Ramsdell, Capt. Alexander, Feb. 28, 1855, age 70 y, 3 m, 8 d.
Ramsdell, Frances A., widow of William G., Nov. 16, 1874, age 69.
Ramsdell, Mary, widow of Alexander, Feb. 13, 1860, age 68 y, 6 m, 12 d.
Ramsdell, William G., July 18, 1855, age 51.
Ramsey, David P., June 28, 1851, age 23; in IA, returning home from CA.
Ramsey, John, Feb. 2, 1877, age 64.
Ramsey, Maggie, Co. Almshouse, Aug. 27, 1879, age 35.
Rand, Calvin G., LaSalle, April 26, 1872, age 39; bur. at Tonawanda.
Rand, Charles T., June 17, 1859, age 57.
Rand, Deborah F., wife of C. T., Dec. 28, 1851, in 44th year.
Rand, Samuel C., brother of Charles T., from Fair Haven, MA, May 28, 1857, in 53d year.
Randall, Adley, Feb. 23, 1876, age 62.
Randall, Eleanor B., wife of W.E., Oct. 12, 1878, age 39.
Randall, Elisha, b. Aug. 29, 1769/61, d. Jan. 4, 1847, bur. Sardinia, NY; Soldier of the Revolution.
Randall, Mrs. Gibbs, Aug. 31, 1852, age 37.
Randall, Capt. Henry, formerly of Buffalo, July 8, 1874, age 72.
Randall, John, March 22, 1874, age 49.
Randall, Lizzie Valldau, wife of Maj. George M., Dec. 9, 1868, age 22; d. in Janesville, WI, bur. Buffalo.
Randall, Rev. Moses, Holland, NY, April 17, 1873, age 80 y, 11 m, 9 d.
Randall, Maj. Gen. Nelson, Feb., 1864; bur. Feb. 28th.
Randall, Miss Phoebe A., Cheektowaga, NY, March 1, 1862, age 26.
Randall, Volney, Aug. 29, 1865, age 63.
Randall, Rev. William H., Williamsville, March 7, 1874, age 56; d. at Lake Maitland, FL, remains brought home.
Raney, Thomas S., May 26, 1844, age 38.
Ranford, Miss Clarissa, Dec. 3, 1822, age 21.
Rankin, Anne, wife of Rev. A. T., Oct. 10, 1865; at Mapleton, Niagara Co., NY.
Rankin, Anne Burt Holland, formerly of Buffalo, April 14, 1873, age 46; d. in Baltimore, MD, bur. Forest Lawn. Wife of Rev. Alexander Taylor Rankin.
Rankin, Annie B., Aug. 14, 1869: bur. with Mary L. & Thomas Rankin in single grave in Forest Lawn. (From cemetery records.)
Rankin, Dr. Francis, March 24, 1872, age 67.
Rankin, George Nichols, formerly an attorney in Walthamstow, Essex, England, East Hamburgh, NY, March 3, 1853, age 63.

Rankin, Hugh, July 28, 1877, age c. 40.
Rankin, Mark, May 13, 1880, age 67.
Rankin, Mary L., Aug. 14, 1869; bur. with Annie B. & Thomas Rankin, Forest Lawn.
Rankin, Thomas, Aug. 14, 1869; bur. with Mary L. & Anne B. Rankin in single grave, Forest Lawn.
Ransler, David, of Buffalo Light Battery, April 3, 1864, age 45; at Camp Barry.
Ransom, Albert F., Clarence, Aug. 21, 1877, age 46.
Ransom, Amasa, Feb. 8, 1851, age 82.
Ransom, Col. Asa, Clarence, NY, March 11, 1835, age 74; d. at Ransom's Grove.
Ransom, Asa Jr., Grand Island, June 8, 1872, age 32.
Ransom, David, Dec. 12, 1872, age 55.
Ransom, Elias, Aug. 1, 1842, age 80.
Ransom, Eunice, widow of Col. Henry B., Clarence, NY, March 17, 1878, age 71; d. in Cleveland, OH, bur. Clarence.
Ransom, Dr. Franklin, March 25, 1873, age 68.
Ransom, Col. Henry B., Clarence, NY, May 17, 1872, age 72.
Ransom, James T., Grand Island, Nov. 11, 1871, age 30.
Ransom, Jane, wife of E. F., Dec. 26, 1866, age 32 y, 5 m.
Ransom, Kezia, widow of Col. Asa, Clarence, June 13, 1837, age 67.
Ransom, Miss Maria E., only dau. of A. R., Oct. 13, 1866.
Ransom, Ruth, widow of Elias, Nov. 20, 1851, age 64.
Ransom, Sally, wife of Elias, Oct. 9, 1820, age 57.
Ranson, Wallace B., Clarence, July 12, 1870, age 42.
Rapp, Joseph, July 8, 1878, age 64 y, 5 m.
Rapp, Maria, wife of Charles, May 23, 1865, age 24 y, 2 m, 8 d.
Rapp, Mrs. Rachel, March 18, 1879, age 78 y, 6 m.
Rasuage, Margaret, wife of George, Dec. 31, 1879, age 64; bur. at Ft. Erie, Ontario.
Ratcliffe, George W., accidental death, July 5, 1875, age 23.
Ratcliffe, Harry, Aug. 8, 1872, age 33.
Rathbone, Amanda, wife of Benjamin, Concord, NY, Sept. 4, 1866.
Rathbone, Anna Diell, wife of Charles T., eldest dau. of the late Rev. John Diell, March 5, 1870, age 36.
Rathbone, Cynthia, wife of Philander, Jr., Hamburgh, NY, Nov. 12, 1840, in 39th year.
Rathbone, George Burwell, April 1, 1874, age 10 months. Res. 660 Niagara St., bur. Forest Lawn on Glenny-Clark Burwell lot beside Anna Burwell Rathbone. (Data from cemtery.)
Rathbone, Harriet, wife of Charles E., formerly of Elmira, April 9, 1860, in 42d year.
Rathbone, Henry A., son of Samuel of Buffalo, late of New Orleans, LA, March 10, 1867; in Paris, France.
Rathbone, Isaac T., youngest son of Samuel, June 12, 1849, age 27; in Cincinnati, OH.
Rathbone, James H., Aug. 17, 1843, in 41st year.
Rathbone, Jane Furey, wife of Charles H., June 25, 1861, age 35.
Rathbone, Mrs. Mary, mother of Mr. C.E., Clarence, Nov. 29, 1868, age 89; bur. in Buffalo.
Rathbone, Roxana, wife of Moses, July 5, 1857, age 64; in Oswego, bur. in Buffalo.
Rathbone, Samuel, Nov. 5, 1865, in 90th year.
Rathbone, Watts S., formerly of Smith and Rathbone, Buffalo, July 7, 1848, in 28th year; d. in Baltimore, MD, bur. at Abbott's Corners, Hamburgh, NY.
Rathbun, Alice, wife of Benjamin, formerly of Buffalo, Oct. 6, 1871; d. in NY City.
Rathbun, Benjamin, formerly of Buffalo, July 20, 1873, age 82; d. at Ft. Washington, NY.
Rethbun, Charles H., July 25, 1879, age 50.
Rathbun, Elizabeth, wife of E. M., July 11, 1855.
Rathbun, Mrs. Elizabeth, East Hamburgh, March 17, 1873, age 81.
Rathbun, Fannie E., late of Atlantic, IA, Arpil 11, 1880; wife of Albert H.
Rathbun, Isaac T., June 1849; body brought to Buffalo for burial in family lot.
Rathbun, Louisa E., wife of E. M., Feb. 18, 1851, in 26th year.
Rathbun, Marie K., widow of Lyman, Nov. 16, 1874, age 70.
Rathbun, (Nathaniel), Moses, May 6, 1860, Batavia, NY, age 89. Born July 25, 1770 in CT, m. Patience James, Charlotte Moore, and Roxanna Bates; father of Benjamin Rathbun, Buffalo builder. (See Cooley, John C., Rathbone Genealogy.)
Rathbun, Nancy Abby, wife of E. M., April 18, 1846, age 33.

Rathbun (or Rathbone), Patience, wife of Moses, mother of Benjamin, Buffalo builder, Oct. 7, 1823, age 53.
Rathbun, Rebecca, wife of Frank A., Dec. 5, 1877, age 26.
Rathbun, Mrs. Sarah, Feb. 7, 1880, age 78.
Rathbun, T. L., son of Benjamin, March 26, 1853; in Detroit, MI.
Rathbun, Thomas, Nov. 14, 1866, age 68.
Ratzforth, Michael, drowned, July 12, 1876, age 30.
Rauch, Jacob, Aug. 1, 1875, age 53.
Rauert, Dora, Feb. 19, 1879, age 57.
Rawley, Mrs., May, 1827, age 73.
Ray, Amos, Cheektowaga, NY, Nov. 20, 1863, age 57.
Ray, Asa M., Nov. 17, 1856, age 45.
Ray, John, formerly of Cumberland, England, Dec. 11, 1871, age 81.
Ray, Patrick G., Jan. 7, 1880, age 34.
Ray, Mrs. Prudence, Cheektowaga, NY, April 19, 1864, age 84.
Ray, Mrs. Ruth, March 3, 1876, age 93.
Ray, Susan, wife of A. M., sister of Mrs. Ann Bishop, Aug. 31, 1849, age 33.
Ray, Thomas, formerly of Buffalo, Oct. 10, 1855; at Union Bar, Butler Co., CA.
Ray, William A., son of the late A. M., Nov. 9, 1868, age 25.
Raymond, Flora Hastings Grannis, wife of A. C., May 28, 1863, age 25; taken to Gowanda, NY.
Rayner, Sarah A., wife of Charles A., formerly of Buffalo, April 25, 1872; d. at Indianapolis.
Raynolds, Henrietta A., formerly of Buffalo, Jan. 17, 1877, age 43; d. at Springfield, MA.
Raynor, Augustus, June 1, 1877, age 72.
Raynor, Frank J., Marilla, Feb. 11, 1877, age 30.
Raynor, Jane, sister of George Gage, May 9, 1857, in 49th year.
Raynor, John, formerly of Buffalo, Clarence, NY, April 9, 1855, age 81.
Raynor, Rachel L., wife of Augustus, only dau. of Margaret Evans, Dec. 20, 1856.
Raze, Elizabeth C., Nov. 4, 1850.
Raze, Jane C., wife of Horatio N., Jan. 26, 1864, age 30.
Raze, Joel S., June 5, 1858, age 46.
Raze, Joseph, Aug. 27, 1879, age 78.
Rea, Sara B., Aug. 9, 1877, wife of W.C., age 24 y, 11 d.
Read, Clarissa, wife of Nelson H., March 25, 1841, age 32.
Read, John, July 18, 1851, age 44.
Read, Louisie [sic], wife of William S., Feb. 13, 1866, age 39 y, 5 m.
Read, Elizabeth, widow of John, April 13, 1875.
Read, Jane E., wife of William, June 14, 1876, age 47.
Read, Mary Ann Bartholomew, wife of William, Jan. 10, 1873, age 44.
Read, Mrs. Mary H., July 18, 1863, age 65; taken to Williamsville, N.Y.
Read, Melvina, wife of A.L., March 12, 1876; d. at Yorkshire, Cattaraugus Co., NY.
Read, Rebecca, wife of William, Jan. 31, 1866, age 40 y, 5 m.
Read, Sarah Hobbs, Feb. 12, 1873, age 92 y, 7 m, 10 d.
Read, Seth W., son of W. S., June 26, 1874, age 22 y, 5 m.
Readdy, Patrick, Almshouse, Aug. 27, 1880, age 50.
Reader, Subima, wife of Thomas J., March 16, 1851, age 39 y, 5 m, 29 d.
Reading (or Redding), Margaret, Dec. 24, 1874, age 31 y, 6 m.
Ready, John, formerly of Buffalo, Dec. 3, 1879; suicide at Bradford, PA.
Ready, Lawrence, employee of Lake Shore & MI Southern RR, Dec. 31, 1870; killed on railroad at Silver Creek, bur. Buffalo.
Reagen, Thomas, accidental death, dock laborer, age 26 (28?) years.
Ream, Victor, railway accident, Cheektowaga, Dec. 22, 1876, age 60.
Reamer, Ann Eliza, wife of Matthew, March 21, 1855, in 39th year.
Reardon, Elizabeth McManus, wife of John, Aug. 11, 1871, age 40.
Reardon, Sister Mary Delphina, Nov. 28, 1878, age 21 y, 11 m.
Reavels, Henry, formerly of NC, July 6, 1863, age 41.
Reaves, Louden, formerly of Buffalo, Hamburgh, NY, April 16, 1859, age 55 y, 4 m.
Rebadow, Louise, May 30, 1880, age 81 y, 10 m, 15 d.
Rebhan, George, laborer, missing since May 3, found drowned May 12 (1880) age 39.
Rebstock, Elias L., Feb. 11, 1862, age 28 y, 6 m, 22 d.

Rebstock, Laurens, Lancaster, Oct. 9, 1873, age 67.
Rebstock, Stephen A., Dec. 1, 1868, age 39.
Rechtenwalt, Peter, Sept. 22, 1868, age 45 y, 9 m.
Recker, Jacob, Hamburg, July 28, 1851, age 80.
Record, Edward A., March 23, 1839, age 21; at Vicksburg, MS.
Record, John, March 21, 1837, age 51.
Record, Margaret, wife of Adam L., July 22, 1831, age 24.
Record, Mrs. Sarah, July 30, 1841, age 49.
Rector, William D., formerly of Buffalo, March 28, 1875, age 55; d. at the hacenda of Joluchuca, Mexico.
Red Jacket, Sa-Go-Ye-Wat-Ha, the celebrated Indian Chief, Seneca Village near Buffalo, Jan. 20, 1830, age 78.
Redden, Patrick, April 25, 1879, age 62.
Redericke, Joseph, April 16, 1871.
Redfield, Homer J., Eden, Jan. 7, 1871, age 64.
Reding, Mrs. Mary C., Sept. 15, 1875, age 71.
Redmond, Arthur, Brant, NY, Co. A, 116th Reg. N.Y. Vol., Jan. 16, 1863, age 23; d. at Chesapeake Hospital, Old Point, VA.
Reece, Mrs., Black Rock, NY, Aug. 1815.
Reed, Abolona, Feb. 18, 1875, age 76.
Reed, Adam or Philip, June 9, 1874, age 72.
Reed, Daniel, Tonawanda, NY, Jan. 21, 1831, age 71.
Reed, Hattie K., dau. of Samuel Roxy M., March 7, 1874, age 20; taken to Hamburgh, NY.
Reed, George W., May 29, 1853, age 29 y, 7 m, 9 d; in Milwaukee, WI.
Reed, Israel, Dec. 30, 1813, at Battle of Black Rock.
Reed, Israel, Willink, NY, killed at the battle of Black Rock, Dec. 30, 1813.
Reed, Capt. John, Chicago, May 9, 1872.
Reed, John S., Aug. 12, 1845, age 37.
Reed, Lavinie, wife of William C., formerly of Buffalo, March 22, 1878, age 57.
Reed, Louisa J., widow of George W., eldest dau. of Capt. Amos Pratt, Aug. 8, 1853, age 23 y, 7 m, 28 d.
Reed, Lucy A. Reeve, wife of William, Feb. 10, 1862, age 26.
Reed, Mrs. Maria, Tonawanda, NY, wife of Capt. Reed, April 8, 1874, age 62.
Reed, Nancy, wife of Loman, late of Milwaukee, WI, Sept. 11, 1846, age 53.
Reed, Peter A., May 13, 1867, age 35.
Reed, Samuel Sr., April 23, 1876, age 80.
Reed, Simeon R., Sept. 4, 1870, age 61; d. in Shamburg, PA, bur. Buffalo.
Reed, Sylvia, widow of Daniel, Tonawanda, Jan. 25, 1832, age 70.
Reed, William W., formerly of Buffalo, Nov. 28, 1859, age 30; in Springville, NY.
Reef, Mrs., Black Rock, NY, May 19, 1872.
Rees, Charles, May, 1856; in Rock Island, IL, bur. in Buffalo May 7th.
Rees, David, July 2, 1834, age 58.
Rees, Mrs. F., Jan. 28, 1873, age 64.
Rees, Mrs. Hannah, Feb. 28, 1880, age 62.
Rees, Sally, widow of David, Nov. 17, 1848, in 68th year.
Rees, William S., 2d male child b. in Buffalo after its permanent settlement, Evans, NY, Aug. 24, 1848, age 43.
Reese, Mr., accidental death, Sept. 20, 1876.
Reese, Eugene M., 2d son of George, Sept. 26, 1876, age 29 y, 24d; taken to Troy.
Reese, Susannah Prower, wife of George, Aug. 18, 1876, age 66, taken to Lockport, NY.
Reese, Rev. William J., Pastor of First Universalist Society, Sept. 6, 1834, age 35.
Reeser, John, Cheektowaga, NY, Nov. 29, 1880, age 78 y, 6 m, 29 d.
Reeson, Miss Dinah, East Aurora, NY, June 13, 1874, age 25.
Reeves, Capt. Charles, Aug. 17, 1866, age 46 y, 8 m, father of Charles E.
Reeves, Elvina, wife of Elisha, dau. of John A. Blauvelt of Buffalo, April 27, 1865, age 29 y, 17 d; in Lodi Center.
Reeves, Lillie O., Aug. 9, 1879, of J.T. (or I.C.).
Regan, John, Oct. 26, 1873, age 55.
Regan, Owen, Sept. 8, 1879, age 35.
Register, John, Oct. 1824, age 47.

Register, Miss Susan, East Hamburgh, NY, Aug. 15, 1860, age 38.
Regler, Louise, wife of William, drowned, Dec. 4, 1877, age 59.
Rehm, George J., Nov. 19, 1863, age 44 y, 4 m, 10 d.
Reiboldt, Elizabeth, wife of Christian, Jan. 13, 1871, age 44.
Reichert, Jacob, Feb. 24, 878, age 60 y, 8 m, 14 d.
Reid, Mrs., widow, Lower Black Rock, NY, July 28, 1880, age 27; suicide or accident at Fort Erie.
Reid, Alexander, Tonawanda, NY, Superintendent of Niagara Iron Works, Dec. 1, 1880, age 65.
Reid, Carrie H., wife of Peter B., Feb. 24, 1880.
Reid, Hannah, April 28, 1874, age 81.
Reid, James, of Aberdeenshire, Scotland, Nov. 4, 1874, age 29.
Reid, L. P., Aurora, Sept. 18, 1876, age 92 y, 5 m., 7 d.
Reid, William, April 22, 1862, age 33.
Reide, Archibald, late of Morayshire, Scotland, Aug. 4, 1851, in 31st year.
Reidpath, Robert D., May 27, 1874, age 43 y, 11 m.
Reif, Anthony, March 28, 1872, age 33.
Reigart, Marcia Caroline Van Deventer, dau. of Maj. Eugene Van Deventer, wife of James Hamilton Reigart, formerly of Buffalo, Oct. 8, 1864, in 24th year; Lancaster, PA.
Reigen, John, Oct. 27, 1880, age 62.
Reilly, Margaret Ann, North Buffalo, NY, wife of John G., Sept. 24, 1860, age 85.
Reilly, Mary A., Nov. 10, 1873, age 53.
Reilly, Rebecca D., dau. of J. G., May 15, 1874, age 21.
Reilly, Thomas, April 19, 1873, age 59.
Reimann, Catherine, wife of Jacob, Sept. 6, 1869, age 35 y, 9 m.
Reimann, Mrs. Margaretha, May 28, 1878, age 58.
Reimann, Maria O., widow of Ludwig, Dec. 15, 1876, age 79.
Reimer, Leonard, accidental death, Nov. 12, 1875.
Reinhardt, Margaret, wife of Philip, July 16, 1874, age 67 y, 8 d.
Reinhardt, Philip J., Jan. 25, 1879, age 68 y, 11 m, 16 d.
Reinhart, Peter L. Jan. 4, 1877, age 43 y, 9 m.
Reinheimer, Lizzie, wife of William, Dec. 24, 1874, age 23 y, 3 m, 14 d.
Reinholt, Catharine, suicide, June 2, 1877, age c. 21.
Reist, John, Jr., April 27, 1853, age 24 y, 5 m, 27 d.
Reist, Rev. John, Bishop of the Mennonite Church, Williamsville, Jan. 18, 1879, age 79.
Relay, Mrs. Selinda, Sept. 19, 1833, age 31.
Relf, George W., Feb. 2, 1855, age 28.
Reif, Mary Ann, wife of George, Feb. 4, 1863, age 59.
Relf, Perry E., 2d son of Thomas, Sept. 10, 1864, age 31 y, 11 m, 20 d.
Relf, Sarah E., wife of George, March 31, 1874, age 49.
Relf, Thomas, Sr., May 7, 1858, age 51 y, 10 m, 7 d.
Relf, Thomas J., son of Thomas, Oct. 9, 1855, age 25.
Relph, Andrew, June 7, 1873, age 85.
Relph, Andrew O., Black Rock, NY, Jan. 19, 1854, age 46.
Relph (or Ralph), Celia, widow of Andrew, Oct. 16, 1875, age 91.
Rembold, Ernest, accidental death, Sept. 1, 1877, age 38.
Rembold, Henry, suicide, Aug. 22, 1877, age 35.
Remington, Caroline Evans, wife of Rev. James, Lancaster, NY, May 3, 1872, age 59; taken to Alden.
Remington, Catherine Jane, oldest dau. of Rev. David of Rye, NY, Aug. 10, 1849, age 26 y, 1 m, 19 d.
Remington, Elizabeth S., wife of W. A., March 12, 1841, age 26.
Remington, Mrs. Experience, Lancaster, NY, June 14, 1843, age 76.
Remington, Frank H., dau. of late Edwin, Dec. 11, 1862.
Remington, Sarah Kingsburn, Alden, NY, dau. of Rev. David, Aug. 7, 1854, age 21; bur. in Buffalo.
Remington, Shadrake, March 22, 1846, age 80; Lancaster, NY.
Remington, Shirmon, Lancaster, NY, April 15, 1880, age 70 y, 10 m, 12 d.
Remington, William A., Oct. 16, 1841, age 31.
Rennewitz (or Bennewitz), Charles, April 30, 1873, age 69.
Renney (or Kenney), John W., Dec. 29, 1876, age 49.

Reno, Christian, Sept. 5, 1875.
Renowden, Susan, wife of William, July 24, 1866, age 29 y, 9 m.
Rensler, John, May 15, 1877, age 21.
Renwick, Mary Jane, wife of Ralph, March 6, 1853, age 21.
Renwick, Thomas, formerly of Buffalo, Sept. 17, 1878, age 37; d. at Point Mackinaw, Lake Huron, bur. Buffalo.
Renz, Mathias, April 1880, age 50; drowned.
Repholtz, Charles, laborer, Sept. 27, 1872, age c. 30.
Reppenhagen, Wilhelm, Sept. 1, 1878, age 53 y, 8 m.
Ressegue, Mrs. Lydia M., mother of Mrs. Capt. Talcott, March 14, 1864, age 78.
Rexford, Elizabeth, May 23, 1868, age 84 y, 9 m.
Reyburn, Mary J., widow of Thomas C., dau. of Gordon Bailey, Dec. 24, 1867.
Reynders, Mary, Sept. 21, 1880, age 20 y, 11 m.
Reynolds, Adaline, wife of David, Dec. 29, 1852, age 25 y, 2 m.
Reynolds, Mrs. Amy, wife of J.N., formerly of Greenwich, RI, June 27, 1833, in 74th year.
Reynolds, E. Burton, Dec. 6, 1866, age 48; at LaSalle, Niagara Co.
Reynolds, Francis, May 11, 1875, age 32.
Reynolds, Grovenor, son of Lynus, Nov. 24, 1866, age 42.
Reynolds, Dr. H. H., May 9, 1862, age 57.
Reynolds, Josiah, Colden, NY, Sept. 11, 1852, age 88.
Reynolds, Julia Ann, widow of Dr. H. H., July 8, 1863, age 55.
Reynolds, Capt. Lynus, Dec. 3, 1868, age 68.
Reynolds, Martha D., wife of A., June 3, 1865, age 40.
Reynolds, Sarah A., wife of William, dau. of Samuel Brown, formerly of Buffalo, March 24, 1863, age 47; San Francisco, CA.
Reynolds, Sarah, Co. Almshouse, Feb. 2, 1878, age 44.
Reynolds, Mrs. Sophia, March 4, 1865, age 82.
Rhodes, Mrs. Lydia, Evans, NY, July 6, 1874, age 103 y, 2 m, 12 d.
Rhodes, Samuel D., formerly of New Haven, CT, Sept. 17, 1861, age 53.
Ribbel, Elizabeth, Oct. 16, 1879, age 79 y, 3 m; widow of J.
Ribbell, J. P., father of C. A., Jan 4, 1874, age 74.
Rice, Lieut., NY Vol., formerly of Madison Co., NY, Sept. 9, 1814.
Rice, Mrs. Almey A., April 23, 1879, age 79.
Rice, Asa, lawyer, May 28, 1823, age 35.
Rice, Barnard, Dec. 17, 1875, age 72.
Rice, Mrs. Catherine, Nov. 17, 1866, age 39.
Rice, Charles B., July 26, 1863, age 58.
Rice, Charles E., April 3, 1872, age 29.
Rice, Elihu, Sardinia, NY, March 22, 1863, age 76.
Rice, Ellen, July 30, 1880, age 68.
Rice, Eva H. C., wife of John, Feb. 11, 1874, age 31 y, 2 m, 24 d.
Rice, Huldah Conklin, wife of Henry, Clarence, NY, April 14, 1878, age 51.
Rice, J.J.H., son-in-law of Elias Weed, formerly of Buffalo, Dec. 9, 1862, age 27; in Wheatland, NY.
Rice, Julia, Alden, NY, Oct. 24, 1875, age 30; d. at Petrolia, bur. Alden.
Rice, Mrs. Lydia, formerly of Marlborough, MA, April 11, 1842, age 65.
Rice, Minnie Lane, Clarence, NY, June 12, 1880, age 23; d. at Warsaw, NY.
Rice, Rhoa, wife of Clark of Watertown, Sept. 14, 1853; taken to Watertown, NY.
Rice, Sarah A., Oct. 16, 1879, age 71.
Rice, Sarah Elizabeth, wife of Capt. John, Nov. 12, 1864, age 25.
Rice, Selina, wife of Asa, Oct. 10, 1825, age 36. D. on a canal packet boat.
Rice, Sophia, wife of J. M., April 3, 1873.
Rice, Tiny B., wife of Josiah, Dec. 1825, age 30.
Rice, Hon. Victor M., Oct. 18, 1869, age 51; d. at Oneida, bur. Buffalo.
Rice, Wilder, Boston, NY, Sept. 11, 1864, age 74.
Rice, William M., Elma, NY, April 28, 1872, age 69.
Rice, Gaius B., Oct. 25, 1861, age 71.
Rice, Hannah Eliza, wife of C.B. Akron, Feb. 13, 1862, age 38.
Rich, Andrew J., Dec. 15, 1870, age 47; d. in NY City, bur. Buffalo.
Rich, Aphia, wife of the late Gaivus B., Feb. 15, 1868, age 75.

Rich, Hon. Charles, Akron, May 16, 1870, in 62d year; found lying dead on the highway.
Rich, Charles Townsend, May 1, 1878, age 30 y, 5 m.
Rich, Gaius B., Oct. 25, 1861, age 71.
Rich, Hannah Eliza, Akron, NY, Feb. 13, 1862, age 38; wife of C.B.
Rich, Ina Belle, wife of Charles T., Oct. 24, 1876, age 25.
Richards, Abel B., Aug. 23, 1850, age 34.
Richards, Benjamin P., East Aurora, NY, April 9, 1863, age 73.
Richards, Caroline, wife of Henry, March 30, 1873, age 73.
Richards, Cathrine Elizabeth, wife of LaFayette, Sept. 14, 1857, age 24 y, 5 m, 27 d.
Richards, Gilbert, late of Cummington, MA, Nov. 1, 1879, age 84.
Richards, Henry, at Homeopathic Hospital, Aug. 5, 1877, age 74.
Richards, Mrs. Kate, March 28, 1872, age 21.
Richards, Salome, wife of Thomas F., Sept. 2, 1832, age 26; d. of cholera.
Richards, Susan, wife of John, Dec. 29, 1863, in 62d year.
Richards, W. L., March 1874, age 24.
Richardson, Caleb, Aurora, June 5, 1837, age 81. [Another card: Richardson, Caleb, E. Aurora, NY, b. 1756, d. June 5, 1837, age 81; Soldier of the Revolution.]
Richardson, Charles B., son of R. H., Dec. 8, 1869, age 35.
Richardson, Fanny Jane, wife of Samuel B., formerly of Nashua, NH, Oct. 20, 1858, in 40th year.
Richardson, Mrs. Frances, of Boston, England, May 4, 1867, age 50.
Richardson, Frances Ella, only dau. of George, April 29, 1856.
Richardson, George, Oct. 19, 1870, age 73; taken to Akron, NY.
Richardson, Jasper F., Co. A, 21st Regt., Sept. 15, 1862; at Fairfax Seminary Hospital from wounds received at second battle of Bull Run. Bur. in Buffalo.
Richardson, John, b. 1766, d. 1841, bur. Lockport (Niagara Co.); Soldier of the Revolution.
Richardson, John, Lancaster, NY, March 11, 1878, age 68.
Richardson, John Lewis, March 13, 1869, age 40.
Richardson, Miss Kate, sister of Mrs. R. L. Perkins or Jenkins, April 4, 1878.
Richardson, Louisa, wife of George, March 18, 1849, age 28.
Richardson, Rufus, Feb. 4, 1878, age 83.
Richardson, S.B., formerly of Buffalo, Dec. 20, 1867, age 53 y, 6 m; at Nashua, NH.
Richardson, Thomas B., Williamsville, NY, Oct. 22, 1877, age 63.
Richardson, William E., suicide, Jan. 17, 1877, age 33.
Richey, Satie Bell, Lancaster, NY, Sept. 7, 1870, age 21.
Richey, William, Lancaster, NY, March 26, 1859, age 70.
Richmond, ex-Lieut. Carlos H., 100th Regt. N.Y., Springville, NY, July 19, 1865, age 26 y, 5 m.
Richmond, Caroline, wife of Charles T., dau. of Capt. James C. Gibson, May 31, 1856, age 27.
Richmond, Charles Y., July 22, 1870, age 46; d. in Chicago, bur. in Buffalo.
Richmond, Dean, Batavia, NY, Aug. 27, 1866, age 62.
Richmond, George, Sardinia, NY, Dec. 25, 1869, age 78.
Richmond, George M., Sardinia, July 25, 1846, age 24.
Richmond, Jewett Merritt, Nov. 14, 1880, age 9th year, son of M. & Geraldine H. Richmond.
Richmond, Mary l., wife of Alfred W., Sept. 2, 1874, age 33 y, 10 m; taken to Batavia.
Richter, August, letter-carrier, Aug. 11, 1872, age 50.
Rickard, Maria F., wife of George, Aug. 22, 1864.
Riddle, Mary A., dau. of Charles C., Boston Center, NY, Jan. 16, 1861, age 20 y, 10 m.
Rider, E. G., Feb. 25, 1849, age 38.
Rider, Capt. Henry, Sept. 1828, age 40.
Rider, Melissa, wife of John A., Aug. 1, 1865, age 43.
Rider, Capt. Reuben, Sardinia, NY, July 24, 1864, age 72.
Ridge, Thomas, July 21, 1873, age 22.
Riebeling, Burkhard, July 23, 1870, age 78.
Riebeling, John J., formerly of Buffalo, Sept. 4, 1878, age 83; d. in Chicago, IL.
Riedy, Mary, wife of John, Aug. 30, 1869.
Riefler, J.C., Feb. 23, 1867, age 36 y, 4 d.
Riehl, George R., May 21, 1869, age 26 y, 10 m, 21 d.
Rielly, Mary, sister of Thomas, June 11, 1878, age 73.

Rieman, Frances H., June 28, 1879, age 65 y, 2 m, 2 d.
Rieman, Martin A., Nov. 12, 1880, age 21 y, 15 d.
Riethenburger (or Rightenburg), George, Railroad accident, Jan. 1, 1878, age 56 (or 52 y, 7 m, 23 d.).
Rigg, Angelica Hubbell, wife of William H., Oct. 1, 1873, age 53.
Riggs, George, drowned off Erie, PA, May 12, 1872.
Riggs, Margaret, widow of William, Aug. 23, 1880.
Riley, Abram, brother of the late Capt. John, formerly of Buffalo, May 30, 1874, age 62; d. at Oak Orchard, Orleans Co., NY.
Riley, Angelett, wife of Col. A., Oct. 12, 1852, age 42.
Riley, Annie S., June 7, 1875, age 21, dau. of William A.; taken to Berlin, CT.
Riley, Bvt. Maj. Gen. Bennett, Col., 1st Regt., U.S. Inf., June 9, 1853, age 66; bur. Forest Lawn Cemetery.
Riley, Emily, dau. of Gen. Aaron, Aurora, March 20, 1857, age 22.
Riley, Rev. Isaac, Oct. 23, 1878, age 44.
Riley, James, Dec. 21, 1875, age 39; taken to Lockport.
Riley, Jane, wife of P., June 16, 1848, age 47.
Riley, Capt. John, Aug. 4, 1865, age 49.
Riley, Julia A. Ryther, wife of Henry W., Holland, NY, Aug. 28, 1871.
Riley, Lucy B., wife of John O., Holland, NY, Aug. 13, 1873, age 54, d. at Elmira.
Riley, William H., Nov. 1867.
Rinck, Bartholomew, June 22, 1871, age 61 y, 10 m.
Rinck, Elizabeth, widow of William, April 15, 1878, age 78.
Rinck, William, Feb. 1, 1854, age 71.
Ring, Mrs. Lydia Brownell, Feb. 14, 1880, age 56.
Ring, Patrick, March 13, 1879, age 75.
Ringer, Anna, wife of G. A., March 8, 1875, age 21.
Ringer (or Ruenger), Charles, accidental death, carpenter, July 20, 1875, age 57.
Rink, William, March 22, 1864, age 35.
Riordan, Mrs. Mary, May 15, 1875, age 48.
Ripley, Cornelia S., wife of Rev. A. P., Aug. 2, 1869, age 48.
Ripley, Deacon Eli, Aurora, NY, May 19, 1830, age 70.
Ripley, Mrs. Eliza L., Nov. 28, 1853, age 43.
Ripley, Huntington, formerly of Windham, CT, Oct. 9, 1852, age 49.
Ripont, Jacques, July 6, 1876, age 67.
Ripont, Peter J., June 8, 1878, age 45 y, 2 m, 18 d.
Ritchie, Catherine T., wife of H.B., Aug. 5, 1860, age 39; in Lewiston, NY, bur. in Buffalo.
Ritchie, Henry B., May 21, 1875, age 62.
Ritchie, Mrs. Mary, Sept. 17, 1865, age 56.
Ritchie, William, Aug. 6, 1849, age 27.
Riter, Philip, March 26, 1874, age 62 y, 10 m.
Riter, Philip Jr., Sept. 10, 1877, age 40 y, 5 m, 8 d.
Riter, Samuel F., July 6, 1878, age 34.
Riter, Washington, May 1879, found drowned at Tonawanda.
Riter, William, Aug. 17, 1875, age 40.
Ritt, Nicholas, father of Gregory and M.L., Nov. 14, 1867.
Rittersbaugh, Michael, Clarence, NY, Oct. 8, 1851, age 38.
Roach, Ellen, April 15, 1880, age 80.
Roach, Henry, May 26, 1880, age 40.
Roach, Joseph, Oct. 15, 1869, age 63.
Roader (or Roaber), Ernst, carver, July 23, 1875, age 33.
Robb, Lizzie, dau. of David, Nov. 2, 1877, age 20.
Robbins, Cornelia L., wife of S.W. of Lower Alton, IL, Dec., 1836, age 34.
Robbins, Franklin, Sept. 26, 1869, age 56.
Robbins, H. C., Aug. 13, 1877, age 76.
Robbins, Henry F., formerly of Buffalo, son of Mrs. Eliza H. Robbins, 1st OH Battery, Dec. 5, 1863, age 34; in hospital at Nashville, TN.
Roberts, Abraham, formerly of Plattsburgh, NY, Aug. 4, 1844, age 48.
Roberts, Adaline, wife of Zacheus, April 8, 1839, age 25.
Roberts, Clara A. Cotter, wife of John, April 27, 1873, age 21 y, 8 m.

Roberts, David, May 13, 1879, age 69.
Roberts, Elizabeth, wife of J. D., Oct. 18, 1851, in 48th year.
Roberts, Mrs. Ellen, March 16, 1871.
Roberts, Enos M., Feb. 3, 1833, age 27.
Roberts, Frank, switchman on Erie Railway, June 11, 1870.
Roberts, Horace C., Dec. 24, 1873, age 57.
Roberts, John K., Oct. 31, 1867, age 58.
Roberts, Leander Hart, Feb. 7, 1843, in 27th year.
Roberts, Gen. Leander J., Dec. 28, 1867, age 78th year.
Roberts, Lois, wife of Elijah, Sept. 14, 1836, age 32.
Roberts, Paul, Tonawanda, NY, Sept. 21, 1872, age 63.
Roberts, Sarah Maria, eldest dau. of Warner, Williamsville, NY, April 6, 1843, in 21st year.
Roberts, Thomas, March 7, 1866, age 44.
Roberts, Warner, Williamsville, NY, April 16, 1846, age 50.
Robertson, Delia, wife of William, May 26, 1878, age 34.
Robertson, Mrs. Mahala, mother of William M., May 6, 1876, age 58.
Robertson, Capt. R. L., Aug. 26, 1850; at Chagres on the *Empire City*. A Lake Captain for many years.
Robertson, Richard L., formerly of Buffalo, Oct. 21, 1867, age 37; at Matamoras, Mexico.
Robertson, William, native of Perth, Scotland, attorney; Nov. 8, 1868, age 58th year.
Robie, Rev. John E., May 26, 1872, age 61; d. at Cowlesville, bur. Buffalo.
Robinet, Theodore, found in the water Aug. 5, 1873; carpenter.
Robinson, Alanson, formerly of Buffalo, May 21, 1870, in 54th year (?); d. in NY City, funeral at Brewster's Station, Putnam Co., NY.
Robinson, Amos, Cheektowaga, NY, May 21, 1875, age 86.
Robinson, Andrew, Feb. 22, 1828, age 22.
Robinson, Asahel, Marilla, NY, Aug. 9, 1874, age 74 y, 10 m; bur. at Aurora.
Robinson, Azel P., Lancaster, NY, Feb. 25, 1846, in 46th year.
Robinson, Caroline, wife of John, April 12, 1861, age 42.
Robinson, Charles, July 7, 1844, age 36.
Robinson, Christopher, Black Rock, NY, March 13, 1848, age 67.
Robinson, Clark, Oct. 30, 1853, age 47.
Robinson, Coleman T., formerly of Buffalo, May 1, 1872, age 33 or 34; son of the late Alanson. D. at Brewster's Station, Putnam Co., NY.
Robinson, Eliza, wife of Nelson, formerly of Buffalo, Sept. 17, 1848, in 35th year; in New York.
Robinson, Mrs. Eliza, Feb. 25, 1875, age 58.
Robinson, Elizabeth, dau. of Robert, Sept. 4, 1867, age 23.
Robinson, Elizabeth, June 17, 1871, age 73.
Robinson, Emma, wife of William, Dec. 13, 1862, age 35.
Robinson, Gain, Aug. 31, 1860, age 32.
Robinson, Henry J., son of Amos, Cheektowaga, NY, Oct. 17, 1853, age 37.
Robinson, Jane, Dec. 30, 1879, age 49 y, 9 m, wife of Hugh.
Robinson, Capt. John, of Steamer *Globe*, Sept. 17, 1850, age 39.
Robinson, Joseph, Jan. 1825, age 46.
Robinson, Mary, wife of John, Wales, NY, June 30, 1844, age 50.
Robinson, Mary, wife of William, Dec. 17, 1878, age 31.
Robinson, Mary E., wife of John A., formerly of Lowell, MA, Feb. 25, 1843, age 23 y, 6 m.
Robinson, Mrs. Mary Law, mother of George N., Jan. 14, 1865, in her 90th year.
Robinson, Morgan L., June 26, 1876, age 58.
Robinson, Moses C., father of A., late of Patterson, Putnam Co., NY, June 8, 1847, in 64th year.
Robinson, Robert, Feb. 4, 1850, in Cincinatti, OH.
Robinson, Ruhamah, wife of Azel P., Lancaster, NY, Nov. 28, 1840, age 33.
Robinson, William F., March 9, 1871, age 50.
Robson, Grace A., wife of John, Dec. 30, 1872, age 35.
Robson, Jennie, widow of John, Oct. 1, 1875, age 28.
Robson, John, Aug. 12, 1874, age 37.
Roche, Mr. late of Demarara, Nov. 9, 1850.
Roche, Richard, Dec. 24, 1869, age 59.

Rochester, Amanda, wife of William B., Jan. 16, 1831, age 32.
Rochester, James U., formerly of Buffalo, March 22, 1860, age 41, in Auburn, NY.
Rockafellow, Christopher, Dec. 1880, age 75.
Rockett, Mrs., mother of Edward and Mary of Tonawanda, NY; Clarence, NY, Dec. 31, 1873, age 52.
Rockland, George, July 3, 1880, age 33.
Rockwell, Frederick S., Jan. 29, 1867, age 60.
Rockwell, Phebe, Nov. 2, 1874, age 22 y, 4 m, 22 d.
Rockwood, Gertrude C. James, wife of Charles D., formerly of Buffalo, Nov. 3, 1873, age 27; d. Kansas City, MO, bur. Buffalo.
Rodenbach, Catharine, wife of Christopher, Jan. 22, 1867, age 48.
Rodgers, Edwin, March 7, 1859.
Rodney, Charles H., son of John, April 4, 1862, age 24 y, 3 m.
Rodney, James Albert, June 20, 1879, age 22 y, 6 m, 7 d.
Roe, Patrick, Jan. 2, 1874, age 22 y, 4 m.
Roesch, Luis, a Frenchman, Oct. 1827, age 20.
Roese, Gesena, Aug. 29, 1865, in 30th year.
Roese, Henry, July 25, 1868, age 30 y, 8 m, 23 d; accidentally drowned.
Roesser, Annie J., eldest dau. of J. & C., Aug. 25, 1869, age 21; d. at Battle Creek, MI, bur. Buffalo.
Roffo, Joseph, Dec. 1872, age 39.
Rogen, John, Jan. 21, 1880, age 52.
Rogers, Miss Abigail, April 21, 1832, age 22.
Rogers, Agnes Hood, Aug. 4, 1871, wife of John.
Rogers, Carey, Dec. 23, 1843, age c. 35.
Rogers, Caroline M., wife of William F., June 16, 1847, in 25th year.
Rogers, Charlotte, wife of James, Alden, NY, Aug. 9, 1833, age 22.
Rogers, Emily, wife of Calvin, Aurora, NY, May 13, 1878, age 78.
Rogers, George, blacksmith, Aug. 8, 1873, age 35.
Rogers, Dr. Gustavus A., father of Sherman S. of Buffalo, Nov. 26, 1872, age 74; d. in Chicago, bur. Buffalo.
Rogers, Capt. Harry, of Arcadia, Wayne Co., NY, and taken there, Sept. 27, 1850, age 46.
Rogers, Hetty Peckham, wife of Jabez J., formerly of Buffalo, March 31, 1864, in 61st year; at Unadilla, Otsego Co., N.Y.
Rogers, James, Aug. 16, 1832, age 24.
Rogers, Jane, wife of Charles, dau. of James Mann of Black Rock, NY, March 27, 1850, age 27.
Rogers, Jennett, wife of Samuel, Sr., mother of H. S. Cunningham of Buffalo, Feb. 3, 1854, age 59.
Rogers, Jerome B., Co. D, 10th Regt., NY Cavalry, North Collins, Nov. 15, 1863, age 29.
Rogers, Deacon John, Feb. 9, 1875, age 70.
Rogers, John C., Alden, NY, Oct. 19, 1871, age 58.
Rogers, Joseph G. M., only son of Mrs. Timothy Paige, Jan. 27, 1864, age 28.
Rogers, Lucy, Holland, NY, Feb. 19, 1873; widow of Albert, age 28 y, 11 m.
Rogers, Marilla, wife of John C., Alden, NY, Nov. 16, 1855, age 38.
Rogers, Mrs. Mary Ann, Sept. 4, 1870, age 53 y, 10 m.
Rogers, Mary Jane, wife of Thomas (or Thompson), Jan. 5, 1875.
Rogers, Nathaniel, proprietor of "Phelps House," Dec. 24, 1852, age 50.
Rogers, Phebe Ann, widow of Nathaniel, formerly of Buffalo, July 23, 1859, age 58; in Albany.
Rogers, Platt, Collins, NY, March 8, 1850, age 28.
Rogers, Sally A., wife of Hon. Wilson, North Collins, NY, Dec. 28, 1866, age 55 y, 1 m, 5 d.
Rogers, Samuel Sen., formerly of Clarence, NY; Tonawanda, NY, Oct. 17, 1873, age 82.
Rogers, Sarah, wife of Frederick, July 18m, 1876, age 47.
Rogers, Sarah S., widow of Samuel, mother of Jabez J. and Henry W. of Buffalo, Alden, NY, Oct. 2, 1850, in 84th year; formerly of Unadilla, NY.
Rogers, Susan Campbell, widow of Dr. G. A., formerly of Buffalo, July 29, 1875: d. in Chicago, IL.
Rogers, Vincent, Lancaster, NY, June 17, 1878, age 75.

Rogers, Warren S., East Aurora, NY, June 9, 1877, age 61.
Rogers, William, May, 1824, age 35.
Rohde, John Frederick, April 4, 1872, age 80.
Rohe, Mrs. Catharine, June 13, 1853, age 23.
Rohe, Catharine, May 22, 1861, age 73 y, 9 m, 9 d.
Rohe, Peter, Feb. 11, 1865, age 72 y, 2 m, 23 d.
Rohl, Louis, March 16, 1871, age c. 45.
Rohmer, George, scalded, July 18, 1876.
Rohr, Kittie M., Oct. 1, 1880, age 22 y, 10 m, 5 d.
Roleiman (or Robinson), J. C., Dec. 17, 1878, age 60.
Roll, W. Amelia, wife of August, Nov. 7, 1873, age 44 y, 4 m.
Rollin, Henry, 1839, bur. on Harry H. Bissell lot in Forest Lawn Cemetery.
Rollin, Peter, supposed poison, Elma, Aug. 8, 1877, age over 60.
Romer, Henrietta D., wife of Alexander, March 21, 1841, in 40th year.
Ronan, Michael, April 22, 1880, age 33 y, 1 m.
Roney, Mathew, Jan. 23, 1878, age 45.
Roneyn, Ann, May 10, 1871, age 38.
Ronian, T., father of Mrs. W. G. Dixon of Buffalo, Boston, NY, May 4, 1873.
Roop, Henry, March 5, 1874, age 69.
Roop, Henry, April 10, 1878, age 28.
Roop, John, killed at Battle of Black Rock, Dec. 30, 1813.
Roop, William C., formerly of Buffalo, Dec. 27, 1846, in 33rd year; at Hanoverston, OH.
Roos, Regina, widow of Jacob, July 13, 1869, age 57.
Roos, Jacob, Nov. 27, 1867, age 59 y, 5 m, 11 d.
Root, Amos, Evans, NY, Oct. 24, 1875, age 77 y, 1 m, 17 d.
Root, Mrs. Caroline A., sister of Mrs. James M. Smith, Aug. 14, 1880; bur. at Oneida Castle.
Root, Christian, Williamsville, June 3, 1877, age 66 y, 3 m, 16 d.
Root, Christiana, wife of John, July 5, 1821, age 43 y, 1 d.
Root, Edward, firm of E. and A. R. Root, Aug. 25, 1858, age 31.
Root, Edward, March 13, 1850, age 61.
Root, Elizabeth J., widow of John, Nov. 10, 1849, in 56th year.
Root, Ellen, wife of Edward, Oct. 30, 1852, age 24; at Elyria, OH.
Root, Henry, Black Rock, NY, Sept. 6, 1853, age 61.
Root, Henry Lungdon, eldest son of the late Edward, formerly of Buffalo, March 25, 1858, age 34; at Laredo, TX.
Root, John, Sept. 16, 1846, age 76.
Root, Dr. John, formerly of Buffalo, Nov. 29, 1876, age 52; d. at Batavia, NY.
Root, Lucius A., Feb. 6, 1871. Killed by accident on Hudson River Railroad at New Hamburgh, bur. in Geneva.
Root, Lucy H., wife of J. S., Sept. 20, 1875, age 68.
Root, Sarah, wife of Charles G., formerly of Buffalo, March 7, 1860, age 24; in Louisville, KY.
Root, Mrs. Sophronia, sister of Zenas Clark, Dec. 18, 1856, in 73rd year; taken to Lancaster, NY.
Root, Temperance, mother of Francis H., March 7, 1845, age 74.
Roots, Ann, wife of John, July 18, 1847, age 28.
Roots, John, June 12, 1879, age 65.
Roscoe, H. S., formerly of Aurora, NY, Jan. 10, 1852, age 32; at Frankfort, Herkimer Co., NY.
Rosa, Matthew W., June 11, 1872, age 82.
Rose, Alexander, May 21, 1861, age 34.
Rose, Amy Urilla, widow of Edwin, Hamburg, NY, April 7, 1880.
Rose, Charles, laborer, June 29, 1880, age 35; drowned in Buffalo River.
Rose, Edward, formerly of Buffalo, Sept., 1853, age c. 40; in Cincinnati, OH.
Rose, Edwin, Jan. 19, 1873, age 68.
Rose, Florence A., wife of Myron P., March 19, 1877, age 28.
Rose, John, March 7, 1836, age 34.
Rose, John, Nov. 18, 1864, age 49.
Rose, John, Nov. 20, 1868, age 5.
Rose, Josiah, Evans, NY, Aug. 19, 1840, age 79.

Rose, Mary, wife of John, April 1, 1862.
Rose, Mary A., wife of A.S.T., Dec. 10, 1875, age 28.
Rose, Miranda, mother of Myron P., Nov. 30, 1875, age 75.
Rose, Myron P., railroad conductor, Dec. 29, 1880, age 40; killed by a locomotive at Silver Creek, NY.
Rose, Thomas, Sept. 1879, age 60.
Rose, Walter, formerly of Buffalo, Alden, NY, May 5, 1867, in 65th year.
Roselle, Thomas, June 1871.
Rosemeyer, John, Jan. 9, 1874, age c. 24.
Rosenberg, William, Almshouse, Nov. 3, 1880, age 39.
Rosenbury, Charles E., Nov. 16, 1880, age 45; d. at Atlanta, GA.
Rosenfelt, Charles, July 6, 1871, age c. 25.
Roskopf, Mrs. Anna Maria, March 5, 1872, age 79.
Roskopf, Elizabeth, wife of Jacob Jr., May 1, 1872, age 31 y, 3 m, 16 d.
Roskopf, Jacob Sr., Dec. 28, 1879, age 77.
Rosner, Mary, wife of Henry, Nov. 1, 1873, age 73.
Ross, Alexander, drowned, mate of the Bark *Tanner*, Aug. 25, 1873, age c. 40.
Ross, Andrew, Almshouse, Dec. 19, 1880, age 78.
Ross, Mrs. Arethuse, formerly of Buffalo, Fan. 17, 1878, age 60; d. in Chicago, IL.
Ross, Benjamin, May 17, 1875, age 59.
Ross, Cassius M., formerly of Buffalo, July 23, 1871, age 27; d. in Utica.
Ross, David P., March 26, 1878, age 47.
Ross, James, Dec. 7, 1873, age 60.
Ross, Jeannie E., wife of James W., formerly of Buffalo, Sept. 9, 1879; d. in Chicago.
Ross, Mr. L. D., formerly of Buffalo, Nov. 23, 1858, in 47th year; at Pennelville, Oswego Co., NY.
Ross, Ruth, wife of Capt. S., dau. of Major M. Case, Sept. 29, 1831, in 25th year.
Ross, Schuyler, June 4, 1846, age 45.
Ross, William, North Collins, NY, Jan. 3, 1870, age 27.
Ross, William, April 27, 1872, age 36.
Rosseel, Charles, late of Buffalo, April 16, 1869; d. in Cananadaigus, bur. in Buffalo.
Rossenbach, John, July 25, 1877.
Rossenblatt, Peter T., March 12, 1858, age 30.
Rosseter, Martin, Nov. 17, 1879, age 64 y, 7 d.
Roth, Anthony, June 10, 1880, age 56 y, 7 m, 3 d.
Roth, Francis Lewis, May 8, 1866, age 80 y, 1 m, 7 d.
Roth, Frederick, Feb. 1, 1872, age 34 y, 9 m.
Roth, John, clerk, Aug. 28, 1870, age 21; drowned in the Erie Basin.
Roth, John G., June 28, 1873, age 60.
Roth, Josephine Julia, wife of John, Jan. 22, 1870, age 25.
Roth, Lorenz, April 1, 1857, age 42d year.
Roth, Mrs. Magdalena, accidental death, Feb. 8, 1875, age 50.
Roth, Michael, May 23, 1866, age 21.
Roth, William, tailor, railroad accident Jan. 24, 1877.
Rothe, Heinrich, suicide, July 10, 1871.
Rother, Auguste E., wife of Gustavus, March 9, 1878, age 55 y, 5 m, 15 .
Rough, Capt. James, a Scotchman, the oldest navigator on the Upper Lakes, Dec. 4, 1828, age 67.
Rounds, George W., May 22, 1871, age 50; taken to Middle Haddam, CT.
Rourke, John, June 5, 1880, age 35; found in Buffalo River June 10. Missing since June 5.
Rouse, Alexander B., Feb. 4, 1875, age 31.
Rousey, Mrs. R. M., Jan. 26, 1868, age 77.
Rous, Perry, Dec. 2, 1853, age 56.
Rouse, Gilbert N., June 10, 1858, age 44.
Rowan, Martin, an old respected citizen, Dec. 28, 1859.
Rowe, Mrs. Eliza, d. at the Church House, Nov. 28, 1876, age 63.
Rowe, Selah, firm of Rowe and Co., Buffalo, April 18, 1852, age 30; in Fair Haven, CT.
Rowen, Patrick, Co. Almshouse, May 9, 1880, age 49.
Rowland (or Boland), James, Oct. 18, 1873, age 41.
Rowland, Mrs. Martha, mother of Mrs. G. E. Waldron, Akron, Sept. 10, 1871, age 88.

Rowley, Cynthia, wife of Charles, Aurora, NY, Nov. 30, 1836, age 36.
Rowley, Eunice, wife of Capt. Thomas, May 16, 1827, age 71.
Rowley, Ezra, Willink, NY, Jan. 1813, age 22.
Rowley, Laurena, wife of Millar, Aurora, NY, Aug. 2, 1856.
Rowley, Capt. Thomas, soldier in the French & Revolutionary Wars, Sept. 13, 1828, age 84.
    [Another card: Rowley, Capt. Thomas, Buffalo, Sept. 13, 1828, b. 1746, age 84.]
Rowley, Washington R., June 23, 1876, age 64.
Roy, Lawrence M., July 8, 1873, age 23.
Royal, Michael (or Nicholas), brakeman on NYC Railroad, April 20, 1873, age 30.
Royce, Mrs. Mary B., Feb. 15, 1870, age 52; taken to Batavia, NY.
Rubens, Mary, widow of Henry, Aug. 23, 1859, age 46.
Rubins, Edward J., Jan. 21, 1872, age 32 y, 8 m.
Rubins, Henry, Dec. 17, 1857, age 47.
Rubins, Simeon H., June 4, 1868, age 33.
Ruble, Andrew, April 25, 1874, age 42 y, 2 m, 26 d.
Ruch, Eliza P., widow of Thomas E., Nov. 22, 1878, age 37.
Ruch, Thomas E., Oct. 13, 1878, age 38.
Ruck, Henery, Locksmith, Feb. 21, 18782, age 47.
Rudd, Horley, North Collins, July 1878.
Rudder, William, Nov. 22, 1863, age 72.
Ruden, Alexander B., oldest son of Emanuel, Oct. 4, 1864, age 28.
Ruden, Emanuel, firm of George W. Rogers and Co. of Buffalo, Aug. 28, 1852, in 44th year.
Ruden, Evelina Rozella, wife of E., Feb. 26, 1841, age 27.
Ruden, Mrs. Rachel, March 14, 1855, in 85th year.
Rudio (or Rudir), Christian, Oct. 10, 1876, age 53.
Rudolf, Caroline Augusta, wife of William, Jan. 12, 1877, age 46 y, 1 m, 24 d.
Rudy, Mrs. Barbara, North Buffalo, NY, Aug. 1, 1867, age 71.
Rudy, Mrs. Barbara, Aug. 1, 1867, age 71.
Rudy, John, North Buffalo, NY, Dec. 24, 1865, age 69th year.
Ruger, Jane Ann, wife of James W., dau. of William Lane of Mattewan, Dutchess Co., Nov. 8,
    1864, age 28 y, 9 m.
Rumer(e)ovoy, Jonathan, b. 1758, d. 1848, bur. Chestnut Ridge (Niagara Co.); Soldier of the
    Revolution.
Rumley, William, Jan. 20, 1874, age 35.
Rumney, Miss Susan, sister of the late Mrs. John W. Beals, Nov. 11, 1875, age 90.
Rumrill, Augusta E., wife of H., May 1, 1852, age 29.
Rumrill, Levi H., Dec. 30, 1876.
Rumrill, Luther, formerly of Utica, Jan. 10, 1855, in 80th year; taken to Utica.
Rumrill, Melissa A., wife of Henry, Dec. 16, 1862, in 33rd year; in Stockbridge, MI, bur.
    in Buffalo.
Rumsey, Aaron, April 6, 1864, age 67.
Rumsey, Mrs. Aaron, April 13, 1870, age 73.
Rumsey, Bradley, Jan. 27, 1868, age 23; d. at LaCrosse, WI.
Rumsey, Dr. Daniel, Nov. 4, 1864, age 85; taken to Silver Creek, NY.
Rumsey, Elizabeth, widow of Fayette, June 29, 1872, age 51.
Rumsey, Elizabeth A., widow of Emmett P., Jan. 29, 1880, age 55 y, 9 m.
Rumsey, Emmet P., March 24, 1873, age 58; d. at Falls City, Dunn Co.
Rumsey, Fayette, Dec. 5, 1862, age 44.
Rumsey, Mary C., widow of Dexter P., May 6, 1859. [NOTE: widow crossed out & wife written
    in.]
Rumsey, Matilda C., wife of Fayette, Dec. 7, 1858, age 36.
Runcie, Mrs. Elizabeth, Feb. 2, 1878, age 95; taken to Brooklyn, NY.
Runcie, Elvira Melissa, wife of William J., Oct. 5, 1872; d. in Brooklyn, NY.
Runcie, James, Feb. 17, 1864, in 49th year.
Rundell, Ann P., dau. of John and Sarah, Alden, NY, Aug. 18, 1857; bur. in Buffalo.
Rundell, John, Alden, NY, Oct. 29, 1872, age 80.
Rundy, Lavina, wife of Sanford, Evans, Feb. 7, 1847, age 64.
Runyan, Rodney, Erie Co. Almshouse, Nov. 6, 1878, age 45.
Runyan, William E., telegrapher, July 25, 1879, age 29.
Rup, Mrs. Barbara, May 19, 1872.

Ruppersberg, Leonora Van Kleeck, wife of Charles F., Jan. 1877, age 36 y, 5 m, 25 d.
Ruppert, Jacob, May 23, 1880, age 81; Almshouse.
Rusco, Lydia K. (or R.), mother of Mrs. Lydia Hall, Oct. 5, 1869, age 78.
Rush, Dyer, Hamburgh, NY, March 10, 1879, age 66.
Russ, Kate M., widow of Wheeler S., June 15, 1873; bur. in Buffalo.
Russell, Mrs., wife of Col. Samuel, Hamburgh, Sept. 1819, age 63.
Russell, Caleb, formerly of Albany, Black Rock, NY, Jan. 31, 1822, age 54.
Russell, Calista Norton, wife of William C., South Wales, NY, Sept. 3, 1873, age 60.
Russell, Caroline A., wife of B. F., June 10, 1879, age 33.
Russell, Clark W., eldest son of William C., South Wales, NY, Sept. 9, 1871; d. in Chicago, bur. in South Wales.
Russell, Elizabeth, Black Rock, NY, dau. of Washington A., Sept. 8, 1853, age 21.
Russell, Elizabeth P., dau. of Robert, Aug. 16, 1854, age 25; at Ash Grove, Iroquois Co., IL.
Russell, Elizabeth, mother-in-law of Cyrus A. Westcott, March 6, 1869, age 74; taken to North Adams.
Russell, F. Elizabeth Barr, Buffalo Plains, NY, wife of W.A., Feb. 13, 1867, age 56.
Russell, Frances S., wife of Robert, Aug. 22, 1847, age 47.
Russell, George, accidental death, Aug. 19 or 20, 1875, erroneously reported as George Wilson.
Russell, George B., South Wales, NY, Jan. 11, 1871, age 73.
Russell, George H., for the firm of Russell & Moulton, June 9, 1874; d. at Gowanda, NY.
Russell, John, late of Falkirk, Scotland, July 27, 1853, age 46.
Russell, John N., son of William C., South Wales, Oct. 9, 1876, age 44; d. in Virginia City, NV.
Russell, Josephine, Cincinnati, formerly of Buffalo, Feb. 23, 1865, age 35.
Russell, Levinia H., wife of George P. of Philadelphia, Oct. 7, 1874, age 35.
Russell, Mrs. Lucie Cary, Aug. 5, 1877, age 82.
Russell, Mrs. Mary, mother of Mrs. Barnes and Mrs. Charles Rees, Dec. 19, 1853, age 85 y, 1 m, 5 d.
Russell, Peter, Jan. 2, 1872, age 29.
Russell, S. S., May 20, 1872, age 39 y, 8 m; d. and bur. in East Penbroke, Genesee Co., NY.
Russell, Hon. Samuel, Postmaster of Buffalo, July 3, 1834, age 74.
Russell, Sophia, wife of John E., Jan. 28, 1847, age 23.
Russell, Susan, wife of Sylvanus, July 12, 1839, age 63.
Russell, Capt. Sylvanus, from Nantucket, MA, Nov. 7, 1846, age 71.
Russell, Washington A., Buffalo Plains, Aug. 1876, age 77.
Russell, Capt. William A., May 16, 1828, age 38.
Russell, Wing, Syracuse, NY, formerly of Buffalo, Sept. 10, 1844; d. in Syracuse.
Ruth, Jacob, Feb. 16, 1878, age 55.
Ruth, John K., March 8, 1873, age 33 y, 7 m.
Rutler, Susan, wife of Thomas, formerly of New York, Dec. 8, 1843, age 49.
Rutter, Samuel, June 26, 1848, age 29; d. at the Hydraulics.
Ruxford, Frederick W., Albion, MI, formerly of Buffalo, Jan. 2, 1852.
Ruxton, William, native of Scotland, June 7, 1842, age 45.
Ruza, J.S., Feb. 1873, age 65.
Ryan, Mrs., May 1871.
Ryan, Elizabeth Anne Agnes, Oct. 21, 1874.
Ryan, Esther Ann, May 20, 1880, age 90.
Ryan, James, Co. Almshouse, Aug. 12, 1878, age 68.
Ryan, James, Nov. 20, 1878, age 67.
Ryan, Capt. John, drowned May 14, 1848, body recovered & bur. July 4, 1848.
Ryan, John, Dec. 6, 1870, age 50.
Ryan, John, April 5, 1871, age 48.
Ryan, John, March 2, 1872, age c. 68.
Ryan, John, Jan. 7, 1877, age 44.
Ryan, John, Nov. 9, 1880, age 39.
Ryan, Margarett, Almshouse, Dec. 12, 1880, age 70.
Ryan, Mrs. Mary, May 9, 1874, age 76.
Ryan, Mrs. Mary, Nov. 10, 1877, age 77.

Ryan, Patrick, May 5, 1870, age 30.
Ryan, Patrick, Aug. 18, 1872, age 33.
Ryan, Patrick, July 1874, drowned in Welland Canal, bur. in Buffalo.
Ryan, Patrick, fireman, March 11, 1880, age between 25 and 30.
Ryan, Paul, cartman, Dec. 8, 1868, age 30.
Ryan, Timothy, Sept. 16, 1873, age 20.
Ryan, Timothy, railroad accident, June 30, 1876, age 67.
Ryan, Winnifred, Jan. 5, 1871, age 30.
Ryerson, George W., June 7, 1876, at Auburn, NY.
Ryneck, Rosella, wife of William A., Feb. 1, 1842, age 32.
Ryno, Ervin D., son of David, April 2, 1877, age 24 y, 4 m, 11 d; d. at Olean, bur. in Buffalo.
Ryon, Miss Emma, Farnham, Feb. 7, 1873, age 21 y, 10 m, 11 d.
Ryther, Miss Alice, Eden, NY, Nov. 27, 1865.
Ryther, Eliza M., wife of John L., Pipestone, Berrien Co., MI., formerly of Eden, NY, Feb. 3, 1858, age 45 y, 11 m.
Ryther, Sarah Josephine, wife of James F., North Evans, NY, Nov. 4, 1873, age 24 y, 9 m, 9 d.
Ryther, Solon B., Eden, NY, Nov. 24, 1860, age 50.

Sabins, Emma Corp, wife of Benjamin, Feb. 23, 1876, age 21.
Sackett, Anne, May 16, 1860.
Sackett, Maria, widow of Reuben, May 27, 1872, age 82.
Sackett, Reuben, Feb. 26, 1837, age 63.
Sackett, Russell, formerly of Buffalo, May 6, 1873, age 63; d. at Los Angeles, CA.
Safford, George, Lancaster, NY, July 25, 1853, age 24.
Safford, H. Emma Bailey, wife of Philo T., March 31, 1857, age 26; taken to Madison, OH.
Safford, Henry L., Nov. 29, 1863, age 59.
Sager, Mrs. Catharine, Lancaster, NY, April 28, 1852, age 90.
Sagermuller, Jacob, Jan. 1872, age c. 50.
Sage, Henry H., Dec. 9, 1874, age 45; d. Philadelphia, bur. in Buffalo.
St. John, ---, d. in Hamburgh, last week, a chid of Mr. St. John.
St. John, Ada, wife of Samuel, Alden, Aug. 8, 1870, age 60 y, 1 m.
St. John, Gamaliel, June 6, 1813, age 47th year. Drowned. Native of Norwalk, CT, b. Sept. 22, 1766. Has dau., Mrs. Hemis.
St. John, John R., formerly of Buffalo, brother of Mrs. P. Sidway and Mrs. Aurelia Bemis, d. at Lockport, NY.
St. John, LeGrand C., Oct. 6, 1870, age 63.
St. John, Margaret K., widow of Gamaliel, April 29, 1847, in 79th year.
St. John, Samuel, Hamburg, NY, Sept. 17, 1819, age 65; Revolutionary Soldier.]
St. John, Soloman, Jan. 23, 1835, age 47.
St. Louis, Edward, formerly of Buffalo, Oct. 28, 1879, age 35; d. at Montreal.
St. Louis, Mary Ann, Feb. 11, 1874, age 27.
St. Ody, Henry, March 5, 1870, age 41st year.
Salisbury, Adah, widow of Edward S., mother of Mrs. Gaius B. Rich, Feb. 27, 1850, in 88th year.
Salisbury, Alvin, Big Tree Corners, Sept. 6, 1878, age 79.
Salisbury, Amanda Malvina, dau. of William J., Jan. 21, 1873.
Salisbury, Ann E., wife of C.B., April 12, 1870, age 31.
Salisbury, Benjamin F., son of Smith H., March 21, 1858, in 41st year.
Salisbury, Betsey, wife of Hezekiah A., Sept. 24, 1827, age 36.
Salisbury, Bowman, Hamburgh, NY, Aug. 2, 1825, age 36.
Salisbury, Guy H., B. Dec. 25, 1811 in Canandaigua, NY. Last seen alive Sept. 1, 1869. Drowned, body found in Buffalo Creek Sept. 5, 1869. Age 57 y, 8 m, 7d. Bur. in Forest Lawn, son of Smith H. Salisbury.
Salisbury, Hezekiah A., March 14, 1856, age 67.
Salisbury, John, youngest son of the late Hezekiah A., Dec. 24, 1875, age 34.
Salisbury, John S., brother of Guy H., Graham, Ontario Co., NY, formerly of Buffalo, Oct. 31, 1850, age 30.
Salisbury, Nancy, wife of S. H., Feb. 13, 1830, age 43.

Salisbury, Phebe Osborn, widow of Hezekiah A., Dec. 9, 1879, age 80.
Salisbury, Smith, Hamburgh, NY, March 28, 1843, age 48.
Salisbury, Smith H., formerly editor of the *Black Rock Gazette and Buffalo Republican*, Jan. 25, 1832, age 46; in Rochester.
Salisbury, Stephen, Hamburg, NY, Nov., 1812, age 19; in Buffalo.
Salisbury, William, Nov. 30, 1845, age 37.
Salles, John, father of Michael, July 6, 1859, age 82 y, 6 m.
Salles, Maggie, wife of John J., March 13, 1873, age 25 y, 5 m, 13 d.
Salls, Harriet, widow of Samuel, Concord, July 26, 1875, age 66.
Salmon, S. J., Nov. 29, 1866, age 34; taken to East Bloomfield, NY.
Salter, Elizabeth R., March 30, 1865, age 24 y, 7 m.
Salter, Josephine LaMotte, Feb. 2, 1868.
Samo, Charles W. Sr., Feb. 10, 1852, in 54th year.
Samo, Charles W., July 14, 1857, in 28th year.
Samo, Isaac, musician, formerly of NY, Oct. 7, 1841, in 84th year.
Samo, Sgt. James A., Co. A, First U.S. Cav., May 6, 1862, age 28; in NY of wounds received at Battle of Williamsburg.
Samo, Mary Ann, widow of Charles W., Aug. 17, 1853, age 42.
Samson, Alice E., dau. of Theodore, Feb. 28, 1878, age 20 y, 10 m, 7 d.
Samson, James, Sept. 13, 1880, age 73.
Samuels, A. N., Oct. 15, 1877, age 34.
Samuels, Leeis, March 13, 1870, age 30.
Sanburn, Enoch, Williamsville, NY, Jan., 1813, age 40.
Sand, Anthony, March 16, 1861, age 20.
Sander, John G., July 5, 1875, age 73.
Sanders, Anny, wife of William, Springville, NY, May 30, 1844, age 41.
Sanders, Helen L., wife of Hohn [sic] W., May 18, 1877, age 42 y, 6 m, 17 .
Sanders, Mrs. Johanna Augusta, April 28, 1877, age 76 y, 7 m, 8 d.
Sanders, Rhoda, wife of Atwell, Hamburgh, NY, March 4, 1869, age 63.
Sandford, Ellen, March 19, 1871, age 24.
Sandrock, George, Sept. 22, 1863, age 55.
Sandrock, Gustavus, March 29, 1871, age 24.
Sands, Mrs. Mary Ann, Aug. 17, 1853, age 42.
Sanford, George G., Cheektowaga, NY, March 25, 1873, age 52.
Sanford, Maj. Isaac, son-in-law of G. W. Bull, Paymaster in U.S. Army, March 19, 1864, in Louisville, KY, while in Army of the Cumberland; bur. in Buffalo.
Sanford, W. H., May 6, 1853, age 25; in Palmyra, NY.
Sangstar, Mary A., wife of Hugh, Nov. 6, 1878.
Sangster, Archibald C., Jan. 16, 1856, age 40.
Sardis, Hobart, Sardinia, NY, July 5, 1873, age 65.
Sargeant, Margaret, wife of Richard, Sept. 13, 1879, age 37, 1 m, 20 d.
Sargeant, Mrs. Olive, Feb. 8, 1861, age 68.
Sargent, Deborah, widow of Timothy, formerly of New Chester, NH, Jan. 7, 1838, age 70.
Sargent, Phineas, formerly of Buffalo, June 7, 1871, age 78.
Sasch, Philip, suicide, Bowmansville, June 13, 1875, age 56.
Sauer, Adam, May 16, 1877, age 41 y, 5 m, 12 .
Sauer, Catharine, wife of A., March 16, 1875, age 37 y, 9 m, 27.
Sauer, Katie, dau. of Adam, Jan. 14, 1877, age 19.
Sauerwein, Mrs. Mary, July 24, 1870, 75 y, 6 m, 26 d.
Sauerwein, Matilda, wife of Henry, Sept. 4, 1880, age 38 y, 6m.
Sauerwein, Philip, April 15, 1879, age 41 y, 9 m, 2 d.
Sauerwine, Rachel, wife of Henry, Feb. 1, 1865, in 22nd year.
Saulpaugh, Sabrina, wife of Peter B., Feb. 14, 1877, age 59 y, 9 m.
Saulters, David, Dec. 20, 1872, age 45.
Saulters, Margaret, wife of Philip, March 16, 1867, age 43.
Saulters, Philip, March 7, 1872, age 51.
Saulters, Philip, March 13, 1879, age 33 y, 3 m.
Saunders, Atwell, Hamburgh, Nov. 1875, age 68; funeral at Abbotts Corners, Sunday, 14th inst.
Saunders, Benjamin, Hamburgh, formerly of Albany, Nov. 30, 1842, age 67.

Saunders, Mrs. Cloe, Hamburg, NY, May 30, 1848, age 62.
Saunders, Edward, Alden, NY, Jan. 1875, age 89 y, 8 m.
Saunders, Henry K., Aug. 29, 1831, age 28.
Saunders, Lavinia, wife of Riley, April 22, 1846, age 22.
Saunders, Miss Mary H., dau. of Joseph of Nelson, N.B., Oct. 23, 1861, age 38.
Saunders, Samuel, Hamburgh, NY, Jan. 27, 1867, age 85.
Savage, Marjery, wife of Thomas, Feb. 3, 1864, age 73.
Savage, Thomas, Aug. 17, 1866, age 68.
Savitz, Walter M., Nov. 28, 1864, age 22 y, 2 m, 7 d.
Sawin, Albert, Jan. 23, 1863, in 49th year.
Sawin, Daniel J., March 4, 1865, age 24.
Sawin, Miss Harriet L., eldest dau. of P. W., Aug. 20, 1856, age 21.
Sawin, Sabre, wife of Rev. Benjamin, formerly of Aurora, NY, Sept. 9, 1845, age 68; Laporte, IA.
Sawin, Silas, May 7, 1863, age 61 y, 6 m, 21 d.
Sawken, William Gustav, Dec. 1, 1878, age 50 y, 7 m, 27 d.
Sawn, Edwin G., Oct. 5, 1878, age 35.
Sawtell, Edmond, late of Clarence, Williamsville, NY, June 18, 1865, age 68.
Sawtell, Edmund, late of Erie, NY, Oct. 28, 1826, age 65.
Sawyer, Arthur, drowned July 23, 1871.
Sawyer, Charlotte O., Jan. 12, 1877, wife of James D.
Sawyer, Emily Cotton, wife of John, Nov. 16, 1879, age 44.
Sawyer, George, Oct. 22, 1872, age 33.
Sawyer, Mrs. James D., Jan. 1877.
Sawyer, Mrs. John, Nov. 1879.
Sawyer, William Babcock, son of James D., Nov. 7, 1880, age 24.
Sayer, Charles A., Oct. 1864.
Sayles, George, July 4, 1880, age 50 y, 3 m, 4 d.
Scanlan, Michael, Dec. 31, 1877, age 55.
Scanmon, John, Sept. 13, 1879, age 50; accidentally killed.
Schabel, Frank, accidental death, April 23, 1880, age 36.
Schabtack, John, Nov. 2, 1879, age 31 y, 9 m.
Schaefer, George F., Nov. 19, 1878, age 48.
Schaefer, Joseph, Oct. 3, 1880, age 39 y, 5 m, 10 d.
Schaefer, Julia H., wife of Christian, Oct. 2, 1873, age 74.
Schaeffer, George, Dec. 28, 1869, age 45.
Schafer, Andrew, Lancaster, Feb. 27, 1877, age 45; suicide.
Schafer, Henry, Aug. 19, 1875, age 32.
Schaff, Joseph, Jan. 2, 1872, age 65 y, 10 m, 216 d.
Schaff, Mary (Mrs. John), April 21, 1879, age 24.
Schaffleiter, Father, Aug. 1856.
Schaftley, John, Nov. 1875, age 42, drowned.
Schaller, Mary, wife of John, Oct. 4, 1871, age 50.
Schalman (or Schallwell), Philip, Williamsville, April 12, 1874.
Schamber, Mrs. Elizabeth, Oct. 1878, age 84 y, 3 m.
Schank, Joseph, June 18, 1867, in 51st year.
Schannahan, Margaret, dau. of B., Jan. 16, 1872, age 27 y, 11 m.
Schanzlin, Maria M., wife of Jacob F. Jr., Nov. 18, 1866, age 25 y, 6 m.
Scharf, Christian, Jan. 21, 1880, age 52; bled to death.
Scharthel (or Schaltel), Stephen, June 1, 1875, age 43.
Schawzlin, Henrietta, wife of Jacob F., Dec. 18, 1876, age 37.
Schedy, John, laborer, May 26, 1873, age 46.
Scheffel, Godfrey, Aug. 27, 1880, age 83 y, 4 m.
Scheffer, Ella Clark, wife of Charles F., Nov. 30, 1873; d. in Schenectady, NY.
Scheffle, Julius, 21st Regt. NY Vols., April 30, 1863; in Hospital at Aquia Creek, VA.
Schelife, WIlliam, Co. Almshouse, Sept. 3, 1876, age 55.
Schell, Warren, Tonawanda, NY, March 20, 1865, age 28.
Schelling, Christiana, wife of Frederick W., Jan. 24, 1877.
Schenck, Jane, wife of Jacob, May 31, 1844, age 20.
Schenck, Nelly, wife of Peter, Aug. 16, 1827, age 30.

Schenk, John G., July 3, 1880, age 51 y, 4 m, 3 d.
Schenkelberger, Martin, April 5, 1878, age 48 y, 10 m.
Schenkelberger, Mary Sophia, Nov. 19, 1872, age 69.
Schenker, Catherine, wife of John M., Nov. 23, 1877, age 75.
Scherer, Jacob, March 18, 1879, age 35 y, 8 m.
Scherer, Peter, Co. Almshouse, April 16, 1877, age 77.
Scherer, Mrs. Teresa, Aug. 31, 1874, age 68.
Schermerhorn, Mrs. Anna C., mother of Isaac M., July 18, 1878, age 82.
Schermerhorn, Henry, formerly of Buffalo, Express Messenger, Jan. 10, 1876; d. at Rotterdam, NY.
Schermerhorn, Marie, wife of Isaac M., April 22, 1856, age 35.
Scheu, Elizabeth, wife of William, May 21, 1867, age 29.
Scheu, Ferdinand, July 18, 1880, age 36 y, 6 m, 18 d.
Scheu, George W., eldest son of Jacob, April 4, 1877, age 29 y, 1 m, 10 d.
Scheu, Georgia L., wife of Augustus F., March 30, 1874, age 19 y, 8 m, 14 d.
Scheu, Henry, Aug. 17, 1871, age 49.
Scheu, Henry J., Oct. 29, 1879, age 25.
Scheu, Jacob Jr., May 20, 1873, age 30.
Scheu, Major Jacob, Lancaster, Jan. 1, 1875, age 44; bur. in Buffalo.
Scheu, Martin Jr., printer, Oct. 9, 1875, age 21 y, 1 d.
Scheu, Mary, wife of Henry, June 19, 1878, age 24 y, 15 d.
Scheu, Philip, April 16, 1868, age 71st year.
Scheu, Solomon P., son of Jacob, Jan. 1, 1879, age 21 y, 7 m, 4 d.
Scheusler (Scheuerle), Christian C., Oct. 19, 1880, age 48 y, 2 m.
Schiess, Conrad, Aug. 1875, age 69.
Schiffhauer, Charles, Sept. 22, 1878, age 50.
Schildt, August, March 2, 1872, age 21.
Schill, Jacob, Oct. 8, 1878, age 21 y, 4 m.
Schinbaum, Philip, accidental death, West Seneca, Oct. 22, 1876, age 65.
Schine (or Schire), Michael, March 5, 1880, age 60; sudden death.
Schintzius, Michael, Nov. 5, 1879.
Schlegel (Schleget), Annie, Almshouse, Aug. 11, 1880, age 60.
Schlegel, George, July 31, 1873, age 33.
Schlegel, Rudolph, July 13, 1876, age c. 43; suicide by drowning.
Schlehr, Peter M., May 5, 1877, age 65; sudden death.
Schlenker, George, Aug. 1876. Member of the old 100th Regt., bur. Aug. 20.
Schleup, Frederick, Feb. 7, 1870; killed by a falling limb of a tree at Port Colborne, Ontario.
Schlosser, Charles, Nov. 24, 1872, age 36; found dead on railroad.
Schlotzer, Barbara, wife of John, North Boston, NY, Sept. 24, 1880, age 51.
Schmall, Kittie, dau. of Louis, April 7, 1877, age 22 y, 9 m, 1 d.
Schmidel, Henry, Sept. 13, 1867, age 29; in New Orleans, bur. Buffalo.
Schmidt, ---, accidental death (coroner's inquest), Feb. 12, 1872.
Schmidt, Mr. A. J., formerly of Buffalo, April 1878, a grocer at Erie; accidental death.
Schmidt, Anthony, June 26, 1880, age 69 y, 2 m, 8 d.
Schmidt, August, Oct. 29, 1871, age 43.
Schmidt, Charles, M.D., July 26, 1848, age 28.
Schmidt, George Edward, son of Joseph, Feb. 22, 1880.
Schmidt, Gertrude, wife of Anthony, April 24, 1871, age 57 y, 8 m.
Schmidt, Hamilton, Williamsville, Nov. 10, 1878, age 71.
Schmidt, William H., Feb. 7, 1879, age 21 y, 6 m, 27 d.
Schmitt, John, Buffalo Plains, Feb. 17, 1879, age 88.
Schnable, Peter, May 28, 1873, age 58; suicide.
Schnaidt, August, formerly of Buffalo, April 1880.
Schnapp, George, laborer, Aug. 21, 1879, age 30; killed on the railroad.
Schneider, Anthony, cooper, July 30, 1879, age 40 (?); drowned near Tonawanda, NY.
Schneider, Frank, suicide, June 9, 1877, age 54.
Schneider, Mrs. Mary, Aug. 1874, age 68.
Schnell, Sophia, wife of Frederick, Aug. 3, 1871, age 27.
Schnopp, Casper, May 9, 1875, age 58; found drowned.

Schnorr, Conrad, laborer, March 16, 1874, age 52.
Schnuberger, Peter, April 26, 1879, age 31.
Schnur, Anna Catharine, widow of Peter, June 30, 1879, age 81 y, 8 m.
Schoefs, Charles, Dec. 11, 1877.
Schoelkopf, John, June 8, 1876, age 34.
Schoellkopf, Henry, Feb. 20, 1880, age 31; d. at Jacksonville, FL.
Schoenacher, Mrs. Magdalena, wife of Jacob, Pine Hill, Feb. 26, 1878, age 88.
Schoene, Christopher, drowned, Aug. 10, 1877, age 62.
Schoenleber, Peter, March 1874.
Schoenthel, Henry, accidental death, Aug. 28, 1875.
Schoernen, John, March 7, 1877, age 32 y, 5 m, 15 d.
Scholl, Jacob, July 1878, age 68.
Schoonthaler, Charles, Co. Almshouse, Feb. 19, 1877, age 67.
Schorodotzki, Frank, railroad accident, Jan. 12, 1879, age 34.
Schorr, Ernest, Dec. 24, 1873, age 70 y, 9 m.
Schott, George, July 22, 1867.
Schrab, Ann M., Pine Hill, Dec. 17, 1875, age 84.
Schraft, Ernst, accidental death, Sept. 9, 1876, age 40.
Schranck, Josephine, April 8, 1879, age 21 y, 4 m, 28 d.
Schrank, Michael, June 1874, age 67.
Schranker, Henrich, Eden, NY, July 18, 1880, age 59; fell dead.
Schreck, F. L., Jan. 20, 1873.
Schreder, Miss Amelia, May 1, 1875; drowned from the schooner *Consuello* off Marbleheads.
Schreiber, Sgt. Jacob, Sept. 1866.
Schriebdinger (or Shuhburger), Alexander, May 2, 1877.
Schrodt, Joseph, Jan. 30, 1854, in 44th year.
Schroeder, Charles Frederick, Oct. 26, 1878, age 63.
Schroeder, Sophia, dau. of Charles F., Dec. 3, 1877, age 26 y, 34 d.
Schroer, Peter, son of Peter and Catherine, May 27, 1874, age 23 y, 5 m.
Schryver, Charity H. Pierson, wife of Allen L., Jan. 4, 1875, age 72.
Schubert, Lewis, May 9, 1878.
Schubkegel, Henry, Feb. 7, 1870, age 40; found dead near Dunville, Ontario.
Schuchardt, Christiana, dau. of Lorenz, April 11, 1869, age 22 y, 5 m, 24 d.
Schudt, Philip, Reserve, Erie Co., NY, May 18, 1879, age 45 y, 6 m; d. at Reserve, Erie Co., NY.
Schuehle, John G., July 18, 1862, in 35th year.
Schuett, Fred, Canal Boat Captain, Aug. 9, 1880, age 48; drowned at Lockport, NY.
Schuler, Frank, March 29, 1873, age 20.
Schuler, William H., May 1, 1877, age 66; found dead in bed.
Schultz, Barbara, widow of Gottfreid, Aug. 1, 1877, age 56.
Schultz, Charles, West Seneca, May 25, 1876, age 29.
Schultz, Dorothea E., April 30, 1844, age 34.
Schultz, Ferdinand, June 14, 1878, accidental death.
Schultz, Frederica, wife of John T., March 29, 1879, age 58.
Schultz, Gottfried, Oct. 1869.
Schultz, Hannah, wife of William, West Seneca, Nov. 28, 1878, age 33 y, 1 m, 16 d.
Schultz, Michael, Williamsville, Oct. 21, 1870, age 63.
Schulyer, Martha C., wife of Daniel, April 18, 1867, age 30th year.
Schum, John, June 2, 1874, age 49 y, 8 m, 9 d.
Schumacher, Regina, wife of Jacob, Jan. 3, 1879, age 36 y, 16 d.
Schumaker, Mrs. Caroline, Feb. 2, 1873, age 56.
Schuman, Albert F., Feb. 9, 1877, age 20 y, 4 m.
Schunk, Elizabeth, Dec. 1, 1869, age 41.
Schuster, Mrs. Caroline, Aug. 28, 1875, age 60.
Schuster, Ferdinand, April 25, 1868, age 59.
Schuster, George, son of Christian, Oct. 28, 1874, age 21 y, 1 m.
Schuster, George, accidental death, June 23, 1875, age 23.
Schuster, Miss Lill A., formerly of Buffalo, Jan. 24, 1879, age 24; d. at East Saginaw, MI, bur. in Buffalo.
Schuster, Michael, Oct. 1878, age 51.

Schuster, Theodore, son of Ferdinand, Oct. 5, 1866 in Meadville, PA, age 20 y, 13 d; bur. in Buffalo.
Schutrum, Valentine, Nov. 15, 1869, age 45 y, 8 m, 15 d.
Schuyler, Rev. Louis S., formerly of Buffalo, Sept. 17, 1878.
Schuyler, Lydia E., wife of Rev. Montgomery, Oct. 10, 1852.
Schuyler, Martha C., wife of Daniel, April 18, 1967, in 30th year. [Not in card file.]
Schwab, Louis, July 4, 1875, age 51.
Schwameyer, Charles April 1874, age 32 y, 2 m.
Schwanz, Vincent, Feb. 16, 1879, age 50 y, 25 d.
Schwartz, Caroline, Co. Almshouse, April 9, 1878, age 55.
Schwartz, Daniel, Nov. 19, 1874, age 51 y, 7 m.
Schwartz, George, Feb. 16, 1870, age 48.
Schwartz, George J. (or G.), Sept. 24, 1877, age 30 y, 1 m, 20 d.
Schwartz, Hannah, wife of William, April 11, 1864, age 26.
Schwartz, Henry, Aug. 30, 1877, age 49.
Schwartz, Jacob, Feb. 2, 1877, age 52 y, 11 m, 16 d.
Schwartz, Jacob, Feb. 22, 1880, age 34.
Schwartz, John Sr., Jan. 31, 1872, age 75.
Schwartz, John, Colden, Oct. 22, 1876; suicide.
Schwartz, William H., Oct. 1872, age 23 y, 2 m, 11 d.
Schweiger, Martin, Dec. 7, 1880, age 78.
Schweigert, Elizabeth, dau. of John, March 2, 1874, age 21.
Schweigert, Hatie, wife of Henry, May 23, 1868, age 21 y, 2 m.
Schweigert, Theresia, wife of A. E., March 23, 1865, in 24th year.
Schweikert, Theodore, Eden Center, April 26, 1873, age 57; Eden Center.
Schweinfurth, George, Lancaster, Oct. 2, 1877; suicide.
Schweitzer, Jacob, Oct. 24, 1873.
Schwier, Henry, railroad accident, Nov. 28, 1877, age c. 28.
Scofield, Augustus, April 22, 1873, age 62.
Scofield, James H., Nov. 28, 1873, age 23; taken to Stamford, CT.
Scofield, John, Almshouse, April 17, 1880, age 30.
Scott, Benjamin, late of Horncastle, Lincolnshire, England, Aug. 15, 1851, in 38th year.
Scott, Benjamin, Town-crier, Sept. 19, 1876, age 77.
Scott, Bethiah, Hamburgh, NY, March 12, 1839, age 89.
Scott, Charles A., eldest son of J. B., Nov. 29, 1866, age 23 y, 10 m.
Scott, Charlotte D., wife of Mather, Dec. 13, 1867, age 56.
Scott, Mrs. Clarence H., Feb. 16, 1862, age 39 y, 1 m, 8 d; taken to Jamesville, NY.
Scott, Edwin, May 31, 1873, age 46.
Scott, Ellen, Aug. 21, 1879.
Scott, Frederick W., Oct. 8, 1878, age 28.
Scott, George W., Aug. 12, 1878, age 55.
Scott, Henrietta Maria, wife of James H., formerly of Buffalo, May 30, 1860, in 27th year; in Brooklyn, NY.
Scott, Henry (colored), Co. Almshouse, Sept. 9, 1877, age 40.
Scott, Henry, April 8, 1879, age 73; d. & bur. at Colden, NY.
Scott, J. Burton, April 29, 1867, age 51.
Scott, Dr. John, May 6, 1839, age 74; father of Dr. William K. A soldier in the Revolution.
Scott, John, April 1847.
Scott, John, Sept. 11, 1880, age 41 y, 4 m, 1 d.
Scott, John S., Jan. 1854, age 28; in Louisville, KY; bur. in Buffalo.
Scott, Maria V. B., wife of James B., June 12, 1872, age 56.
Scott, Mary, wife of Dr. William K., Feb. 18, 1854, age 60.
Scott, Mary, wife of Michael, Feb. 3, 1863, age 40.
Scott, Mary, dau. of the late John, Nov. 24, 1875, age 38.
Scott, Phineas, May 24, 1872, age 76.
Scott, Robert, Nov. 12, 1866.
Scott, Sarah, Black Rock, NY, wife of Robert, May 2, 1865, age 31.
Scott, Sarah A., wife of E. G., Feb. 1, 1873, age 52.
Scott, Dr. William K., Jan. 5, 1879, age 90 y, 1 m, 7 d.
Scott, William M., Black Rock (Plains), NY, Jan. 11, 1850, age 70.

Scott, William Stevenson, Dec. 13, 1876, age 50.
Scott, William Walter, formerly of Rochester, March 8, 1858, age 27.
Scovil, Elizabeth, Hamburg, NY, wife of John, May 13, 1880, age 55 y, 7 m, 5 d.
Scovil, Nelson, Hamburg, NY, April 1880, age 21 y, 2 m.
Scovill, Anna, June 29, 1848, in 73rd year; bur. at White's Corners.
Scovill, Capt. Erastus, May 27, 1869, age 48.
Scovill, Louisa, wife of Erastus, Dec. 1, 1849, age 34.
Scovill, Philo, formerly of Buffalo, June 5, 1875, age 84; d. in Cleveland, OH.
Scovill, R. C., Co. D, 5th Regt., son of Deacon Jonathan, Hamburgh, NY, Feb. 28, 1863, in 35th year; d. at Beaver Dam.
Scoville, James, son of Jasper, Hamburgh, March 21, 1879, age 21.
Scoville, Mathew, Sept. 30, 1871, gae 41.
Scrafford, Charles, b. in Guilderlands, N.Y., d. Aug. 22, 1860, age 80.
Scribbins, Mrs. Eliza, d. April 28, 1879 at "Home of Friendless," age 58.
Scriven, Martha N., wife of Alonzo H., Aug. 25, 1876, age 52.
Scunk (or Schenck), Anna Maria, Sept. 28, 1872, age 73.
Scurr, Sarah, wife of Henry, Feb. 1, 1833, age 33.
Seabrook, Samuel, formerly of Buffalo, Brant, May 5, 1855, age 30.
Segar, E. S., wife of Prof. S., Pastor of Swan St. Methodist Ch., Sept. 3, 1852.
Seager, Rev. Schuyler, D.D., formerly of Buffalo, Oct. 22, 1874, age 68; d. in Lockport.
Seam, Mary, May 1, 1878, age 87.
Seaman, Benajmin, Eden, NY, June 13, 1866, age 79.
Seaman, Mrs. Elizabeth, Tonawanda, NY, sister of Jacob L. Barnes of Buffalo, Aug. 12, 1855, age 52 y, 3 m.
Seaman, Hezekiah, Revolutionary patriot, Amherst, NY, March 15, 1835, age 72d year.
Seaman, Harriet B., wife of Marvin, Lancaster, NY, July 29, 1845, age 21.
Seaman, Mrs. Lydia, mother-in-law of A. R. Torrey, Jan. 8, 1862, age 89.
Seamans, Hezekiah, b. 1763, d. 1835, bur. Bowmansville, Erie Co.; Soldier of the Revolution.
Seamon, Rinda, wife of Edmund, Oct. 18, 1876, age 33.
Seamster, John, Oct. 20, 1876, age 75; suicide.
Searl (or Seal), Sarah Jane, Jan. 23, 1876, age 24 y, 10 m, 20 d.
Searls, Albert G., formerly of Buffalo, July 25, 1877, age 60; d. at Monience, IL.
Sears, J. P., borther of the late Richard, Lancaster, Feb. 9, 1873, age 62.
Sears, John, Lancaster, NY, April 24, 1837, age 41.
Sears, Richard, formerly of Buffalo, May 29, 1870, age 70; d. at Montclair, NJ, bur. in Buffalo.
Sears, Roxcellana Parrish, wife of Frank A., Sept. 6, 1867, age 29.
Sears, Sarah C., widow of Lewis of Danbury, CT, May 31, 1869.
Sears, Selin, March 22, 1867, in 57th year.
Seaters, Joseph, July 4, 1875, age 58.
Seaver, Joseph, father of Thomas, June 16, 1857, age 67.
Seaver, Nicholina M. J., dau. of Thomas, Jan. 22, 1872, age 22 y, 4 m.
Seaver, Mrs. Sophia, April 17, 1878, age 74.
Seaver, Col. William, Aug. 25, 1871, age 82; pioneer resident of Batavia.
Seckler, Mrs. Barbara, wife of John Sr., Nov. 4, 1879, age 72.
Seckler, Barbara, wife of James J., Oct. 12, 1880, age 36.
Seckler, Joseph, butcher, July 24, 1872, age 35.
Secord, Nicholas, May 21, 1875.
Sedorf, Mrs. Charles, near Limestone Hill, Aug. 39 [sic], 1870; killed on Lake Shore Railroad.
See, Abraham, Co. Almshouse, May 31, 1876, age 73.
See, Israel W., son of Rev. John L., June 19, 1857.
Seelbach, Mrs. Louise, Aug. 26, 1875, age 22.
Seelye, John J., Black Rock, NY, Sept. 1815, age 36.
Seelye, Nehemiah, Black Rock, NY, Sept. 12, 1815, in 32nd year.
Seereiter, Jacob A., March 23, 1873, age 23 y, 11 m, 21 d.
Seereiter, Michael, Oct. 29, 1867, age 48.
Seereiter, Peter J., April 6, 1874, age 23.
Seerieter, Joseph, in Chicago from explosion of propeller *Tonawanda*, Oct. 24, 1864, age 44 y, 6 m; bur. in Buffalo.

Seery, Patrick, a foreigner, Jan. 2, 1825, age 35.
Segelhurst, Christopher, Feb. 6, 1880, age 80 y, 3 m, 25 d.
Seib, Jacob, Jan. 7, 1880, age 38.
Seibel, Mr. J. F., May 29, 1866, age 55.
Seibert, Peter P., printer, Jan. 30, 1871.
Seibold, Mrs. Adaline Shultes, formerly of Buffalo, June 11, 1879, age 70; d. at Marilla, NY.
Seibold, Jacob, March 17, 1863, 71st year.
Seibold, John, June 19, 1879, age 54; drowned. Almshouse Hospital.
Seidenstricker, Frances C., wife of H. A., Jan. 26, 1868.
Seigel, Charles, May 2, 1879, age 48.
Seiler, John, Jan. 22, 1880, age 42.
Selden, Henry H., formerly of Buffalo, brother of Mrs. E. S. Hawley, March 19, 1864; in Middle Haddam, CT.
Selden, Miss Julia, March 27, 1825, age 36.
Selke, Catharine, wife of Charles, Sept. 4, 1877, age 43 y, 7 m, 20 d.
Selkirk, John H., Sept. 23, 1878, age 71.
Selle, Theodore R., Nov. 8, 1877, age 26 y, 3 m, 28 d.
Sellers, George W., April 30, 1879, age 25 y, 5 m, 12 d.
Sellstedt, Louise M., wife of L.G., dau. of Mrs. Sarah Lovejoy, 171 East Seneca, Oct. 15, 1850.
Sellstedt, William Scott, son of L. G. and Caroline, Sept. 30, 1869, age 12.
Semans, Isaac P., Winfield, Herkimer Co., NY, Sept. 23, 1844.
Semon, Mary E., wife of G. S., Dec. 27, 1850, in 26th year.
Senn, Christina, formerly of Buffalo, wife of Ferdinand, dau. of Jessie Webb of Buffalo, Nov. 21, 1879; d. in New York.
Service, John, July 18, 1835, age 38.
Service, John, Nov. 7, 1849, in 27th year.
Severance, Eliza F., wife of C. C., Springville, Jan. 1, 1843, age 26.
Severance, Hannah M., wife of C. C., June 2, 1859, age 30.
Seward, Asahel, Jan. 30, 1835, in 54th year.
Sewell, Joseph Kirkland, Black Rock, NY, formerly of Albright, VT, April 8, 1852.
Sexelby, Mrs. Elizabeth, Sept. 28, 1878, age 22; d. at San Francisco, CA, bur. in Buffalo.
Sexton, Jason, Feb. 3, 1873, age 65.
Sexton, Martha Elizabeth, wife of Jason, Jan. 11, 1847, age 29.
Sexton, Walter, South Wales, July 20, 1873, age 70.
Seymour, Barrant Staats (or Barent Staats), Dec. 27, 1873, age 30 y, 1 m, 6 d.
Seymour, C. L., April 16, 1862, in 35th year.
Seymour, Celia M., wife of Erastus E., Aug. 21, 1854, age 42; taken to Batavia.
Seymour, Cornelia J., wife of Charles, Feb. 2, 1865.
Seymour, David, July 22, 1849, in 52nd year.
Seymour, E. Letitia, wife of John, May 4, 1875, age 44 y, 7 m.
Seymour, Elizabeth S., wife of Henry R., Sept. 6, 1817, age 32.
Seymour, Elizabeth S., widow of Horatio, March 15, 1876, age 60.
Seymour, Frank, Aug. 28, 1880, age 21.
Seymour, George, Nov. 3, 1846, age 27.
Seymour, George B., Feb. 13, 1876, age 31 y, 2 m, 12 d.
Seymour, Henry R., Feb. 1851; bur. Feb. 16.
Seymour, Horatio, Sept. 16, 1872, age 58.
Seymour, Mrs. Horatio, March 1876.
Seymour, Horatio Schuyler, son of Horatio, June 5, 1870, age 28.
Seymour, John B., railroad accident, March 4, 1877, age 24.
Seymour, John B., Aug. 11, 1877, age 38; sunstroke.
Seymour, John Spencer, Oct. 25, 1872, age 23 y, 2 m, 2 d.
Seymour, Lucretia Grosvenor, dau. of Henry R., April 16, 1850, age 22.
Seymour, Lucy, widow of C. L., May 24, 1877, age 47.
Seymour, Maria Govers, wife of William, Jan. 1875, age 50 y, 5 m.
Seymour, Mary, Nov. 3, 1876, age 35; dropped dead.
Seymour, Thomas J., Oct. 14, 1876, age 24 y, 5 m, 8 d.

Seymour, William, July 2, 1856; 2d mate of Schooner *Golden Harvest*. Fell overboard and was drowned in Lake Michigan.
Seymour, William H., July 15, 1874, age 26.
Sfitzenmier, Frederick, Sept. 21, 1861, age 37.
Shadrake, Agnes, dau. of the late Frederick, March 26, 1879, age 34 y, 8 m, 20 d.
Shadrake, Mrs. Ann Miriam, widow of Frederick, March 11, 1878, age 70 y, 7 m, 10 d.
Shadrake, Lieut. Edward, Co. K, 1st Regt., US Vols., Ullman's Brigade, June 10, 1863, age 26 y, 3 m, 19 d; in New Orleans, bur. in Buffalo.
Shadrake, Frederick, Aug. 16, 1867, age 65.
Shafer, Frederick, Almshouse, May 20, 1880, age 24.
Shaffer, Peter, Aug. 26, 1866, age 51.
Shaft, William, printer, April 14, 1857, age 34; taken to Lockport.
Shagney, George, late of Chicago, IL, June 26, 1866, age 28.
Shainholdts, Anna, wife of Capt. P., Jan. 6, 1841.
Shainholdts, Capt. Peter, July 19, 1846, age 40.
Shaler, Michael F., July 23, 1875, age 50 y, 5 m.
Shallow, Mrs. Margaret, March 17, 1875, age 50.
Shamback, John C., Aug. 6, 1833, age 36.
Shanahan, Bartholomew, Feb. 21, 1879, age 65 y, 8 m.
Shanahan, John, Feb. 3, 1878, age 65.
Shanahan, Michael, Nov. 29, 1877, age 39.
Shannon, John, Sept. 27, 1875, age 21; accidental death.
Shannon, Michael, June 10, 1880, age 42; drowned.
Shapaker, Joseph, July 15, 1876, age 35.
Sharkey, Patrick, Nov. 17, 1874.
Sharp, Augustus, Aug. 22, 1852, age 73.
Sharp, Benjamin, Feb. 17, 1852, age 49.
Sharp, Cloe, wife of David, Aug. 22, 1821, in 67th year.
Sharp, David, March 10, 1826, in 81st year.
Sharp, DeWitt C., Dec. 18, 1879, age 58.
Sharp, Erastus, July 11, 1814, age 28.
Shassel, Adeline, wife of Jacob, Buffalo Plains, Aug. 18, 1874, age 43; taken to Harris Hill.
Shattuck, Dr. Alvin, Aug. 15, 1872, age 52 y, 4 m.
Shattuck, Cyrus, Jan. 17, 1867, age 73; taken to Fredonia, NY.
Shattuck, William S., Dec. 27, 1867, age 61; taken to Williamstown, MA.
Shaul, Adam (or John), Crittenden, Aug. 3, 1874, age c. 40; suicide.
Shaver, "Auntie," an old negro woman, Aug. 14, 1872.
Shaver, Mary Ellen, wife of Norman J., May 17, 1863, in 23rd year.
Shaver, Norman J., March 26, 1877, age 46.
Shavlin, Daniel, March 3, 1873, age 35; d. in the Penitentiary.
Shaw, Aurelia, J., Brant, March 25, 1872, age 25.
Shaw, Daniel, Springville, NY, Aug. 20, 1846, age 28.
Shaw, Mrs. Hannah B., Feb. 8, 1868, age 81; d. in Oxford, MA.
Shaw, Job, Feb. 24, 1866, age 34.
Shaw, John, April 22, 1879, age 40 y, 7 m.
Shaw, John F., July 14, 1845, age 47.
Shaw, Mary, widow of Timothy, Nov. 12, 1869, age 78; taken to Lewiston.
Shaw, Naomi, widow of J. F., March 3, 1849, age 38.
Shaw, Pamelia W., wife of Charles A., June 5, 1880.
Shaw, Perzina, wife of Col. Joseph, March 28, 1848, age 57.
Shaw, Salmon, Oct. 25, 1834, age 23.
Shaw, Seymour D., formerly of Buffalo, June 9, 1853, age 30; in Chicago, IL.
Shaw, Timothy, father of Mrs. William Fleming, July 4, 1857, age 64; taken to Niagara Co., NY.
Shaw, Thomas, Nov. 8, 1865, age 45.
Shaw, William R., March 4, 1875, age 48th year.
Shawl, Lorenzo D., Dec. 13, 1871, age 49.
Shay, John, Co. Almshouse, Sept. 12, 1876, age 55.
Shay, Patrick, June 17, 1877, age 30.

Shea, Dennis, May 12, 1872.
Shear, Timothy, July 5, 1870, age 35; drowned in Buffalo Creek.
Shearer, Laura B., wife of Albert N. of New York, Sept. 27, 1868.
Shearer, Louisa L., dau. of Noah, Aurora, NY, March 18, 1849, in 33rd year.
Shearer, Noah, formerly of MA, Aurora, June 24, 1849, age 85. [Another card: Shearer, Noah, E. Aurora, NY, b. Sept. 4, 1764, d. June 24, 1849, age 85; Soldier of the Revolution.]
Shearer, Thomas, June 3, 1871, age 33.
Sheares, Donald, father of Daniel, Jan. 26, 1873, age 81.
Shearman, Robert Haight, only son of R. H., Sept. 17, 1853.
Sheather, George W., June 19, 1863 in Baton Rouge [LA]. Co. D., 116th Regt., NY State Vols. D. of wounds received at Port Huron.
Shedd, David, b. 1758, d. April 11, 1841, bur. Sardinia, NY; Soldier of the Revolution.
Sheehan, Cornelius M., clerk, Comptroller's Office, June 27, 1879, age 27 y, 8 m, 10 d.
Sheehan, Hanora, wife of William, May 30, 1873.
Sheehan, Honora, wife of William, Jan. 30, 1878, age 65.
Sheehan, James, Aug. 5, 1875, age 60.
Sheehan, James, Sept. 22, 1880, age 24 y, 6 m.
Sheey, Martin E., April 10, 1880, age 32.
Sheffer, John J., April 15, 1836, age 28.
Sheils, John F., July 1, 1877, age 24 y, 4 m.
Shelden, Miss Adelaide C., dau. of C. H., formerly of Lancaster, NY, April 22, 1855; at Camillus, NY, aged 21 y, 2 m.
Shelden, James, Erie Co., NY, on Bark *Avon*, from Dublin to St. John, New Brunswick, seaman, killed by the falling of a block while fishing the anchor, July 27, 1848. (Mosher, master) Seaman.
Sheldon, Alexander J., March 23, 1876, age 52.
Sheldon, Bethun, wife of Asa C., Boston, NY, Sept. 7, 1866.
Sheldon, Diodorus, Sgt., in Capt. William Hull's Vol., Hamburgh, NY, Aug. 1812, age 27.
Sheldon, Elizabeth C., July 8, 1874, age c. 43; drowned.
Sheldon, Ezekiel, Clarence, NY, July 11, 1825, age 40.
Sheldon, Capt. Henry M., Jan. 18, 1860, age 30.
Sheldon, Horace T., May 29, 1865, age 45; taken to Rochester, NY.
Sheldon, James, formerly of Buffalo, Sept. 12, 1850, age 56; in Utica, NY.
Sheldon, Joshua, July 8, 1874, drowned, age 41.
Sheldon, Miss Lydia P., Jan. 17, 1835, age 44.
Sheldon, Mary Ann, wife of William, dau. of John Jackson, March 15, 1862, age 24.
Sheldon, P. S., Aug. 17, 1840, age 23.
Sheldon, Solomon, formerly of Barnet, Caledonia Co., VT, Seneca Mission near Buffalo, Dec. 8, 1845, in 84th year.
Sheldon, Sylvia, widow of James, May 28, 1862, age 65.
Sheldon, William, April 30, 1879, age 81 y, 2 m, 26 d.
Sheldon, Gen. William B., formerly of Janesville, WI, Oct. 20, 1847, age 49; taken to Racine, WI.
Shell, John, Tonawanda, NY, March 18, 1863, age 67 y, 9 m, 3 d.
Shell, Sarah Maria, wife of Jacob, of Tonawanda, Aug. 27, 1855, age 21.
Shelters, William M., Springville, NY, July 6, 1849, in 61st year.
Shelton, Margaret, formerly of Buffalo, July 23, 1880; sister of Dr. William S. Shelton. D. at Bridgeport, CT.
Shepard, Mrs. Elizabeth, mother of John E., Jan. 21, 1872, age 63.
Shepard, Emeline C., wife of William H., Alden, Oct. 5, 1854, age 25 y, 10 m; at New London, NH.
Shepard, Mrs. Lavinnie, Feb. 26, 1868, age 86.
Shepard, Louise K., wife of Stephen B., Nov. 4, 1877, age 24 y, 4 m, 2 d.
Shepard, Margaret, wife of Benjamin F., April 15, 1871.
Shepard, Mrs. Margaret C., Sept. 10, 1871, age 70 y, 6 m, 4 d; taken to Darien, Genesee Co., NY.
Shepard, Matthias, formerly of Erie Co., March 23, 1879, age 59; d. at Mayville.
Shepard, Ralph, killed by explosion of propeller *Kenosha*, and brought here from Sheboygan for bur. on July 11, 1860, age 35 y, 1 m, 26 d.
Shepard, William L., June 8, 1872, age 48.

Shepard, Mrs., April 1871, age 19; found drowned April 30.
Shephard, Abbey J., wife of J. M., Jan. 9, 1877, age 37.
Shephard, Jeremiah B., formerly of Buffalo, May 30, 1875; d. at Smith's Creek, MI.
Shepherd, Elizabeth, widow of David, North Buffalo, Feb. 5, 1871, age 73.
Sheppard, Caroline, wife of James D., Oct. 2, 1849, in 45th year.
Sheppard, Catharine, wife of Christopher, April 11, 1859, age 57 y, 17 d.
Sheppard, Elizabeth Harriet Snowey, wife of Edward, June 18, 1856, age 34.
Sheppard, Henry, formerly of Aurora, NY, Sept. 23, 1840 (Date of newspaper). D. at Louisville, KY, on Steamboat *Rover*.
Sheppard, John Sr., Englishman, Aug. 14, 1842, in 78th year.
Sheppard, Susan, widow of John of Frome Selwood, Somerset, England, March 17, 1846, in 80th year.
Sheridan, John P., formerly of Buffalo, April 16, 1875, age 37.
Sherman, Almon P., Nov. 24, 1873.
Sherman, Mrs. B., late of New Haven, VT, sister of Mrs. E. R. Jewett of Buffalo, March 16, 1852, age 26; taken to VT.
Sherman, B. F., eldest son of B. F. of this City, formerly of Buffalo, March 11, 1877, age 33; d. in Chicago, IL.
Sherman, Benjamin W., Hamburgh, Feb. 1, 1876, age 69.
Sherman, Mrs. Charles H., April 16, 1880, age 22.
Sherman, David, Tonawanda, May 24, 1874, age 70.
Sherman, Dorcas, Nov. 10, 1869, age 68.
Sherman, Esther H., April 9, 1880, age 74; bur. at Medina, NY.
Sherman, George A., May 31, 1857, age 36.
Sherman, Hannah, wife of Orson, of Broomfield, MA, Sept. 18, 1848, age 30.
Sherman, J. H., Sept. 1865.
Sherman, Jane Eliza Hooker, wife of Bejamin [sic] F., July 13, 1876.
Sherman, Ledrick, North Collins, April 1, 1872, age 32.
Sherman, Louise C., dau. of B. F., late of Chicago, IL, July 23, 1867; at Clifton Springs, bur. in Buffalo.
Sherman, Nellie, Almshouse, May 20, 1880, age 25.
Sherman, Patrick, April 8, 1878, age 63.
Sherman, Paul, May 31, 1868.
Sherriff, Mrs. Mary, Black Rock, Oct. 30, 1868, age 60.
Sherry, Robert, 97th N.Y. Vol., formerly of the 21st NY Vols., Nov. 26, 1863, in 39th year; in Emory Hospital, Washington, DC.
Sherwin, Phineas Bartlett, late of Aurora, NY, April 19, 1843, age 38; d. near Memphis, TN.
Sherwin, Susan F., widow of Phineas B., Aurora, NY, Nov. 16, 1843, age 31.
Sherwood, Adiel, Esq., Sept. 2, 1839, age 55.
Sherwood, Albert, Feb. 14, 1868, age 52.
Sherwood, Mrs. Anna M. A., mother of M. B. Sherwood Esq., Sept. 30, 1840, age 48.
Sherwood, Griffin, eldest son of M. B., Nov. 2, 1878, age 44.
Sherwood, John P., March 17, 1871, age 87; taken to Oneida.
Sherwood, Samuel B., May 26, 1852, age 31. D. on Steamer *Gen. Scott* on Mississippi River; brought to Buffalo June 25.
Sherwood, Sheldon Jr., Dec. 31, 1831, in Pittsburgh, PA.
Sherwood, Thomas T., Aug. 8, 1850, age 58.
Sherwood, Lt. William Lord, formerly of Buffalo, April 14, 1873, age 26; killed by the Modacs.
Shettler, Sarah, wife of J., Cheektowaga, June 26, 1872, age 38.
Sheu, Kate, wife of Henry, July 2, 1869, age 19 y, 3 m.
Shewbrook, Mary E., wife of Benjamin T., April 25, 1879, age 32 y, 6 m, 23 d.
Shick, Margaret, wife of Philip, Jan. 22, 1844, age 30 or 39.
Shields, Thomas C., March 7, 1856, age 38.
Shiels, Andrew, son of George of Dodgeville, WI, Sept. 14, 1862, in 30th year.
Shiels, Charles, June 20, 1874, age 67th year.
Shiels, Joanna, dau. of William of Earlstown, Scotland; niece of Charles Shiels of Buffalo, Feb. 19, 1864.
Shiels, John A., March 2, 1871, age 30.

Shiels, Sarah, dau. of George of Dodgeville, WI, late of Berwickshire, Scotland, Feb. 9, 1867, age 24.
Shier, Peter, Feb. 21, 1875, age 62 y, 4 m, 9 d.
Shifferens, Bernhard, June 19, 1872, age 76 y, 2 m, 12 d.
Shimer, Richard A., Oct. 13, 1867, age 62.
Shiner, Clarisa, March 9, 1869, age 68; taken to Fredonia.
Shinners, Maggie Wall, wife of James, Nov. 15, 1872, age 27.
Shipman, Sarah M., wife of John, Oct. 9, 1847, age 23.
Shirr, George Adam, Aug. 17, 1874.
Shirrell, David, Jan. 1877, age 89; taken to Phelps, NY.
Shisler, Mary, widow of David, Harris Hill, Aug. 25, 1877, age 88.
Shoecraft, Elizabeth Dickerson, wife of James P., Jan. 29, 1866, in 35th year.
Shoecraft, Imogene Oviatt, wife of Ross P., March 13, 1871, age 28 y, 11 m.
Shoecraft, James P., auctioneer, Sept. 1880; found drowned.
Shoemaker, John, of firm Shoemaker, Stewart & Co., Oct. 4, 1861.
Shoemaker, John, Sept. 4, 1875, age 85.
Shoop, Daniel, April 14, 1868, age 69.
Shoop, Letitia, wife of Charles, March 5, 1863, age 34.
Shoop, Mrs. Sarah, Sept. 15, 1873, age 63.
Shope, Benjamin A., only son of Abram, Clarence, Sept. 28, 1872.
Shope, Catharine, widow of Abram, Clarence, NY, Aug. 28, 1865, age 89 y, 10 m, 28 d.
Short, Edward, son of Patrick, March 19, 1879, age 32.
Short, George W., son of Levi E. of Buffalo, Sept. 19, 1867; in New Orleans, LA.
Short, Henry, July 11, 1866, age 25 y, 6 m.
Short, James, father of Patrick, Francis and James, July 26, 1848, age 67.
Short, James, son of James, Sept. 3, 1871, age 28 y, 7 m, 2 d.
Short, Levi, Nov. 26, 1863 in Philadelphia, PA.
Short, Mary Elizabeth, wife of Rev. B. P., South Wales, NY, Sept. 1, 1845.
Shortall, Mrs. Byron, June 18, 1864, age 37.
Shove, Luhi, June 24, 1860, age 40.
Shreve, Corinna H., wife of Charles, of Grand Gulph, MS, Aug. 13, 1850, in 32nd year.
Shriner, Peter, April 29, 1871, age 40 y, 1 m, 27 d.
Shriver, Margaret, wife of Henry, Aug. 31, 1873, age 64.
Shryer, Caroline, wife of John, Sept. 19, 1878, age 31 y, 9 m, 7 d.
Shuetz, Richard C., Aug. 27, 1879, age 57.
Shultes, David, Springville, NY, June 6, 1859, age 80.
Shultes, H., wife of George W., Jan. 12, 1844, age 25.
Shultes, Mary Adelia, wife of George W., formerly of Sidney, Delaware Co., NY, June 22, 1852, age 30.
Shultus, Lucy, wife of David, Springville, NY, Jan. 15, 1848, age 65.
Shultz, Godfried, Feb. 1865; funeral Feb. 26th.
Shultzest, Mrs. Maria, April 29, 1873, age 86.
Shulze, J. D., wife of J. P. of Chicago, formerly of Buffalo, Aug. 21, 1869; d. and bur. at Freistadt, WI.
Shuman, George, Clarence, NY, Aug., 1832, age 45.
Shumway, Anson, Oct. 18, 1847, age 77.
Shumway, Hon. Horatio, July 24, 1871, age 83.
Shumway, Miss Maria, Aug. 11, 1847, age 22.
Shumway, Maria A., wife of Jerome B., April 20, 1876, age 48.
Shuttleworth, William, May 20, 1877, age 58.
Sibley, Benjamin, formerly of Erie Co., NY, May 16, 1851, in 63rd year; in Lyndon, Sheboygan Co., WI.
Sibley, Carrie L., wife of C. L., July 24, 1880, age 21 y, 11 m.
Sibley, Mrs. Dorothea, March 20, 1872, age 68.
Sibley, Emily W., dau. of Clark H., Oct. 21, 1856, age 27 y, 1 d.
Sibley, Dr. Joseph C., Colden, NY, March 17, 1866, age 48.
Sibley, Lillian J., wife of C. L., Jan. 20, 1878, age 25.
Sibley, Mrs. Maria G., widow of Hon. Mark H., May 23, 1877, age 73; taken to Canandaigua.
Sibley, Mark H., Sept. 1852.

Sibley, Mary Augusta, wife of O. E., July 13, 1870, age 62; d. at Rochester, bur. in Buffalo.
Sibley, Mary G., wife of John C., dau. of Henry B. Gibson, Oct. 19, 1866; taken to Canandaigua, NY.
Sibley, Matilda Calhoun, wife of Charles W. H., Feb. 24, 1860, in 21st year; in Toledo, OH.
Sibley, Oscar E., formerly of Buffalo, Dec. 7, 1876, age 71; d. at Elizabeth, NJ, bur. in Buffalo.
Sicherman, Mary M., Sept. 23, 1880, age 55.
Sidway, Elizabeth Danes, widow of William of Goshen, NY, mother of John J. of Buffalo, March 15, 1861, in 73rd year.
Sidway, James, father of Capt. James, May 18, 1836, age 76; a Revolutionary soldier. [Another card: Sidway, James, May 18, 1836, age 76; Revolutionary Soldier.]
Sidway, James H., Jan. 25, 1865, age 25 y, 5 m.
Sidway, Jonathan, b. 1759, d. 1826, bur. Buffalo; Revolutionary Soldier.
Sidway, Jonathan, Jan. 21, 1847, age 63.
Sidway, Mrs. Parnell St. John, widow of Jonathan, April 22, 1879, age 78.
Sidway, Mrs. Rebecca, mother of Jonathan, March 24, 1843, age 84.
Siebold, Catharine, Co. Almshouse, July 10, 1876, age 85.
Siechrist, Catherine, Amherst, NY, mother of A.B. Gantz of Buffalo, April 1865, age 58 y, 10 m, 20 d. Funeral in Williamsville, NY.
Sieffer, Charles, Dec. 2, 1870, age c. 28; accidental death.
Sieffert, Caroline E. A., wife of John C., Aug. 22, 1849, age 36.
Sieffert, Charles, June 7, 1869, age 38.
Sieffert, Ernest G., eldest son of John C., April 27, 1860, in 23rd year; at Jacksonville, FL.
Siefert, John C., May 25, 1873, age 67.
Siegel, Gotleib, tailor, Sept. 23, 1874, age 40.
Siehl, Frederick, Dec. 31, 1878.
Sifkins, Andrew, sailor, April 28, 1872, age 33.
Sigison, George W., former member of the Buffalo Historical Society, April 19, 1880, age 51.
Signer, Charles, May 7, 1873, age 39.
Sigwald, Mrs. Barbara, Dec. 23, 1878, age 76.
Sikes, Clara C., wife of Edwin, Feb. 21, 1867, in 39th year.
Sikes, ELiza, widow of Simeon, North Evans, May 9, 1875, age 69.
Sikes, Samuel D., Feb. 12, 1875, age 46 y, 7 m.
Sikes, Simeon, North Evans, July 7, 1873, age 70.
Silcox, George Henry, formerly of Buffalo, July 7, 1860, age 24; at sea on ship *Panama*, bound for San Francisco, CA.
Sill, Delas E., Feb. 1869.
Sill, Electa, widow of Gurdon, Eden, NY, May 6, 1856, age 60.
Sill, John, b. in Lynn, CT, Alden, May 20, 1869, age 78.
Sill, Joseph, formerly of Black Rock, NY, June 30, 1843; at Jonesville, MI.
Sill, Mary Adelia, dau. of Enoch, Boston, NY, Nov. 9, 1835.
Sill, Richard E., Oct. 27, 1829, age 22.
Sill, Mrs. Sarah, Sept. 26, 1830, age 49.
Sill, Judge Seth Ely, Sept. 15, 1851, age 42.
Sill, Hon. Thomas H., Feb. 1856.
Silsbee, P. P., formerly of Buffalo, March 16, 1847, age 29; at Clarkson, NY.
Simcoe, Mrs. Anna, Feb. 9, 1864, age 75.
Simmons, Alpheus, Sept. 23, 1844, age 27.
Simmons, Mrs. Caroline, Dec. 10, 1875, age 65; taken to Alden, Erie Co., NY.
Simmons, Christopher A., Feb. 26, 1877, age 58; d. at Utica.
Simmons, John, Dec. 2, 1874, age 61; taken to Utica.
Simmons, John H., formerly of Buffalo, Feb. 24, 1863, age 24; at Fort Edward, Washington Co., NY.
Simmons, S. Austin, May 10, 1880, age 21 y, 9 m.
Simonds, Edmon J., Sept. 29, 1872.
Simonds, Roderick, Sardinia, NY, June 17, 1880, age 67.
Simonds, Samuel A., March 23, 1870, age 24 y, 5 m; taken to Susquehanna Co., PA.

Simons, Alice, wife of George, Sardinia, Oct. 28, 1876, age 22.
Simons, Eliza, wife of Dr. Marcius, May 31, 1836, age 42; taken to Forestville.
Simons, Orson D., Sardinia, April 7, 1874, age 60.
Simons, Stark, formerly of Buffalo, Feb. 13, 1852, age 28; in Rochester, NY.
Simpson, Agnes, Almshouse, insane, Dec. 16, 1880, age 63.
Simpson, Agnes Virginia, Feb. 21, 1860, age 20 y, 9 m, 2 d.
Simpson, Charles E. A., April 29, 1879, age 26 y, 1 m, 10 d.
Simpson, Mrs. E. O., Nov. 6, 1868.
Simpson, Edward, June 9, 1872, age c. 60.
Simpson, Elizabeth, March 25, 1871, age 60.
Simpson, George, Jan. 26, 1864, age 38; taken to Caledonia, NY.
Simpson, Rev. Ira W., Springville, NY, Pastor of Baptist Church, Oct. 13, 1867.
Simpson, Jane E., wife of Gen. J. H., dau. of the late Commodore Stephen Champlin, Feb. 24, 1870, age 49.
Simpson, Susanna, Oct. 11, 1862, age 61 y, 6 m, 4 d.
Simpson, William, Oct. 9, 1872, age 35 y, 8 m, 16 d.
Sims, Cornelia, wife of Elias, Nov. 27, 1876.
Simser, Mrs. Elizabeth, Nov. 18, 1879, age 28 y, 9 m.
Simson, William Shipton, accidental death, Nov. 23, 1874, age 22.
Sinclair, Angus A., printer, May 18, 1866, age 25 y, 9 m; taken to Toronto, Canada.
Sinclair, Anna Susanna, widow of W. H., Jan. 7, 1878, age 44 y, 6 m, 23 d.
Sinclair, John, April 22, 1868, age 47.
Sinclair, John H., Aug. 23, 1879, age 27 y, 8 m, 18 d.
Singer, Mary Ann, wife of George H., March 29, 1844, age 31.
Sinnott, John, Jan. 19, 1872, age 29.
Sinton, Thomas E., firm of Candee and Sinton, May 22, 1856; taken to Cuyahoga Falls.
Sippel, George G., suicide at Langford, North Collins, April 7, 1873.
Sirret, Augusta, wife of William B., Oct. 22, 1871, age 35.
Sisco, Mr. J. H., Aug. 19, 1875, age 39 y, 1 m, 24 d; taken to Memphis, Onondaga Co., NY.
Sisler, Lewis, Aurora, NY, June 22, 1851, age 63.
Sissan, Laura, Dec. 22, 1862.
Sisson, Alexander, sailing master, US Navy, Dec. 7, 1812, age 30.
Sisson, Daniel S., Aug. 17, 1879, age 47.
Sisson, George B., Oct. 2, 1878, age 51.
Sisson, Miss Martha A., Brant, Sept. 19, 1871, age 39.
Sisson, Phebe T., wife of Joseph, North Collins, NY, Oct. 25, 1856, age 58 y, 4 m, 4 d.
Sisson, William, Collins, NY, Nov. 1831, age 73; formerly of Westport, MA.
Sisto, Very Rev. Father, St. Patrick's Church in Buffalo, Jan. 4, 1865; in New Orleans, bur. in Buffalo.
Sitter, Anthony, Feb. 14, 1872.
Sittley, J. George, Oct. 12, 1874, age 57th year.
Siver, John, Jan. 7, 1859, age 41.
Siver, Mrs. John, Nov. 11, 1861, age 41.
Sizer, Henry H., June 28, 1849, age 45.
Sizer, HJenry S., Sept. 17, 1870, age 33; d. at Duluth, MN.
Sizer, Louisa, wife of Col. Samuel, Jan. 18, 1867, age 83; sister of the Hon. Thomas C. Love.
Sizer, Mary E., widow of Henry H., Aug. 24, 1874, age 64.
Sizer, Col. Samuel, Feb. 20, 1871, age 88.
Skaats, John E., formerly of Buffalo, Feb. 4, 1861, age 72; in Attica, Wyoming Co., NY.
Skeldon, Lucy Bethya, wife of John, Aug. 29, 1850, age 36.
Skidmore, Beers W., Feb. 1, 1863, age 39 y, 2 m, 27 d.
Skillings, Robert, March 31, 1868, age 62.
Skinner, Mr. C. J., May 23, 1872.
Skinner, Henry C., formerly of Buffalo, Dec. 3, 1859, age 28; in Chicago, IL, bur. in LeRoy, NY.
Skinner, John B. II, Attica, Wyoming Co., NY, Aug. 25, 1870, age 48; d. at Clifton Springs.
Skinner, Hon. John B., June 6, 1871, age 72.
Skinner, Jonathan, b. 1760, d. Aug. 8, 1848, bur. Hamburg, NY; Soldier of the Revolution.

Skinner, Lydia C., wife of Dr. J. S., Oct. 16, 1843, age 23 y, 1 m, 10 d; at Amity, Madison Co., OH, bur. in Buffalo.
Skinner, Mrs. Martha St. John, formerly of Buffalo, March 11, 1880, age 76; d. at Willoughby, OH. Youngest dau. of the late Gamaliel and Margaret K. St. John.
Skinner, Palmer, Hamburgh, May 1877.
Sky, John, a Seneca Chief, Tonawanda, NY, Jan. 27, 1819, age 50.
Slade, Aurora, widow of Samuel, Alden, Dec. 18, 1864, in 76th year.
Slade, Caroline, dau. of Samuel, Alden, NY, Nov. 26, 1832, age 21.
Slade, Elizabeth V., wife of William, Alden, NY, May 25, 1859.
Slade, Harriet, wife of William, Alden, NY, Sept. 22, 1862.
Slade, Harry, May 26, 1854, age 65.
Slade, Helen Aurelia Sutton, wife of William H., July 26, 1866, age 26 y, 3 m, 21 d.
Slade, Samuel, Alden, NY, May 7, 1852, age 71.
Slagle, Peter, Jan. 24, 1879, age 61.
Slaight, Randolph B., Gowanda, NY, July 27, 1849, age 19.
Starke, Thomas, Nov. 20, 1859, age 37.
Slater, John, Englishman, Jan. 15, 1876, age 29.
Slattery, Hannah, Aug. 30, 1880, age 23.
Slauson, Helan, Clarence, Jan. 30, 1877, age 70; railroad accident. Killed at Lancaster, Erie Co., NY.
Slayton, Ann, wife of S. M., July 11, 1854, age 36 y, 3 m, 8 d.
Slayton, Charles Vernon, Nov. 9, 1878, age 21.
Slayton, Samuel V., April 27, 1875, age 56.
Sleeper, John, Holland, NY, July, 1855, age 65.
Sleeper, Rufus, father of Mrs. Clark B. Lacy, Holland, Jan. 12, 1869, age 76.
Sliter, Richard R., June 1861, bur. June 5th.
Sloan, Mrs. Abigail, Lancaster, NY, Sept. 27, 1855, age 68.
Sloan, Barbara, wife of William, April 4, 1853, age 23.
Sloan, Catharine, wife of William M., Jan. 28, 1859, age 38.
Sloan, David Franklin, Feb. 27, 1874, age 35.
Sloan, George O., Oct. 2, 1878, age 35.
Sloan, Capt. James, Black Rock, March 5, 1868, age 80.
Sloan, John, Black Rock, NY, Sept. 17, 1823, age 30.
Sloan, Miss Lydia A., North Collins, NY, April 19, 1863, age 41 y, 5 m, 15 d.
Sloan, Mrs. Matilda Young, wife of Hugh, April 29, 1879, age 45, 7 m.
Sloan, May Young, wife of William, March 21, 1876.
Sloan, Mrs. Nellie, Feb. 5, 1873, age 20.
Sloan, Mrs. Sarah C., Feb. 14, 1867, age 40.
Sloan, Thomas, formerly of Buffalo, Sept. 24, 1878, age 52; d. at Pecatonica, IL.
Sloane, Horace, Lancaster, NY, Nov. 12, 1841, age 62.
Slocum, Giles, Dec. 23, 1874, age 43.
Slocum, Lottie, wife of Oscar A., Jan. 10, 1879; d. at Macedon, NY.
Slosson, Abby, widow of Belden, Aug. 28, 1846, in 59th year.
Slosson, Calista, wife of Helon, Clarence, NY, Oct. 7, 1850, age 40 y, 4 m, 7 d.
Slosson, Caroline, Clarence, NY, dau. of John, May 23, 1846, age 30; at Dixon, IL.
Slosson, John, Clarence, NY, father of Mrs. John Drullard, Nov. 20, 1857, in 93rd year.
Slosson, John S., Lancaster, NY, brother of Mrs. John Drullard, June 3, 1859, age 59.
Slosson, Judith, wife of John, Lancaster, NY, May 21, 1855, age 79.
Slosson, Matilda, wife of Helon, Clarence, NY, Oct. 20, 1875, age 56 y, 3 m, 3 d.
Slotky, Moses, Dec. 16, 1875, age 84.
Sly, Aurelia, dau. of John, West Hamburgh, NY, Nov. 4, 1860, age 24 y, 8 m, 16 d.
Sly, Charles E., son of Gilbert, Evans, NY, March 11, 1863, age 20 y, 5 m, 14 d.
Sly, Mrs. Elizabeth, Feb. 11, 1879, age 77 y, 28 d.
Slyter, Abram, Co. Almshouse, Jan. 1, 1878, age 70.
Small, Ernst, Co. Almshouse, Sept. 28, 1877, age 54.
Small, Henry, May 10, 1872; d. at Milwaukee, bur. Buffalo.
Small, Joseph, May 25, 1863, in 21st year.
Small, Maria L., widow of James H., Feb. 12, 1872, age 32.
Small, Peter Sr., father of Mrs. Oscar A. Lindsay, March 7, 1879, age 63.
Small, Mrs. Sophia, May 4, 1877, age 77.

Smallshaw, Marion F., wife of John, Aug. 12, 1869, age 25 y, 5 m, 18 d.
Smallshaw, Corp. Thomas U., Co. J, 100th Regt., N.Y. State Vol., killed at the charge on
    Fort Gregg, April 2, 1865, age 25.
Smart, Edmund B., Akron, Dec. 26, 1869, age 62.
Smead, George R., son of Horace A., July 14, 1877, age 27.
Smead, Harriet Barnard, wife of Charles, dau. of Lewis Barnard of Worcester, MA, July 12,
    1850, age 31; taken to Worcester.
Smead, Horatio N., formerly of Binghamton, NY, Nov. 7, 1848.
Smead, Polly S., wife of H.B., April 25, 1869, age 35 y, 20 d; taken to Bethany, Genesee
    Co., NY.
Smilie, ---, fell during the war of 1812, Jan. 1812.
Smith, Adah Augusta, dau. of the late John M., Dec. 6, 1873, age 26.
Smith, Addis E., East Hamburgh, Nov. 9, 1870, age 40 y, 9 m.
Smith, Aggie C., dau. of the late John M., June 12, 1876.
Smith, Agnes M., April 5, 1876, age 41; taken to Syracuse, NY.
Smith, Mrs. Albert H., Feb. 9, 1876, age 21 y, 2 m, 9 d.
Smith, Alexander, Aug. 25, 1874, age 40.
Smith, Alfred J., formerly of Buffalo, son of the late Edward W., Dec. 23, 1869, age 27.
    D. at St. Paul, MN, bur. Buffalo.
Smith, Alice Roche, wife of Joseph, of the Lake Shore Hotel, April 21, 1857.
Smith, Almer, East Hamburgh, Nov. 6, 1874, age 74 y, 6 m, 23 d.
Smith, Alva P., formerly of Tonawanda, Feb. 4, 1873; d. in Bay City, bur. in Tonawanda.
Smith, Amanda A., wife of William, Lancaster, NY, Nov. 8, 1851, age 29.
Smith, Amelia, dau. of Amos of Boston, Erie Co., NY, Aug. 26, 1852, age 32.
Smith, Amos, from Worcester, MA, Aug. 17, 1828, age 48.
Smith, Amos, Boston, NY, March 17, 1837, age 62d year.
Smith Andrew, Nov. 24, 1880, age 76, Almshouse.
Smith, Andrew J., farmer, Eden Center, NY, April 30, 1880; suicide.
Smith, Ann, Jan. 1, 1877, age 52.
Smith, Mrs. Ann McCarty, Feb. 9, 1847, age 28.
Smith, Anns, wife of Deacon Ezekiel, Hamburgh, NY, Aug. 20, 1819, age 68.
Smith, Miss Anna M., March 22, 1877.
Smith, Annetta M. Stevens, wife of James R., July 16, 1876, age 35 y, 1 m, 9 d.
Smith, Annie, wife of Griffin, Nov. 8, 1870.
Smith, Archibald M. C., Jan. 18, 1852, age 45.
Smith, Arthur, Evans, May 15, 1874, age 55.
Smith, Arthur F., eldest son of Erasmus H., 116th Regt., N.Y. Vol., Aurora, NY; d. May 27,
    1863, in New Orleans of wounds while leading the charge upon Port Hudson, as one of
    the forlorn hope.
Smith, Augustus, son of Mrs. William, Dec. 16, 1852, in 24th year; in St. Augustine, West
    FL.
Smith, B. Rush, May 14, 1875, age 58.
Smith, Benjamin Franklin, May 4, 1875, age 55.
Smith, Betsey, wife of Alma, Hamburgh, June 8, 1824, age 27.
Smith, Beulah A., widow of Archibald, M.B., July 9, 1877.
Smith, Blanche A., wife of Colton B., Dec. 29, 1876, age 27; lost at the railroad accident
    at Ashtabula, OH.
Smith, Mrs. Catharine, Feb. 23, 1871.
Smith, Celia M., widow of O. B., Sept. 7, 1878, age 58.
Smith, Charity, wife of Philip A., May 26, 1860, age 52.
Smith, Charles, Jan. 6, 1865, age 30.
Smith, Charles, drowned Sept. 17, 1871, age 55.
Smith, Charles C., son of Edward W., Oct. 1, 1860, age 52.
Smith, Charles E. (or R.), June 1, 1878, age 81.
Smith, Charles H., switchman, Oct. 14, 1874, age 19; accidental death.
Smith, Charles H., tobacconist, May 4, 1875, age 62; d. at Jamestown.
Smith, Charles L., May 21, 1870, age 21.
Smith, Charles O., son of the late A.M.C. and Beulah A., d. Dec. 10, 1861, age 20th year;
    at Beverly, WV, bur. in Buffalo. In Quartermaster's Dept. under Gen. Reynolds.

Smith, Charles T., manager of Buffalo Academy of Music, Aug. 19, 1869; formerly 1st Lt. in 7th Regt. OH Vol. Cavalry & Quartermaster on staff of Maj. Gen. George Stoneman.
Smith, Charlotte, wife of John, June 20, 1871, age 72 y, 6 m.
Smith, Charlotte, widow of Nathaniel, East Hamburgh, July 8, 1876.
Smith, Charlotte T., Hamburgh, NY, wife of Harrison W., Dec. 5, 1849, age 31.
Smith, Christopher, Feb. 4, 1879, age 33.
Smith, Conrad, railroad, Cheektowaga, Dec. 22, 1876, age 40.
Smith, Cynthia, wife of Hiram G., Springville, March 13, 1872, age 80.
Smith, Cynthia A., wife of R. W., June 28, 1871, age 35.
Smith, Cynthia B., widow of William W., May 21, 1873, age 72.
Smith, Mrs. Daniel, Hamburgh, NY, March 1819.
Smith, Darius, Dec. 31, 1866, in 66th year.
Smith, David, father of Dr. Ellery P., formerly of Buffalo, Jan. 9, 1856; Albion, Orleans Co., NY.
Smith, David, formerly of Aberdeen, Scotland, Jan. 21, 1862, age 39.
Smith, DeWitt C., March 29, 1877, age 39.
Smith, Diadama, Brant, March 24, 1877, age 52.
Smith, E. L., Nov. 22, 1868, age 47.
Smith, Edmond H. (or Edward), Sept. 24, 1876, age 49.
Smith, Edward Jr., son of the late Edward W., formerly of Buffalo, May 25, 1869, age 33 y, 4 m; d. in San Francisco, CA.
Smith, Edward B., July 3, 1853, in 46th year.
Smith, Edward W. Sr., Dec. 31, 1863, in 70th year.
Smith, Edwin, banker, Aug. 1, 1868, age 50; of the firm of Robinson & Co.
Smith, Eleanor, wife of Eli B., from Chestertown, Warren Co., NY, Dec. 10, 1836, age 26th year.
Smith, Eli, sailor, Aug. 28, 1873, age 23; drowned. Formerly resided at Batavia.
Smith, Mrs. Elisha, Hamburgh, NY, Jan. 1820, wife of Dr. Elisha.
Smith, Eliza, drowned Jan. 1, 1877, age 48.
Smith, Eliza Ann, wife of John and dau. of Peter Cowan, April 21, 1860, age 34.
Smith, Eliza Ann, wife of Abijah, Collins, NY, Feb. 28, 1867, age 63.
Smith, Eliza C., wife of John P., Dec. 13, 1847, age 25.
Smith, Eliza Earl, East Aurora, NY, wife of Jonathan, Jan. 7, 1880, age 73.
Smith, Elizabeth, wife of Elder Gideon, Clarence Hollow, NY, Nov. 27, 1836, age 35 y, 7 m, 19 d.
Smith, Elizabeth, widow of Sheldon, Feb. 20, 1874, age 90.
Smith, Elizabeth Quale, wife of W. W., Oct. 5, 1877, age 57.
Smith, Emily S., dau. of Rev. S. R., Jan. 8, 1853, age 20 y, 15 d.
Smith, Erastus, Sept. 26, 1847, age 55.
Smith, Erlon G., East Hamburgh, NY, Sept. 9, 1880, age 56.
Smith, Ermina A., wife of C. L., April 19, 1877, age 19; taken to Brockport, NY.
Smith, Mrs. Esther, Feb. 16, 1853, age 53.
Smith, Esther, wife of James F., formerly of Buffalo, Jan. 28, 1873, age 63; d. at Suspension Bridge, NY.
Smith, Mrs. Evalina L., East Hamburgh, April 18, 1870, age 40 y, 8 m, 18 d; taken to Aurora.
Smith, Deacon Ezekiel, Hamburgh, NY, Feb. 2, 1828, age 87. [Written in: wife- Anna.]
Smith, Ezra Loomis ("Col. Lum"), Bill-Poster, May 14, 1873, age 39 y, 4 m.
Smith, Fannie, Sept. 3, 1880, age 40 or 45 years; killed by a blow on the head.
Smith, Fanny, wife of Charles, Dec. 23, 1872, age 47.
Smith, Father, Amherst, NY, formerly of Clarence, NY. Minister of the United Brethren in Christ, Sept. 8, 1860, in 87th year; at the residence of his son in West Hempfield, Lancaster Co., PA.
Smith, Francis, Nov. 26, 1880, age 53.
Smith, Frank (Benjamin Franklin), May 4, 1875, age 55.
Smith, Frank, Co. Almshouse, Feb. 27, 1879, age 64.
Smith, Frederick, April 22, 1839, age 31; in Detroit, MI.
Smith, Frederick, formerly of Buffalo, June 8, 1870, age 73; d. at Boise City, Idaho Territory.
Smith, Frederick, Sept. 27, 1879, age 45; found drowned.
Smith, George, Feb. 16, 1822, in 23rd year.

Smith, George, Aug. 22, 1820, age 63.
Smith, George, West Seneca, NY, Oct. 10, 1862, age 49.
Smith, George, accidental death March 27, 1879.
Smith, George Evelyn, wool grower, formerly of Buffalo, July 21, 1879; stabbed in TX.
Smith, George, formerly of Genesee Co., NY, Aug. 14, 1864, age 24; taken to Oakfield, NY.
Smith, George W., law student, May 13, 1837, age 22; at Lyons, Wayne Co., NY.
Smith, George W., formerly of Buffalo, printer, Dec. 12, 1870; d. in NY City.
Smith, George W., youngest son of the late Edward, formerly of Buffalo, Feb. 16, 1871, age 25 y, 11 m; d. at Pittsburgh, PA.
Smith, George W., physician, May 30, 1872, age 58.
Smith, Gerrit, obituary Jan. 5, 1875; tribute from colored citizens of Buffalo.
Smith, Capt. Gilbert of the Brig *Oleander*, March 17, 1861, age 39.
Smith, Mrs. Gilman, Nov. 6, 1828.
Smith, Grisausier, wife of Charles, March 31, 1852, age 32.
Smith, H. K., Crittenden, April 23, 1873.
Smith, Hannah, wife of P., dau. of Mrs. Sally Rees, Nov. 27, 1838, age 35.
Smith, Hannah, widow of Amos, mother of Mrs. Benjamin Dole, Aug. 29, 1846, age 67.
Smith, Hannah C., wife of Narhan, Dec. 31, 1877, age 48.
Smith, Harriet, wife of Alfred, of Pamlico, London, England, May 16, 1850, age 34.
Smith, Harriet M., wife of Charles W., dau. of Alfred W. Wilgus, formerly of Buffalo, Feb. 26, 1854; in Brooklyn, NY, bur. in Buffalo.
Smith, Henry, Boston, NY, Jan. 16, 1867, age 62 y, 4 m, 19 d.
Smith, Rev. Dr. Henry, formerly of Buffalo, Jan. 14, 1879, age 73.
Smith, Henry E., son of Patrick, April 15, 1869, age 31.
Smith, Henry K., lawyer, Sept. 23, 1854.
Smith, Hon. Henry P., July 14, 1874, age 63; La Salle.
Smith, Rev. Henry Ryan, formerly of Buffalo, April 1873; d. in Niagara Co.
Smith, Henry T., July 4, 1858, age 26; in New York, bur. in Buffalo.
Smith, Hiram, Boston, NY, merchant Aug. 1833, in 27th year.
Smith, Hiram, Marilla, Jan. 8, 1876, age 78.
Smith, Hiram G., March 24, 1873, age 76.
Smith, Horace, Aug. 7, 1873, age 28; his parents reside at Little Falls.
Smith, Humphrey, North Collins, Feb. 23, 1877, age 81.
Smith, Isaac, suicide, Springville, July 7, 1876, age 30.
Smith, Isaac S., formerly of Buffalo, July 31, 1860, age 68; in Syracuse, NY.
Smith, Jacob M., Feb. 22, 1880, age 69.
Smith, James, March 30, 1848, age 25.
Smith, James, Dec. 17, 1865, age 47.
Smith, James Sr., July 29, 1872, age 62.
Smith, James, July 10, 1873.
Smith, James, Feb. 12, 1880, age 41 y, 6 m.
Smith, James F., Sept. 23, 1862.
Smith, James H., firm of John J. Smith and Co., Aug. 19, 1849, age 29.
Smith, James M., Hamburgh, NY, Dec. 14, 1847, age 28.
Smith, James P., Nov. 7, 1874, age 56.
Smith, James S., Sept. 3, 1856, age 65; in Lewiston, NY, bur. in Buffalo.
Smith, Jane, wife of James, April 29, 1880, age 58.
Smith, Mrs. Jesse C., formerly of Buffalo, D. in Brooklyn, NY; Nov. 1876.
Smith, Joel L., son of Walter S. and Harriet, Sept. 28, 1873, age 19 y, 9 m, 27 d.
Smith Joel S., Hamburgh, Jan. 20, 1879, age 80.
Smith, John of Live Oak Engine C No. 2, July 2, 1858, age 21; of over-exertion at the fire yesterday.
Smith, John, Sept. 13, 1872, age 73; taken to Freeport, IL.
Smith, John, brother-in-law of Capt. L. Vallier, Sept. 29, 1873, age 20; d. in Chicago, bur. in Buffalo.
Smith, John, Clarence, NY, Jan. 28, 1874, age 64.
Smith (or Schmidt), John, Sept. 4, 1874, age 71.
Smith, John, Sept. 16, 1879, age 60.
Smith, John, Almshouse, Sept. 23, 1880, age 41.
Smith, John H. T., Dec. 5, 1877, age 30; taken to Kendall, NY.

Smith, John M., Oct. 20, 1872, age 72.
Smith, John P., of firm of Smith Brothers, Aug. 11, 1851, in 29th year.
Smith, Joseph, a transient person, July 16, 1818, age 72.
Smith, Joseph, Aug. 6, 1873, age 51.
Smith, Joseph, Co. Almshouse, April 21, 1876, age 20.
Smith, Joseph H., Aug. 9, 1870, age 68.
Smith, Joseph H., West Seneca, NY, Oct. 22, 1878, age 36.
Smith, Joseph K., March 2, 1864, age 41.
Smith, Josie A., formerly of Buffalo, May 17, 1876, wife of Clark J. D. in Boston, MA.
Smith, Julia C., wife of W.L.G., July 19, 1869, age 49 y, 9 m.
Smith, Kate, Aykroyd, wife of Marshall N., Dec. 14, 1879.
Smith, Kohama, mother of T. J., June 19, 1863, age 84.
Smith, L. Dorr (or Dow) only son of Nathaniel, Brant, Nov. 8, 1875, age 29 y, 10 m.
Smith, Mrs. L. H., May 6, 1878.
Smith, Laura J., wife of William N., May 16, 1868, age 24.
Smith, Lawrence, D. Feb. 10, 1846, age 95.
Smith, Loretta, wife of Jose S., Nov. 20, 1871, age 67.
Smith, Lorrian, firm of Smith and Clark, Evans Center, NY, June 13, 1849, age 29.
Smith, Louisa A., wife of Samuel, June 16, 1851, in 29th year.
Smith, Lovina L., wife of Joseph H., Sept. 8, 1854, age 38 y, 6 m.
Smith, Lucian M., Dec. 12, 1851, age 29.
Smith, Capt. Luman, Buffalo Plains, Feb. 4, 1869, age 68.
Smith, M. Catherine, wife of Mathias, June 9, 1877, age 35 y, 3 m, 26 d.
Smith, Magdalena, wife of C. A., May 8, 1873, age 22.
Smith, Margarette Wilson, wife of Edward W., July 7, 1860, age 56 y, 5 m, 22 d.
Smith, Maria, June 24, 1871, age 44.
Smith, Maria C., sister of Rev. S. R. Smith, Aug. 16, 1847, age 43.
Smith, Marshall, Oct. 1828, age 35.
Smith, Martha, wife of James, March 7, 1875, age 60.
Smith, Martha W., wife of James M., May 26, 1841, in 22nd year.
Smith, Mary, wife of Daniel, Hamburgh, NY, Nov. 15, 1829, age 52 y, 10 m.
Smith, Mary (Maky), wife of Samuel, recently of St. Albans, VT, Sept. 12, 1836, in 19th year.
Smith, Mary, dau. of John, Collins, NY, April 15, 1842, age 22.
Smith, Mrs. Mary, July 11, 1849, in 64th year.
Smith, Mary, wife of B. F., dau. of Newton Hayes of New York, Sept. 30, 1859 in St. Catharines, Canada.
Smith, Mrs. Mary, mother of Sidney of Buffalo, Oct. 21, 1863, age 63.
Smith, Mary, Dec. 12, 1871, age 35.
Smith, Mary, wife of George, Oct. 6, 1877, age 20.
Smith, Mrs. Mary, native of London, England, Feb. 8, 1878, age 83; d. at the "Church Home."
Smith, Mrs. Mary Ann, Jan. 21, 1833, age 30.
Smith, Mary Ann, wife of James H., Aug. 13, 1849, age 26.
Smith, Mary Ann, wife of Francis, Dec. 27, 1878, age 61 y, 10 m.
Smith, Mary Ann, Jan. 15, 1880, age 77; sudden death.
Smith, Mary Eliza, wife of Asa P., May 22, 1873, age 53; taken to Grimsby, Ontario.
Smith, Mary F., wife of Joseph, June 28, 1865, age 27 y, 11 m.
Smith, Mary J., wife of Barnard, Nov. 30, 1876, age 75.
Smith, Mary M., wife of Frederick, March 4, 1862, age 62; taken to Collins, NY.
Smith, Michael, formerly of St. Louis, Dec. 8, 1873, age 43.
Smith, Nancy, wife of Thomas G., formerly of Buffalo, March 16, 1866; at St. Joseph, MO.
Smith, Nathaniel K., Aug. 18, 1851, age 72.
Smith, Nehemiah, father of O. B. of Buffalo, East Hamburgh, July 31, 1870, age 76 y, 9 m.
Smith, Olivia, widow of Isaac S., formerly of Buffalo, Jan. 10, 1871, age 72; d. in Syracuse, NY.
Smith, Oran, Jan. 1869.
Smith, Orsamus B., July 15, 1877, age 60.
Smith, Owen, June 14, 1872, age 52.
Smith, Oziel, Williamsville, NY, Jan. 3, 1836, age c. 55.
Smith, Patrick, Feb. 5, 1848, age 49, saddler.

Smith, Peter, Black Rock, NY, Oct. 22, 1850, age 47, formerly of Buffalo.
Smith, Peter, Aug. 23, 1875, age 67.
Smith (Schmitz), Peter, accidental death, June 14, 1879, age 20.
Smith, Pliny, Springville, Jan. 3, 1878, age 73.
Smith, Polly, widow of Jefferson, Dec. 29, 1876, age 70.
Smith, Rachel, wife of G. Smith, formerly of Bungay, Suffolk, England, Jan. 17, 1846, age 31.
Smith, Randolph, Collins, Feb. 4, 1869, age 33 y, 16 d; d. at Effingham, KS.
Smith, Rhoba, widow of Capt. Ezekiel Jr., Hamburgh, NY, Jan. 15, 1860, age 80.
Smith, Robert, March 15, 1872, age 34; d. at London, Ontario, bur. in Buffalo.
Smith, Robert B., Jan. 25, 1865, age 36.
Smith, Rodney B., formerly of Black Rock, May 3, 1873, age 75; d. at Smith's Mills, Hanover, Chautauqua Co.
Smith, Dr. Rufus, Clarence, NY, Jan. 26, 1846, age 63.
Smith, Ruth, wife of Timothy Sr., Collins, NY, March 20, 1835.
Smith, S. Riley, March 1851.
Smith, Samuel, Canal Boatman, Aug. 29, 1870, age 60.
Smith, Samuel, Oct. 18, 1879, age 68.
Smith, Samuel B., Fredonia, NY, Sept. 29, 1864, age 40; bur. in Buffalo.
Smith, Samuel T., son of the late Samuel, Nov. 2, 1876, age 19 y, 9 m, 10 d.
Smith, Sarah, wife of Arlu, eldest dau. of Capt. Alexander Ramsdell, Hamburgh, NY, March 17, 1853, age 40 y, 5 m.
Smith, Mrs. Sarah, Sept. 22, 1857, age 77.
Smith, Sarah, wife of James, Jan. 26, 1866, in 76th year.
Smith, Sarah Ann, wife of Henry K., dau. of Sheldon Thompson, April 15, 1839.
Smith, Sarah Ann, wife of Henry K., formerly of Montgomery Co., NY, dau. of Henry P. Voorhees, April 20, 1836, age 23 y, 5 m.
Smith, Sarah Delia Bellamy, wife of John B., Feb. 11, 1854, age 33.
Smith, Sarah E., wife of W. S., dau. of S. Z. Haven of Buffalo, Aug. 6, 1861, in 31st year; in Harlem, IL.
Smith, Sarah Elizabeth Vallette, wife of Rev. J. Hyatt Smith, July 3, 1855, age 36.
Smith, Sarah J., wife of Levi, June 6, 1878, age 53.
Smith, Sarah Simcoe, wife of John J., Oct. 27, 1864, age 40 y, 9 m.
Smith, Sheldon, lawyer, June 1, 1835, in 47th year.
Smith, Simeon B., Black Rock, NY, late of Syracuse, NY, Sept. 8, 1867, age 58 y, 7 m.
Smith, Mrs. Sophia H., formerly of Buffalo, Feb. 4, 1877, age 32; d. at Pemberville OH, bur. in Buffalo. Dau. of F. Duzen.
Smith, Miss Sophronia, dau. of Abijah, Colden, NY, Jan. 10, 1835, age 27; in Aurora, NY.
Smith, Rev. Stephen Rensselaer, Pastor of First Universalist Church, Buffalo, Feb. 17, 1850, age 62.
Smith, Susan, wife of James, April 29, 1862, age 51.
Smith, Susan, mother of B. R. Smith, Jan. 9, 1863, age 81.
Smith, Susan, Co. Almshouse, May 8, 1876, age 45.
Smith, Theron W., Sardinia, Erie Co., NY, Jan. 19, 1879, age over 80.
Smith, Thomas, Jan. 15, 1847, age 42.
Smith, Thomas, Aug. 6, 1876, age 67.
Smith, Thomas, Nov. 24, 1876, age 22.
Smith, Thomas Jefferson, Buffalo Pains, Oct. 30, 1870, age 66.
Smith, Timothy, Jan. 19, 1833, age 28.
Smith, Timothy, Collins, NY, July 30, 1836, age 78.
Smith, Mrs. W. A., wife of Capt. W. A., Oct. 22, 1873.
Smith, W. H., Nov. 17, 1879, age 46.
Smith, W. L. G., Jan. 31, 1878, age 64 y, 10 m.
Smith, Mr. W. M., Jan. 10, 1846, age 59.
Smith, Walter B., Marilla, June 10, 1871, age 71.
Smith, William, Oct. 28, 1872.
Smith, William Jr., Engineer, April 3, 1880; sudden death.
Smith, William A., July 24, 1850, in 35th year.
Smith, Capt. William A., March 29, 1880, age 43.
Smith, William C., May 21, 1879, age 28 y, 8 m, 22 d.

Smith, William H., Dec. 5, 1868, age 42.
Smith, William H., Oct. 24, 1874, age 39 y, 7 m, 26 d; taken to Cypress Hills, Brooklyn, NY.
Smith, William H. A., formerly of Buffalo, Oct. 13, 1863; at Convalescent Camp, VA.
Smith, Deacon William M., Jan. 10, 1846, age 46 y, 5 m.
Smith, Wilmoth C., Brant, NY, Oct. 13, 1851, age 41.
Smith, Zenas, Williamsville, NY, Feb. 17, 1843, age 75.
Smither, Sarah, wife of Robert, Lancaster, Nov. 10, 1877, age 56.
Smithson, James F., Sept. 12, 1874, age 40.
Smithwick, Averina Purdon, dau. of late William Purdon, July 8, 1855.
Smithwick, Mrs. Prudence B., Jan. 5, 1870, age c. 70; of Stratford, C[anada] W[est].
Smithwick, Prudence Margaret, dau. of late William, July 27, 1854, age 27.
Smithwick, William, late of Grange House, Cashell, County Tipperary, Ireland, July 21, 1854, age 56.
Smyth, Mrs. Jane, Jan. 11, 1859, age 41.
Smyth, Percy I., Dec. 5, 1880, age 29.
Snaith, Eleanor M., wife of John S., Nov. 4, 1878.
Snashell, Mrs. Mary Ann, Griffin's Mills, mother of Mr. J., Feb. 1876, age 80th year.
Snearley, Emmanuel, Williamsville, NY, Aug. 17, 1864, age 25; in battle of Snickerville, VA.
Snearly, Esther, Williamsville, widow of George, Aug. 7, 1877, age 57 y, 6 m.
Snell, Mrs. B., Dec. 1866, age 88 y, 9 m.
Snell, Mrs. Jane, Feb. 18, 1855, age 72.
Snell, Sarah C., wife of William S., July 3, 1875, age 67.
Snider (Schneider), John B., Dec. 31, 1879, age 49.
Sniggs, Kittie, wife of R. F., Nov. 6, 1877, age 26.
Snively, Daniel, Lancaster, NY, Feb. 6, 1846, age 29.
Snow, Augustin T., July 2, 1875, age 65.
Snow, Charlotte, wife of Capt. James, Feb. 11, 1854.
Snow, Frank M., firm of Howard, Whitcomb and Co., Sept. 22, 1861, age 32.
Snow, Harriet Augusta, oldest dau. of Harriet C., Aug. 22, 1872, age 26 y, 9 m.
Snow, Harriet Miller, wife of R. G., Sept. 7, 1866.
Snow, Louisa, wife of William S., Oct. 20, 1866, age 64 y, 8 m, 20 d.
Snow, Mary S., wife of Dr. R. G., Oct. 20, 1853; in Newport, Herkimer Co., NY.
Snow, Persis, wife of A. T., Aug. 15, 1873, age 58.
Snow, Dr. Reuben G., May 25, 1871, age 65.
Snow, Sarah, wife of Dr. George B., Sept. 21, 1878.
Snow, Susan B., wife of Dr. R. G., April 23, 1850; at sea on return from West Indies.
Snow, William, b. Jan. 10, 1753, d. Feb. 18, 1834, bur. Alden, NY; Soldier of the Revolution.
Snow, William S., April 9, 1876, age 78.
Snyder, C. C., Sept. 16, 1876, age c. 50.
Snyder, George, formerly of PA, Sept., 1814, age 73.
Snyder, John, Town Line, March 10, 1879, age 62.
Snyder, Joseph, June 3, 1868, age 60.
Snyder, Mary, widow of George, July 3, 1872, age 80 y, 10 m.
Sole, Rev. Daniel B., Sept. 30, 1850, age 62; taken to Canada.
Sole, Dr. Sidney W., only son of D. B., son-in-law of Col. Peter Relyea of Albany, NY, April 26, 1850, in 34th year; taken to Albany.
Solomon, Godfred, Sept. 4, 1878, age 76.
Somerville, Alice, wife of Dr. William, Sept. 18, 1858, age 41.
Somerville, Elizabeth, widow of John, Nov. 26, 1868, age 75.
Somerville, John, Nov. 23, 1859, age 75.
Somerville, JohnAshton, Nov. 14, 1870, age 22 y, 7 m, 19 d.; d. in Cleveland, OH, bur. Buffalo.
Sommer, Margaret, wife of Andrew, Cheektowaga, Sept. 15, 1874, age 66.
Sommer, Kathrina, Dec. 29, 1872.
Soper, James, H., Hamburgh, Feb. 28, 1875, age 23.
Soutern, John, drowned Nov. 1, 1877, age 31.
Soule, Henry V., Feb. 21, 1877, age 58.

Sourwine, Eleanor Jane, wife of Michael, Jan. 8, 1871, age 50 y, 10 m.
Sourwine, Michael, Feb. 28, 1877, age 57 y, 7 m, 24 d.
Sourwine, Peter, April 19, 1873, age 32.
Sourwine, Sarah Jane, wife of Peter, Feb. 19, 1870, age 29 y, 8 m.
Southard, Capt. A., Nov. 20, 1876, age 36; taken to Newark, OH.
Southard, John B., March 15, 1868, age 26.
Southwick, Dr. William L., Alden, NY, formerly of Colden, Erie Co., NY & Conneaut, OH, Sept. 11, 1853, age 27.
Southworth, Mrs. Almira, mother of Mr. M. C., North Collins, Nov. 8, 1872, age 72.
Southworth, Mrs. D. W., Angola, NY, May 13, 1879, age 60; widow of Dr. D. W. Died of injuries received at burning of her home.
Southworth, Dr. Delos W., physician, Angola, NY, May 8, 1879, age 60-70; burned in his home.
Southworth, George E., July 1, 1880, age 29 y, 2 m, 20 d.
Soven, Mary, wife of Augustus, Aug. 12, 1880, age 50 y, 12 d.
Sowle, Tibbits, Collins, NY, July 21, 1836, age 74.
Spadi, Mary, wife of Conrad, Dec. 7, 1880, age 44 y, 7 m.
Spalding, John, Alden, NY, formerly of Windham, CT, April 11, 1831, age 55.
Spalding, Joseph, formerly of Black Rock, NY, Dec. 3, 1857, age 76; at Addison, Somerset Co., PA.
Spalding, Mercy, Aurora, NY, wife of Roswell S., Sept. 25, 1828, age 45.
Spalding, Rufus, Niagara Falls Village, March 9, 1870, age 98.
Spalding, Sally M., Bowmansville, NY, widow of Dr. Luther, Oct. 29, 1867, age 64.
Spangenberg, Carl, New York City, Oct. 9, 1872, age 38.
Spangenberg, Mrs. Maria K., formerly of Buffalo, Nov. 22, 1850, in 63rd year; in Bethany, PA.
Sparks, Frank H., May 7, 1880, age 28 y, 2 m, 7 d.
Sparks, George P., Nov. 1, 1854, age 24.
Sparks, Jane, widow of William, mother of Mrs. John Sage, Nov. 7, 1857.
Sparks, Miss Mary Ann, Black Rock, NY, June 1825; d. from taking opium.
Sparks, William, step-father of Mrs. J. Sage, Dec. 9, 1854, in 85th year.
Sparrow, Mary Ann, wife of Erastus, Jan. 6, 1843, age 45.
Spath, Mary, Jan. 1, 1877, age c. 50.
Spaulding, Hon. Alexander, formerly of Buffalo, Feb. 20, 1876, age 48; d. in NY City.
Sapulding, Elijah, Griffin's Mills, June 16, 1877, age 72 y, 5 m, 16 d.
Spaulding, Jane Antoinette, wife of Elbridge G., dau. of G. B. Rich, Aug. 1, 1841; at Attica, NY.
Spaulding, John, near Lancaster, June 19, 1871, age 71.
Spaulding, Nancy S., wife of Hon. E. G., May 4, 1852, age 28.
Spayth, David, Williamsville, Feb. 2, 1870, age 77.
Speechly, Ralph, Sept. 15, 1869, age 67.
Speed, William, March 12, 1879, age 48.
Speidel, Christiana, Dec. 23, 1879, age 71.
Speisser, August, June 26, 1875, age 55 y, 9 m.
Spencer, Mrs. A. B., Springville, June 15, 1865, age 54 y, 5 m.
Spencer, Catharine, wife of Hon. Ambrose, dau. of Gen. James Clinton, sister of the late Gov. DeWitt Clinton, Aug. 20, 1837, age 58.
Spencer, Elizabeth F., May 5, 1879, wife of F. D.
Spencer, Mrs. Fanny A., April 3, 1872, age 77.
Spencer, John E., son of James, March 16, 1879, age 50.
Spencer, Mrs. L., Nov. 18, 1880, age 85; d. at Titusville.
Spencer, Lucinda E., wife of Charles N., dau. of John W. Hamlin, formerly of Aurora, Jan. 22, 1866, age 25 y, 4 m; at Titusville, PA; taken to Aurora, NY.
Spencer, Mary, wife of James, March 3, 1866, in 63rd year.
Spencer, Mary A., formerly of Buffalo, Aug. 1, 1879, wife of Burrall; d. in Canandaigua, NY.
Spencer, Michael, suicide, Clarence, NY, April 17, 1874.
Spencer, Miss S. Ann, sister of B. Spencer, July 24, 1867; taken to Rochester, NY.
Spencer, Sarah Eliza, widow of Nelson, June 14, 1874, age 67th year.
Spencer, Sheldon, Nov. 3, 1846, age 53.
Spencer, Solon, Sept. 25, 1857, age 55.

Spencer, Mrs. Solon, July 5, 1872, age 66.
Spencer, Mrs. Sophronia, Lake View, April 15, 1874, age 79; bur. in Buffalo.
Sperry, Charles R., March 4, 1859, age 25.
Sperry, Mrs. Phebe, Sept. 25, 1858, age 52.
Sperry, Mr. W. M., May 14, 1853, in 49th year.
Spertzell, Justus, July 5, 1864, in 44th year.
Spertzell, Mary Ann, widow of Justus, Aug. 23, 1865, age 44.
Spicer, Christiana, widow of Thomas, April 20, 1878, age 69; d. at Aurora, IL, bur. in Buffalo.
Spicer, Isabella, wife of George W., June 12, 1867, age 26.
Spicer, Thomas, Oct. 20, 1875, age 84; d. at Aurora, IL, bur. in Buffalo.
Spicher, Rev. Peter S. J., March 29, 1874, age 63.
Spiegel, Mrs. Babette, Nov. 10, 1880, age 80.
Spike, Louis, teamster, Dec. 7, 1872, age 50.
Spingler, Gottleib, Nov. 10, 1872, age 50.
Spire, George, Nov. 10, 1876, age 39 y, 1 m, 5 d.
Spooner, Dorcas, widow of Lemuel, East Aurora, June 4, 1871, age 83 y, 6 m.
Spooner, Lemuel, East Aurora, NY, Aug. 4, 1864, age 87 y, 7 m.
Spooner, Millard, East Aurora, NY, Sept. 14, 1863, age 41.
Spooner, Phebe Ann, East Aurora, NY, wife of Whipple, Sept. 28, 1866, in 52nd year.
Spoonley, Thomas, Hamburgh, Oct. 18, 1868, age 54.
Spoor, Orsamus, formerly of Clarence, Aug. 31, 1840; at Byron, IL.
Spoor, William, Clarence, NY, Oct. 1828, age 59.
Sprague, Abiah H., wife of Noah P., Sept. 14, 1851, age 48.
Sprague, Dr. Alden Spooner, Jan. 6, 1863, age 61 y, 11 m, 18 d.
Sprague, Charles E., suicide, April 10, 1878, age 41.
Sprague, Ebenezer, Hamburg, Sept. 16, 1837, age 90 y, 1 m, 1 d.
Sprague, Mrs. Horatio, Hamburgh, NY, Aug. 1829.
Sprague, John, Dec. 7, 1874, age 54; funeral at Potters Corners.
Sprague, M. E., May 26, 1872, age 47.
Sprague, Mary Bosworth, widow of Dr. Alden S., June 15, 1877, age 72.
Sprague, Noah P., Aug. 21, 1879, age 80.
Sprague, Susan, wife of W. P., East Hamburgh, May 7, 1875, age 58.
Sprickmann, Joseph, May 14, 1879, age 29 y, 5 m, 26 d.
Springer, Henry, April 1878.
Sprisler, John J., July 8, 1877, age 45.
Sproat, Mrs. Julia, Aug. 22, 1872.
Spurback, Reuben, Alden, NY, Co. E., 49th Regt., N.Y. Vol., Feb. 19, 1863, age 18.
Squeezy, Charles, railroad accident, March 14, 1878, age 21.
Squibb, Edgar J., railroad engineer, June 18, 1879, age 27; killed on the railroad.
Squier, Capt. Abiram H. (Lake Captain), May 5, 1875, age 62.
Squier, Esther Mary, wife of Socrates, April 27, 1878.
Squier, Frederic C., Dec. 1, 1880.
Squier, Capt. John, Jan. 17, 1872, age 80 y, 5 d.
Squier, Sarah Lydia, wife of Henry C., Dec. 9, 1865.
Squier, Socrates, June 29, 1880, age 62.
Staadtlar, Joseph, May 15, 1879, age 96; d. at Co. Almshouse.
Staats, Barent I., April 4, 1830, age 40.
Staats, Mrs. Jane, mother of Jeremiah and Barent, May 22, 1846, age 80.
Staats, Jeremiah F., Aug. 21, 1829, son Barent I., age c. 4 years.
Staats, Lancing, Dec. 28, 1875, age 58.
Staats, Nicholas J., son of Barent I., July 4, 1853.
Staats, Pamelia, widow of Barent I., age 78.
Stabell, Jacob F., Nov. 7, 1880, age 22.
Stabell, Mary Libbie, Nov. 10, 1879, age 23 y, 4 m.
Stable, Mary Herman, wife of John, Dec. 27, 1859, age 21 y, 6 m.
Stacey, Sally, widow of John, Griffin's Mills, NY, Jan. 20, 1858, age 73.
Stack, Patrick, accidental death, Feb. 21, 1876, age c. 29.
Stacy, John, Master Builder, Jan. 7, 1839, age 50.
Stacy, John, drowned Aug. 20, 1874, age 23.

Staebler, George, Dec. 26, 1865, age 64 y, 8 m.
Staedt, John S., June 2, 1876, age 69.
Stafford, Candace O., wife of Samuel, Colden, NY, Aug. 20, 1862, age 32.
Stafford, Darius B., Aurora, NY, April 2, 1841, age 29.
Stafford, David Jr., Aurora, NY, Sept. 28, 1869, age 67.
Stafford, David Sr., Aurora, NY, Oct. 25, 1869, age 88.
Stafford, Egbert E., March 30, 1865, age 45; taken to Aurora, NY.
Stafford, Elizabeth Cadwallader, wife of John F., of Chicago, Nov. 26, 1861, in 32nd year.
Stafford, J. R., Nov. 15, 1873, age 48; taken to Aurora.
Stage, Frank, Newstead, Aug. 19, 1872, age 29.
Stagg, Elizabeth M., widow of Dr. Henry R., dau. of late Hon. Samuel Wilkinson, Sept. 5, 1858, age 54.
Stagg,. Dr. Henry Rutgers, Feb. 29, 1848, age 46.
Stahl, Caddie A., April 1, 1880.
Stahleker, Mary Ann, wife of Frederick L., July 25, 1866, age 32.
Staley, Anna, Eggertsville, Sept. 14, 1876, age 19.
Staley, Franklin, Eggerstville, Aug. 6, 1876, age 22.
Staley, Samuel, Eggertsville, NY, May 21, 1845, age 53 y, 11 m.
Stambach, Frederick, April 27, 1879, age 68 y, 4 m.
Stambach, H. G., July 3, 1858, age 48 y, 9 m, 2 d.
Stambach, Peter C., Dec. 2, 1872, age 50 y, 2 m, 10 d.
Stamm, Catherine, April 26, 1879, age 69.
Stamm, John, Oct. 9, 1853, age 46.
Stamp, Mrs. Jane, Aug. 14, 1862, age 54; taken to West Seneca, NY.
Stanbridge, Thomas Sr., Black Rock, NY, Englishman, Dec. 21, 1859, age 54.
Stanclifft, John, b. 1759, d. 1847, bur. N. Collins; Soldier of the Revolution.
Standart, Sgt. Charles D., Elma, NY, 116th Regt., N.Y. State Vol., killed April 8, 1864 in battle of Sabine Cross Roads.
Standart, De Forest, Elma, NY, Oct. 10, 1864, age 41; at Newberne, NC. Sutler to 23rd NY Battery.
Standart, Dolly, wife of Oliver, formerly of Buffalo, Aug. 31, 1844, age 66; at East Wauwatosa, WI.
Standart, Helen Williams, Elma, wife of John W., July 8, 1874, age 23.
Standart, John W., suicide, Elma, July 7, 1874, age c. 35.
Standart, Olive M., ELma, NY, Aug. 18, 1879, age 77; wife of William.
Standart, Oliver, b. 1765, d. Aug. 2, 1841, bur. Alden, NY; Soldier of the Revolution.
Standart, Oliver, formerly of Buffalo, Aug. 31, 1854, age 62; at East Wauwatosa, WI.
Standart, Stephen W., Clarence, NY, June 17, 1832, age 42; late of Cayuga Creek.
Standish, George William, April 12, 1871, age 24; taken East.
Standish, Samuel, Oct. 9, 1851; en route from Ft. Leavenworth and bound for England.
Standish, Samuel T., Oct. 27, 1844, age 33.
Stanfield, Charles, formerly of Buffalo, Feb. 11, 1850, age 83; in Huntington, OH.
Stanfield (or Sterfield), Maria Tiffany, wife of James C., April 19, 1876, age 36.
Stanfield, Mrs. Polly, April 18, 1869, age 87.
Stanford, George, Sept. 15, 1873, age 78.
Stanford, Harry, accidental death, June 26, 1876, age 44 y, 7 m.
Stang, Adam and his wife Annie, accidental death, May 28, 1875; age he 80, she 81.
Stanley, Frederick G., March 16, 1840, age 38.
Stanley, Harriet Emily, wife of P. S., June 10, 1859, age 20 y, 10 m.
Stanley, Horace, Alden, NY, Aug. 11, 1857, age 67.
Stanley, J. M. (The Artist), formerly of Buffalo, April 10, 1872, age 58; d. in Detroit, MI.
Stanley, Miss Jane, niece of Mrs. Benjamin Bidwell, Aug. 11, 1849, age 28.
Stanley, Mrs. Julia A. F., Dec. 23, 1880, age 71.
Stanley, Mary B., formerly of Buffalo, wife of Eames of Troy, NY, dau. of John Burns of Buffalo, Oct. 28, 1867.
Stanley, Col. Rufus, Feb. 24, 1836, age 42.
Stanley, Sally, wife of Seth, Dec. 18, 1819, age 31.
Stanley, Seth, July 3, 1834, age 50.
Stanley, Mrs. Sophia, Alden, NY, Jan. 5, 1862, age 69.

Stansell, John, Black Rock, NY, Sept. 8, 1812, age 32.
Stanthorp, Thomas, lately from England, July 18, 1830, age 40.
Stanthorp, William, Aug. 30, 1852, age 30.
Stanton, John, Co. Almshouse, July 3, 1877, age 60.
Stanton, Joseph, Holland, April 11, 1868, age 79.
Stanton, Miss Mary Ann, niece of Capt. W. Cleves, Feb. 26, 1848, age 24.
Stapf, Charles, Dec. 27, 1880, age 27 y, 8 m, 15 d.
Starck, Charles, May 22, 1875, age 39.
Staring, Adaline G., wife of Capt. Sylvanus, Hamburgh, NY, Sept. 22, 1853.
Staring, Mary L., wife of John, July 18, 1868, age 51.
Stark, Mrs. Elizabeth, Sept. 14, 1872, age 66.
Stark, Elizabeth, May 10, 1878, age 20.
Stark, George, Holland, farmer, June 21, 1878, age 40.
Stark, Josephine A., Dec. 13, 1879, age 32.
Starkey, Sophia E., wife of Rev. T. A. of Washington, DC, Sept. 4, 1869; d. at residence
    of her son-in-law, P. S. Bemis.
Starkweather, Augustus, April 14, 1878, age 51; taken to Franklinville, NY.
Starkweather, Henry B., only son of the late Rodman, Aug. 3, 1870; d. at Cape Vincent.
Starkweather, Dr. Rodman, March 22, 1858, age 69.
Starr, Ephraim, Deputy Comptroller, State of NY, Aug. 17, 1828, age 50.
Starr, Ezra S., June 15, 1875, age 38.
Starr, Jane E., wife of Albert Jr., Nov. 5, 1840, age 23 y, 9 m.
Starr, Lydia Smith Burr, widow of Samuel, Sept. 30, 1865, in 80th year; taken to Greenwood.
Starring, Gilbert, Jan. 1, 1871, age 51.
Starritt, William, Pilot of *Stillman Witt*, Oct. 29, 1857, age 23.
Start, John, Feb. 15, 1880, age 77 y, 3 m, 7 d.
Staub, Theresse, March 27, 1872.
Stauber, Christopher, July 30, 1870, age c. 50; killed by jumping from 2d story window.
Stauch, Elizabeth, wife of Theobold, April 20, 1864, in 38th year.
Stearnes, Albert B., private US Army, formerly of Buffalo, March 4, 1875, age 23 y, 6 m,
    10 d. D. & bur. at Fort Niagara, Youngstown, NY.
Stearns, David, formerly of Pawlett, VT, May 23, 1854, age 78.
Stearns, Norman, formerly of Buffalo, July 22, 1872, age 49; d. at Nanuet, NY.
Stearns, Philena, wife of Samuel, Aug. 2, 1844, age 49.
Stearns, Samuel, June 1, 1857, age 65.
Stebbins, Alice Skinner, formerly of Buffalo, wife of A. H. of Boston, July 24, 1879. D.
    at Kenwood, IL.
Stebbins, Susan E., wife of C. B., formerly of Buffalo, March 9, 1854, age 37; at Adrian,
    MI.
Stedler, B. Robert, Oct. 7, 1879, age 20 y, 10 m, 7 d.
Stedwell, Gilbert, Brant, NY, Dec. 24, 1865, age 82.
Steedman, John, son of Andrew, March 4, 1867, age 32.
Steedman, Mary, wife of Andrew, Sept. 21, 1875, age 75 y, 6 m.
Steel, Miss Elenor W., late of Buffalo, July 15, 1852, age 24; in Milwaukee, WI.
Steele, Rev. Allen, formerly of Buffalo, Jan. 15, 1873, age 65th year; d. in Barre, Orleans
    Co., NY.
Steele, Austin L., Lancaster, NY, Oct. 8, 1844, age 49.
Steele, Mrs. Calista M., late of Buffalo, Jan. 3, 1857; in Fredonia, NY.
Steele, Capt. Danford, Clarence, NY, Dec. 1830, age 33.
Steele, Miss Elizabeth Lenora, formerly of Lancaster, NY, Aug. 4, 1850, age 21 y, 16 d; in
    Dover, IL.
Steele, Hannah, wife of Horace, Editor of *Buffalo Bulletin*, Dec. 23, 1832, age 39.
Steele, Lieut. Jeduthan Loomis, one of the proprietors of the Bulletin, Oct. 29, 1833, age
    24.
Steele, John, May 13, 1868, age 55.
Steele, Mrs. Oliver G., Aug. 1875.
Steele, Oliver G., Nov. 11, 1879, age 74.
Steele, Peter W., Aug. 6, 1870, age 50; d. in Brooklyn, bur. in Buffalo.
Steele, Sarah E., Aug. 17, 1875, age 63, wife of Oliver G.
Steele, Mrs. Sarah H., native of Boston, MA, Oct. 8, 1844, age 71.

Steele, Seth, May 19, 1837, age 72.
Steener, Leonard, Amherst, NY, May 20, 1850, age 91 y, 3 m, 8 d.
Steffan, Mary Frances, wife of Michael, April 7, 1880, age 66.
Steffan, Rosa Reinagle, wife of Anthony C., Dec. 27, 1879, age 29.
Steger, Frederick, July 12, 1879, age 58 y, 10 m, 25 d.
Stein, Caroline, wife of Charles B., April 14, 1867, age 59 y, 9 m.
Stein, Charles B., formerly of Buffalo, March 3, 1880, age 72 y, 5 m; d. at Geneseo, IL.
Steinberg, Pearl L., April 1866.
Steinborn, Kate, Sept. 4, 1879, age 20 y, 10 m.
Steinford, John, accidental death Nov. 25, 1877, age 50.
Steiniger, Florian, tailor, Aug. 9, 1874, age 51.
Steinner, John, accidental death Aug. 5, 1878.
Stellwagon, John, suicide (?), Jan. 30, 1876, age 49.
Stemler, ---, wife of Philip, July 8, 1879, age 27.
Stephens, Nelson, Rogersville, formerly of Buffalo, Jan. 11, 1838, age 21.
Stephenson, Jane, mother of T., Aug. 11, 1851.
Stephenson, Linai, wife of T., Aug. 14, 1851.
Stephenson, Peter, Jan. 1861.
Sterling, Ambrose S., formerly of Buffalo, July 1, 1880, age 69; bur. at Sharon, CT, July 3.
Sterling, John, Nov. 18, 1880; killed by the cars.
Sterling, Louisa S., wife of A. S., June 26, 1854.
Stern, Mary Ann, widow of Henry, Feb. 23, 1880, age 57 y, 5 m, 23 d.
Sternberg, Col. Chester W., formerly of Buffalo, Nov. 1874, age near 40; d. in Middletown Insane Asylum, bur. in Buffalo.
Sternberg, Ephraim, Dec. 9, 1863, age 60 y, 3 m, 10 d.
Sternberg, Joseph, b. Jan. 24, 1751, d. Feb. 11, 1836, bur. Cambria, NY; Soldier of the Revolution.
Sternberg, Pearl L., b. Jan. 24, 1809, d. April 14, 1866, age 57 y, 2 m, 21 d.
Sternberg, Sophia, widow of Pearl L., March 14, 1869, age 59.
Stetson, Mrs. Lydia, mother of Cyrus Athearn, of MA, Oct. 1, 1850, in 92nd year.
Stettenbenz, Coralie, wife of Anthony, Dec. 4, 1867, age 41 y, 4 m, 21 d.
Stetzel, Francis, found dead Dec. 9, 1876, age 81.
Steuben, Catharine A., wife of W. N., formerly of East Aurora, NY, dau. of Zane A. Hamilton, Nov. 28, 1860; at Visalia, CA.
Steuben, Jonathan, Steuben, Oneida Co., NY, Revolutionary Officer, Jan. 1, 1839, age 82. His name was formerly Arnold, but after the treachery of Benedict Arnold changed his name to Steuben at the request of Baron Steuben.
Steubenger, Caroline, Co. Almshouse, Jan. 18, 1876, age 21.
Stevens, Albert Gallatin, Dec. 13, 1872, age 54.
Stevens, Mrs. Ann, May 11, 1851, in 93rd year.
Stevens, Augustus C., late of Flint, MI, formerly of Buffalo, May 8, 1845, age 42; at the residence of his father-in-law, S. Sidney Breese, Sconondoe, NY.
Stevens, Charles, July 4, 1874, age 30.
Stevens, Charles L., April 2, 1873, age 34.
Stevens, E. J., June 29, 1870, age 64, taken to Albany.
Stevens, Edward, lawyer, July 29, 1868, age 35; d. at Fredonia.
Stevens, Elizabeth, Feb. 24, 1874, age 28.
Stevens, Hon. Frederck P., March 23, 1866, age 55; judge, mayor of Buffalo in 1856.
Stevens, Mrs. Hannah Hastings, mother of Hon. F. P. Stevens, June 28, 1858, age 85; taken to Lockport, NY.
Stevens, Henry, Jan. 12, 1880, age 54; Almshouse.
Stevens, Henry Franklin, Mill Grove, Oct. 26, 1877, age 63.
Stevens, James G., Oct. 22, 1873, age 38.
Stevens, James M., Aurora, NY, Jan. 4, 1830, age 38; in OH.
Stevens, John, late of Colden, NY, Aug. 16, 1845; at Dupage, IL.
Stevens, Juliana H., widow of Edward, formerly of Buffalo, April 7, 1878, age 44; d. in Philadelphia, bur. at Fredonia.
Stevens, Laura V., wife of Harrison B., Holland, July 2, 1868, age 49.
Stevens, Lewis L., Aug. 29, 1873, age 64.

Stevens, Merriam, wife of Moses K., Nov. 13, 1821, age 27.
Stevens, Peabody, Nov. 18, 1862; sudden death. Well known liquor dealer of this city d. suddenly at the General City Hospital last evening.
Stevens, Philip, East Hamburg, NY, March 25, 1880, age 44 y, 8 m.
Stevens, Major. Phineas, Black Rock, NY, Dec. 16, 1812, age 47; taken to Willink, NY.
Stevens, Rodney, only son of Mrs. John Hollister, late of Buffalo, Sept. 26, 1866, age 33; in Chicago.
Stevens, Mrs. Rosina, mother-in-law of George M. Huntley, West Falls, NY, drowned on Steamer *Atlantic*, Sept. 1852, age 63.
Stevens, Sally, wife of Henry B., Wales Center, NY, July 24, 1848, age 58.
Stevens, Sarah C., widow of Albert G., Oct. 2, 1875, age 42 y, 5 m, 28 d.
Stevens, Mrs. Tamson, mother of Milo, Feb. 27, 1867, age 67; taken to Sterling, Cayuga Co., NY.
Stevens, Walter L., formerly of Buffalo, Feb. 11, 1872, age 32; bur. in Buffalo.
Stevenson, Ann, Nov. 7, 1862, age 76; at residence of E. L. Stevenson.
Stevenson, Archibald, Nov. 18, 1874, age 49.
Stevenson, Edward, Oct. 26, 1834, age 67.
Stevenson, Eliza, wife of James J., Jan. 19, 1878, age 55 y, 2 m, 28 d.
Stevenson, George, Sept. 9, 1878, age 32 y, 7 d.
Stevenson, George P., May 17, 1864, age 52 y, 9 m, 4 d.
Stevenson, George P., only son of Edward L., May 23, 1878, age 33 y, 14 d.
Stevenson, Harriet, wife of John S., Aug. 19, 1879, age 65 y, 25 d.
Stevenson, Henry F., May 3, 1835, age 27.
Stevenson, James, Seneca Chief, many years resident of Buffalo Creek Reservation, Cattaraugus Reservation, Dec. 22, 1846, age 81.
Stevenson, Joel T., formerly of Buffalo, July 25, 1877, age 33; d. at Toledo, OH.
Stevenson, Mrs. Margaret, Dec. 7, 1864, age 66.
Stevenson, Ruth Ann, widow of George P., June 29, 1864, age 45.
Stever, Catharine, widow of Jacob, Eggertsville, Aug. 29, 1874, age 69.
Stever, Franklin, 21st Regt., U.S. Vol., Clarence, NY, April 19, 1862; at Alexandria Hospital.
Stevesson, Mrs. Ann, Sept. 16, 1823, age 55.
Steward, John F., only son of late Thomas, Feb. 1857, age 34; in Rock Island IL, bur. in Buffalo Feb. 6.
Steward, Meribah, widow of Thomas, Dec. 29, 1856, age 59.
Steward, Thomas, March 8, 1837, age 40.
Stewart, Andrew, July 24, 1873, age 64.
Stewart, Calvin M., late of Kingsbury, Washington Co., NY, March 1, 1839, age 21.
Stewart, Capt. Charles, LaSalle, Jan. 8, 1878, age 66.
Stewart, Hannah S., wife of Henry, March 28, 1863, age 52 y, 5 m, 2 d.
Stewart, Helen, April 9, 1878, age 67.
Stewart, Henry R., formerly of Buffalo, Oct. 15, 1878, age 33; d. in St. Cloud, MO.
Stewart, Capt. James, Feb. 2, 1870, age 74.
Stewart, Mrs. Jane, mother of J. W., Dec. 2, 1850, age 79.
Stewart, Jerry (colored), July 1873, age 22.
Stewart, John W., Feb. 18, 1867, age 69.
Stewart, Mary A., wife of T. H., formerly of Utica, NY, March 29, 1880.
Stewart, Miss Mary B., formerly of Buffalo, Dec. 29, 1850, age 24; Detroit, MI.
Stewart, Mr. R. W., Hamburgh (Water Valley), NY, Jan. 5, 1847, age 28.
Stewart, Thaddeus, Aug. 7, 1828, age 58.
Stickney, Orin, May 24, 1874.
Stiker, Jean Pierre, Jan. 18, 1878, age 92 y, 2 m.
Stiles, Charles R., Oct. 22, 1856, age 55.
Stiles, Capt. Daniel D., Aurora, Jan. 19, 1869, age 68.
Stiles, Rev. Laren, May 1863.
Still, Mr. J. S., Dec. 12, 1846, age 36.
Stillman, George, East Aurora, NY, Dec. 18, 1870, age 56.
Stillman, Hulda, wife of Horace, dau. of S. A. Stillman of Enfield, CT, June 21, 1844, age 25.
Stillson, James B., Aurora, Feb. 24, 1878, age 69.

Stillson, Jerome B., formerly of Buffalo, Dec. 26, 1880; d. in New York.
Stillwell, Cornelius, brother-in-law of E. Rose, formerly of Buffalo, Wales, NY, Feb. 24, 1849, age 41.
Stillwell, Horace G., East Hamburgh, Nov. 16, 1876, age 32 y, 9 m.
Stimers, Commander Alban C., US Navy, formerly of Buffalo, June 3, 1876, age 49; d. at West brighton, Staten Island, NY.
Stimpson, Eliza W., wife of William, June 7, 1873, age 51.
Stimson, Elizabeth, wife of William, June 17, 1846.
Stinson, Charles, Sept. 13, 1870, age 40 (or 30?) y, 7 m.
Stinson, Margaret, wife of Edward, May 6, 1872, age 40.
Stirling, George, late of Glasgow, Scotland, Dec. 24, 1855, age 61.
Stivers, Edward Milton, son of John G., Feb. 26, 1859, age 29 y, 3 m; at sea on barque *Roebuck*, from Rio Janeiro to NY.
Stock, Elizabeth, wife of Christopher, March 1876, age 24 y, 7 m.
Stock, Henry, Co. Almshouse, Feb. 19, 1877, age 33.
Stocking, George, Jan. 29, 1838, age 4; son of late Joseph.
Stocking, Deacon Joseph, Sept. 4, 1835, age 60.
Stocking, Julia Ann, wife of Thomas R., Nov. 5, 1859, age 45.
Stocking, Sarah B., widow of Deacon Joseph of Buffalo, formerly of Buffalo, Aug. 13, 1869, age 80 y, 10 m; d. at Batavia, bur. in Buffalo.
Stoddard, Charles, formerly of Akron, Dec. 1875, age 32; killed on railroad at Batavia, bur. in Buffalo.
Stoddard, Miss Helen, only child of Moses, formerly of Buffalo, July 3, 1859, age 24; Ann Arbor, MI.
Stoddard, Moses, Dec. 20, 1863, age 53.
Stoddard, Capt. Robert, Nov. 20, 1871, age 42; d. on Lake Michigan, bur. in Buffalo.
Stokes, William, Feb. 8, 1877, age 56.
Stone, Mrs., Eden, NY, Dec. 1812, age 70.
Stone, Miss Adaline, Aurora, NY, Aug. 26, 1842, age 23.
Stone, Mrs. Cornelia M., July 24, 1846, age 31.
Stone, Eli, father of Capt. W. P., May 8, 1853, age 73.
Stone, Francis H., Feb. 25, 1858, age 38.
Stone, Frederick A., July 27, 1875, age 22 y, 6 m.
Stone, Honeyman, Eden, NY, June, 1828, age 50.
Stone, Jesse, June 22, 1857, age 68.
Stone, John B., Master Builder, Oct. 2, 1836, age 51.
Stone, Kezia B., widow of Jesse, Feb. 22, 1858, age 66.
Stone, Sarah, wife of Eli, March 2, 1848, age 54.
Stone, Sophia, widow of John B., Nov. 19, 1843, age 52.
Stone, William, Alden, NY, June 17, 1853, age 39.
Stone, William, drowned Aug. 18, 1876, age 24.
Stone, Capt. William P., Feb. 20, 1853, age 37; in New York.
Stone, William P., Alden, NY, June 3, 1862, age 85.
Stone, William S., Aug. 25, 1879; burned to death.
Stone, William Y., oldest son of John B., Aug. 28, 1833, on his 20th birthday.
Stonebreaker, Mrs. Teresa, Alden, Sept. 11, 1872, age 50.
Stonehouse, Mrs. Isabella, Jan. 27, 1870, age 50.
Stooks, John H., June 7, 1846, age 36.
Stopinsky, Mrs. Augustus, May 16, 1876, age 22.
Storar, Robert, Black Rock, July 22, 1873, age 24.
Storck, Dr. Karl J. Sr., father of Dr. Edward of this City, Jan. 27, 1875, age 79.
Storck, Michael, April 24, 1871, age 26.
Storer, George L., late of NY City, Nov. 1, 1854.
Storm, Calista Ann, wife of George T., Marilla, NY, Aug. 22, 1858, age 26 y, 10 m, 23 d.
Storm, Harriet, wife of Anson, Marilla, NY, May 18, 1855, age 47 y, 10 m, 14 d.
Storm, Serviah, widow of James, Aurora, NY, Aug. 8, 1850, age 75.
Storrs, Gen. Lucius, Aug. 5, 1875, age 86.
Storrs, Susan Young, wife of Lucius, March 26, 1871, age 69.
Storum, Mary A., Oct. 22, 1877, age 63.
Story, Catherine, Dec. 17, 1877, age 60.

Story, Eliza J., wife of Patrick J., Jan. 26, 1879, age 34.
Story, Ellen C., West Concord, NY, June 12, 1866, age 22.
Story, John W., March 22, 1874, age 46 y, 6 m, 10 d.
Stoughton, Mrs. C., Feb. 13, 1868, age 81.
Stout, Algernon, youngest son of William, July 30, 1863, age 21; on gunboat, *Choctaw*.
Stout, Eleanor, wife of William, March 8, 1875, age 68.
Stout, Robert D., formerly of Buffalo, Aug. 12, 1858, age 30; in Dixon, IL.
Stover, George L., late of New York, Nov. 1, 1854.
Stover, Louisa, wife of Theodore, March 10, 1871, age 50.
Stow, George, May 15, 1859, age 75; at residence of William D. Fobes.
Stow, Horatio J., Lewiston, NY, formerly of Buffalo, Feb. 19, 1859 at Clifton Springs, NY.
Stow, James C., only son of George, formerly of Dunkirk, NY, Sept. 1, 1864, age 33.
Stow, Mary W., wife of Col. George, Jan. 5, 1843, age 48.
Stowell, Ralph P., Nov. 1, 1862, age 29; in the Hospital in Yorktown, VA.
Strachan, John, June 7, 1854, age 31.
Stradelick, Joseph, East Buffalo, NY, May 31, 1879, age 35; found drowned.
Straekel, John, accidental death, Aug. 25, 1870, age 64.
Straight, Chester L., Tonawanda, July 26, 1874, age 61 y, 8 m, 6 d.
Straight, Jane E., wife of C. L., April 28, 1860, age 41 y, 1 m, 10 d.
Stranahan, Mrs. Rhodes, Clarence, NY, Oct. 26, 1811.
Stranahan, Betsey, wife of Rhodes, Clarence, NY, March 19, 1821, age 29.
Stranahan, Mary Ann, dau. of Rhodes, Clarence, NY, April 8, 1841, age 21 y, 4 m, 21 d.
Strap, Catherine, co. almshouse, Feb. 27, 1878, age 58.
Strass, Emanuel J., Sept. 26, 1876, age 30 y, 6 m.
Strasser, Frederick, suicide, July 28, 1873, age 50.
Strasson, Henry, March 12, 1871.
Stratford, Alfred, Dec. 5, 1872, age 42.
Strathern, Andrew, Feb. 1875, age 29.
Stratton, Jonathan, Wales, NY, Aug. 3, 1860, age 54.
Straub, George, Feb. 1, 1880, age 85 y, 2 m, 6 d.
Strauss, Anna, wife of Peter, dau. of Jacob Lang, July 22, 1870, age 25 y, 1 d, 10 1/2 hours.
Strausser, Ferdinand, June 2, 1873, age 54; accidently killed on railroad.
Strawn, Mrs. Julia (Charles), formerly of Buffalo, April 4, 1879.
Streb, Mrs. Catharine, March 1878, age 53.
Strebel, Barbara, wife of David, Feb. 13, 1871, age 26 y, 2 m, 13 d.
Strebel, Jacob, April 19, 1876, age 30 y, 6 m.
Strebel, Kate, April 6, 1880, age 73 y, 9 m, 12 d.
Streeter, Alexander, son of Only and Sarah, March 30, 1878, age 29 y, 11 m.
Streeter, Eliza Victoria, wife of Byron L. of Chicago, dau. of William C. Trimlett of Buffalo, June 13, 1862, age 19 y, 11 m; d. in Chicago, IL.
Streeter, Henry, Lancaster, NY, Nov. 14, 1861, age 65.
Streeter, Henry James, Oct. 29, 1863.
Streeter, Jane, wife of Henry, Black Rock, NY, Feb. 28, 1848, age 43; d. near Cold Springs, NY.
Strehle, Joseph, July 18, 1873, age 75.
Streich, John G., July 19, 1879, age 48 y, 7 m, 6 d.
Streicher, John, Feb. 10, 1868, age 47.
Streit, John, formerly of Canton of Berne, Switzerland, Jan. 14, 1832, age 41.
Stressinger, Christian, Jan. 28, 1878, age 48.
Striber, Sarah, wife of Edward, July 19, 1868, age 58.
Strickland, Noah, b. 1760, d. 1829, bur. Beach Ridge (Niagara Co.; Soldier of the Revolution.
Strickler, Jacob, Clarence, NY, March 1836, age 35.
Stridiron, James S., formerly of Buffalo, May 5, 1876, age 52; d. in Detroit, MI.
Stroebel, Thomas, Sept. 10, 1870, age 59.
Stroh, Charles, Dec. 21, 1880, age 53.
Strohauer, Peter, Nov. 8, 1870, age 32 y, 8 m, 6 d.
Strong, Bushnell, June 16, 1849, age 47.

Strong, Carrie, Jan. 27, 1880, age 40; almshouse (insane).
Strong, Eliza Ann, wife of Dr. P. H., June 22, 1869.
Strong, Emory G., Feb. 7, 1872, age 36.
Strong, Isabel P., formerly of Buffalo, March 9, 1875; d. in NY City, bur. in Buffalo.
Strong, Lt. Col. James Clark, May 1862.
Strong, John, Brant, Feb. 4, 1879, age 101 y, 2 m, 11 d.
Strong, John, Aug. 15, 1880, age 45.
Strong, John C., lawyer, July 5, 1879, age over 60.
Strong, Lydia M., wife of J. M., Dec. 18, 1867, age 47.
Strong, Mrs. Marinda, Feb. 16, 1864, age 52; taken to Geneva, NY.
Strong, Nancy, widow of Capt. Strong, Seneca Chief, Cattaraugus Reservation, July 23, 1860,
    age 68; at residence of her son, N. T. Strong.
Strong, Nathaniel T., Brant, NY, Jan. 4, 1872, age 62.
Strong, Samuel, May 19, 1873, age 53.
Strow, Mrs. Betsy, Oct. 12, 1878, age 85.
Strowbridge, William B., Dec. 9, 1836, age 23.
Struby, Louis H., July 23, 1880, age 27 y, 6 m, 10 d.
Strothers, Mary, wife of Thomas, Sept. 10, 1852, age 25; at Lundy's Lane, Canada.
Struthers, William J. (or F.), March 21, 1880, age 44; colored.
Stuart, Charles, late of the Niagara Hotel, March 4, 1849, age 29; taken to Coburg, Canada
    West.
Stuart, Charles Jr., Aug. 16, 1871, age 20 y, 6 m.
Stuart, Margaret, widow of L. of Albany, NY, Feb. 5, 1870.
Stubbs, Abner, April 16, 1856, age 67.
Stubchen, Christian, laborer, Dec. 2, 1880, age 50.
Studdart, Rosa, Co. Almshouse, Aug. 29, 1879, age 30.
Stults, John H., Nov. 23, 1871, age 46.
Stumm, Margaret, wife of William, April 26, 1876, age 27 y, 28 d.
Stuperyski, Mrs. Anna, Oct. 25, 1879.
Sturges, Mary, wife of Edward, dau. of Commodore William Mervine, U.S. Navy, March 4, 1859;
    taken to Utica, NY.
Stuski (or Tuski), John, Nov. 27, 1855, age 43.
Stutor, George, accidental death, Clarence Hollow, May 26, 1877, age c. 23.
Stutz, C. J., Dec. 14, 1880, age 28 y, 6 m, 1 d.
Stutz, Lorenz, Nov. 1, 1877, age 52 y, 6 m.
Stutzman, Frederick, March 2, 1872, age 53.
Stutzman, Henry, sunstroke, Aug. 15, 1878, age 36 y, 3 m, 14 d.
Sudderick, John, Feb. 8, 1878, age 51.
Suess, George S., April 23, 1873, age 64.
Sullivan, Agnes, Co. Almshouse, Nov. 24, 1877, age 34.
Sullivan, Capt. Clement, Black Rock, NY, 14th Reg. U.S. Infantry, Dec. 14, 1812.
Sullivan, Daniel, Feb. 22, 1880, age 35.
Sullivan, Dennis, May 23, 1873, age 28.
Sullivan, Dennis, July 30, 1880, age 54.
Sullivan, James, May 5, 1870, age 75.
Sullivan, Jerry, July 27, 1879, age 37; drowned.
Sullivan, John, Oct. 29, 1877, age 31.
Sullivan, Julia, wife of Eugene, April 1, 1874, age 29 y, 2 m.
Sullivan, Lawrence Jr., Dec. 14, 1880, age 31.
Sullivan, Matilda Rooney, wife of D., April 16, 1872, age 34.
Sullivan, Matthias, July 5, 1873, age 33.
Sullivan, Owen, Sept. 24, 1871, age 70.
Sullivan, Patrick, Nov. 13, 1880, age 60.
Sullivan, Timothy, June 20, 1856, age 20.
Sullivan, Timothy, Aug. 14, 1879, age 37 y, 5 m; d. at Utica.
Sullivan, William, Co. Almshouse, Nov. 2, 1877, age 22.
Sullivan, William, July 29, 1878, age 43.
Sully, Charlotte, widow of Robert, Dec. 15, 1869, age 61.
Sully, James, formerly of Buffalo, July 3, 1862, Wakefield, Canada West.
Sully, Robert Sr., March 8, 1869, age 80.

Summer, Miss Esther, dau. of Daniel, Hamburgh, NY, Aug. 13, 1837, age 23.
Summers, Mrs. Frances, May 31, 1868, age 51.
Summers, George W., Nov. 4, 1880, age 37 y, 1 m, 13 d.
Sumner, Anne, wife of Joshua, formerly of Hamburgh, Sept. 9, 1875, age 71; d. at Lancaster, Grant Co., WI.
Sumner, Mrs. Caroline, formerly of East Hamburgh, Sept. 5, 1871, aged 89 y, 2 m, 13 d; d. in Rockford, IL.
Sumner, Daniel, late of Hamburgh, NY, Oct. 1845; at Koshkonong, WI Territory.
Sumner, Mrs. Deliliah, West Falls, NY, May 19, 1861, in 93rd year.
Sumner, Sarah A., March 4, 1875, age 52; taken to Rochester.
Sunderlin, Mrs. D. W., Feb. 10, 1880, age 85.
Supple, Ann, wife of James, Dec. 12, 1877, age 70 y, 5 m.
Supple, James, May 31, 1879, age 50.
Supple, Mrs. Margaret C., March 30, 1879, age 52 y, 3 m, 5 d.
Surrey, Mrs. Susana, Sept. 18, 1873, age 90.
Sutcliff, John, Aug. 30, 1873, age 48.
Sutcliffe, Elizabeth, wife of William, Feb. 2, 1842, age 28.
Sutcliffe, William, Aug. 12, 1863, age 31 y, 5 m.
Sutfin, Derick, Clarence, NY, Sept. 18, 1831, in 67th year.
Sutherland, Brush, formerly of Buffalo, April 23, 1880, age 69; d. at Mitchellville, IA.
Sutherland, Donald, April 17, 1878, age 29 y, 2 m, 14 d.
Sutherland, Ellen, June 1862, bur. June 16th.
Sutherland, Esther, April 1, 1876, age 41.
Sutherland, Frank W., Sept. 24, 1871, age 21.
Sutherland, John, June 24, 1876, age 60; taken to Owen Sound, Ontario.
Sutherland, Mrs. O. M., Oct. 7, 1876, age 65; taken to Kinderhook.
Sutherland, Mrs. Rachel, mother of A. Sutherland & Mrs. C. H. DeForest, June 23, 1870, age 85.
Sutherland, Sarah A., wife of Anson, April 27, 1862, age 37.
Sutor, Augustus H., Jan. 12, 1871, age 70.
Sutor, Laban, died of accidental injuries, July 25, 1879, age 43.
Sutton, Amelia, wife of William A., Aug. 24, 1852, age 35.
Sutton, Francis, May 1871, age 82 y, 1 m.
Sutton, Margaret, widow of Peter, Aug. 7, 1875, age 43 y, 1 m, 24 d.
Sutton, Peter, April 29, 1874, age 42 y, 11 m, 25 d.
Sutton, Samuel, Sept. 10, 1853, age 20.
Sutton, William A., May 17, 1863, age 58.
Sutton, Mr. Would E., Sept. 8, 1858, age 50th year.
Suydam, Ferdinand, March 23, 1851, age 65; late of New York.
Svegilgus, Bridget, wife of Joseph, July 25, 1864, age 39.
Swain, Mrs. Eleanor, mother-in-law of Palmer Cleveland, Feb. 7, 1855.
Swain, Jacob, E. Aurora, NY, b. March 4, 1757, d. May 23, 1845; Revolutionary Soldier.
Swain, John, April 23, 1874, age 71.
Swain, Mary, widow of Daniel of Boston, NY, Sept. 28, 1859, age 82; taken to Boston, Erie Co., NY.
Swain, Adin, Feb. 10, 1874, age 77 y, 9 m, 7 d; d. in Brooklyn, bur. in Buffalo.
Swan, Adin A., Oct. 27, 1874, age 22 y, 9 m, 20 d.
Swan, Mrs. Mary, Feb. 11, 1877, age 82; taken to Albion.
Swan, Mary A., wife of Russell, Feb. 3, 1879.
Swan, Nancy M., wife of Charles B., dau. of Mrs. Jane K. Harrington, Dec. 31, 1858, aged 22nd year.
Swan, Oscar M., Aug. 10, 1853, age 23 y, 4 m, 24 d.
Swan, William H., Jan. 9, 1874, age 45.
Swander, Aggie C., wife of Alexander F., Jan. 26, 1872, age 22 y, 9 m.
Swannie, Thomas, July 14, 1879, age 53; d. at Chicago. Native of Orkney, Scotland.
Swans (or Swantz/Schwantz), Joseph, Aug. 3, 1873, age c. 20.
Swanton, Mrs. Kate C., June 27, 1880, age 39.
Swanton, William, April 1, 1865, age 63.
Swarty (or Swartz), Michael, Dec. 15, 1872, age 50.
Swartz, Albert R., fell in battle, Aug. 30, 1862, age 20.

Swartz, DeWitt C., son of Samuel, Feb. 20, 1875, age 34 y, 8 m, 5 d.
Swartz, Henry A., accidentally killed, Jan. 19, 1874, age 45.
Swartz, Joseph, March 25, 1874, age 81.
Swartz, Mary Ann, March 5, 1877, age 33.
Swartz, Mary Jane Thornton, wife of Henry A., Nov. 16, 1865, age 28 y, 2 m, 3 d.
Swartz, Samuel C., formerly of Buffalo, brother of Henry A., Dec. 1865 in New York.
Swartz, William J., June 28, 1868, age 33.
Sweeney, Mrs. Edward, Nov. 4, 1876, age 82.
Sweeney, Edward, April 2, 1879, age 80.
Sweeney, George T., Nov. 21, 1877, age 20 y, 5 m.
Sweeney, James, Tonawanda, NY, Jan. 13, 1850, age 59.
Sweeney, John, July 24, 1825, age 80.
Sweeney, Col. John, Tonawanda, NY, Oct. 1854; bur. Oct. 15th.
Sweeney, John, Tonawanda, NY, May 19, 1856, age 29.
Sweeney, Mrs. Margaret, Nov. 24, 1870, age 63.
Sweeney, Mrs. Mary, Oct. 9, 1859, age 58th year.
Sweeney, Miles, Sept. 3, 1861, age 76.
Sweeney, Moica, wife of James, Tonawanda, NY, Sept. 15, 1836, age 38.
Sweeney, Patrick, April 17, 1880, age 69.
Sweeney, Mary Robinson, wife of William, Tonawanda, Feb. 26, 1875, age 62.
Sweet, Abigal, wife of Chester, East Hamburgh, NY, Dec. 15, 1865, age 52 y, 2 m, 24 d.
Sweet, Allan S., formerly of Buffalo, May 31, 1873; d. at Detroit, taken to Rochester.
Sweet, Chester, East Hamburgh, NY, Nov. 11, 1865, age 44 y, 4 m, 17 d.
Sweet, Cornelia C., wife of Charles A., June 11, 1870, age 32.
Sweet, Ellen M., wife of James, Dec. 1, 1855, age 25.
Sweet, Dr. G. J., of Key West, FL, Surgeon US Army, Aug. 12, 1868, age 35.
Sweet, George Horace, July 7, 1875, age 65 y, 6 m; taken to Hume, NY.
Sweet, G. W., March 21, 1861, age 36; taken to Colden, NY.
Sweet, Horace, son of the late George H., formerly of Buffalo, Feb. 8, 1878, age 40; d. at Attica, NY.
Sweet, Jacob, Aug. 10, 1871, age 60.
Sweet, James, Willink, NY, Feb. 1813, age 25.
Sweet, Mrs. Maria, Sept. 4, 1880, age 83.
Sweet, Richard, Colden, father of L. and J. B., Nov. 8, 1873, age 80.
Sweet, Silas, formerly of Buffalo, July 13, 1870; d. at Rockton, CA.
Sweetapple, Corp. John E., Colden, NY, Dec. 21, 1862 in Hospital, Fortress Monroe, VA, age 27. Co. D, 116th NY Vols.
Sweetland, Emma Jane, wife of George Jr., dau. of Judge Aaron Salisbury, Evans, NY, March 29, 1857, age 31.
Swegles, Hiram, Dec. 3, 1869, age 46.
Swegles, Margaret, wife of John, July 13, 1879, age 28.
Swegles, Mrs. Mary, April 27, 1862, age 45 y, 27 d.
Swegles, W. M., June 16, 1862, age 45.
Swegles, William, June 22, 1878, age 84 y, 1 m, 10 d.
Sweitzer, Mrs. Elizabeth, Williamsville, NY, Nov. 9, 1862, age 83.
Sweitzer, Lucinda Ann, Williamsville, NY, wife of George, Oct. 8, 1866, age 37th year.
Swift, Abbey C., Silver Creek, Chautauqua Co., NY, Nov. 23, 1880; wife of C.C.
Swift, Alice M., wife of Charles, Akron, Feb. 27, 1873, age 26 y, 1 m, 6 d.
Swift, Alida, dau. of Orson, East Hamburgh, April 18, 1873, age 20.
Swift, Cushing, East Hamburgh, Dec. 21, 1872, age 87.
Swift, Ephraim, Aug. 28, 1858; late of Norwich, CT.
Swift, Harrison W., Jan. 10, 1874, age 50.
Swift, Mary E., dau. of Orson, East Hamburgh, May 15, 1872, age 22.
Swift, Nathaniel, East Hamburgh, NY, Sept. 24, 1852, age 64 y, 6 m.
Swift, Nathaniel James, East Hamburgh, NY, July 14, 1863 in Baton Rouge, LA, age 25 y, 6 m. 116th Regt., NY Vols., son of Orson.
Swift, Roxa, wife of Simon P., March 5, 1876, age 37; taken to Cuba, Allegany Co., NY.
Sykes, Almeda, wife of Reuben A., Aug. 7, 1868, age 68 y, 4 m.
Sykes, Lyman R., Oct. 2, 1858.
Sylven, James, Feb. 28, 1829, age 32.

Sylvester, Delilah, wife of William, May 22, 1856, age 58.
Sylvester, William, March 5, 1859, age 58.
Syms, Amos W., April 5, 1866, age 39.

Taber, Clarissa Mothe, wife of Martin, Nov. 2, 1844, age 39.
Taber, Helen A. Bramble, wife of James P., Dec. 20, 1875, age 30; taken to Honeoye, NY.
Taber, Helim, Wales, NY, Oct. 27, 1863, age 68.
Taber, Dr. Hiram, Marilla, May 8, 1873, age 46.
Taber, Martin, formerly of Aurora, NY, June 23, 1846, age 45.
Taber, Mrs. Mary D., June 26, 1855, age 76.
Taber, Mary R. D., Feb. 17, 1856, age 41.
Taber, Mason, Springville, Aug. 11, 1872, age 37 y, 9 m, 26 d.
Taber, Sarah, relict of Jesse, Wales Center, June 10, 1868, age 76; d. at Marilla.
Taber, Dr. Wells, Wales Center, NY, Nov. 24, 1861; formerly of Bergan, NY.
Taber, William, Collins, NY, May 13, 1864, age 75.
Tabor, Betsy E., widow of Silas, Akron, Oct. 5, 1878, age 70.
Taff, Deborah C., wife of M. Taff, May 2, 1853 in Darien, Genesee Co., NY; bur. in Buffalo.
Taff, Manuel, June 2, 1869, age 58 y, 7 m, 23 d.
Taff, Mattie, wife of Manuel C., Nov. 28, 1864, age 24th year.
Taff, Samuel S., brother of R. Taff of Buffalo, formerly of Buffalo, June 8, 1872, age 62; d. at London, Ontario.
Taft, Mrs. Mercy P., formerly of Buffalo, Jan. 19, 1878, age 84; d. at Hamburgh, NY.
Taggart, Frances, wife of Moses, May 14, 1832, age 25th year.
Taggart, Hannah C., wife of James H., formerly of Buffalo, June 28, 1874, age 34; d. at LeRoy, NY.
Taggart, James, railroad accident, Nov. 17, 1877.
Taggatz, August, accidental death, Dec. 8, 1878, age 38.
Taintor, Catharine E., wife of Charles, Dec. 18, 1855, age 52.
Taintor, Charles, formerly of CT, March 1827, age 54.
Taintor, Chrles, March 14, 1864, age 58.
Taintor, Edward C., son of late Charles, formerly of Buffalo, May 16, 1878, age 37; d. in Shanghai, China.
Taintor, John S., March 28, 1864, age 48.
Taintor, Mrs. Sally, mother of Charles Taintor, May 9, 1838, age 59.
Taintor, Sarah M., March 29, 1871, age 26; d. in NY City, bur. Buffalo.
Talbot, George, Black Rock, NY, March 26, 1846, age 39.
Talcott, Mrs. M. D., Nov. 13, 1871, age 70.
Talcott, Sarah Williams, wife of William H., formerly of Buffalo, July 26, 1876; dau. of the late Hiram P. Thayer. Died in Brooklyn, NY; bur. at Pittsfield, MA.
Tallcott, Asa G., Sept. 10, 1869, age 73.
Tallman, Charles H., Sept. 9, 1874, age 32.
Tallman, Mrs. Margaret, Sept. 17, 1876, age 49.
Tallman, Polly, wife of John S., Jan. 6, 1863.
Tallman, William H., drowned Dec. 2, 1876, age 43.
Tangloff, George, Cheektowaga, May 13, 1872, age 63 y, 7 m.
Tanner, Amos S., Wales, NY, April 22, 1849, age 54; d. in Buffalo.
Tanner, Elizabeth, wife of Henry, March 12, 1856, age 38 y, 8 m, 24 d.
Tanner, Frank W., Sept. 14, 1865, age 47.
Tanner, James, Clarence, NY, Jan. 1813, age 40.
Tanner, John, Holland, Nov. 25, 1872, age 43.
Tanner, Josephine, wife of Harvey M., May 17, 1868, age 48 y, 10 m.
Tanner, Miss Maria, sister of Henry Tanner of Buffalo, Nov. 3, 1849 in Philadelphia; bur. in Buffalo.
Tanner, Mary, Dec. 9, 1878, age 47 y, 4 m.
Tanner, May Orr, wife of Hiram C., Protection, March 21, 1877, age 39.
Tanner, Orvelle A., wife of Alonzo, July 13, 1852 in Alabama, Genesee Co., NY, age 31.
Tanner, Sally, widow of Amos S., Wales, May 22, 1875, age 78.
Tanner, Wiatt, Clarence, NY, Nov. 6, 1841, age 52 y, 9 m, 27 d.
Tapel, William, Feb. 19, 1874, age 63.
Tapenden, Catharine, May 1, 1875, age 63.

Tapenden, Henry, June 25, 1875, age 36.
Tappenden, Mrs. Louisa V., June 3, 1866 in Aurora, NY; age 27 y, 2 m, 5 d; bur. in Buffalo.
Tappenden, Richard, Nov. 4, 1871, age 20 y, 9 m, 13 d.
Tappert, William, son of Martin and Rosa, April 25, 1874, age 24 y, 7.
Tate, Ella, wife of Charles H., March 8, 1880, age 25.
Tate, Maggie, adopted dau. of James & Susan Wright, May 22, 1858, age 19 y, 3 m, 3 d.
Tate, William, Nov. 4, 1863, age 43d year.
Tatu, Ellen Maria, wife of Sylvester J., April 11, 1879, age 24.
Taturn, Thomas T., Nov. 27, 1846, age 40; barber. Formerly of Nashville, TN.
Taunt, Emory, March 1, 1869, age 65.
Taunt, Martha E., widow of Emory, Sept. 19, 1870, age 62.
Taunt, W. E. S., formerly of Buffalo, April 16, 1877, age 24.
Taylor, Mrs. A. B., Eden Center, NY, April 2, 1880, widow of Rev. Ephraim; age 59 y, 11 m, 22 d.
Taylor, Anna Louise, wife of T. F., Nov. 13, 1872, age 23.
Taylor, Mrs. Betsey, Feb. 24, 1848, age 48.
Taylor, Carrie M., Collins, NY, Nov. 12, 1880, age 28.
Taylor, Miss Celia Emma, dau. of J. J., Jan. 7, 1869, age 20.
Taylor, Charles, formerly of Buffalo, Aug. 8, 1863 in Monroe, MI; age 51.
Taylor, Chalres D., Dec. 26, 1880, age 76.
Taylor, Miss Clara E., Oct. 1864, bur. Oct. 22nd.
Taylor, David, Tonawanda, NY, Aug. 6, 1864, age 90 y, 5 m.
Taylor, Dennis, March 3, 1876.
Taylor, Edward, formerly of Sinclearville, Chautauqua Co., NY, Nov. 29, 1863, age 75.
Taylor, Eliza A., wife of John R., Jan. 21, 1872, age 50.
Taylor, Elizabeth A., widow of Aaron, Dec. 4, 1874, age 79; taken to Alden.
Taylor, Elizabeth Cherry, wife of John, Tonawanda, June 28, 1874, age 49.
Taylor, Emma L., wife of Charles J., Oct. 7, 1872, age 22 y, 5 m, 16 d.
Taylor, Rev. Ephraim, Eden Center, NY, March 28, 1880, age 75 y, 1 m, 18 d.
Taylor, Corp. George, Brant, NY, Feb. 26, 1865, age 21; 116th Regt., NY State Volunteers.
Taylor, Helen M., wife of Cyrus H., Oct. 18, 1877.
Taylor, Jacob, Collins, NY, May 3, 1840, age 84.
Taylor, James, switch tender, killed by cars Aug. 2, 1879.
Taylor, Jennie, suicide, Aug. 24, 1877, age 26.
Taylor, John, Dec. 24, 1843, age 40.
Taylor, John, Co. Almshouse, Jan. 28, 1879, age 38.
Taylor, Mrs. Louisa, June 6, 1867, age 44.
Taylor, Mrs. Lydia Castle, Shirley, NY, Oct. 8, 1866, age 83.
Taylor, Mrs. Margaret, April 11, 1879, age 41.
Taylor, Margarett, June 30, 1852, age 85.
Taylor, Martha Ann, wife of Augustus C., Dec. 25, 1879.
Taylor, Martin, April 3, 1880, age 48 y, 6 m.
Taylor, Mary, wife of John, June 4, 1841, age 36th year.
Taylor, Mary A., wife of A. W., Lancaster, NY, Aug. 2, 1847, age 23.
Taylor, Mrs. Mary A., wife of Robert, June 4, 1879, age 57.
Taylor, Mary Jane, wife of Robert S., Aug. 11, 1872, age 25 y, 4 m.
Taylor, Mary L., wife of Joseph, North Collins, NY, Jan. 17, 1860, age 33 y, 4 m, 1 d.
Taylor, Nancy, wife of David, Tonawanda, NY, Nov. 15, 1860, age 80.
Taylor, Nancy, Buffalo Plains, NY, formerly of Saratoga Springs, NY, April 3, 1867, age 67th year.
Taylor, Noah, Jan. 8, 1835, age 78.
Taylor, Mrs. Robert, formerly of Buffalo, March 25, 1850 in Paisley, Scotland.
Taylor, Ruth, wife of S., Wales, NY, Aug. 30, 1848, age 63.
Taylor, Miss Sarah, dau. of John Taylor, formerly of Saratoga Springs, NY, Feb. 4, 1861, age 69 y, 1 m.
Taylor, Stephen, Oct. 30, 1855, age 77 y, 10 m.
Taylor, Sylvester D., Jan. 24, 1865, Co. F, 24th NY Cavalry.
Taylor, Col. W. F. P., March 4, 1848, age c. 40. [Also found in the Green Bay, WI Terr. *Advocate*.]
Taylor, William, East Hamburgh, NY, Feb. 12, 1863, age 58.

Taylor, William, Aug. 20, 1871, age 45.
Taylor, William F. P., June 15, 1838; firm of Pratt & Taylor. Drowned at the wreck of the Steamer *Pulaski*.
Tayntor, Agnes L., wife of Oscar J., March 27, 1870, age 24.
Tayntor, Sylvina, wife of Adelbert, Jan. 11, 1872.
Teall, Dr. Samuel T., May 17, 1876, age 74 y, 7 m, 24 d.
Tearson (or Feason), Frederick, drowned, Tonawanda, June 18, 1872, age 26.
Teasdill, Dr. John T., April 21, 1873, age c. 86.
Teats, Jesse, Aurora, NY, May 25, 1832, age 45.
Teehan, Cornelius, May 20, 1878, age 70.
Teehan, Lizzie, March 25, 1879, age 28.
Tefft, Caroline M., wife of Pardon, Eden Valley, NY, Aug. 23, 1857.
Tefft, Catharine, wife of J.S., Williamsville, NY, June 21, 1837, age 33.
Tefft, Celinda, Hamburgh, NY, wife of Deacon Royal Tefft, Aug.12, 1858, age 71.
Tefft, Jairus F., Williamsville, June 7, 1872, age 68.
Tefft, James, Williamsville, Dec. 14, 1868, age 67.
Tefft, Royal, Evans, NY, Jan. 23, 1864, age 7 4 y, 23 d.
Tefft, Miss Sophia Barrett, Black Rock, NY, Aug. 21, 1848, age 31; d. at Forestville, NY. Dau. of R. Tefft.
Templeton, Williams, Holland, frozen to death Jan. 7, 1873, age 70.
Tennant, Hattie B. Tinker, wife of Alvin, Aug. 2, 1870; taken to Meadville, PA.
Tenvilliger, ---, canal boatman, June 12, 1880. D. at Albany, NY; had been in Buffalo Almshouse.
Terry, Miss, Black Rock, NY, Aug. 1825, age 40.
Terry, Abel, Aug. 7, 1831, age 50.
Terry, Caroline C., wife of Arthur, Nov. 29, 1863, age 42.
Terry, Charlotte, wife of Joseph, formerly of Buffalo, Feb. 9, 1877; d. at Caledonia, bur. in Buffalo.
Terry, Mrs. Elizabeth S., Dec. 22, 1868, age 51 y, 4 m.
Terry, Gershon, Lancaster, NY, formerly of Coxsackie, NY, Oct. 31, 1840, age 72.
Terry, Jennie A., formerly of Buffalo, accidental death April 19, 1876, age 31; d. at Darien Centre.
Terry, John S., son of Thomas, April 22, 1854 on Steamer *Bunker Hill* near Memphis, TN, age 27th year.
Terry, Mrs. Lucian B., Feb. 10, 1845, age 25.
Terry, Sarah Ann, wife of Thomas, Sept. 22, 1854, age 52.
Terry, Thomas, Aug. 21, 1874, age 79 y, 5 m.
Tester, William, Nov. 12, 1871, age 75.
Tew, Lizzie H., Aug. 15, 1865, age 22.
Tewksbury, Mrs. Sarah Ann, May 12, 1867, age 47.
Thatcher, George, Alden, Nov. 18, 1877, age 75.
Thatcher, John, son of Luther R. of Newark, NJ, Feb. 24, 1848, age 23.
Thayer, Adelia E., wife of Nathan W., dau. of the late Capt. L. Weller, June 17, 1870, age 42.
Thayer, Alfred Augustus, only son of N. W., April 16, 1873, age 23; d. in San Francisco, CA.
Thayer, Hon. Andrew, formerly of Buffalo, April 28, 1873, age 55; d. at Corvallas, Benton Co., OR.
Thayer, E. Selden, formerly of Buffalo, Oct. 18, 1876; d. in Brooklyn, NY; bur. in Buffalo.
Thayer, Edward S., Dec. 16, 1844, age 23; taken to Palmyra, NY.
Thayer, Edwin, May 4, 1877, age 52.
Thayer, George H., Aug. 3, 1872, age 52.
Thayer, Hiram P., Oct. 1, 1866, age 60; taken to Palmyra, NY.
Thayer, Jane, wife of Atherton, Jan. 1, 1833, age 20.
Thayer, Joel, Jan. 28, 1853, age 61st year.
Thayer, Julia A., wife of James C., Hamburgh, Sept. 5, 1873, age 44.
Thayer, Levi Jr., Feb. 11, 1850, age 25; taken to Palmyra, NY.
Thayer, Miss Mary, dau. of Joel, March 8, 1854 in Palmyra, NY, age 30th year; bur. in Buffalo.
Thayer, Milleythiah, wife of Jacob, Collins, NY, Aug. 27, 1849, age 81st year.

Thayer, Nancy F., widow of Joel, Feb. 27, 1866, age 76.
Thayer, Oscar S., formerly of Buffalo, June 12, 1880, age 26; d. at Chicago.
Thayer, Sally, wife of John, May 5, 1832, age 34.
Thayer, Sarah E., widow of Hiram P., formerly of Buffalo, Aug. 17, 1873; d. at Geneva, bur. at Palmyra.
Thayer, Selden E., Oct. 1876.
Thayer, Susan, wife of Levi, July 19, 1850, age 48th year.
Thayer, William A. (or John A.), Sept. 3, 1869, age 56.
Thayer, William Austin, Feb. 17, 1867, age 75th year.
Thede, William, suicide, Boston Corners, June 26, 1876, age 56.
Therot, Anselm, Nov. 25, 1880, age 68.
Theurer, Christian G., April 15, 1876, age 44.
Thiebold, William H., conductor on Erie Railroad, killed by falling between the cars, May 19, 1880, age 40.
Thiel, Elizabeth, widow of Jacob, Feb. 27, 1876, age 77.
Thiele, Hugo, Oct. 13, 1870, age 25; suicide by poison.
Thielen, John, April 28, 1875, age 55.
Thieme, Oscar, suicide, formerly of Buffalo, Aug. 7, 1878; d. at Rochester.
Thomas, Ada F. Nimbs, wife of John H., Jan. 20, 1873, age 18 y, 9 m, 13 d.
Thomas, Alanson S., Jan. 19, 1871, age 45.
Thomas, Alfred A., only surviving son of C.F.S. Thomas, June 16, 1861 in St. Johns, New Brunswick, age 19 y, 8 m; bur. in Buffalo.
Thomas, Augustus, June 1862 in White House Landing, VA, age 17; Co. L, 100th Regt.
Thomas, C.F.S., Springfield, MO, formerly of Buffalo, Sept. 19, 1876, age 69th year. D. in Buffalo.
Thomas, Lt. Calvin Frederick, Feb. 18, 1860, age 26 y, 5 m; US Navy. Eldest son of C. F. S. Thomas.
Thomas, Charles L., formerly of Buffalo, Feb. 11, 1879, age 53 y, 4 m, 5 d.
Thomas, Miss Cordelia, dau. of Rev. Robert E. Thomas, Sardinia, NY, May 27, 1866, age 21.
Thomas, Cornelia L., April 22, 1875, age 47.
Thomas, Cyrus A., brother of Mrs. J. Hawkins, April 15, 1875, age 36; d. in Washington, DC, bur. Buffalo.
Thomas, Dinah Ann, Spring Brook, NY, formerly of Buffalo, Oct. 29, 1862, age 30 y, 5 d.
Thomas, Dorcas, March 25, 1880, age 62. Found dead in bed. [March 26 obit states "arsenic," March 27th "suicide."
Thomas, Ebenezer, Saloon keeper, May 1, 1879, age 66 (or 67).
Thomas, Rev. Eleazer, D.D., formerly of Buffalo, April 11, 1873; massacred by the Modac Indians.
Thomas, Eliza, March 6, 1877, age 62.
Thomas, Elizabeth, widow of Dyre, July 26, 1844, age 68th year.
Thomas, Elizabeth C., widow of W. D., Feb. 16, 1876.
Thomas, Elizabeth P., wife of George H., Feb. 5, 1862, age 34.
Thomas, Ernst, Prussian, suicide, boiler maker, Oct. 12, 1871.
Thomas, Eunice, wife of W. G., July 3, 1853.
Thomas, Harriet F. (T.), wife of Horace, March 9, 1879, age 64.
Thomas, Henry, Spring Brook, NY, Nov. 3, 1862, age 21.
Thomas, Henry, veteran of the War of 1812, Oct. 28, 1875, age 85.
Thomas, Isabella, wife of David, Sept. 12, 1863, age 34.
Thomas, James, Sept. 4, 1873, age 31.
Thomas, John H., formerly of Buffalo, Oct. 11, 1859 in Fulton City, IL, age 27 y, 5 m.
Thomas, Joseph, Jan. 26, 1870, age 65.
Thomas, Mrs. Julia Ann, April 10, 1854, age 94, colored; mother of D. P. Brown.
Thomas, Lavinia, formerly of Buffalo, May 12, 1875, age 24; suicide. [Obituary of May 20 says occurred near Watkins; that of May 21, 22 says "there is an error in the statement."]
Thomas, Lucy, wife of Capt. William, Dec. 29, 1876.
Thomas, Mrs. Margaret, wife of Horace, Sept. 12, 1870, age 78.
Thomas, Mrs. Maria C., June 3, 1841, age 60, mother of C.F.S. Thomas.
Thomas, Martha, wife of Frederick, Black Rock, Nov. 15, 1868, age 23 y, 10 m, 24 d.
Thomas, Mrs. Mary, April 9, 1870, age 68.

Thomas, Widow Meribee, Williamsville, NY, Jan. 1816, age 53.
Thomas, Rebecca Ophelia, wife of Ebenezer, July 9, 1850, age 25.
Thomas, Rosanna, Sept. 9, 1871, age 68; taken to Aurora.
Thomas, William, Aug. 8, 1872, age 30.
Thomas, William A., son of Horace, Oct. 19, 1870, age 30.
Thomas, William D., Jan. 21, 1875, age 46; taken to Springbrook.
Thompson, Abijah Hull, June 18, 1876, age 51.
Thompson, Abraham, Aug. 5, 1841, age 48; d. at Port Burwell, Upper Canaca.
Thompson, Albertus, formerly of Buffalo, Jan. 16, 1871, age 42; d. in Cincinnati, OH.
Thompson, Alfred D., Oct. 6, 1878, age 33; d. in Hernando, MS.
Thompson, Amanda Josephine, wife of Edwin C., Nov. 1, 1854, age 29th year.
Thompson, Amasa, Brandt, NY, formerly of Otsego Co., June 17, 1867, age 88.
Thompson, Angus, Sept. 28, 1880, age 24 y, 2 m.
Thompson, Artemas, formerly of Amherst, NY, 1838 in Mobile, AL.
Thompson, Benoni, Nov. 7, 1858, age 47.
Thompson, Caroline, dau. of Isaac W., Sept. 20, 1853.
Thompson, Catharine, wife of Capt. Sheldon, May 8, 1832, age 39th year.
Thompson, Charles Henry, Feb. 2, 1865, age 25; 2nd NY Cavalry.
Thompson, D.?, Nov. 15, 1880, age 55; Almshouse (from Germany).
Thompson, David, Wales, NY, son of Samuel, May 7, 1839 in Concord, NY, age 30.
Thompson, Dougal, Dec. 11, 1880, age 65; Almshouse.
Thompson, Enos W., Aug. 16, 1876, age 26 y, 8 m.
Thompson, George, Dec. 6, 1879, age 62; colored, dropped dead.
Thompson, Prof. George W., Feb. 1872.
Thompson, Hannah, Black Rock, NY, wife of William, Sept. 2, 1851, age 75th year.
Thompson, Harry, Oct. 27, 1873, age 81.
Thompson, Harry, July 8, 1876, age 48.
Thompson, Henry, Sept. 5, 1876, age 62.
Thompson, Isabella, mother of Mrs. P. Barton, Nov. 5, 1845, age 65.
Thompson, J. Ellen Blossom, wife of Hiram, Dec. 30, 1867; d. at St. Louis.
Thompson, Jacob S., June 16, 1872, age 36; d. at Hornellsville, bur. in Buffalo.
Thompson, James, March 6, 1863, age 54.
Thompson, Jane, wife of Capt. H. D., May 11, 1874, age 55 y, 11 m.
Thompson, Mrs. Jane B., Dec. 22, 1834, age 30.
Thompson, John, Clarence, NY, Dec. 4, 1845, age 22 y, 8 m.
Thompson, John, formerly of Buffalo, July 21, 1875, age c. 25; d. in Prairie City, Jasper Co., IA.
Thompson, John, East Aurora, April 25, 1876, age 85.
Thompson, John, Dec. 8, 1879, age 36; drowned.
Thompson, John, New York City, formerly of Buffalo, Jan. 17, 1880; d. at St. Paul, MN.
Thompson, Kate, wife of N. E., late of Cayuga, Canada West, June 13, 1867.
Thompson, Letitia M., wife of Gilbert, Aug. 5, 1878, age 29.
Thompson, Louisa, wife of Orrin, Aurora, NY, June 9, 1849 in Toronto, Canada West, age 22.
Thompson, Lucy Manning Allen, wife of T. E., formerly of Buffalo, Noc. 3, 1859 in Houston, TX.
Thompson, Margaret, wife of John, Jan. 21, 1866, age 27 y, 3 d.
Thompson, Maria, wife of Henry, July 10, 1857, age 20.
Thompson, Martin, April 15, 1874, age 74 y, 7 m, 13 d.
Thompson, Nancy, wife of A., formerly widow of Warren Dendall, Aug. 2, 1852, age 52.
Thompson, Nicholas, Swedish seaman, June 5, 1845 in the "Seaman's Home," age 42.
Thompson, Mrs. Orilla S., Aurora, NY, Feb. 2, 1863, age 27.
Thompson, Osca F., June 23, 1873, age 55.
Thompson, Pamela, wife of Martin, June 26, 1872, age 75.
Thompson, Mrs. Phebe, Auora, NY, June 18, 1841, age 77.
Thompson, Reuben H., Aug. 18, 1872, age 69.
Thompson, Richard, colored man, Dec. 18, 1826, age 22.
Thompson, Capt. Samuel, Irishman, Nov. 1825, age 60.
Thompson, Samuel F., formerly of Buffalo, sailor, Oct. 12, 1871.
Thompson, Sarah, widow of Andrew, April 11, 1842, age 46.
Thompson, Sarah, wife of James, Oct. 31, 1860.

Thompson, Sarah Virginia, wife of Oscar S., Jan. 18, 1861, age 23.
Thompson, Sheldon, March 13, 1851, age 66th year.
Thompson, Susan Ada, wife of William, Feb. 12, 1863, age 22.
Thompson, Susan Halsey, wife of R. H., mother of Mrs. W. H. Pease and Mrs. Platt of this City, April 2, 1871, age 61.
Thompson, Theodore, April 16, 1880, age 25.
Thompson, Thomas Murray, formerly of Buffalo, native of Stranraer, Wigtonshire, Scotland, Oct. 18, 1870, age 50; d. in Chicago.
Thompson, Walter R., Jan. 4, 1866, age 38.
Thompson, William, Jan. 3, 1865, age 68.
Thompson, Capt. William, formerly of Derby, CT, eldest brother of the late Sheldon Thompson, Harry Thompson, Mrs. Mary Kimberly and Mrs. Betsey Hull of Buffalo. Feb. 17, 1868, age 89.
Thompson, William, b. 1757, d. 1841, bur. Beach Ridge (Niagara Co.); Soldier of the Revolution.
Thompson, William E., June 25, 1874, age 52 y, 7 m.
Thompson, William S., May 1872, age 20 y, 3 m.
Thomson, Prof. George W., Feb. 5, 1872, age 60; taken East.
Thomson, Gertrude, Sept. 13, 1878, age 40.
Thomson, Jennis E., wife of James E., May 20, 1873, age 47 y, 6 m, 25 d.
Thomson, Dr. Lyman, formerly of Grand Island, Jan. 12, 1879, age 73; d. at Dayton, OH.
Thomson, Mary, Aurora, NY, dau. of J., Dec. 23, 1843, age 24.
Thomson, Mary Ann, wife of E. H., formerly of Buffalo, d. 1840 in Flint, MI, age 27.
Thomson, William Alexander, formerly of Buffalo, Oct. 1, 1878, age 62; d. at Glencairn, near Queenstown, Ontario.
Thorn, Charles, shoemaker, Dec. 8, 1877.
Thorn, Frederick, Jan. 27, 1879, age 83.
Thorn, Jacob, son of Jacob, Dec. 28, 1876, age 22 y, 25 d.
Thorn, Wilhelmina, wife of Jacob, March 2, 1875, age 43 y, 3 m.
Thornton, Julia A., wife of James, Oct. 9, 1872, age 59.
Thornton, Mary A., wife of Capt. Samuel, Aug. 13, 1871, age 29.
Thornton, Mary B., wife of Thomas, Dec. 7, 1877, age 67.
Thornton, Stephen, Oct. 7, 1864, age 43d year.
Thornton, Thomas F., Aug. 28, 1865, age 47 y, 2 m, 7 d.
Thorp, Abiel, March 27, 1836, age 39.
Thorp, Capt. H. W., Lake Captain, Dec. 25, 1863, age 44.
Thorp, Harriet Eliza, dau. of N. B., Jan. 22, 1849, age 21.
Thorp, Lucy E., wofe of J. O. Jr., formerly of Buffalo, Dec. 12, 1875, age 33 y, 7 m, 15 d; d. in Brooklyn, bur. in Buffalo.
Thorp, Martin, May 25, 1868, age 57.
Thorp, Philana, wife of Col. N. B., July 14, 1845, age 39.
Thrasher, George, b. 1763, d. 1844, bur. Somerset; Soldier of the Revolution.
Throm, Mary Magdelain, wife of John Martin, Dec. 4, 1879, age 57.
Thules, Mr., Black Rock, NY, June 18, 1831; drowned. Left a wife and six children in Buffalo.
Thum, John, late of Sackett's Harbor, Jan. 14, 1837, age 20.
Thurber, George W., Concord, Jan. 6, 1870, age 65; d. at Boston Corners.
Thurber, Hannah, Glenwood, NY, Nov. 11, 1859, age 46.
Thurber, Thomas, East Hamburgh, NY, Jan. 17 (?), 1880, age 94 y, 4 m, 2 d.
Thurman, Washington, May 31, 1871, age 55.
Thurstin, Silas, May 1832, age 25.
Thurston, Miss Cyrenia V., dau. of Thomas, Aurora, NY, Jan. 26, 1839, age 23 y, 5 m.
Thurston, Daniel, formerly of Aurora, NY, May 21, 1850 in Leona, Jackson Co., MI, age 98th year.
Thurston, Electa, Aurora, NY, wife of Thomas, Nov. 26, 1833, age 41st year.
Thyng, George P., Nov. 30, 1876, age 37.
Thyng, J. S., June 5, 1872, age 78; taken to Jamestown.
Tibbets, William Nelson, May 8, 1864, age 48th year; taken to Lisbon, St. Lawrence Co., NY.
Tibbetts, Charles H., May 19, 1879, age 23; d. in Rochester, bur. in Buffalo.
Tibbetts (or Tibbits), Nelson, Oct. 6, 1875, age 24 y, 3 m.

Tibbits, Charles S., March 14, 1875, age 46.
Tibbits, William C., May 5, 1852; lawyer.
Tice, Mrs. Ann, Feb. 25, 1843, age 55th year.
Tice, Peter, Nov. 9, 1867, age 38 y, 8 m, 2 d.
Tichenor, Calvin, formerly of Buffalo, March 29, 1880; d. at South Lansing, NY.
Tierman, Martin, May 3, 1877, age 53.
Tiers, Edwin M., Dec. 19, 1880, age 45; bur. from Homeopathic Hospital.
Tiffany, Albert W., Clarence, NY, Feb. 20, 1843, age 30th year.
Taffany, Augustus J., April 26, 1858 in Albany, NY, age 47; bur. in Buffalo.
Tiffany, Edward A., formerly of Buffalo, Aug. 9, 1866 in Cincinnati, OH, age 31.
Tiffany, Emily Eliza, wife of A. J., March 31, 1849, age 38.
Tiffany, Miss Julia A., dau. of the late Augustus A., Dec. 29, 1873.
Tiffany, Lois J., wife of L.L., Lancaster, July 17, 1876, age 51 y, 7 m, 18 d.
Tiffany, Lucius F., president of the Pratt Bank, Feb. 11, 1852, age 42.
Tiffany, Maria Louisa, wife of L. F., May 24, 1844, age 34.
Tifft, Clarinda J., wife of A. W., Oct. 8, 1859, age 48.
Tifft, Cynthia S., wife of W. S., Feb. 5, 1873.
Tifft, Elias A., only son of J. S., Williamsville, NY, May 23, 1854, age 24th year.
Tifft, George Henry, Jan. 1865.
Tifft, Mrs. George W., Aug. 21, 1870, age 64.
Tifft, John, Pine Grove, MI, Oct. 20, 1868, age 73; taken to MI.
Tifft, Joseph N., April 22, 1873, age 47.
Tilden, Abby Huntington, Feb. 23, 1865, age 64th year; wife of Thomas B., dau. of Jared Hyde of Franklin, CT.
Tilden, Cyrus, Black Rock Dam, NY, Sept. 19, 1850, age 47.
Tilden, Jasial R. L., son of Gen. Joseph of Lebanon, CT, Sept. 6, 1849, age 21; taken to Lebanon, CT.
Tilden, Thomas Brown, April 2, 1869, age 68.
Tillinghast, Anna E., wife of W. J., Sept. 12, 1875, age 34; taken to Lockport.
Tillinghast, Dyre, March 18, 1862, age 64; attorney, city clerk and superior court clerk.
Tillinghast, H. D., May 30, 1862, age 32; Quarter Master 40th Regt.
Tillinghast, Henry, Aug. 1841.
Tillinghast, Henry D., May 1862.
Tillinghast, Maria, widow of Dyre T., Jan. 8, 1880, age 79.
Tillinghast, Sarah Annie, wife of J. W., Sept. 21, 1866, age 25.
Tillow, Hannah, widow of Joseph, Elma, Aug. 27, 1878, age 82 y, 6 m.
Tilton, Josiah S., May 27, 1867, age 38; taken to Cooperstown, NY.
Tilton, Capt. Luther, Lake vessel master, Brant, NY, March 29, 1863, age 59.
Timmerman, Benjamin, formerly of Buffalo, Feb. 11, 1878; d. at Grinnell, IA.
Timmerman, Henry, eldest son of Benjamin, Oct. 28, 1865, age 22.
Timms, Mrs. Sarah, Sept. 20, 1879, age 68.
Timon, Rt. Rev. John, first Bishop of Buffalo, April 16, 1867, age 72.
Tims, Hannah, wife of William, March 2, 1850, age 34.
Tiphaine, Victor, July 10, 1873, age 74.
Tirrell, Elizabeth, wife of Edward, Sept. 3, 1846.
Tischerdorf, Gustave A., Dec. 17, 1867, age 41.
Tisdale, Mrs. Maria, sister of Josiah B. Bailey, formerly of Buffalo, Feb. 4, 1877; brought to Buffalo.
Titta, The Very Rev. James, formerly of Buffalo, March 11, 1877, age 45; d. in NY City, bur. in Allegany, Cattaraugus Co.
Titus, Mrs. Aurilly, widow of Zebulon, Hamburgh, Dec. 10, 1870, age 91.
Titus, Nathaniel, East Hamburg, NY, born in Buffalo, Aug. 26, 1880, age 78.
Titus, Orrin, East Hamburgh, NY, Dec. 8, 1867, age 25 y, 5 m, 17 d.
Titus, Orrin B., March 19, 1865, age 49.
Titus, Rose M., East Hamburgh, Sept. 4, 1871, age 21 y, 4 m.
Titus, Sara A., widow of Capt. T. J., Nov. 30, 1877, age 62.
Tobias, Rosetta, mother of William Tobias, July 17, 1863, age 67.
Tobin, Charles, accidental death, Nov. 25, 1875, age 25.
Tod, James, only son of Alexander and Jenet C., Sept. 5, 1852, age 70 m.
Todd, Mrs. Robert, Oct. 6, 1874; d. & bur. in Chicago. Wife of Capt. Robert Todd.

Todd, Susan Barnard, wife of H. C., formerly of Williamsville, Oct. 2, 1878, age 36; d. at Kankakee, IL.
Toher (Margaret) Bridget Moran, wife of Thomas, Feb. 29, 1879, age 28.
Toles, Benjamin, June 2, 1880, age 77.
Toles, Mrs. Hannah, mother of Harry & Sheldon Thompson, Black Rock, NY, May 4, 1851, age 91.
Toles, Julia A., wife of B., Aug. 21, 1873, age 50.
Toles, Mary Louisa, wife of Benjamin, Jan. 19, 1846, age 33.
Toles, Nathan, Cold Springs, NY, Sept. 1815, age 36.
Tolfree, Hattie F., wife of J. Herbert, Dec. 30, 1880, age 30 y, 10 m, 7 d.
Tolfree, Jane E., wife of James H., May 1873, age 51; d. at Danville, NY, bur. Buffalo.
Tolles, George H., June 23, 1879, age 52.
Tolsma, Ellen, Black Rock, March 14, 1872, age 26.
Tombertie, Philip, Alden, July 31, 1873, age 28.
Tomlinson, Mrs. Anna S., formerly of Buffalo, wife of Oliver, Nov. 20, 1873, age 67; d. at Fairport, Monroe Co., NY, bur. in Buffalo.
Tomlinson, Mrs. Hannah Griffin, Dec. 4, 1878, age 91.
Tomlinson, Oliver M., Cheektowaga, NY, Sept. 30, 1867, age 73.
Tompkins, Letitia, wife of John, Jan. 18, 1872, age 39.
Tompkins, Patty, wife of Robert, Hamburgh, NY, Oct. 2, 1846, age 40.
Tompkins, Robert, East Hamburgh, NY, Dec. 4, 1863, age 60.
Toms, Rebecca, wife of Joseph P., Jan. 16, 1876, age 54 y, 7 m, 12 d.
Tonius, Mrs. Maria Magdalena, June 2, 1873, age 55.
Tooner, William D., Oct. 21, 1871, age 73.
Topping, Mary E., wife of M. H., formerly of Buffalo, Jan. 28, 1872; d. in NY City.
Torpot, William T., son of Timothy, April 15, 1867, age 24.
Torrance, Harriet H. S., wife of H.B., March 22, 1847, age 23.
Torrance, Hosea B., firm of Hibbard & Torrance, March 20, 1849 in Springfield, OH.
Torrance, Jared S., formerly of Buffalo, lawyer, May 2, 1872, age 56.
Torrance, Mary Elizabeth, June 23, 1880, age 38.
Torrance, Sarah Ann, wife of H. B., Dec. 4, 1844, age 26.
Torrey, A. Wray, Concord, NY, Nov. 11, 1865, age 32.
Torrey, Capt. Asa, Revolutionary officer, Boston, NY, Jan. 1, 1839, age 80.
Torrey, Cyrena Humphrey, dau. of U. Torrey, Aurora, NY, May 24, 1859, age 23.
Torrey, Elbridge G., Aurora, Jan. 19, 1875, age 33.
Torrey, George, son of Capt. Asa, formerly of Lebanon, CT, Boston, NY, Jan. 26, 1830, age 24.
Torrey, Merritt P., Jan. 5, 1878.
Torrey, Sanford, Aurora, NY, son of Urial, March 31, 1864 in St. Paul, MN, age 30.
Torrey, Col. Urial, Aurora, Soldier of the War of 1812, Sept. 10, 1868, age 75.
Tospot, Mary, Dec. 29, 1875, age 69.
Tospot, Timothy, March 22, 1868, age 61 y, 28 d.
Tottman, Joshua (Adj.) (Canadian), fell during the War of 1812, Jan. 1814.
Touger, Mary, wife of Thomas T., July 6, 1871, age 42.
Touhey, Catherine, Dec. 24, 1878, age 73.
Tourney, Elizabeth, March 8, 1878, age 76.
Tourot, Susanne, wife of Frederick, Oct. 17, 1880, age 65.
Towle, Ira S., late of Buffalo, Feb. 18, 1857 in Monmouth, ME, age 29.
Towne, Elijah, May 19, 1873, age 75.
Townsend, Judge Charles, Sept. 14, 1847, age 61.
Townsend, Charles, Sept. 1, 1877, age 47; d. at Haslach, Paden.
Townsend, Charlotte M., wife of Richard, Dec. 13, 1865.
Townsend, Elizabeth, wife of Alexander C., Nov. 15, 1857.
Townsend, Eunice, wife of Jacob, Aug. 2, 1848, age 67.
Townsend, George, Color Sgt., 116th Regt., Nov. 30, 1864 in Hospital in Philadelphia from wounds received at battle of Cedar Creek, Sept. 19th. Age 37.
Townsend, George C., formerly of Buffalo, Jan. 30, 1852, age 30; d. in Columbus, OH.
Townsend, Harriet M., wife of K. W., June 28, 1859, age 27 y, 4 m.
Townsend, Henry C., Jan. 26, 1871; d. in San Francisco, CA, bur. in Buffalo.

Townsend, Jacob, May 7, 1850, age 82d year; formerly a merchant in New Haven, CT. Father-in-law of James C. Evans. Bur. at Lewiston, NY.
Townsend, Jane C., wife of Charles, Nov. 3, 1841, age 40.
Townsend, John F., formerly of Buffalo, July 31, 1865 in Westfield, Chautauqua Co., NY; formerly Secretary of Buffalo Savings Bank.
Townsend, Julia R. Porter, wife of David T., Sept. 18, 1854, age 47th year.
Townsend, Lucius A., Color Sgt., 116th Regt., Nov. 20, 1864 in Winchester Hospital of wounds received at battle of Winchester, Sept. 19, age 42.
Townsend, Mary E., wife of Peter B., April 24, 1850, age 25th year; taken to Duchess Co., NY.
Townsend, Mrs. Olive, Springville, NY, June 4, 1862, age 92.
Townsend, Mrs. Patty, formerly of Concord, in this county, March 17, 1846, age 51.
Townsend, Rebecca Parkman, Dec. 5, 1879, age 79.
Townsend, Robert, March 7, 1878, age 49.
Townsend, Robert G., Black Rock, NY, former Inspector of Customs, July 23, 1849, age 34.
Townsend, Samuel, formerly of Boston, MA, June 24, 1838, age 58.
Townsend, Sarah, eldest dau. of A. C. Townsend, March 5, 1860
Townsend, Sarah, wife of John, July 4, 1865, age 61 y, 1 m.
Townsend, Sophronia, wife of A. C. Townsend, Aug. 4, 1845.
Toy, Catherine, wife of Ernest, dau. of Jacob F. Haller, Dec. 9, 1870, age 27 y, 10 m.
Tracy, Albert Haller, Sept. 19, 1859, age 66.
Tracy, Albert Haller, Jan. 23, 1874, age 40.
Tracy, Mrs. Ann W., Aug. 6, 1863, age 78th year.
Tracy, Esther, formerly of Buffalo, Oct. 23, 1859 in Sinclairville, age 22d year.
Tracy, Harriet F., widow of Albert H., March 16, 1876, age 75.
Tracy, Harvey W., May 6, 1854, age 70.
Tracy, Mrs. John, Dec. 1, 1877, age 50.
Tracy, Kester, Jan. 26, 1880, of Ripley, Chatauqua Co., age 81.
Tracy, Mary Ann, wife of Sanford A., March 3, 1876, age 31.
Tracy, Hon. Phineas L., Dec. 22, 1876, Batavia, NY, age 89; lawyer, judge, congressman.
Trant, Frank Earle, Jan. 1, 1878, age 23.
Trask, Mrs. Jane, Newstead, July 7, 1869, age 57; sister of Mrs. B. Toles of Buffalo.
Trautman, Rosina, Nov. 8, 1875, age 26.
Trautman, William, June 17, 1875, age 75.
Travandusskie (or Levandesski), John, March 5, 1874, age 50.
Traynor, Maria, wife of James, Feb. 1878, age 44.
Treanor, Ann, wife of John, Eden, NY, Aug. 11, 1854, age 41.
Treat, Caroline K., eldest dau. of Henry H. Treat of Buffalo, Feb. 2, 1843, in Providence, RI, age 20.
Treat, John, Concord, NY, Jan. 10, 1864, age 68.
Treat, THomas, b. 1758, d. 1832, bur. Griffins Mills, Erie Co.; Soldier of the Revolution.
Treat, William, MD, Aug. 19, 1861, age 48; b. in Portsmouth, NH.
Tregilgus, Bridge, wife of Joseph, July 25, 1864, age 39.
Tremain, Jay J., Aug. 8, 1868, age 42; taken to Vienna, Oneida Co.
Trenner, Sarah, Aug. 3, 1873, age 88 y, 3 m.
Trent, Thomas, Aurora, NY, Revolutionary soldier, Oct. 10, 1832, age 74.
Trerise, Rev. W. H., Aug. 2, 1873, age 30.
Trescott, Ann, widow of Capt. George (Royal Navy), Dec. 10, 1879.
Trevallee, Amos, July 2, 1878, age 56.
Trevett, Serepta, wife of Lewis, Concord, NY, Feb. 16, 1867, age 74 y, 9 m, 23 d.
Trible, Barbara, wife of J. M., June 17, 1876, age 54.
Trier, Christian, Oct. 8, 1868, age 43.
Trier, Louisa, June 24, 1874, age 74.
Trimlet, Ann Penninnah, wife of William C., Jan. 6, 1851, age 28 y, 9 m.
Trimlett, William C., Dec. 17, 1871, age 56.
Trimmer, Phoebe, Erie Co. Almshouse, April 26, 1876, age 32.
Trinkel, Adam, Almshouse, May 16, 1880, age 53.
Tripp, George, Jan. 6, 1878, age 30 y, 10 m.
Tripp, Joseph P., May 21, 1861, age 53.
Tripp, Mary M., wife of Augustus F., June 15, 1866, age 40 y, 5 m.

Tripp, Noah, North Collins, NY, Oct. 30, 1861, age 72 y, 6 m, 1 d.
Tripp, Pelty, May 1819.
Tripp, Samuel, June 1869, age 57; d. at Jamestown, bur. in Buffalo the 18th.
Trisket, John, killed at the battle of Black Rock Dec. 30, 1813.
Trivette, A. C., formerly of East Hamburgh, July 1872, age 37.
Trotter, James, Dec. 21, 1848, age 22; formerly resident of London, Canada West.
Trowbridge, Ann, wife of E. B., Sept. 16, 1859, age 58.
Trowbridge, Capt. Benjamin, son of Dr. Josiah, Dec. 17, 1857 in NY.
Trowbridge, Benjamin H., Feb. 28, 1852, age 34.
Trowbridge, Daniel, Newstead, NY, Feb. 4, 1850, age 57.
Trowbridge, Capt. Henry W., May 1862.
Trowbridge, James M., funeral Nov. 24, 1846, son of Dr. Trowbridge. Lost last fall from Schooner *Texas*. Brought to this city.
Trowbridge, Josiah, MD, Sept. 18, 1862, age 79th year.
Trowbridge, Lewis B., June 9, 1868, age 50.
Trowbridge, Margaret, widow of Dr. Josiah, Oct. 26, 1863, age 66.
Trowbridge, Sarah, May 9, 1872.
Trowbridge, William, formerly of Buffalo, son of Dr. Josiah, 1862 in Memphis TN, age 44.
Truman, Thomas, Aug. 3, 1865, age 56.
Trumer, Sarah, Aug. 3, 1873, age 88 y, 3 m.
Truscott, George, RN, July 2, 1851.
Tryon, Miss Eliza P., Feb. 16, 1851, age 32nd year.
Tryon, John H., Oct. 13, 1875, age 42 y, 10 m, 27 d.
Tryon, Julia C., East Hamburgh, NY, wife of Isaac C., May 2, 1862, age 35; bur. in Buffalo.
Tryon, Louisa Reynolds, dau. of M. H., April 8, 1877, age 27.
Tryon, Ogden Edwards, March 14, 1873, age 31.
Tryon, Samuel A., son of Amos S. of Lewiston, NY, Sept. 14, 1859, age 32; taken to Lewiston.
Tubbs, Stephen, Colden, NY, July 26, 1831, age 83rd year; Revolutionary soldier, present at the capture of Burgoyne.
Tubbs, William H., March 3, 1878, age 23 y, 9 m, 8 d.
Tubesing, Charles R., Dec. 25, 1868, age 24 y, 4 m, 1 d.
Tubesing, Henry C., May 12, 1874, age 25 y, 5 m, 5 d.
Tucker, Mrs. Ann C., Nov. 12, 1876, age 74.
Tucker, Adeline, wife of William, Jan. 10, 1848, age 33.
Tucker, Mrs. Anna, mother of David, Brant, March 20, 1871, age 91.
Tucker, Annie S., wife of David, Feb. 20, 1878, age 27 y, 10 m, 18 d.
Tucker, Carrie, wife of William, March 20, 1874, age 33; taken to Fitchburg, MA.
Tucker, Chauncey, formerly of Buffalo, April 25, 1874, age 69; d. at LaSalle, NY, bur. Buffalo.
Tucker, Edwin W., North Collins, NY, Nov. 6, 1867, age 28th year.
Tucker, Elvira, wife of William, Colden, May 25, 1874, age 52.
Tucker, Florella C. Risley, widow of Chauncey, formerly of Buffalo, June 4, 1874, age 62; d. at LaSalle, NY, bur. in Buffalo.
Tucker, Hepsibah, wife of Samuel, Collins, NY, April 17, 1839, age 59.
Tucker, Jeannette L., wife of Rev. Levi D.D., formerly of Buffalo, Boston, NY, Oct. 21, 1851.
Tucker, John, formerly of firm of Sage & Tucker, formerly of Buffalo, June 12, 1874, age 37; d. at Chicago, IL.
Tucker, John K., Nov. 10, 1878, age 52.
Tucker, John N. T., formerly of Buffalo, once local editor of the *Daily Republic* of Buffalo, June 29, 1863 in Toledo, OH, age 53.
Tucker, Levi (Rev.), Aug. 1853.
Tucker, Lorenzo D., Oct. 11, 1869, 45 y, 6 d or 42 y, 6 d.
Tucker, Mrs. Mary, May 9, 1880, age 81 y, 3 m, 8 d.
Tucker, Mary M., Aug. 30, 1874, age 63.
Tucker, Moses, Collins, NY, Sept. 16, 1830, age 50.
Tucker, Phoebe T., Brant, NY, wife of Nathaniel, Jan. 6, 1880, age 68.
Tucker, Samuel, Evans, NY, April 12, 1855, age 36.
Tucker, Samuel, North Collins, NY, April 6, 1858, age 79 y, 9 m, 6 d.
Tucker, Samuel G., late of Madison, NY, father of Dezelie, Feb. 18, 1869, age 85.

Tucker, Mrs. Sarah, Lodi, Erie Co., NY, May 11, 1838, age 48.
Tucker, Sarah E., Sept. 27, 1875, age 45; wife of Dezell.
Tucker, Sarah P., wife of S. L., June 2, 1875, age 71.
Tucker, Sarah S., wife of David, April 2, 1852, age 30; taken to Collins, NY.
Tucker, Mrs. Tamor, Evans, NY, May 15, 1844, age 98.
Tucker, William Channing, formerly of Buffalo, Nov. 4, 1855 in Galena, IL, age 21.
Tucker, William F., Sept. 18, 1865, age 55.
Tuggey, Amelia, March 27, 1879, age 43.
Tuggey, William Thomas, blacksmith, Dec. 7, 1880, age 47.
Tully, Charles, suicide, May 25, 1878, age 63.
Tumer, Frederick J., May 18, 1880, age 41 y, 1 m, 13 d.
Tummelty, Margaret, wife of John, March 24, 1874, age 21 y, 7 d.
Tunison, Tunis C., March 24, 1863 in Lyons Farm, NJ, age 27.
Tunison, Tunis C., June 23, 1873, age 54.
Tunkey, Eva E., wife of William, Jan. 3, 1878, age 33 y, 4 m.
Tunnecliffe, Ephraim, Nov. 13, 1841, age 41.
Tunnecliffe, Thomas, March 24, 1825, age 37.
Tuohy (or Tuohey), Rev. John, Jan. 24, 1875, age 65.
Tupper, Col. Elihu, formerly of Canandaigua, NY, Aug. 13, 1832, age 60; d. of cholera.
Tupper, James, White's Corners, NY, July 1858, age 21.
Tupper, Percie, widow of Samuel, Nov. 2, 1828, age 64.
Tupper, Samuel, Dec. 30, 1817, age 52.
Tupper, Sarah W., wife of George W., Evans, NY, July 12, 1844, age 42.
Tupper, Virgil, formerly of Buffalo, Sept. 25, 1859 in Corning, NY, age 38th year.
Turcotte, Capt. Israel, Capt of the barque *Flying Mist*, son of Collis Turcotte of Green Bay, WI, Feb. 7, 1870, age 30; taken to Green Bay.
Turnbull, Isabella, mother of Mrs. John Dowd, Jan. 1, 1867, age 74 y, 8 m.
Turnbull, Mary, wife of Mark, Evans, July 12, 1874, age 56.
Turner, Euphemia Campbell, wife of Adam, Nov. 8, 1877, age 58.
Turner, Dr. Fitzhue W., Nov. 30, 1841 at Poinsett Barracks, age 19. Hospital Steward at Ft. Niagara, son of Dr. William Turner of Buffalo.
Turner, Fran, April 1, 1877, age 62.
Turner, Frank W., formerly of Buffalo, Aug. 1877, age 37; d. in Plymouth, MA.
Turner, Horace S., Aurora, NY, Sept. 24, 1844, age 53.
Turner, Capt. J. E., formerly of Cleveland, OH, Sept. 26, 1873, age c. 45; d. at Trenton, MI.
Turner, Jacob, Wales, NY, Sept. 1820, age 60.
Turner, James, son of Archibald and Jane Fortune, Jan. 22, 1872, age 24th year.
Turner, James G., ex-alderman, Nov. 1, 1867, age 57.
Turner, Jane A., formerly of Hamburgh, NY, wife of Samuel, July 20, 1863 in Rock Island, IL.
Turner, Josiah, Aug. 19, 1826, age 36.
Turner, Libbeus, late of Aurora, NY, Jan. 6, 1865 in Spencertown, Columbia Co., NY, age 88 y, 3 m, 10 d.
Turner, Lucy, East Aurora, Jan. 31, 1879, age 84 y, 9 m.
Turner, Rebecca, wife of Libbeus, Aurora, NY, June 7, 1862, age 83 y, 6 m, 25 d.
Turner, Sarah, Aug. 3, 1873, age 88 y, 3 m.
Turner, Mrs. Sarah, Nov. 9, 1879, age 69; found in Buffalo Creek.
Turner, William, M.D., Englishman, Jan. 29, 1836, age 50.
Turner, William P., Aug. 26, 1862, age 24 y, 6 m.
Turpin, Cornelius, June 1, 1874, age 65.
Tuski, John S., Nov. 27, 1855, age 43.
Tuthill, Mr. A. G. D., late of Buffalo, June 12, 1843 in Montpelier, VT, age 67; artist-pupil of Benjamin West.
Tuthill, Mrs. E. D., April 1880.
Tuthill, Nettie L., wife of E. D., April 1879.
Tuthill, Col. William, July 18, 1844 in Syracuse, NY, age 47; taken to Jamaica, Long Island, NY.
Tuton, Elizabeth V., wife of Harvey, Jan. 6, 1869; taken to North Adams, MA.

Tuton, Harvey, formerly of Buffalo, March 19, 1870; d. at Petersburg, VA, taken to North Adams, MA.
Tuton, Mrs. Jane, mother of Harvey, Dec. 15, 1865, age 68.
Tuttle, Arad, brother of the late David N., formerly of Buffalo, Oct. 27, 1870; d. at Quindaro, KS.
Tuttle, Capt. David, Oct. 1863.
Tuttle, David M., Jan. 17, 1870, age 63.
Tuttle, Capt. David W., July 13, 1863 in Donaldsonville, LA, age 23 y, 2 m, 22 d; 116th Regt., NY Vols., bur. in Buffalo.
Tuttle, Epphemia, wife of David N., April 23, 1865 in Brooklyn, NY, age 54; bur. in Buffalo.
Tuttle, Henry, Eden, NY, Sept. 18, 1820, age 40.
Tuttle, Henry, switchman, railroad, Feb. 25, 1880, age 29; d. from accidental injury, 5 days previous.
Tuttle, Nathan, Dec. 29, 1824, age 60.
Twichell, Collins S., Nov. 24, 1864 in Mt. Pleasant Hospital, Washington D.C., age 26 y, 2 m, 16 d. Co. H, 179th Regt., NY Vols., only son of Abram.
Twichell, Samuel, April 9, 1865, age 86; father of Samuel, Abram & Austin Twichell.
Twichell, Samuel, Feb. 9, 1872, age 64.
Twin, Mrs. Nancy, Clarence, NY, Oct. 1815.
Twohey, John, railroad accident, Jan. 15, 1877, age 20.
Twomley, William J., Almshouse, Feb. 19, 1880, age 61.
Tye, Elizabeth, alias Griffin, Aug. 29, 1873.
Tyler, Alpha, July 30, 1850, age 31.
Tyler, Angeline, wife of Alpha, formerly of Washington Co., NY, Nov. 7, 1845, age 29.
Tyler, Charles R., formerly of Buffalo, Aug. 7, 1872, age 50; d. at City of Green Bay, WI.
Tyler, Miss Elizabeth, dau. of Royal Tyler, late of CT, April 2, 1840.
Tyler, Emily E., formerly of Buffalo, Aug. 9, 1876; d. in Cleveland, OH.
Tyler, Emma S., wife of Joseph, formerly of Buffalo, Feb. 15, 1877, age 45 y, 1 m; d. at Dunkirk, taken to Cazenovia, NY.
Tyler, Eugene O., mechanic, April 2, 1879, age 35; found drowned.
Tyler, Frances, wife of A. S., formerly of Buffalo, March 29, 1848 in Boston, MA, age 28.
Tyler, James L., formerly of Lowville, Lewis Co., NY, March 20, 1861, age 35.
Tyler, Mrs. John, Clarence, NY, Dec. 1812, age 30.
Tyler, John P., form of Eaton & Tyler, formerly of Western, Worcester Co., MA, Nov. 9, 1824, age 22.
Tyler, Joseph K., Nov. 16, 1874, age 60.
Tyler, Mary A., widow of Alpha, May 2, 1877, age 59.
Tynett, William, Nov. 14, 1880, age 84.
Tyrer, James, formerly of Concord, March 6, 1876, age 61.
Tyrrel, Mrs. Susan, dau. of Mrs. S. B. Vandeventer, formerly of Buffalo, Sept. 23, 1873; d. in Clinton, IA, bur. in Buffalo.
Tyrrell, John T., Nov. 28, 1876, age 82 y, 7 m.
Tyrill, Thomas, Oct. 10, 1865, age 71.

Ulrich, John P., suicide, West Seneca, Oct. 1, 1878, age 56.
Umbeck, Jacob, North Buffalo, NY, Oct. 13, 1864.
Umfelbach, Elizabeth, Lancaster, NY, March 29, 1844.
Umpleby, Elizabeth, Co. Almshouse, Aug. 14, 1876, age 47.
Umpleby, Mrs. Sophia Penn, Oct. 29, 1866, age 68.
Underhill, R. Lovina, wife of J. H., Boston Centre, June 10, 1878, age 51 y, 2 d.
Underhill, William G., Dec. 19, 1864, age 58.
Underwood, Lydia, wife of Cyrus, May 1825, age 21.
Underwood, Royal, Sept. 21, 1828, age 20.
Unger, George L., Feb. 5, 1873, age 62.
Upham, Charles Wentworth, April 2, 1860, age 29.
Upham, Mrs. Lathrop, Black Rock, NY, Feb. 20, 1851, age 35.
Upson, Jefferson T., photographer, July 30, 1870, age 40.
Uptegraff, Elvira, wife of William, Clarence, NY, March 21, 1863, age 41st year.
Uptegraff, William, Clarence, NY, April 15, 1837, age 71.
Upton, Ellen, Co. Almshouse, March 21, 1878, age 40.

Upton, Stephen (Steven), May 1, 1880, age 67.
Urban, Henry, Sept. 9, 1856, age 38.
Urban, Jacob, Aug. 24, 1876, age 50.
Urban, Jacob, June 1878.
Urban, Mrs. Louisa, March 18, 1876, age 59.
Urban, Marie Kern, wife of George, Jan. 30, 1879.
Urban, Mary, wife of George, Jan. 30, 1879.
Urban, Philip J., father of George, Jan. 14, 1864, age 78.
Usher, Mrs. Eliza, March 9, 1872, age 68.
Usher, Silas, May 30, 1852, age 54.
Utley, Mrs. Ann, Clarence, NY, Jan. 22, 1866, age 54; sister of N. B. Thorp of Buffalo.
Utley, Anna Eliza, wife of Horace, May 26, 1857, age 30.
Utley, Horace, Dec. 3, 1873, age 63.
Utley, Martha Charlotte, wife of Horace, Sept. 29, 1847, age 22.
Utley, Mary, wife of Charles B., Hamburgh, NY, Jan. 29, 1850, age 70.
Utley, Samuel, Clarence, NY, postmaster, March 3, 1859, age 52.

Vader, Daniel, Aug. 7, 1865, age 66.
Vail, George O., resident member of the Buffalo Historical Society, Oct. 21, 1879, age 62.
Vail, Lindemira, wife of James W., June 24, 1835, age 23.
Vail, Louis, father-in-law of Dr. A. T. Bull, Jan. 10, 1875, age 70; taken to Middletown, Orange Co., NY.
Vail, Panama, wife of Capt. John, formerly of Silver Creek, Chautauqua Co., NY, Jan. 26, 1840, age 32d year.
Vail, Sophronia L., wife of A. R., Sept. 11, 1858.
Valentine, Catharine, wife of William, March 18, 1852, age 38.
Valentine, Charlotte, Aug. 21, 1854, widow of George.
Valentine, Emeline P., wife of Frederick, May 13, 1869, age 43 y, 4 m.
Valentine, George Sr., March 7, 1854, age 69.
Valentine, John, formerly of Buffalo, May 15, 1879, age 62; d. in Chicago, bur. Buffalo.
Valentine, Percilla, Almshouse, insane, Sept. 2, 1880, age 65.
Valentine, William C., formerly of Buffalo, Feb. 5, 1876; d. at San Francisco, CA.
Valentine, William H., June 1871, age 29.
Valeto, Frederick, Co. Almshouse, Oct. 23, 1878, age 74.
Valleau, Mrs. Elizabeth A., Aug. 28, 1847, age 77.
Valleau, William, formerly of Buffalo, brother of Mrs. John T. Lacy, July 8, 1857 in Appalachicola, FL, age 54.
Valley, Rachel, April 28, 1865, age 77.
Van Allen, Cornelius, son of Jacob D., Dec. 8, 1855 in Berwick, Warren Co., IL; age 22 y, 10 m, 14 d.
Van Allen, Tabitha, widow of Jacob D., formerly of Buffalo, Dec. 11, 1878, age 74; d. in Chicago.
Vananden, Mary J., wife of William, May 14, 1874, age 39.
Vanantwerp, Joseph, Springbrook, Feb. 2, 1877, age 59.
Van Antwerp, Joseph B., July 18787, age 69 y, 5 m; taken to Spring Brook.
Van Arnam, Lucy B., Aurora, NY, wife of Daniel W., only dau. of John Nye, Oct. 27, 1864, age 42.
Van Bentheusen, George A. Johnson, son of J. H., Aug. 29, 1859, age 20 y, 9 m.
Van Bergen, P. H., Jan. 22, 1880, age 70 y, 11 m; father-in-law of Joseph M. Blake, bur. at Madison, WI.
Van Buren, Ellen J., wife of S. T., Oct. 31, 1849, age 27th year.
Van Buren, Phebe, Granville, NY, wife of James, May 15, 1865, age 54; bur. in Buffalo.
Van Camp, Abraham, Aug. 14, 1822, age 55.
Van Camp, Cornelius, Four-mile Creek in Buffalo, Aug. 1826, age 35.
Van Campen, Jane M., wife of James M., Aug. 18, 1871.
Van Dalfson, Catharine, Aug. 5, 1876.
Vandebogart, Minnie, wife of H. D., formerly of Buffalo, Sept. 24, 1874, age 23; d. at Alexander, NY.
Vanderburg, Austin, killed by George Marany, Oct. 29, 1875.
Vandermeer, H. John, Jan. 30, 1876, age 70 y, 9 m.

Vanderpoel, Isaac, Co. Almshouse, April 15, 1878, age 58.
Vanderpoel, Isaac V., March 22, 1871, age 57; taken to Kinderhook, Columbia Co., NY.
Vanderpool, D. M., firm of D. Benson & So., July 12, 1851 in Cincinnati, OH, age 43rd year; bur. in Buffalo.
Vandervoort, William, Tonawanda, NY, Oct. 18, 1858 in Dorchester, MA, age 54.
Vanderwerf, Elizabeth, Dec. 29, 1879, age 74.
Van Deusen, Electa Wainwright, Cheektowaga, NY, wife of Mathew, formerly of Great Barrington, MA, Sept. 19, 1840, age 64.
Van Deusen, Mary, wife of H. G., May 23, 1871, age 39.
Van Deusen, Walter E., formerly of Buffalo, Feb. 26, 1879, age 26; d. in Washington, D.C.
Van Deventer, Annie, wife of James T., dau. of Hon. Thomas Burlock of Derby CT, Dec. 19, 1852 in Derby, CT.
Vandeventer, Miss Antoinette Grenelle, April 20, 1862.
Van Deventer, Maj. Eugene, July 3, 1854 in Roslyn, Long Island, NY, age 38; bur. in Buffalo.
Van Deventer, Jeanie C., wife of James T., dau. of Cyrus Clarke, May 8, 1856, age 24.
Vandeventer, Mrs. S.B., formerly of Buffalo, Feb. 12, 1874, d. at Clinton, IA; bur. in Buffalo.
Vandevoort, Charles, Tonawanda, NY, Dec. 11, 1829.
Vandevoort, Dora H. Gowdy, Alden, Oct. 15, 1871, age 20.
Vandevoort, Mrs. Rebecca, Tonawanda, NY, July 28, 1848, age 80.
Vandewater, John, Oct. 26, 1880, age 38.
Van Durer, Lucy, Hillsdale, MI, Dec. 26, 1869, age 24.
Van Dusen, Mathew, Cheektowaga, NY, formerly of Great Barrington, MA, Sept. 15, 1848, age 72 y, 6 m.
Vanduzee, Lucretia M., wife of B. C., March 24, 1848, age 30.
Van Duzen, Hugh Grovenor, June 6, 1855, age 29 y, 9 m; taken to Jamestown, NY.
Van Dyke, Abram, Medina, NY, July 27, 1880; accidentally drowned.
Van Every, Samuel, May 17, 1863.
Van Hattan, Anthony, formerly of Buffalo, Sept. 5, 1879; found dead in the street, Bay City, MI.
Van Hatten, Martin, May 17, 1872, age 42.
Vanhouton, Ann Amelia, wife of J. H., Aug. 6, 1853, age 23 y, 11 m.
Van Husen, Kate, wife of N. K., Nov. 18, 1868, age 28; taken to Caledonia, Livingston Co.
Van Kleeck, Mrs. Elizabeth, Oct. 14, 1848, age 74th year.
Van Kleeck, William H., May 10, 1852, age 38 y, 6 m.
Van Mabzen, Rev. Cornelius, Feb. 15, 1848, age 22.
Van Meeter, T. O. E., drowned at Mt. Clemens, MI, AUg. 29, 1878, age c. 27.
Van Name, Aaron, Hamburgh, NY, Aug. 11, 1867, age 76.
Van Name, Hattie L., wife of A. A., Hamburgh, Oct. 14, 1870, age 23.
Van Natter, Elizabeth, wife of James R., Oct. 16, 1880, age 49 y, 9 m.
Van Nostrand, Lydia, Oct. 9, 1870, age 71.
Vanorman, Charles T., Dec. 5, 1879, age 62.
Van Orman, Cyrus S., Nov. 26, 1866, age 54.
Van Ornam, P. C., formerly of Buffalo, Aug. 25, 1877, age 61; bur. in Buffalo.
Van Ornam, Sarah Ann, wife of P.C., Oct. 19, 1857, age 37.
Vanpoel, Isaac V., March 1871.
Van Quintard, John, Sept. 28, 1853.
Van Rensselaer, Sanders, Sept. 12, 1850, age 35.
Van Sicklen, Charles N., son of James, Sept. 3, 1875, age 20.
Van Sicklen, Hattie S. Knight, wife of Edward H., Dec. 12, 1872, age 26; taken to Silver Creek.
Vanslack, Thurzea Jane, Hamburgh, NY, wife of A. N., Sept. 20, 1851, age 19 y, 6 m.
Van Slyck, Lena, April 30, 1873, age 47.
Van Slyke, Mrs., mother of C. A. Van Slyke, Dec. 5, 1858, age 73.
Van Slyke, Albert, son of the late C. A., Sept. 14, 1878, age 38 y, 8 m, 5 d.
Van Slyke, Cornelius A., Nov. 15, 1869, age 61 y, 4 m, 7 d.
Van Slyke, Jane Ann, wife of Cornelius A., Sept. 6, 1850, age 38.
Van Slyke, Lewis, eldest son of the late C. A., Nov. 25, 1870, age 37.
Van Tine, Abbie, wife of Charles of NY, June 16, 1862 in Brant, NY, age 26; bur. in Brant.
Vantine, Anna, Clarence, NY, wife of Wilder, Aug. 5, 1861, age 21 y, 11 m, 21 d.

Vantine, David, Clarence, NY, April 30, 1879, age 86.
Vantine, Ellenor, wife of David, Clarence, Dec. 21, 1878.
Vantine, Jacob Jr., Clarence, NY, Dec. 30, 1813; killed at the battle of Black Rock.
Van Tine, Mary Mather, Clarence, wife of George K., Sept. 28, 1878, age 43.
Van Valer, Mrs. Margery, Dec. 31, 1871, age 87.
Van Valkenburgh, Julia A., widow of Rev. Daniel, May 9, 1866, age 57th year.
Van Valkenburgh, Mary E. Clark, dau. of Nelson Van Valkenburgh, April 11, 1866, age 22.
Van Valkenburgh, Sarah, widow of William, Sept. 12, 1862, age 71.
Van Velsor, Benjamin, Jan. 11, 1859, age 47.
Van Velsor, Isabella, widow of Benjamin, May 26, 1874, age 60.
Van Vleck, Hannah, Willink, NY, widow of William H., June 6, 1860, age 45th year.
Van Volkenburg, Hiram, Dec. 15, 1874, age 46.
Van Voorhis, Abraham, May 21, 1868, age 74.
Vanwagenen, Radcliffe, suicide, Aug. 11, 1876.
Van Wie, John M., Alden, NY, May 25, 1865 in Tioga, PA, age 24 y, 10 m, 25 d; son of Louis
Van Woert, Martha, Sept. 21, 1865, age 65.
Varey, Capt. Samuel, Jan. 14, 1856, age 45.
Vary, Daniel W., Nov. 1866, age 36; bur. Nov. 29th.
Vaugan, Mrs. Jessey, Cheektowaga, Dec. 25, 1874, age 80 y, 20 d.
Vaughan, Jesse, Cheektowaga, Jan. 18, 1877, age 80.
Vaughan, Almara B. Swain, Springville, NY, wife of Eugene A., July 25, 1866, age 22d year.
Vaughn, Betsey, mother of D. G. C. Vanghn, Sept. 22, 1862, age 80th year.
Vaughn, George C., Oct. 3, 1863, age 51.
Vaughn, John, merchant, Aug. 27, 1852.
Vaughn, Mary A., widow of Dr. G. C., Jan. 10, 1874.
Vaughn, Col. Otis, Sept. 4, 1869, age 67.
Vaun, Elizabeth, Oct. 24, 1871.
Vaux, John P., June 6, 1874, age 64; taken to East Aurora.
Vedder, Albert A., Feb. 17, 1868, age 88; d. at Schenectady, NY.
Vedder, Jacob S., March 25, 1860, age 31.
Vedder, Mrs. Mary A., April 10, 1877, age 47.
Veder, Isaac, Alden, NY, Aug. 10, 1840, age 21.
Vedder, John, Marilla, March 31, 1877, age 82.
Vallacott, Bessie J., wife of J. R., July 25, 1880, age 26.
Venn, Eliza, wife of Robert, suicide, June 9, 1874, age 26.
Verplanck, Major Abram G., formerly of Buffalo, March 9, 1880, age 38, at Washington, D.C.
Verplanck, Judge Isaac A., April 15, 1873, age 61.
Verplanck, Laura Allen, widow of Isaac A., May 11, 1879, age 63.
Verrinder, Benjamin Antill, formerly of Buffalo, eldest son of Rev. William of Jersey City,
    NJ, Dec. 30, 1861 at Camp Kearney, VA, age 21st year.
Verson (or Varson), Michael, Dec. 23, 1873, age 33; drowned.
Vetter, Charles, Nov. 5, 1878, age 69.
Vetter, George, Feb. 25, 1873, age 28.
Vetter, Katharine, wife of Charles, March 6, 1873, age 62 y, 3 m, 16 d.
Vickery, Mary, wife of William R., Nov. 3, 1869, age 69 y, 5 m.
Vickery, William, formerly of Buffalo, Jan. 22, 1851 in Cleveland, OH, age 26.
Victory, Stephan, Co. Almshouse, April 1876, age 74.
Viger, Capt. E. R., Lake Captain, formerly of Buffalo, Nov. 14, 1874, age 45; d. in Detroit.
Vincent, Martin, residence unknown (Swedish), sailor, Sept. 23, 1876, age c. 35.
Vincent, Richard, switchman, Nov. 26, 1880, killed by rail train; bur. at Elmira.
Vine, Emily Russell, dau. of H. Russell Vine, April 5, 1864.
Vine, Mrs. Mary, West Seneca, Feb. 13, 1879, age 81.
Vine, Mary A., wife of George, Dec. 30, 1862, age 34.
Vining, Emily H., wife of G. W., June 29, 1864, age 42.
Vining, George W., teacher of music, formerly of Buffalo, April 28, 1879, age 57; d. in
    Denver, CO.
Vinton, Elizabeth, wife of Henry, Aug. 31, 1849, age 34.
Vircoulon, Henry Frasser, native of Bordeaux, France, Sept. 10, 1866, age 31 y, 6 m.
Voak, Abram, Newstead, NY, Dec. 19, 1849, age 86.
Voas, Carrie S., Elma, wife of Robert W., Aug. 27, 1873, age 37.

Voelker, Mrs. Catherine Louisa, lamp accident, March 9, 1879, age 33.
Vogel, George, suicide, May 21, 1877, age 56.
Vought, Sarah Tillinghast, wife of Casper, July 17, 1877, age 49 y, 1 m, 21 d.
Vogt, Andrew, Dec. 30, 1874, age 65.
Vogt, Frederique, wife of Rev. G. S., March 26, 1873, age 37 y, 4 m, 15 d.
Volger, Edward F., Feb. 1, 1860, age 47 y, 11 m.
Volker, Mrs. Aug. 22, 1873, age 70.
Volkman, Christian, accidental death, Hamburgh, Sept. 20, 1870, age 59.
Vollert, Joseph, July 1878, age 69.
Volliard, Charlotte, May 13, 1878, age 94.
Vollmer, Capser, March 2, 1858, age 42 y, 4 m, 15 d.
Vollmer, George, Oct. 6, 1878, age 76.
Vollmer, Joseph, Aug. 23, 1879.
Vollmer, Mrs. Margaret, mother of Casper, April 9, 1848, age 73 y, 3 m, 11 d.
Volmer, Mrs. Lavinia, Oct. 16, 1871, age 67.
Volmer, William H., Feb. 15, 1873, age 32 y, 2 m, 5 d.
Voltz, George, Nov. 25, 1868, age 62.
Voltz, Henrietta Caroline, wife of George, March 6, 1866, age 45.
Voltz, Matthew, father of A. W., J.S. & C. G., Dec. 6, 1872, age 60.
Von Brautwein, John Wolfgang, Tonawanda, Aug. 5, 1870, age 71; found dead on the farm of Christian Rudio.
Von Holst, Marius, April 1, 1875, age 35 y, 10 m.
Voorhees, Harriet, widow of Commander Ralph of US Navy, June 7, 1872; taken to New Haven, CT.
Vordtriede, Helen, wife of Julius, Aug. 5, 1872, age 43.
Vosturg, Abram, Oct. 9, 1879, age 44; d. in County Almshouse.
Vosburgh, C. Estella Woodward, wife of William H., Jan. 5, 1879.
Vosburgh, Frances Mary Addington, wife of William, Dec. 8, 1864, age 31 y, 10 m, 4 d.
Vosburgh, John, Gowanda, Feb. 28, 1872.
Vosburgh, Myndert Arthur, eldest son of P. M., Aug. 27, 1861 in Cincinnati, OH, age 22 y, 7 m; bur. in Buffalo.
Vosburgh, Col. N., Nov. 23, 1847, age 55th year.
Vosburgh, Peter H., Feb. 6, 1871, accidentally killed on Hudson River Railroad.
Vosburgh, Peter M., Dec. 12, 1864, age 95 y, 3 m, 4 d.
Vosburgh, Robert, Feb. 6 1871, accidentally killed on Hudson River Railroad.
Vosburgh, Ruth, wife of Col. Nathaniel, Feb. 3, 1845, age 48.
Vosburgh, Tennis H., son of P. M., Aug. 23, 1865 in Townville, PA, age 25th year; bur. in Buffalo.
Voss, Juliette H., wife of Robert, Sept. 22, 1867, age 34.
Voss, Mrs. Wilhelmina, April 20, 1876, age 65.
Vosseler, Jacob, April 19, 1877, age 31; body found in Hamburg Cana.
Vosseller, Racilia Dynehart, dau. of Nathan, Sept. 19, 1877, age 42 y, 4 m, 27 d.
Voyle, Priscilla, wife of P. J., late of Teuby, South Wales, Dec. 22, 1851.

Wackerman, Charles, Cheektowaga, accident, April 6, 1875, age 20.
Wackerman, Francis, Dec. 29, 1851, age 24; attached to the 3rd Art. in the Mexican War.
Wackerman, Michael, Cheektowaga, NY, Sept. 18, 1860, age 80th year.
Wade, Elizabeth L., wife of James, Aug. 12, 1858, age 59th year.
Wade, Frances A. Flint, wife of Frank A., Aug. 20, 1868.
Wade, Mrs. Isabella, May 21, 1860, age 80th year.
Wade, James, Jan. 7, 1866, age 65.
Wade, Mary, wife of Peleg, July 15, 1852, age 43.
Wade, Schuyler, Dec. 25, 1878, age 72.
Wadsworth, Ann, wife of Richard, Springville, NY, Oct. 15, 1859, age 72 y, 4 m.
Wadsworth, Gerard, April 7, 1836, age 31.
Wadsworth, John, July 11, 1841.
Wadsworth, Miss Lavina Sacketts, dau. of John, Oct. 1, 1838 in Talbatton, GA, age 20th year.
Wadsworth, Mrs. Nancy Davenport, Jan. 8, 1863, age 73; mother of Mrs. Henry Lamb.
Wageman, Adam, Aug. 21, 1874, age c. 35.
Wagenlauer, Mrs. Louise, Hamburg, May 1878, age c. 70.

Waggoner, Mrs. Lucretia, formerly Mrs. Peter Lake, formerly of Buffalo, Oct. 27, 1872; d. at Seneca, Lenawee Co., MI.
Wagner, Lena, Co. Almshouse, March 3, 1876, age 58.
Wagner, Mary Frances, widow of Joseph, March 31, 1876, age 82 y, 5 m, 19 d.
Wagner, Philip A., March 14, 1875, age 50.
Wagner, William, drowned Sept. 2, 1872, age 22.
Wahl, Julia, wife of Frederick J., May 8, 1878.
Wainwright, Mrs. Mary E., East Aurora, March 24, 1879, age 37; taken to Syracuse.
Wait, Alexander, brother of William, July 17, 1878, age 34 y, 8 m, 9 d.
Wait, Eliza, wife of Hiram, Sept. 2, 1860, age 42.
Wait, Hiram, Sept. 15, 1878, age 69 y, 7 m, 15 d.
Waite, Charle Henry, Nov. 9, 1865, age 44 y, 10 m.
Waite, Daniel E., July 1, 1875; suicide, killed himself at his father's residence in Batavia, NY.
Waite, Harriet H., wife of Charles H., April 27, 1862, age 40.
Waite, Joseph, Clarence, NY, Feb. 3, 1815, age 74; formerly of Lyme, CT.
Waite, Mary, wife of Benjamin, May 31, 1843, age 31.
Waite, Richard (Maj.), May 1857.
Waite, Stephen, Holland, NY, May 16, 1849, age 65.
Waith, Mrs. Sarah Goodman, widow of Rev. William, Lancaster, NY, April 26, 1879, age 89.
Wake, Phillip, April 23, 1857, age 27.
Wakefield, Richard, May 16, 1860, age 51.
Wakelee, Clement, Lancaster, NY, Sept. 20, 1863, age 70.
Wakelee, Harriet, wife of Clement, Clarence, NY, June 17, 1832, age 37.
Wakelee, Sally, Lancaster, NY, wife of Clement, dau. of A. Scovill of Columbia, CT, Feb. 4, 1842, age 40.
Wakelee, Sarah, wife of Charles M., dau. of Benjamin Bidwell, Jan. 29, 1861, age 38th year.
Wakelee, Susan J., wife of Henry P., Sept. 23, 1848, age 20.
Wakeman, Stephen, b. 1761, d. 1852, bur. Lockport (Niagara Co.); Soldier of the Revolution.
Walbridge, Charles E., formerly of Buffalo, brother of George B., Feb. 4, 1841 in Erie, PA, age 20th year.
Walbridge, Mrs. Esther, Oct. 2, 1842, age 79th year.
Walbridge, George B., Aug. 30, 1852, age 38.
Walbridge, Mrs. Ruth, mother of the late George B., Oct. 14, 1853, age 68; taken to Erie, PA.
Walbridge, Sarah Louisa, only dau. of Wells D., Aug. 11, 1864 in New Bedford, MA; bur. in Buffalo.
Walbridge, Wells D., formerly of Buffalo, April 29, 1880, age 54; d. in NY City.
Walcott, Mr., found drowned Aug. 4, 1873, age c. 30.
Walden, Hon. E., Hamburgh, NY, Nov. 10, 1857, age 80.
Walden, Judge Ebenezer (Niagara), Nov. 1857.
Walden, Edward, son of Hon. E., law-student, Hamburgh, NY, July 20, 1854, age 22.
Walden, Helen Elizabeth, eldest dau. of E. Walden, March 7, 1843.
Walden, James W., son of Mrs. Judge Walden, April 10, 1871, age c. 40; bur. at Lake View.
Walden, Susan, widow of Judge E., Lake View, July 7, 1873, age 79.
Waldron, Adele D., wife of J. Ferris Waldron of Albany, late Adele D. Myner of Buffalo; Dec. 1862.
Waldron, Cornelius A., June 23, 1879, age 79 y, 2 m, 7 d.
Waldron, Mrs. E. C., widow of C. A., Feb. 20, 1868.
Waldron, Elizabeth, widow of Peter A., Aug. 28, 1857, age 56.
Waldron, Mrs. Hannah, March 21, 1849, age 82.
Waldron, Isaac Ferris, son of C. A. Waldron of Buffalo, Oct. 13, 1866 in Chicago, IL, age 33; bur. in Buffalo.
Waldron, James H., son of C. A., Dec. 23, 1856, age 28 y, 3 m.
Waldron, Halsey, April 13, 1875, age 45.
Waldron, Margaret, widow of Gilbert, formerly of Honesdale, PA, July 16, 1847, age 66.
Waldron, Peter A., March 31, 1842, age 44.
Waldsmith, Christopher, Aug. 7, 1876, age 55.
Walfe, Nathaniel H., Jan. 1873.
Walker, Amanda B., wife of George, Jan. 29, 1874, age 56 y, 7 m.

Walker, Capt. Augustus, Feb. 6, 1865, age 65.
Walker, Benjamin, of English birth, Dec. 29, 1873, age 75.
Walker, Mrs. Caroline A., wife of Richard, eldest dau. of Joseph Adams, June 26, 1846, age 24th year.
Walker, Catherine, March 4, 1879, age 20.
Walker, Charles, Feb. 15, 1880, age 37.
Walker, Charles R., March 5, 1872, age 49.
Walker, Charles S., son of Capt. Augustus, April 30, 1862, age 35 y, 7 m, 21 d.
Walker, Christian, father of Stephen A., Black Rock, NY, April 20, 1866.
Walker, Christopher, only brother of Stephen A., Oct. 2, 1870, age 35 y, 6 m.
Walker, David, 1843 at sea on packet ship *Wellington*, from NY to London, merchant.
Walker, Electa M., wife of Russell, Juy 3, 1880, age 52 y, 2 m, 21 d.
Walker, Deacon Elihu, father of Joel L., Aurora, NY, July 13, 1866, age 83 y, 7 m, 14 d.
Walker, Elizabeth, wife of Elihu & mother of Joel L., Aurora, NY, Dec. 2, 1863, age 74.
Walker, George, Oct. 21, 1875, age 62.
Walker, George Anna (or Georgia Emma), Dec. 2, 1876, age 40.
Walker, George H., youngest son of Capt. Augustus, March 25, 1864 in Washington, D.C., age 31 y, 6 m, 16 d; bur. in Buffalo.
Walker, George J., Jan. 4, 1872, age 24.
Walker, George M., May 11, 1859 in Chicago, age 28; bur. Buffalo.
Walker, Harriet, dau. of John, May 21, 1859, age 29.
Walker, Mrs. Harriet N., Dec. 2, 1876, age 77.
Walker, Henry, late of Richmond, VA, Feb. 13, 1850.
Walker, Isaac C., firm of H. C. Walker & Co., May 31, 1858, age 34.
Walker, James, May 7, 1877, age 33; found in the Canal.
Walker, Hon. Jesse, County Judge of Erie Co., Sept. 6, 1852, age 40.
Walker, John, father of S. N., Dec. 31, 1865, age 78th year.
Walker, John M., June 12, 1877, age 40; d. at Utica, NY, bur. in Buffalo.
Walker, Mariah L., wife of George, Nov. 4, 1861 in Berlin, Erie Co., OH.
Walker, Matilda J. Bingham, wife of Jeremiah W., Jan. 15, 1865, age 23 y, 11 m, 24 d.
Walker, Rebecca, wife of James W., Tonawanda, NY, March 16, 1830, age 21.
Walker, Reuben, Williamsville, NY, Dec. 7, 1812, age 40.
Walker, Sally, widow of the late Stephen, Feb. 8, 1868, age 78 y, 5 m, 6 d.
Walker, Sally, wife of Ashley, East Hamburg, July 25, 1879, age 72.
Walker, Samuel G., July 21, 1857, age 57.
Walker, Mrs. Sarah A. R., April 12, 1855, age 23rd year.
Walker, Stephen, Dec. 16, 1864, age 71.
Walker, Stephen, fisherman, May 10, 1879, age 28; found dead in bed.
Walker, Walter, formerly of PA, Oct. 22, 1834, age 67.
Walker, Mrs. William, late Mrs. M. Coyl, March 22, 1866, age 32.
Walker, Capt. William R., April 2, 1862, age 40.
Walkly, Samuel, Nov. 14, 1867, age 46.
Wall, Miss Anna, Nov. 24, 1866, age 74.
Wall, Anthony, Co. Almshouse, March 20, 1877, age 75.
Wall, Caroline, July 1, 1880, age 45 y, 11 m, 6 d.
Wall, Frank, letter carrier, Oct. 2, 1880, age 50; crushed to death between cars.
Wall, James W., Sept. 1, 1861, age 71st year.
Wall, Samuel canaler, Oct. 29, 1879, age 25.
Wallaber, David, April 5, 1863, age 27 y, 1 m, 20 d.
Wallace, Beckie McLane, wife of Ezra H., Sept. 5, 1880.
Wallace, Caroline, wife of Dr. Erastus, Aurora, NY, May 1831.
Wallace, Egbert B., Nov. 3, 1861 in VA, age 19 y, 10 m, 8 d. Sgt., Co. B, 21st Regt. NY Vols., bur. in Buffalo.
Wallace, Ellen, wife of Frederick K., June 23, 1873.
Wallace, Eunice B., widow of Robert A., June 25, 1879.
Wallace, Isabella Gordon Nelson, wife of William, Aug. 13, 1868, age 26.
Wallace, James, Nov. 22, 1852, age 90; taken to Rochester, NY.
Wallace, Julia, wife of Robert A., May 23, 1867, age 49.
Wallace, Mary, wife of James, Nov. 13, 1852, age 80; taken to Rochester, NY.
Wallace, Robert A., April 8, 1878, age 60.

Wallace, Serj. Andrew, b. 1730, d. 1835; Soldier of the Revolution. Obituary Jan. 31, 1835.
Wallace, Thomas, Hamburgh, July 27, 1873, age 35.
Wallace, William Alexander, born in Paisley, Scotland Aug. 1797; d. Aug. 10, 1867, age 70.
Wallace, William H., formerly of Buffalo, April 25, 1879; d. at Columbus, TX, 1st Sgt. Co. B., 65th Regt.
Wallbridge, Henrica Hallaway, wife of Samuel Shelly, formerly of Buffalo, Nov. 25, 1879, age 27 y, 3 m; d. at Ontario, Canada.
Wallenhorst, Elizabeth, wife of Frank H., May 26, 1880, age 55 y, 5 m.
Wallingford, Kate, wife of John A., sister of Mrs. A. G. Chester of Buffalo, Aug. 31, 1860 in Cincinnati, OH, age 24; bur. in Buffalo.
Wallis, Dr. Erastus, Aurora, NY, Jan. 24, 1862, age 59.
Walls, Mrs. Bridget, Nov. 13, 1876, age 78.
Walls, Hannah, wife of John, April 2, 1871, age 48.
Walls, Mrs. Joanna Currie, mother of John, Sept. 17, 1874, age 70.
Walls, Thomas, July 27, 1874, age 77.
Walsh, Catharine, wife of Timothy, Oct. 14, 1878, age 66 y, 5 m.
Walsh, Mrs. Catharine, Oct. 5, 1880, age 70.
Walsh, Catherine, wife of James, Jan. 11, 1865, age 38.
Walsh, Edward, drowned, missing since Oct. 17, Nov. 1875, age 30.
Walsh, James, March 30, 1873, age 52.
Walsh, James P., May 5, 1869, age 21.
Walsh, John, March 16, 1876, age 32.
Walsh, John, May 22, 1878, age 72.
Walsh, John, Feb. 10, 1880, age 20; burned to death at Tarport, PA.
Walsh, Lydia E., wife of John, Aug. 24, 1864, age 41 y, 3 m, 21 d.
Walsh, Margaret, widow of John, Sept. 13, 1878, age 70.
Walsh, Martin, July 13, 1873, ge 44.
Walsh, Mary, mother of John and Michael, Oct. 5, 1857, age 65.
Walsh, Mary, Jan. 27, 1873, age 50; suicide.
Walsh, Michael, Oct. 30, 1867, age 64.
Walsh, Michael, Aug. 20, 1873.
Walsh, Nicholas, Nov. 30, 1870, age 23 y, 6 m.
Walsh, Nicholas M.D., Oct. 28, 1873, age 55.
Walsh, Patrick, Sept. 19, 1875, age 53.
Walsh, Peter, Jan. 15, 1877, age 53.
Walsh, William, Dec. 27, 1872, age 20.
Walsh, William, Aug. 5, 1880, age 72.
Walter, David, March 31, 1860, age 45.
Walter, Frank J., March 25, 1879, age 20 y, 4 m, 24 d.
Walter, Martin, June 19, 1875, age 68.
Walter, Mary Ann, wife of Hugh, July 26, 1850, age 47th year.
Walters, John, hod carrier, June 20, 1872, age 55.
Walters, John, May 19, 1873, age 57.
Waltman, Frederick, Clarence, NY, May 14, 1814, age 30.
Wandell, Timothy S., July 19, 1849; Co. K, 1st Regt., NY Vols.
Wannamaker, John, murdered, formerly of Buffalo, Nov. 28, 1876; killed about 40 miles from Fort Reno, Indian Territory.
Wannemacher, Christina, wife of Peter, Nov. 9, 1876, age 35.
Wannop, John, Aug. 25, 1874, age 55 y, 9 m, 2 d.
Wappurty, William, laborer, accidental death Oct. 27, 1880.
Warburton, Wright, from Huddersfield, Yorkshire, England, d. at Hamburgh June 22, 1880, age 33.
Ward, Daniel H., Dec. 1, 1833, age 24.
Ward, John D., son-in-law of Mrs. J. S. Newkirk, Dec. 1868; bur. Dec. 30.
Ward, Letitia N., wife of Hiram P., March 13, 1851, age 26.
Ward, Miss Maggie, Nov. 22, 1861, taken to Rochester, NY.
Ward, Sophia Langdon, formerly of Buffalo, wife of William R. L., dau. of Hon. John Langdon, Feb. 4, 1855 in Salem, MA.
Ward, Capt. William W., late of Killingworth, CT, Springville, NY, June 26, 1828, age 34.
Wardwell, Maggie, wife of Allen, dau. of Robert Skillings, Feb. 17, 1865.

Wardwell, Mary Hawes, wife of William F., July 11, 1862, age 64th year.
Wardwell, William, father of George S., Sept. 29, 1876, age 78.
Ware, E. R., Aug. 27, 1832, age 37; d. of cholera.
Ware, Jesse, b. 1750, d. 1829, bur. Niagara Falls; Soldier of the Revolution.
Ware, John C., March 26, 1873, age 26 y, 6 m, 18 d.
Warhus, Mary Ann, wife of Henry F., Sept. 11, 1849, age 28.
Waring, C. R., merchant, March 12, 1828, age 40.
Warner, Abby W., wife of John F., March 11, 1868, d. at Jacksonville, FL.
Warner, Amri, Wales, NY, Revolutionary soldier, Dec. 20, 1841, age 82.
Warner, Asa B., Sept. 29, 1859, age 36; d. in Bolton, NY.
Warner, Bertha, dau. of John and Sarah, Oct. 22, 1878, age 19.
Warner, Charles, April 26, 1878, age 50 y, 7 m, 20 d; taken to Alden.
Warner, Cynthia, Cheektowaga, NY, wife of James, Dec. 9, 1841, age 51.
Warner, Ezra N., Feb. 15, 1865, age 33 y, 11 m, 13 d; taken to Collins Center, NY.
Warner, Frances S. Phelps, wife of Samuel C., May 14, 1874.
Warner, George, South Wales, NY, May 31, 1865, age 25 y, 2 m, 4 d.
Warner, Harriet, wife of Thomas N., March 10, 1852, age 23d year.
Warner, Jacob, June 3, 1880, age 72.
Warner, Jesse, Dec. 13, 1879, age 46.
Warner, Jonathan, South Wales, NY, Revolutionary soldier, Jan. 14, 1845, age 85.
Warner, Mrs. Mary, formerly of Sand-lake, NY, May 2, 1835 at house of James Sloan, age 68.
Warner, Dr. N. H., June 24, 1860 in Swamscott, MA, age 53d year; bur. Buffalo.
Warner, Mrs. Noah H., widow of Dr. Noah H., Jan. 31, 1876, age 68 y, 8 m; d. at Groton, MA, bur. in Buffalo.
Warner, Omri, b. 1762, d. 1841, bur. Strykersville (Wyoming Co.); Soldier of the Revolution.
Warner, Pardon P., son of James, Cheektowaga, NY, Oct. 1, 1846, age 28.
Warner, Rebecca, widow of Aaron, South Wales, NY, Aug. 10, 1853, age 69.
Warner, Samuel C., Dec. 23, 1875, age 59.
Warren, Adaline, wife of Gen. William, Aurora, Feb. 16, 1869, age 68.
Warren, Miss Alvira, dau. of Mrs. E. A. Warren, Jan. 15, 1852, age 21st year.
Warren, Anna, wife of Col. Asa, Eden, NY, Jan. 21, 1822.
Warren, Asa, Eden Centre, NY, July 16, 1866, age 73d year.
Warren, B. M., formerly of Buffalo, May 1, 1874; d. at Ft. Erie, Ontario.
Warren, Miss Betsey, dau. of Orsamus, Clarence, NY, Feb. 8, 1850 in Lockport, NY.
Warren, Betsey G., widow of Horatio, Nov. 29, 1869, age 63.
Warren, Charles, Clarence, NY, May 7, 1833, age 23d year.
Warren, Edward Stevens, son of Gen. Hastings Warren, May 20, 1863, age 49.
Warren, Mrs. Eliza A., May 13, 1879, age 70.
Warren, Evarts E. S., July 26, 1880; died on trip up lakes for his health. Secretary of Courier Co.
Warren, Fannie, wife of John, Feb. 13, 1879, age 27 y, 1 m, 22 d.
Warren, Gilbert Holland, July 1869.
Warren, Harriet T., wife of Orsamus, Sept. 27, 1875, age 72 y, 10 m, 19 d; taken to Clarence.
Warren, Henrietta L., wife of Melvin F., Nov. 17, 1876, age 25.
Warren, Henry J., formerly of Buffalo, Oct. 26, 1853 in Rutland, VT.
Warren, Mrs. Horatio, July 27, 1830.
Warren, Horatio, Oct. 24, 1862 in Lyondonville, Orleans Co., NY, age 64; bur. in Buffalo.
Warren, Ira, Boston, NY, March 8, 1864.
Warren, Jabisle (Jabez), b. 1761, d. April 28, 1810, bur. East Aurora, NY; Soldier of the Revolution. Father of Gen. William Warren.
Warren, Jane A., wife of Edward D., Jan. 12, 1854, age 22.
Warren, Mrs. John, Dec. 25, 1829, age 54.
Warren, John, Feb. 17, 1874, age 79; taken to Canada.
Warren, Joseph, Sept. 30, 1876, age 48.
Warren, Lafayette Franklin, Cheektowaga, NY, Aug. 15, 1861, age 22.
Warren, Lathrop, Aurora, NY, Sept. 6, 1850, age 28.
Warren, Laura, Clarence Hollow, NY, wife of James D., Oct. 14, 1850, age 28th year.
Warren, Lemuel D., son of N. D., Jan. 14, 1872, age 21 y, 8 m; d. in NY City, bur. in Buffalo.

Warren, Life, Colden, NY, father of Mrs. Orlando McCumber, May 8, 1856, age 67.
Warren, Lois, wife of Dr. John D., June 27, 1865.
Warren, Mrs. Margaret E., Aurora, NY, March 3, 1848, age 88.
Warren, Martha, Eden, NY, widow of Col. Asa, April 4, 1867, age 75th year.
Warren, Martin D., April 26, 1849, age 42.
Warren, Mattie M., Dec. 23, 1865.
Warren, Mrs. Orsamus, Clarence, NY, July 7, 1843.
Warren, Orsamus, Feb. 16, 1876, age 76; taken to Clarence, NY.
Warren, Mrs. Phebe, mother of Horatio, Oct. 11, 1852, age 77.
Warren, Philetus S., Aurora, NY, April 6, 1839, age 28.
Warren, Robert, late of Macroone, Cork Co., Ireland, Feb. 18, 1852, age 55 or 60.
Warren, Sabin, Hamburgh, NY, Feb. 24, 1826, age 24.
Warren, Sally, wife of Gen. William, Aurora, NY, July 5, 1849, age 76.
Warren, Miss Selena, Feb. 16, 1835 in Hamburgh, NY, age 23d year.
Warren, Thomas W., Colden, April 11, 1876, age 78.
Warren, Gen. William, formerly of Aurora, NY, June 21, 1879, age 95.
Warrick, Henry, Englishman, March 5, 1836, age 46.
Warriner, Charles, formerly of Springfield, MA, Feb. 8, 1847, age 28.
Warriner, Julia Ann, wife of Capt. J. C., July 24, 1840, age 29.
Warring, M. J., Oct. 4, 1864, age 42.
Warwick, Mrs. Sarah, mother of W. and J. Galligan, May 29, 1843, age 54.
Washburn, Alonzo, Wales, NY, eldest son of J. R., May 1, 1862, age 27th year.
Washburn, George, drowned Sept. 7, 1874.
Washburn, Hannah, widow of William, East Hamburgh, Jan. 28, 1876, age 84 y, 7 m, 6 d.
Washburn, Hiram, Feb. 7, 1879.
Washburn, Mrs. James, Aurora, NY, April 29, 1836, age 66.
Washburn, Mary A., wife of Dr. S. F., March 15, 1873, age 47; taken to Rome, Bradford Co., PA.
Washburn, Melinda, formerly of Boston, widow of Salmon, Aug. 15, 1872, age 72; d. in Niagara Co.
Washburn, Nathaniel, b. 1758, d. Oct. 2, 1837, bur. Sardinia, NY; Soldier of the Revolution.
Washburn, Salmon, formerly of Boston, April 3, 1869; brother-in-law of Dr. T. T. Lockwood of Buffalo. Died at Newfane, Niagara Co., NY.
Washburn, Samuel, May 19, 1852, age 40.
Washburn, Sarah M., wife of N. S., sister of Mr. A. Robinson, March 14, 1849, in Albany, NY, age 27.
Washburn, William, East Hamburgh, NY, Dec. 25, 1864, age 74 y, 10 m, 10 d.
Washburne, Lydia, wife of Alanson, June 8, 1867, age 55.
Washburne, Mrs. Temperance Root, April 16, 1866, age 70.
Washington, James, 1850; lost on the *Griffith*; bur. June 19, 1850.
Waslofski, Frances, accident, Nov. 29, 1877, age 23.
Wasser, Gertrude, wife of A., April 18, 1874, age 51 y, 6 m, 17 d.
Wasson, Eliza Jane, June 2, 1875; taken to Perry Center, Wyoming Co.
Wasson, John, East Hamburgh, NY, Jan. 3, 1865, age 79th year.
Wasson, Stephen M., West Seneca, Sept. 23, 1877, age 68.
Wasson, Thomas, Hamburgh, NY, 1837; d. some weeks since.
Wasson, William, Aug. 30, 1875, age 66.
Water, Matthew M., eldest son of Peter, April 1869, age 28; d. at Fort Stockton, TX.
Waterbury, Catharine, wife of Henry, Sept. 28, 1873, age 23 y, 7 m, 2 d.
Waterman, Darias, b. Aug. 12, 1760, d. Jan. 26, 1846, bur. Alden, NY; Soldier of the Revolution.
Waterman, David, b. June 10, 1760, d. March 28, 1845, bur. Johnson's Creek, NY; Soldier of the Revolution
Waterman, Miss Mary, dau. of Joseph of Thompson, CT, Aug. 30, 1836, age 22nd year.
Waterman, Mrs. Polly, May 9, 1867, age 74.
Waters, Albert E., only son of Levi J., Nov. 8, 1869, age 28; d. in Chicago, bur. in Buffalo.
Waters, David, b. 1748, d. 1834, bur. Java (Wyoming Co.); Soldier of the Revolution.
Waters (or Walters), Elizabeth B., wife of Levi, April 21, 1872, age 64.
Waters, Frank (or A. Frank), Oct. 26, 1874, age 34; taken to Rochester, NY.

Waters, George S., Nov. 18, 1874, age 45.
Waters, Hannah, widow of John D., May 12, 1873, age 62.
Waters, John Davies, formerly of Burlington Quay, Yorkshire, England, Sept. 19, 1864, age
    72 y, 4 m, 13 d.
Waters, Lucy Ann, wife of William S., Jan. 17, 1841, age 31 y, 8 m, 11 d.
Waters, Mary, Elma, Nov. 27, 1875, age 22.
Waters, Theodore H., Dec. 18, 1870, age 27.
Waters, William S., Oct. 24, 1843, age 44.
Waterworth, George R., son of Thomas, Sept. 30, 1869, age 28.
Waterworth, Thomas, Jan. 1, 1874, age 64.
Watkins, Charles, Dec. 6, 1848, age 29.
Watkins, Edward (colored), June 25, 1871.
Watkins, Fidelia L., wife of George, Aug. 23, 1874, age 41 y, 7 m, 12 d.
Watrous, Edwin, Dec. 10, 1875; taken to Tonawanda.
Watson, Ana, widow of Chauncy, Feb. 16, 1879; taken to Geneseo.
Watson, Caroline, wife of Basil, Jan. 13, 1853, age 30 y, 7 m.
Watson, Elizabeth Hall, wife of George H., March 23, 1874.
Watson, Mrs. Ellen, April 13, 1875, age 75.
Watson, George H., Nov. 13, 1876.
Watson, Mrs. Hannah, Oct. 24, 1877, age 74.
Watson, Joseph M., Dec. 25, 1859, age 26.
Watson, Sarah, Wales, NY, wife of Dr. Ira G., Sept. 14, 1833, age 38.
Watson, Stephen V. R., June 15, 1880, age 63.
Wattles, Abby, East Hamburgh, NY, wife of Myrtle Wattles, Aug. 4, 1857, age 36.
Wattles, Hannah Eaton, wife of A., July 19, 1846 in Plainfield, CT, age 25.
Wattles, Nathaniel, July 29, 1846, age 38.
Watts, Mrs. Elizabeth, Oct. 24, 1872, age 76 y, 7 m, 7 d; taken to Springfield, Lucas Co.,
    OH.
Watts, George, July 28, 1864 in US Hospital, Newark, NJ, age 31; Co. C, 3rd NY Cavalry.
Watts, John B., Nov. 8, 1878, age 57.
Watts, Joseph X., Nov. 11, 1863, age 70.
Watts, Mrs. Mary Frances, May 28, 1866, age 68th year.
Watts, Matilda, Co. Almshouse, Feb. 11, 1877.
Watts, Rebecca, wife of Horace O., Dec. 13, 1879, age 33.
Watts, Sarah, wife of William, Oct. 14, 1868, age 25; d. at Northeast, PA, bur. in Buffalo.
Watts, Thomas, father of Robert of Buffalo, d. at Holland, Lucas Co. [OH?], June 25, 1871,
    age 97.
Watts, Walter H., formerly of Buffalo, March 23, 1871; accidentally killed at State Line
    Station, MO.
Watts, William, Jan. 28, 1859.
Watts, Xavier Joseph, Nov. 1863.
Wand, Mary, wife of Edward, July 21, 1852.
Waud, Nettie, wife of Thomas S., May 24, 1874, age 23.
Waver, Orsamus, July 14, 1878, age 73 y, 7 m.
Wayland, Mrs. Elizabeth, April 22, 1872.
Wayland, Frank, Sept. 7, 1872, age 29.
Weatherly, Joseph L., Jan. 29, 1866, age 60th year.
Weaver, Anthony, railroad accident, Aug. 11, 1878, age 45.
Weaver, Ephraim, Hamburgh, NY, Sept. 18, 1819, age 25.
Weaver, George, from Earl Township, Lancaster Co., PA, Williamsville, NY, Jan. 11, 1842,
    age 82[?] year.
Weaver, Joseph, Amherst, July 24, 1873, age c. 70.
Weaver, Mrs. Lizzie, East Hamburg, July 17, 1875, age 27.
Webb, Benjamin, Washington, DC, formerly of Buffalo, printer, Nov. 11, 1880, age 33.
Webb, Christopher, Grand Island, Dec. 11, 1880, age 50.
Webb, Jesse Sr., Dec. 18, 1879, age 59 y, 2 m, 23 d.
Webb, Mrs. Keturah, Home of the Friendless, Dec. 30, 1878, age 70.
Webb, Mrs. Mary, formerly of Buffalo, Dec. 9, 1878, age 78.
Webb, Peter J., Dec. 14, 1865, age 50.
Webb, William, March 24, 1857, age 44th year.

Webber, Charles Richard, Feb. 23, 1870, age 27; suicide.
Webber, Mary, Dec. 30, 1872, age 31.
Weber, Bernhardt, near Boston Corners, March 3, 1873, age 50.
Weber, Catharine, wife of John J., Feb. 11, 1878, age 55 y, 4 m.
Weber, Daniel, New York, May 23, 1877; body found in Canal at Black Rock.
Weber, Elizabeth, wife of Nicholas, May 25, 1844, age 27.
Weber, Frederick Jacob, May 4, 1880, age 76.
Weber, Henry, Aug. 23, 1873, age 71; suicide.
Weber, Herman, Nov. 23, 1874, age 38 y, 9 m.
Weber, Herman Jr., Oct. 30, 1878, age 26; d. in Denver, CO, bur. in Buffalo.
Weber, Herman, Oct. 21, 1880, age 54.
Weber (or Weaver), Jacob, carpenter, May 15, 1872, age 55.
Weber, John, May 25, 1876, age 60.
Weber, John, suicide, Jan. 1, 1877, age 28.
Weber, Mrs. John, Nov. 4, 1879.
Weber, Mary E., widow, June 22, 1871, age 80.
Weber, Peter, Sept. 26, 1870, age 61.
Weber, Philip J., father of Col. John B., Aug. 9, 1878, age 74.
Weber, Philip J., Aug. 5, 1879, age 40.
Weber, Wilhelmina, wife of Jacob, Jan. 29, 1844, age 22 y, 2 m.
Webster, Alanson, Sept. 17, 1880, age 73.
Webster, Ammon F., May 10, 1873, age 38; taken to Niagara Co.
Webster, Ann Eliza, East Hamburgh, NY, dau. of John, March 22, 1852, age 25 y, 3 m, 11 d.
Webster, Byron, Webster's Corners, Oct. 2, 1876.
Webster, Caroline, wife of David B., April 28, 1847, age 42.
Webster, Charles H., son of William C., March 18, 1865, age 20 y, 11 m, 12 d.
Webster, Daniel, father of Hugh, Eden, March 29, 1869.
Webster, Daniel J., brother of Hugh, March 15, 1878, age 48 y, 6 m, 24 d.
Webster, David, Dec. 4, 1853, age 45 y, 11 m, 4 d.
Webster, Edward, Eden, NY, Sept. 26, 1865, age 72.
Webster, Eliza A., East Hamburgh, NY, wife of Eli, March 24, 1859.
Webster, Emma C., East Hamburgh, NY, Feb. 19, 1880, age 21 y, 9 m, 16 d.
Webster, Esther L., Hamburg, NY, widow of Thomas S., April 24, 1879, age 73 y, 11 m.
Webster, George B., April 3, 1857, age 58.
Webster, George C., son of the late George B., Feb. 1, 1873, age 50.
Webster, Mr. H. M., formerly of Buffalo, March 13, 1877, age c. 41; d. at Petrolia.
Webster, Hannah Joy, widow of George B., Dec. 21, 1878, age 62.
Webster, Mrs. Isabella B., Feb. 17, 1873, age 68.
Webster, John, Alden, NY, Jan. 6, 1859, age 80.
Webster, John, East Hamburgh, NY, Oct. 9, 1860, age 73d year.
Webster, John, near Alden, March 25, 1880, age 70 y, 1 m, 20 d.
Webster, Joseph, East Hamburgh, NY, Aug. 30, 1847, age 78th year.
Webster, Joseph, Eden, Dec. 10, 1878, age 58 y, 8 m, 11 d.
Webster, Julia Allen, Feb. 16, 1880, age 23.
Webster, Margaret M., wife of Hugh, April 2, 1856, age 39 y, 2 m, 10 d.
Webster, Mary A., Aurora, wife of Hiram, July 7, 1879.
Webster, Mary Rockwood, wife of Levi, Eden, June 21, 1877.
Webster, Rachel, East Hamburg, wife of Charles, Jan. 27, 1880, age 84.
Webster, Salinda, Eden, NY, wife of Daniel, March 23, 1839, age 40.
Webster, Samuel W., East Hamburgh, July 18, 1876.
Webster, Miss Sarah Ann, Eden, NY, dau. of Daniel, March 16, 1851, age 23.
Webster, THomas S., East Hamburgh, NY, Nov. 1, 1866, age 67.
Webster, William, formerly of East Hamburgh, NY, Dec. 19, 1853 in Poplar Grove, IL, age 61.
Weckly (or Wechly), George, Aug. 20, 1877, age 36.
Weed, Alsop C., Feb. 24, 1877; d. at Morris, IL, bur. Buffalo.
Weed, Betty, wife of John D., mother of Joseph and Elias, April 2, 1844, age 64.
Weed, DeWitt Chapin, Nov. 16, 1876, age 53.
Weed, Elias, Aug. 9, 1862.
Weed, George, Aug. 23, 1828 in Auburn, NY, age 40.
Weed, George T., July 9, 1853, age 24; drowned.

Weed, Hannah Willis, wife of Elias, dau. of Rev. Jabez B. Hyde, Feb. 19, 1844, age 29.
Weed, Helen E., Jan. 27, 1879, age 61.
Weed, James, formerly of Buffalo, Jan. 30, 1846 in Troy, NY, age 35.
Weed, Jane Elizabeth, wife of Joseph, Wales, NY, Jan. 15, 1844, age 27.
Weed, Joseph, Wales, NY, Dec. 6, 1862, age 51.
Weed, Mrs. Matilda, Feb. 11, 1876, age 80.
Weed, Thaddeus, Feb. 4, 1846, age 54.
Weed, Hon. William W., July 3, 1860, age 66.
Weeden, Mrs. Charity, sister of Mrs. E. N. Hatch, Aug. 27, 1866; funeral at Boston Corners, NY.
Weeden, Eleazer M., Springville, NY, June 28, 1861, age 36 y, 3 m, 13 d.
Weeks, Zebedee, father of John L., March 23, 1862.
Wehrley, AUgust, May 5, 1879, age 35?; found dead.
Wehrung, Catharine C., wife of Adam, Aug. 21, 1875, age 28.
Weich, John, Oct. 8, 1871, age 57.
Weidinger, John, March 21, 1878, age 23 y, 6 m, 10 d.
Weidt, John, Feb. 10, 1878, age 56.
Weig, George, Feb. 1, 1876, age 43.
Weigel, Peter, Sept. 30, 1879, age 60 y, 9 m.
Weil, Aaron, Feb. 3, 1879, age 80 y, 4 m.
Weil, Albert, Dec. 4, 1880, age 63.
Weil, Caroline, June 5, 1879, age 76.
Weil, George, Nov. 15, 1880, age 42 y, 1 m, 15 d.
Weil, Miriam, Aug. 18, 1879, age 82 y, 5 m, 13 d.
Weilbeck, Engelhardt, Nov. 1, 1872, age 25.
Weimer, Eva C., widow, Feb. 25, 1878, age 82 y, 1 m.
Weimer, Agnes, wife of John G., Aug. 30, 1874, age 43.
Weimer, Mary C., June 27, 1872, age 56.
Weingartner, Michael, Co. Almshouse, July 21, 1876, age 72.
Weinheimer, George, June 10, 1875, age 19; accident. Killed by explosion of the Tug *R. R. Hefford*.
Weinmann, Edward J., May 26, 1879, age 38.
Weir, George Jr., March 21, 1865, age 42 y, 4 m, 18 d.
Weir, Jacob, Jan. 31, 1873, age 79.
Weir, James, Aug. 31, 1862, age 42.
Weir, Mary E. Weed, formerly of Spring Brook, wife of Neil, Jan. 16, 1880, age 26; d. at Chicago.
Weisenborn, Mrs. Elizabeth, July 2, 1874, age 62.
Weishuhn, Cyrenius H., Dec. 27, 1849, age 31.
Weishuhn, Harry, Sept. 11, 1848, age 34.
Weishuhn, Martin, Dec. 21, 1868, age 45.
Weishuhn, Ruth, wife of Philip H., April 20, 1858, age 71st year.
Weisleder, Christopher A., Oct. 19, 1858, age 39.
Weisner, Charles J. L., Feb. 16, 1858 in Fort Erie, Canada West, age 59; bur. in Buffalo.
Weisner, Mrs. Helen, Nov. 20, 1873, age 62.
Weiss, Abram, June 18, 1858.
Weiss, John W., April 8, 1871, age 22.
Weissenberger, John, June 20, 1874, age 55.
Weisser, Christina, wife of Henry, May 30, 1880, age 69 y, 8 m.
Weissgerber, Stephen, Oct. 24, 1879, age 72.
Welbasky, Lydia C., March 13, 1849, age 34.
Welch, Mrs., June 22, 1880, age 66.
Welch, Gen. Benjamin Jr., formerly of Buffalo, April 14, 1863 in Clifton Springs, NY.
Welch, Harriet, wife of Franklin, late of Eden, NY, Dec. 20, 1864.
Welch, Miss Ida M., Sept. 17, 1878, age 19.
Welch, James, son of Peter, Aug. 20, 1854, age 23 y, 11 m.
Welch, Nathaniel B., Nov. 27, 1863, age 33.
Welch, Philip, Sept. 15, 1863, age 33.
Welch, Mrs. Sylvia, Lancaster, July 18, 1876, age 78 y, 5 m, 4 d.

Welch, Thomas Cary, lawyer, June 13, 1864 in Liverpool, England, age 44; bur. in Buffalo July 2, 1864.
Welchi, Serena, North Buffalo, NY, wife of Samuel, dau. of John Rody, March 18, 1864, age 40.
Weldy, Nellie Edith, wife of S. E., formerly of Lancaster, June 18, 1877, age 20; d. at West Philadelphia, PA, bur. at Lancaster, NY.
Wellberry, Mrs. Mary, May 18, 1877, age 90.
Wellbery, George, late of Cooper Falls, L.S. MI, Jan. 27, 1870, age 39.
Weller, Emily, formerly of Buffalo, wife of Leander, Dec. 1, 1852 in Ashtabula, OH, age 46.
Weller, Capt. Leander, July 17, 1860, age 65.
Weller, Louisa E., wife of Louis, dau. of George Denny, Oct. 28, 1870, age 27.
Weller, Mary Olivia, Oct. 1870.
Weller, Peter Jr., Oct. 7, 1876, age 41 y, 2 m, 7 d.
Wellmasn, Manly P., Dec. 1, 1879, age 79 y, 9 m.
Welis, Aldridge, June 3, 1849, age 46; said to be the first male born in Buffalo.
Wells, Ann A., wife of Charles F., Aug. 17, 1876; taken to Silver Creek.
Wells, Dalia Sherwood, widow of Richard H., formerly of Buffalo, May 28, 1877, age 51; d. in Rochester, bur. in Buffalo.
Wells, Elijah, Dec. 23, 1874, age 75.
Wells, Ezra, Hamburgh, NY, June 9, 1836, age 25.
Wells, Fannie E., wife of Moses D., formerly of Buffalo, March 7, 1873; d. in Chicago.
Wells, Henry, founder of Wells College, formerly of Buffalo, Dec. 10, 1878 in Glasgow, Scotland, age 73. Bur. at Aurora, Cayuga Co., NY.
Wells, John G., brother of William and Aldrich, March 21, 1848, age 43d year.
Wells, Maj. Joseph, Sept. 15, 1834, age 64.
Wells, Mrs. M. A., Nov. 8, 1873, age 63.
Wells, Orange, formerly of Buffalo, Oct. 19, 1871, age 89; d. at Paw Paw, Van Buren Co., MI.
Wells, Prudence, formerly of Buffalo, widow of Joseph, mother of William, Chandler J., and Chauncey of Buffalo, Aug. 27, 1855 in Bellevue, MI, age 85; bur. in Buffalo.
Wells, Richard H., Jan. 4, 1868, age 52.
Wells, Miss Sarah Emily, Jan. 11, 1859, age 21st year.
Wells, Mrs. Sophronia, mother of David B., North Evans, Dec. 26, 1875, age 71 y, 9 m, 7 d.
Wellsteed, John, late of Dorset, England, May 19, 1874, age 83.
Wellsteed, Mary, March 30, 1878, age 78 y, 11 m.
Welsch, Mary, Co. Almshouse, May 8, 1878, age 30.
Welsh, Catherine, Nov. 23, 1870, age 70.
Welsh, John, b. 1758, d. 1839, bur. Eden Valley; Soldier of the Revolution.
Welsh, James, accident, June 16, 1875. Killed by the cars, near Merrinton Station, Canada, bur. in Buffalo.
Welsh, Thomas, July 11, 1858, age 42 y, 7 m, 12 d.
Welty, Jacob, Feb. 9, 1836, age 22; bur. in Williamsville, NY.
Wendel, Daniel W., eldest son of Daniel, July 25, 1861, age 19 y, 8 m, 11 d.
Wendell, Daniel W., Sept. 18, 1878, age 62.
Wendt, William, Nov. 18, 1877, age 63 y, 7 m, 26 d.
Wentworth, Lucius, Nov. 26, 1851, age 34.
Wentworth, Lucy Ann, formerly of Buffalo, wife of Delavan, July 13, 1862 in Washington, Erie Co., PA, age 33 y, 9 m, 11 d.
Wentworth, Mary Ann, wife of Allen D., July 21, 1853, age 29.
Wenz, Dr. James, Sept. 1, 1874, age 58; d. in New Orleans.
Weppner, Annie M., oldest dau. of Arnold, Jan. 26, 1877, age 24 y, 3 m, 14 d; d. at Santa Barbara, CA, bur. in Buffalo.
Weppner, Augustus, March 14, 1869, age 84 y, 2 m, 23 d.
Weppner, Barbara, wife of Augustus, Sept. 17, 1858, age 61.
Werle, Caroline, wife of Anthony, April 12, 1864, age 47 y, 4 m.
Werle, Mary E., wife of George A., Jan. 30, 1863, age 32.
Werneke, Hyman M., M.D., Aug. 6, 1880, age 46.
Werner, Joseph, formerly of Buffalo, March 22, 1874, age 28.
Werner, William, suicide by hanging, Aug. 23, 1870, age 53.
Werrick, Magdalena, wife of John, Sept. 11, 1874, age 53.

Wesch, George, father of Fred., July 15, 1877, age 72.
Wescott, Alden, July 15, 1861 in Columbus, OH, age 42; bur. in Buffalo.
Wescott, Catharine, wife of R., June 4, 1850, age 23.
Wescott, Mary A., wife of Ira, Jan. 29, 1875, age 50 y, 6 m; taken to Manlius, NY.
Wesley (or Welsey), Julia A., wife of W. K., July 6, 1845, age 26.
Wesley, Mary B., mother of A. and Mrs. E. B. W. Drew of this city. Died at Portchester, NY, late of Buffalo, Dec. 6, 1869, age 84.
West, Annie Louisa, wife of Isaac, June 24, 1871, age 24; d. at Hamburgh, NY.
West, Elizabeth Green Giles, wife of Charles Edwin, Sept. 7, 1864 (or 1863).
West, Miss Elizabeth L., formerly of Buffalo, dau. of Dr. West of the US Army, Dec. 24, 1846 in Porter, Niagara Co., NY, age 40.
West, Elvira Tracy, wife of Stephen, Angola, Jan. 15, 1873, age 73 y, 5 d.
West, Emory, Feb. 1866.
West, Miss Jane, dau. of Dr. West of the US Army, Dec. 14, 1837.
West, John, Dec. 22, 1880, age 71; Almshouse.
West, Morgan L., Brant, April 22, 1877, age 72 y, 4 m, 22 d.
West, Nathan, lately from OH, May 26, 1827, age 40.
West, Peter, Aug. 16, 1838, age 80.
West, Silence, wife of Peter, Aug. 12, 1821, age 65.
West, W. W., May 9, 1880, age 54 y, 10 m, 9 d.
Westcott, Charles C., Sept. 10, 1854, age 30; taken to Rochester, NY.
Westcott, Mrs. Jennie A. Barker, wife of Byron H., April 26, 1879, age 24 y, 13 m.
Westcott, Mrs. Mary, Aurora, NY, Dec. 22, 1837, age 72.
Westcott, Mary Ann, wife of Rufus R., Sept. 8, 1854, age 23.
Westerhold, John H., Aug. 18, 1870, age 65 y, 3 m.
Westerman, Joseph, Dec. 4, 1880, age 58; Almshouse.
Westlake, Thomas, May 13, 1874, age 26.
Weston, Charles, formerly of London, England, May 25, 1867, age 55.
Weston, Mrs. Eliza, mother of William, May 20, 1869, age 61.
Weston, John L., July 20, 1873, age 36.
Weston, Laura Tiffany, wife of Henry James, Oct. 2, 1869, age 36.
Weston, Mary, widow of William, formerly of Coventry, England, Nov. 16, 1859 in King's Heath, England.
Weston, Mary, wife of W. H., Jan. 25, 1874, age 36.
Weston, Sophia P., Black Rock, NY, wife of H. J., Feb. 12, 1865, age 49.
Weston, William, April 13, 1850, age 47.
Weston, William, Dec. 14, 1879, age 43.
Weter, Anna Maria, wife of Peter, Jan. 14, 1859, age 81st year.
Weter, Annie, wife of Peter, Oct. 28, 1876, age 60.
Weter, Joseph, March 11, 1864, age 37 y, 4 m.
Wetherell, Hon. Benjamin F. H., June 26, 1867.
Wetmore, Mary E., wife of Dr. S. W., Sept. 1, 1876, age 47.
Wetmore, Timothy, Alden, NY, July 25, 1848, age 68.
Wetmore, Viscount S., son of Parsons Wetmore, Aug. 17, 1840, age 24.
Wetzel, George, laborer, accidentally killed July 20, 1874, age 54.
Wey, Rufus Stanley, May 8, 1869, age 53.
Whalen, Edward, Co. Almshouse, May 11, 1876, age 24.
Whalen, Patrick, Co. Almshouse, June 24, 1877, age 65.
Whaples, Julia Ann, wife of Reuben, Sept. 29, 1832, age 19.
Wheeler, Mrs., Clarence, NY, Dec. 1812, age 65.
Wheeler, Asa, Feb. 18, 1866, age 54.
Wheeler, Betsey, wife of Charles, Dec. 3, 1839, age 25; in Chicago, IL.
Wheeler, Betsey, Feb. 25, 1862, age 58; wife of William H. Taken to Schaghticoke, Rensselaer Co., NY.
Wheeler, Cornelia B., wife of Isaac G., May 4, 1864; in Chicago, IL, bur. in Buffalo.
Wheeler, Daniel P., July 25, 1860, age 41.
Wheeler, Ebenezer, March 7, 1858, age 81 y, 3 m.
Wheeler, Electa, wife of Ira P., May 1, 1860, age 48 y, 10 m.
Wheeler, Emily T., wife of Charles W., May 24, 1831, age 19 y, 5 m.
Wheeler, Francis, proprietor of Wheeler's Hotel, Dec. 10, 1848, age 40.

Wheeler, Capt. Frederick S., Jan. 19, 1854, age 39.
Wheeler, George L., March 8, 1865, age 40.
Wheeler, Hannah, wife of Paul, East Hamburgh, NY, Aug. 5, 1866, age 59 y, 9 m, 5 d.
Wheeler, Hannah C., wife of Paul, East Hamburgh, Aug. 30, 1878, age 53; d. at Provincetown, MA.
Wheeler, Isaac, Evans, formerly of Buffalo, Oct. 14, 1880, age 70; over 50 years res. in Buffalo.
Wheeler, Jane, wife of Isaac, Aug. 7, 1844, age 39.
Wheeler, John H. H., May 5, 1869, age 61.
Wheeler, Josiah, Clarence, NY, Dec. 1812, age 70.
Wheeler, Josiah Jr., Clarence, NY, Dec. 1812, age 35.
Wheeler, Loring B., Dec. 2, 1879, age 32 y, 9 m, 17 d.
Wheeler, Margaret, wife of Rufus, Nov. 16, 1862, age 45 y, 4 m.
Wheeler, Maria C., only dau. of the late John H., Oct. 1, 1869; d. in Chicago, bur. Buffalo.
Wheeler, Mrs. Rebecca, Feb. 28, 1860, age 75.
Wheeler, Rufus, May 14, 1865, age 47 y, 3 m, 8 d.
Wheeler, Rufus, son of the late Rufus, Feb. 24, 1867, age 23; in Ontonagan, MI, bur. in Buffalo.
Wheeler, Stephen, Hamburgh, NY, Aug. 1829, age 42.
Wheeler, Mrs. Susan, April 17, 1853, age 72; mother of Isaac and Joel & Mrs. C. J. Wells.
Wheeler, Mrs. Susan, East Hamburgh, Nov. 26, 1877, age 88 y, 7 m.
Wheeler, William, March 1830 on canal near Columbusk OH, age 30; said to have belonged in this vicinity.
Wheelock, Charles, son of N. of Bridport, VT, Sept. 24, 1850, age 35.
Wheelock, Miss Charlotte, dau. of John G., Lancaster, NY, May 11, 1854, age 34; d. in Buffalo.
Wheelock, John, March 2, 1874, age 55.
Wheelock, Lavinia, wife of John E., Lancaster, NY, Sept. 13, 1853.
Wheelock, Martha L., wife of Milton, Hamburgh, NY, Nov. 21, 1865, age 22; d. in Boston, NY.
Whelan, Ann, mother of Justice Whelan, Aug. 19, 1880, age 80.
Whelan, Kate, suicide, Sept. 29, 1877, age 21.
Whelan, Mrs. Margaret, Sept. 7, 1875, age 83.
Whelan, Martin, native of Queen's County, Ireland, Sept. 21, 1871, age 58.
Whelan, Patrick, Oct. 12, 1873, age 69.
Whelan, Rev. William, pastor of St. Patricks, Buffalo, April 27, 1847.
Whelock, Sarah, Brant, May 10, 1875, age 85 y, 7 m, 20 d.
Wherrell, Mary Jane, wife of John, April 23, 1869, age 28.
Whatmore, Mrs. Nellie, wife of Daniel, May 13, 1879, age 79.
Whiffen, Uridge, teacher of select school in Buffalo, April 30, 1838, age 36; in Slayton's Bush, Oneida Co., NY, at his father's.
Whinham, Robert, formerly of Buffalo, Feb. 10, 1880, age 66; d. at Caledonia, Livingston Co., NY.
Whipple, Mrs. Charlotte, July 18, 1878, age 83.
Whipple, James S., Black Rock, NY, Jan. 28, 1843, age 26.
Whipple, Job, Clarence, Dec. 19, 1874, age 86 y, 8 m, 15 d.
Whiston, Terese Grace, wife of John W., March 12, 1876, age 38.
Whitaker, Alanson, postmaster, d. of cholera, Hamburgh, NY, July 28, 1832, age 35.
Whitaker, Chauncey, Jan. 9, 1865, age 37.
Whitaker, Edward, formerly of Buffalo, Nov. 8, 1856, age 29; in Terrecoupe, IN.
Whitaker, Miss Polly, Hamburgh, NY, Dec. 10, 1827, age 63.
Whitaker, Obediah, Holland, NY, March 23, 1863, age 75.
Whitcomb, Everett K., son of George, May 26, 1872, age 21; drowned in New York Harbor.
Whitcomg, Louisa, Almshouse, Dec. 10, 1879, age 34.
Whitcomb, Louise, Oct. 1, 1866, wife of George.
Whitcomb, Mary Ann, wife of Dr. Nathan, Aug. 14, 1854, age 32.
Whitcomb, Sarah C., wife of George, Angola, Sept. 12, 1879, age 52 y, 3 m, 28 d.
White, Albert A., brother of Dr. James P., East Hamburgh, Jan. 16, 1875, age 61.
White, Mrs. Ann, late of Ballygillan, Co. Wexford, Ireland, May 21, 1869.
White, Mrs. Ann Quayle, wife of H. G., Aug. 1, 1860, age 39.
White, Ann Eliza, only dau. of Henry G., June 6, 1867, age 20.

White, Ansel, accidentally killed, Crittenden, Dec. 6, 1873, age 72.
White, Rev. Ansley D., brother of the late Isaac D., formerly of Buffalo, Sept. 23, 1877; d. in Trenton, NJ.
White, Betsey, wife of David P., mother of James P. M.D. of Buffalo, East Hamburgh, NY, June 15, 1867, age 80.
White, Betsey E., wife of Truman, June 29, 1852, age 67 y, 11 m.
White, Catharine B., wife of Hubbard T., Aug. 19, 1865, age 38.
White, Daniel D., Feb. 6, 1874, age 67.
White, David Pierson, East Hamburgh, May 2, 1868, age 80.
White, Dewitt C., eldest son of J. B., March 20, 1865, age 33 y, 11 m.
White, Dorothy S., wife of Joseph L., July 31, 1865, age 64; taken to Schenectady, NY.
White, Elizabeth, wife of J.J., Nov. 20, 1863, age 35.
White, Elizabeth Margaretta, wife of Rev. R. M. of Savannah, GA, dau. of Judge Stryker, formerly of Buffalo, July 16, 1850, age 31; in Talbotton, GA.
White, Emily R., Sept. 13, 1864, age 50.
White, Emma N., wife of Joel S. of Eden, NY, April 4, 1845, age 35.
White, Frances, Feb. 28, 1874, age 22.
White, Frances Helena, wife of William H., Nov. 27, 1878, age 43.
White, Francis, White Haven, Grand Island, NY, brother of Stephen, Feb. 13, 1841, age 52.
White, George, Hamburgh, NY, merchant, Jan. 1826, age 28.
White, George, formerly of Buffalo, Sept. 24, 1849, age 20; in Fredonia, NY.
White, George C., May 30, 1869, age 64.
White, Mrs. Hamilton, April 1867, formerly of Buffalo.
White, Hannah M., wife of A. W., Collins Centre, July 17, 1875, age 46 y, 4 d, bur. in Buffalo.
White, Mrs. Hattie M., dau. of Joseph Harris, March 4, 1876, age 35; d. in St. Catharines, Ontario, bur. in Buffalo.
White, Henry, formerly of Franklin, Delaware Co., NY, Aug. 25, 1832, age 38.
White, Henry, lawyer, April 13, 1845, age 24; d. in Fredonia, NY, bur. in Buffalo.
White, Henry A., Sept. 4, 1870, age 56 y, 4 m.
White, Hollis, formerly of Buffalo, Sept. 30, 1875; d. at Sioux City, IA.
White, Humphrey, North Collins, NY, May 6, 1863, age 65.
White, I. J., for the firm of L. & I.J., Feb. 2, 1879, age 64.
White, Isaac D., Lancaster, Oct. 12, 1875, age 54.
White, Mrs. Jacob, Springville, NY, May 30, 1844.
White, Dr. James, Black Rock, NY, Feb. 26, 1854, age 67.
White, James, April 7, 1855, age 39.
White, James, Black Rock, April 4, 1869, age 48.
White, James, Tonawanda, April 4, 1869, age 40.
White, James J., March 3, 1876, age 30 y, 2 m.
White, Jessie A., 2d dau. of John, Nov. 28, 1880, age 37; d. suddenly at Geneva.
White, Laura A., wife of Hoel, Hamburgh, Oct. 10, 1874, age 55.
White, Lemuel, May 5, 1840, age 45.
White, Margaret, wife of William, April 8, 1871, age 47.
White, Marie, dau. of Homer, Springville, NY, Sept. 13, 1862, age 29.
White, Marion, wife of Horace K., formerly of Buffalo, June 29, 1875; d. in Syracuse, NY.
White, Marmaduke H., formerly of the Eagle Street Theatre, Buffalo, Oct. 23, 1845, age 36; d. in New York.
White, Mary, Dec. 2, 1873, age 36.
White, Nathaniel, Erie Co., NY, Feb. 27, 1830, age 78; Revolutionary pensioner.
White, Norman, son of Amos G., South Wales, Feb. 9, 1872, age 20.
White, Phebe B., Dec. 8, 1879, age 76.
White, Reuben, Collins, NY, Aug. 10, 1841, age 72.
White, Roderick R., Oct. 16, 1862, age 39.
White, Mrs. Rosamond, Sept. 22, 1859, age 74; d. in Palmyra, NY, bur. Buffalo.
White, Rev. Rufus M., formerly of Buffalo, Nov. 6, 1854; d. in Petersburgh, VA, bur. Buffalo.
White, Mrs. S. A., Jan. 31, 1869.
White, S. N. Prince, infant son of H. G. and the late Susan N. P. White, Feb. 15, 1864.
White, Samuel, March 31, 1851, age 64.

White, Stephen Thorn, Collins Centre, March 26, 1872, age 45 y, 5 m, 26 d.
White, Susan Nickles Prince, wife of H. G., Jan. 13, 1864.
White, Thomas, June 27, 1873, age 65.
White, Thomas T., Town Supervisor, Hamburgh, NY, June 1825.
White, Col. Truman, Hamburgh, Jan. 26, 1869, age 88.
White, Weltha Maria Cobb, wife of Leonard, Sept. 19, 1857, age 38.
White, William C., formerly of firm of Moores & White, son-in-law of William P. Moores, Dec. 13, 1868, age 28.
White, William C., Jan. 2, 1872, age 52.
White, William Henry, June 26, 1879, age 52.
White, William M., North Collins, Sept. 16, 1877, age 49.
White, Williston, May 25, 1848, age 23.
Whitefield, Joseph Jr., 14th RI Heavy Artillery, eldest son of Joseph H., March 1, 1864, age 22 y, 5 m; d. in Hospital at Dutch Island.
Whiteley, John W., formerly of Philadelphia, PA, Jan. 30, 1821, age 37.
Whiteman, Mrs. Isaac, Wales, NY, Dec. 22, 1831, age 36.
Whiteman, Zachariah, Evans, Feb. 29, 1880, age 74.
Whiteneck, Elizabeth, wife of Peter, Clarence, NY, June 7, 1815, age 28.
Whitfield, J. W., Feb. 2, 1870, age 55 y, 2 m, 2 d.
Whitier, Mitchell, Oct. 12, 1848, age 73.
Whiting, Abijah A., 27th NY Battery, Jan. 27, 1863, age 22 y, 9 m; d. in Washington.
Whiting, Ammi, Boston, Feb. 2, 1877, age 71.
Whiting, Amos, Boston, NY, Dec. 6, 1842.
Whiting, Arthur, Feb. 5, 1870, age 23; taken to Greenwood.
Whiting, Eva, only dau. of Sanford E., April 10, 1877, age 22 y, 10 m.
Whiting, George, Feb. 16, 1862, age 58; d. in Brooklyn, NY, bur. in Buffalo.
Whiting, Mrs. Hannah, Black Rock, NY, Sept. 16, 1848, age 59.
Whiting, Joseph S., Tonawanda, NY, March 28, 1854, age 66.
Whiting, Lucy Tifft, wife of Charles R., Feb. 27, 1869, age 32.
Whiting, Matilda, wife of Thomas, Dec. 8, 1877, age 30.
Whiting, Nellie, Co. Almshouse, May 26, 1877, age 33.
Whitney, Alice, wife of Milo A., Jan. 22, 1874, age 39.
Whitney, Dr. Benajah T., Jan. 1872, age 58 y, 2 m, 10 d.
Whitney, Delihah, wife of William M., Aurora, NY, May 21, 1866, age 64.
Whitney, Ezra, Black Rock, NY, Sgt. in Capt. Elias Hull's Co., from Ontario Co., NY, Aug. 1812, age 30.
Whitney, George J. (or A.), formerly of Buffalo, Dec. 31, 1878; d. in Rochester.
Whitney, Henry, Aurora, NY, Aug. 9, 1853, age 74.
Whitney, Henry, Aurora, NY, Jan. 11, 1863. Co. D, 14th Regt., PA Vols. D. in Hospital in Washington of wounds received in battle of Fredericksburg, aged 28. Bur. in Buffalo.
Whitney, Henry, March 6, 1878.
Whitney, Henry L., Lewiston, Jan. 22, 1878, age 41.
Whitney, Joseph W., formerly of Buffalo, May 20, 1879, age 53; d. at Arcadia, WI.
Whitney, Gen. Parkhurst (Niagara Falls), April 1862.
Whitney, Sarah E., widow of Dr. B. T., formerly of Buffalo, July 1872; d. at Solon, Courtland Co., NY.
Whittaker, ANn, wife of John, Wales, March 10, 1870, age 56 y, 5 m.
Whittaker, John, Wales, Jan. 27, 1873, age 65 y, 20 d.
Whittaker, Sarah B., March 20, 1839, age 32; wife of William H., dau. of the late Col. Asa Ransom of Clarence, NY.
Whittemore, Rhoda, wife of Capt. Asa, Aug. 12, 1877, age 71 y, 11 m, 1 d.
Whittet, Elizabeth, widow of James, mother of Mrs. William C. Davison, Jan. 13, 1863, age 80.
Whittet, Joseph, Nov. 26, 1869, age 50.
Whittman, Henry, Dec. 27, 1880, age 26.
Whitton, Frank, railroad accident, Feb. 5, 1879, age 31.
Whitton, Susie Maxfield, June 16, 1880, age 34.
Wickes, Mrs. Elizabeth, March 28, 1872, age 30 y, 11 d.
Wickham, Ann, Oct. 10, 1872, age 31.
Wicks, Mr. Comfort, Aug. 1, 1834, age 40.

Wickes, Jane, widow of Comfort, formerly of Buffalo, April 23, 1863, age 68; in Clinton, NY.
Wickson, Margaret Jane Thomas, wife of John B., Aug. 27, 1880, age 38.
Wickwire, Lewis R., July 22, 1869, age 34.
Widmer, Joseph, Aug. 17, 1869, age 55 y, 5 m.
Wiedrich, Maria, wife of Michael, April 27, 1879, age 55 y, 3 m, 3 d.
Wiemann, Magdalena, wife of Andrew, Jan. 4, 1880, age 42 y, 8 m, 20 d.
Wiering (or Weiring), Benjamin, July 2, 1878, age 20 y, 9 m.
Wiggins, Benjamin I., father of Dr. D.B., Aug. 15, 1870, age 87.
Wiggins, Emily, wife of William, Aurora, NY, Feb. 16, 1840, age 55; d. in New York.
Wiggins, Mary, wife of Benjamin L. and mother of Dr. D. B., April 22, 1869, age 83.
Wiggins, Miss Minerva, sister of Dr. D. B., April 16, 1869.
Wiggins, William, Aurora, NY, June 24, 1860, age 75; taken to New York.
Wight, Clarissa A., eldest dau. of Capt. John F. of Erie, PA, Aug. 12, 1849, age 25.
Wightman, Eliza, wife of George D., May 18, 1875, age 42.
Wightmans, Amos, Jan. 1813, age 21.
Wilber, Champlin, Nov. 1, 1812, age 55.
Wilber, Mrs. Champlin, widow, Dec. 1812, age 50.
Wilber, Miss Frances P., Aug. 4, 1849, age 20.
Wilber, Mary Ann, July 20, 1873, age 81.
Wilbor, Isaac, Collins, NY, July 26, 1835, age 87.
Wilbur, Mrs. Ednah S., March 10, 1873, age 64.
Wilbur, Margaret, wife of Joshua M., March 4, 1842, age 28.
Wilbur, Norman, Oct. 1880, age 57; found drowned at Tonawanda. "Had him in hospital."
Wilbur, Philip, Feb. 12, 1856, age 65.
Wilcox, Amanda B., wife of William, Jan. 16, 1877, age 25.
Wilcox, Birdsey, formerly of Hartford, CT, April 8, 1861, age 62.
Wilcox, Charles H., M.D., surgeon, 21st Regt. NY State Volunteers, Nov. 6, 1862, age 49.
Wilcox, Cornelia Coburn Rumsey, wife of Ansley, Dec. 21, 1880.
Wilcox, Elisha, May 13, 1865, age 74.
Wilcox, Emeline Jemima, formerly of Buffalo, wife of H. W., architect, Feb. 21, 1860; d. in Erie, PA.
Wilcox, Emma, wife of Edmund, Nov. 9, 1868, age 26.
Wilcox, Frank B., youngest son of the late Birdseye, formerly of Buffalo, April 29, 1873, age 22; d. in Philadelphia, bur. in Buffalo.
Wilcox, Hannah, wife of David, Clarence, NY, Aug. 16, 1821, age 39.
Wilcox, Henrietta M., widow of Dr. Charles H., Sept. 22, 1867, age 40.
Wilcox, Herry, wife of Roswell D., Dec. 23, 1875, age 57 y, 11 d.
Wilcox, Lt. Isreal of the US Volunteers, Clarence, NY, May 1813, age 35.
Wilcox, Jenny A., wife of Robert S., dau. of Darius Smith, April 30, 1857, age 22 y, 4 m.
Wilcox, Joseph, Clarence Hollow, NY, Sept. 13, 1834, age 20.
Wilcox, Lewis, Jan. 21, 1861.
Wilcox, Mary, widow of Col. Benjamin J. of Madison, CT, Oct. 26, 1847, age 84.
Wilcox, Mrs. Mary E., Dec. 1, 1870, age 38.
Wilcox, Norris S., Angola, Dec. 2, 1879, age 22.
Wilcox, Robert S., Jan. 1868.
Wilcox, Susan C. Barrill, wife of John F., Angola, Aug. 2, 1880, age 62.
Wilcox, William W., Oct. 1, 1880, age 62; bur. at Lockport.
Wild, Andrew, son of George, Oct. 1, 1872, age 20 y, 3 m.
Wilder, Ruth D., wife of Milton, Nov. 7, 1873, age 58; taken to Attica.
Wilds, Ellen B., eldest dau. of Electa and H. N., May 29, 1862, age 25.
Wiley, Capt. John, Nov. 16, 1854, age 39th year.
Wiley, Michael, Black Rock, April 26, 1868, age 92.
Wiley, Richard, accidentally shot, Colden, Nov. 24, 1873, age 37.
Wilford, E. Sr., b. in Boston, England, May 4, 1863, age 59.
Wilganz, Christopher, Sept. 1, 1873, age 66.
Wilgus, Alfred W., Nov. 11, 1862, age 67.
Wilgus, Charles H., June 27, 1857, son of Alfred W. of Tampico, Mexico, age 34.
Wilgus, Friend Humphrey, son of A. W., Oct. 19, 1859, age 30.
Wilgus, Jairus A., July 13, 1863, age 28.

Wilgus, John B., youngest son of Nathaniel, Aug. 11, 1854; d. in Stockton, CA.
Wilgus, Juliana, wife of Capt. Nathaniel, Sept. 2, 1830, age 32.
Wilgus, Lavenia, widow of Alfred W., Feb. 25, 1878, age 80.
Wilgus, Lucia K., wife of Nathaniel, Nov. 10, 1849, age 44.
Wilgus, Lewis L., son of Alfred, June 27, 1865, age 38.
Wilgus, Lucy, wife of Nathaniel, July 21, 1834, age 23.
Wilgus, Mary Ann, wife of N., Jan. 7, 1837, age 29th year.
Wilgus, Nathaniel, March 28, 1873, age 80.
Wilgus, Miss Sarah, sister of N. and A.W., May 29, 1849, age 60.
Wilgus, William, b. Aug. 20, 1755, d. April 13, 1817, bur. Buffalo; Soldier of the Revolution.
Wilgus, William H., son of Nathaniel, Aug. 1, 1862, age 48; d. in Minneapolis, MN.
Wilgus, William J., artist, July 23, 1853, age 34.
Wilhelm, David, Lancaster, Oct. 22, 1875, age 43 y, 6 m, 22 d.
Wilhelm, John, Lancaster, April 11, 1873, age 75 y, 3 m, 1 d.
Wilhelm, John N. Jr., Millgrove, March 5, 1878, age 23 y, 6 m, 25 d.
Wilhelm, Louis, March 15, 1874, age 53 y, 4 m.
Wilkenson, Betsy, wife of Ansel, East Hamburgh, NY, March 1, 1851, age 51 y, 5 m.
Wilkes, Helen Marion, Dec. 26, 1866, age 24 y, 6 m, 9 d; wife of George H. of Brantford, Canada West, eldest dau. of E. St. John Bemis of Buffalo.
Wilkeson, Lt. Bayard, July 1863; bur. July 11th.
Wilkeson, Eli R., 2d son of the late Samuel, April 13, 1849, age 40th year.
Wilkeson, Jane, wife of Samuel, April 6, 1819, age 35.
Wilkeson, Lt. John, June 1862; remains brought to Buffalo for burial July 1863.
Wilkeson, John E., painter, drowned June 28, 1874, age c. 29.
Wilkeson, Maria Louisa, wife of John, Oct. 7, 1843, age 29.
Wilkeson, Mary P., wife of Hon. Samuel, Aug. 25, 1847, age 52d yr.
Wilkeson, Hon. Samuel, July 7, 1848, age 67; d. in Kingston, TN; bur. Forest Lawn, John Wilkeson lot owner. [From cemetery records, 1958.]
Wilkeson, Sarah St. John, April 21, 1836. Wife of Hon. Samuel, Mayor of the City, d. in Buffalo, aged 39.
Wilkins, Ann Elizabeth Ebbs, wife of George W. of Erie, PA, June 2, 1865, age 28th year.
Wilkins, Clarissa, widow of S.P., Alden, April 14, 1870, age 61.
Wilkins, Jonathan S., father of Mrs. E. Weston, March 11, 1869, age 84.
Wilkins, Julia A., wife of George P., Alden, April 1873, age 20.
Wilkins, Mrs. Nancy Jane, Oct. 27, 1865, age 76.
Wilkins, Stillman P., formerly of Reading, Windsor Co., VT, Alden, NY, March 14, 1857, age 28.
Wilkins, capt. Thomas, Erie, PA, Dec. 1870.
Wilkinson, Rev. Charles, Akron, Feb. 24, 1872, age 41.
Wilkinson, Capt. David, Perrysburg, OH, Sept. 8, 1873, age 74.
Wilkinson, Mary Ann, Aug. 16, 1873, age 27.
Wilkinson, William, bricklayer, July 11, 1868, age 63; sunstroke.
Wilkinson, William, July 24, 1870, age 30; drowned.
Willard, Helen Kimberly, wife of Nelson, Feb. 16, 1847, age 33.
Willard, James M., formerly of Buffalo, Oct. 28, 1869, age 56; d. at Oriskany Falls, Oneida Co., NY.
Willard, John, Willink, March 20, 1871, age 59.
Willard, Nelson, June 18, 1871, age 68.
Willard, Timothy, May 12, 1837, age 55; d. in Sheldon Centre, Genesee Co., NY.
Willcox, Thomas R., printer, Aug. 29, 1838, age 32; in Arkwright, Chautauqua Co., NY.
Willcox, William, Sept. 5, 1866, age 77; taken to Palmyra, NY.
Willets, William, Cincinnati, OH, June 13, 1846, at the American Hotel, age 27; taken to Skaneateles, NY.
Willett, Mrs. Christiana, formerly of Buffalo, Feb. 27, 1878, age 57; d. in Detroit.
Willett, James, b. Oct. 10, 1831, d. June 6, 1877.
Williams, Abner M., killed in action of war 1812; Sept. 1813.
Williams, Addison G., July 15, 1873, age 59; d. in Aiken SC, bur. in Buffalo.
Williams, Capt. Alexander John, Aug. 15, 1814, in 24th year. Killed in the night attack by the British on Fort Erie, Aug. 14-15, 1814. Bur. in Forest Lawn.

Williams, Alfred M. Sr., Aug. 14, 1861, age 49.
Williams, Alonzo M., Boston, NY, April 21, 1853, age 33.
Williams, America Pinckney, wife of Capt. William G. of the US Topographical Engineers, April 25, 1842, age 38.
Williams, Betsey, wife of John F., May 15, 1860, age 43.
Williams, Betsey, widow of Charles, Dec. 20, 1879, age 84 y, 9 m.
Williams, Caleb, Newstead, May 25, 1873, age 72 y, 6 m, 14 d.
Williams, Catherine, wife of O.V., May 7, 1862, age 42 y, 6 m.
Williams, Catharine, wife of Watkins, July 30, 1873, age 68.
Williams, Charles, brother of Judge Nathan Williams of Utica, NY, Jan. 12, 1861, age 74.
Williams, Charles, sailor, drowned, Aug., 7, 1874, age c. 30.
Williams, Charles, Co. Almshouse, Oct. 29, 1876, age 22.
Williams, Charles H., May 18, 1875, age 60.
Williams, Clara A., Nov. 19, 1879, age 27 y, 2 m, 5 d.
Williams, Miss Clarissa, sister of William Williams, dau. of Samuel of Bolton, CT, Sept. 28, 1852.
Williams, Daniel, Black Rock, NY, Aug. 1826, age 35.
Williams, Daniel B., East Buffalo, NY, Feb. 4, 1866, age 39 y, 8 m; taken to Stockbridge.
Williams, Dudley D., father of Benjamin H., March 3, 1875, age 71.
Williams, Mrs. E. A., formerly of Buffalo, Feb. 4, 1872; d. at Elizabeth, NJ.
Williams, ELijah P., Jan. 26, 1871, age 65.
Williams, Eliza Bostwick, wife of George A., Aug. 14, 1876, age 29.
Williams, Eliza, Aug. 1, 1849, age 55; in Niagara Falls, NY.
Williams, Eliza Watson, wife of Horace, Dec. 24, 1871, age 39.
Williams, Mrs. Elizabeth, April 15, 1862, age 82d yr.; taken to Palmyra, NY.
Williams, Elizabeth F., widow of Alfred M., Feb. 28, 1878, age 65 y, 7 m, 13 d.
Williams, Ellen E., wife of Isaiah T., formerly of Buffalo, Feb. 14, 1877; d. in NY City.
Williams, Emily B., wife of Daniel, July 14, 1867, age 50.
Williams, Frances E., wife of Howell C., June 20, 1872, age 33 y, 8 m; d. in Williamsville, NY.
Williams, Frank H., July 4, 1872, age 39.
Williams, Capt. George, Nov. 19, 1867, age 51 y, 4 m, 19 d.
Williams, George W., April 23, 1866, age 35.
Williams, Mrs. Hannah, March 21, 1849, age 55.
Williams, Hannah, wife of E. P., Oct. 29, 1866, age 54.
Williams, Helen C. Moore, wife of Edward W., April 21, 1866, age 31.
Williams, Helen E. Gilman, wife of V.R., June 1, 1871, age 33.
Williams, Helen M., wife of Albert B., Tonawanda, March 25, 1870, age 30.
Williams, Henry, railroad accident, Aug. 28, 1876, age 33.
Williams, Henry R., formerly of Buffalo, July 19, 1853, age 43, d. in Buffalo; resident of Grand Rapids, MI.
Williams, James, March 3, 1872, age c. 30.
Williams, James, May 4, 1875, age 47 y, 19 d.
Williams, James, Sept. 24, 1876, age 65.
Williams, John, formerly of Buffalo, Nov. 24, 1864, age 21. Shot himself in Kent Co., MI. Youngest son of William Williams of Buffalo. Adopted son of Levi and Sarah Hodges.
Williams, John, Co. Almshouse, July 25, 1878, age 66.
Williams, John B., Aug. 12, 1852, age 32.
Williams, John F., Jan. 24, 1865, age 45.
Williams, John R., Aug. 12, 1849, age 40.
Williams, Jonas, Williamsville, NY, Oct. 22, 1819, age 36.
Williams, Jonathan B., Aug. 20, 1871, age 50; taken to Fredonia.
Williams, Julia, wife of George H., Oct. 22, 1866, age 34; taken to Hamilton, Madison Co., NY.
Williams, Laura S., wife of Ortis B., Sept. 13, 1853, age 24.
Williams, Levi S., Nov. 24, 1872, age 40 y, 2 m, 21 d.
Williams, Lorin L., Aug. 26, 1859, age 30.
Williams, Louisa, widow of John R. Williams, May 13, 1863, age 58.
Williams, Louise M., wife of W. A., June 16, 1878, age 32 y, 2 m, 10 d.
Williams, Lucinda, Boston, NY, wife of Joseph, April 8, 1853, age 55.

Williams, Lucy, wife of William, late cashier Niagara Bank, Aug. 30, 1829, age 20.
Williams, Lucy Clark, wife of L.H., July 26, 1868, age 49.
Williams, Lydia C., East Hamburgh, wife of Lt. Henry R., US Army, Sept. 3, 1878.
Williams, Marian Porter, wife of George, March 29, 1866, age 31; in Titusville, PA; bur. Lewiston, Niagara Co., NY.
Williams, Marion, wife of Thomas, Sept. 27, 1872, age 23.
Williams, Martha Rochelle, wife of William H., May 26, 1858, age 23.
Williams, Mary, Sept. 24, 1864, age 55, wife of Watkins.
Williams, Mary, wife of Deacon Thomas, Colden, Sept. 24, 1817, age 66 y, 11 m.
Williams, Mrs. Mary, March 23, 1877, age 64.
Williams, Mrs. Mary, mother of O.G., March 6, 1879, age 79.
Williams, Mary D., widow of Deacon Ashley, June 16, 1866, age 84.
Williams, Mary Isabel, wife of John L., dau. of E. Hadley, April 16, 1870, age 31.
Williams, Miss Morgeania B., Boston, NY, May 5, 1854, age 32.
Williams, Mortimer H., formerly of Buffalo, Jan. 6, 1879; d. at Augusta, GA, bur. in Buffalo.
Williams, Nathan Roberts, May 2, 1880, age 32.
Williams, Oliver, formerly of Buffalo, proprietor of the Eagle Tavern, April 5, 1841, age 40; in Perry, Genesee Co., NY.
Williams, Oliver H., formerly of West Falls, Nov. 30, 1868; d. at Six Corners, MI.
Williams, Oscar V., May 19, 1862, age 46 y, 1 m, 19 d.
Williams, Otis, formerly from Hartford, CT, May 12, 1831, age 30.
Williams, Priscilla, May 3, 1869, age 29.
Williams, Ralph, March 30, 1873, age 64.
Williams, Richard, March 1862.
Williams, Sarah Ann, wife of O.H.P., July 28, 1852, age 27.
Williams, Mrs. Susan Storrs, formerly of Buffalo, dau. of the late Lucius Storrs of Buffalo, June 3, 1878, age 46; d. in Chicago.
Williams, Thomas, father of Mrs. B. Lyman, Sept. 19, 1863, age 60.
Williams, Thomas, May 14, 1878, age 27.
Williams, Thomas P., formerly of Buffalo, Nov. 16, 1857, age 33; d. in Milwaukee, WI.
Williams, Thomas T., formerly of Buffalo, 1853 in New Orleans, recently; taken to Cincinnati, OH.
Williams, THomas W., formerly of Buffalo, July 27, 1861, age 51; d. in Emerald Grove, WI.
Williams, Watkins, formerly of Buffalo, March 24, 1871, age 68.
Williams, William, Aug. 1, 1849, druggist, age 55; in Niagara Falls, NY.
Williams, William, Nov. 27, 1853, age 53.
Williams, William, Sept. 10, 1876, age 61.
Williams, William G., Capt., Corps of Topographical Engineers, US Army, Sept. 21, 1846, age 45. Bur. Forest Lawn.
Williams, Windsor L., Sept. 23, 1867, age 24th year; at General Hospital.
Williams, Zerviah, wife of Oliver, formerly of Utica, NY, Oct. 27, 1840, age 35th year.
Williamson, Elizabeth, wife of Eli, Feb. 8, 1849, age 33.
Williamson, Elizabeth, wife of Capt. Robert, Jan. 17, 1848, age 22.
Williamson, Jane, mother of E. of Buffalo Steam Engine Works, July 25, 1848, age 67.
Williamson, Mary, wife of Lewis, Oct. 30, 1877.
Willink, Wilhelm, May 1841.
Willis, Betsey Amelia, wife of Nathan, Alden, NY, March 23, 1825, age 28th year.
Willis, Charles, only son of Charles, formerly of Buffalo, March 30, 1872, age 29 y, 2 m; d. at Bosanquet, Ontario.
Willis, Juliana, wife of M.H., April 4, 1863.
Willis, Lt. Lander, Ullman's Brigade, Alden, NY, Oct. 20, 1864, age 24.
Willis, Nathan, Alden, NY, Jan. 9, 1865, age 79.
Willis, WIlliam Pitts, A.M., M.D., Alden, NY, Jan. 7, 1866, age 31.
Willson, Abijah, Hamburgh, NY, Jan. 1813, age 30.
Willson, John C., Feb. 11, 1851, age 28.
Willson, Joseph, Hamburgh, NY, Jan. 1813, age 40.
Willson, Juliette, wife of Abner, March 28, 1874, age 36.
Willson, Sarah S., wife of Henry, April 14, 1873, age 20.
Willyoung, Maria Kittinger, wife of John, Aug. 4, 1873, age 32.

Willyoung, Michael, Cheektowaga, April 25, 1877, age 82 y, 2 m, 12 d.
Wilson, ---, (Bloomfield), fell during War of 1812, Jan. 1814.
Wilson, Mr., stone cutter, Williamsville, NY, Aug. 9, 1823, age 21.
Wilson, Mrs. A. E., May 26, 1866, age 29.
Wilson, Alfred, March 24, 1876, age 47.
Wilson, Andrew, late of Fife Shire, Scotland, July 25, 1854, age 46.
Wilson, Mrs. Ann, June 25, 1874, age 58 y, 11 m.
Wilson, Charles A., March 5, 1847, age 46; Commercial Reporter of the *Buffalo Commercial Advertiser*.
Wilson, Cordelia, North Buffalo, NY, wife of Samuel, May 2, 1866, age 57.
Wilson, Elizabeth, widow of Andrew, Jan. 15, 1878, age 78.
Wilson, Frances, wife of James R., Jan. 22, 1859, age 30; in Batavia, NY.
Wilson, Francis W., Jan. 15, 1876, age 21 y, 3 m.
Wilson, George, May 23, 1874, age 50.
Wilson, Guilford Reed, Feb. 18, 1877, age 64.
Wilson, James, Aug. 25, 1864, age 64.
Wilson, Jeanie C., March 1864; bur. March 19th.
Wilson, John, July 1, 1878, age 26 y, 6 m, 24 d.
Wilson, John A., Brant, Dec. 27, 1874, age c. 30.
Wilson, John A., probable suicide, Ridgway, Ontario, March 28, 1875, age 51.
Wilson, John Q. A., Nov. 6, 1875, age 50.
Wilson, John Tanner, formerly of Buffalo, April 25, 1872; d. in New Orleans.
Wilson, Jonathan B., brother of Mrs. D. Belden, Alden, NY, Jan. 26, 1852.
Wilson, Josephine E., wife of Alfred, March 27, 1879, age 38 y, 4 m.
Wilson, Julia A., widow of Charles A., April 29, 1869, age 68.
Wilson, Louisa, wife of D.W., Dec. 22, 1870, age 28.
Wilson, Lucy, Hamburgh, NY, wife of Abner, June 10, 1826, age 47.
Wilson, Maggie Rose, wife of M.P., Jan. 1, 1872.
Wilson, Marion L., Aurora, NY, wife of Charles W., Sept. 28, 1858, age 29.
Wilson, Marmaduke P., Jan. 5, 1872.
Wilson, Mary, formerly of Sardinia, wife of Benjamin W., Feb. 7, 1874, age 51 y, 2 m, 21 d; d. at Hartland, NY.
Wilson, Mary Ann S., formerly of Buffalo, wife of Matthew, Dec. 2, 1860; d. in Brooklyn, NY.
Wilson, Mrs. Minerva, March 19, 1873, age 73.
Wilson, Dr. Peter (De jeh non da weh hoh), Cattaragus Reservation, March 1872.
Wilson, Phebe, wife of John, May 20, 1854, age 55.
Wilson, Samuel, Black Rock, NY, formerly of Mings Clave Hants, England, Aug. 10, 1852, age 34.
Wilson, Mrs. Sarah A., Dec. 5, 1865, age 53.
Wilson, Stephen, Williamsville, June 13, 1875, age 70.
Wilson, Thomas B., formerly of Buffalo, newphew of James Franklin, killed by gas explosion in Topeka, KS, June 21, 1870.
Wilson, William, seaman, lost on the Schooner *LaPetite*, Nov. 1874.
Wilson, William Thomas, formerly of Buffalo, shot in Memphis, TN, Sept. 30, 1863, age 34th year.
Wiltse, Jeremiah, Clarence, NY, July 10, 1844, age 64.
Wimple, Miss F., Jan. 18, 1845, age 69.
Winant, A.S., formerly of Buffalo, Sept. 20, 1879; drowned in Milwaukee.
Winants, Mrs. Esther, mother of Warren and George Bryant, June 28, 1871, age 90.
Winch, Mrs. Nancy, July 6, 1866, age 54; taken to Watertown, NY.
Winchell, Mary Elizabeth, dau. of Joseph W. Winchell, July 7, 1860, age 28 y, 6 m; taken to Erie.
Winchester, Dr. Elijah C., Sept. 8, 1862, age 45.
Wine, William, sailor, Oct. 10, 1847.
Winfield, Elizabeth, Dec. 15, 1879, age 54.
Wing, Abigail, Concord Center, NY, wife of Benjamin, June 2, 1839, age 56.
Wing, Albert G., formerly of Buffalo, Dec. 22, 1879, age 37; d. at Burlington, VT.
Wing, Alexander Hamilton, formerly of Buffalo, April 12, 1877, age 60; d. in Chicago, bur. in Buffalo.

Wing, Almanza, formerly of Buffalo, wife of George F., Feb. 26, 1865, age 44th year; d. in Brooklyn, NY.
Wing, Sgt. Charles, June 1862.
Wing, George R., April 20, 1869, age 24.
Wing, Halsey R., formerly of Buffalo, Jan. 26, 1870, age 61; d. at Glens Falls, NY.
Wing, Horace, formerly of Buffalo, Jan. 20, 1867, age 77; in Burlington, VT.
Wing, Horace Jr., Sept. 22, 1858, age 34 y, 6 m, 22 d.
Wing, M. A., wife of J. G., Jan. 7, 1847, age 29th year.
Wing, Ruth K., wife of Stephen, Collins, NY, March 24, 1866, age 58.
Wing, Stephen, formerly of Collins, Sept. 13, 1873, age 73; d. at Plattsburgh, NY, bur. at North Collins.
Wingels (or Minels), Gerhardt, laborer, drowned in canal, June 29, 1879, age 54.
Wingfield, Walter Fay, son of Mrs. Eli Cook, Feb. 9, 1861, age 25; d. in Brooklyn, NY; bur. in Buffalo.
Winne, Dr. Charles, May 1877.
Winne, Jellis D., printer, brother of Isaac of Albany, NY, late of Buffalo, Oct. 6, 1839, age 29; d. in Savannah, GA.
Winne, Charles, M.D., May 9, 1877, age 65; taken to Albany.
Winship, Aaron N., Oct. 25, 1878, age 59.
Winship, Ezra T., Evans, NY, March 21, 1864, age 70.
Winship, Sally B., widow of Ezra T., Evans, NY, March 1866, age 62.
Winship, Sarah A., wife of A.N., July 16, 1878, age 58.
Winslow, Altheda, wife of Myron D., Evans, NY, June 2, 1846, age 34.
Winslow, Henry C., Dec. 14, 1876, age 36.
Winslow, Julia Ann, Evans Centre, NY, wife of A.D., Feb. 24, 1845, age 32.
Winslow, Nathan C., formerly of Buffalo, June 9, 1880, age 67.
Winspear, William, Elma, June 21, 1878, age 66; taken to Lancaster.
Winter, Ann, wife of George, Dec. 17, 1879, age 43.
Winter, Matilda, June 28, 1880, age 70 y, 3 m, 24 d.
Winterling, Frederick, Nov. 6, 1879, age 50 y, 9 m, 6 d.
Winters, Henry, suicide, Dec. 21, 1876, age 40.
Winters, James, Aurora, Dec. 9, 1874, age 75.
Winters, John, Sept. 8, 1873, age 66.
Wire, Annie, Tonawanda, Jan. 30, 1872, age 91.
Wirt, Harriet E., wife of Hiram, Sept. 20, 1851, age 26.
Wirt, Hiram, Sept. 11, 1852, age 31; in Montreal.
Wishuhn, Philip H., May 14, 1863, age 75th year.
Wisner, Charles H., Dec. 6, 1865, age 25; d. in Chicago, IL, bur. in Buffalo.
Wisner, David, b. 1758, d. 1840, bur. Olcott; Soldier of the Revolution.
Wisner, John, Oct. 26, 1869.
Wisner, Rev. William C., D.D., formerly of Buffalo, July 14, 1880, age 71 y, 7 m, 7 d; d. at Lockport.
Wisskirchen, Christian, M.D., Aug. 2, 1878, age 55.
Wiswell, Daniel H., Dec. 21, 1866, age 65.
Witbeck, Mathew, formerly of Buffalo, March 3, 1876, age 56; d. at St. Catharines, Ontario.
Withers, William, June 11, 1872, age 62.
Witter, Mrs. Lucy B., wife of M.E., Oct. 9, 1866, age 42; taken to Leroy, NY.
Wogan, Mary, eldest dau. of Thomas, Sept. 21, 1862, age 33.
Wohlfart, Peter, June 30, 1874, age 53.
Wolcott, Miss Abby Caroline, Aurora, NY, dau. of Augustus Wolcott, formerly of MA, May 26, 1843, age 22.
Wolcott, Jennie, Clarence, NY, wife of W.F. of Adrian, MI, youngest dau. of Duty Corwin, Esq., June 24, 1854, age 19.
Wolcott, Martha A., formerly of Buffalo, wife of Horatio G., dau. of Gen. Abner Hubbard of Westchester Co., NY, Nov. 22, 1856; d. in Clifton Springs, NY, taken to Covington, KY.
Wolcott, Mary C., Aurora, NY, formerly from MA, May 26, 1843.
Wolcott, Susan H., wife of Joseph W., March 19, 1872, age 41; taken to Northeast.
Woleben, Mrs. Lephy, May 23, 1869, age 78; taken to Fredonia.
Wolf, Anna Mary, wife of Joseph, March 27, 1878, age 37 y, 2 m.

Wolf, Christian, Sept. 27, 1863, age 39.
Wolf, Henry, Jan. 1879, age 23.
Wolf, John J., Oct. 10, 1869, age 59.
Wolf, Mary, wife of Michael, Sept. 5, 1878, age 48 y, 6 m, 27 d.
Wolf, Sarah M., May 7, 1879, age 35.
Wolfe, Barbara, July 27, 1874, age 68.
Wolff, Barbara, wife of Christian, Sept. 11, 1859, age 46 y, 4 m.
Wolff, Catherine Anna, wife of Charles, June 15, 1858, age 23.
Wolff, Charles, only son of Christian, April 11, 1864, age 28 y, 25 d.
Wolff, Christian, June 6, 1865, age 56 y, 11 m.
Wolfe, Gottlieb J., Nov. 27, 1876.
Wolford, Mary, Almshouse, insane, May 19, 1880, age 67.
Wolgemuth, Michael, Erie Co. Almshouse, June 2, 1877, age 55.
Wollaber, Jacob D., June 26, 1877, age 47.
Wolven, Godfrey J., Feb. 14, 1860, age 86.
Wolverton, Capt. George W., formerly of Buffalo, Jan. 12, 1876; d. in Detroit, MI.
Wolvin, Sgt. Oliver, Co. C, 100th Regt., June 14, 1862 in the Hospital, Annapolis, MD, of
    wounds received at the battle of Fair Oaks, near Richmond.
Wolz, George, suicide, Nov. 22, 1874, age 50.
Wood, Capt. Alfred C., April 30, 1860, age 27.
Wood, Asa D., Jan. 26, 1868, age 57 y, 2 d; d. at Farley Brundy Station, VA.
Wood, Bersheba, Water Valley, NY, widow of Welcome Wood, Feb. 8, 1867, age 87.
Wood, Deborah, Hamburgh, NY, wife of Daniel, March 17, 1841, age 72d year.
Wood, Eli, Aug. 20, 1815, age 34.
Wood, Mrs. Eliza, Feb. 19, 1867, age 90.
Wood, Elizabeth, formerly of Buffalo, oldest dau. of William B., Sept. 16, 1875, age 45;
    d. in Chicago, bur. in Buffalo.
Wood, Elizabeth Merrill, Dec. 18, 1857, age 34; wife of F. P.
Wood, Mrs. Emily Steele, formerly of Buffalo, dau. of O.G. Steele, March 31, 1862, age 25;
    in San Francisco, CA.
Wood, Grace, Co. Almshouse, insane, Sept. 18, 1879, age 30.
Wood, Helen A., wife of A.J., Oct. 19, 1878, age 40; taken to Cleveland, OH
Wood, Henrietta W., Jan. 17, 1855, age 21.
Wood, Huldah, Alden, NY, wife of Sewall, Feb. 4, 1860, age 76th year.
Wood, Mrs. Huldah, Brant, April 7, 1873, age 94 y, 7 m, 23 d.
Wood, James, Wales, March 19, 1876, age 85.
Wood, Jemima, wife of John, Dec. 21, 1880, age 46 y, 7 m, 16 d.
Wood, John, Lancaster, NY, native of Lincolnshire, England, April 1, 1861, age 76th year.
Wood, John, Co. Almshouse, native of England, May 26, 1876, age 27.
Wood, Mrs. John D., March 18, 1865, age 23.
Wood, John D., formerly of Buffalo, Jan. 23, 1877; d. at Cincinnati, OH.
Wood, Joseph, Collins, NY, Oct. 10, 1830, age 77.
Wood, Julia A., sister of Mrs. P.B. Eaton, Aug. 25, 1867.
Wood, Linus R., son of John, Lancaster, NY, Aug. 1, 1864, age 18 y, 12 d; d. in US Hospital,
    City Point.
Wood, Mary Kempshall, Cardiff, South Wales, wife of William Wood, 2d dau. of Willis
    Kempshall, formerly of Buffalo, Aug. 30, 1864, age 25.
Wood, Mrs. Oliver P., Nov. 1862; bur. Nov. 2d.
Wood, Philander, Oct. 3, 1851, age 34.
Wood, Richard, June 25, 1879, age 81.
Wood, Samuel, May 26, 1880, age 61.
Wood, Sarah St. John, wife of W.W., Jan. 23, 1861, age 26 y, 3 m; taken to Monroe, MI.
Wood, Miss Sarah W., dau. of William, Lancaster, NY, NOv. 5, 1847, age 21.
Wood, Silas F., formerly of Chautauqua, NY, March 19, 1848, age 42d year.
Wood, Solon L., Aug. 14, 1853, age 22.
Wood, Sophia M., wife of W.W., May 25, 1854, age 35 y, 7 m, 22 d; taken to Adams, NY.
Wood, Willard W., June 1, 1867, age 49; taken to Monroe, MI.
Wood, Willis E., March 1879, age 50.
Woodall, John, late of England, March 26, 1867, age 52.
Woodard, Adelaide Maria Ordway, wife of Barnet, July 11, 1867, age 39.

Woodard, Mrs. Mary, mother of Mrs. James Jackson, Hamburgh, NY, Feb. 6, 1855, age 86.
Woodbury, Dr. Lucius, formerly of NH, recently of the city of Mexico, Sept. 12, 1829, age 35.
Woodbury, Marjorie Ella, formerly of Black Rock, NY, wife of A. B., dau. of Mrs. Levi Love, Nov. 12, 1862, age 31; d. in Des Moines, IA.
Woodbury, Sophia, wife of Hiram, May 28, 1875.
Wooderson, Capt. E., Aug. 17, 1847, age 51.
Woodhams, Isaac, late of Buffalo and New York, July 4, 1858, age 42; in Springfield, IL.
Woodhouse, Leonard, Hamburgh, NY, April 6, 1841, age 39.
Woodhouse, Mary L., wife of James W., formerly of White's Corners, July 30, 1870, age 34; d. at Brandon, WI.
Woodruff, Mrs. Amanda, Aurora, NY, Sept. 2, 1863, age 68.
Woodruff, Curran Clark, Nov. 9, 1878, age 41.
Woodruff, Cynthia L., wife of William, Jan. 31, 1878, age 61; d. at Minneapolis, MN.
Woodruff, Eli, Aurora, NY, Aug. 8, 1859, age 6? (Last figure not printed.)
Woodruff, Mrs. Elizabeth, March 22, 1848, age 61.
Woodruff, Ephraim, Aurora, NY, June 5, 1840, age 69.
Woodruff, Harriet, dau. of Eli, Aurora, NY, Oct. 1, 1845, age 30.
Woodruff, Henry S., formerly of Buffalo, Oct. 31, 1865, age 42d year; in Franklinville, Cattaraugus, Co., NY.
Woodruff, Inez L., Colden, Aug. 12, 1880, age 22.
Woodruff, Isaac, April 20, 1832, age 55; colored man.
Woodruff, Bvt. Gen. Israel Carl, formerly of Buffalo, Dec. 10, 1878.
Woodruff, John, East Aurora, NY, date of death unknown, age 79. (May 5, 1879)
Woodruff, Josiah, May 29, 1847, age 57.
Woodruff, Lawrence J., Aurora, NY, Jan. 14, 1838, age 44.
Woodruff, Lucy R. Olden, Griffins Mills, Aug. 2, 1872, age 36 y, 3 m, 11 d.
Woodruff, Mr. Romanta, Colden, Aug. 17, 1880, age 87 y, 5 m, 15 d.
Woodruff, Samuel, Sept. 12, 1870, age 73.
Woodruff, Taylor, Aurora, NY, June 17, 1848, age 50.
Woods, Ananias, Jan. 4, 1876, age 43; colored.
Woods, Annie, dau. of Patrick, Sept. 18, 1871, age 26 y, 8 m.
Woods, David, May 31, 1875.
Woods, Ellen, July 22, 1875, age 71.
Woods, John, late of Holbeach, Lincolnshire, England, Nov. 14, 1856, age 56.
Woods, Patrick, Aug. 26, 1878, age 64.
Woods, Thomas, March 21, 1875, age 44.
Woodward, Mrs. Anna C., Dec. 25, 1872, age 64.
Woodward, Anna Jane, wife of David M., Jan. 11, 1869, age 38.
Woodward, David M., April 19, 1871, age 48; taken to Concord, Erie Co., NY.
Woodward, Elizabeth, Aurora, NY, widow of Timothy T., June 3, 1858, age 97 y, 1 m.
Woodward, Frederick, Oct. 27, 1850, age 20.
Woodward, James S. D., Oct. 24, 1854, age 23 y, 11 m.
Woodward, Jane, adopted dau. of H.B., Evans, Aug. 28, 1874, age 24.
Woodward, Jenny M., wife of William H., dau. of Nathan Farrington of Franklin, MA, Aug. 3, 1855; taken to Franklin, MA.
Woodward, Oscar B., Oct. 4, 1872, age 59.
Woodward, Vashti, wife of Jonathan, Alden, Sept. 15, 1872, age 70.
Woodward, Walter S., brother of the late S.W., Nov. 25, 1873, age 68; d. at Hudson City, NJ, bur. in Buffalo.
Woodward, William H., suicide, Jan. 6, 1876, age 50.
Woodworth, Hiram, June 19, 1877, age 67.
Woodworth, Maria M., Oct. 7, 1852, age 23; taken to Herkimer, NY.
Woodworth, Rial N., Dec. 17, 1836, age 55.
Woolcott, James, Aurora, NY, June 1848, age 65.
Woolcott, Wyatt, formerly of Aurora, March 31, 1869, age 69; d. in Boone Co., IL.
Woolfenden, Edward, Jan. 15, 1867, age 51.
Woolley, Martha, Feb. 1, 1873, taken to Toronto.
Woolley, William P., Sept. 7, 1850, late of Louisville, KY.
Woolsey, Myron H., May 20, 1875, age 38; taken to Abbott's Corners.

Woolson, Hon. Theron W., formerly of Tonawanda, Nov. 1872; d. at Mt. Pleasant, Henry Co., IA.
Woolworth, Frances J., dau. of Hon. Richard, formerly of Buffalo, March 23, 1878; d. in Syracuse.
Worcester, Caroline T., widow of Capt. Jacob, March 4, 1872, age 57.
Worcester, Capt. Jacob, Nov. 3, 1852, age 50.
Workeron, John, accident, Pine Hill, Feb. 23, 1877, age 23.
Workman, Edwin, Aug. 8, 1876, age 41 y, 4 m.
Worley (or Werle), Frank M., suicide, Aug. 19, 1873, age 20.
Wormwood, Mrs., Sept. 11, 1875; d. at the Church Home.
Worth, Mrs. Leonard, April 2, 1871, age 62.
Worthington, Lotta E., widow of Richard P., Feb. 15, 1879, age 26.
Worthington, Richard P., Sept. 19, 1878, age 40.
Wren, Alice, formerly of Buffalo, March 1877. Killed at Cape Town, Cape of Good Hope, Africa, by savages. (Account denied in April 3d.)
Wright, Alvin, Wales Centre, NY, Feb. 21, 1861, age 61.
Wright, Hon. Amos, Clarence, NY, Oct. 20, 1850, age 55.
Wright, Ansel, civil engineer, Aug. 17, 1872; d. in Port Sarnia, Ontario, bur. in Buffalo.
Wright, Rev. Asher, Missionary to the Seneca Indians, April 13, 1875 at the Seneca Mission House on the Cattaraugus Reservation; age 74th year.
Wright, Austin Hume, late of Clarence, NY, Aug. 16, 1845, age 32d year; d. in East Troy, WI Territory.
Wright, Bridget, wife of Matthew, April 15, 1879, age 68.
Wright, Mrs. Catharine, March 30, 1877, age 77.
Wright, Charles, Erie Co. Almshouse, March 6, 1876, age 42.
Wright, Chauncey L., brother of M.C.F., formerly of Buffalo, Feb. 19, 1869, age 64; d. at Waukegan, IL.
Wright, Miss Cynthia, late of St. Albans, VT, April 12, 1850, age 49th year.
Wright, Eliza C., widow of Hon. George W., of Genesee Co., March 30, 1876, age 66.
Wright, Mrs. Elizabeth, April 12, 1847, age 75 y, 7 m.
Wright, Elizabeth Ellen, wife of John Edward, May 20, 1853, age 27.
Wright, Ellen, wife of Malden, formerly of Buffalo, Aug. 10, 1856, age 44 y, 24 d; in Davenport, IA.
Wright, George, formerly of Wootton Waven, Warwickshire, England, Jan. 30, 1868.
Wright, Henry A., May 22, 1879, age 66 y, 3 m.
Wright, Henry C., only child of Judge Wright, Clarence, NY, Oct. 18, 1852, age 27.
Wright, Horatio N., April 16, 1848, age 35th year.
Wright, Isabelle, Springville, NY, Dec. 30, 1861, age 19 y, 4 m.
Wright, James, West Seneca, March 10, 1879, age 79.
Wright, Miss Jane Eliza, Jan. 10, 1860, age 22.
Wright, John E., Feb. 16, 1856, age 90 y, 4m.
Wright, Joseph, First Mate of the *Erastus Corning*, July 6, 1873, age 39 y, 2 m, 17 d; bur. in Milwaukee, WI.
Wright, Miss Julia A., Dec. 30, 1871, age 28.
Wright, Lavinia L., March 9, 1880, wife of A.P.
Wright, Lucinda, widow of Hon. Amos, Clarence, NY, Oct. 18, 1852, age 52.
Wright, M. Alonzo, Aug. 2, 1880, age 54.
Wright, Mary, April 13, 1875, age 20.
Wright, Mary, Dec. 27, 1880, age 56; widow of Willis.
Wright, Mary L. Thomas, wife of William, Aug. 31, 1876.
Wright, Mary S. Thomas, wife of William, Aug. 29, 1876.
Wright, Patrick, Almshouse, Nov. 20, 1879, age 65.
Wright, Rebecca, wife of C.F., Jan. 9, 1865, age 58.
Wright, Sally, widow of Alvin, Wales Center, Sept. 26, 1877, age 80 y, 6 m, 21 d.
Wright, Sue Lu, wife of J.J.H., Nov. 17, 1878; d. at Kirkwood, MO.
Wright, Susan Haywood, wife of H.O., April 18, 1876, age 52.
Wright, Dr. William B., March 30, 1880, age 41 y, 7 m; d. at Atlanta, GA.
Wright, William E., formerly of Buffalo, Feb. 22, 1878, age 37; at East Bethany, Genesee Co., NY.
Wright, Willis, Nov. 26, 1860, age 34 y, 3 m; d. in Terre Haute, IN, bur. Buffalo.

Wright, Rev. Worthington, Oct. 28, 1873, age 89.
Wuerthner, Ehrhard, March 1, 1875.
Wuest, Margaretha, wife of Frederick, Nov. 21, 1880, age 71 y, 2 m.
Wuest, Frederick, Feb. 4, 1871, age 20.
Wurste, George, Aug. 17, 1870, age 48 y, 5 m.
Wurster, Frederick, Jan. 28, 1880, age 55 y, 11 m, 16 d.
Wurts, Landon J., Aug. 8, 1866, step-father of Mrs. S. A. Walker of Buffalo, age 67.
Wurts, Mrs. Persis M., Jan. 14, 1875, age 71.
Wurtz, Mrs. Catherine, March 20, 1878, age 66.
Wurtzel, Joseph, Oct. 6, 1872; taken to Williamsville.
Wurtzer, Charles M., Oct. 17, 1836, age 30; ex-policeman.
Wuster, Joseph F., accidentally choked, March 11, 1878, age 60.
Wyckoff, Fanny H., June 27, 1869, age 43, wife of Dr. C. Age stated by Dr. Wyckoff Jan. 23, 1874.

Yaeger, Mrs., Alden, June 16, 1877, age 77.
Yarwood, Mrs. Susan M., mother of George A. Phillips, Nov. 28, 1870.
Yates, Capt. John, Lake Captain, June 30, 1849, age 58; in Newcastle, DE.
Yates, Mary Ann, formerly of Buffalo, Oct. 27, 1878; d. in Lockport, NY.
Yates, Philetus S., Feb. 24, 1853, age 39 y, 5 m.
Yaw, Ambrose P., Feb. 18, 1867, age 64.
Yaw, Ambrose S., Boston, Nov. 5, 1869, age 37.
Yaw, Hiram, Boston, NY, Feb. 26, 1859, age 63.
Yaw, Hiram, Boston, Erie Co., NY, June 9, 1880, age 50.
Yax, Jacob Jr., April 26, 1873, age 26.
Yax, Jacob, June 25, 1877, age 60.
Yax, Josephine, May 8, 1887, age 39 y, 10 m.
Yax, Nicholas, Aug. 20, 1852, age 31.
Yearsley, Mrs. Maria, dau. of John Bodamer, Sept. 26, 1873.
Yeoman, Peter D., Sept. 15, 1871, age 46; taken to Monroeville, OH.
Yeomans, William H., Feb. 25, 1871, age 35.
Yonke (or Gonke), Henry, suicide, Oct. 12, 1876, age 46.
York, Harvey, Cattaraugus Indian Reservation, March 17, 1848, age 115.
Yosburgh, Peter M., Dec. 1864.
Young, Abraham, Aug. 6, 1871, age 71.
Young, Amelia B., wife of William F., Feb. 8, 1874, age 56 y, 9 m, 6 d.
Young, Aurora M., wife of Charles E., June 24, 1863, age 42.
Young, Catherine Livingston, wife of William C., April 5, 1872, age 73; taken to Albany.
Young, Eli, July 23, 1875, age 69.
Young, Elizabeth, wife of Peter, July 4, 1880, age 41.
Young, Foster, Jan. 9, 1851, age 68.
Young, Frances Henrietta, wife of William, dau. of James Gray of Gray's Village, Tioga CO., PA. April 21, 1851, age 23.
Young, Francis H., bookbinder, Feb. 20, 1843, age 28.
Young, John, March 4, 1880, age 47.
Young, Joseph, Nov. 30, 1862, age 29.
Young, Kate E., July 3, 1875, age 26; taken to Batavia, NY.
Young, Michael, Aug. 14, 1865, age 28.
Young, Michael, April 4, 1874, age 68.
Young, Peter, March 19, 1874, age 34 y, 8 m, 16 d.
Young, Thomas E., July 17, 1870, age 31 y, 8 m.
Young, Valentine, March 26, 1880.
Young, Walter Morris, April 23, 1875; taken to Albany.
Young, King (Gaw-yeh-gwa-doh), Reservation, May 3, 1835; a Seneca Chief. Bur. by the side of his ancient friend Red Jacket.
Younglove, Mrs. Abby, Sept. 14, 1874, age 65.
Younglove, Robert, formerly of Buffalo, Jan. 29, 1865, age 33; in St. Louis.
Younglove, Elbridge G., Feb. 10, 1878, age 48.
Younglove, Oliver, May 26, 1851, age 50.
Younglove, Rufus H., Dec. 1, 1877, age 36.

Youngs, James, April 29, 1880, age 42; d. at Fairhaven, NY.
Yuncker, Rosa, Alden, NY, wife of Jacob P., May 12, 1864, age 24 y, 18 d.
Yunge, Charles, Oct. 29, 1871, age 50 y, 6 m.
Yurann, George, Lancaster, April 6, 1877, age 82.

Zacher, Clara, dau. of C.D., Sept. 11, 1876.
Zacher, Susanna, Nov. 18, 1877, age 73.
Zahm, Michael, Feb. 19, 1865, age 88 y, 8 m, 17 d.
Zamy, William, son of Patrick, drowned, Sept. 2, 1878, age 25.
Zarchus, Sarah A., June 21, 1875; bur. Forest Lawn.
Zarchus, Sarah Ann, June 21, 1875, age 60.
Zeen, Yocum, suicide, Eden, Oct. 8, 1875, age 84.
Zeidler, Emil, Erie Co. Almshouse, June 12, 1876, age 41.
Zeigler, Mrs. Elizabeth, Dec. 27, 1874, age 57.
Zeller, Frederick, Aug. 6, 1872, age 28 y, 11 m, 22 d.
Zettler, August, Sept. 20, 1879, age 27.
Zuegele, Catharine Dorothea, wife of Albert, June 30, 1873.
Ziemer, Mrs. Louis, Nov. 3, 1879, age 52 y, 3 m.
Zillig, Barbara, APril 10, 1880, age 52 y, 10 m.
Zimmer, Charlotte Caroline, wife of Eustavus, Aug. 20, 1872.
Zimmer, Joseph, Jan. 22, 1874, age 78.
Zimmer, Michael, Dec. 9, 1879, age 45; accidental death.
Zimmer, Rudolph, Clarence, Jan. 6, 1879, age 81.
Zimmerman, George, son of William, June 7, 1874, age 20 y, 6 m; d. in El Passo, IL, bur. Buffalo.
Zimmerman, Jacob, Dec. 25, 1865, age 27 y, 6 m; in Indianapolis, IN, bur. Buffalo.
Zimmerman, Martin, May 1, 1871, age 71; suicide.
Zimmerman, Miss Mary, Tonawanda, NY, Feb. 25, 1846, age 26.
Zimmers, Angelina, Oct. 8, 1879, age 21 y, 11 m, 9 d.
Zimpfer, Martin, July 21, 1877, age 71 y, 26 d.
Zing, Michael, March 16, 1877.
Zink, Victoria, widow of George, Sept. 16, 1871, age 58 y, 8 m, 23 d.
Zink, Xavier, accident, March 31, 1878.
Zintl, Mrs. Margareta, March 31, 1878, age 94 y, 7 m.
Zittel, Lydia R., formerly of Buffalo, wife of Frederick, June 19, 1865, age 28th year; in New York.
Zoank (or Zang), Michael, accident, June 3, 1878.
Zoeller, J. C. August, near Millgrove, NY, farmer, April 10, 1879, age 64.
Zook, Charlotte Ann, wife of Daniel M., dau. of Jacob Lyon, June 4, 1856, age 20 y, 8 m, 20 d.
Zook, Margaret, March 27, 1865, dau. of David, age 44 y, 10 m, 7 d.
Zuidema, J. H., Lancaster, Feb. 11, 1879, age 56.
Zurbrick, Christina, wife of Peter, Cheektowaga, May 22, 1874, age 42.
Zwerger, Rev. Leo, April 10, 1878, age 48 y, 6 m.
Zwisken, Jacob, Nov. 3, 1880, age 82.

GAZETTEER

ERIE COUNTY, NEW YORK

The references below are taken from *Gazetteer of the State of New York*, by J. H. French, Syracuse, NY, 1860.

Erie County was formed from Niagara, April 2, 1821. It lies upon Lake Erie and Niagara River in western New York state. Buffalo is the county seat. Towns in the county are:

ALDEN-- formed from Clarence, 1823, and part of Marilla was taken off in 1853. On the east border of the county, northeast of the center. Also a station on the B. & N.Y. R.R. Also listed under Alden: Alden Center, Mill Grove, Alden (Crittenden p.o.) and Wende, stations on the railroad. This area was first settled in 1810 by Moses Fenno. Among the first settlers were Joseph Freeman, John Eastabrook, William Snow and Arunah Hibbard, who came in 1810. Samuel Slade, James Crocker, Samuel Huntington and Jonas Stickney came in 1811; William Dayton came in 1812.

AMHERST-- formed from Buffalo, 1818; Cheektowaga taken off in 1839. On the northern border of the county, between Clarence and Tonawanda. Also listed under Amherst are Williamsville (inc. in 1850), Eggertsville, Getzville, East Amherst and Westwood post offices. First area settlement in 1804 by Timothy S. Hopkins and Elias Ransom, from Great Barrington, MA. Other early settlers were William Maltbury, Jonas Williams, James Harmon, Horatio Kelsey, Seth Canfield, Enos A. Armstrong and James Harris.

AURORA-- formed from Batavia, as "Willink," 1804; name changed 1818. Clarence taken off in 1808, Buffalo in 1810, Concord, Hamburgh and Eden in 1812, Holland and Wales in 1818, and part of Elma in 1857. Central Erie County. Also listed under Aurora are Willink (inc. 1840), East Aurora, West Falls and Griffins Mills. First settled in 1803 by Jabez Warren, Henry Godfrey and Nathaniel Emerson; followed by Joel & John Adams, Tabor Earlle, and Humphrey Smith in 1804 and William Warren, Thomas Tracy, Christopher Stone and Luther Hibbard in 1805.

BOSTON-- formed from Eden in 1817, in central Erie County. Also listed under Boston are Boston Center and North Boston. First settlement was by Didemus Kinney in 1803. Oliver and Charles Johnson settled in the town in 1805; Richard Cary and Samuel Eaton in 1807.

BRANDT-- formed from Collins and Evans in 1839. On the shore of Lake Erie in southwest corner of the county. Also listed under Brandt are Mill Branch (Farnham post office) and Saw Mill Station on the railroad. First settled in 1817 by Moses Tucker. John, Robert and Major Campbell and John West settled in the town in 1808, and Ansel Smith, Robert and William Grannis, and Benjamin Olmstead in 1819.

BUFFALO CITY-- formed as a town from Clarence in 1810. Amherst taken off in 1818, and Tonawanda in 1836. Buffalo Village inc. 1813, and inc. as a city in 1832. In 1853 the town of "Black Rock" was included within the city limits. The earliest notice of the site of the city of Buffalo is found in the travels of Baron La Hontan, who visited this locality in 1687. No white settlers located here until after the American Revolution.

CHEEKTOWAGA-- formed from Amherst in 1839, and a part of West Seneca was taken off in 1851. Lies north of center in the county. Post offices listed include Cheektowaga and Four Mile Creek. First settlement was made by Apollos Hitchcock in 1808. Among other early settlers were Samuel Lasure, Roswell Judson, Abraham Hatch and Maj. Noble.

CLARENCE-- formed from "Willink" (now Aurora) in 1808; Buffalo was taken off in 1810, Alden in 1823, and Lancaster in 1833. On the north border of the county, east of the center. Post offices in the area include Clarence Hollow, Clarence Center, Harris

Hill and North Clarence. First settlement was made at Clarence Hollow in 1799 by Asa Ransom. Gen. Timothy Hopkins settled in 1797; Asa Chapman, Timothy James, William Updegraff, Christopher Saddler, Levi Felton, Abraham Shope, John Haines and John Gardner in 1801; Andrew Durnet, George Shurman, Bera Ensign and Jacob Shope in 1803; and Daniel Bailey in 1804.

COLDEN-- formed from Holland in 1827, an interior town, lying south of the center of the county. Postal villages are Colden and Glenwood. First settled in 1810 by Richard Buffum. Thomas Pope, Josiah Brown and L. Owen settled in 1810, and Jesse Southwick, Richard Sweet, Nathaniel Bowen and Silas Lewis in 1811.

COLLINS-- formed from Concord in 1821. A part of Brandt was taken off in 1839 and North Collins in 1852. Lies on the southern border of the county. Post offices are Collins Center, Angola and Gowanda. First settled in 1806 by Jacob Taylor. Joshua Palmerton, Stephen Peters, Turner Aldrich and Stephen Lapham settled in 1810, and Stephen Wilbur and Sylvanus Bates in 1811.

CONCORD-- formed from "Willink" (now Aurora) in 1812; Collins and Sardinia taken off in 1821 and part of Sardinia annexed in 1822. On the southern border of the county. Postal villages include Springville (inc. 1834), Mortons Corners and Woodwards Hollow. First settlement was in 1808 by Christopher Stone. John Albro and John Russell settled also in 1808; Rufus Eaton, Joseph Adams, Alva Plumb and David Shultiez in 1810.

EAST HAMBURGH-- formed from Hamburgh as "Ellicott" in 1850. Part of West Seneca, as "Seneca," taken off in 1851. Name changed in 1852. An interior town, lying near center of the county. Postal villages are East Hamburgh and Ellicott. First settlement was in 1803 by David Eddy from Rutland, VT. Ezekiel Cook and Zenas Smith settled in 1803, and Amos Colvin and Ezekiel and Daniel Smith in 1804.

EDEN-- formed from "Willink," (now Aurora) in 1812. Boston taken off in 1817 and Evans in 1821. An interior town, southwest of center of the county. Postal villages include Eden, Eden Valley, Clarksburgh and East Eden. First settled in 1808 by Benjamin Joseph and Samuel Tubbs. Among the first settlers were John Marsh, Silas Este and Calvin Thompson who came in 1809; Daniel and Edward Webster in 1810.

EVANS-- formed from Eden in 1821; part of Hamburgh annexed in 1826 and part of Brandt taken off in 1839. In the southern part of the county. Postal villages include Evans, Angola, North Evans, East Evans and Pontiac. First settled in 1804 by Joel Harvey. --- Fisk and --- Worder settled in 1808; Aaron Salisbury and Aaron Cash in 1809, and Andrew Tyler and Elijah Gates in 1810.

GRAND ISLAND-- formed from Tonwanda as a town in 1852. In northwest corner of the county. First settlers were squatters who located soon after the War of 1812.

HAMBURGH-- formed from "Willink" (now Aurora) in 1812. Part of Evans taken off in 1826, East Hamburgh in 1850, and part of West Seneca ("Seneca") in 1851. Named for Hamburgh, Germany. On the shore of Lake Erie. Postal villages are Whites Corners, Water Valley, Abbotts Corners, Big Tree Corners and Hamburgh-on-the-Lake. First settled in 1804 by Nathaniel Titus and Dr. Rufus Belden. Benjamin, Enos and Joseph Sheldon settled in 1806; John Fox and Elisha and David Clark in 1806.

HOLLAND-- formed from "Willink" (now Aurora) in 1818; Colden taken off in 1827. On the eastern border of the county. First settled in 1807 by Jared Scott, Abner Currier and Arthur Humphrey from VT. Followed by Daniel McKean and Ezekiel and Harvey Colby the same year; and by Increase Richardson, Samuel Miller, Theophilus Baldwin and Sandford Porter in 1808.

LANCASTER-- formed from Clarence, March 20, 1833. Part of West Seneca taken off in 1851 and part of Elma in 1857. An interior town in the northeast center of the county.

Postal villages are Lancaster (inc. 1849), Bowmansville, Town Line, Winspear and Looneyville. First settlement in 1803 by James and Asa Woodward. Other early settlers were Alanson Eggleston and David Hamlin who came in 1804; Joel Parmalee in 1805; Warren Hamlin in 1806; William Blackman, Peter Pratt, --- Kerney and Elisha Cox in 1807 and Elias Bissell, Pardon Peckham and Benjamin Clark in 1808.

MARILLA-- formed from Alden and Wales in 1853, near the center of the eastern border of the county. First settlement was by Jerry and Joseph Carpenter in 1829. Rice Wilder, Cyrus Finney and Rodman Day settled in the town in 1831.

NEWSTEAD-- formed from Batavia (Genesee Co.) as "Erie" in 1804; name changed in 1831. The northeast corner town of the county. Hamlets include Akron (inc. 1850) and Falkirk. First settlement made in early 1800's by Otis Ingalls, David Cully, Peter Van de Venter, Samuel Miles, John Felton, Charles Barney, Aaron Beard, Robert Durham, Tobias Cole and Samuel, Silas, John and Thomas Hill.

NORTH COLLINS-- formed from Collins in 1852 as "Shirley." Name changed in 1853. An interior town lying in the southwest part of the county. Post offices include North Collins, Shirley, Langford, New Oregon and Marshfield. First settlers were Stephen Sisson, Abram Tucker and Enos Southwick, from Warren Co., who moved into the town in 1810.

SARDINIA-- formed from Concord, March 16, 1821. Part of Concord was taken off in 1822. It is the southeast corner town of the county. Post offices are Sardinia and Protection. First settlement was made by George Richmond from VT. Other early settlers were Ezra Nott, Henry Godfrey, and Josiah Sumner. Elisha Rice and Giles Briggs settled in the town in 1810.

TONAWANDA-- formed from Buffalo in 1836; Grand Island was taken off in 1852. In the northwest part of the county, situated on the canal. Alex. Logan, John King and John Hersey settled in the town in 1805; Emanuel Winter, Joseph Haywood, Oliver Standard, John Cunningham, Josiah Guthrie, Ebenezer Coon, Thomas Honnan and Joseph Hersey in 1806; Henry Anguish in 1808; and Frederick Buck in 1809.

WALES-- formed from Aurora in 1818; part of Marilla taken off in 1853. Near the center of the eastern border of the county. Postal villages are Wales Center, Wales and South Wales. First settlement was made in 1805 by Oliver Pettengill. Ethan and William Allen and Jacob Turner settled here in 1806; Charles and Alex. McKay, Ebenezer Holmes and William Hoyt in 1807.

WEST SENECA-- formed as "Seneca" from Cheektowaga, Hamburgh and East Hamburgh, and Lancaster in 1851; name changed in 1852. On the shore of Lake Erie, near the center of the western border of the county. Towns include Middle Ebenezer, Lower Ebenezer, New Ebenezer, Reserve, West Seneca Center and West Seneca. First settlement was by Reuben Sackett in 1826. Other early settlers were Artemus W. Baker, John G. Wells, Isaac Earlle and George Hooper, who located in 1828.

INDEX

Abbey, Austin 1
Abbott, Daniel 1
  G. S. 1
  James 1
  Samuel 1
Abell, C. 1
  Thomas G. 1
  William H. 1
Ackerman, P. I. 1
Adams, A. B. 2
  Asahel 2
  B. C. 2
  Caroline A. 281
  E. C. 2
  Elijah 2
  George 2
  John 1
  John I. 2
  Joseph 281
  Luther 2
  N. H. 2
  W. H. 2
Addington, Isaac 2
  Samuel H. 2
Agen, James 3
Agins, David 3
Ahearn, Thomas 3
Ahlheim, John 3
Albertson, William F. 3
Albro, Louisa 108
  Stephen 108
Alexander, S. 3
Alger, John 3
Allbury, Robert 3
Allen, Archibald 3
  B. 3
  Charles H. 4
  Crayton 4
  Ethan B. 93
  George B., Mrs. 83
  George E. 3
  George W. 3, 4, 172
  Henry E. 4
  Horace 3
  Jacob 4
  James 4
  James, Mrs. 91
  Job 3
  John 4
  John P. 3
  Julia A. 93
  Levi 3, 4
  Lewis F. 4, 52
  Lucy A. 130
  Mary Louisa 172
  Orlando 3, 4, 130
  Philo 3
  Ralph 4

Allen, Stephen 3
  W. P. 4
  William R. 3
Allman, Elizabeth 96
  George F. 96
  John 96
Allmendinger, Charles F. 4
Alport, E. S. 4
Altman, Jacob 5
Amann, Christine 5
Amsden, Ira R. 5
Anderson, Cyrus H. 5
  Cyrus K. 5
  H. S. 5
  James 5
  Robert H. 5
Andrews, Jonathan 142
  R. 5
  Rachel A. 142
  Richard 5
  Sybil 142
  William A. 5
  William H. 5
Angeles, S., Mrs. 214
Ansteth, M. 6
Appleby, James 6
Arey, Charles 6
Argus, Joseph 6
Armitage, James 6
Arms, Richard A. 6
Armstrong, B. 6
  Charles 6
  Christopher 6
  Hiram I. 6
  William H. 6
Arnold, Daniel 6
  George 6
  Jacob 6
  Jonathan 257
  Lewis 6
  Oliver H. 6
  W. W. 6
  William W. 6
Ashley, William M. 6
Atkins, Asahel 7
  Barton 7
  Samuel 7
  Samuel R. 7
Atloff, John 170
Atwater, Moses 7
Atwood, Henry 7
Ault, James 7
Aumock, A. P. 7
Aurere, James R. 7
Austin, B. H., Mrs. 49, 157
  Benj. H. 7
  Benjamin H. 7
  John 7

Austin, Seth 7
Averell, James M. 7
Avery, C. L. 8
  George 7
Ayer, Charles 8
  Ira 8
Ayers, George B. 8
Aylsworth, George 8
Ayrault, Nicholas 8
Ayres, William B. 8
Baade, William F. 8
Babcock, George R. 8
  James 8
  John D. 8
Bachman, Adam 8
Backus, D. C. 8
Bacon, Charles E. 8
  Henry 8
Baetzhold, Augus 9
Bagnall, Benjamin 9
  Samuel 9
Bailey, George W. 9
  Gordon 9, 223
  Horace 9
  Josiah B. 270
  Maria 270
  Mary J. 223
  Samuel 9
Bain, Alexander 9
Baker, Albert L. 10
  Alfred 10
  C. S. 9
  Chauncey 9
  Clifford A. 10
  Daniel 10
  Darius O. 9, 10
  Elisha 10
  Elizabeth 187
  Freeman 10
  Geo. W. 10
  George L. 10
  George P. 10
  George W. 10
  Isaac 10
  Isaac E. 9
  Israel 10
  James H. 10
  Moses 9, 187
  Moses Seneca 9
  Obadiah 10
  S. O. 10
  Theophilus 9
  William 10
  William H. 9, 10
Balcam, Vine 10
Balch, Dan 10
Balcom, Abijah W. 10
  Philo A. 11

Baldwin, C. H. 11
  Cynthia S. 35
  Daniel 11
  Ira 11
  Isaac 11
  James 35
  Wm. M. 11
Baldy, C. M. 11
  Wm. 11
Bale, George T. 11
Balfour, William 11
Ball, G. H. 11
  Joseph 11
  Timothy 11
Ballou, Levi 11
Baltz, George 11
Banks, Levi A. 11
Bannister, John 11
Barber, Daniel 12
  Rowell 12
Barckley, William 12
Bardwell, Smead 12
Barker, Catharine Ann 38
  D. B. 12
  George B. 12
  George W. 12
  Gideon 12
  Jacob A. 12
  Louisa Augusta 58
  Michael H. 12
  Nathan B. 12
  P. A. 152
  Pierre A. 12, 38, 58
  William 12
  Z. 12
  Zenas 12
Barnard, Albert 12
  Edward C. 13
  Frank 12
  Harriet 247
  Ira 12
  Lewis 247
  Othniel FitzHenry 13
  Selah 12, 13
Barnes, Bradford 13
  Elizabeth 238
  George M. 13
  Irvina 13
  J. L., Mrs. 18
  Jacob L. 13, 238
  Jacob L., Mrs. 18
  Joseph 13
  Josiah 13
  Seth 13
  W. T. 13
Barnett, James 13
Barnum, Austin 13, 216
  E. S. 13
  Ellen 13
  George G. 13

Barnum, Juliette E. 216
  S. O. 13
Barr, Augustus 13
  Charles 13
  Rudolph 14
  William 13
Barras, Chas. M. 14
Barrett, Patrick 14
Barritt, Ransom 14
Barrow, James 14
Barrows, A. Z. 14
Barry, Augustus B. 14
  John M. 14
  Mathew 14
  William F. 14
Barth, A. J. 14
  Catherine 14
Bartholomew, Chauncey 14, 55
  Julia H. 55
Bartlett, Allen 14
  Elliott 14
  F. W. 14, 136
  J. M. 14
Bartley, Samuel 15
Barton, James L. 15
  L. H. 15
  P., Mrs. 268
  Phineas 15
  Pliny F. 15
  Theodore D. 15
Bartram, Henry 15
Basinger, Jacob B. 15
Bassett, Gustavus 15
  Jason 15
  Thomas 15
Bates, John 15
  Phineas P. 15
  Roxanna 219
  Thomas 15
Battel, Henry 15
Batty, David 15
Bauer, George F. 16
  Peter 16
Bautz, Elizabeth 152
Baxter, John 16
  Peter 16
Beach, Harry 16
Beales, William John 16
Beals, John W., Mrs. 230
Bean, Aaron 16
  Dixon 16
  William M. 16
Beard, David 16
  Wm. H. 16
Beardsley, Hazard 16
Beattie, John 17
Beatty, Charles 17
Beaugrand, John B. 17
Beaver, Nicholas 17

Becker, Anthony 17
Beckley, John 17
Beckwith, James L. 17
Bedford, John 17
Beebee, Ebenezer 17
  Erastus 17
Beecher, Eneas 17
  Hiram L. 17
  James C. 17
Beeman, Joshua 17
  Samuel 17
Beers, Seth P. 17
Behan, Michael 17
Beiser, Adolph 18
Belden, D., Mrs. 297
  Dexter 18
Bell, David 18
  Lafayette W. 18
  William 18
Bellinger, Peter P. E. 18
Beltz, W. H. 18
Bemis, Asaph S. 189
  Aurelia, Mrs. 232
  E. St. John 294
  Helen Marion 294
  Maria 189
  P. S. 256
Bender, Louis L. 18
  P. H. 18
  Ph. H. 18
Benedict, Alfred 18
  D. V. 18
  George C. 18
  Joel H. 18
Bennet, James 19
  Philander 19
  Seymour 19
Bennett, Andrew 19
  D. Chapin 19
  Joseph 19
Benny, Francis 19
Benson, D. D. 19
  E. W. 19
  John 19
  John, Mrs. 3
  O. P. 19
Bentel, Charles 19
Berry, Hattie 71
  J. 71
  James 19
  Joseph 19
  Matthew 19
Berryman, James 20
  John 20
Bertling, Reinhard 20
Bertrand, Michael 20
Besse, John 20
Besser, Ernst 20
  Johann G. 20
Best, Joseph 20

Best, R. H. 13, 20
  R. R., Mrs. 178
  William 20
  William F. 20
Bestow, Job 20
Bettinger, Stephen 20
Bettis, Stephen 20
Bettys, G. 20
Beveridge, Robert C. 20
Beyer, Philip 20
  William H. 20
Bibaman, Jacob 20
Bickerstaff, Francis 20
Bidwell, B. S. 21
  Benjamin 20, 61, 280
  Benjamin, Mrs. 255
  Charles H. 20
  Daniel D. 21
  Daniel Davidson 20
  J. N. 21
  Jane A. 61
  John H. 20, 21
  Sarah 280
Bigden, Robert 21
Bigelow, E. A. 21
  Samuel A. 4
  W. H. 21
Bigham, John 21
Bignell, John 21
Billings, Charles F. 21
  Henry F. 21
  J. A. 21
  Theodore D. 21
Billyard, Francis 21
Bingeman, John 21
Bird, George W. 21
  W. A. 21, 206
Birk, Jacob 22
Bishop, Albert W. 22
  Amelia 104
  Ann 220
  Christopher F. 22
  DeFrancis T. 22
  Nathaniel 22
  William 104
Bissell, Elias 22
  Elihu 22
  Harry H. 122, 228
Bivins, Homer 22
Bixby, James 22
  Robert S. 22
Black, Braddock 22
  Lytle 22
  Robert 22
Blackmond, Edwin T. 22
Blackmore, John 22
Blackmur, Edward 22
Blackwood, Hannah 198
Blain, Oscar 22
Blake, Joseph M. 276

Blakeley, Joseph 23
Blakely, Erastus 23
  Joseph 23
  Robert 23
  William 23
Blakeslee, G. W. 23
Blanchard, A. A. 23
  G. G. 23
Blauvelt, Elvina 221
  John 23
  John A. 221
Bleiler, Casper 23
Bliss, John 23
  John H. 23
  John Horace 23
Blocher, John 23
Blodget, Isaac 23
Blodgett, Lewis 23
  William H. 23
Blood, David 23
  Ira D. 23, 24
Bloomfield, N. J. 24
Blossom, I. A. 133
  Ira 24
  Ira A. 24
  Ira H. 24
  Thomas 24
Boardman, John 24
  Samuel 24
  William G. 24
Bodamer, John 302
  Maria 302
Bodine, Abram 24
  Cornelius 24
Bodkin, Patrick 24
Bogert, C. C., Mrs. 156
  James B. 24
  L. K. 24
Boggiano, Anthony 24
Boggis, William 24
Bogue, H. P. B. 24
Boice, Isaac 24
Boies, Horace 25
  Joel 25
Boke, James Wilson 63
  Janet 63
Boland, William 25
Bole, C. F. H. 25
Bond, Oliver 25
  Oliver D. 25
  William W. 25
Boniface, Georgia 25
Bonnar, William H. 25
Bonner, T. E. 25
Bonney, David 25
  Zoroaster 25
Booker, B. W. 25
Booman, John W. 25
Boomer, Samuel 25
Boorman, Richard 25

Bordwell, Dennice 25
Boston, William 26
Bosworth, Benjamin 26
  Samuel 26
Botsford, Jerome 26
Bourkhart, Frank 26
Bourner, C. 31
Bouyon, Paul 26
Bovington, E. E. 26
Bowan, Jason 26
Bowen, Anna M. 201
  D. A., Mrs. 19
  Daniel 21, 26, 201
  Daniel A. 26
  Dennis 26
  Fanny E. B. 21
  George W. 26
  Goodrich J. 26
  Isaac 26
  Jason T. 26
  John 26
  Jonathan 26
  Lucius M. 26
  Palmer 26
  Samuel W. 26
  Thomas 26
Bower, Jacob 26
  Philip 26
Bowes, John 26
Bowie, William D. 27
Bowles, Charles I. 27
Bowman, Benjamin 27
  Eli H. 27
  George 27
Boyd, David 27
  Wm. 27
Boynton, Charles 27
  T. N. 27
Bozze, Dominick 27
Brace, Curtis 27
  Lester 27
  Orange 27
  Tamma 27
Bradford, Thomas 27
Bradish, John 27
Bradley, Benjamin 28
  Elias A. 28
  Philo 28
Brady, John R. 28
Bragg, Ellen S. 194
  George 28
  George S. 28
  Maynard 194
Braids, William 28
Brainard, J. G. 28
Brand, Gardner 28
Brathwaite, John C. 28
Brayman, Daniel 28
  Henry 28
Brayton, Charles E. 28

Breckenridge, John 213
　Mary 213
Breed, F. W. 28
Breese, S. Sidney 257
Brett, John 29
Bretton, Thomas 29
Brick, Anthony 29
Brideson, Augustus C. 29
Bridgman, J. W. 29
Brierley, William 29
Briggs, Alexander J. 29
　Ebenezer G. 29
　Morey P. 29
　Thomas 29
Brigs, Isaac 29
Brimmer, Martin 29
Brinkman, Henry 29
Brintnal, Phineas 30
Bristol, C. C. 30
　Cyrenius C. 30
　Daniel 30
　T. M. 30
Brittan, John 30
Brittin, Lewis 30
Britton, Andrew 30
　N. 30
Broad, Thomas 30
Brock, Henry E. 30
Brodie, James 30
Bronson, Isaac C. 30
Brooks, George 30
　Sheldon 30
　Wells 30
　Wells, Mrs. 181
Brosart, Charles L. 31
Brothers, John L. 31
Brouner, George L. 31
Brown, A. W., Mrs. 171
　Alexander H. 31, 32
　Alvah 31
　C. Wheeler 31, 32
　Charles 31
　Cody S. 32
　D. P. 267
　David Paul 31
　Dexter 192
　E. D. 31
　Edward 31
　Eleazer 31
　Enos R. 32
　George 32
　George E. 32
　George V. 31, 32
　Henry 31
　Horace 32
　J. C. 31
　J. F. 32
　J. J. 32
　James C. 31
　Jeremiah 31

Brown, John D. 32
　John F. 32
　John M. 31
　John S. 32
　Joseph E. 31
　Joseph W. 31
　Lorenzo 32
　Lucy J. 192
　Neil 31
　Noah H. 31
　Orange T. 31
　Phebe 32
　Phebe P. 31
　R. R. 32
　Robert 31
　Samuel 32, 223
　Sarah 23
　Sarah A. 223
　Sylvester 31
　Thomas 31
　William 31
　William D. 32
　William O. 32, 50
　Wm. 32
Brownell, Isaac W. 33
Browning, Barnard B. 33
　Potter 33
　Thomas H. 33
Bruce, B. 33
　E. K. 33, 141
　E. K., Mrs. 125, 161
　George 33
　Jacob 33
　R. F. 33
Brundige, C. G., Mrs. 201
Brush, Alexander 33
　Henry B. 33
　Hiram 33
　John 33
Bryant, Abner 33
　Isaac F. 33
　Warren 33
　William C. 33
Bryson, William 34
Bubell, Michael 34
Buchanan, R. G. 202
　Robert S. 34
Buchser, Jacob 34
Buck, H. T. 34
　Thomas 34
Buckland, Andrew I. 34
Buddenburg, J. B. J. 34
Buehl, Christian 34
Buffam, Richard 34
Bugbee, A. W. 34
　Alvin W. 34
　O. 34
Bull, A. T. 35, 276
　Absalom 34
　Charles 34

Bull, E. C. 35
　Eleanor 10
　G. W. 233
　George B. 34
　George W. 34
　Hugh L. 34
　J. B. 35
　Jabez 35
　Jabez B. 34
　Milton 10
Bullis, Hiram 35
Bullock, Samuel 35
Bullson, Daniel R. 35
Bullymore, Joseph 35
　Richard 35
　Thomas R. 35
Bulson, D. B. 35
Bump, Jonathan 35
Bundy, Sanford 35
Bunker, A. B. 35
Bunnell, Levi 35
Bunting, Joseph 35
　Lucinda 35
Burchill, Susan 35
Burdett, James D. 35
Burdette, John 35
Burg, John 35
Burgard, John 35
Burgess, Henry 36
　R. W. 35
Burk, Eliza J. 184
　John A. 184
Burke, Charles G. 36
　John 36
　Michael 36
　Ulic 36
　William 36
Burkshaw, George 36
Burlin, J. 36
Burlock, Annie 277
　Thomas 277
Burmell, Jacob 36
Burnell, Alfred 38
　B. 38
　Elliott 38
Burnett, H. S. 36
Burns, Alexander 37
　Daniel 36
　George L. 36
　James 36
　John 36
　John C. 36
　Michael 37
　Robert 36
　Theodore 36, 176
　W. P. 36
Burnside, Arthur 37
Burr, Emmet D. 37
　Levi C. 37
　Moses 37

Burroughs, Joseph 37
Burrows, L. A. 37
  Roswell S. 37
Burrus, L. G. 37
Burt, George L. 37
  H. B. 37
  Henry B. 37
Burtis, Arthur 37
Burton, J. H. 37
  Silas 37
Burts, Robert 38
Burwell, Bryant 38
Busbridge, John 38
Bush, Ephraim 38
  G. Webster 38
  John 38
  John, Mrs. 111
  W. 38
Busher, F. W. 38
Bussmann, Anton 38
Butler, Ann 201
  Charles W. 38
  Frederick J. 38
  James 38
  Morris 38
  Samuel M. 38
  Theodore 38
Butman, Charles A. 39
  William 38
Butterfield, Robert 39
Butters, John 39
Buttolph, John P. 39
Butts, S. B. 39
Buxton, Braley K. 39
Byers, Robert L. 39
Byrne, John 39
Cadwallader, Michenor 39
Cahill, Joseph 39
  Thomas 39
Cain, Jesse 39
Caldwell, Samuel 39
Calhoun, Nathan 61
Caligan, Charles 39
  John E. 39
Calkins, Delavan 39
  Moses 39
Callahan, Cornelius 40
  Michael 39
  Richard 40
  William 39
Callard, A. 40
  George 40
Callender, Amos 40
  Samuel N. 40
Cameron, Walter 40
Camp, H. B. 40
  John G. 40
  L. 40
Campbell, Alexander 40
  Augustus T. 40

Campbell, C. J. 41
  Charles J. 41
  Colin 40
  Daniel 40
  Henry C. 40
  James 40
  M. A. 40
  Maurice 40
  Robert 40
  Rufus H. 40
  Walter 41
Candee, Charles E. 41
  Joseph 41
Candell, Henry 41
Candler, William 41
Caney, David 41
Canfield, Jared 41
Cannell, Thomas 41
Cannon, George S. 41
  Peter 41
Canty, Eugene 41
  John C. 41
Card, William 41
Carey, John 42
  Murray B. 41
  Richard J. 41
  Samuel 41
Carhart, Jeremiah 42
Carl, Peter 42
Carlisle, T. 4
Carney, John 42
  Wm. 42
Carpenter, Frank S. 42
  Isaac 42
  John 42
  John H. 42
  M. D. 42
  S. W. 42
  William A. 42
Carr, Charles 43
  Clark M. 42
  E. M. 42
  George 43
  John 42
  Peter 43
  Thos., Mrs. 5
Carrier, David 43
Carroll, J. W. 43
  James 43
  Patrick 43
  Thomas 43
Carruthers, George 43
Carson, Joseph 43
Carswell, Allen 43
Carter, John P. 43
Cartwright, Burr E. 43
  E. 43
Carver, Jerome G. 43
  Lafayette 43
Cary, Asa 43

Cary, Truman 44
Caryl, Benj. 44
  Jonathan 44
Case, A. J. 44
  Hugh M. 44
  Joseph G. 44
  M. 229
  Manning 44
  Nehemiah, Mrs. 198
  Patrick 44
  Ruth 229
  S. S. 44
  Whitney A. 44
Cash, Whiting 44
Cass, William S. 44
Castle, D. B. 44
  Lewis S. 45
Caswell, William 68
Cation, John 45
Caulfield, Peter 45
Cavanah, John 45
Cavanaugh, Daniel 45
  Jeremiah 45
Cemeron, Gilbert 40
Chadduck, David 155
  Davis S. 45
  Emma 1
  Mary 155
Chadwick, Edmund 45
Chaffee, Freelon 45
Chalker, Randolph W. 45
Chamberlain, Alonzo J. 46
  J. M., Mrs. 131
  John 46
  Jonathan 45
  Sylvester 45, 93
Chamberlayne, E. L. 46
Chamberlin, Asahel 46
  John 46
Chambers, Hiram 46
Chamot, Frederick 46
Champlin, Jane E. 245
  Lydia Minerva 83
  O. H. P. 46
  Stephen 46, 83, 245
  Thos. A. T. 46
Chandler, A. W. 46
  Isaac 46
  James D. 46
  Louise 46
  Lyman 46
  O. 46
  Oira 46
Chapin, Cooley S. 46
  Cyrenius 47, 129
  Daniel 46
  E. D. 47
  Henry 46
  R. 46
  Seth 47

Chapin, William 46
Chapman, E. W. 47
  George L. 47
Chappell, R. C. 47
Chard, William 47
Chase, Alanson 47
  Charles E. 47
  David V. R. 47
  Edward 47
  George L. 47
  J. L. 47
  Jacob 47
  Thomas B. 47
  William H. 47
Cheney, Orlando W. 47
Chester, A. G., Mrs. 282
  A. T. 48
  Augustus 48
  Charles 48
Chew, Francis W. 48
Chichester, J. L. 48
Chilcott, Amos 48
Child, Jonathan 48
  Perley A. 48
Childs, Isaac 48
Chipman, John B. 48
Choate, E. W. 48
  R. M. 48
  W. H. 48
Chowings, Henry C. 48
Chretien, George 48
  Joseph 48
Christ, Carl 48
Christey, Arthur 36, 48
  Joseph 36
Christoph, E. G. 48
Church, Alvah 49
  Ralph 49
Churchill, C. P., Mrs. 72
  Charles 49
  Emmet L. 49
  F. G. 49
  Frank P. 49
  John 49
  Julius M. 49
  M. A. 49
  Putnam 49
Churchyard, Joseph 49
Clabo, Peter 49
Clancy, P. J. 49
Clapp, A. M. 49
  Charles P., Mrs. 34
  Lewis 49
Claraluna, Cartholomew 49
Clark, Alexander L. 51
  Alfred 50
  Almond 51
  Benjamin 51
  Charles 51
  Charles S. 51

Clark, D. N. 50
  Daniel 50
  E. E., Mrs. 7
  Edward 50
  Erastus 50, 51
  G. W., Mrs. 181
  Geo. R. 50
  Harvey 50
  Henry 50
  Horace 50, 51
  J. W. 51
  James 50
  John 50, 51
  Justus 51
  Minerva 170
  Myron H. 50
  Orange W. 51
  Orton S. 50
  Orville 170
  Richard W. 50
  Satterlee 50
  Seth 3
  Sophronia 228
  Staley N. 50
  Stephen 50, 51
  Sylvester 51
  W. A. 50
  W. S. 50
  William 50
  William A. 50
  Zenas 49, 51, 228
Clarke, Charles E. 51
  Charles S. 51
  Cyrus 51, 277
  Dudley 51
  E. J. 96
  Jeanie C. 277
  John 51
Clarkson, George P. 51
Clement, Jesse 52
Clemons, Alfred 52
  Ann 167
  Frances 167
Cleveland, Margaret 52
  Palmer 52, 262
  William 52
Cleves, W. 256
Cliff, John W. 52
Clifford, James 52
  John 52
Clingen, William 52
Clink, George 52
Clinton, Catharine 253
  DeWitt 253
  George W. 52
  James 253
  Spencer 52
Clor, Michael 52
Close, Emery 52
  Jerome B. 52

Clough, Horace 52
Coates, James J. 52
Coatsworth, C. 52
  Caleb 52
Cobb, A. R. 53
  Carlos 53
  E. B. 173
  Eliza P. 173
  Francis 53
  Frank 53
  John 53
  Oscar 53
  Zenas 53
Cobley, Oliver 53
Coburn, Theodore 53
Cochrane, A. C. 212
  A. G. C. 53
  Lucy 212
Codd, Robert 53
  Thomas 216
  Thomas F. 53
Coe, Thomas D. 53
Cogswell, Henry F. 53
  Henry T. 53
Coit, George 54
  George, Mrs. 15
Coke, John 54
Colborn, R. H. 54
Colburn, George C. 54
  James 54
  William M. 54
Colden, Harriet Sophronia 120
  William H. 120
Cole, John 54
  William W. 54
Colegrove, B. H. 54
Coleman, Charles H. 54
  Jeremiah 54
  John C. 54
  William 54
Coles, Henry 54
Colie, Oliver S. 55
  Samuel 55
  Samuel D. 54
Collard, Nathan 55
Collette, L. 161
  Lambert 55
Colley, D. D. 55
Collignon, John C. 55
Collins, Chas. H. 10
  Daniel 55
  Dennis 55
  Frank 55
  Jeremiah 55
  John 55
  John J. 55
  Moses 10
  Patrick 55
  Thomas 55

Colquhoun, John 55
Colson, Augustus 55
  Frederick 55
Colston, James 55
Colton, Henry 55
  Joseph 55
  Manly 55
  R. P. 55
Colvin, Amos 56
  Luther 56
  Zina 56
Colyer, Charles W. 56
Comesford, H. G. 56
Compton, Lewis 56
Comstock, George 56
  Marcus L. 56
  Martin 56
Conant, Allen E. 56
  R. M. 56
Concklin, Mathew 56
Congdon, John 56
Conger, Noel 56
Conkey, David S. 56
Conkling, Aureilian 56
Conley, Terence 56
Conlon, Thomas R. 119
Conly, William R. 56
Connelly, Edward 56
Conner, Michael 56
Connoly, Thomas 57
Cook, Benjamin 163
  Charles L. 57
  David 57
  E. W. 57
  Eli 49, 57
  Eli, Mrs. 298
  James 57
  John 57
  Jonathan 57
  Joseph 57
  Josiah 57
  Lucy A. 127
  Maggie 163
  Raphael 57
  Seyman 57
  William 57, 127
  William H. 57
Cooley, John C. 219
Coons, George 58
Cooper, Charlotte 2
  John 2
  Joseph 58
  P. H. 58
  William 58
  Young 58
Coots, William A. 58
Coppock, W. R. 58
Corbett, Elijah 58
  William G. 58
Corbin, Caroline S. 14

Corbin, John 58
  Peter 58
  W. H. 58
  Wm. H. 14
Corcoran, Martin 58
  Michael, Mrs. 181
Cormick, Joseph 59
Cornell, George E. 59
  S. G. 59
Corning, Jasper 59
Cornwall, W. W. 59
Cornwell, Francis E. 59
  W. C. 59
Corwin, Duty 298
  Jennie 298
Cosgrove, William 59
Costello, Thomas 59
Cott, George 59
Cotti, Jacob 59
Cottier, Hugh 60
Cotton, Daniel H. 60
  Elisha G. 60
  Rowland 60
Coughlin, Michael 60
Cousins, William 60
Covell, Ezra M. 60
Coveny, Robert 60
Coville, Peter 60
Cowan, Charles H. 60
  Eliza Ann 248
  Peter 248
  Robert 60
Cowing, E. H. 60
  H. O. 60
  John 60
Cowles, E. W. 60
  Samuel H. 60
  Seth G. 60
Coyl, M., Mrs. 281
Crafts, Willard 61
Craig, A. F. 49
  F. S. 49
  Francis S. 61
  Sarah P. 49
  William H. 61
Cramer, Peter 61
  Samuel, Mrs. 30
Crane, George B. 61
  Ruth 61
  Thomas 61
  Willie J. 61
Crary, L. P. 61
  Oscar F. 61
  Spencer 61
Crate, James 61
Crawford, Charles 61
  Julia A. 117
  William 117
Crego, Francis 61
Cremer, James 61

Criqui, Anthony 62
  Joseph 91
Crocker, James 62
  John 62
  William 62
Crolius, John 62
Cronin, James 62
  Patrick 62
Crook, Benjamin 62
Crooker, Erastus 62
  George 62
  William 62
Crosby, Chanucey 62
  O. T. 62
Crosier, John M. 62
Crosman, Irwin H. 62
Cross, Aviral 62
  Daniel 62
  E. T. 62
  Joseph 62
  William 62
Croswell, Jacob 63
Crow, Almond 63
  Olive 63
Crowder, Jacob 63
Crowe, Patrick 63
Crowley, J. G. 63
  Michael 63
  Timothy 63
Cruinkshank, John K. 63
Crumb, W. R. 67
Crump, Benjamin 63
Culbertson, J. J., Mrs. 136
  James A. 63
Culliman, Michael 63
Cullinan, Michael 63
Cumming, James 63
Cummings, A. A. 64
  B. L. 63
  Frank 63
  Haffiel 64
  U. 63
  William S. 64
Cunningham, H. S. 227
  Layton 64
Curran, James 64
Curren, Thomas 64
Currie, Alexander 64
  Sarah 64
Currier, Abner 64
Curry, F. F. 64
  William C. 64
Cursons, Josiah 64
Curtenius, John L. 64
Curtis, Edward, Mrs. 96
  Ja. A. 64
  O. 64
  Robert C. 64
Curtiss, Frederick A. 64
  Harriet Cowles 132

Curtiss, Henry A. 64
  Peter 64, 132
  R. I. 64
  William H. M. D. 64
Cushing, Alanson S. 64
  Lysander 64
Cushman, Josiah 64
Cutler, Abner 65
  Asa 65
  Clara 15
  S. J. 65
  Samuel J. 65
Cutter, A. 134
  A. W. 65
  Sarah 134
Cutting, Harvey T. 65
  Julia 139
  T. S. 139
  Thomas C. 65
  Thomas S. 65
Daetsch, Conrad 65
Daley, Charles 65
  Julia 100
  Louisa 34
  Martin 34, 65, 100
  Martin, Mrs. 159
Daly, James 65
Dalzell, William 65
Damon, Hiram 65
Danahy, Dennis 66
Danforth, J. B. 66
  Loring 66, 186
  Mary 186
Daniel, J. M. 66
Daniels, Charles 66
  Henry 66
  William 66
Danser, Jacob 66
Darbee, John C. 66
  Nathan N. 66
  W. L. 187
  Wallace L. 66
Darby, John C. 66
Dark, John 66
Darling, Jonathan 66
Darrow, Avery 66
  George W. 66
  Harvey C. 66
Dart, Freeman 67
  Joseph 66
  Joseph, Mrs. 70
Dashide, John R. 67
Dashiell, John R. 67
Daul, Andrew 67
Davidson, Douglas N. 67
  Edgar 67
  John B. 67
  Samuel 67
Davis, A. 68
  George 68

Davis, Jacob 67
  John 67
  John H. 68
  Laura 67
  Louis 67
  Noah 67
  Orion L. 67
  W. 67
  William 67
  William H. 68
Davison, B. F. 68
  William C. 68
  William C., Mrs. 292
Daw, Henry 68
  William 68
Day, David F. 68
  David M. 68
  Ebenezer 68
  Elijah 68
  Elizabeth 133
  Eunice S. 213
  George 133
  Hiram C. 68
  John 68
  Lester 213
  Thomas 68, 69
  William A. 69
Dayton, L. P. 69
  M. W. 69
Deacon, Jacob 69
Dean, Jonathan 69
  Stephen 69
Decker, Billens 69
Deeves, William 69
DeForest, C. H. 69
  C. H., Mrs. 262
Degner, Charles 69
Delaney, Arteruina 69
  Thomas 69
Delano, David B. 70
  Elisha D. 70
Dellenbaugh, Frederick 70
Dellury, Thomas 70
Delong, John 70
Demarest, James 70
  James F. 70
  James, Mrs. 44
  William C. 70
Dembach, E. W. 65
Demond, Alpheus 70
Dendall, Nancy 268
  Warren 268
Denham, J. B. 70
Denison, E. H. 70
Dennis, Arad 70
  Daniel 70
Dennison, John M. 70
  William 70
Denny, George 70, 288
  Louisa E. 288

Densham, J. B. 70
  John A. 70
Denter, Lewis A. 70
Derr, John L. 71
Derrick, B. L. 71
  B. L., Mrs. 62
Deshler, D. W. 71
  John G. 71
DeSpies, Gustate 71
DeTamble, Peter 71
Deters, John 102
Deuel, Charles 71
  Isaac 71
  Joseph 71
  Merrit 71
  Merritt 71
  Samuel L. 71
Deuther, George A. 71
DeVeaux, Samuel 71
Devening, Daniel 71
Devenport, Horace 71
Deveraux, Catherine 19
  Elisha S. 71
Deverell, T. 72
Devereux, Julia 141
DeVine, Charles H. 72
Devine, Thomas 72
Devlin, Mercy 72
Dewein, Frederick 72
Dewel, Benjamin 72
Dewey, Norman R. 72
  S. B. 72
Dewitt, Edward 72
Dibble, Clark 72
  R. E. 72
Dick, Robert 72
  W. H. 72
Dickerson, William 72
Dickes, Ralph 72
Dickey, A., Mrs. 90
  Anderson 72
  Benjamin 160
  John 37
  Mary Jane 37
Dickie, J. G. 72
Dickinson, A. B. 72
Dickson, Wm. 72
  Wm. D. 73
Dieboldt, Bernard 73
Diebolt, George 73
Diell, Anna 219
  John 219
Dietz, Julius 73
Dietzer, Daniel 73
Dillane, James 73
Dillon, James 73
  John 73
Dimond, Charles A. 73
  Henry S. 73
Dinkel, Thomas 73

Dinnin, J. R. 73
Dinsmore, A. 73
Dislar, John Burke 73
Dissett, H. 73
 Joseph 73
Dixon, W. G., Mrs. 228
Dizard, James 74
Dodd, William 74
Dodge, Alma 2
 Alvan 2, 60
 Alvan L. 74
 Camantha 60
 Elam 74
 Hampton 74
 Harry 74
 J. W. 74
 Leonard 74
 Wayne 74
Dodsworth, William 74
Doelman, Myron 74
Dolan, James D. 74
Dole, Anthony 74
 Benjamin 74
 Benjamin, Mrs. 249
 Francis 74
 John A. 74
Dominoes, Edward 75
Donaldson, Eliza Jane 190
 James 190
Doney, Henry 75
 Loring 75
Donn, Nicholas 75
Donoghue, Hugh 75
Donovan, Dennis J. 75
 S. E. 75
Doolittle, Charles 75
 Justus 75
Dorr, Frank J. 75
 John N. 75
Dorris, Philo W. 75
Dorsheimer, P. 76
 Philip 76
Dorst, Jacob 76
 Philip 76
Doty, Rufus 76
Dougherty, Alexander F. 76
Douglass, Robert 76
Dover, George 76
 John H. 76
Dow, William F. 76
Dowd, Bernard 76
 John, Mrs. 274
Downs, Edward 76
Doyle, Timothy 76
Drake, John 77
 Marcus M. 77
Drew, E. B. W., Mrs. 289
 Edward 77
 John 77
Driggs, Roswell W. 77

Driggs, Uriel 77
Drullard, Francis 77
 George 77
 John, Mrs. 246
 Soloman 77
Dubois, J. B. 77
 James B. 77
 Philo 77
Duchene, Lucius 77
Duck, D. 77
Dudley, H. P. 5
 H. P., Mrs. 5
 Joseph D. 78
 Stephen 77
 Thomas J. 77
Duel, Benjamin 78
Duer, Edward 78
 William 78
Duff, A. M. 78
 Frank 78
Dumont, Waldron 78
Dumoulin, Joseph 78
 Mary A. 78
Dunbar, Edwin 79
 George W. 78
 Julia M. 134
 Lyman 78, 134
 Robert 78
 Thomas 78
Duncan, John 79
Dunkel, Jacob A. 79
Dunlap, Horace 195
 Lottie 195
Dunlop, James 79
Dunmeyer, Louis 79
Dunn, Taylor 79
Dunning, Martin D. 79
 William R. 79
Durfee, Philo 79
Durick, James 79
Durkee, Dwight 79
 George 79
 George B. 79
 Phebe H. 79
 Rudney 79
 Ziba 79
Durrie, Horace 79
Dusenbury, E. F. 80
 Erastus 79
Duthie, James 80
Dutton, Carlton 80
 James 80
 Wert O. 80
Dwight, T. C. 80
Dwyer, Michael 80
Dygert, J. W. 80
Eagan, John C. 80
Easley, William T. 80
East, James 80
 William R. 80

Eastman, Sanford 80
Easton, James T. 80
Eaton, C. S. 80
 Lewis 81
 P. B., Mrs. 299
 R. 81
Eckhardt, John 81
Eckhart, Jacob 81
Eddy, Amazi 81
 David 81
 Hosea 81
Edes, Alonzo B. 81
Edgarton, Orrin 81
Edge, Edward 81
Edgerton, Julius 81
 Orrin 81
Edmonds, Thomas 81
Edmunds, James J. 81
 Nelson W. 81
Edwards, Emma 1
 L. B. 81
 W. 81
Eeles, William A. 82
Efner, E. 82
 E. D., Mrs. 75
Egelston, Alanson 82
 E. 82
 Eri 82
 Lanson 82
Eggers, Ernest 82
 Ernst 82
Eggleston, Seth 82
Ehle, Melvin 82
Ehrlich, Jacob 82
Eighme, Isaac 82
Elderkin, Alamath 82
 William 82
Eldridge, Benjamin 82
 John R. 83
 Samuel 82
 Solomon 83
 Zoeth 83
Ellas, F. S. 83
Eller, Christian 83
Ellicott, Andrew 23
 Letitia Matilda 23
 Sarah 23
Elliott, Bernard 83
 John B. 83
Ellsworth, Daniel P. 83
Elsesser, John 83
Ely, E. Selden 83
 Israel N. 83
 Samuel 83
Emeigh, Michael 83
Emerick, Jacob 83
Emerson, Charles A. 83
 Charles D. 83
 Nathaniel 83
 Nelson 84

Emery, Edson F. 84
  Josiah 84
Emmons, A. H. 84
  Carlos 84
Emslie, George 84
  Peter 84
English, Abel 84
  William 84
Enos, E. M. 84
  Elisha 84
  Harvey 84
Ensfield, George 84
Ensign, E. W. 84
  Elisha 84
Erickson, Allen 84
Ernst, Christian 84
  J. Frederick 84
Erwin, Henry C. 84
Eustaphieve, Alexander A. 85
Eva, Adam 85
Evans, Edwin T. 85
  Evan B. 85
  H. B. 300
  Henry B. 85
  James C. 85, 272
  Lewis E. 85
  Margaret 220
  O. M. 85
  Rachel L. 220
  Richard 85
  Robert M. 85
Evarts, Henry 85
Evens, Richard 85
Everhart, Jacob 85
Ewing, Benjamin 85
Extein, Hiram, Mrs. 1
Failing, R. 85
Fairbanks, Willard 86
Fairchild, Caleb 86
Fales, Henry 86
Falvery, Michael 86
Fargo, Francis F. 86
  Jerome F. 86
  William G. 86
Farmer, Edward 37
  William G. 86
Farnham, J. B. 86
  Maria A. 112
  Thomas 86, 112
  Walter R. 86
Farnsworth, Levi 86
  Thomas 86
Farr, J. S. 87
  Rinaldo 86
Farrand, Augustus 87
Farrell, C. J. 87
  Michael 87
  Timothy 87
Farrington, Jenny M. 300

Farrington, Nathan 300
Farron, Augustus 87
Farthing, James 178
  Mary Frances 178
Farwell, Eldridge 87
  Henry D. 87
Fassett, A. D. 87
Fattey, George L. 87
Faul, Gottfried 87
Faulkner, George 87
  Morgan L. 87
Faver, Peter 87
Favor, James 87
Faxon, Charles 87
Fay, Amos F. 87
  Ward 87
Feeney, John 87
Feil, Gottleib 87
Feist, John 87
Fellner, Louis 88
Fellows, Abram 88
  Adrian W. 88
  John 88
  William R. 88
Feltes, Nicholas 88
Felthousen, Isaac D. 44
  Margaret 44
Felton, Charles E. 88
  Nicholas 88
Fenner, Seth 88
Fenton, Solomon 88
Ferguson, Alonzo 88
  Andrew 88
  Wm., Mrs. 11
Fero, J. R., Mrs. 190
  R. 128
  Robert 88
Ferrell, John 88
Ferris, Charles D. 88
  Christopher 88
  H. A. 88
  Isaac W. 88
  Nathaniel P. 88
Feyl, F., Mrs. 99
Fiedler, Francis 89
Field, Asa 89
  Charles 89
  James 89
  Jesse H. A. 115
  Jessie A. 115
  M. D. 89
Fielder, Alexander 89
Fields, Robert 1
  Rosana 1
Fillmore, Calvin 89
  Millard 89
  Nathaniel 89
  Sherlock 89
  Simeon 89
Finch, Andrew J. 89

Finch, Daniel 177
  Ephraim 89
  Thasa Maria 177
Findlay, James 89
Finkenstaedt, R. 90
Finley, James 90
Finney, Isabella 57
  John 57
Fish, Anson 90
  Anson T. 90
  Edward P. 90
  James M. 90
  S. S., Mrs. 8
Fisher, D. 90
  Jacob P. 90
  James 90
  James H. 90
  Martin 90
  Michael 90
Fisk, Harvey 90
  William 90
Fiske, William 91
Fitch, Augustus B. 91
  Francis S. 91
  Henry S. 115
  Rosabella N. 115
  William 91
  William C. 91
Fitzpatrick, Thomas 91
Flach, Richard 91
Flagg, Edmund 91
  John B. 91
Fleeharty, John 91
Fleeman, Adam 91, 92
Flegemaker, Joseph A. 87
Fleming, Emmet 92
  John 92
  William, Mrs. 240
Flershein, George B. 92
Flett, John 92
Flint, Austin 96
  Charles G. 92
Flynn, James 170
  Lucy 170
Fobes, S. A., Mrs. 66
  William D. 260
Foley, Bernard 92
Folger, T. P. 92
Follett, O. 92
Folsom, D. E. 92
Folwell, William W. 93
Fones, W. 93
Fontaine, Eli 93
Foot, Star 93
Foote, Clinton C. 93
  John C. 93
  R. S. 93
  Thomas 93
  Thomas M. 93
  William 93

Forbes, C. 93
　D. S. 93
Forbush, Amos B. 93
　B. G. 93
　E. B., Mrs. 3
Ford, E. 93
　Elijah 93, 114
　Mary A. 114
Forde, Matthew 93
Forester, O. 93
Forsyth, James G. 94
　Joseph 94
Fortheringham, Alexander 94
Fortier, David H. A. 94
　James 94
　P. J. 94
Forward, Oliver 94
Fosdick, Soloman 94
Foster, E. 94
　Edward J. 94
　H. A. 94
　Joseph 94
　Manning 94
Fougeron, Simon 95
Fowler, Benjamin 95
　Henry 95
　James S. 95
Fox, A. R. 95
　Charles J. 95
　Christopher G. 95
　Henry 95
　J. H. 95
　Jacob 70
　Simeon 95
Frame, Alexander N. 95
Frampton, Edward 95
Francis, Calvin 95
　Daniel 95
　Julius E. 95
　Lysander 95
　Peter B. 95
Frank, Abraham I. 95
　John 96
　Martin 95
Franke, L. A. 96
Franklin, James 96, 297
Frary, R. A. 96
Fraser, John 96
Fredenberg, Mitchell W. 96
Frederick, Peter C. 96
Frederickson, Christian 96
Freeman, Elias 96
　James 96
　James M. 96
　Joseph 96
　Lansing 96
　Noah 96
French, Harlow 21, 96
　Susan 21
　Wallace W. 96

Freshour, George W. 97
Frick, C. Z. 97
Friedlander, Samuel 97
Friedman, Charles B. 97
Frost, Frederick J. 97
　Ransom M. 97
Fuller, Hosea 97
　James E. 97
　Jerome 97
　Samuel 97
　William O. 97
Fullerton, George 98
　J. C. 98
　James C. 98
　John 98
Furleck, T. W. 98
Furlong, Joseph 98
Fursman, Samuel 98
Gaffney, Anthony 98
　John 85
Gage, G. C. 155
　George 98, 220
　Jane 220
　Ladoiska M. 155
Gager, Charles L. 98
　F. 113
　Sarah E. 113
Gaige, S. P. 98
Gail, Lockwood 98
Gallagher, Edward 98
　F. B. 98
　M. J. 98
Galligan, J. 284
　W. 284
　William 99
Gallivan, Martin 99
Galloway, Alexander R. 99
Galvin, Patrick 99
Gangloff, Peter 99
Ganson, Cornelius B. 99
　Holton 99
　James 99
　Joseph 99
Gantz, A. B. 99, 159, 244
Gardiner, Abraham 99
　Henry 99
Gardner, Charles 99
　D. W. 99
　E. C. 99
　John 99
　John T. 99
　Joseph B. 99
　N. H. 99
　Noah H. 99
Garland, J. G. 99
　Samuel 99
Garner, George 100
Garretson, O. S. 100
Garrett, Cuyler 100
Garrigan, Matthew 100

Garrison, Eugene H. 100
Garvin, Isaac 100
Gastell, George 100
Gastinel, Arthur 100
Gates, Daniel 100
　George B. 100
　Horatio 100
　J. H. 100
　Levi S. 100
　Sigismund J. 100
Gault, James 100
　Thomas 100
Gazley, John F. 100
Gelston, Samuel F. 101
George, J. C. 101
Georger, Charles 101
Gerard, Porter 46
Gerber, Charles 101
Gering, George J. 101
Germain, C. C. 101
　Charles 101
　Ira V. 101
　James 101
　John C. 101
　Rollin 101
Gerring, George B. 101
Getz, Joseph 101
Gibbons, Charles 102
　John J. 101
　Patrick 102
Gibbs, Artemas 102
　Asgill 102
Gibbsons, John J., Mrs. 79
Gibson, A. B. 102
　Caroline 224
　Henry B. 244
　James C. 224
　Mary G. 244
Gidding, A. H. 102
Gifford, Lewis 102
Gilbert, David 102
　E. F. 102
　Erastus 102
　Luzerne 102
Gilchrist, John 102
Gillespie, Anthony 103
Gillet, Caleb 103
　Caleb G. 103
　Henry T. 103
　Israel 103
　Noel 103
Gillett, Helen Shaw 67
　Henry T. 67
　Israel 33
　Israel T. 103
Gillig, Charles 103
　Lorenz 103
Gilman, James W. 103
　Oscar F. 103
Gire, Austin 103

Gleason, Cyrenius 104
  G. B. 103
  W. H. 104
Glennan, James 104
Glynn, E. B. 104
Gockel, Michael 104
Godard, Alvan 104
Godfrey, Charles E. 104
  E. W. 104
  James J. 104
  R. T. 104
Goetz, Joseph 104
Goffe, William 104
Gold, Charles R. 104
  William B. 104
Golden, William 116
Good, John 104
Goodale, Daniel 104
Goodall, W. A. 104
  William N. 104
Goodell, Jabez 104
Goodhue, William H. 105
Gooding, Rodney 105
Goodrich, Chauncey A. 105
  E. H. 105
  Guy H. 105
  Levi 105
Gordon, Charles A. 105
Gorham, Benjamin L. 105
  George 105
Gould, Aaron 106
  Asa 105, 106
  Benjamin 105
  E. S. 106
  Frank J. 106
  George L. 105
  Royal A. 106
  William C. 105
Gowans, Peter 106
Graham, Amasa 106
  John A. 106
  Philip 106
  Samuel 106
Granby, John 106
Granger, Erastus 106
  Seth 106
  Warren 106
Grant, A. P. 107
Grau, F. W. 107
Graves, Constant 107
  S. V. R. 107
Gray, David 107
  Frances Henrietta 302
  James 302
  John 107
  Joseph 107
  William 107
Greek, George 107
  Nicholas 107
Green, Elias 107

Green, Elias, Mrs. 131
  G. B. 107
  George B. 107
  Hiram T. 107
  J. C. 107
  John 107
  Samuel 107
  Thomas 107
  William S. 107
Greene, Charles 107
Greenleaf, W. R. 108
Greenman, James L. 108
Greenshields, John 108
Greer, J. F. 108
Gregg, Benjamin 108
  Charles 108
  George H. 108
Gregory, Amos S. 108
  Esther Antoinette 164
  F. H. 164
  Moses 164
Greiner, Frederick 108
  John 108
Greisen, John P. 108
Grey, Robert 108
Grider, Catharine G. 26
  Daniel 26, 108
Gridley, Clement 108
  F., Mrs. 167
  Frederick 108
Grierson, John P. 108
Griesman, Jacob 108
Griffeth, Jonathan 108
Griffin, Alanson C. 109
  Henry 108
  Hiram 109
  John 109
Griffith, Henry L. 109
  John M. 109
  Thomas C., Mrs. 40
Grimes, William H. 109
Grimmell, Jeremiah P. 109
Griswold, E. A. 109
  Isaac 109
Groning, C. A. 109
Gross, Thomas 109
Grosvenor, Godfrey 214
  Lucien 110
  Mary Lobdell 214
  Seth B., Mrs. 32
Groundwater, James 110
Grove, John 110
Guenther, Francis H. 110
  John G. 110
Guernsey, E. B. 110
Guild, Charles W. 110
  Joseph 110
Guinn, Obed 110
Guiteau, John L. 110
Gunn, Jefferson S. 110

Guthrie, E. B. 110
Gwin, Thomas 110
Gwinn, William R. 110
Haack, Christian 110
Haberly, Martin 111
Haberstro, Joseph 111
Hachmann, Frederick William 111
Hackley, C. 111
Haddock, C. C. 65, 144
  Charles C. 204
  Joseph E. 65, 111
  L. K. 111
  Sarah K. 204
Hadley, E. 296
  James 111
  Mary Isabel 296
Haehn, Mary Emilie 162
  O. F. 162
Hagan, Michael 111
Hager, Raymond 111
Hagle, Michael 111
Haight, C. 111
  Irving 111
Haines, Ann M. 111
  Benjamin 111
  Emmor 111
  Frances E. 84
  Samuel 84, 111
Halbart, Norman A. 112
Haldane, James 112
Hale, C. S. 112
  Ebenezer 112
  Henry H. 112
  Nathan 112
Haley, James 112
  John 112
Hall, A. A. 112, 113
  Andrew A. 112, 113
  Emily H. 105
  Jacob 112
  James H. 113
  Joel 113
  Johnson 112
  Joseph B. 112
  Lydia 231
  N. K. 105, 112
  N. K., Mrs. 215
  Rowland 113
  S. M. 112
Hallack, Joshua 113
Hallenbeck, G. S. 113
Haller, Catherine 272
  Jacob F. 272
Hallock, Benjah 113
Halloran, B., Mrs. 93
Halloway, Isaac 3
Hambleton, Orlando 113
  Samuel A. 113
Hambujer, E. 113

Hamilton, C. N. 113
  Catharine A. 257
  Frank H. 113
  Henry 114
  L. H. F. 113
  Sarah S. 139
  Theodore B. 113
  W. S. 113
  William 113
  Z. A. 139
  Zane A. 257
Hamlin, Daniel R. 114
  Frank 114
  J. W. 114
  John W. 114, 253
  Lucinda E. 253
Hammellman, Paul 114
Hammond, Edwin F. 114
  Ellen J. 114
  Robert 114
Hampton, Ellis C. 114
  Thomas 218
Handel, Francis J. 114
Hanna, Samuel 115
Hannegan, F. B. 115
Hanny, John 115
Hanrahan, James 115
  Patrick 115
Hanson, A. T. 115
  Henry H. 115
  John 115
Harding, Leonard 115
  William T. 115
Hardings, S. L., Mrs. 115
Hardy, Thomas L. 115
Harlow, Augustus 115
Harmon, E. F. 115
Harper, Comer 115
  Joseph 115
Harraden, James 115
Harrett, Elsie Ann 54
  Jeremiah 54
Harrington, C. B., Mrs. 142
  Isaac R. 116
  Jane K. 262
  Seth 116
  Whitford 116
Harris, Adelaide 217
  Asa P. 116
  Emma E. 210
  F. L. 116
  Hattie M. 291
  Ira 169
  James 210
  Jesse 116
  Joseph 116, 291
  L. E. 116
  Linus E. 116
  P., Mrs. 116
  Peyton 116, 217

Harris, Peyton, Mrs. 162
  R., Mrs. 116
  S. W. 116
  William 104
  William H. 116
Harrison, Alfred 116
  Joseph 116
  Richard B. 116
Hart, Henry S. 117
  Osias 117
  William A. 117
Hartman, Joseph 117
Harty, John D. 117
Harvey, Benjamin F. 117
  F. B. 117
  James 117
  John C. 117
  S. D. 117
Hascall, George 117
Haskell, Norman F. 117
Haskins, John F. 118
  R. W. 117
  William P. 118
Hass, Louis F. 118
Hastings, C. J. 118
  E. 118
  William 118
Hatch, Albert G. 118
  E. N., Mrs. 287
  E. P. 118
  Edward 118
  Ephraim 118
  Israel 118
  Israel T. 118
  Junius H. 118
  William B. 118
Hathaway, Arthur S. 118
  Obed 118
Hatton, John 118
Hausauer, Michael 118
Haven, S. Z. 119, 251
  Sarah E. 251
Havens, E. S. 119
  Hiram 119
  Selah W. 119
Hawkins, David 67
  David Henry 119
  Henrietta 67
  J., Mrs. 267
  Samuel 119
  Theodore A. 119
  William 119
Hawks, A. Y. 119
  C. S. 119
  J. D. 119
  T. S. 119
  Z. 119
  Zadock 119
Hawley, Alonzo 119
  E. S., Mrs. 239

Hawley, Edward S. 119
  J. H. 120
  Lucian 119
  Lucien 119
  M. S. 119
  Patrick 133
Hayden, Albert 119, 120
Hayes, George E. 119, 120
  J. E. 120
  J. L. H. 120
  Robert P. 120
  William H. 120
Hayner, Warren S. 120
Hayward, Plato B. 120
  S. H. 120
Haywood, Russell H. 120
Hazard, Edward E. 120
  John H. 120
  M., Mrs. 191
  Maria B. 120
  Morris 120
Heacock, Grosvenor 60
  Grosvenor R. 120
  R. 120
  Reuben B. 120
  Seth G. 120
Head, James 120
  Joseph A. 120
Healy, George W. 120
  Samuel 120
Heaton, Luther 120
Hebard, Andrew 121
  John H., Mrs. 61
Hecox, Samuel 121
  William H. 121
Hedge, Charles L. 121
  George F. 121
Hedstrom, E. 121
Heeb, Charles H. 121
Heellriegel, Conrad 121
Heerdt, August 121
Heilbeck, Louis 121
Heinicke, John 121
Heinold, Michael 121
Heins, Bernhard 121
Heinz, Bernhard 121
Heinze, Charles G. 121
Heiser, Godfrey 121
Heisser, Godfried 122
Hellriegel, Elizabeth C. 66
  Henry 122
  J. 66
Hemenway, Edwin C. 122
  Henry B. 122
  Silas 122
Hemmingway, Rufus 122
Hemstreet, Abram 122
Henderson, Albert N. 122
  Edward 122
  John J. 122

Hendrick, James 122
Henrich, John 122
Henry, James 122
  Louis W. 122
Henshaw, Eveline 182
  Isaac 123
  James H. 182
  James S. 122, 123
  Jefferson 123
  Manuel 123
  N. 123
  Nathaniel 123
Hepworth, Joseph 123
  William H. 123
Hermann, Charles E. 123
Herold, Nicholas 123
Herr, Emanuel 123
Herring, John H. 123
Herron, John 123
Hersee, James William 123
Hertel, John 123
Herter, John 123
Hervey, R. G. 124
Hesket, Samuel 124
Heth, Franklin 124
Hetz, David 124
Heussy, Casper E. 124
Heywood, R. 124
  R. H. 124
  R. H., Mrs. 151
Hibbard, Daniel 79, 124
  John 124
  Lester D. 124
  Luther 124
  Mary Elizabeth 79
Hibsch, Michael 124
Hickey, Hugh 124
  Patrick 124
Hickman, Arthur 124
  Arthur W. 124
Hickox, Frances A. 140
  Ithiel 140
Hicks, John 125
  John B. 124
Higgins, Edward 125
  Frincie 125
  James H. 125
  Matthew 125
  Zenas, Mrs. 117
Higham, John B. 125
Higinbotham, Thomas 125
Hildreth, Thomas 125
  Thomas H. 125
Hill, Eli 125
  Frederick C. 125
  H. M. 125
  Henry 125
  James B. 125
  M. W. 126
  William 125

Hills, Geo. M. 126
  Horace 126
Hines, Bernhard 121
Hingston, William 126
Hinkley, N. P. 126
Hinman, Hiram 126
  Hoel 126
  J. B. 126
Hinson, William A. 126
Hitchcock, Apollos 127
  James 127
Hitchcox, Hiram 127
Hitzel, Albert T. 127
Hives, Timothy 127
Hoag, Hiram 127
Hobson, James H. 127
Hodge, Benj. 8
  Benjamin 127
  Benjamin, Mrs. 205
  Dwight W. 127
  George, Mrs. 186
  Loring 127
  Philander, Mrs. 12
  William 127
Hodges, Corydon A. 127
  Levi 295
  Sarah 295
Hodgkins, George 127
  James 127
Hodgson, George 127
Hoepfner, Henry A. 128
Hofeller, Lehman 128
Hoff, David 128
Hofheins, George F. 128
Hogaboom, John T. 128
Holbrook, D. O. 128
  Marston 128
  Ora L. 128
Holcomb, Charles G. 128
Holley, Elizabeth Doris 151
  Grace 69
  Myron 69, 128, 151
Hollingshead, John 129
Hollister, James 129
  John 129
  John, Mrs. 258
  Robert 129
  William 129
Holloway, Isaac 129
Holman, Edward D. 129
Holmes, Benjamin 129
  Ebenezer 129
  Elkanah 129
  Isaac 129
  J. B. 129
  Seth 129
  W. 129
Holser, Jacob 129
Holt, Elijah 129
  H. N. 129

Holt, John 129
Holtz, William 129
Honk, Philip 130
Hooker, Charles M. 130
Hooper, F. G. 130
Hoople, Charles M. 130
Hoover, George H. 130
  Silas 130
Hope, Edward 130
Hopkins, A. T. 130
  Charles M. 130
  Charles W., Mrs. 22
  Henry 157
  Ichabod 130
  John A. 130
  Nelson 130
  Nelson K. 130
  Otis R. 130
  R. H. M. 130
  Robert 130
  Submet 130
  T. S. 130
  Thomas N. 130
Horton, Joseph G. 131
Hose, David 131
Hosmer, A., Mrs. 202
  Gustavus P. 131
  H. L. 131
  Silas 131
  Theodore M. 131
Hotchkiss, Frederick A. 131
  George C. 131
  Wheeler 131
Hottinger, M., Mrs. 89
Houck, Michael 131
  V. W. 131
Hough, D. C. 131
  Hannah 41
  Robert 41
Houghton, Alfred A. 131
  Emory H. 131
House, Charles A. 132
  Garrett 132
  Hamilton 131
  Hiram 131
  Joseph 131
Hovey, Darius A. 132
  Josiah 132
How, C. 132
Howard, Austin A. 132
  Catharine 33
  Catherine 132
  Charles 132
  D. H. 132
  E. A. 132
  E. H. 132
  E. H., Mrs. 190
  Eddy 132
  Edward D. 132
  Eunice Abzina 137

Howard, George 132
  Henry 33, 132
  Hiram E. 132
  J. P. 212
  Lloyd 132
  R. L. 132
  Rufus 132, 137
  Simeon 132
Howden, William 132
Howe, A. S. 132
  Estes 132
  J. D. 132
Howell, Stephen W. 133
  William W. 133
Howells, Thomas 133
  William 133
Howes, Abner 133
Howley, Patrick 133
Hoxie, David 133
Hoyt, Jonathan 133
  Joseph 133
  Joseph D. 133
  P. W. 133
  William 133
Hubbard, Abner 298
  Alonzo 133
  C. J. 133
  Charles J. 133
  George 133
  H. H. 133
  Martha A. 298
Hubbell, Elnathan 134
  Thomas 134
Hubby, Frank W. 134
Huber, Peter 134
Hucker, N. 134
Huddleston, T. R. 134
Hudson, Benoni 134
  Clark 134
  John T. 134
  M. 134
  N. L. 134
  Sarah 134
Huff, David 128
  H. D. 140
  Isaac 134
  M. W. 134
  Silas 134
  W. 140
Huftill, William 134
Hughes, J. H. 135
  John 134
  John E. 134
  John S. 134
  Mathew D. 134
  Peter 134
Hughson, Egbert E. 135
Hugson, Frank 135
Hulbert, Milton A. 135
Hull, Betsey 269

Hull, D. B. 135
  E. 135
  Edmund 135
  Edmund C. 135
  Elias 292
  Robert B. 135
  Warren 135
  Willard J. 135
  William 241
Humberstone, John 135
Hummell, Frederick 135
Humphrey, James M. 135
  Richard 135
Humphreys, George 135
Hunt, Emory W. 135
  John 136
Hunter, George 136
  James 28, 136
  John B. 136
  Maria 28
  Mary 136
Huntington, J. G. 136
  John 136
Huntley, George M. 258
Hurd, Cyrus 136
  J. C. 136
  Russel 136
Hurlbart, Abijah 136
Hurley, Timothy 136
Hussey, John 136
Hussy, John 137
Husted, Emeline T. 137
  Ezekiel 137
Hutchinson, David 137
  Elisha 137
  John 137
  John M. 137
  Joseph 137
  Thomas M. 137
Huwerth, H. K. 137
Hyatt, George 137
  Gilbert, Mrs. 130
Hyde, Abby Huntington 270
  E. R. 137
  Hannah 287
  J. W. 137
  Jabez B. 287
  James 137
  Jared 270
  Paris P. 137
  R. A. G. 137
Hyman, Ellis 137
Hynes, Michael 137
  Thomas 137
Illig, Peter J. 137
Illingworth, Edwin 137
Ingalls, Otis 138
Ingersoll, Edward 138
  John 138
  William H. 138

Inglis, James 138
Ingram, Daniel 138
  John C. 138
Inman, George H. 138
Ireland, P. A. 138
Ireson, John 138
  William 138
Irish, Arthur 138
  Atwood T. 138
  Charles G. 138
  Edward 138
  Ira E. 138
  Mary M. 62
  R. 62
Irons, J. B. 138
Isherwood, H. 138
Islet, Charles 138
Ittell, John 139
Jackson, Amansel 139
  Charles P. 139
  James, Mrs. 300
  John 241
  Joshua S. 139
  Mary Ann 241
  R. 139
  T. J. 139
  Thomas 139
  William 139
  William L. 139
Jacus, W. C. 139
James, Aaron 139
  Freeman 139
  Joseph 139
  Patience 219
  Thomas 139
Jamison, James 139
  William 139
Jangraw, Nicholas 140
Jaques, Henry 140
Jebb, Thomas A. 140
Jehle, Charles 140
  Edward 140
  Louisa 140
Jendevine, Henry 140
Jenkins, Lewis 140
  William H. 140
Jenks, William 140
Jennings, Benjamin 140
  Selden 140
Jerauld, Nancy H. 42
  Niles 42
Jessemin, Charles 140
  James 140
Jewett, E. R. 140
  E. R., Mrs. 242
  Edward M. 140
  George W. 140
  James H. 140
  Sherman S. 140
Jewitt, Caleb 140

Johnson, A. M. 141
  Alexander 141
  Augustus 141
  Burdette J. 142
  Chas. 140
  David 140
  E. 141, 142
  E. T. 142
  Ebenezer 142
  George 142
  George W. 142
  Gilbert 141
  Henry 141
  Henry W. 141
  J. B. 141, 142
  John J. 142
  John W. 142
  Joseph 141
  Julia 141
  Mortimer F. 141
  N. B. 141
  Robert B. 141
  Samuel 141, 142
  Thomas M. 141
  Wallace 142
  William 142
  William H. 142
  Zerah 141
Johnston, William 142
Jones, Arthur W. 143
  Frederick S. 142
  G. B. 143
  George 143
  George B. 143
  George H. 143
  H. P. 143
  Howard P. 142
  Isaac A. 143
  Isabella 143
  John 143
  Miles 143
  R. I. 142
  Smith 143
  Thomas 142
  Wakely 143
  William D. 143
Jordon, M. 144
  Matthew 144
  P. 144
Josephs, Joseph 144
Joslyn, D. M. 144
Josselyn, Samuel 144
Joy, Lewis 144
  Lewis B. 144
  Thaddeus 144
  Walter 217
Judd, Orvan K. 144
  William 144
Judge, Henry 144
Judson, B. M. 144

Judson, L. P. 144
Julier, H. S. 144
Jungken, Frederick H. 144
Justin, Reuben 144
  Thomas 145
Kaden, John 145
Kaene, Robert 145
  William 145
Kaffert, Jacob 145
Kalbfleisch, Henry 145
Kamerling, A. 145
Kamper, Charles 145
Kane, James 145
  Michael 145
Kaneen, William 145
Karr, James N. 145
Kasson, W. M. 145
  William M. 145
Kast, Joseph 145
Kautz, Christian J. 145
Kearn, Patrick 146
Kearney, John 146
Keating, Robert 146
Keays, W. J. 146
Keech, George 146
Keel, Charles A. 146
  James O. 146
Keeler, E. W. 146
  James 146
Keena, Peter 146
Keenan, John 146
Keene, G. B. 146
Keese, George 146
Kelley, John 147
  John M. 147
  M. 147
  Richard D. 147
  Thomas J. 147
Kellogg, S. S. 147
  William H. 147
Kelly, Dennis 147
  Jesse 147
  John 147
  John P. 147
Kelsey, Daniel 147
Kelty, Michael 147
Kemberle, Jacob 147
Kemp, William 147
Kempshall, Mary 299
  Willis 299
Kenaga, John 148
Kendall, C. 148
  Frederick 148
  J. M. 148
Kendrick, Rodney 148
Kenedy, James 148
Kenefick, John 148
Kennedy, Lester E. 148
  Thomas 148
Kenney, Elijah 148

Kent, Granger D. 148
  Henry M. 148
  John 148
  Warren 148
Kenton, N. W. 149
Kenyon, L. M. 149
  Robert 149
Kerdel, John 149
Kernick, John 149
Kerr, Elijah 149
  George 149
  John 149
  Robert 149
Kessler, John 149
Kester, Benjamin H. 149
  Irving 149
  James 149
  John 149
  Stephen 149
Ketcham, Emily B. 11
  Emma R. 29
  Jesse 29
  William 11
Ketchum, Jesse 149
  John 149
  W. F., Mrs. 114
  William 149
  William F. 149
  Zebulon 149
Kibbe, George R. 150
Kibbey, F. M. 150
Kiefer, Charles 150
Kilderhouse, Thomas 150
Kilpeck, Bartholomew 150
Kimball, Daniel F. 150
  L. M. 150
  L. T. 150
  Smith 150
  William 150
Kimberly, John L. 150
  Lucius 150
  Mary 269
  Trumball C. 150
King, Alexander 151
  Calvin E. 151
  Calvin W. 151
  Charles M. 151
  Cyrus 151
  Elisha 151
  Francis C. 151
  George 151
  James 151
  John S. 151
  S. B. 151
  William 151
  William J. 151
Kingman, George G. 151
  George, Mrs. 151
Kingscott, William 151
Kingsley, A. F. 151

Kingsley, A. S., Mrs. 8
　Phineas 151
　S., Mrs. 61
Kinney, D. 152
　Richard C. 152
Kinsley, A. S. 152
　William 152
Kinyon, George W. M. 152
Kip, Elbert 152
　Gardner J. 152
　Henry 152
　Thomas 152
Kirby, William A. 152
Kirkover, Oliver 152
Kissock, Emanuel 152
Kitching, Henry 152
Kittle, S. P., Mrs. 158
Klas, John 153
Klein, Mathew 153
Klicker, Jacob C. 153
Kline, Charles J. 153
Klinger, Charles W. 153
Knapp, Stephen L. 153
Knauber, Michael 153
Knecht, Edward 153
Kneeland, E. Y. 153
　Elisha Y. 153
Kniffle, Frederick 153
　Philip 153
Knight, Nathaniel 193
　Sarah Ann 193
　William M. 153
Knippel, Frederick 153
　Philip 153
Knowles, T. C. 153
Knowlton, C. C. 154
　Henry 154
Koch, Jacob 154
　John 154
Kolb, Frank Anthony 154
　Jacob 154
Krafferd, Jacob 145
Krauss, Godfrey 154
Krefe, Frederick 104
　Julia 104
Kreiner, George 154
Kress, Frederick 154
Krettner, Jacob 155
Kretz, Edward 155
　Michael 155
Krutzelmann, Frederick 155
Kurtz, Charles 155
　Joseph 155
Kyle, William 155
Lace, Jacob 155
Lacey, John T., Mrs. 95
Lacke, Warren 155
Lacy, Clark B., Mrs. 246
　Edgar D. 155
　John T. 155

Lacy, John T., Mrs. 276
Lafferty, Dewitt C. 155
LaFlam, Anna 161
　Joseph 161
LaForce, Charles 155
Laible, Christopher 155
Lake, Cortland 156
　Lucretia 280
　Peter 280
LaMassh, Edward 156
Lamb, Henry 156
　Henry, Mrs. 279
　John 156
　Thomas 156
　William 156
Lambert, J. G. 156
Lamphear, H. H. 156
Lamphier, Edward A. 156
Lamprie, Michael 156
Lancaster, A. H. 190
　Abby 190
Lander, James 156
　William P. 156
Landon, Horace 156
　Luther B. 156
Lane, Alexander 156
　George 156
　Jane Ann 230
　John 156
　William 230
Lang, Abram 156
　Anna 260
　Jacob 260
Langanhadir, Herman H. 156
　John F. 156
Langdon, George W. 156
　John 282
　Sophia 282
Langner, J. G. 157
Lanior, Peter 157
Lansing, Garrett 157
　Henry L. 157
　Stephen 157
Lapey, John 157
Lapham, G. H. 157
Lapp, Christian 157
　Isaac S. 157
　Jacob 157
Larish, J. W. 157
Larkin, Levi H. 157
Larned, H. S. 157
Larraux, Noel 157
Laselle, Chauncey 158
Lasher, John E. 158
Latham, George H. 26
　Obadiah B. 158
　Susan A. 26
Lathrop, Denison 158
　John 158
　Joseph B. 158

Lathrop, L. L., Mrs. 158
　Paul B. 158
　Rufus 158
　Septimius 158
Lathrope, Charlotte 158
Latta, Robert 158
Laughlin, Martin 158
Laury, John 158
Lauterman, David 158
Lautz, F. C. M. 158
Laux, Martin 158
Lavake, Thomas 158
Laverack, William 158
Law, James 158
　Prentiss 159
Lawrence, John 159
　Richard T. 159
Lawson, Richard 159
Lay, Charles 159
　John 159
　Nathaniel 159
Laycock, Thomas 159
Layton, John 159
Leach, Elijah 159
　George 159
　J. W., Mrs. 35
Learmouth, Hugh 159
LeClear, Hiram 159
LeCouteulx, Louis Stephen 159
Lee, D. P. 160
　Daniel P. 160
　Edward 160
　Elisha 160
　James H. 160
　John R. 160
　P. A. 160
　Richard Hargrave 160
　Royal 160
　Samuel 160
　Samuel W. 160
　William G. 160
Leech, Elijah 160
　J. H., Mrs. 99
Leichtnam, Joseph 161
Leigh, James 161
Leighton, Walter H. 161
Leitch, John 161
Lenhard, Jacob 161
Lenhart, John W. 161
Leonard, B. 161
　John J. 161
　Patrick B. 161
LePage, Remie 161
Lerock, James 161
Lesuer, Nathan 161
Letchworth, Josiah 161
Letson, Isaiah 161
Levi, Emanuel 162
Levy, S. N. 162

Levyn, Siegmund 110
Lewin, William 162
Lewis, Dio 162
  Franklin 162
  George W. 162
  Hiram A. 162
  Irving H. 162
  John 162
  L. L. 162
  Lovell 162
  Richard H. 162
  William, Mrs. 139
Libby, James 162
  John 162
Lichtenstein, Barnett 162
Lichtensten, Barnett 82
  Bertha 82
Linder, William 162
Lindley, Nathaniel 162
Lindsay, Oscar A. 163
  Oscar A., Mrs. 246
Little, Guy 163
Littlefield, L. B. 163
  Leason C. 163
  Linsing B. 163
  Wray S. 163
Lloyd, Henry 163
Lock, Harriet L. 15
  J. 15
  John 15
Locke, Charles H. 163
  E. A. 163
  Franklin D. 163
  John 163
  W. C. 163
Lockwood, Ebenezer 163
  Philo 164
  Philo D. 164
  Ralph 164
  Stephen 164
  T. T. 163, 284
  William 164
Lodge, Thomas 164
Loersch, J. Philip 164
Long, Alfred H. 164
  Benjamin 123
  Christian 165
  Fanny 123
  George 164, 165
  Isaac 164
  Lucius 165
  Lucius S. 164
  M. 165
  Macall 165
  Walter R. 165
Longnecker, Christian 165
  John 165
Loomis, Charles K. 165
  H. N. 165
  Harvey 165

Loomis, N. H. 165
Loosen, Frederick 165
Loper, Samuel 165
  Samuel W. 165
Lord, Andrew P. 165
  John 142
  Lucy E. 142
  T. D. 165
Lorenz, Frederick 166
  John 166
Loring, William N. 166
Losee, Simeon 166
Losehand, B. C. 166
Love, Levi 166, 217, 300
  Louisa 245
  Marjorie Ella 300
  Mary E. 217
  Robert J. 166
  Solomon 166
  Thomas C. 166, 245
Loveday, J. H. 166
Lovejoy, Joshua 166
  Sarah 239
Loveland, M. R. 166
Loveridge, A. A. 166
  A. A., Mrs. 207, 208
  E. D. 166
Lovering, Mary 23
  William 166
  Wm. 23
Lowe, John C. 166
Lowell, George 166
Lowry, George 167
Lucas, L. D. 167
  Lorenzo D. 167
Luce, Alfred 167
  Orlando 167
  Truman 167
Ludlow, Charles H. 167
  Ebenezer 167
  Myron M. 167
Luesenhop, Adolph 167
Luke, Marvin S. 167
Lusk, William 167
Lutted, James 167
Lyall, Alexander 167
Lyman, B., Mrs. 296
  Loomis 167
  Nathan 167
  P. Stephen 167
Lymburner, Hamilton M. 167
Lynch, Edward 168
  Michael T. 168
  Patrick 168
Lynde, Albertus L. 6
Lynn, John E. 168
  Thomas 168
Lyon, Charlotte Ann 303
  Jacob 168, 303
  William 168

Lyons, Cornelius 168
  Freeman 168
  Jacob 42
  Jane Eliza 42
  Stephen W. 168
Lytle, Andrew 168
MacCabe, John 168
Mack, W. J. 125
Mackay, Edward 168
Mackenroth, J. C. 169
MacNoe, George 169
Macomber, C. S., Mrs. 163
  E. 169
  Luke 169
Macy, John B. 169
  Samuel H. 169
Madison, James H. 169
  William 75, 169
Magee, John H. 169
Mager, C. S. 169
Maharg, John 169
Maher, Martin 169
  Patrick 169
Mahon, Samuel 169
Mahoney, Dennis 169
Mahony, James 169
Main, Miles 170
Mallon, Daniel 170
  Hugh 170
Mallory, James A. 170
Malone, Patrick 170
Maltbie, Isaac F. 170
Maltby, Benjamin 150
  F. A. 170
  Isaac 170
  Lucinda M. 150
Manay, A. 170
Manchester, Bradford A. 170
Mane, John 170
Manghan, James 170
Manhart, Jacob 170
Manley, William R. 170
Mann, C. J. 171
  Charles J. 171
  David 171
  James 227
  Jane 227
  William B. 171
  William W. 170
Manser, Thomas 171
Mansfield, Orange 171
  W. Q. 171
Mapes, Josiah 171
  Stephen 171
Marany, George 276
Marcy, D. G. 171
Markham, G. T. 171
Marsh, George D. 172
  L. W. 171
  LeRoy W. 172

Marshall, John 172
  John E. 172
  Orsamus H. 172
Martin, Alexander 59
  E. M. 172
  Frederick S. 172
  George A. 172
  Isaac H. 172
  Jesse 172
  John 172
  John M. 172
  William 172
  William N. 172
Martine, Joseph Z. 172
Martyn, William T. 173
Marvel, Charles 173
Marvin, Asa 173
  George L. 173
  Henry 173
  Le Grand 173
  Sylvanus 173
  Z. H. 173
Mary, Charles 173
Mason, Amasa 173
  Andrew S. 173
  Charles R. 173
  Daniel 173
  David H. 173
  Frank B. 173
  John 173
  Joseph 173
  Robert 173
Masters, Robert 173
Mathews, Sylvester 174
Matteson, H. H. 174
  Henry H. 174
Matthews, L. B. 174
  Sylvester 174
Mattison, Charles T. 174
  William 174
Mattson, John C. 174
Maugham, Elizabeth 174
  James 174
Mauke, Carl 7
Maurer, John 174
Maxwell, Joshua 174
May, Patrick 174
  William J. 174
Mayberry, George 174
Mayer, C. S. 169
  George C. 174
Maynard, R. H., Mrs. 37
  Robert H. 174
Mayne, Richard T. 175
Mayo, Charles P. 175
  E. 175
McAllester, Ebenezer 175
McArthur, Arthur 175
McAuliffe, Daniel 175
McBeth, John 175

McBride, William 175
McBurney, John 175
McCabe, Hugh 175
McCall, Ira 175
McCarthy, Cornelius 176
  John 175
  Richard 176
McCarty, John 176
McClure, A. B. 176
  Heman 176
  Joseph 176
McCollum, Otis 176
McComb, Robert 176
McCool, James 176
McCourt, John 176
McCoy, J. A. 177
McCready, James 177
McCredie, W. B. 177
McCrowell, Henry 177
McCumber, Orlando 177
  Orlando, Mrs. 284
McDearborn, Joseph 177
McDermot, William 177
McDonald, C. R. 177
  Rosanna 79
  William 177
  William H. 177
McDonnell, Martin 178
McDowell, Henry 178
McElvany, Charles T. 178
McElwain, W. D. 178
McEvoy, Elizabeth 178
  Thomas 178
McEwen, Henry 178
  Hugh C. 178
  Stephen 178
  Timothy 178
  William B. 178
McFarland, Levi 178
McFaul, Thomas 178
McFee, Peter 178
McGillivray, William 178
McGinness, James, Mrs. 21
McGloin, J. D. 178
McGorry, Bernhard 178
McGowan, Andrew 178
  Henry H. 178
  John 178
McGraw, Michael 178
McIlwreth, Andrew 179
McIntyre, Robert J. 179
McKay, Alexander 179
  D. T. 179
  James 179
  Robert 179
McKean, John 179
McKee, Joshua 179
  Thomas 179
McKeen, Almira 179
  Robert 179

McKelip, Robert 179
McKenna, James 179
McKeon, Michael 179
McKibbin, Hugh 179
  Robert H. 179
McKinley, Edward 179
McKinney, O. W. 180
McKnight, James 180
  James, Mrs. 86
McLain, Andrew 180
McLane, Henry 180
McLaren, William 180
McLaughlin, S. J. 180
McLean, Alexander 180
McLeish, Archibald 180
  Charles G. 180
  James 180
McMahon, James 180
McManus, John 180
McMartin, Peter 180
McMichael, William J. 180
McMillen, Daniel H. 180
  Hugh 180
McNamara, James 181
  Joseph 181
McNeal, Andrew 181
  John W. 181
  William 181
McNish, William 181
McPherson, Samuel 181
McQuenn, Alexander 181
McWilliams, Francis 181
Meacham, George 181
Mead, Alfred 181
  Hiram 181
  William 181
Meads, Willis H. 181
Meech, Henry T. 182
  S. L., Mrs. 115
  Samuel G. 182
Meeks, James C. 182
Meeney, Bessie 182
  John 182
Meldrum, Robert O. 182
Mellon, N. 182
Mensch, Valentine 182
Mergenhagen, Joseph 182
Merrill, Frederick B. 183
  George W. 183
  Ira 183
  William H. 183
Merritt, G. H. 183
  J. 183
  Peter 183
Mervine, Mary 261
  William 261
Mesmer, Peter 183
Messer, Christian 183
Metz, Abraham 183
  C. 183

Metz, John 183
Metzger, Nicholas 183
Meyer, Frank X. 183
  J. W. A. 183
Meyers, F. A. 184
Middleditch, Alonzo 184
Miles, Peter E. 184
Millar, Allan P. 184
  Thomas 184
Miller, A. D. A. 185
  Adam 185
  Benjamin 184, 185
  C. 185
  C. F., Mrs. 10
  Charles 185
  Charles G. 184
  Daniel 184
  Elizabeth 195
  F. 184
  Frank J. 184
  Frederick S. 185
  Jacob 185
  Jacob S. 184, 185
  James 185
  John U. 185
  Joseph 184
  Luman A. 184
  Myron H. 184
  Peter P. 184
  Philip 184, 185, 195
  Richard 185
  Robert W. 184
  Thomas C. 185
  W. F. 184
  W. G. 185
  William T. 184
Milligan, Martin 185
Millington, Joseph 185
Mills, Ansel 24, 185
  C. J. 185
  Calvin 75, 186
  Charles R. 186
  Cyrus 186
  George 185
  James H. 121, 186
  John 185
  Kate S. 121
  Louisa M. 24
  Lucy E. 75
  M. C. 185
  S. J. 185
  William M. 186
Milnor, Robert 186
  William 186
Milton, Patrick 186
Mintler, Andrew 186
Minton, Jones 186
Mitchell, George B. 186
  J. R. 186
  James 186

Mitchell, John 186
  Joshua 186
  Robert 186
  Thomas 186
  William 186
  William H. 186
Moffat, James 187
  William 187
Molter, Jacob 187
Monforte, Joseph C. 187
Monteath, William 187
Montgomery, G. W. 187
  H. M. 187
  Robert 187
Moodie, John W. 187
Moon, M. A. 187
Mooney, John 187
  John A. 187
Moore, Andrew B. 188
  Charlotte 219
  Emily Elizabeth 41
  James 41, 188
  John 188
  John O. 188
  William 55
  William H. 188
Moores, W. P. 188
Mooses, W. P., Mrs. 211
Morehouse, Thaddeus 188
Morey, Amzi 188
  H. G. 188
Morgan, A. G. 188
  A. R. 188
  Amos 188
  Edward 188
  Richard 188
Moriarty, B. J. 189
Morin, William 189
Morrasay, Michael 189
Morris, Henry 189
  Rees T. 189
  Warren 189
Morrison, J. W. 189
  William 189
  William P. 189
Morrow, Elisha 189
  Hugh 189
Morse, Alanson 189
  Alfred 189
  C. W. 189
  Charles 190
  Parker 189
Morton, James 190
  O. C. 190
Moseley, William A. 190
Moses, William 190
Mosher, Daniel E. 78
  David 190
  Hezekiah 190
Mosier, John 190

Mosier, Louis 190
Moss, Jacob 190
Motteler, Frederick 190
Mount, Francis 190
  George 190
Movius, Julius 190
Moxley, Henry 190
Muehlhauser, George J. 191
Mugridge, Adrian E. 191
  George 191
Mulcahy, William 191
Mulhall, Stephen J. 191
Mullen, James 191
Mullett, Elnathan 191
Mulligan, Eugene 191
  Samuel 191
Munce, James 191
Munger, Edward H. 191
  Orrin 191
Munro, Peter G. 191
Munroe, Charles H. 191
Murbach, Casper 191
Murdock, Jasper 191
Murphy, Edward 191
  James 192
  John 191
  John Francis 192
  Michael E. 191
  Stephen 191
Murray, Anna E. 192
  Francis P. 192
  Hubert 192
  Hugh 192
  James A. 192
  James C. 192
  John 192
  Samuel 192
  Thomas 192
  W. G. 192
Musson, Henry W. 192
Myer, Henry 192
Myers, Eugene 192
  Francis H. 193
  Jacob 193
  O. T. 193
Myner, Adele D. 280
Nagel, John C. 193
  John M. 193
Napier, Peter 193
Nash, Peter 193
  Richard 193
  Thomas 193
Naughton, James 193
  William 193
Near, Peter 193
Nechter, James 193
  M. A. 193
  Mary A. 78
Needham, C. H., Mrs. 207
  Joseph P. 193

Neeper, James 193
Neeve, John 193
Negus, J. G. 193
  John 193
  John G. 193
Nehin, John 193
Nellany, Michael 193
Nelson, Charles 193
Nesbitt, Margaret 210
  Samuel 210
Netcher, Louis 194
Nevitt, C. R. 194
New, Thomas 194
Newell, Raphael 194
  V. C. 194
Newkirk, J. S., Mrs. 282
  J. W., Mrs. 74
Newland, Hannah 194
  John 194
Newman, Henry 194
  James M. 194
  John 194
  Sumner 194
Newton, D. R. 195
  James 194
  O. O., Mrs. 16
Nichols, A. P. 48
  Daniel 195
  David 195
  Levi 195
  Merritt 195
  Silas C. 195
Nickerson, Alfred 195
Niederlander, N. F. 195
Niemann, A. D. 195
Niergarth, Frederick 195
Niles, Jeremiah 195
Noble, James 195
  W. 196
Nolan, Bartholomew 196
  Edward 196
Nolton, Hiram G. 196
Norris, Abram 196
  James 196
North, James 196
  Walter 196
Norton, Charles D. 196
  Enoch B. H. 196
  J. S. 196
  James M. 196
  Joseph G. 196
  M. B. 196
  Walter 197
Noye, John T. 197
  R. 197
Noyes, Daniel 197
Nuhn, J. A. 197
Nutting, Abner F. 197
Nye, Barton 197
  John 276

Nye, Lucy B. 276
O'Brian, John 198
  John P. 198
  Matthew 198
  Patrick 198
  Thomas 198
O'Brien, John 198
  Martin 198
  Thomas James 198
  William Lloyd 198
O'Bryan, Patrick 198
O'Connor, D. M. 198
  Daniel 198
  John 198
O'Day, Edward 198
O'Grady, Thomas 199
O'Keefe, John 199
O'Leary, Michael 199
O'Malley, Patrick 200
O'Shea, Daniel 200
Oades, James 197
Oakes, Samuel 197
Oakley, R. 165
  Theresa P. 165
Oaks, Ira 197
  Samuel 198
  Samuel F. 197
Oberist, Samuel 198
Ochs, George 183
Odell, A. 199
  Daniel 199
Odelum, James 199
Oehmig, Charles 199
  Frederick N. 199
Offenbacher, Valentine 199
Ogden, William Jones 199
Ohlmer, Harmon 199
Olliver, W. W. 199
Olmstead, John 199
Olver, Nicholas 200
Ongley, William H. 200
Ord, Robert 200
Orr, C. A. 200
  George 200
Osborn, Elias 200
Osgood, David R. 200
Ostrander, A. K. 201
  Amasa K. 201
Otis, Ceylon 201
  Chandler 201
  Jabez 62, 151
  Naoma 151
  Nathaniel T. 201
  Sophia 62
Ottenot, Louis J. 201
  Nicholas 201
Otto, Jacob S. 201
  James W. 201
  William E. 201
Ovens, Robert 201

Owen, John 201
  Joseph 201
Owens, Joshua 201
Packard, S. 201
Paddock, Julia E. 201
Page, David P. 201
  Timothy 202
Paige, Timothy 202
  Timothy, Mrs. 227
Paine, James M. 202
Palmer, Alanson 52, 202, 211
  Bartlett 202
  Cynthia J. 64
  E. J. 202
  Edward D. 202
  Edward W. 202
  Elias W. 144, 202
  Elizabeth 52
  Everard 202
  George 64, 202
  J. H. 202
  Mary 144
  N. B. 202
  William J. 202
Papes, Jimmy 177
Parish, Charles G. 203
  Joshua L. 203
Park, Edgar 203
  Paul 203
Parker, Aaron 94, 203
  Andrew 203
  Charles 203
  Francis B. 203
  George W. 203
  Jason 203
  John 203
  John K. 203
  John P. 203
  Joseph 203
  P. 203
  Perry G. 203
  Raymond J. 203
  T. L. 203
  Thomas R. 203
  Wing T. 203
Parkhurst, Abram W. 203
  Lemuel 203
Parkinson, James 204
  Reuben 203
Parmelee, Edward F. 204
  Lemuel 204
  Roswell 204
Parson, Francis J. 204
Parsons, Charles W. 204
  G. 204
  Galusha 204
  H. A. 204
  Lewis B. 204
  Silas 204

Partridge, Joseph 204
  Mason 204
Patchin, A. T. 204
  Aaron D. 204
  Talcott 204
Pattengill, A. O. 205
Patterson, C. H. 205
  F. G. 205
  James 205
  John 205
  Mary Ann 143
  Robert 13, 143, 205
  Susan A. 13
  William W. 205
Paul, Abijah 206
  Adams 206
  James C. 205
  Joseph 206
  Mathias 205
Pauly, Frederick 206
Paxon, William 206
  William L. 206
Paxson, James 206
  John 206
  Minerva P. 87
  William 87
Paxton, Ahaz 206
  Thomas 206
Payne, C. 206
  Cynthia 215
  F. A. 206
  George J. 206
  L. S. 206
  Truman B. 206
  William 206
Peabody, John M. 206
  Joseph 206
Peace, William 206
Peacock, Henry 206
  James 207
  William 206
Peak, George 207
Pearson, C. 207
  Christopher 207
  Joseph 207
  Thomas 207
Pease, Alvan 207
  Arthur W. 207
  F. S., Mrs. 104
  Gideon 207
  John 207
  John, Mrs. 131
  W. H., Mrs. 269
  William 207
Peate, John 207
Peck, Charles E. 207
  Daniel 207
  Hiram 207
  Jacob P. 207
  Jesse 207

Peck, Jesse S. 207
  John 207
  William B. 207
Peckham, Philip 207
Peek, John S. 207
  Samuel 208
Peirce, John 208
Peitch, Thomas 208
Pells, George H. 208
Pembroke, Kerin 208
Penfield, Daniel 208
  George W. 208
  T. V. N. 208
  William 208
Penfold, Charles 208
  Frank 208
Pennell, G. C. 208
Pepper, Calvin 208
Perham, B. 208
Perine, Benjamin 208
  R. B. G. 208
Perkins, C. H. B. 208
  L. P. 208
  Nelson 208
  Philetus 208
  R. L., Mrs. 224
  Thomas 208
  Waterman 46
  William 208
Perrie, George 208
Perry, H. A. 209
  Isaac 209
  J. H. 131
  Louisa E. 131
  Philip 209
Persch, H. C. 8
  Louisa A. 8
Person, Robert 209
Persons, Byron D. 209
Peter, James F. 209
  John S. 209
Peters, John 201
  Samuel 209
Petrie, Alexander 209
  William 209
Pettes, William H. 209
Pfeifer, George F. 209
Pfeiffer, George 210
Pfeil, Peter 210
  Philip 210
Phelps, C. B. 210
  George E. 210
  Oliver 210
  Orson 210
  Orson, Mrs. 90
Phillips, Andrew W. 210
  Edward 210
  George A. 302
  J. H. 210
  P. H. 210

Phillips, Richard 210
  Seneca 210
  Sophia 210
  Stephen 210
  Thomas 210
Phillipson, Isaac 210
Philpot, J. N. 210
  William S. 210
Pickering, D. 211
  Thomas 211
Pierce, Calvin 211
  Charles L. 211
  Charles S. 211
  Clark 211
  Cornelius H. 211
  Eugene 211
  F. D. 211
  James 211
  Jerome 211
  John 211
  Loring 211
  Loring, Mrs. 66
  Oliver 211
  Pardon 211
  Sanford B. 211
Pierson, Gordon 211
  Gurdon 211
Pike, Stafford 212
Pilliard, Frederick 212
Pine, Samuel 212
Pingree, John T. 212
Pinkney, John 212
  Joseph 212
Pinner, Debby 212
  James N. 212
  M., Mrs. 94
  Michael 212
Pinney, Austin 212
Piregry, Aquilla 212
Pitkin, J. F. 212
Pitts, John A. 212
Plato, J. D. 212
Platt, L. B. 212
Playter, Charles G. 212
Pleuthner, John 212
Plimpton, Daniel 212
Plumb, Miles D. 212
Plumley, Allen S. 212
Poh, Louis 213
Pollard, B. F. 213
  John 213
  John O. 213
Polley, John H. 213
Pollock, Joseph M. 213
Pomeroy, Emerson C. 213
  Helen Sophia 162
  Isaac 162
  J. A. 213
  Oliver 213
  Robert 213

Pond, Lawrence 213
Poole, C. O. 213
Porcher, A. J. 213
Porter, Augustus 213
　Augustus S. 214
　Fannie E. 141
　J. J. 213
　James 213
　James E. 213
　Peter A. 213
　Peter B. 213
　Peter Buell 213
　Stephen B. 213
　Walter 141
Porth, Henry 214
Poseiner, Jacob 214
Post, William 214
Poth, George H. 214
Potter, Allen 214
　Elizabeth M. 107
　Frederick A. 214
　George R. 214
　George S. 214
　Gilbert 214
　H. B. 214
　Heman B. 107, 214
　Jacob 214
　Joshua 214
　Levi 214
　Milton 214
　Samuel 214
Pound, J. 214
　L. S. 206
　Rebecca 206
Powell, David 215
　Elisha 214
　John 214
　M. H. 214
　N. O. 214
Powellson, B. F. 215
Powers, Averill 215
　Lydia 80
　O. T. 215
　P. W. 136
　William 215
Pratt, Amos 215, 221
　Anson B. 215
　Asabel 215
　Benjamin 215
　Byron F. 215
　Elon G. 215
　Helen M. 48
　Hiram 215
　John C. 215
　Louisa J. 221
　Lucius H. 215
　Luke M. 215
　Marilla Adeline 4
　Pascal P. 215
　Pascall P. 48

Pratt, Rachel 215
　Samuel 215
Prenatt, Augustus 215
Presbrey, O. F. 216
Prescott, William 216
　William C. 216
Preston, John R. 216
Price, Charles 216
Pride, J. B. 216
　John B. 216
Prince, Alpheus 216
　George A. 216
　George I. 216
　Hamilton 216
　J. R. 216
　John R. 216
Pring, William J. 216
Proper, John 216
Prosser, E. S. 216
Prouty, James 216
　Wallace 216
Provoost, David 216
　James P. 216
Provost, Samuel A. 217
　William K. 217
Prozeller, Joseph M. 217
Puninton, A. J. 217
Purdey, John 217
Purdie, John 217
Purdon, Averina 252
　William 252
Purdy, Samuel 217
Purrington, A. J. 217
　George A. 217
Pursel, J. N. 217
Putnam, Henry 217
　James O. 217
　John S. 217
　Timothy 217
Quick, William H. 217
Quigley, Patrick 217
Quinlan, John D. 217
Quinn, Joseph 217
Radcliffe, Jerry 217
Raichle, Charles 218
Ralph, Edward 218
　Fesse 218
　Reuben L. 218
Ramage, George 218
Ramsdell, Alexander 218, 251
　O. P. 218
　Sarah 251
　William G. 218
Rand, C. T. 218
　Charles T. 218
　Chas. T. 183
　Mary Ann 183
Randall, George M. 218
　W. E. 218

Rankin, A. T. 218
　Alexander Taylor 218
　Anne B. 219
　Annie B. 219
　Mary L. 218, 219
　Thomas 218, 219
Ransom, A. R. 219
　Asa 219, 292
　E. F. 219
　Elias 219
　Henry B. 219
　Sarah B. 292
　Sophia 183
Rapp, Charles 219
Rasuage, George 219
Rathbone, Anna Burwell 219
　Benjamin 219
　C. E. 219
　Charles E. 219
　Charles H. 219
　Charles T. 219
　Moses 219
　Philander 219
　Samuel 219
Rathbun, Albert H. 219
　Benjamin 219, 220
　Charlotte 219
　E. M. 219
　Frances Maria 207
　Frank A. 220
　Lyman 207, 219
　Mary Ann 83
　Moses 220
　Patience 219
　Roxanna 219
　Thomas 83
Ray, A. M. 220
Raymond, A. C. 220
Rayner, Charles A. 220
Raynor, Augustus 220
Raze, Horatio N. 220
Rea, W. C. 220
Read, A. L. 220
　John 220
　Nelson H. 220
　W. S. 220
　William 220
　William S. 220
Reader, Thomas J. 220
Reamer, Mathew 220
Reardon, John 220
Record, Adam L. 221
Redfield, Elizabeth 216
　Reuben 216
Reed, Daniel 221
　George W. 221
　Loman 221
　Samuel Roxy M. 221
　William 221
　William C. 221

Rees, Charles, Mrs. 231
  David 221
  Sally 249
Reese, George 221
Reeve, Walter, Mrs. 43
Reeves, Charles E. 221
  Elisha 221
Regler, William 222
Reiboldt, Christian 222
Reid, Peter B. 222
Reif, George 222
  Thomas 222
Reigart, James Hamilton 222
Reilly, J. G. 222
  John G. 222
Reimann, Jacob 222
  Ludwig 222
Reinhardt, Philip 222
Reinheimer, William 222
Relf, George 222
  Thomas 222
Relph, Andrew 222
Relyea, Peter 252
Remington, David 222
  Edwin 223
  James 222
  W. A. 223
Renowden, William 223
Renwick, Ralph 223
Reyburn, Thomas C. 223
Reynolds, A. 223
  David 223
  H. H. 223
  J. N. 223
  Lynus 223
  William 223
Ribbell, C. A. 223
Rice, Asa 223
  C. B. 223
  Clark 223
  Henry 223
  J. M. 223
  John 223
  Josiah 223
Rich, Charles T. 224
  G. B. 191, 253
  Gaius B., Mrs. 232
  Gaivus B. 223
  Harriet 191
  Jane Antoinette 253
Richards, Henry 224
  John 224
  LaFayette 224
  Thomas F. 224
Richardson, George 224
  R. H. 224
  Samuel B. 224
Richmond, Alfred W. 224
  Charles T. 224
  Geraldine H. 224

Richmond, M. 224
Rickard, George 224
Riddle, Charles C. 224
Rider, John A. 224
Riedy, John 224
Rielly, Thomas 224
Rigg, William H. 225
Riggs, William 225
Riley, A. 225
  Aaron 225
  Henry W. 225
  John 225
  John O. 225
  P. 225
  William A. 225
Rinck, William 225
Ringer, G. A. 225
Ripley, A. P. 225
Risley, J. 179
Ritchie, H. B. 225
Ritt, Gregory 225
  M. L. 225
Robb, David 225
Robbins, Eliza H. 225
  S. W. 225
Roberts, E., Mrs. 1
  Elijah 226
  Elmira 49
  J. D. 226
  John 225
  John, Mrs. 35
  L. I. 49
  Paul 148
  Warner 226
  Zacheus 225
Robertson, William 226
  William M. 226
Robinson, A. 32, 226, 284
  Alanson 226
  Amos 226
  Azel P. 226
  George N. 226
  John 226
  John A. 226
  Mary E. 32
  Nelson 226
  Robert 226
  Sarah M. 284
  William 226
Robson, John 226
Rochester, Harriet L. 34
  William B. 227
Rockett, Edward 227
  Mary 227
Rockwood, Charles D. 227
Rodenbach, Christopher 227
Rodney, John 227
Rody, John 288
  Serena 288
Roesser, C. 227

Roesser, J. 227
Rogers, Albert 227
  Calvin 227
  Charles 227
  Frederick 227
  G. A. 227
  Henry W. 227
  Jabez J. 227
  James 227
  John 227
  John C. 227
  Nathaniel 227
  Samuel 227
  Sherman S. 227
  Thomas 227
  Thompson 227
  William F. 227
  Wilson 227
Roll, August 228
Romer, Alexander 228
Roop, H. 83
Roos, Jacob 228
Root, Amos 183
  Carissa H. 183
  Charles G. 228
  Edward 228
  Francis H. 228
  J. S. 228
  John 228
Roots, John 228
Rose, A. S. T. 229
  E. 259
  Edwin 228
  John 229
  Myron P. 228
Roskopf, Jacob 229
Rosner, Henry 229
Ross, James W. 229
  S. 229
Roth, John 229
Rother, Gustavus 229
Rowan, Josephine 180
  Martin 180
Rowley, Charles 230
  Millar 230
  Thomas 230
Rubens, Henry 230
Ruch, Thomas E. 230
Ruden, E. 230
  Emanuel 230
Rudio, Christian 279
Rudolf, William 230
Ruger, James W. 230
Rumrill, H. 230
  Henry 230
Rumsey, Aaron 49, 62
  B. C., Mrs. 112
  Dexter P. 230
  Emmett P. 230
  Fayette 230

Rumsey, Olive 49
Runcie, William J. 230
Rundell, John 230
  Sarah 230
Rundy, Sanford 230
Russ, Wheeler S. 231
Russell, B. F. 231
  Elihu 188
  George P. 231
  H. P., Mrs. 192
  Jane Ann 188
  John E. 231
  Robert 231
  Samuel 231
  Sylvanus 231
  W. A. 231
  Washington A. 231
  William C. 231
Rutler, Thomas 231
Rutterfield, J. H. 11
  Jennie A. 11
Ryneck, William A. 232
Ryno, David 232
Ryther, James F. 232
  John L. 232
Sabins, Benjamin 232
Sackett, Reuben 232
Safford, Philo T. 232
Sage, John, Mrs. 253
Salisbury, Aaron 263
  C. B. 232
  Edward S. 232
  Emma Jane 263
  Guy H. 137, 232
  H. A., Mrs. 200
  Hezekiah A. 232
  Hezekial A. 215
  Rachel S. 215
  S. H. 232
  Smith H. 215, 232
  William J. 232
Salies, John J. 233
  Michael 233
Salls, Samuel 233
Samo, Charles W. 233
Samson, Theodore 233
Sanders, Atwell 233
  Hohn 233
  William 233
Sangstar, Hugh 233
Sargeant, Richard 233
Sargent, Timothy 233
Sauer, A. 233
  Adam 233
Sauerwein, Henry 233
Saulpaugh, Peter B. 233
Saulters, Philip 233
Saunders, Joseph 234
  Riley 234
Savage, Thomas 234

Sawin, Benjamin 234
  P. W. 234
  Silas, Mrs. 163
Sawyer, James D. 234
  John 234
Schaefer, Christian 234
Schaller, John 234
Schannahan, B. 234
Schanzlin, Jacob F. 234
Schawzlin, Jacob F. 234
Scheffer, Charles F. 234
Schelling, Frederick W. 234
Schenck, Jacob 234
  Peter 234
Schenker, John M. 235
Schermerhorn, Isaac M. 235
Scheu, Augusutus F. 235
  Henry 235
  Jacob 235
  William 235
Schlotzer, John 235
Schmall, Louis 235
Schmidt, Anthony 235
  Carrie 76
  Joseph 235
Schnell, Frederick 235
Schnur, Peter 236
Schoenacher, Jacob 236
Schroeder, Charles F. 236
Schroer, Catherine 236
  Peter 236
Schryver, Allen L. 236
Schuchardt, Lorenz 236
Schultz, Gottfreid 236
  John T. 236
  William 236
Schulyer, Daniel 236
Schumacher, Jacob 236
Schuster, Christian 236
  Ferdinand 237
Schuyler, Daniel 237
  Montgomery 237
Schwartz, William 237
Schweigert, A. E. 237
  Henry 237
  John 237
Scott, E. G. 237
  I. B., Mrs. 7
  J. B. 237
  James B. 237
  James H. 237
  John 237
  Mather 237
  Michael 237
  Robert 237
  William K. 237
Scovil, John 238
Scovill, A. 280
  Erastus 238
  Jonathan 238

Scovill, Sally 280
Scoville, Jasper 238
Scriven, Alonzo H. 238
Scurr, Henry 238
Seaman, Marvin 238
Seamon, Edmund 238
Searls, Maria E. 172
  S. J. 172
Sears, Frank A. 238
  Lewis 238
  Richard 238
Seaver, Thomas 238
Seckler, James J. 238
  John 238
See, John L. 238
Segar, S. 238
Seidenstricker, H. A. 239
Selke, Charles 239
Sellstedt, Caroline 239
  L. G. 239
Semon, G. S. 239
Senn, Ferdinand 239
Severance, C. C. 239
Sexton, Jason 239
Seymour, Abby G. 129
  C. L. 239
  Charles 239
  E. B. 3
  Erastus E. 239
  Harriet E. 3
  Henry R. 129, 239
  Horatio 239
  John 239
  William 239
Shadrake, Frederick 240
Shainholdts, P. 240
Sharp, David 240
Shassel, Jacob 240
Shaver, Norman J. 240
Shaw, Charles A. 240
  Ellen Rebecca 132
  J. F. 240
  John P. 132
  Joseph 240
  Timothy 240
Shearer, Albert N. 241
  Noah 241
Sheares, Daniel 241
Shearman, R. H. 241
Sheehan, William 241
Shelden, C. H. 241
Sheldon, Asa C. 241
  James 241
  William 241
Shell, Jacob 241
Shelton, William S. 241
Shepard, Benjamin F. 241
  John E. 241
  Stephen B. 241
  William H. 241

Shephard, J. M. 242
Shepherd, David 242
Sheppard, Christopher 242
  Edward 242
  James D. 242
  John 242
Sherman, B. F. 242
  Bejamin 242
  Orson 242
Sherwin, Phineas B. 242
Sherwood, Adiel 32
  Juliette 32
  M. B. 242
Shettler, J. 242
Sheu, Henry 242
Shewbrook, Benjamin T. 242
Shick, Philip 242
Shiels, Charles 242
  George 37, 242, 243
  Margaret 37
  William 242
Shinners, James 243
Shipman, John 243
Shisler, David 243
Shoecraft, James P. 243
  Ross P. 243
Shoop, Charles 243
Shope, Abram 243
Short, B. P. 243
  Francis 243
  James 243
  Levi E. 243
  Patrick 243
Shreve, Charles 243
Shriver, Henry 243
Shryer, John 243
Shultes, George W. 243
Shultus, David 243
Shulze, J. P. 243
Shumway, Jerome B. 243
Shuster, Emily 10
  F. 10
Sibley, C. L. 243
  Charles W. H. 244
  Clark H. 243
  John C. 244
  Mark H. 243
  O. E. 244
Sidway, James 244
  Jonathan 244
  P., Mrs. 232
  William 244
Sieffert, John C. 244
Sikes, Edwin 244
  Simeon 244
Sill, Enoch 244
  Gurdon 244
Simons, George 245
  Marcius 245
Simpson, J. H. 245

Sims, Elias 245
Sinclair, W. H. 245
Singer, George H. 245
Sirret, William B. 245
Sisson, Joseph 245
Sizer, Henry H. 245
  Samuel 245
Skeldon, John 245
Skillings, Maggie 282
  Robert 282
Skinner, J. S. 246
  John B. 161
  Mary R. 161
Slade, H. 174
  Samuel 246
  William 246
  William H. 246
Slayton, S. M. 246
Sloan, Hugh 246
  James 283
  William 246
  William M. 246
Slocum, Oscar A. 246
Slosson, Belden 246
  Helon 246
  John 246
Sly, Gilbert 246
  John 246
Small, Harriet L. 160
  James H. 246
  Mary Ann 160
Smallshaw, John 247
Smead, Charles 247
  H. B. 247
  Horace A. 247
Smith, A. M. C. 247
  Abijah 248, 251
  Alfred 249
  Alma 247
  Amanda L. 99
  Amos 247, 249
  Archibald M. B. 247
  Arlu 251
  Asa P. 250
  B. F. 250
  B. R. 251
  Barnard 250
  Beulah A. 247
  C. A. 250
  C. L. 248
  C. L., Mrs. 135
  Charles 248, 249
  Charles W. 249
  Clark J. 250
  Colton B. 247
  Daniel 250
  Darius 293
  Edward 249
  Edward W. 247, 248, 250
  Eli B. 248

Smith, Elisha 248
  Ellery P. 248
  Erasmus H. 247
  Ezekiel 247, 251
  Francis 250
  Frederick 250
  G. 251
  George 250
  George W., Mrs. 125
  Gideon 248
  Harriet 249
  Harrison W. 248
  Henry K. 251
  Hiram 10
  Hiram G. 248
  Isaac S. 250
  J. Hyatt 251
  James 250, 251
  James F. 248
  James H. 250
  James M. 250
  James M., Mrs. 228
  James R. 247
  Jefferson 251
  Jenny A. 293
  John 89, 248, 250
  John B. 251
  John J. 251
  John M. 247
  John P. 248
  Jonathan 248
  Jose S. 250
  Joseph 247, 250
  Joseph H. 250
  Levi 251
  Louise 89
  Lucius 99
  Marshall N. 250
  Mary Ann 10
  Mathias 250
  Narhan 249
  Nathaniel 248, 250
  O. B. 247, 250
  P. 249
  Patrick 249
  Philip A. 247
  R. W. 248
  S. R. 248, 250
  Samuel 250, 251
  Sheldon 248
  Sidney 250
  T. J. 250
  Thomas G. 250
  Timothy 251
  W. A. 251
  W. L. G. 250
  W. S. 251
  W. W. 248
  Walter S. 249
  William 247

Smith, William N. 250
  William W. 248
  William, Mrs. 247
Smither, Robert 252
Smithwick, William 252
Snaith, John S. 252
Snashell, J. 252
Snearly, George 252
Snell, William S. 252
Sniggs, R. F. 252
Snow, A. T. 252
  George B. 252
  Harriet C. 252
  James 252
  R. G. 252
  William S. 252
Snyder, George 252
Soldan, C. F. 20
  Henrietta S. 20
Sole, D. B. 252
Somerville, John 252
  William 252
Sommer, Andrew 252
Sourwine, Michael 253
  Peter 253
Southworth, D. W. 253
  M. C. 253
Soven, Augustus 253
Spadi, Conrad 253
Spalding, Luther 253
  Roswell S. 253
Sparks, William 253
Sparrow, Erastus 54, 217, 253
  Louisa H. 54
  Mary J. 217
Spaulding, E. G. 253
  Elbridge G. 253
Spencer, Ambrose 253
  B. 253
  Burrall 253
  Charles N. 253
  E. A., Mrs. 152
  James 253
  Nelson 253
Spertzell, Justus 254
Spicer, George W. 254
  Thomas 254
Spooner, Julia E. 147
  Lemuel 147, 254
  Whipple 254
Sprague, A. S. 172
  Alden S. 254
  Martha O. 172
  Noah P. 172, 254
  W. P. 254
Squier, Henry C. 254
  Socrates 254
St. John, Gamaliel 90, 232, 246

St. John, Margaret K. 246
  Maria 90
  Martha 246
  Samuel 232
Staats, Barent 254
  Barent I. 254
  Jeremiah 254
Stable, John 254
Stacey, John 254
Stafford, John F. 255
  Samuel 255
Stagg, Henry R. 255
Stahleker, Frederick L. 255
Standart, John W. 255
  Oliver 255
  William 255
Stanfield, James C. 255
Stang, Annie 255
Stanley, Eames 255
  Horace, Mrs. 72
  P. S. 255
  Seth 255
Staring, John 256
  Sylvanus 256
Starkey, T. A. 256
Starkweather, Rodman 256
Starr, Albert 256
  Samuel 256
Stauch, Theobald 256
Stearns, Samuel 256
Stebbins, A. H. 256
  C. B. 256
Steedman, Andrew 256
Steele, Daniel 79
  Eliza D. S. 207
  Emily 299
  Horace 256
  Johanna 79
  Lucy A. 87
  O. G. 87, 299
  Oliver G. 207, 256
Steffan, Anthony C. 257
  Michael 257
Stein, Charles B. 257
Stemler, Philip 257
Stephenson, Emma Curtis 144
  T. 257
  Thomas 144
Sterling, A. S. 257
Stern, Henry 257
Sternberg, Pearl L. 257
Stetson, Cyrus Athearn 257
Stettenbenz, Anthony 257
Steuben, W. N. 257
Stevens, Albert G. 258
  Edward 257
  F. P. 257
  Harrison B. 257
  Henry B. 258
  Milo 258

Stevens, Moses K. 258
Stevenson, E. L. 100, 258
  Edward L. 258
  George P. 258
  James J. 258
  John S. 258
Stever, Jacob 258
Steward, Thomas 258
Stewart, Henry 258
  J. W. 258
  T. H. 258
Stillman, Horace 258
  S. A. 258
Stimpson, William 160, 259
Stimson, William 259
Stinson, Edward 259
Stivers, John G. 259
Stock, Christopher 259
Stocking, Joseph 259
  Thomas R. 259
Stoddard, Moses 259
Stone, Eli 259
  J. G. 28
  Jesse 259
  John B. 259
  W. P. 28, 259
Stoneman, George 248
Storck, Edward 259
Storm, Anson 259
  George T. 259
  James 259
Storrs, Lucius 259, 296
  Susan 296
Story, Patrick J. 260
Stout, William 260
Stover, Theodore 260
Stow, George 260
Straight, C. L. 260
Stranahan, Rhodes 260
Strauss, Peter 260
Strebel, David 260
Streeter, Ann M. 120
  Byron L. 260
  Henry 120, 260
  Only 260
  Sarah 260
Streiber, Sarah 106
Striber, Edward 260
Strong, J. M. 261
  N. T. 261
  P. H. 261
Strothers, Thomas 261
Stryker, Elizabeth Margaretta 291
Stuart, L. 261
Stumm, William 261
Sturges, Edward 261
Sullivan, D. 261
  Eugene 261
Sully, Robert 261

Summer, Daniel 262
Sumner, Credulia 133
  Daniel 133
  Joshua 262
Supple, James 262
Sutcliffe, William 262
Sutherland, A. 262
  Anson 262
Sutton, Peter 262
  William A. 262
Svegilgus, Joseph 262
Swain, Daniel 262
  J., Mrs. 143
Swan, Charles B. 262
  Russell 262
Swander, Alexander F. 262
Swartz, Ellen D. 213
  Henry A. 263
  John 213
  Samuel 263
Sweeney, James 263
  William 263
Sweet, Charles A. 263
  Chester 263
  George H. 263
  J. B. 263
  James 263
  L. 263
Sweetland, George 263
Swegles, John 263
Sweitzer, George 263
Swift, C. C. 263
  Charles 263
  Orson 263
  Orson, Mrs. 119
  Simon P. 263
Sykes, Reuben A. 263
Sylvester, William 264
Taber, James P. 264
  Jesse 264
  Martin 264
Tabor, Silas 264
Taff, M. 264
  Manuel C. 264
  R. 264
Taggart, James H. 264
  Moses 264
Taintor, Charles 264
Talcott, William H. 264
Tallman, John S. 264
Tanner, Alonzo 264
  Amos S. 264
  Harvey M. 264
  Henry 264
  Hiram C. 264
Tappert, Martin 265
  Rosa 265
Tate, Charles H. 265
Tatu, Sylvester J. 265
Taunt, Emory 265

Taylor, A. W. 265
  Aaron 265
  Augustus C. 265
  Charles J. 265
  Cyrus H. 265
  David 265
  Dorothy 12
  Ephraim 265
  J. J. 265
  John 265
  John R. 265
  Joseph 265
  Othniel 12
  Robert 265
  Robert S. 265
  S. 265
  T. F. 265
  W. F. P. 16
Tayntor, Adelbert 266
  Oscar J. 266
Tefft, J. S. 266
  Pardon 266
  R. 266
  Royal 266
Tennant, Alvin 266
Terry, Arthur 266
  Joseph 266
  Thomas 266
Thatcher, Luther R. 266
Thayer, Atherton 266
  Hiram P. 264, 267
  Jacob 266
  James C. 266
  Joel 266
  John 267
  Levi 267
  N. W. 266
  Nathan W. 266
  Sarah 264
Thiel, Jacob 267
Thomas, C. F. S. 267
  David 267
  Dyre 267
  Ebenezer 268
  Frederick 267
  George H. 267
  Horace 267
  John H. 267
  Robert E. 267
  W. D. 267
  W. G. 267
  Wealthy, Mrs. 133
  William 267
Thompson, A. 268
  Andrew 268
  Edwin C. 268
  Gilbert 268
  H. D. 268
  Hannah 271
  Harry 269, 271

Thompson, Henry 268
  Hiram 268
  Isaac W. 215, 268
  James 268
  John 268
  Martin 268
  N. E. 268
  Orrin 268
  Oscar S. 269
  R. H. 269
  Samuel 268
  Sarah Ann 251
  Sheldon 251, 268, 269, 271
  T. E. 268
  William 268, 269
Thomson, E. H. 269
  J. 269
  James E. 269
Thorn, Jacob 269
Thornton, James 269
  Samuel 269
  Thomas 269
Thorp, J. O. 269
  N. B. 79, 269, 276
Throm, John Martin 269
Thurston, Thomas 269
Tiffany, A. J. 270
  Augustus A. 270
  L. F. 270
  L. L. 270
Tifft, A. W. 270
  J. S. 270
  W. S. 270
Tilden, Joseph 270
  Thomas B. 270
Tillinghast, Dyre T. 270
  J. W. 270
  W. J. 270
Tillow, Joseph 270
Timmerman, Benjamin 270
Tims, William 270
Tirrell, Edward 270
Titus, Hester 92
  John F. 92
  O. B., Mrs. 211
  T. J. 270
  Zebulon 270
Tobias, William 270
Tod, Alexander 270
  Jenet C. 270
Todd, H. C. 271
  Robert 270
  William H. 147
Toher, Thomas 271
Toles, B. 271
  B., Mrs. 272
  Benjamin 271
Tolfree, J. Herbert 271
  James H. 271
Tomlinson, Oliver 271

Tompkins, John 271
  Robert 271
Toms, Joseph P. 271
Topping, M. H. 271
Topspot, Sarah M. 139
  Timothy 139
Torpot, Timothy 271
Torrance, H. B. 271
Torrey, A. R. 238
  Asa 271
  U. 271
  Urial 271
Touger, Thomas T. 271
Tourot, Frederick 271
Townsend, A. C. 272
  Alexander C. 271
  Charles 272
  David T. 272
  Jacob 271
  John 272
  K. W. 271
  Peter B. 272
  Richard 271
Toy, Ernest 272
Tracy, Albert H. 196, 272
  Sanford A. 272
Traynor, James 272
Treanor, John 272
Treat, Henry H. 272
  William, Mrs. 89
Tregilgus, Joseph 272
Trescott, George 272
Trevett, Lewis 272
Trible, J. M. 272
Trimlet, William C. 272
Trimlett, Eliza Victoria 260
  William C. 260
Tripp, Augustus F. 272
Trowbridge, E. B. 273
  Josiah 273
Tryon, Amos S. 273
  Isaac C. 273
  M. H. 273
Tucker, Chauncey 273
  David 273, 274
  Dezelle 273
  Levi 273
  Nathaniel 273
  S. L. 274
  Samuel 273
  William 273
Tummelty, John 274
Tunkey, William 274
Tupper, George W. 274
  Samuel 274
Turcotte, Collis 274
Turnbull, Mark 274
Turner, Adam 274
  Archibald 274

Turner, Chester P. 34
  Jane Fortune 274
  Julia A. 34
  Libbeus 274
  Samuel 274
  William 274
Tuthill, E. D. 274
Tuton, Harvey 274, 275
Tuttle, D. N., Mrs. 76
  David N. 275
Twichel, Abraham, Mrs. 94
  Samuel, Mrs. 94
Twichell, Abram 275
  Austin 275
  Samuel 275
Tyler, A. S. 275
  Alpha 202, 275
  Joseph 275
  Mary E. 202
  Royal 275
Underhill, J. H. 275
Underwood, Cyrus 275
Uptegraff, William 275
Urban, George 276
Usher, Elizabeth 36
  Sila 36
Utley, Charles B. 276
  Horace 276
Vail, A. R. 276
  James W. 276
  John 276
Valentine, Frederick 276
  George 276
  William 276
Vallacott, J. R. 278
Vallier, L. 249
Van Allen, Jacob D. 276
Van Arnam, Daniel W. 276
Van Bentheusen, J. H. 276
Van Buren, James 276
  S. T. 276
Van Campen, James M. 276
Van Deusen, H. G. 277
  Mathew 277
Van Deventer, Eugene 222
  James T. 277
  Marcia Caroline 222
Van Husen, N. K. 277
Van Kleeck, Charles F. 231
Van Name, A. A. 277
Van Natter, James R. 277
Van Ornam, P. C. 277
Van Sicklen, Edward H. 277
  James 277
Van Slyke, A., Mrs. 6
  C. A. 277
  Cornelius A. 277
Van Tine, Charles 277
  George K. 278
Van Valkenburgh, Daniel 278

Van Valkenburgh, Nelson 278
  William 278
Van Velsor, Benjamin 278
Van Vleck, William H. 278
Vananden, William 276
Vandebogart, H. D. 276
Vandeventer, S. B., Mrs. 275
Vanduzee, B. C. 277
Vanhouton, J. H. 277
Vanslack, A. N. 277
Vantine, David 278
  Wilder 277
Vaughan, Eugene A. 278
Vaughn, D. G. C. 278
  G. C. 278
Venn, Robert 278
Verplanck, Isaac A. 278
Verrinder, William 278
Vetter, Charles 278
Vickery, William R. 278
Vine, George 107, 278
  H. Russell 278
Vining, G. W. 278
Vinton, Henry 278
Voas, Robert W. 278
Vogt, G. S. 279
Vollmer, Casper 279
Voltz, A. W. 279
  C. G. 279
  George 34, 279
  J. S. 279
  Louisa M. 34
Voorhees, Henry P. 251
  Ralph 279
  Sarah Ann 251
Vortriede, Julius 279
Vosburgh, Nathaniel 279
  P. M. 279
  William 279
  William H. 279
Voss, Robert 279
Vosseller, Nathan 279
Vought, Casper 279
Voyle, P. J. 279
Wade, Frank A. 279
  James 279
  Peleg 279
Wadsworth, Harriet 29
  James 29
  John 279
  Richard 279
Wagner, Joseph 280
Wahl, Frederick J. 280
Wait, Hiram 280
  William 280
Waite, Benjamin 280
  Charles H. 62, 280
  Ellen 62
Waith, William 280

Wakelee, Charles M. 280
  Clement 280
  Henry P. 280
Wakely, Maria 97
  Platt 97
Walbridge, George B. 280
  Wells D. 280
Wald, Hattie 170
  John S. 170
Walden, E. 280
Waldron, C. A. 280
  G. E., Mrs. 229
  Gilbert 280
  J. Ferris 280
  Peter A. 280
Walker, Ashley 281
  Augustus 281
  Elihu 281
  George 280, 281
  James W. 281
  Jeremiah W. 281
  Joel L. 281
  John 281
  Richard 281
  Russell 281
  S. A., Mrs. 302
  S. N. 281
  Stephen 281
  Stephen A. 281
Wallace, Erastus 209, 281
  Ezra H. 281
  Frederick K. 281
  James 281
  Marion B. 209
  Robert A. 281
  William 281
Wallbridge, Samuel Shelly 282
Wallenhorst, Frank H. 282
Wallingford, John A. 282
Walls, John 282
Walsh, James 282
  John 282
  Michael 282
  Timothy 282
Walter, Hugh 282
Wand, Edward 285
Wannemacher, Peter 282
Ward, Hiram P. 282
  William R. L. 282
Wardwell, Allen 282
  George S. 283
  William F. 283
Warhus, Henry F. 283
Warner, Aaron 283
  James 283
  John 283
  John F. 283
  Noah H. 283
  Samuel C. 283

Warner, Sarah 283
  Thomas N. 283
Warren, Asa 283
  E. A., Mrs. 283
  Edward D. 283
  Hastings 283
  Horatio 283, 284
  James D. 283
  John 283
  John D. 284
  Melvin F. 283
  N. D. 283
  Orsamus 283
  William 283, 284
Warriner, J. C. 284
Washburn, J. R. 284
  N. S. 284
  S. F. 284
  Salmon 284
  William 284
Washburne, Alanson 284
Wasser, A. 284
Water, Peter 284
Waterbury, Henry 284
Waterman, Joseph 284
  Polly 208
Waters, John D. 285
  Levi 284
  Levi J. 284
  William S. 285
Waterworth, Thomas 285
Watkins, George 285
Watson, Basil 285
  Chauncy 285
  George H. 285
  Ira G. 285
Wattles, A. 285
  Myrtle 285
Watts, Horace G. 285
  Robert 285
  William 285
Waud, Thomas S. 285
Webb, Christina 239
  Jessie 239
Weber, Jacob 286
  John B. 286
  John J. 286
  Nicholas 286
Webster, Charles 286
  Daniel 286
  David B. 286
  Eli 286
  George B. 286
  Hiram 286
  Hugh 286
  John 286
  Levi 286
  Thomas S. 286
  William C. 286
Wechter, James 193

Wechter, M. A. 193
Weed, Elias 223, 286, 287
  Joseph 286, 287
Weeks, John L. 287
Wehrung, Adam 287
Weimer, John G. 287
Weir, Neil 287
Weishuhn, Philip H. 287
Weisser, Henry 287
Welch, Franklin 287
  Peter 287
Welchi, Samuel 288
Weldy, S. E. 288
Weller, Adelia E. 266
  L. 266
  Leander 288
  Louis 288
Wells, Aldrich 288
  C., Mrs. 290
  Chandler J. 288
  Charles F. 288
  Chauncey 288
  David B. 288
  Emily A. 110
  Harriet 47
  Joel 290
  Joseph 288
  Moses D. 288
  Richard H. 288
  Sarah A. 202
  William 202, 288
  William H. 110
  William, Mrs. 132
Wendel, Daniel 288
Wentworth, Allen D. 288
  Delavan 288
Weppner, Arnold 288
  Augustus 288
Werle, Anthony 288
  George A. 288
Werrick, John 288
Wesch, Fred. 289
Wescott, Ira 289
  R. 289
Wesley, A. 289
  W. K. 289
West, Benjamin 274
  Charles Edwin 289
  Isaac 289
  Peter 289
  Stephen 289
Westcott, Byron H. 289
  Cyrus A. 231
  Rufus R. 289
Weston, E., Mrs. 294
  H. J. 289
  Henry James 289
  W. H. 289
  William 289
Weter, Peter 289

Wetmore, Parsons 289
  S. W. 289
Whaples, Reuben 289
Whatmore, Daniel 290
Wheeler, Charles 289
  Charles W. 289
  Ira P. 289
  Isaac 290
  Isaac G. 289
  John H. 290
  Lucy Ann 172
  Paul 290
  Philander 172
  Rufus 290
  William H. 289
Wheelock, John E. 290
  John G. 290
  Milton 290
  N. 290
Wherrell, John 290
Whiston, John W. 290
Whitcomb, George 290
  Lucia Caroline 133
  Nathan 290
  T. F. 133
White, A. W. 291
  Amos G. 291
  David P. 291
  H. G. 290, 291
  Henry A. 60
  Henry G. 290
  Hoel 291
  Homer 291
  Horace K. 291
  Hubbard T. 291
  Isaac D. 291
  J. B. 291
  J. J. 291
  James P. 290, 291
  Joel S. 291
  John 291
  Joseph L. 291
  Leonard 292
  M., Mrs. 19
  R. M. 291
  Sarah A. 61
  Stephen 291
  Susan N. P. 291
  Truman 291
  William 291
  William H. 291
Whitefield, Joseph H. 292
Whiteneck, Peter 292
Whiting, Charles R. 292
  Sanford E. 292
  Thomas 292
Whitney, B. T. 292
  Milo A. 292
  William M. 292
Whittaker, John 292

Whittaker, William H. 292
Whittemore, Asa 292
Whittet, James 292
Wickes, Comfort 293
Wickson, John B. 293
Wiedrich, Michael 293
Wiemann, Andrew 293
Wiggins, Benjamin L. 293
  D. B. 293
  William 293
Wight, John F. 293
Wightman, George D. 293
Wilber, Daniel 135
Wilbur, Joshua M. 293
Wilcox, Ansley 293
  Benjamin J. 293
  Birdseye 293
  Charles H. 293
  David 293
  H. W. 293
  John F. 293
  Robert S. 293
  Roswell D. 293
  William 293
Wild, George 293
Wilder, Milton 293
Wilds, Electa 293
  H. N. 293
Wilgus, Alfred W. 34, 249, 293
  Grace B. 202
  Harriet M. 249
  James H., Mrs. 171
  Jane A. 34
  Nathaniel 294
Wilkenson, Ansel 294
Wilkes, George H. 294
Wilkeson, John 294
  Louisa 142
  Samuel 141, 294
Wilkins, George P. 294
  George W. 294
  S. P. 294
Wilkinson, Elizabeth M. 255
  Samuel 255
Willard, Nelson 294
William, Wells 47
Williams, Albert B. 295
  Alfred M. 295
  Ashley 296
  Benjamin H. 143, 295
  Charles 295
  Charles G., Mrs. 133
  Daniel 295
  E. P. 295
  Edward W. 295
  George 296
  George A. 295
  George H. 295
  Gibson T. 132

Williams, Henry R. 296
  Horace 295
  Howell C. 295
  Isaiah T. 295
  John F. 295
  John L. 296
  John R. 295
  Joseph 295
  L. H. 296
  Nathan 295
  O. G. 296
  O. H. P. 296
  O. V. 295
  Oliver 296
  Ortis B. 295
  Samuel 295
  Thomas 296
  V. R. 295
  W. A. 295
  Watkins 295, 296
  William 295, 296
  William G. 295
  William H. 296
Williamson, E. 296
  Eli 296
  Lewis 296
  Robert 296
Willis, Charles 296
  M. H. 296
  Nathan 296
Willson, Abner 296
  Henry 296
Willyoung, John 296
Wilson, Abner 297
  Alfred 297
  Andrew 297
  Benjamin W. 297
  Charles A. 297
  Charles W. 297
  D. W. 297
  James R. 297
  John 297
  M. P. 297
  Matthew 297
  Samuel 297
Winants, George Bryant 297
  Warren 297
Winchell, Joseph W. 297
Wing, Anna E. 8
  Benjamin 297
  George F. 298
  J. G. 298
  Stephen 298
Winne, Isaac 298
Winship, A. N. 298
  Ezra T. 298
Winslow, A. D. 298
  Myron D. 298
Winter, George 298
Wirt, Hiram 298

Witter, M. E. 298
Wogan, Thomas 298
Wolcott, Augustus 298
  Horatio G. 298
  Joseph W. 298
  W. F. 298
Wolf, Jacob 115
  Joseph 298
  Marian 115
  Michael 299
Wolff, Charles 299
  Christian 299
Wood, A. J. 299
  Daniel 299
  F. P. 299
  John 299
  Sewall 299
  W. W. 299
  Welcome 299
  William 299
  William B. 299
Woodard, Barnet 299
Woodbury, A. B. 300

Woodbury, Hiram 300
Woodhouse, James H. 300
Woodruff, Eli 300
  William 300
Woods, Patrick 300
Woodward, David M. 300
  Jonathan 300
  S. W. 300
  Timothy T. 300
  William H. 300
Woolworth, Richard 301
Worcester, Jacob 301
Worthington, Richard P. 301
Wright, Alvin 301
  Amos 301
  C. F. 301
  George W. 301
  H. O. 301
  J. J. H. 301
  James 265
  John Edward 301
  M. C. F. 301
  Malden 301
  Matthew 301

Wright, Susan 265
  William 301
Wuest, Frederick 302
Wyckoff, C. 302
  C. C., Mrs. 118
Yax, John 153
Young, Charles E. 302
  Peter 302
  William 302
  William C. 302
  William F. 302
Yox, John 106
Yuncker, Jacob P. 303
Zacher, C. D. 303
Zamy, Patrick 303
Zimmer, Eustavus 303
Zimmerman, William 303
Zink, George 303
Zittel, Frederick 303
Zook, Daniel M. 303
  David 303
Zuegele, Albert 303
Zurbrick, Peter 303

Other Heritage Books by Martha and Bill Reamy:

*Erie County, New York Obituaries as Found in the Files of
The Buffalo and Erie County Historical Society*

*Genealogical Abstracts from Biographical and
Genealogical History of the State of Delaware
Volumes 1 and 2*

History and Roster of Maryland Volunteers, War of 1861-1865, Index

Immigrant Ancestors of Marylanders, as Found in Local Histories

Pioneer Families of Orange County, New York

*Records of St. Paul's Parish, [Baltimore, Maryland]
Volumes 1 and 2*

St. George's Parish Register [Harford County, Maryland], 1689-1793

St. James' Parish Registers, 1787-1815

St. Thomas' Parish Register, 1732-1850

The Index of Scharf's History of Baltimore City and County [Maryland]

Other Heritage Books by Martha Reamy

*1860 Census Baltimore City: Volume 1, 1st and 2nd Wards
(Fells Point and Canton Waterfront Areas)*

*Abstracts of South Central Pennsylvania Newspapers
Volume 2, 1791-1795*

Early Families of Otsego County, New York, Volume 1

Early Church Records of Chester County, Pennsylvania, Volume 2
Martha Reamy and Charlotte Meldrum

Abstracts of Carroll County Newspapers, 1831-1846
Martha Reamy and Marlene Bates

www.ingramcontent.com/pod-product-compliance
Lightning Source LLC
Chambersburg PA
CBHW080728300426
44114CB00019B/2509